Amsco's Preparing for the Regents Examination
Mathematics B

Ann Davidian
Mathematics Department Chair
General Douglas MacArthur High School
Levittown, New York

Christine T. Healy
Mathematics Teacher
Bethpage High School
Bethpage, New York

AMSCO SCHOOL PUBLICATIONS, INC.
315 Hudson Street, New York, N.Y. 10013

Dedication

To Dr. Joyce Bernstein with thanks for your encouragement and faith in us.

To John and Michael—thanks so much for all of your love and support.

To Rosemary Kaste in appreciation of your pioneering our problems and sharing your opinions and reactions.

For Kelly, Kathleen, Maria, and all the students who will use this book. Good luck on your Regents!

Text and Cover Design: One Dot Inc.
Composition: Nesbitt Graphics, Inc.
Art: Hadel Studio

Please visit our Web site at: *www.amscopub.com*

When ordering this book, please specify:
Either **R 761 W** *or* PREPARING FOR THE REGENTS EXAMINATION MATHEMATICS B

ISBN 978-1-56765-556-8
NYC Item: 56765-556-7

10   07

Preface

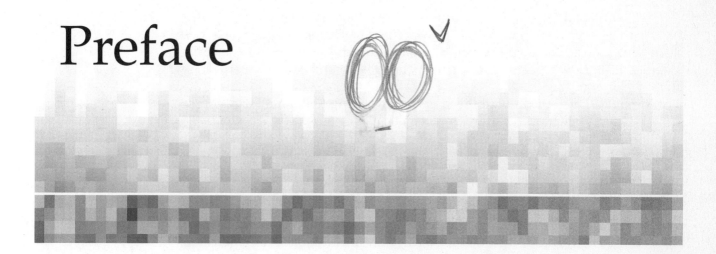

Welcome to *Preparing for the Regents Examination Mathematics B,* written for you, the student. In recent years New York State has changed the Regents Examinations in many subject areas. Sequential Mathematics I, II, and III are being replaced with Mathematics A and B Regents Examinations and the format of these tests is much more hands-on than were previous Regents. The curriculum covered in these two exams comes from the Key Ideas and Performance Indicators listed in the New York State Core Curriculum. We hope that in this review book, we have offered you a sufficient number of explanations and problems to fully acquaint you with the format and type of questions you can expect to see on the Math B Regents Examination.

Preparing for the Regents Examination Mathematics B contains topic reviews with Model Problems, Practice, Chapter Reviews, and Cumulative Reviews to help you study. The problems in these sections incorporate both content and problem-solving situations that are similar to those found in the Core Curriculum and on the Regents examinations already given. The book also contains copies of three previously given Mathematics B Regents Examinations so you can use them to practice before taking the real thing. In addition, *Preparing for the Regents Examination Mathematics B* also contains what we call **FYI,** For Your Information, sections at the conclusion of many chapters to introduce you to the mechanics of your TI-83+ calculator. Some of the questions on the Math B Regents can be more easily solved if you are comfortable performing operations on the calculator, not only to solve problems, but to check those you are required to solve showing all your work.

How to Use This Book

- **Read** the material that is presented. This book was written for you to read.
- **Do the Model Problems.** Don't just read them. Use paper and pencil to work the problems out. When you are finished, see how your solution and your answer compare with the method shown in the book. Remember there are often alternative ways of solving many of these problems, but you should arrive at the same answer.
- **Do the Practice Problems and the Chapter Reviews.** Sometimes it is helpful to work with a friend. Remember, mathematics is not a spectator sport—you learn by doing.

- **Use the Cumulative Reviews** to refresh your memory on many topics. You can either do each Cumulative Review as you finish the chapter, or save them all until you have finished the book. Since the Regents Examination is cumulative, you must constantly review concepts that were previously covered.
- **Do the Regents Examinations** that are provided in the back of the book. These are copies of actual examinations that have already been given. Answering these questions will enable you to get a good idea of how you may perform on a real examination.
- **Start NOW!** Do not wait until the last minute, hoping to cram all of the information into your head. Learning mathematics takes time! Many concepts are built from concepts previously learned and you cannot comprehend all of this at once.

Test-Taking Strategies

- **Become familiar with the directions and format of the test** ahead of time. The Mathematics B Regents Examination has four parts with a total of 34 questions. You must answer *all* of the questions. There are 20 multiple-choice questions and 14 questions where you must show your work. For each of the 14 open-ended questions, you must show the steps you used to solve the problem, including formulas, diagrams, graphs, charts, and so forth, where appropriate.
- **Be aware of how the test is scored.** Part I consists of 20 multiple-choice questions, worth 2 points each. There is no partial credit and you must answer every one of them. Part II contains 6 questions worth 2 points each. Part III contains 6 questions worth 4 points each. Part IV contains 2 questions worth 6 points each. For Parts II, III, and IV, you must show your work and answer all of the questions in each part. A correct numerical answer without the appropriate work will receive only 1 point. The entire test is worth 88 points. The test is then scaled to produce a numerical grade equivalent to the score out of 100 points.
- **Pace yourself.** Remember that you have three hours to answer 34 questions. Do not race to answer every question immediately. On the other hand, do not linger over any problem too long. Keep in mind that you will need more time to complete Parts II, III, and IV. You do not have to get every problem correct to score well on this test.
- **Practice, Practice, Practice.** The more you practice, the more comfortable you will be with the material.
- **Write in the test booklet.** Scrap paper is not permitted for any part of the Regents examination. You must use the blank spaces in the booklet as your scrap paper. A sheet of *scrap* graph paper is provided at the end of the booklet. Be aware that any work done on the graph paper will *not* be scored.
- **Keep track of your place on the answer sheet.** A separate answer sheet is provided for Part I. If you find yourself bogged down on a problem, skip it and come back to it later. Make a note in the margin of the test booklet so that you can locate the skipped problem easily. Be careful when you skip a problem. Be sure to leave the answer line blank that corresponds to the question you skipped.

If you follow these strategies, you will become comfortable with the material, and will do your best on the test. Good luck! We hope our book helps you ace the exam!

Ann Davidian & Christine T. Healy

Contents

Chapter 4 Quadratic Equations and Inequalities   74

Chapter 5 Absolute Value and Rational Expressions   105

Assessment: Cumulative Reviews and Regents Examinations

CHAPTER 1

Geometric Proofs

1.1 Definitions of Key Geometric Terms

The material contained in this section was covered in Math A. It is presented again here as a quick review.

There are three undefined terms in geometry. These are **point, line,** and **plane.** Although these basic terms cannot be defined, we can describe the concept of each.

Point: a position in space. A point has no dimensions, it has only a position. A point is represented with a dot and named with a capital letter, such as point P.

Line: an infinite set of points extending in two directions. A line is named using two of its points, such as $\overleftrightarrow{AB}$, or by using a single lowercase script letter, such as line l.

Plane: a set of points extending infinitely in all directions. A plane is named with a capital letter, such as plane P.

It is important to know some of the terms that are used in geometry.

Points that are contained on the same line are said to be **collinear,** while points that are contained on the same plane are **coplanar.**

To prove statements in geometry we use postulates and theorems. A **postulate** is a statement that is assumed to be true. A **theorem** is a statement that can be proven by deductive reasoning.

If two figures are **congruent,** they have the same size and shape. The symbol for congruent is ≅, meaning that the figures are equal (=) in measure and similar (~) in shape.

An **angle** is the union of two rays that share a common endpoint. The two rays form the **sides** of the angle and the intersection of the two rays is the **vertex** of the angle. An angle can be named by the capital letter located at its vertex; by three capital letters, the middle letter being the vertex, and each of the other letters naming a point on a different ray; by a lowercase letter or a number placed inside the angle.

For example:

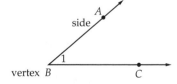

We can call this angle ∠B or ∠ABC or ∠1.

A **bisector** of an angle is a ray whose endpoint is the vertex of the angle, which divides the angle into two congruent angles.

Adjacent angles are two coplanar angles that share a common vertex and a common side, but have no interior points in common.

Complementary angles are two angles, the sum of whose degree measures is 90. **Supplementary angles** are two angles, the sum of whose degree measures is 180. Complementary and supplementary angles can be adjacent or nonadjacent.

A **linear pair of angles** is a pair of two adjacent angles whose sum is a straight angle.

A **line segment** is the set of points containing two points on a line, called the endpoints of the line segment, and all points on the line between the endpoints. Because a line segment has two endpoints, it has a definite length.

The **midpoint** of a line segment is the point that divides the segment into two congruent segments.

The **bisector** of a line segment is the line (or part of a line) that intersects the segment at its midpoint, dividing the segment into two congruent line segments.

Perpendicular lines are two lines that intersect to form right angles. If $\overleftrightarrow{AB}$ is perpendicular to $\overleftrightarrow{CD}$, we write $\overleftrightarrow{AB} \perp \overleftrightarrow{CD}$.

The **perpendicular bisector** of a line segment is a line (or part of a line) that is perpendicular to the line segment, intersecting the line segment at its midpoint.

A **polygon** is a closed figure formed by coplanar line segments that are joined at their endpoints. The word *polygon* comes from the Greek words *polys*, meaning "many," and *gonia,* meaning "angle." A **regular polygon** is both equilateral and equiangular, that is, all its sides are congruent and all its angles are congruent.

A **triangle** is a polygon that has exactly three sides.
Triangles can be classified by their angles:

- An **acute triangle** has three acute angles (all angles measure $< 90°$).

- A **right triangle** has one right angle (one $90°$ angle) and two acute angles. In a right triangle, the two sides that form the right angle are called **legs,** and the side opposite the right angle is called the **hypotenuse.**

- An **obtuse triangle** has one obtuse angle (one angle $> 90°$) and two acute angles.

Triangles can also be classified by their sides:

- An **equilateral triangle** has three congruent sides. An equilateral triangle is also equiangular, so it is a regular polygon.

- An **isosceles triangle** has at least two congruent sides. In an isosceles triangle, the two congruent sides are called **legs,** and the third side is called the **base.** The angles located at the base (opposite the congruent sides) are called **base angles** and are congruent. The angle opposite the base is called the **vertex angle.**

- A **scalene triangle** has no congruent sides.

The **altitude** of a triangle is the line segment drawn from any vertex of the triangle, perpendicular to the opposite side.

The **median** of a triangle is the line segment drawn from any vertex of the triangle to the midpoint of the opposite side.

A **quadrilateral** is a four-sided polygon. The most important quadrilaterals that we will study are parallelograms and trapezoids.

A **parallelogram** is a quadrilateral whose opposite sides are parallel. A **rectangle** is a parallelogram containing four right angles. A **rhombus** is a parallelogram with four congruent sides. A **square** can be described as a rhombus with four right angles or as a rectangle with four congruent sides. A square is equilateral and equiangular, so it is a **regular** quadrilateral.

A **trapezoid** has only one pair of parallel sides, called the bases. The non-parallel sides are the legs of the trapezoid. In an **isosceles trapezoid,** the legs are congruent.

1.2 Helpful Hints for Proofs

Helpful Hints for Direct Proofs

One of the more difficult concepts in formulating a proof is determining how to use the given information.

The table below is designed to help you over this hurdle.

If you are given:	You can conclude:
M is the midpoint of $\overline{AB}$. 	$\overline{AM} \cong \overline{MB}$. A midpoint divides the line segment into two congruent line segments.
$\overleftrightarrow{CD}$ bisects $\overline{AB}$ at P. 	$\overline{AP} \cong \overline{PB}$. When a line segment is bisected, two congruent line segments are formed.
$\overrightarrow{BE}$ bisects $\angle ABC$. 	$\angle ABE \cong \angle EBC$. When an angle is bisected, two congruent angles are formed.
$\overleftrightarrow{AB}$ and $\overleftrightarrow{CD}$ intersect at E. 	$\angle AEC \cong \angle DEB$ and $\angle AED \cong \angle CEB$. Vertical angles are congruent.

If you are given:	You can conclude:
$\overline{CD} \perp \overline{AB}$ at D. ![diagram: C above, vertical segment CD meeting horizontal line with A, D, B; right angle at D] C A D B	$\angle CDA$ and $\angle CDB$ are right angles. Perpendicular lines form right angles. - $\angle CDA \cong \angle CDB$. All right angles are congruent.
$\overline{CD}$ is the perpendicular bisector of $\overline{AB}$. C A D B	$\angle CDA$ and $\angle CDB$ are right angles. Perpendicular lines form right angles. $\angle CDA \cong \angle CDB$. All right angles are congruent. *and* $\overline{AD} \cong \overline{DB}$. A bisector divides a line segment into two congruent line segments.
$\overleftrightarrow{AB}$ is parallel to $\overleftrightarrow{CD}$ and is cut by transversal $\overleftrightarrow{EF}$. E 1 2 A 3 4 B 5 6 C D 7 8 F	$\angle 3 \cong \angle 6$ and $\angle 4 \cong \angle 5$ are in the *interior* of the parallel lines on *alternate* sides of the transversal. *Alternate interior* angles are congruent. - $\angle 1 \cong \angle 8$ and $\angle 2 \cong \angle 7$ are in the *exterior* of the parallel lines on *alternate* sides of the transversal. *Alternate exterior* angles are congruent. - $\angle 1 \cong \angle 5$ and $\angle 2 \cong \angle 6$ and $\angle 3 \cong \angle 7$ and $\angle 4 \cong \angle 8$ are pairs on the same side of the transversal, one angle is in the interior, and the other angle is in the exterior. *Corresponding* angles are congruent. - $\angle 1 \cong \angle 4$ and $\angle 2 \cong \angle 3$ and $\angle 5 \cong \angle 8$ and $\angle 6 \cong \angle 7$ are pairs of *vertical* angles. Vertical angles are congruent.
$\angle ABC$ is a right angle. A 1 2 B C	$\angle 1$ and $\angle 2$ are complementary. Complementary angles are two angles, the sum of whose degree measure is 90.
$\overleftrightarrow{AB}$ is a straight line. 1 2 A B	$\angle 1$ and $\angle 2$ are supplementary. Supplementary angles are two angles, the sum of whose degree measure is 180.

If you are given:	You can conclude:
Triangle *ABC*, with $\overline{BA} \cong \overline{BC}$. 	$\angle A \cong \angle C$. If two sides of a triangle are congruent, the angles opposite them are congruent.
Triangle *ABC* is isosceles, with $\overline{BA} \cong \overline{BC}$. 	$\angle A \cong \angle C$. The base angles of an isosceles triangle are congruent.
Triangle *ABC*, with $\angle A \cong \angle C$. 	$\overline{BA} \cong \overline{BC}$. If two angles of a triangle are congruent, the sides opposite them are congruent. $\triangle ABC$ is isosceles, since it has two congruent sides.
Triangle *ABC*, $\overline{BD}$ the altitude. 	$\angle ADB$ and $\angle CDB$ are right angles. An altitude is perpendicular to the base forming right angles with the base. $\angle ADB \cong \angle CDB$ since all right angles are congruent.
Triangle *ABC*, with $\overline{BE}$ the median to *AC*. 	$\overline{AE} \cong \overline{EC}$. A median, like a midpoint, divides a line segment into two congruent segments.

Helpful Hints for Indirect Proofs

In a direct proof, the argument proceeds directly from hypothesis to conclusion. In an indirect proof, you begin by assuming that the hypothesis is true and also assuming the negation of the conclusion. Then you proceed to show that this assumption leads to a contradiction.

To write an indirect proof:

• Accept the given information as true.

• Assume the opposite of what you want to prove is true. That is, assume the negation of the conclusion is true.

• Continue with your argument until you obtain a contradiction of a known fact, such as the given information or a theorem.

• Conclude that the initial assumption is false.

• Conclude that the statement to be proved must be true.

• Use an indirect proof when there seems to be no clear way to prove a statement directly.

 **MODEL PROOF**

Given: Triangle *ABC*.

Prove: Triangle *ABC* can contain at most one right angle.

Proof:

Statements	Reasons
1. Triangle *ABC*.	1. Given.
2. Triangle *ABC* contains more than one right angle. Call the angles $\angle A$ and $\angle B$.	2. Assumed.
3. $m\angle A = m\angle B = 90$.	3. Definition of a right angle.
4. $m\angle A + m\angle B + m\angle C > 180$.	4. Since $m\angle A = m\angle B = 90$, the sum of all three angles will be greater than 180°.
5. $\angle A$ and $\angle B$ are not both right angles.	5. Contradiction from statement 4—the sum of the angles of a triangle is 180°. Therefore, the assumption in statement 2 is false and the conclusion is true.

Practice

1. Assume that each of the following is a statement that is to be proved. If you were using an indirect proof, how would you begin your proof?

   a. Triangle *ABC* is isosceles.
   b. $\overline{DR} \parallel \overline{MD}$.
   c. $\overline{HE} \perp \overline{LP}$.
   d. $\angle FUN$ is a right angle.
   e. $\angle A \cong \angle B$.

In 2–10, write an appropriate statement and reason, given the following information.

Given	Statement	Reason
2. Triangle *ABC*, with $\overline{AD} \perp \overline{BC}$.		
3. Triangle *DEF* with $\overline{DG}$ the bisector of $\angle EDF$.		
4. $\overline{AN}$ and $\overline{RB}$ intersect at *F*.		
5. Quadrilateral *ABCD*, $\overline{AD} \parallel \overline{BC}$.		
6. Triangles *ABC* and *DEC*, with $\overline{AE}$ the bisector of $\overline{DB}$.		
7. $\overleftrightarrow{LIN}$ is a straight line.		

Given	Statement	Reason
8. Triangles ABC and DBC, $\overline{DB} \cong \overline{DC}$.		
9. Triangle ART, $\overline{AM}$ is the median to $\overline{RT}$.		
10. Given isoceles triangle ISO, with $\overline{IS} \cong \overline{OS}$.		

1.3 Geometric Proof

A geometric "proof" is a demonstration that a specific statement in geometry is true. A sequence of true statements that include the given, definitions, or other statements that have been proved previously are linked by sound reasoning from one to another until the desired conclusion is reached.

A proof consists of five parts: the diagram, the given statement, the prove statement, the statements, and the reasons. We write a geometric proof in two columns; the left column is for statements and the right column is for the reasons the statements are true.

One of the most basic geometric proofs is that of **congruent triangles,** triangles that are shown to be equal in size and shape. Showing that of the six parts of any triangle, three sides and three angles, at least half of the corresponding parts of the two triangles are equivalent often proves congruence.

The following chart demonstrates methods of proving triangles congruent.

Type of Congruence	Sample Diagram	Given Information	Conclusions
Side-Angle-Side (S.A.S.) If two sides and the included angle of a triangle are congruent to two sides and the included angle of a second triangle, the triangles are congruent by S.A.S.		Given: $\overline{AB} \cong \overline{AC}$. $\angle BAD \cong \angle CAD$.	Since you are given one congruent side and one congruent angle in each triangle, all that remains is the second congruent side. $\overline{AD} \cong \overline{AD}$ by identity, so $\triangle ABD \cong \triangle ACD$ by S.A.S. $\cong$ S.A.S.
Side-Side-Side (S.S.S.) If three sides of a triangle are congruent to three sides of a second triangle, the triangles are congruent by S.S.S.		Given: $\overline{KL} \cong \overline{KM}$. N is the midpoint of $\overline{LM}$.	You are given one congruent side in each triangle and a midpoint. Since a midpoint forms two congruent line segments, you can say $\overline{LN} \cong \overline{MN}$. By identity $\overline{KN} \cong \overline{KN}$, so $\triangle KLN \cong \triangle KMN$ by S.S.S. $\cong$ S.S.S.
Angle-Side-Angle (A.S.A.) If two angles and the included side of a triangle are congruent to two angles and the included side of a second triangle, the triangles are congruent by A.S.A.		Given: $\angle N \cong \angle M$. $\overline{PQ}$ is a perpendicular bisector of $\overline{NM}$.	You are given one congruent angle in each triangle. Since $\overline{PQ}$ is a perpendicular bisector of $\overline{NM}$, it makes $\overline{NQ} \cong \overline{MQ}$ and it forms right angles at Q. All right angles are congruent; so $\angle PQN \cong \angle PQM$ and $\triangle PQN \cong \triangle PQM$ by A.S.A. $\cong$ A.S.A.
Angle-Angle-Side (A.A.S.) If two angles and a side of a triangle are congruent to two angles and the nonincluded side of a second triangle, the triangles are congruent by A.A.S.		Given: $\angle C \cong \angle T$. $\overline{AH}$ bisects $\angle CHT$.	You are given one congruent angle in each triangle; $\overline{AH} \cong \overline{AH}$ by identity; and because $\overline{AH}$ bisects $\angle CHT$, we know that $\angle CHA \cong \angle THA$, so $\triangle CHA \cong \triangle THA$ by A.A.S. $\cong$ A.A.S.

Type of Congruence	Sample Diagram	Given Information	Conclusions
Hypotenuse-Leg (Hyp.-leg) With right triangles, if the hypotenuse and one leg of one triangle are congruent to the hypotenuse and one leg of the other triangle, the triangles are congruent by hyp.-leg.		Given: $\overline{AB} \cong \overline{CB}$. $\overline{BD} \perp \overline{AC}$.	Since you are given perpendicular segments, you know $\angle ADB$ and $\angle CDB$ are right angles. Therefore, $\overline{AB}$ and $\overline{CB}$ are the congruent hypotenuses of the triangles. Since $\overline{BD} \cong \overline{BD}$ by identity, $\triangle ABD \cong \triangle CBD$ by hyp.-leg $\cong$ hyp.-leg.

Remember: When you write a proof, each statement should be dependent on the statement that came before. Each reason should follow logically from the statement beside it, using the key word in that statement. Mark corresponding parts of the diagram congruent as you progress through the proof.

 MODEL PROOFS

1. Given: $\triangle ABC$; $\overline{AD}$ is a perpendicular bisector of $\overline{BC}$.

   Prove: $\triangle ABD \cong \triangle ACD$.

Statements

1. $\overline{AD}$ is a $\perp$ bisector of $\overline{BC}$.
2. $\overline{BD} \cong \overline{DC}$.

3. $\angle BDA$ and $\angle CDA$ are right angles.
4. $\angle BDA \cong \angle CDA$.
5. $\overline{AD} \cong \overline{AD}$.
6. $\triangle ABD \cong \triangle ACD$.

Reasons

1. Given.
2. A perpendicular bisector divides a line segment into two congruent line segments.
3. Perpendicular lines form right angles.
4. All right angles are congruent.
5. Identity (Reflexive Postulate)
6. S.A.S. $\cong$ S.A.S.

Note: Sometimes, instead of just being asked for a proof of congruence, you may be required to prove other angles or line segments of the triangles congruent. That automatically happens once the triangles are proved congruent, because:

Corresponding parts of congruent triangles are congruent.

This is often abbreviated C.P.C.T.C.

2. Given: $\triangle MNP$ with Q the midpoint of $\overline{NP}$.
$\overline{MN} \cong \overline{MP}$.

Prove: $\angle NMQ \cong \angle PMQ$.

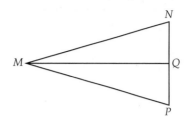

Statements	Reasons
1. Q is the midpoint of $\overline{NP}$; $\overline{MN} \cong \overline{MP}$.	1. Given.
2. $\overline{QN} \cong \overline{QP}$.	2. A midpoint divides a line segment into two congruent line segments.
3. $\overline{MQ} \cong \overline{MQ}$.	3. Identity (Reflexive Postulate)
4. $\triangle MPQ \cong \triangle MNQ$.	4. S.S.S. $\cong$ S.S.S
5. $\angle NMQ \cong \angle PMQ$.	5. Corresponding parts of congruent triangles are congruent. (C.P.C.T.C.)

3. Given: M is the midpoint of $\overline{CH}$.
$\overline{MA} \perp \overline{CT}$, $\overline{MD} \perp \overline{HT}$, and $\overline{AM} \cong \overline{DM}$.

Prove: $\angle TCH \cong \angle THC$.

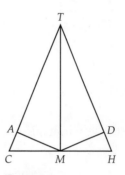

Statements	Reasons
1. M is the midpoint of $\overline{CH}$. $\overline{MA} \perp \overline{CT}$, $\overline{MD} \perp \overline{HT}$, $\overline{AM} \cong \overline{DM}$.	1. Given.
2. $\overline{MC} \cong \overline{MH}$.	2. A midpoint divides a line segment into two congruent line segments.
3. $\angle MAC$ and $\angle MDH$ are right angles.	3. Perpendicular lines form right angles.
4. $\triangle MAC$ and $\triangle MDH$ are right triangles.	4. Right triangles contain one right angle.
5. $\triangle MAC \cong \triangle MDH$.	5. Hypotenuse-leg $\cong$ hypotenuse-leg.
6. $\angle TCH \cong \angle THC$.	6. Corresponding parts of congruent triangles are congruent.

Practice

1. Given: $\triangle KLM$ with $\overline{LN}$ the bisector of $\angle KLM$.
$\angle LKM \cong \angle LMK$.

Prove: $\overline{NM} \cong \overline{NK}$.

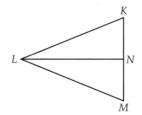

2. Given: $\triangle MNP$; $\overline{MN} \cong \overline{MP}$; $\overline{MR}$ bisects $\overline{NP}$ at Q.

Prove: $\angle NQM \cong \angle PQM$.

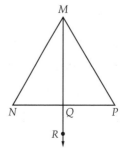

3. Given: △MTH with $\overline{HA} \perp \overline{MT}$.
   ∠HMA ≅ ∠HTA.
   Prove: △MAH ≅ △TAH.

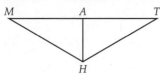

4. Given: $\overrightarrow{SRZ}$ and $\overrightarrow{STP}$ intersecting at S.
   ∠1 ≅ ∠2. $\overline{SM} \perp \overline{RT}$
   Prove: $\overline{SR} \cong \overline{ST}$.

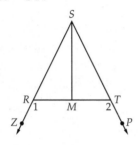

5. Given: $\overline{AB} \perp \overline{BD}$; $\overline{ED} \perp \overline{DB}$.
   $\overline{AE}$ bisects $\overline{BD}$.
   Prove: $\overline{AB} \cong \overline{ED}$.

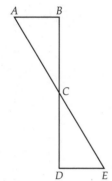

6. Given: $\overline{DO} \perp \overline{OA}$; $\overline{TA} \perp \overline{OA}$.
   $\overline{DO} \cong \overline{TA}$; $\overline{OC} \cong \overline{AG}$.
   Prove: $\overline{DG} \cong \overline{TC}$.

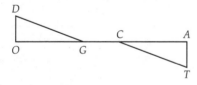

7. Given: $\overline{PS} \cong \overline{PQ}$. T is the midpoint of $\overline{SQ}$.
   Prove: ∠PSR ≅ ∠PQR.

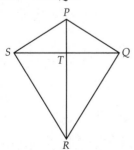

8. Given: $\overline{MH} \cong \overline{AT}$. ∠1 ≅ ∠2.
   Prove: △MAT ≅ △THM.

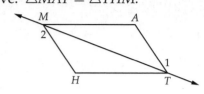

9. Given: △MNP; $\overline{MR} \cong \overline{MP}$.
   $\overline{QM}$ bisects ∠PMR.
   Prove: $\overline{PQ} \cong \overline{RQ}$.

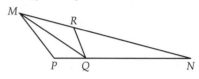

10. Given: $\overline{ML} \cong \overline{AW}$; $\overline{KT} \cong \overline{MA}$; ∠1 ≅ ∠2.
    Prove: $\overline{KL} \cong \overline{TW}$.

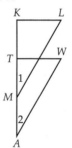

11. Given: $\overline{MI} \perp \overline{TG}$; $\overline{ME} \perp \overline{RG}$; $\overline{MI} \cong \overline{ME}$.
    Prove: ∠TGP ≅ ∠RGP.

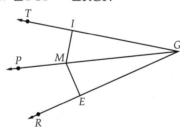

12. Given: △CTH with $\overline{CT} \cong \overline{CH}$.
    $\overline{CX}$ bisects ∠TCH.
    Prove: ∠HTX ≅ ∠THX.

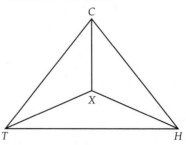

13. Given: $\triangle ABC$; $\angle ADB \cong \angle AEC$. $\overline{AE} \cong \overline{AD}$.
Prove: $\triangle ACE \cong \triangle ABD$. $\triangle DBC \cong \triangle ECB$.

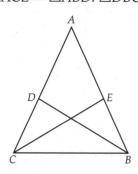

14. Given: $\overline{AC} \cong \overline{EC}$. $\overline{CB} \cong \overline{CD}$. $\overline{AF} \cong \overline{GE}$.
Prove: $\overline{BF} \cong \overline{DG}$.
$\overline{GH} \cong \overline{FH}$.

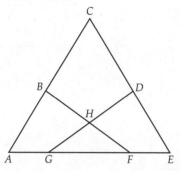

15. Given: $\triangle MNP$; $\overline{ML}$ is a perpendicular bisector of $\overline{NP}$.
Prove: $\triangle KPL \cong \triangle KNL$.
$\angle MNK \cong \angle MPK$.

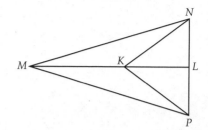

16. Given: $AB \neq BC$; $\overline{AD} \cong \overline{DC}$.
Prove: $\overline{BD}$ is not perpendicular to $\overline{AC}$.

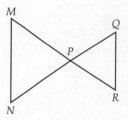

17. Given: $MN \neq QR$; $\overline{MR}$ and $\overline{NQ}$ are straight lines.
Prove: $\overline{MR}$ and $\overline{NQ}$ do not bisect each other.

1.4 Quadrilaterals

A quadrilateral is any four-sided figure, like those shown below.

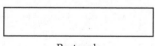

Rectangle

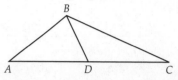

Parallelogram

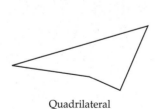

Quadrilateral

Isosceles trapezoid

Recall that one type of quadrilateral is the trapezoid, shown above. A trapezoid is a quadrilateral that has two parallel sides and two nonparallel sides. In an isosceles trapezoid, the nonparallel sides are congruent.

Mathematically, however, we are often concerned with special quadrilaterals known as parallelograms. Recall that a parallelogram is a quadrilateral with opposite sides parallel and congruent. Within the family of parallelograms are the rectangle, the rhombus, and the square, each of which has certain special characteristics, detailed in the chart below.

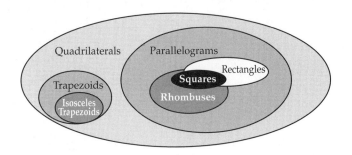

Properties of Quadrilaterals

Property	Parallelo-gram	Rectangle	Rhombus	Square	Trapezoid	Isosceles Trapezoid
Opposite sides congruent	Yes	Yes	Yes	Yes	No	Two non-parallel sides are congruent.
Opposite sides parallel	Yes	Yes	Yes	Yes	Only two sides are parallel.	Two non-congruent sides are parallel.
Opposite angles congruent	Yes	Yes	Yes	Yes	No	No
Diagonals bisect each other	Yes	Yes	Yes	Yes	No	No
Consecutive angles supplementary	Yes	Yes	Yes	Yes	No	No
All angles congruent	No	Yes	No	Yes	No	No
All right angles	No	Yes	No	Yes	No	No
All sides congruent	No	No	Yes	Yes	No	No
Diagonals congruent	No	Yes	No	Yes	No	Yes
Diagonals bisect angles	No	No	Yes	Yes	No	No

Property	Parallelo-gram	Rectangle	Rhombus	Square	Trapezoid	Isosceles Trapezoid
Diagonals perpendicular to each other	No	No	Yes	Yes	No	No
Base angles congruent	No	All angles congruent	No	All angles congruent	No	Yes

To prove that a quadrilateral is a parallelogram, you may do any of the following:

- Prove two pairs of opposite sides parallel.

- Prove two pairs of opposite sides congruent.

- Prove one pair of opposite sides both parallel and congruent.

- Prove the diagonals of the figure bisect each other.

MODEL PROOFS

1. Given: Quadrilateral *MATH*.
   $\overline{AH}$ bisects $\overline{MT}$ at Q.
   ∠*TMA* ≅ ∠*MTH*.
   Prove: *MATH* is a parallelogram.

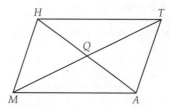

Statements

1. $\overline{AH}$ bisects $\overline{MT}$ at Q.
2. $\overline{MQ} \cong \overline{QT}$.
3. ∠*TMA* ≅ ∠*MTH*.
4. $\overline{MA} \parallel \overline{HT}$.

5. ∠*MQA* ≅ ∠*HQT*.
6. △*MQA* ≅ △*TQH*.
7. $\overline{MA} \cong \overline{HT}$.
8. *MATH* is a parallelogram.

Reasons

1. Given.
2. A bisector forms two equal line segments.
3. Given.
4. If alternate interior angles are congruent when lines are cut by a transversal, the lines are parallel.
5. Vertical angles are congruent.
6. A.S.A. ≅ A.S.A.
7. C.P.C.T.C.
8. If one pair of opposite sides of a quadrilateral is both parallel and congruent, the quadrilateral is a parallelogram.

To prove a quadrilateral is a rectangle, first prove the figure is a parallelogram and then use one of these approaches:

- Prove sides are perpendicular.

- Prove one angle is a right angle.

- Prove diagonals are congruent.

2. Given: Right triangle *ABC* with right angle
ABC. $\overline{BE}$ is a median; $\overline{BE} \cong \overline{ED}$.

Prove: *ABCD* is a rectangle.

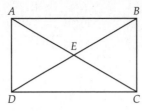

Statements	Reasons
1. Right triangle *ABC* with right angle *ABC*. $\overline{BE}$ is a median; $\overline{BE} \cong \overline{ED}$.	**1.** Given.
2. $\overline{AE} \cong \overline{EC}$.	**2.** A median divides a line segment into two congruent line segments.
3. *ABCD* is a parallelogram.	**3.** If the diagonals of a quadrilateral bisect each other, the quadrilateral is a parallelogram.
4. *ABCD* is a rectangle.	**4.** A rectangle is a parallelogram with one right angle.

To prove a quadrilateral is a rhombus, first prove it is a parallelogram and then use one of the following approaches:

- Prove one pair of consecutive sides congruent.

- Prove diagonals bisect the angles.

- Prove diagonals are perpendicular to each other.

To prove a quadrilateral is a square, first prove it is a parallelogram and then use one of the following approaches:

- Prove one pair of consecutive sides congruent and at least one right angle is present.

- Prove diagonals are congruent and one pair of consecutive sides are congruent.

- Prove diagonals are congruent and perpendicular to each other.

- Prove diagonals bisect the angles and one pair of consecutive sides are congruent.

In some proofs, you will be given a parallelogram and asked to prove another fact. In these cases, it is important to know and apply the characteristics of parallelograms detailed in the chart on pages 14–15.

3. Given: *PQRS* is a parallelogram.
$\overline{YQ}$ bisects ∠*PQR*.
$\overline{XS}$ bisects ∠*PSR*.

Prove: $\overline{SY} \cong \overline{XQ}$.

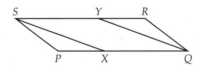

Statements	Reasons
1. *PQRS* is a parallelogram.	**1.** Given.
2. $\overline{PQ} \cong \overline{SR}$; $\overline{SP} \cong \overline{RQ}$.	**2.** Opposite sides of a parallelogram are congruent.
3. ∠*PQR* ≅ ∠*PSR*. ∠*SPQ* ≅ ∠*SRQ*.	**3.** Opposite angles of a parallelogram are congruent.
4. $\overline{YQ}$ bisects ∠*PQR*. $\overline{XS}$ bisects ∠*PSR*.	**4.** Given.

5. ∠PSX is one half ∠PSR.
∠YQR is one half ∠PQR.

6. ∠PSX ≅ ∠RQY.

7. △PSX ≅ △YQR.

8. $\overline{PX}$ ≅ $\overline{RY}$.

9. $\overline{SY}$ ≅ $\overline{XQ}$.

5. Angle bisectors divide an angle in half.

6. Halves of equals are equal.

7. A.S.A. ≅ A.S.A.

8. C.P.C.T.C.

9. Subtraction Postulate (When equals are subtracted from equals, the results are equal.)

 Practice

1. Given: Parallelogram *LOVE*.
∠*OAV* ≅ ∠*EBL*.

Prove: △*OAV* ≅ △*EBL*.
AVBL is a parallelogram.

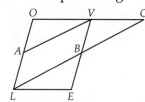

2. Given: $\overline{AC}$ is a diagonal in parallelogram *ABCD*. $\overline{AF}$ ≅ $\overline{CE}$.

Prove: $\overline{DE} \parallel \overline{BF}$.

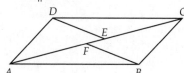

3. Given: *JUNE* is a quadrilateral.
K is the midpoint of $\overline{JE}$. *L* is the midpoint of $\overline{UN}$.
$\overline{KL}$ and $\overline{EU}$ bisect each other at *M*.

Prove: *JUNE* is a parallelogram.

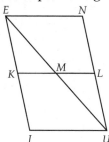

4. Given: *ABCD* is a parallelogram.
$\overline{DE} \perp \overline{AF}$. $\overline{CF} \perp \overline{AF}$.

Prove: $\overline{DE}$ ≅ $\overline{CF}$.

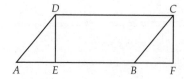

5. Given: Quadrilateral *HELP*.
$\overline{PE}$ bisects $\overline{HL}$ at *M*.
∠*EPL* ≅ ∠*PEH*.

Prove: *HELP* is a parallelogram.

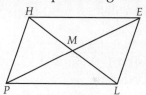

6. Given: Rhombus *ABCD*.

Prove: △*ACE* is isosceles.

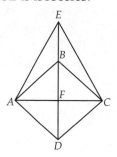

7. Given: Parallelogram *ABCD* with *H* and *F* the midpoints of $\overline{AB}$ and $\overline{DC}$ respectively.
$\overline{HG} \perp \overline{AC}$. $\overline{FE} \perp \overline{AC}$.

Prove: $\overline{HG}$ ≅ $\overline{FE}$.

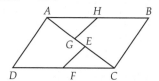

8. Given: Rectangle $ABCD$, $\overline{BNPC}$, $\overline{AEP}$, $\overline{DEN}$.
$\overline{AP} \cong \overline{DN}$.

Prove: $\triangle ABP \cong \triangle DCN$.
$\overline{AE} \cong \overline{DE}$.

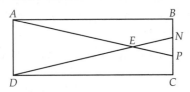

9. Given: Quadrilateral $PQRT$.
$\overline{QSV}$, $\overline{RST}$, $\overline{PTV}$. $\overline{QV}$ bisects $\overline{RT}$.
$\overline{QR} \parallel \overline{PV}$; $\overline{PT} \cong \overline{TV}$.

Prove: $PQRT$ is a parallelogram.

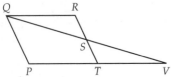

10. Given: Parallelogram $ABCD$.
$\overline{DFEB}$, $\overline{DF} \cong \overline{BE}$.

Prove: $AECF$ is a parallelogram.

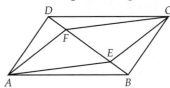

11. Given: $MATH$ is a rectangle with $YT \neq AX$.

Prove: $MY \neq HX$.

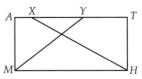

1.5 Similar Triangles

Two triangles that are the same shape, but are not necessarily the same size, are said to be **similar** ($\sim$). Similar triangles have angles that are congruent and sides that are proportional.

To prove two triangles similar, it is not necessary to prove all three angles of one triangle congruent to all three angles of the other triangle. If two angles of one triangle are congruent to two angles of another triangle, the third angles are also congruent. Thus, we can prove two triangles similar if two angles of one triangle are congruent to two angles of another triangle (A.A. Theorem).

Once the triangles are proved similar, we can find sides in one triangle proportional to corresponding sides of the other triangle.

MODEL PROOFS

1. Given: $\triangle ABC$, D is a point on $\overline{AB}$ and E is a point on $\overline{AC}$ such that $\overline{DE} \parallel \overline{BC}$.

Prove: **a.** $\triangle ADE \sim \triangle ABC$.
b. $AD \cdot AC = AB \cdot AE$.

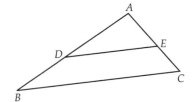

Statements	Reasons
1. $\triangle ABC$ with $\overline{DE} \parallel \overline{BC}$.	1. Given.
2. $\angle ADE \cong \angle ABC$ and $\angle AED \cong \angle ACB$.	2. If two parallel lines are cut by a transversal, the corresponding angles are congruent.
3. $\triangle ADE \sim \triangle ABC$.	3. A.A. Theorem
4. $\dfrac{AD}{AB} = \dfrac{AE}{AC}$.	4. Corresponding sides of similar triangles are in proportion.
5. $AD \cdot AC = AB \cdot AE$.	5. In a proportion, the product of the means equals the product of the extremes.

Sometimes it is difficult to decide which two triangles to use in a proof. Model Proof 2 contains several triangles. If you have difficulty identifying which triangles to prove similar, look at what needs to be proved and work backward.

Since you are ultimately asked to prove $AB \cdot AC = AD \cdot AE$, the previous step must involve a proportion. Ask yourself, "What proportion could produce the required product?" Certainly the proportion $\dfrac{AB}{AD} = \dfrac{AE}{AC}$ is a possibility.

Now, look at the four line segments involved in the proportion. (Perhaps mark them on the diagram by using two different-colored markers.) Ask yourself, "What two triangles involve these four line segments?" Now, you are ready to begin your proof.

2. Given: $\triangle ACE$, B is a point on $\overline{AC}$, D is a point on $\overline{AE}$. $\overline{BE}$ and $\overline{DC}$ intersect at F.
   $\angle ABE \cong \angle ADC$.

   Prove: $AB \cdot AC = AD \cdot AE$.

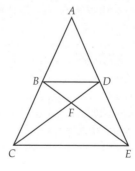

Statements	Reasons
1. $\angle ABE \cong \angle ADC$.	1. Given.
2. $\angle A \cong \angle A$.	2. Reflexive Postulate
3. $\triangle ABE \sim \triangle ADC$.	3. A.A. Theorem
4. $\dfrac{AB}{AD} = \dfrac{AE}{AC}$.	4. Corresponding sides of similar triangles are in proportion.
5. $AB \cdot AC = AD \cdot AE$.	5. In a proportion, the product of the means equals the product of the extremes.

1. Given: Right triangle MAH, with $\angle A$ a right angle, $\overline{UT} \perp \overline{AH}$.

Prove: $\dfrac{MA}{UT} = \dfrac{AH}{TH}$.

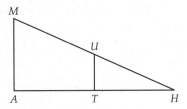

2. Given: $\overline{AB} \parallel \overline{DE}$.

Prove: $\dfrac{AB}{ED} = \dfrac{AC}{EC}$.

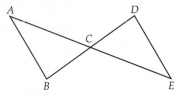

3. Given: Isosceles triangle ACE with $\overline{AC} \cong \overline{AE}$. $\angle EBA \cong \angle CDA$.

Prove: $BC \cdot DC = DE \cdot BE$.

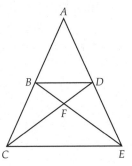

4. Given: $\triangle ACE$, B is a point on $\overline{AC}$, D is a point on $\overline{AE}$, $\angle EBC \cong \angle CDE$.

Prove: $\dfrac{FB}{FD} = \dfrac{FC}{FE}$.

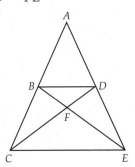

5. Given: $\overline{AE} \perp \overline{BC}$, $\angle DAC \cong \angle DEC$.

Prove: $AD \cdot EC = AC \cdot ED$.

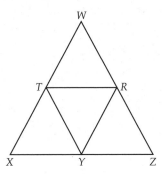

6. Given: Isosceles triangle WXZ with $\overline{WX} \cong \overline{WZ}$, and $\angle YTW \cong \angle YRW$.

Prove: $\dfrac{YT}{YR} = \dfrac{XY}{ZY}$.

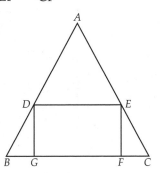

7. Given: Isosceles triangle ADE with $\overline{AD} \cong \overline{AE}$. Rectangle $DEFG$, $\overline{ADB}$, $\overline{AEC}$, $\overline{BGFC}$.

Prove: $\dfrac{DG}{EF} = \dfrac{BG}{CF}$.

8. Given: $\triangle ABC$. D, E, and F are points on $\overline{AC}$, $\overline{BC}$, and $\overline{AB}$ respectively. $\overline{AC} \parallel \overline{FE}$.

Prove: $DG \cdot FG = EG \cdot CG$.

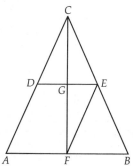

9. Given: Trapezoid $JKNM$ with bases $\overline{MN}$ and $\overline{JK}$.

Prove: $MN \cdot LJ = JK \cdot LM$.

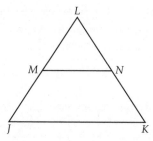

10. Given: Parallelogram $ABCD$, $\overline{CE} \perp \overline{AB}$, $\overline{CF} \perp \overline{AD}$.

Prove: $\dfrac{CF}{CE} = \dfrac{FD}{EB}$.

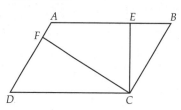

11. Given: Parallelogram $ABCD$, $\overline{BA}$ is extended through A to E, $\overline{DC}$ is extended through C to F.

Prove: $\triangle EAH \sim \triangle FCG$.

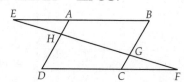

1.6 Direct Analytic Proofs

Before you begin to practice your analytic proofs, it is necessary to review a few important items.

The letter m is used to indicate the slope of a line. The **slope** is defined as the ratio of the rise of the line (the change in the y-values) to the run of the line (the change in the x-values). You should be familiar with the formula for the slope of the line connecting points (x_1, y_1) and (x_2, y_2): $m = \dfrac{\Delta y}{\Delta x} = \dfrac{y_2 - y_1}{x_2 - x_1}$.

You should also recall that, if two lines are parallel, their slopes are equal. If two lines are perpendicular, their slopes are negative reciprocals (that is, $m_1 \cdot m_2 = -1$). The converse of each of these statements also holds true: If the slopes of two lines are equal, the lines are parallel, and if the slopes of two lines are negative reciprocals, the lines are perpendicular.

You will also be using the midpoint formula in your proofs. The **midpoint** of a line segment with endpoints (x_1, y_1) and (x_2, y_2) is the point whose coordinates are the *average* of the x-coordinates and the y-coordinates of the given endpoints. The formula is

$$(x_M, y_M) = \left(\frac{x_1 + x_2}{2}, \frac{y_1 + y_2}{2} \right)$$

The distance formula is also helpful in coordinate geometry proofs. The formula for the distance, d, between any two points (x_1, y_1) and (x_2, y_2) is

$$d = \sqrt{(x_2 - x_1)^2 + (y_2 - y_1)^2}$$

There are often many correct ways to complete coordinate geometry proofs. The following chart will provide you with some ideas on how to begin your proofs.

If you are asked to prove:	Suggestions on how to do this:
Two lines parallel	*Use* the slope formula twice. (Find the slopes of the two lines.) *Determine* that the slopes are equal, therefore the lines are parallel.
Two lines perpendicular	*Use* the slope formula twice. (Find the slopes of the two lines.) *Determine* that the slopes are negative reciprocals of each other, therefore the lines are perpendicular.
A triangle is a right triangle	*Use* the slope formula twice. (Find the slopes of the legs.) *Determine* that since the slopes are negative reciprocals of each other, the lines are perpendicular, forming a right angle. This makes the triangle a right triangle. <div align="center">OR</div> *Use* the distance formula three times. (Find the lengths of the three sides.) *Determine* that the square of the length of the hypotenuse (the longest side) is equal to the sum of the squares of the lengths of the two adjacent legs, that is, use the Pythagorean theorem: ($c^2 = a^2 + b^2$).
A triangle is isosceles	*Use* the distance formula twice. (Find the lengths of two congruent sides.) *Determine* that since the lengths of two sides are equal, the triangle is isosceles.
A triangle is an isosceles right triangle	*Use* the distance formula three times. (Find right triangle the lengths of the three sides.) *Determine* that since the lengths of two sides are equal and that the square of the length of the hypotenuse is equal to the sum of the squares of the lengths of the two adjacent legs ($c^2 = a^2 + b^2$), the triangle is an isosceles right triangle. <div align="center">OR</div> *Use* the slope formula twice and the distance formula twice. (Find the slopes and the lengths of the two legs.) First, prove the triangle is a right triangle (see above), and then use the distance formula to find the lengths of the two legs of the triangle. Since the lengths of two sides are equal, the triangle is isosceles. Thus, the triangle is an isosceles right triangle.
A quadrilateral is a parallelogram	*Use* the slope formula four times. (Find the slopes of the four sides.) *Determine* that since the slopes of both pairs of opposite sides are equal, which makes both pairs of opposite sides parallel, the quadrilateral is a parallelogram. <div align="center">OR</div> *Use* the distance formula four times. (Find the lengths of the four sides.) *Determine* that since the lengths of both pairs of opposite sides are equal, the quadrilateral is a parallelogram. <div align="center">OR</div> *Use* the slope formula twice and the distance formula twice (on the same pair of opposite sides).

If you are asked to prove:	Suggestions on how to do this:
A quadrilateral is a parallelogram	*Determine* that since the slopes of one pair of opposite sides are equal, the sides are parallel. Also determine that the same pair of opposite sides have equal lengths. Since one pair of opposite sides is both parallel and equal, the quadrilateral is a parallelogram. <div align="center">OR</div>*Use* the midpoint formula twice. (Find the midpoints of the diagonals.) *Determine* that the midpoints of the diagonals are the same. Thus, the diagonals bisect each other and the quadrilateral is a parallelogram.
A quadrilateral is a rectangle	*Use* the slope formula four times. (Find the slopes of the four sides.) *Determine* that since the slopes of each pair of adjacent sides are negative reciprocals, the lines are perpendicular, which form right angles. A quadrilateral with four right angles is a rectangle. <div align="center">OR</div>First prove that the quadrilateral is a parallelogram. Then use the distance formula twice. (Find the lengths of the diagonals.) *Determine* that the parallelogram has congruent diagonals, which makes it a rectangle. <div align="center">OR</div>First prove that the quadrilateral is a parallelogram. Then use the slope formula twice. (Find the slopes of two adjacent sides.) *Determine* that the slopes of the sides are negative reciprocals, of each other, which show that they are perpendicular. Thus, the parallelogram has one right angle, which makes it a rectangle.
A quadrilateral is a rhombus	*Use* the distance formula four times. (Find the lengths of the four sides.) *Determine* that the quadrilateral is equilateral, which makes it a rhombus. <div align="center">OR</div>First prove the quadrilateral is a parallelogram and then *Use* the slope formula twice. (Find the slopes of the diagonals.) *Determine* that the quadrilateral is a parallelogram whose diagonals are perpendicular, which makes it a rhombus.
A quadrilateral is a square	*Use* the distance formula six times. (Find the lengths of the four sides and the diagonals.) *Determine* that the quadrilateral is a rhombus (since it is equilateral) with congruent diagonals, making it a square. <div align="center">OR</div>First prove the quadrilateral is a rectangle and then *Use* the distance formula twice. (Find the lengths of two adjacent sides.) *Determine* that the quadrilateral is a rectangle with one pair of congruent adjacent sides, which makes it a square. <div align="center">OR</div>First prove the quadrilateral is a rectangle and then *Use* the slope formula twice. (Find the slopes of the diagonals.) *Determine* that the quadrilateral is a rectangle whose diagonals are perpendicular, which makes it a square.

If you are asked to prove:	Suggestions on how to do this:
A quadrilateral is a trapezoid	*Use* the slope formula four times. (Find the slopes of the four sides.) *Determine* that one pair of opposite sides is parallel (the slopes are the same) and one pair of opposite sides is not parallel (the slopes are not the same).
A quadrilateral is an isosceles trapezoid	First prove the quadrilateral is a trapezoid and then *Use* the distance formula twice. (Find the lengths of the nonparallel sides.) *Determine* that the quadrilateral is a trapezoid whose nonparallel sides are equal, which makes it an isosceles trapezoid.

Note: Before beginning a proof, use graph paper to graph the given information.

1. The coordinates of the vertices of quadrilateral $ABCD$ are $A(2, 0)$, $B(6, -4)$, $C(10, 0)$, and $D(6, 4)$. Prove that quadrilateral $ABCD$ is a square.

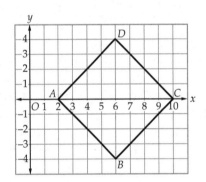

SOLUTION

Find the length of each side.

Distance formula: $d = \sqrt{(x_2 - x_1)^2 + (y_2 - y_1)^2}$

$$AB = \sqrt{(2 - 6)^2 + [0 - (-4)]^2}$$
$$= \sqrt{(-4)^2 + (4)^2}$$
$$= \sqrt{16 + 16}$$
$$= \sqrt{32}$$

$$BC = \sqrt{(6 - 10)^2 + (-4 - 0)^2}$$
$$= \sqrt{(-4)^2 + (-4)^2}$$
$$= \sqrt{16 + 16}$$
$$= \sqrt{32}$$

$CD = \sqrt{(10 - 6)^2 + (0 - 4)^2}$

$\quad = \sqrt{(4)^2 + (-4)^2}$
$\quad = \sqrt{16 + 16}$
$\quad = \sqrt{32}$

$DA = \sqrt{(6 - 2)^2 + (4 - 0)^2}$
$\quad = \sqrt{(4)^2 + (4)^2}$
$\quad = \sqrt{16 + 16}$
$\quad = \sqrt{32}$

$ABCD$ is a rhombus because all four sides are equal.
$AC = |10 - 2| = 8$
$DB = |4 - (-4)| = 8$
$ABCD$ is a square since it is a rhombus with congruent diagonals.

2. Quadrilateral $DEFG$ has vertices $D(a, b)$, $E(a + c, b)$, $F(a + c + d, b + e)$, and $G(a + d, b + e)$. Use coordinate geometry to prove that quadrilateral $ABCD$ is a parallelogram.

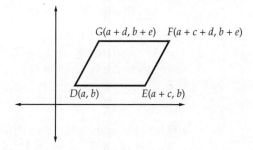

SOLUTION

Find the slope of each side.

$$m_{DE} = \frac{b - b}{(a + c) - a} = \frac{0}{c} = 0$$

$$m_{GF} = \frac{(b + e) - (b + e)}{(a + c + d) - (a + d)} = \frac{0}{c} = 0$$

Since the slopes of $\overline{DE}$ and $\overline{GF}$ are equal, we know that $\overline{DE} \parallel \overline{GF}$.

$$m_{DG} = \frac{(b + e) - b}{(a + d) - a} = \frac{e}{d}$$

$$m_{EF} = \frac{(b + e) - b}{(a + c + d) - (a + c)} = \frac{e}{d}$$

Since the slopes of $\overline{DG}$ and $\overline{EF}$ are equal, we know that $\overline{DG} \parallel \overline{EF}$.

Quadrilateral $DEFG$ is a parallelogram because both pairs of opposite sides are parallel.

1. Triangle *TRI* has vertices *T*(15, 6), *R*(5, 1), and *I*(5, 11). Use coordinate geometry to prove that triangle *TRI* is isosceles.

2. Triangle *DAN* has coordinates *D*(−10, 4), *A*(−4, 1), and *N*(−2, 5). Using coordinate geometry, prove that triangle *DAN* is a right triangle.

3. The vertices of triangle *JEN* are *J*(2, 10), *E*(6, 4), and *N*(12, 8). Use coordinate geometry to prove that triangle *JEN* is an isosceles right triangle.

4. The coordinates of the vertices of triangle *SUE* are *S*(−2, −4), *U*(2, −1) and *E*(8, −9). Using coordinate geometry, prove that
   a. triangle *SUE* is a right triangle.
   b. triangle *SUE* is *not* an isosceles right triangle.

5. Triangle *ART* has vertices *A*(*a*, *b*), *R*(*a* + *c*, *b*), and *T*(*a* + $\frac{c}{2}$, *b* + *d*). Use coordinate geometry to prove that triangle *ART* is isosceles.

6. The vertices of quadrilateral *JOHN* are *J*(−3, 1), *O*(3, 3), *H*(5, 7), and *N*(−1, 5). Use coordinate geometry to prove that quadrilateral *JOHN* is a parallelogram.

7. Quadrilateral *MIKE* has vertices *M*(4, 1), *I*(6, 4), *K*(12, 0), *E*(10, −3). Use coordinate geometry to prove that quadrilateral *MIKE* is a rectangle.

8. The coordinates of the vertices of quadrilateral *DIAN* are *D*(0, 5), *I*(3, 6), *A*(4, 3), and *N*(1, 2). Use coordinate geometry to prove that quadrilateral *DIAN* is a square.

9. Quadrilateral *NORA* has vertices *N*(3, 2), *O*(7, 0), *R*(11, 2), and *A*(7, 4).
   Use coordinate geometry to prove that
   a. quadrilateral *NORA* is a rhombus.
   b. quadrilateral *NORA* is *not* a square.

10. The vertices of quadrilateral *KAIT* are *K*(0, 0), *A*(*a*, 0), *I*(*a* + *b*, *c*), and *T*(*b*, *c*). Use coordinate geometry to prove that quadrilateral *KAIT* is a parallelogram.

11. Quadrilateral *JACK* has vertices *J*(1, −4), *A*(10, 2), *C*(8, 5), and *K*(2, 1). Use coordinate geometry to prove that
    a. quadrilateral *JACK* is a trapezoid.
    b. quadrilateral *JACK* is *not* isosceles.

12. The vertices of quadrilateral *MARY* are *M*(−3, 3), *A*(7, 3), *R*(3, 6), and *Y*(1, 6). Use coordinate geometry to prove that quadrilateral *MARY* is an isosceles trapezoid.

CHAPTER REVIEW

1. In the figure below, $\overline{EA} \perp \overline{AC}$, $\overline{DC} \perp \overline{AC}$.

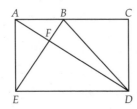

Draw as many geometric conclusions as possible based on this information.

2. Given: $\overline{AC} \cong \overline{CB}$; $\overline{CDE} \perp \overline{ADB}$; $\overline{EB} \parallel \overline{AC}$.
   Prove: $\angle ACD \cong \angle BCD$.
   $\overline{CD} \cong \overline{ED}$.

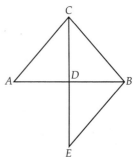

3. Given: $\overline{ABCD}$, $\overline{AB} \cong \overline{CD}$. $\angle EBC \cong \angle ECB$.

   Prove: $\triangle EAD$ is isosceles.

4. Given: Quadrilateral $ABCD$.
   Diagonal AEC bisects $\angle DAB$.
   $\angle ABE \cong \angle ADE$.

   Prove: $\overline{BC} \cong \overline{DC}$.

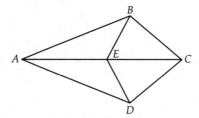

5. Given: $\triangle ABC$, $\overline{CDA}$, $\overline{CEB}$, $\overline{DFB}$,
   $\overline{EFA}$, $\overline{AD} \cong \overline{BE}$, and $\overline{AE} \cong \overline{BD}$.

   Prove: $\angle BDE \cong \angle AED$.
   $\angle FAB \cong \angle FBA$.

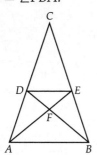

6. Given: $\triangle ABC$, $\angle ACB$ is a right angle.
   $\overline{CD} \perp \overline{AB}$.

   Prove: $\dfrac{AC}{CD} = \dfrac{BC}{BD}$.

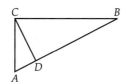

7. Given: $ABCD$ is a parallelogram.
   $\overline{BFE}$, $\overline{CDE}$, and $\overline{AFD}$.

   Prove: $AF \cdot EF = DF \cdot BF$.

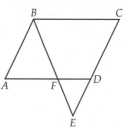

8. Given: Isosceles triangle ABC with
   $\overline{BA} \cong \overline{BC}$, $\overline{BDA}$, $\overline{CEA}$, and
   altitudes $\overline{BE}$ *and* $\overline{CD}$.

   Prove: $BC \cdot DA = CA \cdot EC$.

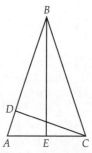

9. Given: Quadrilateral $ABCD$, diagonal $\overline{AFEC}$.
   $\overline{DE} \perp \overline{AC}$; $\overline{BF} \perp \overline{AC}$.
   $\overline{AE} \cong \overline{CF}$; $\overline{DE} \cong \overline{BF}$.

   Prove: $ABCD$ is a parallelogram.

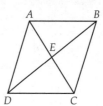

10. Given: Quadrilateral $ABCD$ with diagonals
   $\overline{AC}$ and $\overline{BD}$.
   $\overline{BD}$ bisects $\overline{AC}$ at E; $\angle CAD \cong \angle BCA$.

   Prove: $ABCD$ is a parallelogram.

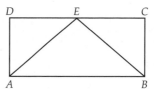

11. Given: Rectangle $ABCD$ with E the midpoint
   of $\overline{DC}$.

   Prove: $\angle EAB \cong \angle EBA$.

12. Given: Parallelogram *MATH* with $\overline{HFT}$ and
$\overline{MEA}$.
$\overline{EH}$ bisects $\angle MHT$; $\overline{FA}$ bisects $\angle MAT$.
Prove: $\overline{EA} \cong \overline{HF}$.

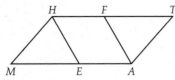

13. The points *W*(−2, 1), *X*(2, 5), *Y*(6, −1), and
Z(4, −7) form a quadrilateral. The points
A, *B*, *C*, and *D* are the midpoints of sides
$\overline{WX}$, $\overline{XY}$, $\overline{YZ}$, and $\overline{ZW}$ respectively. Using coordinate geometry, prove *ABCD* is a parallel-
ogram.

14. Given: △*ABC* with vertices *A*(1, 2), *B*(7, 0),
and *C*(3, −2).
Using coordinate geometry, prove that
△*ABC* is an isosceles right triangle.

15. Quadrilateral *QRST* has vertices *Q*(*a*, *b*), *R*(0, 0),
S(*c*, 0), and *T*(*a* + *c*, *b*). Using coordinate geometry, prove that *QRST* is a parallelogram.

16. The vertices of △*ABC* are *A*(−2, 3), *B*(0, −3),
and *C*(4, 1). Prove, by means of coordinate
geometry, that
a. △*ABC* is isosceles.
b. the median to side $\overline{BC}$ is also the altitude
to side $\overline{BC}$.

17. Quadrilateral *MATH* has vertices *M*(2, 5),
A(7, 1), *T*(2, −3), and *H*(−3, 1). Prove, by
means of coordinate geometry, that *MATH* is
a rhombus.

18. Quadrilateral *NOPE* has coordinates *N*(0, −6),
O(5, −1), *P*(3, 3), and *E*(−1, 1).
Using coordinate geometry, prove that
a. *at least* two sides are *not* congruent.
b. the diagonals, $\overline{EO}$ and $\overline{PN}$, are perpendicular.

19. Given: $\overline{TX}$ bisects $\angle CTH$; $\overline{TX}$ is not perpendicular to $\overline{CH}$.
Prove: $\angle TCH \neq \angle THC$.

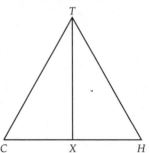

CHAPTER 2

Circles

2.1 Angles and Arcs

A **circle** is the locus of all points equidistant from a fixed point, known as the center of the circle.

A line segment from the center to any point on the circle is a **radius**. All radii of the same circle are congruent. Two circles with congruent radii are congruent.

A **chord** connects any point on the circle with any other point on the circle.

A **diameter** is a chord that passes through the center of the circle. The length of a diameter is twice the length of a radius of the circle: $d = 2r$.

In the figure at the right, $\overline{AOB}$ is a diameter, $\overline{OC}$ is a radius, and $\overline{DB}$ is a chord.

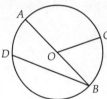

Because a circle contains 360°, the sum of the arcs around the circle must total 360°. When a diameter is drawn, it bisects the 360° of the circle into two arcs, each containing 180°.

In circle O, with diameter $\overline{AB}$ drawn, $m\overarc{ACB} = m\overarc{BHA} = 180$.

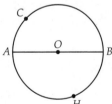

In circle O, $m\angle PON < 180$.
$\overarc{PN}$ is the minor arc with endpoints P and N.
$\overarc{PQN}$ is the major arc with endpoints P and N.

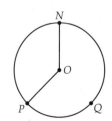

Type of Angle	Identifying Elements	Diagram	Formula	Example
Central angle	Its vertex is the center of the circle and its sides are radii.	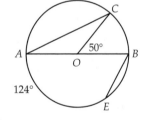	Measure of a central angle is equal to the degree measure of the intercepted arc. $m\angle AOB = m\widehat{AB}$	If $m\widehat{AB} = 74$, then $m\angle AOB = 74$.
Inscribed angle	Its vertex is on the circle; its sides are chords.		Measure of an inscribed angle is one-half the measure of the intercepted arc. $m\angle PRQ = \frac{1}{2} m\widehat{PQ}$	If $m\widehat{PQ} = 74$, $m\angle PRQ = \frac{1}{2}(74)$. $m\angle PRQ = 37$

To find the measure of an angle in a circle:

 Step 1: Locate the angle.

 Step 2: Identify the line segments that form the angle.

 Step 3: Determine which formula is needed to find the measure of the angle. (See chart above.)

 Step 4: Find the measure(s) of the arc(s) intercepted by the sides of the angle.

 MODEL PROBLEM

Given: Circle O with diameter $\overline{AOB}$, radius $\overline{OC}$, chords $\overline{BE}$, $\overline{AC}$
   $m\widehat{AE} = 124$; $m\angle COB = 50$.

Find:

a. $m\widehat{BE}$

b. $m\widehat{CB}$

c. $m\widehat{AC}$

d. $m\angle ABE$

e. $m\angle AOC$

f. $m\angle BAC$

SOLUTIONS

a. Since $\overline{AOB}$ is a diameter, $m\widehat{BE} = 180 - m\widehat{AE}$. $m\widehat{BE} = 180 - 124 = 56$.

b. Since $\angle COB$ is a central angle, the measure of the intercepted arc equals the measure of the angle. So, $m\widehat{CB} = 50$.

c. Since $\overline{AOB}$ is a diameter, $m\widehat{AC} = 180 - m\widehat{CB}$. $m\widehat{AC} = 180 - 50 = 130$.

d. Since $\angle ABE$ is an inscribed angle, its measure equals half its intercepted arc.

$$m\angle ABE = \frac{1}{2}\widehat{AE}$$
$$= \frac{1}{2}(124)$$
$$= 62$$

e. Since $\angle AOC$ is a central angle, its measure equals the measure of its intercepted arc. $m\angle AOC = m\widehat{AC} = 130$.

f. Since $\angle BAC$ is an inscribed angle, its measure is half the measure of its intercepted arc.

$$m\angle BAC = \frac{1}{2}m\widehat{CB}$$
$$= \frac{1}{2}(50)$$
$$= 25$$

Practice

In 1–6, select the numeral preceding the word or expression that best completes the sentence or answers the question.

1. In circle O, radii $\overline{OA}$ and $\overline{OB}$ are drawn. Central angle AOB measures 68. The measure of $\widehat{AB}$ is
(1) 34   (3) 112
(2) 68   (4) 136

2. In circle O, radii $\overline{OA}$ and $\overline{OB}$ are drawn. If $\widehat{AB}$ measures 122, the measure of $\angle AOB$ is
(1) 58   (3) 122
(2) 61   (4) 244

For problems 3 and 4, in circle O below, radii $\overline{OA}$ and $\overline{OB}$ and chords $\overline{AC}$ and $\overline{BC}$ are drawn.

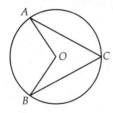

3. If $m\widehat{AB} = 86$, the measure of $\angle ACB$ equals
(1) 43   (3) 86
(2) 62   (4) 172

4. If $m\widehat{AB} = 86$, the measure of $\angle AOB$ is
(1) 43   (3) 86
(2) 62   (4) 172

5. If a central angle and an inscribed angle intercept the same arc, the ratio of the measure of the central angle to the measure of the inscribed angle is
(1) 1:1   (3) 1:2
(2) 2:1   (4) 2:2

6. Triangle XYZ is inscribed in circle O. If $m\angle XYZ = 67$ and the measure of $\widehat{XY} = 144$, which of the following is the measure of $\angle ZXY$?
(1) 82   (3) 108
(2) 162   (4) 41

7. In the diagram of circle O below, diameters $\overline{AOB}$ and $\overline{COD}$ are drawn as well as chords $\overline{AC}$, $\overline{BC}$, and $\overline{DB}$; $m\angle ACD = 32$; $m\widehat{AC} = 116$.

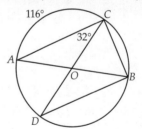

Find:
a. $m\widehat{AD}$
b. $m\widehat{BD}$
c. $m\widehat{BC}$
d. $m\angle AOC$
e. $m\angle ABD$
f. $m\angle CDB$
g. $m\angle BOD$
h. $m\angle ACB$

2.2 Angles Formed by Tangents, Secants, and Chords

There are other angles that fall inside and outside the circle, formed by various rays and line segments that intersect the circle.

A **tangent** is a line or ray that intersects the circle at exactly one point. In the diagram at the right, $\overrightarrow{PA}$ is a tangent to the circle.

A **secant** is a line or ray that passes through the circle, intersecting the circle at two points. In the figure, $\overrightarrow{PBC}$ is a secant of the circle.

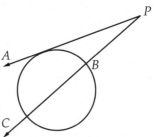

The different angles formed by such lines and rays are detailed below.

Type of Angle	Identifying Elements	Diagram	Formula	Example
Angle formed by tangent and chord	The vertex is on the circle at the point of tangency; one side is a chord; one is a tangent.		Measure of the angle is one-half the intercepted arc. $m\angle PBC = \frac{1}{2}\,m\widehat{BC}$	If $m\widehat{BC} = 110$, $m\angle PBC = \frac{1}{2}(110)$. $m\angle PBC = 55$
Angle formed by a secant and chord	The vertex is on the circle but one side of the angle lies inside the circle and one side lies outside. Angle formulas cannot be used.		Measure of the angle equals 180 − the measure of the adjacent inscribed angle. $\angle CTP$ is a straight angle, therefore, $m\angle PTH = 180 - m\angle CTH.$	If $m\widehat{CH} = 116$, $m\angle CTH = \frac{1}{2}\,\widehat{CH}$ $= \frac{1}{2}(116)$ $= 58.$ $m\angle PTH = 180 - 58$ $= 122$
Angle formed by two chords intersecting within a circle	Its vertex is inside the circle, its sides are parts of chords. The chords form vertical angles.		Measure of an angle formed by two intersecting chords equals one-half the sum of the measures of the intercepted arcs of the angle and its vertical angle. $m\angle MEJ = \frac{1}{2}(m\widehat{MJ} + m\widehat{KN})$	If $m\widehat{MJ} = 56$ and $m\widehat{KN} = 164$, $m\angle MEJ = \frac{56 + 164}{2}$ $= \frac{1}{2}(220)$ $= 110$

Type of Angle	Identifying Elements	Diagram	Formula	Example
Angle formed by a tangent and a radius	The vertex is on the circle at the point of tangency.		Angle formed is always a right angle. $m\angle OAB = 90$	$m\angle OAB = 90$
Angle formed by two tangents intersecting outside the circle	The vertex is outside the circle and the sides of the angle are tangents. The tangents divide the circle's 360° into two arcs.		Measure of the angle formed by two tangents equals one-half the difference of the measure of the intercepted arcs. $m\angle QPR = \frac{1}{2}(m\widehat{QTR} - m\widehat{QR})$ OR The angle formed by two tangents outside the circle is supplementary to the measure of the minor arc of the circle. $m\angle QPR = 180 - m\widehat{QR}$	If $m\widehat{QR} = 114$, then $m\widehat{QTR} = 360 - 114 = 246$. $m\angle QPR = \frac{246 - 114}{2} = \frac{1}{2}(132) = 66.$ If $m\widehat{QR} = 114$, then $m\angle QPR = 180 - 114 = 66$. Note: The result is the same as above. Either approach can be used.
Angle formed by two secants intersecting outside the circle	The vertex is outside the circle and the sides of the angle are secants.		The measure of an angle formed by two secants equals one-half the difference of the measures of the intercepted arcs. $m\angle RPS = \frac{1}{2}(m\widehat{SR} - m\widehat{QV})$	If $m\widehat{SR} = 128$ and $m\widehat{QV} = 32$, then $m\angle RPS = \frac{128 - 32}{2} = \frac{1}{2}(96) = 48$
Angle formed by a secant and a tangent intersecting outside the circle	The vertex is outside the circle. One ray of the angle is a secant and one is a tangent.		The measure of the angle formed by a secant and a tangent equals one-half the difference of the measures of the intercepted arcs. $m\angle APC = \frac{1}{2}(m\widehat{CA} - m\widehat{AB})$	If $m\widehat{CA} = 140$ and $m\widehat{AB} = 52$, then $m\angle APC = \frac{140 - 52}{2} = \frac{1}{2}(88) = 44$

1. Two tangents are drawn to a circle from the same external point. The major arc intercepted by the tangents measures 220. Find the measure of the angle formed by the two tangents outside the circle.

SOLUTION

We first draw the diagram, based on the description in the problem.

Two tangents are drawn to a circle from the same external point.

Once we have a simple diagram, we label the tangents $\overline{PA}$ and $\overline{PB}$. We add a point C to indicate the major arc $\overset{\frown}{ACB}$. If $m\overset{\frown}{ACB} = 220$, then $m\overset{\frown}{AB} = 360 - 220 = 140$.

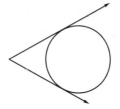 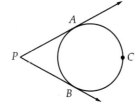

Since $\angle APB$ is formed by two tangents intersecting outside the circle, the measure of the angle is equal to one-half the difference of the major and minor arcs.

$$m\angle APB = \frac{1}{2}(m\overset{\frown}{ACB} - m\overset{\frown}{AB})$$

$$= \frac{1}{2}(220 - 140)$$

$$= \frac{1}{2}(80)$$

$$m\angle APB = 40$$

This problem can also be done by recognizing that the angle formed by two tangents is always supplementary to the minor arc formed by the two tangents.

$$m\angle APB = 180 - \overset{\frown}{AB}$$
$$= 180 - 140$$
$$m\angle APB = 40$$

2. Given: Circle O with tangent $\overrightarrow{CBA}$, secant $\overline{CDG}$.
   Chords $\overline{BE}$, $\overline{FG}$, and $\overline{EF}$. $m\angle BEF = 60$,
   $m\overset{\frown}{BE} = 110$, $m\overset{\frown}{GE} = 60$, $m\angle BCG = 50$.

   Find: **a.** $m\overset{\frown}{BDF}$ **c.** $m\overset{\frown}{BD}$ **e.** $m\angle CHE$
   b. $m\overset{\frown}{FG}$ **d.** $m\angle DGF$ **f.** $m\angle ABE$

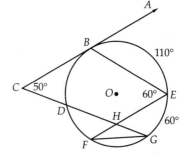

SOLUTION

a. Since $\angle BEF$ is an inscribed angle, its measure is half the measure of its intercepted arc.

$$m\overset{\frown}{BDF} = 2 \cdot m\angle BEF$$
$$m\overset{\frown}{BDF} = 2 \cdot 60$$
$$m\overset{\frown}{BDF} = 120$$

b. To find the measure of the remaining arc, recall that the total of the measures of all arcs of a circle must equal 360. $m\overset{\frown}{FG} = 360 - (m\overset{\frown}{BE} + m\overset{\frown}{EG} + m\overset{\frown}{BF})$.

$$m\overset{\frown}{FG} = 360 - (110 + 60 + 120)$$
$$m\overset{\frown}{FG} = 360 - 290$$
$$m\overset{\frown}{FG} = 70$$

c. $\angle ACG$ is formed by a tangent and a secant so its measure is equal to one half the difference of the measures of the intercepted arcs.

$$m\angle ACG = \tfrac{1}{2}(m\overset{\frown}{BEG} - m\overset{\frown}{BD})$$
$$50 = \tfrac{1}{2}(170 - m\overset{\frown}{BD})$$
$$100 = 170 - m\overset{\frown}{BD}$$
$$m\overset{\frown}{BD} = 70$$

d. Since $\angle DGF$ is an inscribed angle, its measure is equal to half the measure of its intercepted arc.

$$m\overset{\frown}{BDF} = 120$$
$$m\overset{\frown}{BD} = 70$$
$$m\overset{\frown}{DF} = 120 - 70$$
$$m\overset{\frown}{DF} = 50$$
$$m\angle DGF = \tfrac{1}{2}m\overset{\frown}{DF}$$
$$= \tfrac{1}{2}(50) = 25$$

e. $\angle CHE$ is an angle formed by two intersecting chords, therefore its measure is equal to half the sum of the measures of the intercepted arcs of the angle and its vertical angle.

$$m\angle CHE = \tfrac{1}{2}(m\overset{\frown}{DBE} + m\overset{\frown}{FG})$$
$$m\angle CHE = \tfrac{1}{2}(180 + 70)$$
$$= \tfrac{1}{2}(250)$$
$$m\angle CHE = 125$$

f. $\angle ABE$ is an angle formed by a tangent and a chord. Its measure is equal to one-half the measure of the intercepted arc.

$$m\angle ABE = \tfrac{1}{2}m\overset{\frown}{BE}$$
$$m\angle ABE = \tfrac{1}{2}(110)$$
$$m\angle ABE = 55$$

In 1–6, select the numeral preceding the word or expression that best completes the sentence or answers the question.

1. Chords $\overline{MN}$ and $\overline{PQ}$ intersect at point R in circle O. If $m\widehat{MQ} = 112$ and $m\widehat{PN} = 80$, what is the measure of $\angle MRQ$?
   (1) 32   (3) 112
   (2) 96   (4) 192

2. From an external point, two tangents are drawn to a circle. If the tangent intercepts a major arc of 204°, the measure of the angle formed by the tangents is
   (1) 24   (3) 102
   (2) 48   (4) 156

3.

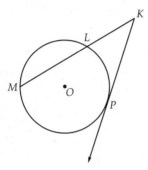

   In the diagram above, secant $\overline{KLM}$ and tangent $\overline{KP}$ are drawn to circle O. If the measure of $\widehat{LP}$ is 50 and the measure of $\angle PKM$ is 47, the measure of $\widehat{MP}$ is
   (1) 94   (3) 188
   (2) 144   (4) 310

4.

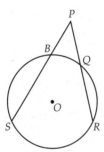

   In circle O, secants $\overline{PBS}$ and $\overline{PQR}$ are drawn. If $m\angle SPR$ is 65 and the measure of $\widehat{BQ}$ is 43, the measure of $\widehat{SR}$ is
   (1) 87   (3) 130
   (2) 107   (4) 173

5. In circle O chords $\overline{CH}$ and $\overline{AD}$ intersect at point Q inside the circle. If $m\angle AQH = 51$ and the measure of $\widehat{CD}$ is 64, the measure of $\widehat{AH}$ is
   (1) 38   (3) 102
   (2) 51   (4) 115

6. In circle O tangent $\overline{PB}$ intersects radius $\overline{OB}$. The measure of $\angle OBP$ is
   (1) 90   (3) equal to the intercepted arc.
   (2) 45   (4) unable to be determined.

7. In circle O tangent $\overline{PA}$, secant $\overline{PBC}$, diameter $\overline{AOC}$, and chords $\overline{AD}$ and $\overline{DC}$ are drawn. $m\angle APC = 57$; $m\widehat{DC} = 34$.

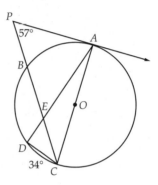

   Find:
   a. $m\widehat{BA}$
   b. $m\widehat{BD}$
   c. $m\angle ACD$
   d. $m\angle BED$
   e. $m\angle PCA$
   f. $m\angle PAD$

2.3 Measurement of Tangents, Secants, and Chords

Not only can we find the measure of angles in a circle, we can also determine the length of line segments within the circle, given certain information. To do this, we make use of key formulas based on the concepts of similar triangles.

- Two tangents drawn to a circle from the same external point are congruent at the point of tangency.

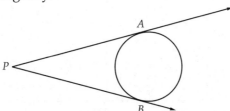

That is, $\overline{PA} \cong \overline{PB}$. (If the tangents continue past the circle, the continued lengths are not necessarily congruent.)

This concept is often used in perimeter problems involving circles inscribed in polygons.

 MODEL PROBLEM

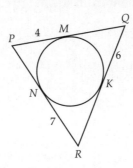

If $PM = 4$, $QK = 6$, and $RN = 7$, find the perimeter of $\triangle PQR$.

SOLUTION
Since $\overline{PM}$ and $\overline{PN}$, as well as $\overline{QK}$ and $\overline{QM}$, and $\overline{RN}$ and $\overline{RK}$ are tangents drawn from the same external point, $\overline{PM} \cong \overline{PN}$; $\overline{QK} \cong \overline{QM}$; $\overline{RN} \cong \overline{RK}$.

Therefore, the perimeter of $\triangle PQR$ is double the length of the tangents already given.

$$\text{Perimeter of } \triangle PQR = 2(PM + QK + RN)$$
$$= 2(4 + 6 + 7) = 34$$

Or, you could add the lengths of all six segments to find the perimeter.

$$\text{Perimeter of } \triangle PQR = PM + PN + QK + QM + RN + RK$$
$$= 4 + 4 + 6 + 6 + 7 + 7$$
$$= 34$$

- If a tangent and a secant are drawn to a circle from the same external point, the product of the lengths of the whole secant and its external segment will equal the square of the length of the tangent.

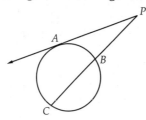

In other words, $PC \cdot PB = (PA)^2$.

MODEL PROBLEMS

1. If $PA = 6$, $PB = 4$ in the diagram above, find the length of PC.

SOLUTION

$$PC \cdot PB = (PA)^2$$
$$PC \cdot 4 = 6^2$$
$$4PC = 36$$
$$PC = 9$$

Note: Sometimes you may be asked for the length of the secant's internal segment. In that case, subtract the length of the external segment from the length of the whole secant.

2. Secant $\overline{PEQ}$ and tangent $\overline{PF}$ are drawn to circle O.

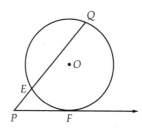

Not drawn to scale.

If $PF = 12$ and $PE = 8$, find the length of QE.

SOLUTION

Since the length of the internal segment of the secant, QE, is not a part of the traditional formula, we need to solve for the length of PQ and subtract the length of PE to find the length of QE.

$$PQ \cdot PE = (PF)^2 \qquad\qquad QE = PQ - PE$$
$$PQ \cdot 8 = 12^2 \qquad\qquad\quad QE = 18 - 8$$
$$8PQ = 144 \qquad\qquad\qquad QE = 10$$
$$PQ = 18$$

- If two secants are drawn to a circle from the same external point, the product of the length of the whole secant and the length of the external segment of one secant equals the product of the length of the whole secant and the length of the external segment of the second secant.

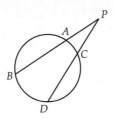

In other words, $PD \cdot PC = PB \cdot PA$.

 MODEL PROBLEM

If $PD = 15$, $PB = 12$, and $PA = 5$, find the length of PC.

$$PD \cdot PC = PB \cdot PA$$
$$15 \cdot PC = 12 \cdot 5$$
$$15 \cdot PC = 60$$
$$PC = 4$$

- If two chords intersect in a circle, the product of the lengths of the segments of one chord equals the product of the lengths of the segments of the other chord.
$$AE \cdot EB = CE \cdot ED$$

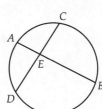

 MODEL PROBLEMS

1. In the circle above (not drawn to scale), chords $\overline{AB}$ and $\overline{CD}$ intersect at E. $AE = 6$ and $EB = 8$. If $CE = 4$, find the length of ED.

SOLUTION

$$AE \cdot EB = CE \cdot ED$$
$$6 \cdot 8 = 4 \cdot ED$$
$$48 = 4 \cdot ED$$
$$12 = ED$$

Sometimes these problems give rise to quadratic equations when the length of the whole chord rather than a segment of the chord is given, as in the problem on the next page.

2. In circle O, chords $\overline{MN}$ and $\overline{KL}$ intersect at Q. If $MN = 16$, $KQ = 6$, and $LQ = 8$, find the length of MQ, given that $MQ < NQ$.

SOLUTION
Draw and label a diagram.

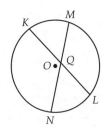

Let $MQ = x$
Let $NQ = 16 - x$

$$MQ \cdot NQ = KQ \cdot LQ$$
$$x(16 - x) = 6 \cdot 8$$
$$16x - x^2 = 48$$
$$0 = x^2 - 16x + 48$$
$$0 = (x - 12)(x - 4)$$
$$0 = x - 12 \quad 0 = x - 4$$
$$x = 12 \qquad x = 4$$

Since $MQ < NQ$, $MQ = 4$.

- If the diameter of a circle is perpendicular to a chord, it bisects the chord.

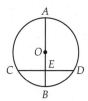

In other words, in circle O, if diameter $\overline{AOB} \perp$ chord $\overline{CD}$ at E, $CE = ED$.

1. In circle O above, if diameter $\overline{AOB} \perp$ chord $\overline{CD}$ at E and $CD = 16$, find the length of CE.

SOLUTION
Since $\overline{AOB}$ bisects $\overline{CD}$, $CE = ED = 8$.

Note: Since perpendicular lines form right angles, if the radii $\overline{CO}$ and $\overline{DO}$ are drawn, right triangles are formed as in the figure on the next page. This setup gives rise to problems that can be solved using the Pythagorean formula.

2. In circle O, diameter $\overline{MON} \perp$ chord $\overline{QR}$ at T, $MN = 34$ and $QR = 30$. Find the length of OT.

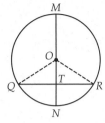

SOLUTION

Since $\overline{MN}$ is a diameter, the length of any radius is half MN, so $OQ = OR = ON = 17$.
Chord $\overline{QR}$ is bisected by the diameter, so $QT = TR = 15$. Using the Pythagorean formula,

$$QO^2 = QT^2 + OT^2$$
$$17^2 = 15^2 + OT^2$$
$$289 = 225 + OT^2$$
$$64 = OT^2$$
$$8 = OT$$

Practice

In 1–11, select the numeral preceding the word or expression that best completes the sentence or answers the question.

1. In circle O, chords $\overline{AB}$ and $\overline{CD}$ intersect at E. If $AE = 6$; $BE = 16$; $CE = 12$, which of the following is the length of $\overline{CD}$?
(1) 8   (3) 18
(2) 12   (4) 20

2. In the accompanying diagram, circle O is inscribed in triangle ABC so that the circle is tangent to $\overline{AB}$ at F, to $\overline{BC}$ at E, and to $\overline{AC}$ at D.

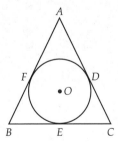

If $AD = 6$, $BF = 7$, and $CE = 10$, what is the perimeter of triangle ABC?
(1) 23   (3) 69
(2) 46   (4) 23π

3. In circle O in the accompanying diagram, the length of $\overline{OE}$ is 8 and the length of chord $\overline{AB}$ is 30.

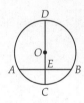

If $\overline{CD}$ is perpendicular to $\overline{AB}$ at E, the length of $\overline{CO}$ is which of the following?
(1) 17   (3) 12
(2) 16   (4) 8

4. Secant $\overline{ADC}$ and tangent $\overline{AB}$ are drawn to circle O from external point A. If $AB = 12$ and $AD = 6$, the length of AC is
(1) 12   (3) 24
(2) 18   (4) 30

5. Secants $\overline{PAB}$ and $\overline{PCD}$ are drawn to a circle from an external point P. If $PA = 4$, $AB = 16$, and $PC = 8$, the length of $\overline{PCD}$ is which of the following?
(1) 8   (3) 20
(2) 10   (4) 80

6. In a circle, a chord of 30 centimeters bisects a chord of 18 centimeters. The length of the shorter segment of the 30-centimeter chord is
   (1) 3   (3) 12
   (2) 10   (4) 27

7. In the accompanying diagram, $\overline{PC}$ is tangent to circle O at C and $\overline{PAB}$ is a secant.

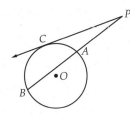

   If $PC = 10$ and $PA = 4$, the length of $\overline{PAB}$ equals
   (1) 6   (3) 25
   (2) 21   (4) 40

8. In circle O, chords $\overline{CH}$ and $\overline{AD}$ intersect at Z. If $AZ = a$, $ZH = z$, and $CZ = c$, what is the length of $\overline{DZ}$ in terms of a, z, and c?
   (1) azc (3) $\frac{cz}{a}$
   (2) $\frac{az}{c}$ (4) $\frac{ac}{z}$

9. In circle O, chords $\overline{AB}$ and $\overline{CD}$ intersect at E. If $AE = 6$, $BE = 12$, and $CE = 8$, CD measures
   (1) 4   (3) 17
   (2) 9   (4) 18

10. $\overline{PA}$ and $\overline{PB}$ are tangents drawn to circle O from external point P. If $PA = 8r - 7$ and $PB = 4r + 13$, PA equals
    (1) 5   (3) 33
    (2) 7   (4) 41

11. In circle O below, the length of the radius is 41 and the length of chord $\overline{AEB}$ is 80.

    If $\overline{CO}$ is perpendicular to $\overline{AEB}$ at E, find the length of $\overline{EO}$.
    (1) 9   (3) 20.5
    (2) 20   (4) 39

12. Secant $\overline{XYZ}$ and tangent $\overline{XA}$ are drawn to circle O from external point X. If $XA = 16$ and $XY = 8$, find the length of $\overline{YZ}$.

13. Secants $\overline{PAB}$ and $\overline{PCD}$ are drawn to a circle from an external point P. If $PA = 5$, $AB = 25$, and $PC = 6$, find the length of $\overline{CD}$.

14. In a circle, a chord of 50 centimeters bisects a chord of 40 centimeters. Find the length of the shorter segment of the 50-centimeter chord.

15. Quadrilateral $PADB$ circumscribes circle O. If $PM = 4$, $AC = 7$, $DN = 6$, and $BQ = 5$, find the perimeter of $PADB$.

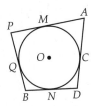

16. Tangent $\overline{PA}$ and secant $\overline{PBC}$ are drawn to circle O from external point P. If $PC = 24$ and $PB = 6$, find the length of $\overline{PA}$.

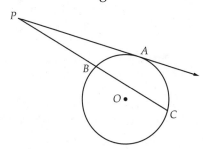

17. In circle O, diameter $\overline{AOB} \perp$ chord $\overline{CD}$ at E. If $AOB = 40$ and $ED = 12$, find the length of $\overline{OE}$.

18. In circle O, chords $\overline{LM}$ and $\overline{NP}$ intersect at Q. If $LQ = 12$, $QM = 8$, and $NP = 22$, find the lengths of $\overline{NQ}$ and $\overline{QP}$ given that $NQ < QP$.

19. Chords $\overline{GH}$ and $\overline{JK}$ in circle O intersect at W. If $GW = x$, $WH = x + 8$, $JW = 6$, and $KW = 8$, find the value of x and the length of $\overline{GH}$.

20. In circle O, diameter $\overline{AOB}$ and chord $\overline{WZ}$ are drawn. They intersect at X. If $AX = 20$, $XB = 5$, $XW = 10$, and $XZ = 10$, determine whether or not $\overline{AOB} \perp \overline{WZ}$. Explain your reasoning.

2.4 Circle Proofs

Circles not only contain various angles, chords, radii, and diameters, but often congruent or similar triangles.

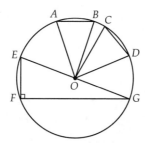

Triangles within circles have the same properties and applicable theorems as triangles outside of circles. In addition to the theorems for congruence and similarities covered in Chapter 1, the following theorems are often used in circle proofs:

- All radii of a circle are congruent.
- In a circle, congruent chords have congruent arcs.
- In a circle, congruent arcs have congruent chords.
- In a circle, congruent central angles have congruent arcs.
- In a circle, inscribed angles that intercept the same arc are congruent.
- In a circle, inscribed angles that intercept equal arcs are congruent.
- Two circles with congruent radii are congruent.
- A triangle inscribed in a semicircle is a right triangle.
- An angle inscribed in a semicircle is a right angle.

MODEL PROOFS

1. *Congruent Triangles*

Given: Circle O with diameters $\overline{AOB}$ and $\overline{COD}$, and chords $\overline{AC}$ and $\overline{DB}$.
Prove: $\overline{AC} \cong \overline{DB}$.

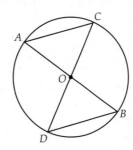

Statements	Reasons
1. Circle O with diameters $\overline{AOB}$ and $\overline{COD}$, and chords $\overline{AC}$ and $\overline{DB}$.	1. Given.
2. $\overline{OA} \cong \overline{OB} \cong \overline{OC} \cong \overline{OD}$.	2. All radii of a circle are congruent.
3. $\angle AOC \cong \angle DOB$.	3. Vertical angles are congruent.
4. $\triangle AOC \cong \triangle BOD$.	4. S.A.S. $\cong$ S.A.S.
5. $\overline{AC} \cong \overline{DB}$.	5. Corresponding parts of congruent triangles are congruent. (C.P.C.T.C.)

2. *Similar Triangles*

Given: Circle O with diameter $\overline{AOD}$,
tangent $\overrightarrow{CA}$; $m\widehat{AB} = 2m\widehat{AE}$.

Prove: a. $\triangle OAC \sim \triangle DBA$.

       b. $AD \cdot AC = OC \cdot BD$.

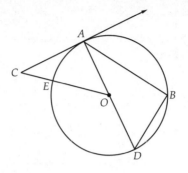

Statements	Reasons
1. Circle O; diameter $\overline{AOD}$, tangent $\overrightarrow{CA}$; $m\widehat{AB} = 2m\widehat{AE}$.	1. Given.
2. $m\angle AOC = m\widehat{AE}$.	2. The measure of a central angle equals the measure of its intercepted arc.
3. $m\widehat{AE} = \frac{1}{2}m\widehat{AB}$.	3. Equals divided by equals are equal.
4. $m\angle AOC = \frac{1}{2}m\widehat{AB}$.	4. Transitive postulate.
5. $m\angle BDA = \frac{1}{2}m\widehat{AB}$.	5. The measure of an inscribed angle equals half the measure of its intercepted arc.
6. $m\angle AOC = m\angle BDA$.	6. Quantities equal to equal quantities are equal.
7. $\overrightarrow{DA} \perp \overrightarrow{CA}$.	7. A tangent is perpendicular to a diameter at point of tangency.
8. $\angle OAC$ is a right angle.	8. Perpendiculars form right angles.
9. $\angle DBA$ is a right angle.	9. An angle inscribed in a semicircle is a right angle.
10. $\angle OAC \cong \angle DBA$.	10. All right angles are congruent.
11. $\triangle OAC \sim \triangle DBA$.	11. A.A. $\cong$ A.A.
12. $\dfrac{CO}{DA} = \dfrac{AC}{AB}$.	12. Corresponding sides of similar triangles are proportional.
13. $AD \cdot AC = OC \cdot BD$	13. In a proportion, the product of the means equals the product of the extremes.

Practice

1.

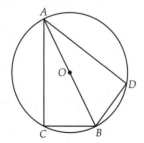

Given: A is the midpoint of $\widehat{CD}$; $\overline{AOB}$ is a diameter.

Prove: $\overline{CB} \cong \overline{DB}$.

2.

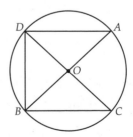

Given: Circle O, with chords $\overline{DA}$, $\overline{AB}$, $\overline{DC}$, $\overline{DB}$, and $\overline{BC}$. $\overline{AD} \cong \overline{CB}$.

Prove: $\overline{AB} \cong \overline{CD}$.

3.

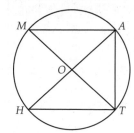

Given: Circle O with diameters $\overline{MOT}$ and $\overline{AOH}$.
Prove: $\overline{MA} \cong \overline{HT}$.

4.

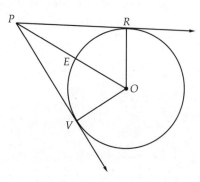

Given: Circle O, tangents $\overrightarrow{PR}$, $\overrightarrow{PV}$.
Prove: $\angle RPO \cong \angle VPO$.

5.

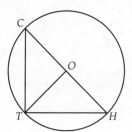

Given: Circle O with T as the midpoint of $\overarc{CH}$.
Prove: $\dfrac{CT}{CH} = \dfrac{TO}{TH}$.

6.

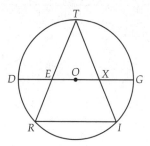

Given: Circle O with diameter $\overline{DOG}$; $\overarc{DR} \cong \overarc{GI}$.
Prove: $TX \cdot RI = EX \cdot TI$.

7.

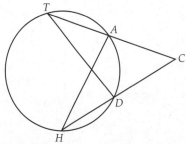

Given: $CT \ne CH$.
Prove: $HA \ne TD$.

CHAPTER REVIEW

In 1–6, select the numeral preceding the choice that best answers the question.

1. In circle O, find the measure of angle x.

(1) 20   (3) 50
(2) 25   (4) 100

2. In circle O, chords $\overline{AB}$ and $\overline{CD}$ intersect at E. If AE is 2 inches longer than EB, $CE = 8$ inches, and $ED = 3$ inches, find the length of AB.
(1) 4 in.   (3) 10 in.
(2) 6 in.   (4) 24 in.

3. In circle O, m$\overset{\frown}{BC}$ = 55. Find m$\angle AOB$.

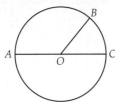

    (1) 27.5   (3) 125
    (2) 55   (4) 135

4. In circle O, chords $\overline{AB}$ and $\overline{CD}$ intersect at E. If m$\overset{\frown}{AC}$ = 100, and m$\angle AEC$ = 70, find m$\overset{\frown}{BD}$.
    (1) 40   (3) 100
    (2) 70   (4) 150

5. Isosceles triangle ABC is inscribed in circle O. If the measure of the vertex angle $\angle ABC$ is 80, find the measure of minor arc $\overset{\frown}{AB}$.
    (1) 40   (3) 80
    (2) 50   (4) 100

6. In the given figure, tangents $\overline{PA}$ and $\overline{PB}$ are drawn to circle O. If m$\angle APB$ = 50, find m$\overset{\frown}{ACB}$.

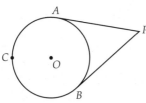

    (1) 260   (3) 130
    (2) 230   (4) 100

7. In a circle, diameter $\overline{RS}$ is extended through S to an external point T. Secant $\overline{TUV}$ is then drawn. If RS = 18, ST = 6, and UT = 9, find TV.

8. Find m$\angle QRS$.

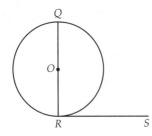

9. If $\angle MTB$ = 23 and m$\overset{\frown}{AH}$ = 58, find m$\overset{\frown}{MB}$.

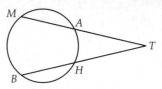

10. Two tangents are drawn to circle O from an external point P. If the major arc has a measure of 200°, find the measure of angle P.

11. If TA = 6, AN = 8 and EG = 10, find the perimeter of triangle TNE.

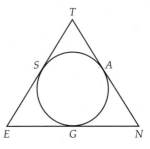

12. In circle O, tangent $\overline{PC}$ and secant $\overline{PAB}$ are drawn from external point P. If PA = 9 and AB = 7, find PC.

13. Given: Circle O with diameter $\overline{FE}$ extended to point C. Secant $\overline{CBA}$, tangent $\overline{CD}$, chord $\overline{FA}$, and diameter $\overline{GOB}$ are drawn. m$\overset{\frown}{AF}$ = 100, m$\overset{\frown}{ED}$ = 55, B is the midpoint of $\overset{\frown}{AE}$, $\overline{FA}\|\overline{GB}$.

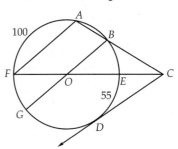

Find: **a.** m$\overset{\frown}{AB}$ **e.** m$\angle FAC$
        b. m$\overset{\frown}{FG}$ **f.** m$\angle GBC$
        c. m$\angle BOE$ **g.** m$\angle FCD$
        d. m$\angle AFE$

14. Given: Circle O, secants $\overline{MJE}$ and $\overline{MKA}$ are drawn. Chord $\overline{FB}$ intersects secants $\overline{MJE}$ and $\overline{MKA}$ in points G and C respectively. Chord $\overline{BK}$ and tangent $\overline{KL}$ are drawn. $\overline{EJ}\perp\overline{FB}$, $m\widehat{EF} = 30$, $m\widehat{FJ} = m\widehat{EA}$, $m\angle AKB = 20$, and $m\angle ACB = 65$.

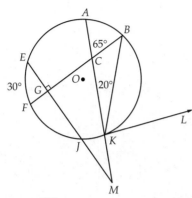

Find: **a.** $m\widehat{AB}$ **d.** $m\angle FBK$
      b. $m\widehat{FJ}$ **e.** $m\angle EMA$
      c. $m\widehat{JK}$ **f.** $m\angle BKL$

15. Given: Circle O, diameter $\overline{AB}$ is extended through B to point C, secant $\overline{CED}$ and chords $\overline{AE}$, $\overline{AF}$, and $\overline{FB}$ are drawn. $m\widehat{EB} = 2\cdot m\widehat{DE}$, and $m\widehat{AD} = 3\cdot m\widehat{DE}$.

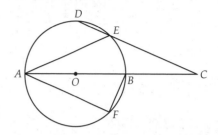

Find: **a.** $m\widehat{DE}$ **d.** $m\angle AEC$
      b. $m\angle DEA$ **e.** $m\angle AFB$
      c. $m\angle DCA$

CHAPTER 3

The Complex Number System

3.1 Types of Numbers

Probably the first numbers you learned about were the **counting numbers**: 1, 2, 3, . . . (The three dots indicate that the numbers continue forever.) Another name for counting numbers is **natural numbers**. If we include zero, we get the set of **whole numbers**. The whole numbers are: 0, 1, 2, 3, . . .

By extending the set of whole numbers in the opposite direction, we now have the set of **integers**. The integers are . . . $-3, -2, -1, 0, 1, 2, 3, \ldots$ Notice the three dots to the right of 3 and to the left of -3. This indicates that the set of integers continues in both directions.

To include numbers between integers, we define the set of rational numbers. A **rational number** is a number in the form $\frac{a}{b}$, where a and b are both integers, and $b \neq 0$. Note that the set of rational numbers also includes the set of integers, since every integer a can be expressed as $\frac{a}{1}$.

If a number is not rational, it is said to be irrational. We can see that an irrational number is a number that cannot be expressed in the form $\frac{a}{b}$, where a and b are both integers, and $b \neq 0$. However, rather than stating what irrational numbers are not, it is better to state what irrational numbers are. An **irrational number** is a nonrepeating, nonterminating decimal. Examples of irrational numbers include π, $\sqrt{2}$, $\sqrt{5}$, 0.12112211122211112222 . . . These numbers never end and never repeat.

Note: Although we often use $\frac{22}{7}$ as an approximation for π, it is only an approximation since π is an irrational number.

A calculator can be used to find the approximate rational value of many irrational numbers.

Enter: (2nd) $\sqrt{}$ 3 (ENTER)
Display: 1.732050808

The value can be rounded to ten-thousandths to give
   $\sqrt{3} \approx 1.7321$.

Real Numbers

The set of **real numbers** is the union of the set of rational numbers and the set of irrational numbers. Every real number can be associated with a point on the number line and every point on the number line can be associated with a real number. On the number line, numbers increase from left to right.

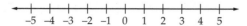

Looking at the number line, we can see that the set of real numbers contains more points than are illustrated in the figure above. The **Property of Density** assures us that there is always another real number between any two real numbers.

For example, the number -1.34 lies between -1 and -2. The fraction $\frac{19}{4}$ can be changed to the decimal 4.75, which lies between 4 and 5. Since $\sqrt{7} \approx 2.645751311$, it lies between 2 and 3. We know that $\pi \approx 3.141592654$, so it lies between 3 and 4. The positions of these numbers on the number line are illustrated below.

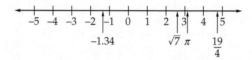

 MODEL PROBLEM

Match each point with the letter on the number line that shows its position.

$$\sqrt{10},\ -\frac{4}{9},\ \sqrt{2},\ -\sqrt{15},\ 4.6,\ -\frac{9}{5},\ \sqrt{22}$$

SOLUTION

The easiest way to determine the placement of each of the points on the number line is to change it to a decimal.

Use a calculator to approximate each value.

$\sqrt{10} \approx 3.16227766$ This point lies between 3 and 4 and matches point E.

$-\frac{4}{9} \approx -0.44444444$ This point lies between 0 and -1 and matches point C

$\sqrt{2} \approx 1.414213562$ This point lies between 1 and 2 and matches point D.

$-\sqrt{15} \approx -3.872983346$ This point lies between -3 and -4 and matches point A.

4.6   This point lies between 4 and 5. Since there are two points indicated between 3 and 4, we'll have to wait to see which point matches which letter.

$-\frac{9}{5} = -1.8$ This point lies between -1 and -2 and matches point B.

$\sqrt{22} \approx 4.6904156$ This point is larger than 4.6, so 4.6 matches point F and $\sqrt{22}$ matches point G.

Properties of the Real Numbers

For all real numbers a, b, and c

Commutative Property of Addition	$a + b = b + a$
Commutative Property of Multiplication	$ab = ba$
Associative Property of Addition	$(a + b) + c = a + (b + c)$
Associative Property of Multiplication	$(ab)c = a(bc)$
Distributive Property	$a(b + c) = ab + ac$
Addition Property of Zero	$a + 0 = 0 + a = a$ (0 is the *additive identity*)
Multiplication Property of Zero	$a \cdot 0 = 0 \cdot a = 0$
Multiplication Property of One	$a \cdot 1 = 1 \cdot a = a$ (1 is the *multiplicative identity*)
Additive Inverse	$a + (-a) = 0$
Multiplicative Inverse	$a \cdot \frac{1}{a} = 1$
Closure	$a + b$ is a real number ab is a real number

 Practice

In 1–8, determine whether the number is rational or irrational. Justify each answer.

1. -0.5

2. $0.45454545\ldots$

3. $\sqrt{25}$

4. $\sqrt{35}$

5. 0

6. $0.12345678\ldots$

7. π

8. $\sqrt{\dfrac{1}{2}}$

In 9–15, determine whether the statement is true or false. Explain your reasoning.

9. All rational numbers are real numbers.
10. All real numbers are rational numbers.
11. All counting numbers are whole numbers.
12. All whole numbers are counting numbers.
13. A number can be both rational and irrational.
14. A number can be both real and irrational.
15. The set of whole numbers is the same as the set of natural numbers.

In 16–19, name two consecutive integers between which each number is located.

16. π
17. $\sqrt{2}$
18. $\sqrt{\dfrac{1}{2}}$
19. $\sqrt{101}$

In 20–25, arrange each set of numbers in order from the least to the greatest. If two numbers are equal to each other, state that they are equal.

20. $0.4, 4.4, 0.444, 0.404$

21. $\sqrt{5}, 2\sqrt{2}, \dfrac{\sqrt{8}}{2}, \dfrac{8}{\sqrt{5}}$

22. $\frac{7}{3}, \sqrt{7}, \sqrt{\frac{7}{3}}, \sqrt{3\cdot7}$

23. $\frac{1}{2}, \sqrt{\frac{1}{2}}, \frac{1}{\sqrt{2}}, \sqrt{2}$

24. $\pi, \frac{22}{7}, 3.14$

25. $\frac{1}{3}, \frac{3}{10}, 0.33333, 0.\overline{3}, \frac{31}{100}$

26. Which letter on the number line corresponds to $\sqrt{\frac{7}{3}}$?

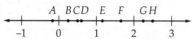

27. Name the letter on the number line that corresponds to each number.

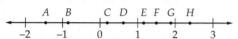

    a. $\frac{1}{4}$

    b. $\sqrt{\frac{1}{4}}$

    c. $\sqrt{3}$

    d. $\sqrt{\frac{1}{3}}$

28. The letters are equally spaced on the number line. H corresponds to 0 and L corresponds to 1. For each number, find the corresponding letter on the number line. If the number lies between two points, name both letters.

    a. $-\frac{7}{16}$

    b. $\sqrt{2}$

    c. $-\sqrt{3}$

    d. -1.65

    e. $\pi - 1$

    f. $\frac{8}{3}$

    g. $\sqrt{2.25}$

29. Write a number between 0.201 and 0.202.

30. Are the integers dense? Use an example to explain your answer.

31. Use the distributive property to find $12 \cdot 37$.

In 32 and 33, select the numeral preceding the word or expression that best answers the question.

32. Which equation illustrates the commutative property of multiplication?
(1) $2 + 3 = 3 + 2$
(2) $2(3 \cdot 4) = (2 \cdot 3)(4)$
(3) $(2 \cdot 3)4 = 4(2 \cdot 3)$
(4) $2(3 + 4) = 2 \cdot 3 + 2 \cdot 4$

33. What is the best sequence of names to identify the elements of this set of numbers?
$$\left\{0.67, 3\frac{1}{9}, -\sqrt{4}, \sqrt{8}, 0.1\overline{4}\right\}$$
(1) real, rational, irrational, irrational, irrational
(2) rational, real, integer, irrational, irrational
(3) rational, rational, real, real, irrational
(4) rational, rational, integer, irrational, rational

34. Is the set of integers closed under division? Use an example to explain your answer.

35. **a.** What is the additive inverse of $\frac{2}{3}$?

    b. What is the multiplicative inverse of $\frac{2}{3}$?

3.2 The Imaginary Unit and Powers of i

An equation such as $x = \sqrt{-9}$ has no solution in the real number system. However, a solution does exist in the system of imaginary numbers. By definition, $\sqrt{-1}$ is defined as i, the imaginary unit. Since $\sqrt{-9} = \sqrt{9}\sqrt{-1}$, and we know that $\sqrt{-1} = i$, we can simplify $\sqrt{-9}$ as $3i$. In other words, $\sqrt{-b^2} = \sqrt{b^2}\sqrt{-1} = bi$ where $b > 0$.

Similarly, $\sqrt{-5} = \sqrt{5}\sqrt{-1} = \sqrt{5}i = i\sqrt{5}$. We generally write $i\sqrt{5}$ rather than $\sqrt{5}i$ to make it clear that i is not under the radical sign.

 **MODEL PROBLEM**

Simplify each number and express it in terms of i.

Problem	Solution
a. $\sqrt{-100}$	a. $\sqrt{-100} = \sqrt{100}\sqrt{-1} = 10i$
b. $\sqrt{-18}$	b. $\sqrt{-18} = \sqrt{-9}\sqrt{2} = 3i\sqrt{2}$
c. $5\sqrt{-12}$	c. $5\sqrt{-12} = 5\sqrt{-4}\sqrt{3} = 5(2i)\sqrt{3} = 10i\sqrt{3}$

Since $i = \sqrt{-1}$, by squaring both sides of the equation, we get $i^2 = -1$. Continuing with this process we get: $i^3 = (i^2)(i) = -1i = -i$; $i^4 = (i^2)(i^2) = (-1)(-1) = 1$; $i^5 = (i^4)(i) = i$; $i^6 = (i^4)(i^2) = (1)(-1) = -1$, and so on. By definition $i^0 = 1$.

Putting this all together, we get:

$i^0 = 1$	$i^4 = 1$	$i^8 = 1$	$i^{12} = 1$
$i^1 = i$	$i^5 = i$	$i^9 = i$	$i^{13} = i$
$i^2 = -1$	$i^6 = -1$	$i^{10} = -1$	$i^{14} = -1$
$i^3 = -i$	$i^7 = -i$	$i^{11} = -i$	$i^{15} = -i$

Look at the pattern in the powers of i. They all simplify to either 1, i, -1, or $-i$. Any power of i that is a multiple of 4 (such as i^4, i^8, i^{12}, . . .) will simplify to 1. To simplify other powers of i, divide the exponent by 4, and find the remainder. Then find the value of i to that power. By learning that $i^1 = i$, $i^2 = -1$, and $i^3 = -i$, you can then determine the value of any power of i.

 MODEL PROBLEM

Write i^{43} as a power of i in simplest terms.

SOLUTION
When 43 is divided by 4, the remainder is 3, so $i^{43} = (1)(i^3) = -i$.

To help you remember the basic powers of i, you can use the following information. Remember: I won, I won, plus, minus, minus, plus. Then, write in a vertical column:

I won, I won, plus, minus, minus, plus.	Fill in the signs: +, −, −, +	Then, fill in the appropriate powers of i to complete your "i chart."
i	$+i$	$i^1 = i$
1	-1	$i^2 = -1$
i	$-i$	$i^3 = -i$
1	$+1$	$i^4 = 1$

MODEL PROBLEMS

1. Write i^{22} as a power of i in simplest terms.

SOLUTION
When 22 is divided by 4, the remainder is 2, so $i^{22} = (1)(i^2)$.
We know that $i^2 = -1$.
Thus, $i^{22} = (1)(i^2) = (1)(-1) = -1$.
Once you know the powers of i, you will be able to perform various operations on imaginary numbers.

2. What is the sum of $7i^7$ and $15i^{15}$?

SOLUTION
$$7i^7 + 15i^{15} = 7i^4i^3 + 15i^{12}i^3$$
$$= 7(1)(-i) + 15(1)(-i)$$
$$= -7i - 15i$$
$$= -22i$$

3. What is the product of $4i^{20}$ and $6i^{13}$?

SOLUTION
Since 20 is a multiple of 4, $i^{20} = 1$. Then,
$$4i^{20} \cdot 6i^{13} = (4)(1) \cdot 6i^{12}i^1$$
$$= 4 \cdot 6(1)(i)$$
$$= 4 \cdot 6i$$
$$= 24i$$

Note: You can simplify and then multiply, or multiply and then simplify.

In 1–12, express each number in terms of i.

1. $\sqrt{-49}$

2. $8\sqrt{-121}$

3. $\frac{1}{2}\sqrt{-64}$

4. $-\frac{7}{10}\sqrt{-100}$

5. $4\sqrt{-5}$

6. $-4\sqrt{-20}$

7. $6\sqrt{-44}$

8. $\frac{4}{5}\sqrt{-200}$

9. $\sqrt{-\frac{1}{4}}$

10. $\frac{2}{3}\sqrt{-27}$

11. $6\sqrt{-\frac{25}{36}}$

12. $8\sqrt{-\frac{3}{8}}$

In 13–20, write the given power of i *in simplest terms.*

13. i^7

14. i^{33}

15. i^{49}

16. i^{103}

17. i^{24}

18. i^{66}

19. i^{201}

20. i^{18}

In 21–24, simplify each expression.

21. $(4i^6) \cdot (3i^{11})$

22. $16i^5 + 13i^{23}$

23. $32i^{32} - 40i^{10}$

24. $-\dfrac{20i^{23}}{10i^{16}}$

In 25–30, select the numeral preceding the expression that best completes the statement or answers the question.

25. The sum of $6i^6$ and $13i^{34}$ is
    (1) $-19i$ (3) -19
    (2) $19i$ (4) 19

26. Find the product of $10i^{18}$ and $7i^{33}$.
    (1) $-70i$ (3) -70
    (2) $70i$ (4) 70

27. Simplify $(10i^{13})^2$.
    (1) $-100i$ (3) -100
    (2) $100i$ (4) 100

28. Which of the following is *not* equal to the other three?
    (1) i^{19} (3) i^{27}
    (2) i^9 (4) i^{35}

29. When $6i^{18}$ is multiplied by $8i^6$, the product is
    (1) $-48i$ (3) -48
    (2) $48i$ (4) 48

30. The expression $\frac{3}{4}\sqrt{-48}$ is equivalent to
    (1) $-3\sqrt{3}$
    (2) $3i\sqrt{3}$
    (3) $-3i\sqrt{3}$
    (4) $-\frac{3}{2}i\sqrt{3}$

3.3 Operations with Radicals

We will quickly review the rules for operations with radicals, and then extend these rules to radicals containing negative numbers.

When adding and subtracting radicals, make sure that the radicals are alike. That is, the **radicands** (the numbers under the radical sign) must be the same. Also, the radicals must be of the same index. (The **index** is the integer that indicates what root is to be taken.) Then, add or subtract the coefficients of the radicands. These are the same rules you use when adding or subtracting algebraic expressions. For example, $2a + 6a = 8a$. Thus, $2\sqrt{5} + 6\sqrt{5} = 8\sqrt{5}$. Also, $2a - 6a = -4a$ and $2\sqrt{5} - 6\sqrt{5} = -4\sqrt{5}$.

If the radicands are not the same, check if you can simplify them. At first glance, it does not appear that you can add $2\sqrt{3}$ and $6\sqrt{12}$. However, if you look carefully, you will notice that $6\sqrt{12}$ can be simplified. Notice what happens after the simplification:

$$
\begin{aligned}
2\sqrt{3} + 6\sqrt{12} &= 2\sqrt{3} + 6\sqrt{4}\sqrt{3} \\
&= 2\sqrt{3} + 6 \cdot 2\sqrt{3} \\
&= 2\sqrt{3} + 12\sqrt{3} \\
&= 14\sqrt{3}
\end{aligned}
$$

Similarly,

$$
\begin{aligned}
2\sqrt{-3} + 6\sqrt{-12} &= 2\sqrt{-1}\sqrt{3} + 6\sqrt{-4}\sqrt{3} \\
&= 2i\sqrt{3} + 6 \cdot 2i\sqrt{3} \\
&= 2i\sqrt{3} + 12i\sqrt{3} \\
&= 14i\sqrt{3}
\end{aligned}
$$

When multiplying and dividing radicals, the radicands do not have to be the same as long as the indexes are the same. For example, $\sqrt{2} \cdot \sqrt{3} = \sqrt{2 \cdot 3} = \sqrt{6}$ and $4\sqrt{2} \cdot 5\sqrt{3} = 20\sqrt{2 \cdot 3} = 20\sqrt{6}$. This is the same as when we multiply monomials: $4a \cdot 5b = 20ab$.

When multiplying or dividing radicals containing negative numbers, it is necessary to simplify before you multiply. For example,

$$
\begin{aligned}
\sqrt{-2}\sqrt{-3} &= (\sqrt{-1}\sqrt{2})(\sqrt{-1}\sqrt{3}) \\
&= (i\sqrt{2})(i\sqrt{3}) \\
&= i^2\sqrt{6} \\
&= -\sqrt{6}
\end{aligned}
$$

Remember: When multiplying or dividing radicals containing negative numbers, "take out your i's" first!

To simplify the quotient of radicals:

- If the numerator is a multiple of the denominator, just divide the numerator by the denominator.

Example: $\dfrac{18\sqrt{6}}{9\sqrt{3}} = 2\sqrt{2}$

- If either radical contains a negative number, it is necessary to simplify before you divide.

Example: $\dfrac{18\sqrt{-6}}{9\sqrt{-3}} = \dfrac{18\sqrt{-1}\sqrt{6}}{9\sqrt{-1}\sqrt{3}}$

$$
\begin{aligned}
&= \dfrac{18i\sqrt{6}}{9i\sqrt{3}} \\
&= 2\sqrt{2}
\end{aligned}
$$

- If the numerator is not a multiple of the denominator, to simplify the quotient, multiply numerator and denominator by a radical that will make the denominator a perfect square (rationalize the denominator).

  For example, to simplify $\dfrac{2\sqrt{5}}{5\sqrt{2}}$, multiply numerator and denominator by $\sqrt{2}$.

$$\frac{2\sqrt{5}}{5\sqrt{2}} = \frac{2\sqrt{5}}{5\sqrt{2}} \cdot \frac{\sqrt{2}}{\sqrt{2}}$$

$$= \frac{2\sqrt{10}}{5 \cdot 2} \qquad \text{Divide both numerator and denominator by 2.}$$

$$= \frac{\sqrt{10}}{5}$$

The same rules would apply if the radicals contained negative numbers. Always factor out the $\sqrt{-1}$, and never leave an i in the denominator.

Example:

$$\frac{2\sqrt{5}}{5\sqrt{-2}} = \frac{2\sqrt{5}}{5i\sqrt{2}}$$

$$= \frac{2\sqrt{5}}{5i\sqrt{2}} \cdot \frac{i\sqrt{2}}{i\sqrt{2}}$$

$$= \frac{2i\sqrt{10}}{5 \cdot 2i^2}$$

$$= \frac{2i\sqrt{10}}{5(-2)}$$

$$= \frac{-i\sqrt{10}}{5}$$

A radical in simplest form also cannot contain a fraction. To simplify such a radical, first separate the fraction, and then rationalize it.

Example:

$$\sqrt{\frac{1}{2}} = \frac{\sqrt{1}}{\sqrt{2}}$$

$$= \frac{1}{\sqrt{2}}$$

$$= \frac{1}{\sqrt{2}} \cdot \frac{\sqrt{2}}{\sqrt{2}}$$

$$= \frac{\sqrt{2}}{2}$$

The same process holds true for radicals containing negative numbers.

Example:

$$\sqrt{-\frac{2}{3}} = \frac{\sqrt{-2}}{\sqrt{3}}$$

$$= \frac{i\sqrt{2}}{\sqrt{3}} \cdot \frac{\sqrt{3}}{\sqrt{3}}$$

$$= \frac{i\sqrt{6}}{3}$$

Perform the indicated operations, and simplify your answer:

a. $2\sqrt{-75} + 4\sqrt{-27}$

b. $(4\sqrt{-50})(2\sqrt{-200})$

SOLUTION

a. $2\sqrt{-75} + 4\sqrt{-27} = 2\sqrt{-25}\sqrt{3} + 4\sqrt{-9}\sqrt{3}$

$$= 2(5i\sqrt{3}) + 4(3i\sqrt{3})$$

$$= 10i\sqrt{3} + 12i\sqrt{3}$$

$$= 22i\sqrt{3}$$

b. $(4\sqrt{-50})(2\sqrt{-200}) = (4\sqrt{-25}\sqrt{2})(2\sqrt{-100}\sqrt{2})$

$$= (4 \cdot 5i\sqrt{2})(2 \cdot 10i\sqrt{2})$$

$$= (20i\sqrt{2})(20i\sqrt{2})$$

$$= 400i^2(2)$$

$$= 800i^2$$

$$= -800$$

Practice

In 1–15, perform the indicated operations, and simplify where possible.

1. $4\sqrt{-25} + 2\sqrt{-36}$

2. $3\sqrt{-4} - 4\sqrt{-81}$

3. $(2\sqrt{-16})(3\sqrt{-9})$

4. $\dfrac{2\sqrt{-100}}{6\sqrt{-4}}$

5. $5\sqrt{-24} + 2\sqrt{-54}$

6. $3\sqrt{-12} - 4\sqrt{-27}$

7. $(2\sqrt{-18})(-3\sqrt{-32})$

8. $(-4\sqrt{5})(3\sqrt{-5})$

9. $(2\sqrt{-50})(-2\sqrt{-27})$

10. $(3\sqrt{-100})(4\sqrt{-200})$

11. $\dfrac{6\sqrt{-300}}{2\sqrt{-100}}$

12. $\dfrac{6\sqrt{-16}}{12\sqrt{4}}$

13. $\sqrt{-\dfrac{3}{4}}$

14. $\dfrac{2}{3}\sqrt{-\dfrac{3}{2}}$

15. $\dfrac{10\sqrt{18}}{3\sqrt{-50}}$

In 16–25, select the numeral preceding the expression that best completes the statement or answers the question.

16. Express $4\sqrt{-36} + 5\sqrt{-4}$ as a monomial in terms of i.
(1) $10i$ (3) $34i$
(2) $24i$ (4) $44i$

17. What is the product of $6\sqrt{-4}$ and $2\sqrt{-9}$?
(1) -72 (3) $-72i$
(2) 72 (4) $72i$

18. When $(\sqrt{-32} + \sqrt{-8})$ is divided by $\sqrt{2}$, the result is
(1) $20i$ (3) $6i$
(2) $i\sqrt{20}$ (4) $6i\sqrt{2}$

19. Simplify: $4\sqrt{-12} - 5\sqrt{-48}$.
   (1) $28i\sqrt{3}$ (3) $-12i\sqrt{3}$
   (2) $-4i\sqrt{3}$ (4) $-32i\sqrt{3}$

20. Simplify: $8\sqrt{\dfrac{-3}{8}}$.

   (1) $-2i\sqrt{6}$ (3) $2i\sqrt{6}$
   (2) -3 (4) $6i\sqrt{2}$

21. What is the quotient when $2\sqrt{-24}$ is divided by $4\sqrt{-6}$?
   (1) 1 (3) $-i$
   (2) -1 (4) i

22. Express as a monomial: $(\sqrt{-2})(6\sqrt{-72})$.
   (1) 72 (3) $-36i\sqrt{2}$
   (2) $36i\sqrt{2}$ (4) -72

23. Express the sum of $2\sqrt{-64}$ and $4\sqrt{-25}$ in simplest form in terms of i.
   (1) -36 (3) $36i$
   (2) $-36i$ (4) 36

24. Simplify: $5\sqrt{-63} - 2\sqrt{-28}$.
   (1) $-11\sqrt{7}$ (3) $3i\sqrt{35}$
   (2) $11i\sqrt{7}$ (4) $3i\sqrt{91}$

25. Perform the indicated operation and simplify: $\dfrac{16\sqrt{24}}{4\sqrt{-3}}$.
   (1) $-8i\sqrt{2}$ (3) $8i\sqrt{2}$
   (2) $-8\sqrt{2}$ (4) $8\sqrt{2}$

3.4 Solving Radical Equations

A **radical equation** is an equation in which the variable is contained in a radical. To solve a radical equation, first isolate the radical. If the radical is a square root, square both sides. If the radical is a cube root, then cube both sides, and so on. After you solve the derived equation, be sure to check that your solution works in the original equation.

MODEL PROBLEMS

1. Solve: $\sqrt{3x + 6} - 2 = 7$.

SOLUTION

$$\sqrt{3x + 6} = 9 \qquad \text{Isolate the radical.}$$
$$(\sqrt{3x + 6})^2 = 9^2 \qquad \text{Square both sides.}$$
$$3x + 6 = 81 \qquad \text{Solve the derived equation.}$$
$$3x = 75$$
$$x = 25$$

Check the solution in the original equation.
$$\sqrt{3x + 6} - 2 = 7$$
$$\sqrt{3(25) + 6} - 2 \stackrel{?}{=} 7$$
$$\sqrt{81} - 2 \stackrel{?}{=} 7$$
$$7 = 7 \text{ (True)}$$

Thus, $x = 25$.

2. Solve: $2\sqrt{2x - 6} + 8 = 4$.

SOLUTION

$$2\sqrt{2x - 6} = -4$$
$$\sqrt{2x - 6} = -2$$
$$(\sqrt{2x - 6})^2 = (-2)^2$$
$$2x - 6 = 4$$
$$2x = 10$$
$$x = 5$$

Check:

$$2\sqrt{2x - 6} + 8 = 4$$
$$2\sqrt{2(5) - 6} + 8 \stackrel{?}{=} 4$$
$$2\sqrt{4} + 8 \stackrel{?}{=} 4$$
$$4 + 8 \stackrel{?}{=} 4$$
$$12 \neq 4$$

Since $x = 5$ is an *extraneous* root, we must reject it. This equation has no solution. The answer is $\varnothing$ or { }. Once we obtained $\sqrt{2x - 6} = -2$ in the solution above, we could have realized that this equation has no solution.

3. Solve: $\sqrt[5]{3x - 1} = 2$.

SOLUTION

$$(\sqrt[5]{3x - 1})^5 = 2^5$$
$$3x - 1 = 32$$
$$3x = 33$$
$$x = 11$$

Check:

$$\sqrt[5]{3x - 1} = 2$$
$$\sqrt[5]{3(11) - 1} \stackrel{?}{=} 2$$
$$\sqrt[5]{32} \stackrel{?}{=} 2$$
$$2 = 2 \text{ (True)}$$

Thus, $x = 11$.

4. Solve: $2\sqrt{4a - 6} = 6\sqrt{a - 4}$.

SOLUTION
First, isolate one of the radicals by dividing both sides of the equation by 2.
$$\sqrt{4a - 6} = 3\sqrt{a - 4}$$

Now, square both sides.

$$(\sqrt{4a - 6})^2 = (3\sqrt{a - 4})^2$$
$$4a - 6 = 9(a - 4)$$
$$4a - 6 = 9a - 36$$
$$30 = 5a$$
$$a = 6$$

Check:

$$2\sqrt{4a - 6} = 6\sqrt{a - 4}$$
$$2\sqrt{4(6) - 6} \stackrel{?}{=} 6\sqrt{6 - 4}$$
$$2\sqrt{18} \stackrel{?}{=} 6\sqrt{2}$$
$$2\sqrt{9}\sqrt{2} \stackrel{?}{=} 6\sqrt{2}$$
$$6\sqrt{2} = 6\sqrt{2}$$

Thus, $a = 6$.

Practice

Solve each equation.

1. $\sqrt{x - 4} = 6$

2. $\sqrt{3x + 7} = 5$

3. $\sqrt[3]{2x - 5} = 3$

4. $\sqrt{5x - 1} + 4 = 12$

5. $3\sqrt{x - 9} = 21$

6. $\sqrt{6x - 2} = \sqrt{3x + 10}$

7. $5\sqrt{4x - 8} + 2 = 12$

8. $3\sqrt{5a - 1} + 12 = 6$

9. $4\sqrt{6b + 1} - 5 = 15$

10. $\sqrt[3]{4x + 1} = 5$

11. $\frac{2}{3}\sqrt{9x + 27} = 6$

12. $5\sqrt{5a + 6} = 10\sqrt{3a - 2}$

13. $3\sqrt{2x + 6} + 22 = 4$

14. $4\sqrt{5a + 16} = 24$

15. $\sqrt[3]{2x - 3} + 1 = 4$

3.5 Complex Numbers

A **complex number** is any number that can be expressed in the form $a + bi$, where a and b are real numbers, and $i = \sqrt{-1}$. The number a is the real part and bi is the imaginary part of the complex number. Examples of complex numbers are $3 + 2i$, $4 - 6i$, $-5 - 2i$, $9 + 0i = 9$, and $0 + 7i = 7i$. When $b = 0$, the complex number is a real number. Thus, the set of real numbers is a subset of the set of complex numbers. When $a = 0$, the complex number becomes a pure imaginary number. Thus, the set of imaginary numbers is also a subset of the set of complex numbers.

We can now complete our number system, which is illustrated this in the chart.

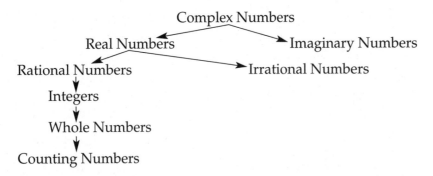

Complex numbers are used in the study of electricity, specifically, electricity involving alternate currents.

Two complex numbers are equal if and only if their real parts are equal and their imaginary parts are also equal.

If $(c + d) + ci = 5 + 3i$, find d.

SOLUTION

Since the two numbers are equal, we know that the real parts of both numbers are equal, that is, $c + d = 5$. The imaginary parts of the numbers are also equal. Thus, $c = 3$. Substituting the value of 3 for c into our first equation, we determine that $d = 2$.

Just as every real number can be represented on a number line, every complex number can be represented on the complex plane. (The complex plane is sometimes called the Argand plane after the Swiss mathematician Jean Robert Argand.)

In the complex plane, the horizontal axis is the real axis (the x-axis) and the vertical axis is the imaginary axis (the yi-axis). To plot the point $2 + 3i$, we go 2 units right and 3 units up. The number $5 + 0i$ would be plotted by proceeding 5 units right on the real axis. This illustrates graphically that the number $5 + 0i$ is a real number, since its graph lies on the real axis. The number $0 + 4i$ is plotted by proceeding 4 units up on the imaginary axis. This illustrates graphically that the number $0 + 4i$ is a pure imaginary number since its graph lies on the imaginary axis. A complex number such as $-3 + 2i$ can be simply called an imaginary number since it is represented by a point on the complex plane that is not on the real number axis.

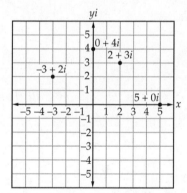

Note: Complex numbers of the form $a + bi$, where $a \neq 0$, cannot be ordered.

Besides being represented by a point in the complex number plane, a complex number can also be represented by a vector in the complex number plane. Vectors are written using their endpoints $\overrightarrow{OA}$, $\overrightarrow{OB}$, and $\overrightarrow{OC}$.

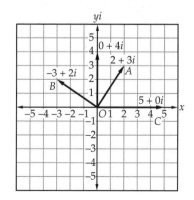

In 1–7, find the real numbers a *and* b *that will make the equation true.*

1. $a + bi = 2 + 5i$

2. $a + bi = 7i$

3. $a + bi = 12$

4. $(a - 2b) + bi = -3 + 7i$

5. $a + (a - b)i = 6 + 4i$

6. $2a + 3bi = 10 - 6i$

7. $a + bi = 2 + 5i - 4 + 7i$

In 8–12, write each number in standard a + bi *form.*

8. $6 + \sqrt{-25}$

9. $3 + \sqrt{-49} - 5$

10. $7 - \sqrt{-27}$

11. $5 + 3\sqrt{-8}$

12. $4i + 6i^2$

In 13–18, tell whether the statement is true or false, and explain your reasoning.

13. All real numbers are complex numbers.
14. All complex numbers are real numbers.
15. All integers are complex numbers.
16. A real number cannot be an imaginary number.
17. An imaginary number cannot be a complex number.
18. A complex number cannot be imaginary.

19. What complex number does each point in the accompanying diagram represent?

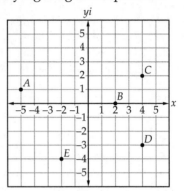

20. What complex number does each vector in the accompanying diagram represent?

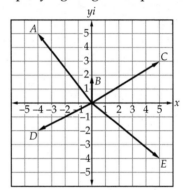

In 21–25, name all the sets of numbers to which each number belongs.

21. -6

22. $3i$

23. π

24. $0.\overline{3}$

25. 8

3.6 Addition and Subtraction of Complex Numbers

Adding and subtracting complex numbers is very similar to adding and subtracting binomials—we simply combine like terms. For example, to add $3 + 5i$ to $4 + 7i$, we add the real components 3 and 4 and the imaginary components $5i$ and $7i$ to get $7 + 12i$.

To subtract $3 + 5i$ from $4 + 7i$, we can add the inverse.

$(4 + 7i) - (3 + 5i)$
$= (4 + 7i) + (-3 - 5i)$
$= 4 + 7i - 3 - 5i$
$= (4 - 3) + (7i - 5i)$
$= 1 + 2i$

 **MODEL PROBLEM**

Perform the indicated operation and express the answer in simplest $a + bi$ form

Problem	Solution
a. $(2 + 4i) + (-5 - 6i)$	$(2 + 4i) + (-5 - 6i) = (2 - 5) + (4i - 6i)$ $= -3 - 2i$
b. $(-3 - 8i) - (-2 + 4i)$	$(-3 - 8i) - (-2 + 4i) = -3 - 8i + 2 - 4i$ $= (-3 + 2) + (-8i - 4i)$ $= -1 - 12i$
c. $(4 + \sqrt{-9}) - (\sqrt{-25})$	$(4 + \sqrt{-9}) - (\sqrt{-25}) = (4 + 3i) - (5i)$ $= 4 + 3i - 5i$ $= 4 - 2i$
d. $(5 - 2\sqrt{-12}) + (4 + \sqrt{-27})$	$(5 - 2\sqrt{-12}) + (4 + \sqrt{-27})$ $= (5 - 2\sqrt{-4}\sqrt{3}) + (4 + \sqrt{-9}\sqrt{3})$ $= (5 - 2 \cdot 2i\sqrt{3}) + (4 + 3i\sqrt{3})$ $= (5 - 4i\sqrt{3}) + (4 + 3i\sqrt{3})$ $= (5 + 4) + (-4i\sqrt{3} + 3i\sqrt{3})$ $= 9 - i\sqrt{3}$
e. $(2 - \sqrt{-8}) - (-4 - 3\sqrt{-32})$	$(2 - \sqrt{-8}) - (-4 - 3\sqrt{-32})$ $= (2 - \sqrt{-4}\sqrt{2}) - (-4 - 3\sqrt{-16}\sqrt{2})$ $= (2 - 2i\sqrt{2}) - (-4 - 3(4i)\sqrt{2})$ $= (2 - 2i\sqrt{2}) - (-4 - 12i\sqrt{2})$ $= 2 - 2i\sqrt{2} + 4 + 12i\sqrt{2}$ $= 6 + 10i\sqrt{2}$

We can use vector addition to graphically illustrate how to add and subtract complex numbers. To add two complex numbers, we represent each complex number by a vector in the complex plane. The sum of the two vectors is the resultant vector (that is, the diagonal of the parallelogram determined by the two vectors).

📖 **MODEL PROBLEM**

Let $Z_1 = 1 + 5i$ and $Z_2 = 6 + 2i$.
a. Graph the sum of Z_1 and Z_2.
b. Express the sum of Z_1 and Z_2 as a complex number.

SOLUTION

a. Graph Z_1 and Z_2. Then draw the parallelogram determined by the two vectors. The sum of the two vectors is the resultant vector (that is, the diagonal of the parallelogram).

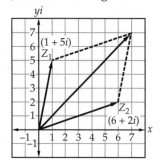

b. From the graph, we can see that the resultant vector represents the number $7 + 7i$.

Since subtraction is simply the addition of an additive inverse, we can also subtract complex numbers using vector addition. To subtract one complex number from another, rewrite the difference as the sum of the first complex numbers and the additive inverse of the second. Then, proceed in the same manner as illustrated above.

📖 **MODEL PROBLEM**

Let $Z_3 = 3 - 4i$ and $Z_4 = -3 + i$.
a. Graph the difference $Z_3 - Z_4$.
b. Express the difference $Z_3 - Z_4$ as a complex number.

SOLUTION

a. $Z_3 - Z_4 = (3 - 4i) - (-3 + i)$
To subtract the two complex numbers, we rewrite the difference and add the additive inverse of the second number.

$(3 - 4i) - (-3 + i) = (3 - 4i) + (3 - i)$

Graph $(3 - 4i)$ and $(3 - i)$. Draw the parallelogram determined by the two vectors. The sum of the two vectors is the resultant vector (that is, the diagonal of the parallelogram).

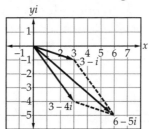

b. From the graph, we can see that the resultant vector represents the number $6 - 5i$.

Practice

In 1–10, simplify each expression.

1. $(-6 + 5i) + (6 - i)$

2. $(6 - 2i) + (-4 + 5i)$

3. $(3 - 5i) - (2 - 4i)$

4. $(-1 + 8i) - (-5 - 2i)$

5. $(6 + \sqrt{-49}) + (3 + \sqrt{-64})$

6. $(-11 + \sqrt{-25}) - (-4 + 5\sqrt{-81})$

7. $(2 + \sqrt{-18}) + (5 + \sqrt{-200})$

8. $(-1 + 2\sqrt{-12}) - (8 + 5\sqrt{-48})$

9. $(11 + 6\sqrt{-45}) - (-3 - 2\sqrt{-20})$

10. $\left(-5 + \frac{2}{3}\sqrt{-27}\right) + \left(-2 + \frac{3}{2}\sqrt{-12}\right)$

In 11–14, find values for a and b that will make each statement true.

11. $(a + bi) + (4 + 6i) = 9 + 11i$

12. $(3 - 4i) + (a + bi) = 7 - 6i$

13. $(a + bi) - (2 + 5i) = 8 - 3i$

14. $(10 + 3i) - (a + bi) = 7 - 6i$

In 15–18, select the numeral preceding the word or expression that best answers the question.

15. Express the sum of $(-5 - 6i)$ and $(10 - 4i)$ in simplest $a + bi$ form.

(1) $-5 - 10i$ (3) $5 - 2i$
(2) $15 - 2i$ (4) $5 - 10i$

16. In which quadrant does the sum of $(4 + 7i)$ and $(-3 - 5i)$ lie?

(1) I   (3) III
(2) II   (4) IV

17. If $(a + bi) - (2 + 4i) = 6 + 8i$, find the sum of a and b.

(1) 20   (3) 8
(2) 14   (4) 6

18. In which quadrant does the difference $(-5 + 11i) - (-2 + 7i)$ lie?

(1) I   (3) III
(2) II   (4) IV

In 19–22,

a. Graph each of the following pairs of numbers, Z_1 and Z_2.

b. Graph the sum of Z_1 and Z_2 and express the sum of Z_1 and Z_2 as a complex number.

c. Graph the difference $Z_1 - Z_2$ and express the difference as a complex number.

19. $Z_1 = -2 + i$, $Z_2 = 1 - 4i$

20. $Z_1 = 1 + 2i$, $Z_2 = 3 + 3i$

21. $Z_1 = 4 - i$, $Z_2 = -2 + 5i$

22. $Z_1 = 2 + 2i$, $Z_2 = -2 + 4i$

23. When is the sum of the two complex numbers **a.** a real number? **b.** a purely imaginary number?

3.7 Multiplication and Division of Complex Numbers

Multiplying complex numbers is very similar to multiplying binomials—we multiply the binomials, simplify, and combine like terms. For example, to multiply $(2 + 3i)$ by $(4 + 5i)$, multiplying the binomials gives us: $8 + 10i + 12i + 15i^2$. Since $i^2 = -1$, we can rewrite this as $8 + 10i + 12i + 15(-1) = 8 + 10i + 12i - 15 = -7 + 22i$.

To multiply $(3 - 6i)$ by $2i$, we distribute the $2i$, that is, $2i(3 - 6i) = 6i - 12i^2$. Since $i^2 = -1$, we can simplify this as $6i - 12(-1) = 6i + 12$. We can rewrite this as $12 + 6i$.

To multiply binomials containing radicals, be sure to simplify before multiplying.

 **MODEL PROBLEMS**

1. Multiply $(6 + \sqrt{-100})$ by $(3 + \sqrt{-4})$.

SOLUTION

$$
\begin{aligned}
(6 + \sqrt{-100})(3 + \sqrt{-4}) &= (6 + 10i)(3 + 2i) \\
&= 18 + 12i + 30i + 20i^2 \\
&= 18 + 42i + 20(-1) \\
&= 18 + 42i - 20 \\
&= -2 + 42i
\end{aligned}
$$

2. Find the product of $(2 + 3\sqrt{-8})$ and $(-1 + \sqrt{-18})$.

SOLUTION

$$
\begin{aligned}
(2 + 3\sqrt{-8})(-1 + \sqrt{-18}) &= (2 + 3\sqrt{-4}\sqrt{2})(-1 + \sqrt{-9}\sqrt{2}) \\
&= (2 + 3(2i)\sqrt{2})(-1 + 3i\sqrt{2}) \\
&= (2 + 6i\sqrt{2})(-1 + 3i\sqrt{2}) \\
&= -2 + 6i\sqrt{2} - 6i\sqrt{2} + 18i^2(2) \\
&= -2 + 36i^2 \\
&= -2 - 36 \\
&= -38
\end{aligned}
$$

Note: The conjugate of the complex number $a + bi$ is the number $a - bi$. For example, the conjugate of $4 + 9i$ is the number $4 - 9i$.

Multiply $6 - 4i$ by its conjugate.

SOLUTION

The conjugate of $6 - 4i$ is $6 + 4i$. Thus, we must find the product $(6 - 4i)(6 + 4i)$.

$$(6 - 4i)(6 + 4i) = 36 + 24i - 24i - 16i^2$$
$$= 36 - 16(-1)$$
$$= 36 + 16$$
$$= 52$$

Note: The product of a complex number and its conjugate is always a real number.

Complex conjugates are used to divide complex numbers.

Perform the indicated division and express your answer in simplest $a + bi$ form.
$$\frac{1 + 2i}{2 + 3i}$$

SOLUTION

This is very similar to rationalizing the denominator of a fraction. Multiply numerator and denominator by the conjugate of the denominator.

$$\frac{1 + 2i}{2 + 3i} = \left(\frac{1 + 2i}{2 + 3i}\right)\left(\frac{2 - 3i}{2 - 3i}\right)$$

Note: $2 - 3i$ is the conjugate of $2 + 3i$.

$$= \frac{2 - 3i + 4i - 6i^2}{4 - 6i + 6i - 9i^2}$$
$$= \frac{2 + i - 6(-1)}{4 - 9(-1)}$$
$$= \frac{2 + i + 6}{4 + 9}$$
$$= \frac{8 + i}{13}$$
$$= \frac{8}{13} + \frac{1}{13}i$$

Notice that we needed to break the fraction $\frac{8 + i}{13}$ into $\frac{8}{13} + \frac{1}{13}i$ to satisfy the requirement to express the answer in "simplest $a + bi$ form."

When dividing radicals containing negatives, be sure to "take out your i's" before you begin.

MODEL PROBLEM

Perform the indicated division and express your answer in simplest $a + bi$ form.

$$\frac{2 + \sqrt{-3}}{3 + \sqrt{-3}}$$

SOLUTION

Be sure to simplify before you begin.

$$\frac{2 + \sqrt{-3}}{3 + \sqrt{-3}} = \frac{2 + \sqrt{-1}\sqrt{3}}{3 + \sqrt{-1}\sqrt{3}}$$

$$= \frac{2 + i\sqrt{3}}{3 + i\sqrt{3}}$$

$$= \frac{2 + i\sqrt{3}}{3 + i\sqrt{3}} \cdot \frac{3 - i\sqrt{3}}{3 - i\sqrt{3}}$$

Note: $3 - i\sqrt{3}$ is the conjugate of $3 + i\sqrt{3}$.

$$= \frac{6 - 2i\sqrt{3} + 3i\sqrt{3} - 3i^2}{9 - 3i^2}$$

$$= \frac{6 + i\sqrt{3} - 3(-1)}{9 - 3(-1)}$$

$$= \frac{6 + i\sqrt{3} + 3}{12}$$

$$= \frac{9 + i\sqrt{3}}{12}$$

$$= \frac{9}{12} + \frac{i\sqrt{3}}{12}$$

$$= \frac{3}{4} + \frac{i\sqrt{3}}{12}$$

Practice

In 1–15, perform the indicated operations, and express your answer in simplest a + bi *form.*

1. $(2 - 5i)(6 + 7i)$

2. $\dfrac{2 - i}{3 + i}$

3. $3i(2i^2 + 4i - 6)$

4. $\dfrac{4 - 6i}{5i}$

5. $(3 + 4i)(-1 - 9i)$

6. $(7 + 3i)^2$

7. $(2 - \sqrt{-9})(3 + \sqrt{-16})$

8. $\dfrac{1}{2 - 5i}$

9. $4i^2(6 + 8i + 5i^2 - 3i^4)$

10. $\dfrac{1 + \sqrt{-4}}{2 + \sqrt{-9}}$

11. $(3 - i)(1 + 2i) + (1 - i)(2 + i)$

12. $\dfrac{5 + i}{3 - 4i}$

13. $(3 - \sqrt{-8})(1 - \sqrt{-18})$

14. $\dfrac{3 - 2i}{2i}$

15. $(4 - \sqrt{-27})(3 + \sqrt{-12})$

16. Find the product of $6 + 8i$ and its conjugate.

17. What is the multiplicative inverse of $5 + 3i$?

In 18–21, select the numeral preceding the expression that best completes the statement or answers the question.

18. The expression $\dfrac{1}{7 - 4i}$ is equivalent to

(1) $\dfrac{7 - 4i}{65}$ (3) $\dfrac{7 + 4i}{65}$

(2) $\dfrac{7 - 4i}{33}$ (4) $\dfrac{7 + 4i}{33}$

19. What is the product of $6 - 7i$ and its conjugate?

(1) -13 (3) 13

(2) 0 (4) 85

20. The expression $(2 + i)^2$ is equivalent to

(1) $3 + 4i$ (3) 3

(2) $3 - 4i$ (4) 5

21. Express $\dfrac{3}{2 + 2i}$ in simplest $a + bi$ form.

(1) $\dfrac{3}{2} + \dfrac{3}{2}i$ (3) $\dfrac{3}{4} + \dfrac{3}{4}i$

(2) $\dfrac{3}{2} - \dfrac{3}{2}i$ (4) $\dfrac{3}{4} - \dfrac{3}{4}i$

22. Find the multiplicative inverse of the complex number $a + bi$ where $a + bi \neq 0 + 0i$. Write the answer in simplest $a + bi$ form.

3.8 Absolute Value of Complex Numbers

The absolute value of a real number is its distance from the origin on a number line. Similarly, the absolute value of a complex number is its distance from the origin in the complex plane. To find $|a + bi|$, connect the point to the origin, and then use the Pythagorean theorem. The distance (also called the **magnitude** or the **modulus**) is written as $|a + bi| = \sqrt{a^2 + b^2}$.

We can sketch the graph of the complex number $a + bi$.

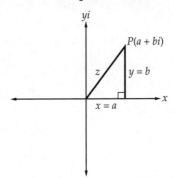

Let P represent point P whose x-coordinate is a and the yi-coordinate is b. By dropping a perpendicular from P we can form a right triangle, and use the Pythagorean theorem.

$$z^2 = x^2 + y^2$$
$$z^2 = a^2 + b^2$$
$$z = \sqrt{a^2 + b^2}$$

1. Find $|3 + 4i|$.

SOLUTION

$$\begin{aligned}
|3 + 4i| &= \sqrt{3^2 + 4^2} \\
&= \sqrt{9 + 16} \\
&= \sqrt{25} \\
&= 5
\end{aligned}$$

2. Express in simplest radical form: $|2 + 4i|$

SOLUTION

$$\begin{aligned}
|2 + 4i| &= \sqrt{2^2 + 4^2} \\
&= \sqrt{4 + 16} \\
&= \sqrt{20} \\
&= \sqrt{4}\sqrt{5} \\
&= 2\sqrt{5}
\end{aligned}$$

✏️ Practice

In 1–10, write each expression in simplest form.

1. $|1 + 2i|$

2. $|8 + 15i|$

3. $|6i|$

4. $|7 - 3i|$

5. $|-4 + 6i|$

6. $|-3 - 3i|$

7. $|4 + \sqrt{-9}|$

8. $|2 - \sqrt{-36}|$

9. $|1 + \sqrt{-8}|$

10. $|3 - \sqrt{-12}|$

11. a. Plot points $O = (0, 0)$, $P = 3 + 5i$, $Q = 7 + i$, and $R = P + Q$.
   b. Draw quadrilateral $OPRQ$.
   c. Express R as a complex number.
   d. Is $|P| + |Q| = |R|$? Explain your reasoning.

12. If $w = 6 + 8i$ and $z = 5 + 12i$, find
   a. $|w| + |z|$.
   b. $|w + z|$.

13. a. Plot points $O = (0, 0)$, $P = 1 + 5i$, $Q = 1 - 5i$, and $R = P + Q$.
   b. Draw quadrilateral $OPRQ$.
   c. Find $|1 + 5i|$ and $|1 - 5i|$.
   d. What kind of quadrilateral is $OPRQ$? Justify your answer.

14. Find $|8 + 6i|$, $|8 - 6i|$, $|-8 + 6i|$, and $|-8 - 6i|$. What do you notice? Why?

15. If $w = 2 + 5i$ and $z = 7 + 2i$, find
   a. $|w| + |z|$.
   b. $|w + z|$.

CHAPTER REVIEW

In 1–20, select the numeral preceding the word or expression that best completes the statement or answers the question.

1. $2i^6 - 3i^2$ equals
   - (1) $-1i^4$
   - (2) -1
   - (3) 1
   - (4) $-6i^{12}$

2. Which of the following represents the product of $3 - 4i$ and its conjugate?
   - (1) -7
   - (2) $\frac{3 + 4i}{25}$
   - (3) $\frac{25}{3 + 4i}$
   - (4) 25

3. $i^3 + i(2 - i)$ is equivalent to
   - (1) $-1 + 3i$
   - (2) $1 - i$
   - (3) $1 + i$
   - (4) $1 + 3i$

4. The value of $\sqrt{-9} \cdot \sqrt{-16}$ is
   - (1) -12
   - (2) 12
   - (3) $12i$
   - (4) ± 12

5. In which quadrant would you find the sum $(2 - \sqrt{-4}) + (-5 + \sqrt{-36})$?
   - (1) I
   - (2) II
   - (3) III
   - (4) IV

6. The expression $\frac{3}{2 + 3i}$ is equivalent to which of the following?
   - (1) $\frac{6 - 9i}{13}$
   - (2) $\frac{-6 + 9i}{13}$
   - (3) $-\frac{6 - 9i}{5}$
   - (4) $\frac{2 - 3i}{3}$

7. Which of the following is the solution to $\sqrt{3x + 1} - 2 = 2$?
   - (1) 5
   - (2) 3
   - (3) 1
   - (4) $\varnothing$

8. Which expression represents a real number?
   - (1) $-5 + 3i$
   - (2) $5i\sqrt{2}$
   - (3) $2 - \sqrt{5}$
   - (4) $0 - 7i$

9. The reciprocal of $12 - 3i$ is
   - (1) $12 + 3i$
   - (2) $-9i$
   - (3) $\frac{12 + 3i}{153}$
   - (4) $\frac{12 + 3i}{135}$

10. $\frac{\sqrt{-50}}{\sqrt{-2}}$ is equivalent to
    - (1) 5
    - (2) $5i$
    - (3) -5
    - (4) $-5i$

11. When simplified, $(1 + 2i)^2 - 4i$ equals
    - (1) $1 + 4i$
    - (2) 5
    - (3) $1 - 4i^2$
    - (4) -3

12. Which of the following is an irrational number?
    - (1) $\frac{1}{2}$
    - (2) $\sqrt{81}$
    - (3) $\sqrt{11}$
    - (4) -14

13. The product of $12i^7 \cdot 3i^3$ is
    - (1) -36
    - (2) $36i$
    - (3) 36
    - (4) $-36i$

14. The sum of $3\sqrt{12} + \frac{1}{2}\sqrt{48}$ is
    - (1) $\frac{7}{2}\sqrt{60}$
    - (2) $20\sqrt{3}$
    - (3) $8\sqrt{3}$
    - (4) $8i\sqrt{3}$

15. Which of the following is the solution to the equation $\sqrt{2x - 1} = 7$?
    - (1) 25
    - (2) 5
    - (3) 4
    - (4) 2.65

16. When simplified, $(4 - 3\sqrt{-2})(4 + 3\sqrt{-2})$ is
    - (1) 52
    - (2) 34
    - (3) -14
    - (4) $16 - 18i$

17. When combined as a monomial in terms of i, $4\sqrt{-18} + \frac{3}{2}\sqrt{-32}$ becomes
    - (1) $18i\sqrt{2}$
    - (2) $36i$
    - (3) $6i\sqrt{50}$
    - (4) $36i\sqrt{2}$

18. In which quadrant would you find the difference $(4 - 2\sqrt{-9}) - (5 + 3\sqrt{-4})$?
    - (1) I
    - (2) II
    - (3) III
    - (4) IV

19. Express $|5 - 12i|$ in simplest form
    - (1) $-7i$
    - (2) $7i$
    - (3) 13
    - (4) $13i$

20. Which of these numbers is a distance of 25 units from the origin?
    - (1) $|12 + 13i|$
    - (2) $|7 - 24i|$
    - (3) $|15 + 10i|$
    - (4) $|5 - 5i|$

In 21–25, show all your work and simplify your answer.

21. If $Z_1 = 5 - 2i$ and $Z_2 = -3 - 5i$,
   a. graphically show the vectors Z_1 and Z_2.
   b. graphically show the sum of Z_1 and Z_2.
   c. Evaluate $|Z_1 + Z_2|$.

22. Simplify $\dfrac{3 - 2i}{-1 + 2i}$.

23. Express in simplest $a + bi$ form: $(4 - i)^2 + 5i^2 - 4i(3 + 2i^3)$.

24. Solve for x: $\sqrt{2x - 3} + 2 = 1$.

25. a. Plot the points O $(0, 0)$, $R = 2 + 4i$, and $K = 7 + 4i$.
   b. If *WORK* is a parallelogram with $RK = WO$, find vector W.
   c. Draw quadrilateral *WORK*.
   d. Find the length of diagonal *OK* in simplest radical form.

Many of the calculations we have done in this chapter can be performed using a graphing calculator. This section will illustrate how to utilize the TI-83 graphing calculator to perform some of these computations.

First, press (MODE) and then select $a + bi$ as shown below.

```
Normal Sci Eng
Float 012456789
Radian Degree
Func Par Pol Seq
Connected Dot
Sequential Simul
Real a+bi re^θi
Full Horiz G–T
```

(Note: Although for some of your calculations it is not necessary to be in complex mode, this setting is needed for other calculations.)

To add, subtract, multiply, or divide two complex numbers, simply enter the numbers with the operation symbol. (Note: the symbol for i is located on the bottom row of the calculator above the decimal point. Since it is in yellow, you must enter (2nd) (.).)

The following screen illustrates how to enter into your calculator several operations with complex numbers.

```
(2–6i)+(–5–9i)
                    –3–15i
(1+7i)(2–4i)
                    30+10i
(3+i)/(2–i)
                    1+i
```

For some added features, go to the MATH CPX menu by pressing (MATH) (▶) (▶).

Option 1: conj(returns the complex conjugate of a complex number.

The example below illustrates how to use the TI-83 to find the conjugate of $3 + 5i$.

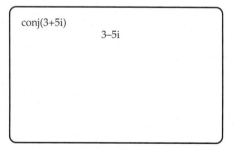

```
conj(3+5i)
                    3–5i
```

Thus, we can utilize the calculator to multiply a complex number by its conjugate. Type in the information as shown in the screen below.

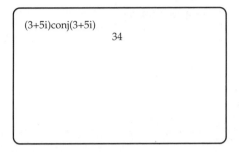

Option 2: real(returns the real part of a complex number.

Option 3: imag(returns the imaginary part of a complex number.

These are illustrated in the screen below.

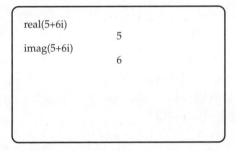

Option 4: angle(returns the polar angle. (This is beyond the scope of this course.)

Option 5: abs(returns the absolute value (also called modulus or magnitude) of a complex number.

An example of this is given below.

abs(5+12i)
                    13

You can also obtain the absolute value of a complex number by using the absolute value function of the calculator. This can easily be obtained by going to the catalog (2nd) (0) and selecting abs(as illustrated below.

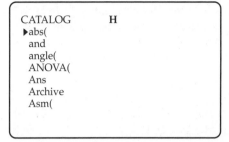

We will not utilize Options 6 or 7 for this course.

Limitations: The TI-83 can help with many of your calculations. However, look at the two examples given below.

(2+√(–9))+(5+√(–
4))
                    7+5i
(2+√(–5))+(5+√(–
20))
         7+6.708203932i

The first example: $(2 + \sqrt{-9}) + (5 + \sqrt{-4})$ is easily computed as $7 + 5i$ by the calculator. However, the answer to the second example $(2 + \sqrt{-5}) + (5 + \sqrt{-20})$ is given as a decimal equivalent to the exact answer of $7 + 3i\sqrt{5}$. Please be aware that, if you are asked for an exact answer, a decimal equivalent will be marked wrong.

Remember: Master the skills in this (and every) chapter. Your calculator is a valuable tool. Learn how to use the calculator, but more importantly, learn when to use it, and when not to use it.

Practice

Go back over the problems from the Chapter Review. See how the calculator can assist you in answering some of the questions, and identify when the calculator should not be used.

CHAPTER 4

Quadratic Equations and Inequalities

4.1 Methods of Solving Quadratic Equations

Quadratic equations are equations in the general form $ax^2 + bx + c = 0$ where $a \neq 0$, and a and b are coefficients and c is a constant. Any equation with only one unknown, in which the highest exponent is 2, is a quadratic equation, such as

$$3x^2 - 4x + 1 = 0$$
$$10x - 21 = x^2$$
$$x^2 - 4 = 3x$$

When you solve quadratic equations, set the equation equal to zero: $ax^2 + bx + c = 0$, and solve by the most reliable method for that equation: factoring, graphing, completing the square, or using the quadratic formula, all of which will be reviewed in this section.

Method One: Factoring Trinomials

To factor a trinomial, remember these rules:

- The factors of the first term and the factors of the last term combine to produce the middle term, which is the sum of the outer and inner products.

- When $a \neq 1$, you must take extra care to consider the sum of the outer and inner products to find the correct combination of factors.

- If the sign of the last term in the trinomial is positive, both factors take the same sign as the middle term of the trinomial.

- If the sign of the last term in the trinomial is negative, there is one positive factor and one negative factor. If $a = 1$, the larger of the two factors takes the sign of the middle term of the trinomial.

- Once the trinomial is factored, set each factor equal to zero and solve.

For example, the table below gives some sample quadratic expressions, the first and last terms that must be factored to form the middle term, and the solutions.

Quadratic Expression	First Term	Last Term	Factored Term
$x^2 + 4x - 5$	x^2	-5	$(x + 5)(x - 1)$
$x^2 - 3x - 10$	x^2	-10	$(x + 2)(x - 5)$
$x^2 + 7x + 12$	x^2	12	$(x + 3)(x + 4)$
$2x^2 - 7x + 3$	$2x^2$	3	$(2x - 1)(x - 3)$
$3x^2 + 5x - 2$	$3x^2$	-2	$(3x - 1)(x + 2)$

After you have factored the equation $3x^2 + 5x - 2 = 0$, you have two binomials: $(3x - 1)$ and $(x + 2)$. Since their product is zero, at least one binomial must equal zero. Therefore, set each individual factor equal to zero and solve for its variable.

$$(3x - 1) = 0 \qquad (x + 2) = 0$$
$$3x = 1 \qquad\qquad x = -2$$
$$x = \frac{1}{3}$$

Check both answers by substituting them into the original equation.

$$3x^2 + 5x - 2 = 0$$

$$3\left(\frac{1}{3}\right)^2 + 5\left(\frac{1}{3}\right) - 2 \overset{?}{=} 0 \qquad 3(-2)^2 + 5(-2) - 2 \overset{?}{=} 0$$

$$3\left(\frac{1}{9}\right) + \frac{5}{3} - 2 \overset{?}{=} 0 \qquad\qquad 3(4) - 10 - 2 \overset{?}{=} 0$$

$$\frac{3}{9} + \frac{5}{3} - 2 \overset{?}{=} 0 \qquad\qquad 12 - 10 - 2 \overset{?}{=} 0$$

$$\frac{18}{9} - 2 \overset{?}{=} 0 \qquad\qquad 12 - 12 \overset{?}{=} 0$$

$$0 = 0 \checkmark \qquad\qquad 0 = 0 \checkmark$$

Both solutions are valid since they check.

Note: Sometimes it is necessary to rearrange an equation to get it into factorable form.

 MODEL PROBLEM

Solve for x: $4x - 5 = \frac{6}{x}$.

SOLUTION

Step 1. Multiply each term by the LCD, x, to eliminate the fraction. $\qquad 4x^2 - 5x = 6$
Step 2. Set the quadratic equation equal to zero. $\qquad 4x^2 - 5x - 6 = 0$
Step 3. Factor. $\qquad (4x + 3)(x - 2) = 0$

Step 4. Set each factor equal to zero.

$$4x + 3 = 0 \qquad x - 2 = 0$$

Step 5. Solve each equation for x.

$$x = -\frac{3}{4} \qquad x = 2$$

Step 6. Check each solution in the original equation.

$$4x - 5 = \frac{6}{x}$$

$$4\left(-\frac{3}{4}\right) - 5 \overset{?}{=} \frac{6}{-\frac{3}{4}} \qquad\qquad 4(2) - 5 \overset{?}{=} \frac{6}{2}$$

$$-3 - 5 \overset{?}{=} -\frac{24}{3} \qquad\qquad 8 - 5 \overset{?}{=} 3$$

$$-8 = -8 \checkmark \qquad\qquad 3 = 3 \checkmark$$

Answer: The solution of $4x - 5 = \frac{6}{x}$ is $\left\{x \mid x = -\frac{3}{4} \text{ and } x = 2\right\}$. $\left(\text{Read "} x, \text{such that, } x \text{ equals } -\frac{3}{4}\right.$ and x equals 2."$\Big)$

 **Practice**

Solve each equation for x *and check the solution.*

1. $x^2 - 14 = 5x$

2. $2x^2 + 1 = \frac{11x}{3}$

3. $5x^2 = 8x + 4$

4. $7 - 4x = 3x^2$

5. $2x^2 - x = 15$

6. $\frac{8x^2}{3} = 2x + 3$

Method Two: Graphing

A quadratic equation can also be solved by plotting the quadratic function, $y = ax^2 + bx + c$, always a parabola, and finding the x-intercepts or the roots by examining the graph. The roots of the function are the solutions of the equation. The difficulty with this method is that not all solutions are integers, so not all solutions will be readily identifiable on the coordinate plane.

For example, to solve the quadratic equation $2x^2 - 3x - 5 = 0$, we could set up a table of values and graph the function. Since the axis of symmetry is $x = \frac{-b}{2a} = \frac{3}{4}$, we would choose x-values to the left and right of the axis of symmetry.

x	y
-2.25	11.875
-1.25	1.875
-0.25	-4.125
0.75	-6.125
1.75	-4.125
2.75	1.875
3.75	11.875

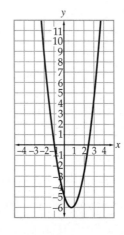

On the graph above, it appears that one root is -1, but the positive root is difficult to discern unless you're looking at the graph on a graphing calculator. (On a TI-83, you can insert the equation in ⟨Y=⟩, graph and use the ⟨2nd⟩ ⟨TRACE⟩ (CALC) –Zero function that will identify one root at a time, as requested. You will be asked for the left and right bounds of the root; be sure the window includes appropriate positive and negative values for y or you will get an error message.)

Without a graphing calculator, in this example, factoring yields better results.

$$2x^2 - 3x - 5 = 0$$
$$(2x - 5)(x + 1) = 0$$

$$2x - 5 = 0 \qquad x + 1 = 0$$
$$x = \frac{5}{2} \qquad x = -1$$

 **Practice**

Solve each equation by graphing.

1. $y = x^2 - 3x - 10$

2. $y = 2x^2 - 9x + 4$

3. $y = -x^2 + 6x - 8$

4. $-\frac{1}{2}x^2 + 2x = 1$

5. $4x^2 = x + 3$

6. $3x^2 - x = 10$

Method Three: Completing the Square

Another method of solving quadratic equations is forcing the quadratic to be a perfect square trinomial, thereby simplifying the analysis and solution. A disadvantage of this method is that a must equal 1 for its use, and when b is an odd number you must deal with fractions. Completing the square will, however, find both rational and irrational solutions exactly.

For example, the equation $x^2 + 6x - 11 = 0$ is clearly not factorable, so we shall use the completing the square method.

Step 1. Arrange the equation to be in the form $ax^2 + bx = c$. $\qquad x^2 + 6x = 11$

(**Note:** If $a \neq 1$, divide each term of the equation by a to make $a = 1$.)

Step 2. Take $\frac{1}{2}b$ and square it. $\qquad\qquad \frac{1}{2}(6) = 3 \qquad 3^2 = 9$

Step 3. Add $\left(\frac{1}{2}b\right)^2$ to both sides of the equation. $\qquad x^2 + 6x + 9 = 20$

Step 4. Write the trinomial as a perfect square in factored form. $\qquad (x + 3)^2 = 20$

Step 5. Take the square root of each side of the equation. $\left(\text{For the trinomial, this}\right.$
value will always be $x \pm \frac{1}{2}b.\left.\right)$ $x + 3 = \pm\sqrt{20}$

Step 6. Solve for x. $\qquad\qquad x = -3 \pm \sqrt{20}$

Step 7. Simplify, if possible. $\qquad\qquad x = -3 \pm 2\sqrt{5}$

1. Find all the roots of the equation $3x^2 - 12x - 21 = 0$.

SOLUTION

Divide by 3 to get an equivalent equation, $x^2 - 4x - 7 = 0$, and complete the square.

$$x^2 - 4x = 7$$
$$x^2 - 4x + 4 = 11$$
$$(x - 2)^2 = 11$$
$$x - 2 = \pm\sqrt{11}$$
$$x = 2 \pm \sqrt{11}$$

Answer: The roots of the equation are $\{2 + \sqrt{11}, 2 - \sqrt{11}\}$.

Note: Again, these points would not be easily identifiable on a graph, but are clear when solved by completing the square. Completing the square also identifies complex roots.

2. Find all the roots of the equation $x^2 + 4x + 13 = 0$.

SOLUTION

$$x^2 + 4x = -13$$
$$x^2 + 4x + 4 = -9$$
$$(x + 2)^2 = -9$$
$$x + 2 = \pm 3i$$
$$x = -2 \pm 3i$$

Answer: The roots of the equation are $\{-2 + 3i, -2 - 3i\}$.

Practice

Solve each quadratic equation by completing the square.

1. $x^2 + 6x + 10 = 0$

2. $2x^2 - 18x = 14$

3. $3x^2 = 6x - 15$

4. $\frac{1}{2}x^2 - 3x = -9$

5. $x^2 + 6x - 7 = 0$

6. $\frac{23}{x} = x - 10$

Method Four: The Quadratic Formula

Quadratic equations can always be solved by using the **quadratic formula,** $x = \frac{-b \pm \sqrt{b^2 - 4ac}}{2a}$. It does not matter whether the roots are real or imaginary, rational or irrational, the quadratic formula can be used to find the solutions. The formula is derived from the general equation of a quadratic by completing the square as shown below.

$$ax^2 + bx + c = 0$$

$$ax^2 + bx = -c$$

$$x^2 + \frac{b}{a}x = -\frac{c}{a}$$

$$x^2 + \frac{b}{a}x + \left(\frac{1b}{2a}\right)^2 = \left(\frac{1b}{2a}\right)^2 - \frac{c}{a}$$

$$x^2 + \frac{b}{a}x + \frac{b^2}{4a^2} = \frac{b^2}{4a^2} - \frac{c}{a}$$

$$x^2 + \frac{b}{a}x + \frac{b^2}{4a^2} = \frac{b^2 - 4ac}{4a^2}$$

$$\left(x + \frac{b}{2a}\right)^2 = \frac{b^2 - 4ac}{4a^2}$$

$$x + \frac{b}{2a} = \pm\frac{\sqrt{b^2 - 4ac}}{2a}$$

$$x = \frac{-b \pm \sqrt{b^2 - 4ac}}{2a}$$

To solve an equation using the quadratic formula, simply substitute the a, b, and c values from the equation and simplify the radical expression as much as possible. If instructed, find the answer to the nearest tenth or hundredth of a unit.

MODEL PROBLEMS

1. Find all roots of the equation $2x^2 - 3x - 2 = 0$.

SOLUTION

$$a = 2 \qquad b = -3 \qquad c = -2$$

$$x = \frac{-b \pm \sqrt{b^2 - 4ac}}{2a}$$

$$x = \frac{-(-3) \pm \sqrt{(-3)^2 - 4(2)(-2)}}{2(2)}$$

$$x = \frac{3 \pm \sqrt{9 - (8)(-2)}}{4}$$

$$x = \frac{3 \pm \sqrt{25}}{4}$$

$$x = \frac{3 \pm 5}{4}$$

$$x_1 = \frac{3 + 5}{4} \qquad\qquad x_2 = \frac{3 - 5}{4}$$

$$x_1 = 2 \qquad\qquad x_2 = -\frac{1}{2}$$

Answer: The solutions to this equation are $\left\{-\frac{1}{2}, 2\right\}$.

2. Find the roots of $x - 6 = -\frac{11}{x}$.

SOLUTION

$$x^2 - 6x = -11$$
$$x^2 - 6x + 11 = 0$$
$$a = 1 \qquad b = -6 \qquad c = 11$$

$$x = \frac{-b \pm \sqrt{b^2 - 4ac}}{2a}$$

$$x = \frac{-(-6) \pm \sqrt{(-6)^2 - 4(1)(11)}}{2(1)}$$

$$x = \frac{6 \pm \sqrt{36 - 44}}{2}$$

$$x = \frac{6 \pm \sqrt{-8}}{2}$$

$$x = \frac{6 \pm 2i\sqrt{2}}{2}$$

$$x = 3 \pm i\sqrt{2}$$

Answer: The solutions to this equation are $\{3 + i\sqrt{2}, 3 - i\sqrt{2}\}$.

3. Solve: $4x^2 - 12x + 25 = 0$.

SOLUTION

$$a = 4 \qquad b = -12 \qquad c = 25$$

$$x = \frac{-b \pm \sqrt{b^2 - 4ac}}{2a}$$

$$x = \frac{-(-12) \pm \sqrt{(-12)^2 - 4(4)(25)}}{2(4)}$$

$$x = \frac{12 \pm \sqrt{144 - 400}}{8}$$

$$x = \frac{12 \pm \sqrt{-256}}{8}$$

$$x = \frac{12 \pm 16i}{8}$$

$$x = \frac{3 \pm 4i}{2} = \frac{3}{2} \pm 2i$$

Answer: The roots of this equation are $\left\{\frac{3}{2} + 2i, \frac{3}{2} - 2i\right\}$.

You may also encounter radical equations. The most important rule to remember in solving radical equations is to isolate the radical before you square both sides of the equation.

Solve for all values of x: $\sqrt{4x + 1} - 1 = x$.

SOLUTION

First, isolate the radical by adding 1 to each side of the equation.

$$\sqrt{4x + 1} = x + 1$$

Square each side of the equation.

$$(\sqrt{4x + 1})^2 = (x + 1)^2$$
$$4x + 1 = x^2 + 2x + 1$$

Solve the resulting equation.

$$0 = x^2 - 2x$$
$$0 = x(x - 2)$$
$$x = 0 \qquad x - 2 = 0$$
$$x = 2$$

Check your solutions in the original equation to be certain the values are not extraneous roots.

$$\sqrt{4x + 1} - 1 = x$$

$$\sqrt{4(0) + 1} - 1 \overset{?}{=} 0 \qquad \sqrt{4(2) + 1} - 1 \overset{?}{=} 2$$
$$\sqrt{1} - 1 \overset{?}{=} 0 \qquad \sqrt{9} - 1 \overset{?}{=} 2$$
$$0 \overset{?}{=} 0 \checkmark \qquad 3 - 1 \overset{?}{=} 2$$
$$2 = 2 \checkmark$$

Both solutions check.

Practice

In 1–9, solve each equation using the quadratic formula.

1. $x^2 + 1 = 4x$

2. $x - 2 = \dfrac{-5}{4x}$

3. $3x^2 + 2 = 7x$

4. $\dfrac{1}{2}x^2 - 3x + 2 = 0$

5. $x^2 - 4 = \dfrac{15x}{2}$

6. $5x^2 - 3x + 1 = 0$

7. $\sqrt{3x - 5} = x - 1$

8. $\sqrt{2x + 7} - 3 = x - 7$

9. $\sqrt{5x + 1} - 2 = x - 3$

In 10–15, solve each equation by whichever method you choose.

10. $x^2 - 6 = \dfrac{5x}{2}$

11. $x^2 - 6x = -11$

12. $2(x + 4) = 3x^2$

13. $\sqrt{10 - 2x} - 7 = x$

14. $3x^2 + 5x + 2 = 0$

15. $2x - 1 = -\dfrac{5}{2x}$

4.2 Applying the Quadratic Formula

Nature of the Roots and the Discriminant

The graph of a quadratic equation, $y = ax^2 + bx + c$, may have four different appearances, depending on what kind of roots the equation has.

The graphs of quadratic functions with imaginary roots will not intersect the x-axis at all but remain totally above or below it, as shown in the figure below, depending on the positive or negative value of a. When a is positive, the parabola opens upward with a minimum point, and when a is negative, the parabola opens downward with a maximum point. The two roots of each of these functions are nonreal or imaginary numbers.

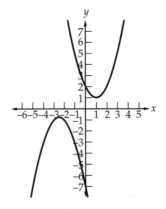

The graph of a quadratic function in which both roots are equal will be tangent to the x-axis, intersecting it at just one point, as shown in the figure below. In this case, the roots will be real but may be either rational or irrational.

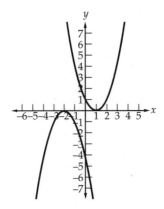

The graph of a quadratic function in which the roots are real and rational but not equal will intersect the x-axis in two distinct points, as shown below, whether the equation of the parabola has a positive or a negative a. These roots may or may not be readily identified on the graph.

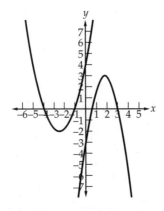

The graph of a quadratic function with two unequal, real, irrational roots will also intersect the x-axis at two distinct points. Because x is an irrational coordinate, its value is not easily identified. While the roots might appear to be 0.8 and 3.2 for the downward parabola, they could just as easily be $\sqrt{0.75}$ or $\sqrt{11}$.

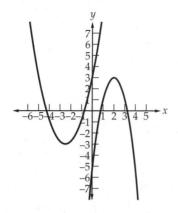

The **discriminant** is an expression that will determine the nature of the roots of the quadratic and, by extension, the best means of solving that particular quadratic equation. The formula for the discriminant is $b^2 - 4ac$, the radicand of the quadratic formula. If you know the nature of the roots from examining the discriminant, you can choose the most efficient method of solving the quadratic to find those roots. This information is summarized in the table below.

If the discriminant is	The roots will be	Best method of solution is
a negative number	imaginary	completing the square or quadratic formula
zero	real, equal, rational	factoring, graphing, completing the square, or quadratic formula
positive perfect square	real, unequal, rational	factoring, completing the square, or quadratic formula
positive nonperfect square	real, unequal, irrational	completing the square or quadratic formula

MODEL PROBLEMS

1. Describe the roots of the quadratic equation $2x^2 - 3x + 4 = 0$.

SOLUTION
Rather than solving the equation, find the discriminant and interpret it.

$$a = 2 \qquad b = -3 \qquad c = 4$$
$$\begin{aligned} \text{discriminant} &= b^2 - 4ac \\ &= (-3)^2 - 4(2)(4) \\ &= 9 - 32 \\ &= -23 \end{aligned}$$

Since -23 is a negative number, there are two unequal, imaginary roots, meaning the parabola does not cross the x-axis. In this case, the graph lies entirely above the x-axis. The solutions can best be found by completing the square or by using the quadratic formula.

2. Given the quadratic $3x^2 - 2x = 4$, which of the following best describes its roots?
   (1) unequal, imaginary roots
   (2) real, unequal, irrational roots
   (3) real, equal, rational roots
   (4) real, unequal, rational roots

SOLUTION
Set the equation equal to zero, find the discriminant, and interpret it.

$$a = 3 \qquad b = -2 \qquad c = -4$$
$$\begin{aligned} \text{discriminant} &= b^2 - 4ac \\ &= (-2)^2 - 4(3)(-4) \\ &= 4 - (-48) \\ &= 52 \end{aligned}$$

Since 52 is not a perfect square, the roots are real, unequal, and irrational (choice 2).

3. If the parabola $y = ax^2 + bx + c$, $a \neq 0$, has two equal roots, what can be said about its graph?
   (1) The graph does not intersect the x-axis.
   (2) The graph is tangent to the x-axis.
   (3) The graph intersects the x-axis at two points.
   (4) The graph is totally above the x-axis.

SOLUTION
Since the equation has two equal roots, the discriminant must be zero. Therefore, the graph is tangent to the x-axis.

4. Find the smallest possible integral value of c such that $6x^2 - 4x + c = 0$ will have imaginary roots.

SOLUTION
For an equation to have imaginary roots, its discriminant must be negative. Set the discriminant, $b^2 - 4ac$, to be less than zero, substitute the values of a and b, and solve for c.

$$a = 6 \qquad b = -4$$
$$b^2 - 4ac < 0$$
$$(-4)^2 - 4(6)c < 0$$
$$16 - 24c < 0$$
$$-24c < -16$$
$$c > \frac{-16}{-24}$$
$$c > \frac{2}{3}$$

To find *the smallest possible integral value of c* as requested in the problem, we look for the smallest integer greater than $\frac{2}{3}$. Therefore c would equal 1.

Remember: When multiplying or dividing by -1, the inequality sign reverses direction.

In 1–6, find the discriminant for each equation and explain its significance.

1. $3x^2 + 7 = -2x$

2. $10 - 3x = x^2$

3. $\dfrac{2x + 1}{x} = \dfrac{3x - 4}{2}$

4. $4x - 1 = \dfrac{-9}{x}$

5. $\dfrac{1}{3}x^2 - x = 6$

6. $4x = \dfrac{12x - 9}{x}$

In 7–15, select the numeral preceding the choice that best answers the question.

7. Which of the following equations has a discriminant of 64?
   (1) $x^2 - 4x - 11 = 0$
   (2) $3x^2 - 2x = 5$
   (3) $2x^2 - x + 7 = 0$
   (4) $6 - 4x = 3x^2$

8. Which method(s) of solution would produce exact solutions to $x^2 + 25 = 6x$?
   (1) graphing
   (2) completing the square
   (3) quadratic formula
   (4) factoring

9. For what integer value of a would $ax^2 - 6x + 8 = 0$ produce imaginary roots?
   (1) 1   (3) 0
   (2) 2   (4) −1

10. Which of the following describes the graph of $4x^2 - 3x - 1 = 0$?
    (1) The parabola would be tangent to the x-axis.
    (2) The parabola would lie entirely above the x-axis.
    (3) The parabola would lie entirely below the x-axis.
    (4) The parabola would intersect the x-axis at two distinct points.

11. Which of the following equations has real, rational, and equal roots?
    (1) $9x^2 + 6x + 1 = 0$
    (2) $2x^2 + 7x - 10 = 0$
    (3) $4x^2 - 9 = 0$
    (4) $5x^2 - 25 = 0$

12. If the discriminant of an equation equals 17, what can be said of the roots?
    (1) two real, unequal, irrational roots
    (2) two real, equal, rational roots
    (3) two imaginary, unequal roots
    (4) two real, unequal, rational roots

13. Which of the following might be the discriminant of a parabola that does not intersect the x-axis?
    (1) 143   (3) 0
    (2) 36   (4) −11

14. For what value of b will the roots of $2x^2 - bx + 9 = 0$ produce two real, unequal, rational roots?
    (1) −1   (3) 5
    (2) 0   (4) 9

15. Find the largest integral value of k for which the roots of $2x^2 + 7x + k = 0$ are real.
    (1) 7   (3) 0
    (2) 6   (4) −2

In 16–21, use any method you choose to solve each equation.

16. $2x^2 - 7x + 3 = 0$

17. $x - 8 = \dfrac{-20}{x}$

18. $\sqrt{2x - 1} - x = -2$

19. $4x(x + 1) = 2(4x - 5)$

20. $x^2 = 2(7x - 12)$

21. $x - 3 = \dfrac{5}{2x}$

Sum and Product of the Roots

Knowing the roots of an equation, we can work backward to find the equation. If the roots of the equation are 3 and -2, we know the factors of the equation are $(x - 3)$ and $(x + 2)$. The product of $(x - 3)(x + 2)$ is $x^2 - x - 6$, so the equation would be $y = x^2 - x - 6$. Sometimes, however, the roots are not rational and the equations are more complicated to discover, such as one with roots of $3 + 2\sqrt{5}$ and $3 - 2\sqrt{5}$.

Another method of finding the equation would be to use formulas for the sum and product of the roots derived from the quadratic formula. We know that the roots of any quadratic equation are

$$\frac{-b}{2a} + \frac{\sqrt{b^2 - 4ac}}{2a} \quad \text{and} \quad \frac{-b}{2a} - \frac{\sqrt{b^2 - 4ac}}{2a}.$$

When irrational or complex, the roots $\frac{-b}{2a} + \frac{\sqrt{b^2 - 4ac}}{2a}$ and $\frac{-b}{2a} - \frac{\sqrt{b^2 - 4ac}}{2a}$ are called **conjugates.**

Adding these roots we get $\frac{-2b}{2a}$ or $\frac{-b}{a}$. Therefore, for any quadratic equation, the sum of the roots would be $\frac{-b}{a}$.

Multiplying the two roots, we get

$$\frac{b^2}{4a^2} - \frac{b\sqrt{b^2 - 4ac}}{4a^2} + \frac{b\sqrt{b^2 - 4ac}}{4a^2} - \frac{b^2 - 4ac}{4a^2}$$

$$= \frac{b^2}{4a^2} - \frac{b^2 - 4ac}{4a^2}$$

$$= \frac{b^2 - b^2 + 4ac}{4a^2}$$

$$= \frac{4ac}{4a^2}$$

$$= \frac{c}{a}$$

Therefore, the product of the roots of any quadratic equation is $\frac{c}{a}$.

To find any quadratic equation given its roots, find the sum of the roots and the product of the roots to determine the values of a, b, and c. Then insert the values into the general form of the quadratic equation, $ax^2 + bx + c = 0$.

MODEL PROBLEMS

1. Find the quadratic equation whose roots are $3 + \sqrt{2}$ and $3 - \sqrt{2}$.

SOLUTION

Sum of the roots: $3 + \sqrt{2} + 3 - \sqrt{2} = 6$ Hence, $\frac{-b}{a} = \frac{6}{1}$, so $b = -6$.

Product of the roots: $(3 + \sqrt{2})(3 - \sqrt{2}) = 9 + 3\sqrt{2} - 3\sqrt{2} - 2 = 7$ Hence, $\frac{c}{a} = \frac{7}{1}$, so $c = 7$.

Since $a = 1$, $b = -6$, and $c = 7$, the equation is $x^2 - 6x + 7 = 0$.

2. Find the quadratic equation whose roots are $5 + 2i$ and $5 - 2i$.

SOLUTION

Sum of the roots: $\dfrac{-b}{a} = \dfrac{10}{1}$

Product of the roots: $25 - 4i^2 = 25 - 4(-1) = 25 + 4 = \dfrac{29}{1} = \dfrac{c}{a}$

Since $a = 1$, $b = -10$, and $c = 29$, the equation is $x^2 - 10x + 29 = 0$.

3. If one root of a quadratic equation is $2 - i\sqrt{3}$, find the other root and write the quadratic equation which would produce these roots.

SOLUTION

Since complex roots always appear as a pair of conjugates, the second root must be $2 + i\sqrt{3}$.

Sum of the roots: $\dfrac{-b}{a} = \dfrac{4}{1}$

Product of roots: $4 - 3i^2 = 4 - 3(-1) = 4 + 3 = \dfrac{7}{1} = \dfrac{c}{a}$

Therefore, $a = 1$, $b = -4$, and $c = 7$. The equation is $x^2 - 4x + 7 = 0$.

 Practice

1. Find the sum and product of the roots of the equation: $2x^2 - 6x + 10 = 0$.

2. If one root of an equation is $6 + 2i$, find the other root and the equation.

3. If $x^2 - 12x + k = 28$ and one root is 2, find the other root and the value of k.

4. Write the quadratic equation whose roots are $\left\{\dfrac{2}{9} + \dfrac{i}{9}, \dfrac{2}{9} - \dfrac{i}{9}\right\}$.

5. If $r_1 = 2 - \sqrt{5}$, find the other root and the quadratic equation from which these roots are derived.

6. Find the sum and product of the roots of the equation: $4x^2 - 12 = 3x$.

7. If the sum of two roots is 12 and one root is 5, find the other root and the pertinent quadratic equation.

8. If one root of the equation $2x^2 + kx - 5 = 0$ is $\dfrac{1}{2}$, find the other root and k.

9. Write the equation of the quadratic whose roots are $-\dfrac{1}{3}$ and 4.

10. Write the equation of the quadratic whose roots are $3 - 4i$ and $3 + 4i$.

4.3 Systems of Equations

A **system of equations** is two or more equations that may share a common solution. When graphed on the same set of axes, the equations sometimes intersect at one or more points, that is, they may share at least one x- and y-coordinate, such as the graphs shown on page 88.

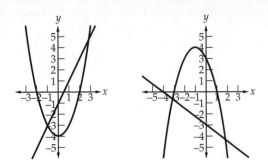

In this section we will limit the systems investigated to linear systems and linear-quadratic systems. The common solution to any system may be found using either algebraic or graphic means, and we will explore both methods.

Algebraic Solutions to Systems

To solve a system of equations algebraically, we must restructure the system so that an equation contains only one variable rather than two. One way to do this is to solve one of the equations in terms of one variable and substitute that definition of the variable into the other equation. That way, the second equation contains only one variable and can be solved by factoring, completing the square, or the quadratic formula. We can also solve a system of equations by adding or subtracting the two equations so that one variable is eliminated.

 **MODEL PROBLEMS**

1. Solve the system of equations.

$$3x - 2y = 1$$
$$2x + y = 10$$

SOLUTION
We can multiply the second equation by 2 and use the elimination process, eliminating one variable and solving for the other.

$$3x - 2y = 1$$
$$+ \; \underline{4x + 2y = 20}$$
$$7x = 21$$
$$x = 3$$

Once you know the value of one variable, substitute and solve for the other.

$$3(3) - 2y = 1$$
$$9 - 2y = 1$$
$$-2y = -8$$
$$y = 4$$

The coordinate point of intersection on a graph is $(3, 4)$.

2. Solve the system of equations.

$$y = x^2 - 2x - 8$$
$$y + 8 = x$$

SOLUTION

The second equation is already solved for x, but it would be simpler to replace y in the quadratic equation to avoid squaring the binomial $(y + 8)$. If $y + 8 = x$, then $y = x - 8$. If y equals both $x - 8$ and $x^2 - 2x - 8$, then

$$x - 8 = x^2 - 2x - 8$$
$$0 = x^2 - 3x$$
$$0 = x(x - 3)$$
$$x = 0 \qquad x - 3 = 0$$
$$x = 3$$

To find the y-values of the coordinate points, substitute the x-values in either equation.

$$y + 8 = x$$
$$y + 8 = 0 \qquad y + 8 = 3$$
$$y = -8 \qquad y = -5$$

The coordinate points at which these quadratic and linear equations intersect are, therefore, $(0, -8)$ and $(3, -5)$. To verify these solutions, it is necessary to check both pairs of points in both equations.

Check:

$$y = x^2 - 2x - 8$$
$$-8 = 0^2 - 2(0) - 8 \qquad -5 = (3)^2 - 2(3) - 8$$
$$-8 = -8 \checkmark \qquad -5 = 9 - 6 - 8$$
$$-5 = -5 \checkmark$$

$$y + 8 = x$$
$$-8 + 8 = 0 \qquad -5 + 8 = 3$$
$$0 = 0 \checkmark \qquad 3 = 3 \checkmark$$

Practice

Solve each system algebraically.

1. $4c - 2h = 10$
   $c = 4 + h$

2. $5m + 3n = 4$
   $m - 3n = 8$

3. $6a + 8b = -2$
   $3a + 5b = 1$

4. $y + 13 = x$
   $y + 3 = x^2 - 6x$

5. $2x^2 - y = 10$
   $y = -2x^2 - 3x + 12$

6. $y - x = 2$
   $y = x^2 - 2x + 4$

7. $y = 2 - x$
   $y + 1 = x^2 + x - 5$

8. $x^2 = y + 10 - 3x$
   $y + 4 = 2x$

9. $y = 2x^2 - 7x + 3$
   $x - 3 = y$

10. $y = x^2 - 5x + 6$
    $y + 1 = 3x$

11. $y + 2x^2 = 4x + 7$
    $y + 4x = x^2 + 4$

12. $y = x^2 + 1$
    $2x + 3 + y = 3x^2$

Graphic Solutions to Systems

To solve systems graphically, you can graph the equations by hand using graph paper or use a graphing calculator such as the TI-83. In either method, the common solution must be checked in both equations.

To solve using a graphing calculator, follow these steps:

- Press the $\boxed{Y=}$ key on the upper left of the calculator.

- Enter the first equation in Y_1, the second equation in Y_2.

Note: the equations must be solved for y in order to graph them on a TI-83.

- Go to the $\boxed{WINDOW}$ key and set reasonable boundaries for x and y. You will be asked to enter X Min and X Max as well as Y Min and Y Max. (At times, it is convenient to use $\boxed{ZOOM}$ 6 to graph. This produces a window that is 10 units in each direction around the graph. This approach will not always include the solution.)

- Once the equations are shown on the screen, if the window is not appropriate, go back to the window settings and adjust the x- and y-values so you can see the full graph of both equations. Remember, you are looking for their intersection.

- To locate the intersection of the graphs, press the $\boxed{2nd}$ function key and the $\boxed{TRACE}$ key, which will give you the CALCULATE screen.

- Scroll to "5:intersect" or press $\boxed{5}$. You will be asked to verify the curves being explored. Press $\boxed{ENTER}$ after each question: First curve? $\boxed{ENTER}$. Second curve? $\boxed{ENTER}$. Guess? $\boxed{ENTER}$. The calculator will then locate one of the solutions. To find the other solution, return to the CALCULATE screen and press 5 again. This time, move the cursor closer to the other intersection point shown when you are asked about the curves. Use these steps to follow the model problem below.

MODEL PROBLEM

Solve the system of equations.

$$y = x^2 + x - 6$$
$$y = x - 5$$

SOLUTION

Step 1: Enter the equations in Y_1 and Y_2.

```
 Plot1  Plot2  Plot3
\Y1 = X²+X–6
\Y2 = X–5
\Y3 =
\Y4 =
\Y5 =
\Y6 =
\Y7 =
```

Step 2: ZOOM 6 for a standard window.

```
ZOOM   MEMORY
1 : ZBox
2 : Zoom In
3 : Zoom Out
4 : ZDecimal
5 : ZSquare
6 : ZStandard
7↓ ZTrig
```

Step 3: Check the graphs to be sure they are visible in the standard window.

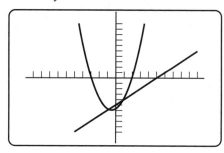

Step 4: (2nd) (TRACE) gives you the CALCULATE screen

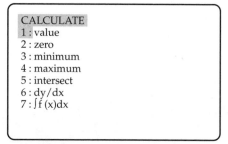

Step 5: Press "5:intersect"; (ENTER), (ENTER), (ENTER) to have the calculator display the first solution.

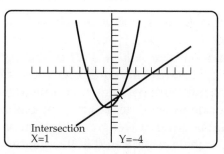

Step 6: Move the cursor closer to the other intersection with the (TRACE) and (◄) keys. Then repeat steps 4 and 5 to find the second solution.

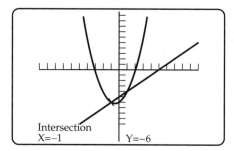

As you have discovered, the solutions to this system are the points whose coordinates are $(1, -4)$ and $(-1, -6)$. Again, the solutions should be checked in each of the equations.

In 1–6, solve each system by graphing.

1. $x + 2 = y$
$y = -x^2 - 3x + 7$

2. $y = 3x^2 - 2x + 4$
$x + y = 6$

3. $y = 2x^2 - 5x + 1$
$y = 1 - x$

4. $y = x^2 - 4x$
$y = \frac{1}{2}x - 2$

5. $y + 3 = x^2 - x$
$y = 2x - 3$

6. $x^2 - y = 3x - 2$
$x + y = 5$

In 7–12, solve each system by whichever method you prefer.

7. $y = x^2 - 2x + 5$
$y - 2 = 2x$

8. $y + x^2 = x + 6$
$y = x^2 - 4x + 3$

9. $y = 2x^2 - 3x - 2$
$x^2 + y = 4$

10. $y = \frac{1}{2}x^2 - 6x - 9$
$y + 2x = 1$

11. $y + 5x + 3 = 2x^2$
$y + 7 = x$

12. $y = 3x^2 + 5x - 2$
$3x + y = 1$

4.4 Parameters of Quadratic Functions

The general form of a quadratic equation is $ax^2 + bx + c = 0$ where $a \neq 0$. When we want to graph a quadratic function, we consider the equation to be $y = ax^2 + bx + c$, $a \neq 0$. The coefficient a exerts great influence over the quadratic determining, as discussed previously, the upward or downward direction of the parabola dependent on its positive or negative value. Yet, even if we ignore the sign of a, the coefficient a also alters the shape of the parabola as indicated in the diagrams below.

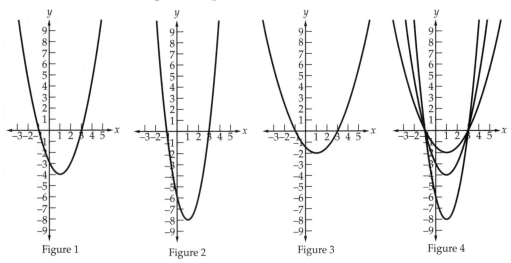

Figure 1   Figure 2   Figure 3   Figure 4

In Figure 1, $a = 1$, while in Figure 2, $a = 2$, and in Figure 3, $a = \frac{1}{2}$. The fourth figure combines the graphs of all three equations so you can see the differences in the shapes of the parabolas. (Since a negative value of a achieves the same effects in a downward direction, we will consider the absolute value of a in the following examples.)

Graph the three equations on the same axes.

$$y_1 = x^2 \qquad y_2 = 2x^2 \qquad y_3 = \frac{1}{2}x^2$$

Discuss the similarities and differences in the appearance of these parabolas.

SOLUTION

When calculated, the coordinate points for each equation are shown in the table below.

$y_1 = x^2$		$y_2 = 2x^2$		$y_3 = \frac{1}{2}x^2$	
x	y	x	y	x	y
−3	9	−3	18	−3	4.5
−2	4	−2	8	−2	2
−1	1	−1	2	−1	0.5
0	0	0	0	0	0
1	1	1	2	1	0.5
2	4	2	8	2	2
3	9	3	18	3	4.5

Notice the effect of the coefficients 2 and $\frac{1}{2}$ on the y-values in the second and third equations. In the equation $y_2 = 2x^2$ the y-values are twice the original y-values in the equation $y_1 = x^2$. In the equation $y_3 = \frac{1}{2}x^2$, the y-values are one-half the original y-values in the equation $y = x^2$. Obviously, then, the leading coefficient of a parabola directly affects the y-values.

These charts of values produce the graphs shown below.

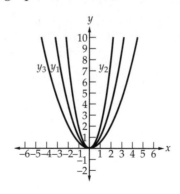

As is seen in the graph above, the larger the absolute value of a, the more steeply the parabola rises and the narrower it appears. The smaller the absolute value of a, the less steeply the parabola rises and the wider it appears, with a flatter appearance at the vertex. In all three cases, the turning point or vertex of the parabola remains the same, as does the axis of symmetry, $x = 0$.

MODEL PROBLEMS

1. Graph the parabolas $y_1 = x^2$, $y_2 = (x - 2)^2$, and $y_3 = x^2 - 2$ on the same set of axes. What similarities and differences occur in the axes of symmetry, the vertices, and the shapes of the parabolas?

SOLUTION

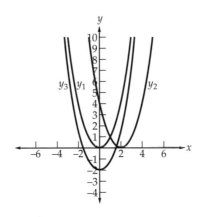

As seen in the diagram above, y_1 has an axis of symmetry of $x = 0$ as does y_3, but they have different vertices. y_1 has a turning point of $(0, 0)$ while y_3 has a vertex of $(0, -2)$. It would appear that y_3 is the graph of y_1 shifted 2 units down. The axis of symmetry of y_2 is $x = 2$ and its vertex is $(2, 0)$. It seems that y_2 is the original parabola moved 2 units to the right. The shape of all of the parabolas is the same.

2. Complete the square of the equation $y = x^2 - 2x - 3$ and then graph it. What do you notice about the equation you completed and graphed?

SOLUTION

$$y = x^2 - 2x - 3$$
$$y + 3 = x^2 - 2x$$
$$y + 3 + 1 = x^2 - 2x + 1$$
$$y + 4 = x^2 - 2x + 1$$
$$y + 4 = (x - 1)^2$$
$$y = (x - 1)^2 - 4$$

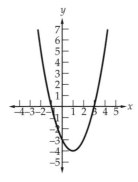

Note: The axis of symmetry is $x = 1$ and the vertex is $(1, -4)$, information revealed in the vertex form of the parabola $y = (x - h)^2 + k$, where (h, k) is the vertex and $x = h$ is the axis of symmetry.

1. Graph the equations $y_1 = x^2$, $y_2 = (x + 4)^2$, and $y_3 = x^2 + 3$ on the same set of axes and discuss their similarities and differences.

2. Graph the equations $y_1 = x^2$, $y_2 = (x - 3)^2$, and $y_3 = (x - 3)^2 + 3$ on the same set of axes and discuss their similarities and differences.

3. Complete the square of the equation $y = x^2 - 6x + 8$ and then graph the parabola. What do you notice about the axis of symmetry and the vertex?

4. Graph the equations $y_1 = (x - 1)^2$, $y_2 = 4(x - 1)^2$, and $y_3 = \frac{1}{2}(x - 1)^2$ on the same set of axes and discuss their similarities and differences.

4.5 Applications of the Quadratic Equation

Geometric Applications

Many of the concepts studied in geometry can produce quadratic equations that are solvable by various means.

 MODEL PROBLEMS

1. In right triangle CTH, hypotenuse $CT = 6$, $TH = x$, and $CH = 8 - x$.
   a. Write an equation in terms of x that can be used to find TH.
   b. Solve the equation for x. (Answer may be left in radical form.)

SOLUTION
First, sketch the triangle described.

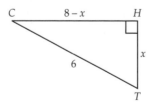

Analyze what options for solutions are available. Since CTH is a right triangle, we can use the Pythagorean formula to solve for x.

$$x^2 + (8 - x)^2 = 6^2$$
$$x^2 + 64 - 16x + x^2 = 36$$
$$2x^2 - 16x + 28 = 0$$
$$x^2 - 8x + 14 = 0$$

Since this equation is not factorable, we must use the quadratic formula to find the roots.

$$a = 1, b = -8, \text{ and } c = 14$$

$$x = \frac{-b \pm \sqrt{b^2 - 4ac}}{2a}$$

$$x = \frac{-(-8) \pm \sqrt{(-8)^2 - 4(1)(14)}}{2(1)}$$

$$x = \frac{8 \pm \sqrt{64 - 56}}{2}$$

$$x = \frac{8 \pm \sqrt{8}}{2}$$

$$x = \frac{8}{2} \pm \frac{2\sqrt{2}}{2}$$

$$x = 4 \pm \sqrt{2}$$

In this problem we are asked to find the length of x, the side of triangle CTH, so a negative solution would have no meaning and would be rejected. In this case, neither $4 + \sqrt{2}$ nor $4 - \sqrt{2}$ is a negative number, so both solutions are valid.

2. A square and a rectangle have the same area. The length of the rectangle is 5 inches more than twice the length of a side of the square. The width of the rectangle is 6 inches less than the length of a side of the square. Find the length of a side of the square.

SOLUTION
First, sketch and label a diagram that fits the situation in the problem.

Since the problem tells us the areas of the two figures are equal, we can set up the equation that states this algebraically.

$$x^2 = (2x + 5)(x - 6)$$
$$x^2 = 2x^2 - 7x - 30$$
$$0 = x^2 - 7x - 30$$

Since the equation is factorable, we can factor, use the quadratic formula, or solve by finding the roots or x-intercepts on the graph. With any method, $x = 10$ or $x = -3$, but the -3 must be discarded since we are finding the length of a side of a square, which cannot be negative.

Real-World Applications

Some situations in the real world offer problems that involve quadratic equations. Some may be solved algebraically or graphically, but others are much easier to solve using the graphing calculator.

Abigail, who has a bionic arm, is crossing a bridge over a small gorge and decides to toss a coin into the stream below for luck. The distance of the coin above the water can be modeled by the function $y = -16x^2 + 96x + 112$, where x measures time in seconds and y measures the height, in feet, above the water.

a. Find the greatest height the coin reaches before it drops into the water below.
b. Find the time at which the coin hits the water.

SOLUTION

a. Graph the function and find the maximum value of the graph.

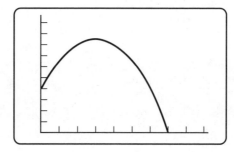

Use (2nd) (TRACE) (CALCULATE) to find the vertex point (3, 256). The coin is at its greatest height 3 seconds after being tossed and at that time it is 256 feet above the water.

b. The coin hits the water when its height equals zero. Therefore, we set the equation equal to zero and solve by factoring. We can simplify the equation by dividing through by -16,

$$-16x^2 + 96x + 112 = 0$$
$$x^2 - 6x - 7 = 0$$
$$(x - 7)(x + 1) = 0$$
$$x = 7 \qquad x = -1 \qquad \text{Reject } -1 \text{ since it refers to time before the coin was tossed.}$$

This solution could also have been determined using the calculator to find the zeros of the function. Use the CALCULATE screen again ((2nd) (TRACE)) but this time, press or scroll down to 2, zero. Indicate the left and right bounds of your answer, being certain to have your y-value be both positive and negative, and then hit (ENTER). Your solution will be the x-value of the coordinate shown in this case, since you are solving for time.

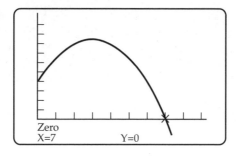

Zero
X=7   Y=0

The coin hits the water 7 seconds after it was tossed.

1. The profits of Mr. Unlucky's company can be represented by the equation $y = -3x^2 + 18x - 4$, where y is the amount of profit in hundreds of thousands of dollars and x is the number of years of operation. He realizes his company is on the downturn and wishes to sell it before he ends up in debt.
   a. When will Unlucky's business show the maximum profit?
   b. What is that maximum profit?
   c. At what time will it be too late to sell his business? (When will he start losing money?)

2. The altitude to the hypotenuse of a right triangle measures 12 inches. If the entire hypotenuse measures 25 inches, find the lengths of the two segments of the hypotenuse created by the altitude.

3. At a swim meet, Janet dives from a diving board that is 48 feet high. Her position above the water is represented by the equation $y = -16x^2 + 24x + 40$, where x represents the time in seconds and y represents the height above the water.
   a. After how many seconds does Janet enter the water? (Hint: the height above the water would equal zero.)
   b. What is the greatest height that Janet reaches in her dive?

4. In $\triangle CTH$ shown below, $\overline{XA} \parallel \overline{CH}$; $CH = 20$; $XA = c + 4$; $TH = 4c - 1$, and $TA = c + 2$. Find the value of c and the lengths of $\overline{TH}$, $\overline{TA}$, and $\overline{XA}$.

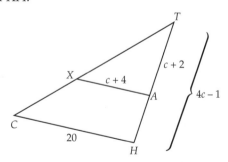

5. The hypotenuse of a right triangle is 3 less than 4 times the smaller leg. The other leg measures 3 more than 3 times the smaller leg. Find the lengths of all sides of the triangle.

6. American astronauts working on a space station on the moon toss a ball into the air. The height of the ball is represented by the equa-

tion $y = -2.7x^2 + 13.5x + 14$, where x represents the number of seconds since the ball was thrown and y represents the height of the ball in feet.
   a. To the nearest hundredth of a second, after how much time does the ball hit the ground?
   b. To the nearest tenth of a foot, what is the greatest height the ball achieves?

7. The length of Mr. McGregor's rectangular carrot patch is 2 less than twice its width. The area of the garden is 420 square feet, but in order to sabotage Peter Cottontail's annoying thefts from the garden, Mr. McGregor wants to install a 2-foot-wide irrigation ditch all the way around the garden.
   a. Find the dimensions of the garden.
   b. Find the perimeter of the garden's planned irrigation ditch.

8. Pierre throws a coin into the air from the top of the Eiffel Tower in Paris. The coin's motion is described by the equation $y = -4.9x^2 + 19x + 300$, where y represents the height in meters and x represents the time in seconds.
   a. How long after being thrown upward does the coin land, to the nearest tenth of a second?
   b. What is the coin's maximum height to the nearest tenth of a meter?

9. Jocelyn and Kelly built rockets from assembly kits and are going to launch them at the same time to see whose rocket flies higher. If Jocelyn's rocket's height, in feet, can be described by the equation $y = -16x^2 + 180x$ while Kelly's is represented by $y = -16x^2 + 240x$,
   a. who wins the rocket race? (What is the maximum height each rocket achieves?)
   b. after how many seconds does each rocket land?

10. a. A trapezoid has bases of $2x - 1$ and $x + 7$. If the height of the trapezoid is 6 units, write a formula for the area of the trapezoid.
    b. A rectangle has the same area as the trapezoid and its length is $2x - 3$ while its width is $x + 4$. Write an expression to represent the area of the rectangle.
    c. If the areas of the trapezoid and rectangle are equal, find the value of x and the dimensions of each figure.

4.6 Quadratic Inequalities

Having spent some time working on quadratic equations, we now consider quadratic inequalities. Given: $y = x^2 - x - 6$. By graphing the function, we can see that when $y = 0$, $x = 3$ or $x = -2$. Thus, we say that $x = 3$ and $x = -2$ are the *zeros* or the *roots* of the function.

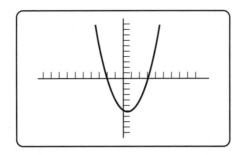

To solve the inequality $x^2 - x - 6 < 0$ graphically, look at which x-values produce negative y-values (that is, values of $y < 0$). We can see this occurs when $-2 < x < 3$. Now let us find the solution of $x^2 - x - 6 < 0$ algebraically. Our inequality translates into finding x-values that will make the quadratic negative (that is, less than zero). The next question is how to solve this inequality.

First, factor the inequality: $(x - 3)(x + 2) < 0$. Now, we know that $(x - 3)(x + 2) = 0$ when $x = 3$ or $x = -2$. We can put this information on a number line.

Think of the number line as divided into three regions $x < -2$, $-2 < x < 3$, and $x > 3$. In other words, numbers to the left of -2, numbers between -2 and 3, and numbers to the right of 3. Choose a number in each of these regions. For example, in the region $x < -2$, you might choose -5. Substitute this number into the inequality to determine whether your answer is positive or negative.

$$(x - 3)(x + 2) < 0 \rightarrow (-5 - 3)(-5 + 2) < 0$$

We obtain $(-8)(-3)$, which gives us $+24$.

Note: The actual *value* of your answer is not important. All that matters in this case is the sign of your answer, $(-)(-) = +$.

By choosing a number in the region $-2 < x < 3$, we get $(-)(+) = -$. In the region $x > 3$, we get $(+)(+) = +$. We put all of this information on our number line as shown below.

Since we are looking for values of x that will produce a negative answer, we choose the region where our answers are negative, that is, $-2 < x < 3$.

If we had wanted values of x such that $x^2 - x - 6 > 0$, we could have proceeded in a similar manner. Graphically, we would look for x-values that would produce positive y-values (that is values of $y > 0$). We can see that our solution is $x < -2$ or $x > 3$.

Algebraically, we must solve $x^2 - x - 6 > 0$. Looking at the number line above, we are interested in obtaining x-values that will make the inequality positive (greater than 0). So, we choose $x < -2$ or $x > 3$.

Given: $x^2 - 2x - 20 > 4$.
a. Find the solution set.   b. Graph the solution set on a number line.

SOLUTION

a. First, rewrite the inequality so 0 is on one side.

$$x^2 - 2x - 20 > 4$$
$$x^2 - 2x - 24 > 0$$

Next, solve this inequality algebraically.
Factor: $(x - 6)(x + 4) > 0$.

b. Plot the zeros on a number line.

Choose a value for x in each region and substitute these values for x in the inequality. Determine whether the answer you obtain is positive or negative, and mark this on your number line, as shown below.

Since we want to solve $x^2 - 2x - 24 > 0$, we are looking for positive x-values (values of $x > 0$). Thus, our solution is $x < -4$ or $x > 6$.

ALTERNATIVE SOLUTION

a. To solve the inequality graphically, graph $y = x^2 - 2x - 24$, as shown below.

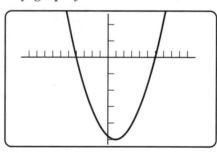

Since we want $x^2 - 2x - 24 > 0$, we are looking for positive y-values ($y > 0$). This occurs when $x < -4$ or $x > 6$.

b. To graph the solution set, we shade in the region less than -4 and also the region greater than 6. The solution set is all values in the shaded area.

Note: If we were asked to solve $x^2 - 2x - 24 \geq 0$, we would also shade in the circles at -4 and 6.

In 1–10, find the solution set for the inequality and graph the solution set.

1. $x^2 - x - 56 > 0$

2. $x^2 - 9 \geq 0$

3. $x^2 - 3x - 3 < 7$

4. $x^2 + 3x \geq -2x - 4$

5. $2x^2 + 7x + 3 > 0$

6. $x^2 \leq -4x + 12$

7. $3x^2 \geq -4x - 1$

8. $4x^2 < 9$

9. $x^2 + 32 > 12x$

10. $x^2 - 4x \leq x$

In 11–16, select the numeral preceding the expression or the diagram that best completes the sentence or answers the question.

11. The solution set of $x^2 - 3x > 18$ is
    (1) $-3 < x < 6$
    (2) $-6 < x < 3$
    (3) $x < -3$ or $x > 6$
    (4) $x < -6$ or $x > 3$

12. The solution set of $x^2 - 36 \leq 0$ is
    (1) $x \leq 6$ or $x \geq -6$
    (2) $x \leq -6$ or $x \geq 6$
    (3) $-6 \leq x \leq 6$
    (4) $-36 \leq x \leq 36$

13. The accompanying graph shows the solution to
    (1) $x^2 - 4x - 21 \geq 0$
    (2) $x^2 - 4x - 21 \leq 0$
    (3) $x^2 + 4x - 21 \leq 0$
    (4) $x^2 + 4x - 21 \geq 0$

14. Which of the following is the solution set of $x^2 \leq 3x$?
    (1)
    (2)
    (3)
    (4)

15. The graph of the solution set of $x^2 - 4x - 6 > 2x + 10$ is
    (1)
    (2)
    (3)
    (4)

16. What is the solution set of $x^2 + x - 2 < 12x - 32$?
    (1) $\{x \mid x < -6 \text{ or } x > 5\}$
    (2) $\{x \mid x < 5 \text{ or } x > 6\}$
    (3) $\{x \mid -6 < x < -5\}$
    (4) $\{x \mid 5 < x < 6\}$

CHAPTER REVIEW

1. Solve each equation by factoring.
   a. $x^2 + 15x + 56 = 0$
   b. $x^2 - 3x + 7 = x + 52$
   c. $2x^2 - 5x = x^2 + 3x$
   d. $2x^2 + 3x = 5$

2. Solve each equation by graphing.
   a. $x^2 + 2x - 24 = 0$
   b. $x^2 - 6x = x$
   c. $x^2 + 12x = 2x - 7$
   d. $2x^2 + 6x = x - 1$

3. Solve each equation by completing the square.
   a. $x^2 - 6x + 5 = 0$
   b. $x^2 - 2x + 3 = 2x + 6$
   c. $x^2 + 3x = x + 7$

4. Solve each equation by using the quadratic formula.
   a. $x^2 - 10x + 5 = 0$
   b. $x^2 + 2x - 4 = 3x - 8$
   c. $2x^2 = 3x - 10$

5. Solve each equation by using any method you prefer.
   a. $x^2 - 3x + 2 = 0$
   b. $x^2 + x + 5 = 0$
   c. $x^2 + 4x + 1 = 0$
   d. $x^2 - 4x = 2$
   e. $2x^2 - x = x^2 + 2x + 40$
   f. $2x^2 + 5x = x - 4$
   g. $3x^2 - 2x + 1 = 4$

6. Explain how you can determine the vertex of the parabola $y = (x - 2)^2 + 5$ by simply looking at the equation.

7. Olive Math is standing on the 102nd floor of the Empire State Building, thinking about mathematics. She realizes that, if she were able to throw a ball from her present position, the height of the ball in feet, h, at time t seconds could be modeled by the equation:

$$h = -16t^2 + 64t + 1,224.$$

   a. How high above the ground is the 102nd floor?
   b. What is the greatest height the ball would reach?
   c. How long would it take to reach that height?
   d. How long would it take the ball to hit the ground?

In 8–10, select the numeral preceding the word or expression that best completes the sentence or answers the question.

8. What is the product of the roots of the equation $x^2 - 6x - 2 = 0$?
   (1) −6   (3) 2
   (2) −2   (4) 6

9. What is the solution set for the inequality $x^2 - 6x - 2 < x - 8$?
   (1) $\{x | -6 < x < -1\}$
   (2) $\{x | 1 < x < 6\}$
   (3) $\{x | x < -6 \text{ or } x > -1\}$
   (4) $\{x | x < 1 \text{ or } x > 6\}$

10. The roots of the quadratic equation $3x^2 - x - 3 = x^2 + 7 - 5$ are
    (1) real, rational, and equal
    (2) real, rational, and unequal
    (3) real, irrational and unequal
    (4) imaginary

11. If a quadratic equation with real coefficients has a discriminant of 12, then the two roots must be
    (1) real, rational, and equal
    (2) real, rational, and unequal
    (3) real, irrational and unequal
    (4) imaginary

12. Solve each equation for x and y, and check.
    a. $y = x^2 + 2x + 7$
       $y = x + 13$
    b. $y^2 - x^2 = 11$
       $y = x + 1$
    c. $y = 2x^2 + 6x + 3$
       $y = x^2 - x - 7$

13. Express the roots of the equation $x^2 + 5x = 3x - 3$ in simplest $a + bi$ form.

14. Solve for x: $\sqrt{4x - 4} = x - 4$.

15. Compare the graphs of $y = x^2$, $y = x^2 + 3$, and $y = (x + 3)^2$.

16. Given: $y = x^2 - 6x - 3$. Complete the square to determine the vertex of the parabola.

17. Write an equation whose roots are −8 and 6.

18. On a number line, graph the solution of the inequality $2x^2 - 7x \geq x^2 - 7x + 9$.

19. Find the solution, to the nearest tenth, of $x - 4 = \sqrt{x + 4}$.

20. The Verrazano-Narrows Bridge, which connects Brooklyn to Staten Island, is the sixth longest suspension bridge in the world. The length of the main span is 4,260 feet. The roadway is suspended by cables that are

supported by two towers that are 700 feet tall. The clearance at the center is 228 feet.

a. The parabola graphed below represents the height of the cables above the water. The y-axis represents the center of the bridge. What are the coordinates of point P? What do these coordinates represent?

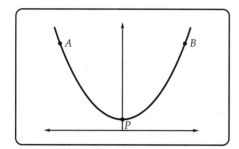

b. Points A and B represent the height of each of the two towers. What are the coordinates of points A and B?

c. The height of the cables above the water can be represented by the equation $y = 0.000104x^2 + 228$, where x is the distance from the center of the bridge. What do the coordinates (100, 229.04) represent?

d. Find y when $x = 1{,}000$. Explain what x and y represent.

e. Find y when $x = -1{,}000$. Explain what x and y represent.

f. Find x when $y = 500$. Explain what x and y represent.

21. Express the roots of the equation $3x^2 + 8x = 5x - 5$ in simplest $a + bi$ form.

In 22–25, select the numeral preceding the expression that best answers the question.

22. Which of the following is the solution set for the equation $\sqrt{17 - x} = x + 3$?
    (1) $\{x \mid x = -8 \text{ or } x = 1\}$
    (2) $\{x \mid x = -8 \text{ and } x = 1\}$
    (3) $\{x \mid x = -8\}$
    (4) $\{x \mid x = 1\}$

23. Which of the following might be the value of the discriminant of a parabola that lies entirely above the x-axis?
    (1) -10 (3) $\sqrt{12}$
    (2) 0   (4) 6

24. For which value of k will the roots of $3x^2 + kx + 2 = 1$ be real?
    (1) 1   (3) 3
    (2) 2   (4) 4

25. What is the solution set of the equation $x^2 + 25 = 0$?
    (1) $\{\ \}$ (3) $\{5i\}$
    (2) $\{-5i\}$ (4) $\{-5i, 5i\}$

26. What is the sum of the roots of the equation $3x^2 - x = x^2 - 5$?

27. Write an equation that has a root of $3 + 4i$.

The following TI-83 calculator program will solve quadratic equations using the quadratic formula. Many thanks to Tom Lutz for creating this program.

ClrHome

Disp "ENTER THE", "COEFFICIENTS", "OF THE QUADRATIC", "Y = AX^2 + BX + C"

Input "A:",A

Input "B:",B

Input "C:",C

B^2 − 4AC→D

FnOff

AxesOff

PlotsOff

Zstandard

ClrDraw

Text(0,0,"−",B,"+/−√ (",B,"^{2} − 4*",A, "*",C,")")

Line(−10,7.8,2,7.8)

Text(8,15,"2*",A)

Text(16,0,"−",B, "+/−√ (",D,")")

Line(−10,2.6, −2,2.6)

Text(24,12,2*A)

If D≥0

Then

Text(30,0,"REAL")

Text(36,0,"X=",(−B+√ (D))/(2A))

Text(42,0,"X=",(−B−√ (D))/(2A))

Else

Text(30,0,"IMAGINARY")

End

Note: This program will be helpful in checking your solution to a quadratic equation. However, be aware that calculator memories are cleared before the Math B Regents Examination. Therefore, you will not be able to use the program during the examination.

CHAPTER 5

Absolute Value and Rational Expressions

5.1 Absolute Value Equations

The absolute value of a number n is the distance from n to the origin on a number line. The symbol for the absolute value of n is $|n|$. Thus, $|5| = 5$ and $|-5| = 5$ since the distance from both positive 5 and negative 5 to 0 is 5. Algebraically,

$$\begin{cases} n \text{ if } n \geq 0 \\ -n \text{ if } n < 0 \end{cases}$$

 **MODEL PROBLEM**

Solve for x: $|x| = 8$.

SOLUTION
We must think about what number(s) are at a distance of 8 units from the origin. Since both 8 and -8 are 8 units from the origin, our solution is $x = 8$ or $x = -8$.

Answer: $x = 8, x = -8$

 **MODEL PROBLEMS**

1. Solve for x: $|x + 2| = 9$.

SOLUTION
We know that the expression on the inside of the absolute value bars must equal 9 or -9. Therefore, we set up two equations.

$$\begin{array}{ll} x + 2 = 9 & x + 2 = -9 \\ x = 7 & x = -11 \end{array}$$

We must now check if the solutions of our derived equations make the original equation true.

Check:

$$
\begin{array}{ll}
x = 7 & x = -11 \\
|x + 2| = 9 & |x + 2| = 9 \\
|7 + 2| \overset{?}{=} 9 & |-11 + 2| \overset{?}{=} 9 \\
|9| \overset{?}{=} 9 & |-9| \overset{?}{=} 9 \\
9 = 9 \checkmark & 9 = 9 \checkmark
\end{array}
$$

Answer: $x = 7$ or $x = -11$

2. Find the solution set: $|2a - 4| = 10$.

SOLUTION

$$
\begin{array}{ll}
2a - 4 = 10 & 2a - 4 = -10 \\
2a = 14 & 2a = -6 \\
a = 7 & a = -3
\end{array}
$$

Check:

$$
\begin{array}{ll}
a = 7 & a = -3 \\
|2a - 4| = 10 & |2a - 4| = 10 \\
|2(7) - 4| \overset{?}{=} 10 & |2(-3) - 4| \overset{?}{=} 10 \\
|14 - 4| \overset{?}{=} 10 & |-6 - 4| \overset{?}{=} 10 \\
|10| \overset{?}{=} 10 & |-10| \overset{?}{=} 10 \\
10 = 10 \checkmark & 10 = 10 \checkmark
\end{array}
$$

Answer: $\{-3, 7\}$

3. Solve: $|5n - 4| + 18 = 8$.

SOLUTION
First, isolate the absolute value.

$$|5n - 4| = -10$$

Answer: There is no number whose absolute value is negative. Therefore, the solution is $\{\ \}$.

4. Solve, and graph the solution on a number line: $|x + 6| - 18 = 2x$.

SOLUTION

First, isolate the absolute value.

$$|x + 6| = 2x + 18$$

$x + 6 = 2x + 18$	$x + 6 = -(2x + 18)$
$6 = x + 18$	$x + 6 = -2x - 18$
$x = -12$	$6 = -3x - 18$
	$-3x = 24$
	$x = -8$

Check:

$x = -12$	$x = -8$
$\|x + 6\| - 18 = 2x$	$\|x + 6\| - 18 = 2x$
$\|-12 + 6\| - 18 \overset{?}{=} 2(-12)$	$\|-8 + 6\| - 18 \overset{?}{=} 2(-8)$
$\|-6\| - 18 \overset{?}{=} -24$	$\|-2\| - 18 \overset{?}{=} -16$
$6 - 18 \overset{?}{=} -24$	$2 - 18 \overset{?}{=} -16$
$-12 = -24$ Doesn't check	$-16 = -16$ ✓

Answer: Thus, our solution set is $\{-8\}$.

Practice

In 1–6, solve each equation and check your answer.

1. $|3x - 6| = 12$

2. $|2y + 5| = 11$

3. $5 + |8 - 4z| = 13$

4. $|5n - 10| - 4 = 11$

5. $|c - 6| = 2c - 3$

6. $|4r + 5| + 3r = 10$

In 7–12, select the numeral preceding the word or expression that best answers the question.

7. What is the solution set of $|4n + 8| = 16$?
(1) $\{-6\}$
(2) $\{2\}$
(3) $\{-6, 2\}$
(4) $\{\}$

8. What is the solution set of $|2 - y| = 3$?
(1) $\{-5, -1\}$
(2) $\{-5, 1\}$
(3) $\{-1, 5\}$
(4) $\{1, 5\}$

9. Solve for x: $|2x - 6| - x = 3$.
(1) $x = 1$ or $x = 9$
(2) $x = 9$ or $x = -1$
(3) $x = 1$
(4) $x = 9$

10. Which of the following equations has no solution?
(1) $|2x - 3| - 4 = 7$
(2) $|2x + 3| - 4x = 7$
(3) $|4 - x| = 5$
(4) $|4 - x| + 10 = 4$

11. Which of the following would represent a number whose distance from 7 is 6 units?
(1) $x - 7 = 6$
(2) $|x - 7| = 6$
(3) $x - 6 = 7$
(4) $|x - 6| = 7$

12. A manufacturer produces metal rods 10 centimeters long. A rod can differ from the perfect 10-centimeter length by 0.001 centimeter and still be acceptable. Which of the following equations could be used to represent this situation?
(1) $|x + 10| = 0.001$
(2) $|x - 10| = 0.001$
(3) $|10 + 0.001| = x$
(4) $|x - 0.001| = 10$

13. The distance from a number, x, to the number 10 is seven units on the number line.
    a. Write an absolute value equation that could be used to express this information.
    b. Solve the equation written in a to find possible value(s) for x.

14. The distance from a point P to the origin is 5 more than twice the value of P.
    a. Write an absolute value equation that could be used to express this information.
    b. Solve the equation found in a to find possible value(s) for P.

15. Normal body temperature is 98.6°F. However, body temperature will normally fluctuate during the course of a day.

    a. If your body temperature, t, could differ from 98.6 by 1.4°F and still be considered normal, write an absolute value equation that could be used to express this information.
    b. Solve the equation written in a to find t.

16. The average age of a student in Juanita's math class is 16 years old. However, the difference between a student's age, a, and the average age of 16 is half a year.
    a. Write an equation involving absolute value that could be used to express this information.
    b. Solve the equation found in a to find a.

5.2 Linear and Absolute Value Inequalities

Linear Inequalities

An inequality in one variable involves two expressions, at least one of which contains a variable, and an inequality sign. Solving a linear inequality is similar to solving a linear equation.

 **MODEL PROBLEMS**

---

1. Solve for x: $7x - 10 \geq 39$.

SOLUTION

$$7x - 10 \geq 39$$

Add 10 to both sides. $\qquad 7x \geq 49$
Divide by 7. $\qquad x \geq 7$

We can graph this on a number line.

Note: A solid dot is shown for the number 7. This indicates that the 7 is included in the solution set, since we are looking for all values of x that are greater than or equal to 7. In solving linear inequalities, we have to be careful when we multiply or divide by a negative number.

2. Solve for n: $-2n < 6$.
When we divide by -2, we have to change the direction of the inequality sign, giving us

$$n > -3$$

We must do this to produce a solution set that will work in the original inequality. If we had not changed the direction of the inequality, we would have obtained $n < -3$. Substituting a value of n less than -3 would give us a result that is not true. For example, try substituting -4 for n. We would obtain $-2(-4) < 6$ or $8 < 6$, which is a false statement. Now, try substituting a value of n greater than -3 to see what happens. For example, try substituting -1 for n. We would obtain $-2(-1) < 6$ or $2 < 6$, which is a true statement.

Remember: When you multiply or divide an inequality by a negative number, change EVERY sign, the positive or negative signs, AND the sign of the inequality.

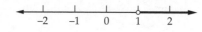

Practice

In 1–7, solve each inequality and graph the solution on a number line.

1. $5x - 4 < 16$

2. $7y + 8 \geq -20$

3. $-4z - 6 \leq 10$

4. $2a - 4 > 12 - 6a$

5. $7 + 3b \geq -14 - 4b$

6. $5c - 4 + 2c < 2c - 7$ 7. $4d + 7 > 2d$

In 8 and 9, select the numeral preceding the expression that best answers the question.

8. Which inequality could be graphed below?

(1) $2x + 3 < 5$ (3) $2x + 3 \leq 5$
(2) $2x + 3 > 5$ (4) $2x + 3 \geq 5$

9. Which inequality could be graphed below?

(1) $3x + 4 < -2x - 1$ (3) $-6x - 2 \leq 4x + 8$
(2) $3x + 4 > -2x - 1$ (4) $-6x - 2 \geq 4x + 8$

10. Fay Lingmath is doing poorly in mathematics and, if her final average is less than 65 points, she will have to go to summer school. Her final average consists of the average of her first quarter, second quarter, third quarter, fourth quarter, and Math B Regents exam grades. Her grades are given in the table in the next column.

First Quarter	60
Second Quarter	55
Third Quarter	60
Fourth Quarter	50
Math B Regents Exam	x

What grade must Fay receive on her Math B exam to avoid summer school?

11. Diane is finally going to fulfill her life-long dream of touring Europe during spring break. When she checked the Internet for what temperature to expect, she found that the temperature varied from approximately $10°$ to $20°$ Celsius. Since Diane lives in Red Hook, New York and is unfamiliar with the Celsius scale, she would like to convert these temperatures to Fahrenheit. Using the formula $F = \frac{9}{5}C + 32$, calculate the temperatures, T, Diane can expect during her vacation and write the answer as an inequality.

12. Iluv Toski is vacationing at a ski resort in the Catskill Mountains. The temperature for the weekend is forecast to range from $5°$ to $23°$F. Since Iluv is from Europe, he would like to convert this forecast from Fahrenheit to Celsius, which he understands better. Using the formula $C = \frac{5}{9}(F - 32)$, what would the temperature, T, be in degree Celsius? Express the answer as an inequality.

Absolute Value Inequalities

In solving an absolute value inequality, we must consider the range of numbers that will give a true inequality. To find the solution for $|x| = 5$, we must remember that the solution set is $x = 5$ and $x = -5$. Given $|x| < 5$, we must also consider both 5 and -5. The solution would include all values of x between these two numbers, $-5 < x < 5$. Given $|x| > 5$, we must again consider both 5 and -5. However, in this case we need the numbers whose absolute values are greater than 5. Thus, our solution set is $x > 5$ or $x < -5$.

MODEL PROBLEMS

1. Solve and graph each inequality on a number line.

a. $|x + 3| < 5$　　　　　　　　**b.** $|5x - 2| \geq 18$

SOLUTION

a. $|x + 3| < 5$

Again we must consider the two cases.

$$x + 3 < 5 \qquad x + 3 > -5$$

Solve.

$$x < 2 \qquad x > -8$$

Combining the two solutions, we obtain $-8 < x < 2$.

We can actually do all of this work at once.

$$|x + 3| < 5$$

When we consider the two cases

$$x + 3 < 5 \qquad x + 3 > -5$$

we are looking for values of x *between* -5 and 5. Therefore, we can put this all together and get the compound inequality

$$-5 < x + 3 < 5.$$

Subtracting 3 from all three parts of the inequality gives us

$$-8 < x < 2.$$

On a number line the solution would look like this:

b. $|5x - 2| \geq 18$

SOLUTION

Set up the two inequalities and solve.

$$
\begin{array}{ll}
5x - 2 \geq 18 & 5x - 2 \leq -18 \\
5x \geq 20 & 5x \leq -16 \\
x \geq 4 & x \leq -3.2
\end{array}
$$

Thus, our solution set is $\{x \mid x \leq -3.2 \text{ or } x \geq 4\}$.

The graph is:

Note: When we are looking for values like $x \geq 18$ or $x \leq -18$, there is no point of intersection. Therefore, we cannot solve this as a single compound inequality.

2. The "average" twenty-five-year-old female in the United States measures 5 feet 4 inches.
    a. If most twenty-five-year-old women measure within 2 inches of this height, use an absolute value inequality to express this fact. (First convert 5 feet 4 inches to inches.)
    b. Determine the range of heights that satisfy this inequality. Express your answer in feet and inches.
    c. Graph the solution on a number line, using inches as your unit of measure.

SOLUTION

a. First, we do the conversion. Since there are 12 inches to a foot, 5 feet = 12(5) = 60 inches. 60 inches + 4 inches = 64 inches. Thus, the average twenty-five-year-old female is 64 inches tall.

Now, let h represent the height of the twenty-five-year-old women. The difference between the women's heights and the average height falls within 2 inches.

Thus, $|h - 64| \leq 2$.

We must consider the two cases, $h - 64 \leq 2$ and $h - 64 \geq -2$.

Set up the compound inequality and solve.

$$-2 \leq h - 64 \leq 2$$
$$62 \leq h \leq 66$$

Answer: $62 \leq h \leq 66$

b. We can see that most twenty-five-year-old women are between 62 inches and 66 inches tall. To convert to feet and inches, we divide each of these numbers by 12, to obtain an answer of between 5 feet 2 inches and 5 feet 6 inches tall.
c. The number line looks like this:

Note: If $|x| \leq n$, where $n > 0$, then $-n \leq x \leq n$.
    If $|x| \geq n$, where $n > 0$, then $x \leq -n$ or $x \geq n$.

In 1–8, solve each absolute value inequality and graph the solution set.

1. $|x - 2| > 7$

2. $|2a| + 4 \le 24$

3. $|3x - 6| < 21$

4. $|5d + 2| \le 22$

5. $\left|\dfrac{x + 4}{3}\right| \ge 5$

6. $\left|\dfrac{n}{2} - 4\right| > 3$

7. $|7y| - 2 < 12$

8. $|3m - 6| + 4 \ge 22$

In 9–14, select the numeral preceding the expression or the diagram that best completes the sentence or answers the question.

9. Which is the graph of the solution set of $|10x - 20| \ge 30$?

(1)
   -6 -5 -4 -3 -2 -1 0 1 2

(2)
   -6 -5 -4 -3 -2 -1 0 1 2

(3)
   -2 -1 0 1 2 3 4 5 6

(4)
   -2 -1 0 1 2 3 4 5 6

10. Which inequality has the solution set represented by the graph?

   -2 -1 0 1 2

(1) $|4x - 2| - 6 \le 8$
(2) $|4x + 2| - 6 \le 8$
(3) $|4x - 2| + 6 \le 8$
(4) $|4x + 2| + 6 \le 8$

11. The solution set of $|8x - 4| > 20$ is
(1) $\{x \mid x < -2 \text{ or } x > 3\}$
(2) $\{x \mid x < -3 \text{ or } x > 2\}$
(3) $\{x \mid -2 < x < 3\}$
(4) $\{x \mid -3 < x < 2\}$

12. The solution set of $|6x - 3| < 21$ is
(1) $\{x \mid x < -4 \text{ or } x > 3\}$
(2) $\{x \mid x < -3 \text{ or } x > 4\}$
(3) $\{x \mid -4 < x < 3\}$
(4) $\{x \mid -3 < x < 4\}$

13. At Jennifer's sweet sixteen party, all of her friends were within 6 months of her age. Using a to represent the age of Jennifer's friends, in years, which of the following inequalities would represent this statement?
(1) $a - 16 \le 6$
(2) $a - 16 \le 0.5$
(3) $|a - 16| \le 6$
(4) $|a - 16| \le 0.5$

14. The average IQ for people of all ages is said to be approximately 100. If most people's IQ falls within 15 points of the average, which of the following inequalities would represent this statement? (Use I to represent a person's IQ.)
(1) $I - 15 \le 100$
(2) $I - 100 \le 15$
(3) $|I - 100| \le 15$
(4) $|I - 100| \ge 15$

15. Normal human body temperature is 98.6°F.
   a. If a person is considered unhealthy if his or her body temperature, t, differs from 98.6°F by 1.4° or more, express this as an absolute value inequality.
   b. Solve the absolute value inequality to determine what body temperatures would be considered unhealthy.

16. Con Sistent is an excellent baseball player. His batting average, a, always falls within 10 points of 500.
   a. Write an absolute value inequality that will express this fact.
   b. Solve the absolute value inequality to determine Con's batting average.
   c. Graph the solution on a number line.

17. When an oven is set to 350°, the temperature, t, varies slightly from this setting. When the temperature varies by more than 7°, the oven will turn on (or off) until it reaches 350° again.
   a. Write an absolute value inequality that will express this fact.
   b. Solve the absolute value inequality to determine when the oven will turn on or off.
   c. Graph the solution on a number line.

5.3 Reducing Rational Expressions

As we discussed in Section 3.1, a **rational number** is a number in the form $\frac{a}{b}$, where a and b are both integers and $b \neq 0$. Similarly, a **rational expression** is a fraction in the form $\frac{P_1}{P_2}$ where P_1 and P_2 are both polynomials and $P_2 \neq 0$. Examples of rational expressions include $\frac{5}{7}, \frac{x}{6}, \frac{3}{x}, \frac{11}{x-2}, \frac{a-3}{a^2-7a-9}$, and so on.

Just as a rational number is undefined if its denominator is zero, a rational expression is said to be **undefined** if its denominator is zero.

Why is division by zero said to be undefined? Look at these examples.

$$\frac{24}{4} = 6 \text{ because } 4(6) = 24$$

$$\frac{18}{9} = 2 \text{ because } 9(2) = 18$$

$$\frac{0}{5} = 0 \text{ because } 5(0) = 0$$

BUT:

What can we do with $\frac{3}{0}$? This division has no solution because there is no number that you can multiply by 0 to get 3. Thus, we say that $\frac{3}{0}$ is undefined.

Note: Division by 0 is undefined.

 MODEL PROBLEMS

1. For what value(s) of x is the rational expression undefined?

    a. $\frac{5}{x}$ **b.** $\frac{11}{x-7}$ **c.** $\frac{x-2}{x^2-9}$ **d.** $\frac{x^2-x-12}{x^2-7x+10}$

SOLUTION

A rational expression is undefined when the denominator is equal to zero. To solve problem, set the denominator equal to zero and solve for x.

a. $\frac{5}{x}$

    $x = 0$

b. $\frac{11}{x-7}$

    $x - 7 = 0$
        $x = 7$

c. $\frac{x-2}{x^2-9}$

    $x^2 - 9 = 0$
  $(x+3)(x-3) = 0$

  $x + 3 = 0 \qquad x - 3 = 0$
      $x = -3 \qquad\quad x = 3$
      $x = -3 \quad$ or $\quad x = 3$

d. $\frac{x^2-x-12}{x^2-7x+10}$

    $x^2 - 7x + 10 = 0$
  $(x-5)(x-2) = 0$

  $x - 5 = 0 \qquad x - 2 = 0$
      $x = 5 \qquad\quad x = 2$
      $x = 5 \quad$ or $\quad x = 2$

A rational expression is said to be in **simplest form** or **reduced to lowest terms** if its numerator and denominator do not have a common factor other than 1 or -1. To reduce a rational expression to **lowest terms** (or express a rational expression in **simplest form**), factor both numerator and denominator and divide numerator and denominator by the greatest common factor (GCF). This is very similar to reducing rational numbers to lowest terms.

---

2. Express each expression in simplest form.

a. $\dfrac{16x^4y^3z^6}{24x^3yz^{10}}$ b. $\dfrac{x^2 - 25}{x^2 - 5x}$ c. $\dfrac{6x + 18}{x^2 + x - 6}$ d. $\dfrac{24 - 6x}{x^2 - 7x + 12}$

SOLUTION

a. $\dfrac{16x^4y^3z^6}{24x^3yz^{10}}$

To reduce this expression to its lowest terms, divide numerator and denominator by its GCF. Take each individual term of the expression and find the GCF of that term in both the numerator and denominator.

The GCF of 16 and 24 is 8, so divide numerator and denominator by 8.

The GCF of x^4 and x^3 is x^3, so divide numerator and denominator by x^3.

The GCF of y^3 and y is y, so divide numerator and denominator by y.

The GCF of z^6 and z^{10} is z^6, so divide numerator and denominator by z^6.

Thus, $\dfrac{16x^4y^3z^6}{24x^3yz^{10}} = \dfrac{2xy^2}{3z^4}$.

b. $\dfrac{x^2 - 25}{x^2 - 5x}$

First, factor numerator and denominator.

$$\frac{x^2 - 25}{x^2 - 5x} = \frac{(x + 5)(x - 5)}{x(x - 5)}$$

Since the $x - 5$ is common to both numerator and denominator, divide both numerator and denominator by $x - 5$. Sometimes we say "cancel out" the $x - 5$.

Thus, $\dfrac{x^2 - 25}{x^2 - 5x} = \dfrac{(x + 5)\cancel{(x - 5)}}{x\cancel{(x - 5)}} = \dfrac{x + 5}{x}$.

Exclude values for which the original fraction is undefined: $x = 0$ and $x = 5$.

Answer: $\dfrac{x + 5}{x}$ $(x \neq 0, 5)$

Remember: You can reduce fractions only by dividing numerator and denominator by their GCF. You *cannot* cancel addends. Thus, you cannot cancel the x's in the rational expression $\dfrac{x + 5}{x}$. It is already in simplest form.

c. $\dfrac{6x + 18}{x^2 + x - 6}$

Factor numerator and denominator and divide both by their GCF.

$$\frac{6x + 18}{x^2 + x - 6} = \frac{6\cancel{(x + 3)}}{\cancel{(x + 3)}(x - 2)} = \frac{6}{x - 2} \qquad (x \neq 2, -3)$$

---

d. $\dfrac{24 - 6x}{x^2 - 7x + 12}$

Factor numerator and denominator.

$$\frac{24 - 6x}{x^2 - 7x + 12} = \frac{6(4 - x)}{(x - 4)(x - 3)}$$

Note: We have a $(4 - x)$ in the numerator and an $(x - 4)$ in the denominator. Since $(4 - x)$ is the additive inverse of $(x - 4)$, we can rewrite $(4 - x)$ as $-(x - 4)$ and then "cancel."

$$\frac{24 - 6x}{x^2 - 7x + 12} = \frac{6(4 - x)}{(x - 4)(x - 3)} = \frac{-6\cancel{(x - 4)}}{\cancel{(x - 4)}(x - 3)} = \frac{-6}{x - 3} \qquad (x \neq 3, 4)$$

One way to check if your reduced fraction is equivalent to the original fraction is to graph both fractions and see if the two graphs are identical. For example, enter the original fraction given above, $\dfrac{24 - 6x}{x^2 - 7x + 12}$, into Y_1 and the reduced fraction, $\dfrac{-6}{x - 3}$, into Y_2 as shown in the figure below. Be sure to put parentheses around the numerator and denominator of each fraction!

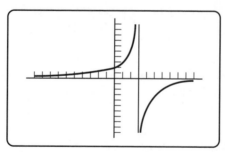

Now, graph both equations. The window shown in the figure below is the Standard Viewing Window, which is $[-10, 10] \times [-10, 10]$. (You can obtain this window by selecting (ZOOM) (6) on your calculator.)

You will notice that you cannot see the second graph at all. That is because the second fraction is equivalent to the first. To be sure that the second fraction is being drawn, you can return to the (Y=) screen, and move your cursor over to the \, to the left of Y_2. Continue to hit (ENTER) until you get the ball with the tail, as shown in the figure below.

Now, when you graph the two equations you'll be able to see the second graph being drawn.

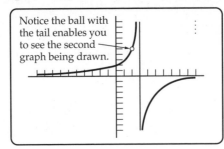

Notice the ball with the tail enables you to see the second graph being drawn.

Note: This method will show you only that your fraction is equivalent to the given one, it will *not* ensure you that your fraction is reduced to lowest terms.

Practice

In 1–6, find the value(s) of x for which the fraction is undefined.

1. $\dfrac{23}{6x}$

2. $\dfrac{12}{x - 2}$

3. $\dfrac{4}{x^2 - 5x}$

4. $\dfrac{x - 2}{x + 9}$

5. $\dfrac{x^2 - 25}{x^2 + 6x + 8}$

6. $\dfrac{6x - 12}{3x + 15}$

In 7–15, reduce the rational expression to lowest terms.

7. $\dfrac{21a^3bc^6}{28a^2b^4c^6}$

8. $\dfrac{8x^3y^7z^{10}}{4x^2y^6}$

9. $\dfrac{5x}{10x^2 + 20x}$

10. $\dfrac{6 - 2x}{x - 3}$

11. $\dfrac{x - 5}{x^2 - 25}$

12. $\dfrac{x^2 - 2x - 24}{x^2 - 16}$

13. $\dfrac{x^2 + 8x + 15}{x^2 + 3x}$

14. $\dfrac{y^4 - 16}{y - 2}$

15. $\dfrac{7x - x^2}{x^2 - 10x + 21}$

In 16–20, select the numeral preceding the expression that best completes the statement or answers the question.

16. Which expression is defined for all real numbers?

(1) $\dfrac{x + 3}{x^2}$

(3) $\dfrac{5}{(x + 2)^2}$

(2) $\dfrac{4}{(x - 2)^2}$

(4) $\dfrac{7}{x^2 + 3}$

17. The expression $\dfrac{10 - 2x}{x^2 - 25}$ is equivalent to

(1) $\dfrac{-2}{x + 5}$

(3) $\dfrac{-2}{5 - x}$

(2) $\dfrac{-2}{x - 5}$

(4) $\dfrac{2}{5 + x}$

18. Which rational expression is in simplest form?

(1) $\dfrac{x^2 + 4x}{4x}$

(3) $\dfrac{x^2 + 4x}{x}$

(2) $\dfrac{x^2 + 4x}{4}$

(4) None of them

19. For what value(s) of x is the rational expression $\dfrac{x - 4}{x^2 - 6x}$ undefined?

(1) $x = 0, x = 4, x = 6$ (3) $x = 6$
(2) $x = 4$ (4) $x = 0, x = 6$

20. Which expression is equivalent to $\dfrac{x^3 - 16x}{x^3 + 12x^2 + 32x}$?

(1) $\dfrac{-1}{2}$

(3) $\dfrac{x + 4}{x + 8}$

(2) $\dfrac{x - 4}{x + 8}$

(4) $\dfrac{x(x - 4)}{x - 8}$

5.4 Multiplying and Dividing Rational Expressions

Multiplying two rational expressions is similar to multiplying two rational numbers.

- Factor the numerators and denominators.

- Divide numerators and denominators by all common factors.

- Multiply remaining factors in the numerators and remaining factors in the denominators.

Remember: You can "cancel" any numerator with any denominator. However, you cannot cancel two numerators or two denominators.

 MODEL PROBLEMS

1. Multiply and express the product in simplest form.

   a. $\dfrac{3x^4}{25y^2} \cdot \dfrac{35y}{9x^3}$ **b.** $\dfrac{x^2 - 25}{2x + 10} \cdot \dfrac{4x + 12}{x^2 - 2x - 15}$ **c.** $\dfrac{x^2 - 6x}{6 - x} \cdot \dfrac{2x + 8}{x^2 + 4x}$

SOLUTION

a. $\dfrac{3x^4}{25y^2} \cdot \dfrac{35y}{9x^3}$

Since we have monomials in all numerators and denominators, there is no factoring to be done. We can simply divide 3 into 3 and into 9, divide 5 into 25 and 35, divide y into y and y^2, and divide x^3 into x^3 and x^4.

Thus, we get $\dfrac{3x^4}{25y^2} \cdot \dfrac{35y}{9x^3} = \dfrac{x}{5y} \cdot \dfrac{7}{3} = \dfrac{7x}{15y}.$ $(x \neq 0, y \neq 0)$

b. $\dfrac{x^2 - 25}{2x + 10} \cdot \dfrac{4x + 12}{x^2 - 2x - 15}$

Factor all numerators and denominators and "cancel out" like factors.

$$\dfrac{x^2 - 25}{2x + 10} \cdot \dfrac{4x + 12}{x^2 - 2x - 15} = \dfrac{\cancel{(x+5)}\cancel{(x-5)}}{2\cancel{(x+5)}} \cdot \dfrac{\overset{2}{\cancel{4}}\cancel{(x+3)}}{\cancel{(x-5)}\cancel{(x+3)}} = 2 \quad (x \neq -5, -3, 5)$$

c. $\dfrac{x^2 - 6x}{6 - x} \cdot \dfrac{2x + 8}{x^2 + 4x}$

Factor all numerators and denominators and cancel like factors.

Remember: $(x - 6) = -1(6 - x)$.

$$\dfrac{x^2 - 6x}{6 - x} \cdot \dfrac{2x + 8}{x^2 + 4x} = \dfrac{x(x - 6)}{6 - x} \cdot \dfrac{2(x + 4)}{x(x + 4)} = \dfrac{-1x\cancel{(6 - x)}}{\cancel{6 - x}} \cdot \dfrac{2\cancel{(x + 4)}}{x\cancel{(x + 4)}} = -2 \quad (x \neq 0, -4, 6)$$

Dividing two rational expressions is similar to dividing two rational numbers. Multiply the dividend by the *reciprocal* of the divisor and then follow the rules for multiplication.

Remember: To divide two rational expressions, leave the first fraction alone, and "flip" the second fraction. Then, follow the rules for multiplication.

2. Divide and express the quotient in simplest terms.

a. $\dfrac{4a^2b^3}{25ab} \div \dfrac{8ab^3}{35a^2b^4}$

b. $\dfrac{x^2-64}{x^2+8x} \div \dfrac{8x-64}{4x+4}$

SOLUTION

a. $\dfrac{4a^2b^3}{25ab} \div \dfrac{8ab^3}{35a^2b^4}$

First, multiply the dividend by the reciprocal of the divisor.

$$\frac{4a^2b^3}{25ab} \div \frac{8ab^3}{35a^2b^4} = \frac{4a^2b^3}{25ab} \cdot \frac{35a^2b^4}{8ab^3}$$

Now, follow the rules for multiplication by dividing numerators and denominators by common factors.

$$\frac{4a^2b^3}{25ab} \div \frac{8ab^3}{35a^2b^4} = \frac{4a^2b^3}{\underset{5}{25\,a\,b}} \cdot \frac{\overset{7}{35}\,a^2\,b^4}{\underset{2}{8}\,a\,b^3} = \frac{a^2b^3}{5} \cdot \frac{7}{2} = \frac{7a^2b^3}{10} \qquad (a \neq 0, b \neq 0)$$

b. $\dfrac{x^2-64}{x^2+8x} \div \dfrac{8x-64}{4x+4}$

First, multiply the dividend by the reciprocal of the divisor.

$$\frac{x^2-64}{x^2+8x} \div \frac{8x-64}{4x+4} = \frac{x^2-64}{x^2+8x} \cdot \frac{4x+4}{8x-64}$$

Now, factor all numerators and denominators and follow the rules for multiplication by dividing numerators and denominators by common factors.

$$\frac{x^2-64}{x^2+8x} \div \frac{8x-64}{4x+4} = \frac{x^2-64}{x^2+8x} \cdot \frac{4x+4}{8x-64} = \frac{\cancel{(x+8)}(x-8)}{x\cancel{(x+8)}} \cdot \frac{4(x+1)}{\underset{2}{8}\,\cancel{(x-8)}} = \frac{x+1}{2x} \qquad (x \neq 0, -1, -8, 8)$$

Note: Any number that makes a denominator zero, or the numerator of the divisor zero, must be excluded.

Practice

In 1–15, perform the indicated operation. Reduce your answer to lowest terms.

1. $\dfrac{4a^3b}{6b^2c^5} \cdot \dfrac{8abc^5}{24ac^3}$

2. $\dfrac{15x^4y^5}{25xyz} \div \dfrac{10x^3y^2}{30xz}$

3. $\dfrac{x^2-4}{6x} \div \dfrac{x+2}{3x-6}$

4. $\dfrac{6x+6y}{12xy} \cdot \dfrac{24x^2}{x^2+xy}$

5. $\dfrac{a^2-9}{9-3a} \div \dfrac{a^2+5a+6}{6a+12}$

6. $\dfrac{7x}{7x+7} \cdot \dfrac{x^2-1}{x^2-x}$

7. $\dfrac{a^2-ab}{a^2-b^2} \cdot \dfrac{3a+3b}{6a^2}$

8. $\dfrac{x^2-x-12}{4x+12} \div \dfrac{x^2-2x-8}{6x+12}$

9. $\dfrac{18-6a}{a^2-9a+18} \div \dfrac{4a}{2a-12}$

10. $\dfrac{a^3-4a}{a^2-7a+10} \cdot \dfrac{a^2-8a+15}{a^2+5a+6}$

11. $\dfrac{4w^2-1}{2w^2+3w-2} \cdot \dfrac{4w+8}{4w+2}$

12. $\dfrac{64 - d^2}{8d + 64} \div \dfrac{4d - 32}{16d}$

13. $\dfrac{3x^2 - x - 2}{6x + 4} \div \dfrac{x^2 - 1}{4x + 4}$

14. $\dfrac{y^2 - y - 12}{y^2 + y - 20} \cdot \dfrac{y^2 + 11y + 30}{y^3 + 9y^2 + 18y}$

15. $\dfrac{7 - z}{z^3 - 49z} \cdot \dfrac{z^2 + 10z + 21}{3 + z}$

In 16–20, select the numeral preceding the expression that best completes the sentence.

16. The product of $\dfrac{x^2 - 9}{3 - x}$ and $\dfrac{4x + 16}{x^2 + 7x + 12}$ is

    (1) −4   (3) 1
    (2) −1   (4) 4

17. The quotient $\dfrac{x^2 + 4x + 3}{6x + 6} \div \dfrac{x^2 + 3x}{6x} = 1$ for
    all values of x where
    (1) $x \ne -1$
    (2) $x \ne 0$
    (3) $x \ne -1$ or $x \ne 0$
    (4) $x \ne -3$ or $x \ne -1$ or $x \ne 0$

18. If the length of a rectangle is equal to $\dfrac{x + 1}{x + 2}$ and the area of the rectangle is $\dfrac{4x + 4}{2x + 4}$, the width of the rectangle is

    (1) 1   (3) $\dfrac{x + 2}{x + 1}$
    (2) 2   (4) 4

19. If the length of a rectangle is $\dfrac{3x + 3}{4x^2 - 4}$ and the width of the rectangle is $\dfrac{8x - 8}{6}$, the area of the rectangle is

    (1) 1   (3) $\dfrac{x + 1}{x - 1}$
    (2) 2   (4) 4

20. If the length of a rectangular solid is x, the width is $\dfrac{x + 1}{x + 2}$, and the height is $\dfrac{3x + 6}{x^2 + x}$, the volume is

    (1) 1   (3) 3
    (2) 2   (4) 4

5.5 Adding and Subtracting Rational Expressions

Expressions with Like Denominators

Adding and subtracting rational expressions is similar to adding and subtracting rational numbers. First make sure that the denominators are the same, then keep the denominator and simply add (or subtract) the numerators. If the denominators are not the same, you must get a common denominator. When you have completed the addition (or subtraction), be sure to reduce the resulting fraction to lowest terms.

MODEL PROBLEM

Perform the indicated operation. Reduce your answers to lowest terms.

a. $\dfrac{3}{2a} + \dfrac{5}{2a}$ b. $\dfrac{2x}{x - 1} - \dfrac{2}{x - 1}$ c. $\dfrac{x^2}{4x + 12} - \dfrac{9}{4x + 12}$

d. $\dfrac{y^2 + 2y}{y^2 + 7y + 12} + \dfrac{3y + 4}{y^2 + 7y + 12}$ e. $\dfrac{z^2 + 5z}{z^2 + 8z} - \dfrac{2z + 40}{z^2 + 8z}$

SOLUTION

In each of the above cases, both rational expressions have the same denominator. So, all we need to do is keep the denominator and add (or subtract) the numerators.

a. $\dfrac{3}{2a} + \dfrac{5}{2a} = \dfrac{3+5}{2a} = \dfrac{8}{2a}$ Divide numerator and denominator by 2.

$$= \dfrac{4}{a} \qquad (a \neq 0)$$

b. $\dfrac{2x}{x-1} - \dfrac{2}{x-1}$

Since both denominators are the same, keep the common denominator and rewrite the two rational expressions as one large fraction.

$$\dfrac{2x}{x-1} - \dfrac{2}{x-1} = \dfrac{2x-2}{x-1} \qquad \text{Factor the numerator and reduce the fraction.}$$

$$= \dfrac{2\cancel{(x-1)}}{\cancel{x-1}} = 2 \qquad (x \neq 1)$$

c. $\dfrac{x^2}{4x+12} - \dfrac{9}{4x+12} = \dfrac{x^2-9}{4x+12} = \dfrac{\cancel{(x+3)}(x-3)}{4\cancel{(x+3)}} = \dfrac{x-3}{4} \qquad (x \neq -3)$

d. $\dfrac{y^2+2y}{y^2+7y+12} + \dfrac{3y+4}{y^2+7y+12}$

$$= \dfrac{y^2+2y+3y+4}{y^2+7y+12} = \dfrac{y^2+5y+4}{y^2+7y+12}$$

$$= \dfrac{\cancel{(y+4)}(y+1)}{(y+3)\cancel{(y+4)}} = \dfrac{y+1}{y+3} \qquad (y \neq -3, -4)$$

e. $\dfrac{z^2+5z}{z^2+8z} - \dfrac{2z+40}{z^2+8z}$

We have to be *very* careful when we are subtracting rational expressions. Remember when we subtract, we are adding the additive inverse of the second rational expression. Be sure to change *all* the signs in the numerator of the fraction immediately following the subtraction sign!

$$\dfrac{z^2+5z}{z^2+8z} - \dfrac{2z+40}{z^2+8z} = \dfrac{z^2+5z-2z-40}{z^2+8z} = \dfrac{z^2+3z-40}{z^2+8z} = \dfrac{\cancel{(z+8)}(z-5)}{z\cancel{(z+8)}} = \dfrac{z-5}{z} \qquad (z \neq 0, -8)$$

Remember: When you are adding (or subtracting) rational expressions that have a common denominator:

- Keep the denominator the same.
- Rewrite the expressions as one large fraction.
- Combine like terms.
- Factor.
- Reduce.

Perform the indicated operation. Express your answer in simplest form.

1. $\dfrac{4}{3a} + \dfrac{5}{3a}$

2. $\dfrac{5x}{x-2} - \dfrac{10}{x-2}$

3. $\dfrac{6x}{11} + \dfrac{5x}{11}$

4. $\dfrac{4x}{x^2 - 2x} - \dfrac{8}{x^2 - 2x}$

5. $\dfrac{3x+5}{x^2 - 5x - 24} + \dfrac{4}{x^2 - 5x - 24}$

6. $\dfrac{2y^2 + 2y}{y^2 - y - 56} - \dfrac{y^2 + 35}{y^2 - y - 56}$

7. $\dfrac{z^2}{z^2 - z} - \dfrac{3z - 2}{z^2 - z}$

8. $\dfrac{3}{a^2 - a - 6} - \dfrac{a}{a^2 - a - 6}$

9. $\dfrac{b^2 + 2b}{2b + 10} + \dfrac{4b + 5}{2b + 10}$

10. $\dfrac{n^3 - n^2 - 2n}{2n^2 - 4n} + \dfrac{n^3 + n^2 - 6n}{2n^2 - 4n}$

Expressions with Different Denominators

Adding (or subtracting) rational expressions that have different denominators is similar to adding (or subtracting) rational numbers with different denominators. Rewrite the fractions as equivalent fractions with the same denominator (use the least common denominator or LCD), then keep the common denominator and add (or subtract) the numerators.

 **MODEL PROBLEM**

Perform the indicated operation. Express your answer in simplest form.

a. $\dfrac{a}{3} + \dfrac{3a}{2}$ **b.** $\dfrac{7}{3b} - \dfrac{5}{b}$ **c.** $\dfrac{2x}{x-4} + \dfrac{8}{4-x}$

d. $\dfrac{x}{x-3} - \dfrac{18}{x^2 - 9}$ **e.** $\dfrac{3}{x+1} - \dfrac{2}{x}$ **f.** $\dfrac{1}{x^2 + 3x + 2} + \dfrac{2}{x^2 - 1}$

SOLUTION

a. $\dfrac{a}{3} + \dfrac{3a}{2}$

First, we must find a common denominator. Since 3 and 2 are each factors of 6, our common denominator is 6. We multiply numerator and denominator of the first fraction by 2, and numerator and denominator of the second fraction by 3.

$$\frac{a}{3} + \frac{3a}{2} = \frac{a}{3} \cdot \frac{2}{2} + \frac{3a}{2} \cdot \frac{3}{3}$$

Once again, rewrite the expressions as one large fraction, and combine like terms.

$$\frac{a}{3} + \frac{3a}{2} = \frac{a}{3} \cdot \frac{2}{2} + \frac{3a}{2} \cdot \frac{3}{3} = \frac{2a + 9a}{6} = \frac{11a}{6}$$

b. $\dfrac{7}{3b} - \dfrac{5}{b}$

The common denominator is $3b$. The first fraction is fine. We must multiply numerator and denominator of the second fraction by 3.

$$\frac{7}{3b} - \frac{5}{b} = \frac{7}{3b} - \frac{5}{b} \cdot \frac{3}{3} = \frac{7-15}{3b} = \frac{-8}{3b} \qquad (b \neq 0)$$

c. $\dfrac{2x}{x-4} + \dfrac{8}{4-x}$

Notice that the denominator of the second fraction is the additive inverse of the denominator of the first fraction. We can rewrite $(4-x)$ as $-(x-4)$. To simplify matters, we will put the negative sign between the two fractions.

$$\frac{2x}{x-4} + \frac{8}{4-x} = \frac{2x}{x-4} - \frac{8}{x-4} = \frac{2x-8}{x-4} = \frac{2\cancel{(x-4)}}{\cancel{x-4}} = 2 \qquad (x \neq 4)$$

d. $\dfrac{x}{x-3} - \dfrac{18}{x^2-9}$

To begin this example, we must factor the denominator of the second expression.

$$\frac{x}{x-3} - \frac{18}{x^2-9} = \frac{x}{x-3} - \frac{18}{(x+3)(x-3)}$$

Now, we can see that our common denominator is $(x+3)(x-3)$. Multiply the numerator and denominator of the first expression by $(x+3)$, rewrite as one large fraction, factor, and reduce.

$$\frac{x}{x-3} - \frac{18}{x^2-9} = \frac{x}{x-3} - \frac{18}{(x+3)(x-3)}$$

$$= \frac{x}{x-3} \cdot \frac{x+3}{x+3} - \frac{18}{(x+3)(x-3)}$$

$$= \frac{x(x+3)-18}{(x+3)(x-3)}$$

$$= \frac{x^2+3x-18}{(x+3)(x-3)}$$

$$= \frac{(x+6)\cancel{(x-3)}}{(x+3)\cancel{(x-3)}}$$

$$= \frac{x+6}{x+3} \qquad (x \neq -3, 3)$$

e. $\dfrac{3}{x+1} - \dfrac{2}{x}$

To get a common denominator we have to find the least common multiple of $x+1$ and x. Thus, we have to *multiply* one or both of these expressions by something. Since they have no common factors, the least common multiple is $x(x+1)$. We multiply numerator and denominator of the first fraction by x, and numerator and denominator of the second fraction by $x+1$.

Remember: We can get a common denominator only by multiplying.

$$\frac{3}{x+1} - \frac{2}{x} = \frac{3}{x+1} \cdot \frac{x}{x} - \frac{2}{x} \cdot \frac{x+1}{x+1}$$

$$= \frac{3x - 2(x+1)}{x(x+1)} \qquad \text{Be careful to distribute the } -2.$$

$$= \frac{3x - 2x - 2}{x(x+1)}$$

$$= \frac{x-2}{x(x+1)} \qquad (x \neq 0, -1)$$

f. $\dfrac{1}{x^2 + 3x + 2} + \dfrac{2}{x^2 - 1}$

To begin, factor the denominators of both expressions.

$$\frac{1}{x^2 + 3x + 2} + \frac{2}{x^2 - 1} = \frac{1}{(x+2)(x+1)} + \frac{2}{(x+1)(x-1)}$$

Our common denominator is $(x+2)(x+1)(x-1)$.

Multiply numerator and denominator of the first expression by $x - 1$.

Multiply numerator and denominator of the second expression by $x + 2$.

$$\frac{1}{x^2 + 3x + 2} + \frac{2}{x^2 - 1} = \frac{1}{(x+2)(x+1)} + \frac{2}{(x+1)(x-1)}$$

$$= \frac{1}{(x+2)(x+1)} \cdot \frac{x-1}{x-1} + \frac{2}{(x+1)(x-1)} \cdot \frac{x+2}{x+2}$$

$$= \frac{1(x-1) + 2(x+2)}{(x+2)(x+1)(x-1)}$$

$$= \frac{x - 1 + 2x + 4}{(x+2)(x+1)(x-1)}$$

$$= \frac{3x + 3}{(x+2)(x+1)(x-1)}$$

$$= \frac{3\cancel{(x+1)}}{(x+2)\cancel{(x+1)}(x-1)}$$

$$= \frac{3}{(x+2)(x-1)} \qquad (x \neq -2, -1, 1)$$

Just as there are mixed numbers such as $2\frac{1}{3}$, there are mixed expressions such as $2x + \frac{1}{x}$. A mixed expression can be written as a rational expression.

MODEL PROBLEM

Transform the mixed expression $a - 2 + \dfrac{5}{a}$ into a rational expression.

SOLUTION

$$a - 2 + \frac{5}{a}$$

This expression is made up of three separate rational expressions, two of which have denominators of 1.

$$a - 2 + \frac{5}{a} = \frac{a}{1} - \frac{2}{1} + \frac{5}{a}$$

The common denominator is a. Multiply numerator and denominator of the first two fractions by a, and follow the procedure as explained above.

$$a - 2 + \frac{5}{a} = \frac{a}{1} - \frac{2}{1} + \frac{5}{a}$$

$$= \frac{a}{1} \cdot \frac{a}{a} - \frac{2}{1} \cdot \frac{a}{a} + \frac{5}{a}$$

$$= \frac{a^2 - 2a + 5}{a} \qquad (a \neq 0)$$

Practice

In 1–15, perform the indicated operation. Express your answer in simplest form.

1. $\dfrac{2x}{7} - \dfrac{x}{3}$

2. $\dfrac{4}{5x} + \dfrac{2}{x}$

3. $\dfrac{3}{x^2} - \dfrac{2}{x}$

4. $\dfrac{5}{a^2} - \dfrac{3}{2a}$

5. $\dfrac{3c}{c - 5} + \dfrac{15}{5 - c}$

6. $\dfrac{x}{x^2 - 16} + \dfrac{4}{x - 4}$

7. $\dfrac{5}{2x + 6} - \dfrac{2}{5x + 15}$

8. $\dfrac{2}{x^2 - 1} + \dfrac{3}{x^2 - x}$

9. $\dfrac{6}{x} - \dfrac{6}{x + 2}$

10. $\dfrac{y + 2}{y^2 - y - 2} + \dfrac{1}{3y + 3}$

11. $\dfrac{6}{x^2 + 4x + 3} + \dfrac{3}{x^2 + 7x + 12}$

12. $\dfrac{3}{x^2 + 5x - 14} - \dfrac{2}{x^2 + 8x + 7}$

13. $\dfrac{x}{x^2 + 9x + 18} - \dfrac{3}{x^2 + 3x}$

14. $\dfrac{x + 2}{x^2 + 7x + 12} + \dfrac{2}{x + 4} + \dfrac{1}{x + 3}$

15. $\dfrac{x - 3}{x^2 - 1} + \dfrac{3}{x - 1} - \dfrac{4}{2x + 2}$

In 16–18, transform the mixed expression into a rational expression.

16. $n + \dfrac{n}{3}$

17. $a + 2 + \dfrac{a}{5}$

18. $r + 2 + \dfrac{3}{r}$

In 19–22, select the numeral preceding the expression that best completes the statement or answers the question.

19. To find the sum of $\dfrac{x + 2}{x}$ and $\dfrac{x}{x + 3}$, the common denominator is

(1) x

(3) $x^2 + 3x$

(2) $x + 3$

(4) $x^2 + 2x$

20. On the first day of her hike into the mountains, Courtney walked one-third of the distance to base camp. The next day, she walked one-fourth of the original distance to base camp. If the distance to base camps is m miles, what is the total number of miles that Courtney has walked?

(1) $\dfrac{1}{7}m$

(3) $\dfrac{5}{12}m$

(2) $\dfrac{2}{7}m$

(4) $\dfrac{7}{12}m$

21. If the length of a rectangle is $\dfrac{x+1}{x}$ and its width is $\dfrac{x+2}{2}$, which of the following would represent the perimeter of the rectangle?

(1) $\dfrac{x^2 + 4x + 2}{x}$ (3) $\dfrac{x^2 + 4x + 2}{2x}$

(2) $\dfrac{x^2 + 4x + 2}{2}$ (4) $\dfrac{x^2 + 8x + 4}{2x}$

22. Mrs. Rose has p papers to mark. She marks $\dfrac{2}{5}$ of them before supper, and $\dfrac{1}{3}$ of them after supper. Which of the following would represent the amount of papers that Mrs. Rose has left to mark?

(1) $\dfrac{2}{15}p$ (3) $\dfrac{11}{15}p$

(2) $\dfrac{4}{15}p$ (4) $\dfrac{3}{8}p$

5.6 Complex Fractions and Complex Rational Expressions

A complex fraction is a fraction that contains other fractions. Examples of complex fractions are $\dfrac{\frac{5}{6}}{\frac{2}{3}}$, $\dfrac{2\frac{1}{2}}{5}$, and $\dfrac{4}{1\frac{1}{3}}$.

A complex rational expression is a rational expression that contains other rational expressions. Examples of complex rational expressions are $\dfrac{\frac{2}{3x}}{\frac{1}{x}}$, $\dfrac{x - \frac{1}{x}}{x + 1}$, and $\dfrac{x + 2}{1 + \frac{5}{x} + \frac{6}{x^2}}$.

The procedure for simplifying a complex fraction or a complex rational expression is basically the same. There are two methods that are commonly used. We will demonstrate both methods. Utilize the method that looks more familiar to you. (If neither method looks familiar, chose a method that looks easier to you.)

 MODEL PROBLEMS

1. Simplify each complex fraction.

     a. $\dfrac{\frac{5}{6}}{\frac{2}{3}}$ **b.** $\dfrac{2\frac{1}{2}}{5}$ **c.** $\dfrac{4}{1\frac{1}{3}}$

SOLUTION

We will demonstrate both methods for part **a** and then use one method for part **b** and the other method for part **c**.

     a. $\dfrac{\frac{5}{6}}{\frac{2}{3}}$

Method 1

Look at the complex fraction as a division problem. It says to divide $\frac{5}{6}$ by $\frac{2}{3}$. Therefore, we can rewrite the complex fraction as a division problem, and utilize the rules for division.

$$\frac{\frac{5}{6}}{\frac{2}{3}} = \frac{5}{6} \div \frac{2}{3} = \frac{5}{\overset{}{6}} \cdot \frac{\overset{1}{3}}{2} = \frac{5}{4}$$

Method 2

Multiply the entire complex fraction by the least common denominator of all of the denominators in the complex fraction. In this case, the common denominator of $\frac{5}{6}$ and $\frac{2}{3}$ is 6, so we multiply both $\frac{5}{6}$ and $\frac{2}{3}$ by 6 and simplify if possible.

$$\frac{\frac{5}{6}}{\frac{2}{3}} = \frac{\frac{5}{6}}{\frac{2}{3}} \cdot \frac{6}{6} = \frac{\frac{5}{6} \cdot 6}{\frac{2}{3} \cdot 6} = \frac{5}{4}$$

b. $\dfrac{2\frac{1}{2}}{5}$

Use Method 1 to simplify this complex fraction. First, rewrite $2\frac{1}{2}$ as the improper fraction $\frac{5}{2}$, then rewrite the entire problem as a division problem, and follow the rules for division.

$$\frac{2\frac{1}{2}}{5} = \frac{\frac{5}{2}}{5} = \frac{5}{2} \div \frac{5}{1} = \frac{\overset{1}{5}}{2} \cdot \frac{1}{\underset{1}{5}} = \frac{1}{2}$$

c. $\dfrac{4}{1\frac{1}{3}}$

Use Method 2 to simplify this complex fraction. First rewrite $1\frac{1}{3}$ as the improper fraction $\frac{4}{3}$ and find the LCD of $\frac{4}{1}$ and $\frac{4}{3}$, which is 3. Then multiply numerator and denominator by 3, and simplify.

$$\frac{4}{1\frac{1}{3}} = \frac{\frac{4}{1}}{\frac{4}{3}} = \frac{\frac{4}{1}}{\frac{4}{3}} \cdot \frac{3}{3} = \frac{\frac{4}{1} \cdot 3}{\frac{4}{3} \cdot 3} = \frac{12}{4} = 3$$

The same methods can be used to simplify complex rational expressions.

2. Express each rational expression in simplest form.

   a. $\dfrac{\frac{2}{3x}}{\frac{1}{x}}$ **b.** $\dfrac{x - \frac{1}{x}}{x + 1}$ **c.** $\dfrac{x + 2}{1 + \frac{5}{x} + \frac{6}{x^2}}$

SOLUTION

We will demonstrate both methods for part **a** and then use one method for part **b** and the other method for part **c**.

a. $\dfrac{\frac{2}{3x}}{\frac{1}{x}}$

Method 1

Look at the complex rational expression as a division problem that says to divide $\frac{2}{3x}$ by $\frac{1}{x}$. Therefore, rewrite the complex fraction as a division problem, and utilize the rules for division.

$$\frac{\frac{2}{3x}}{\frac{1}{x}} = \frac{2}{3x} \div \frac{1}{x} = \frac{2}{3\cancel{x}} \cdot \frac{\cancel{x}}{1} = \frac{2}{3} \quad (x \neq 0)$$

Method 2

Multiply the entire complex fraction by the LCD of all of the denominators in the complex fraction. In this case, the common denominator of $\frac{2}{3x}$ and $\frac{1}{x}$ is $3x$, so multiply both $\frac{2}{3x}$ and $\frac{1}{x}$ by $3x$.

$$\frac{\frac{2}{3x}}{\frac{1}{x}} = \frac{\frac{2}{3x}}{\frac{1}{x}} \cdot \frac{3x}{3x} = \frac{\frac{2}{3\cancel{x}} \cdot 3\cancel{x}}{\frac{1}{\cancel{x}} \cdot 3\cancel{x}} = \frac{2}{3} \quad (x \neq 0)$$

b. $\dfrac{x - \frac{1}{x}}{x + 1}$

Use Method 1 to simplify this complex rational expression. First, rewrite the numerator and denominator with a single fraction in each. Then, rewrite the entire problem as a division problem and follow the rules for division.

$$\frac{x - \frac{1}{x}}{x + 1} = \frac{\frac{x}{1} - \frac{1}{x}}{x + 1} = \frac{\frac{x^2 - 1}{x}}{\frac{x + 1}{1}}$$

$$= \frac{x^2 - 1}{x} \div \frac{x + 1}{1} = \frac{x^2 - 1}{x} \cdot \frac{1}{x + 1}$$

$$= \frac{\cancel{(x + 1)}(x - 1)}{x} \cdot \frac{1}{\cancel{x + 1}} = \frac{x - 1}{x} \quad (x \neq 0, 1, -1)$$

c. $\dfrac{x + 2}{1 + \frac{5}{x} + \frac{6}{x^2}}$

Use Method 2 to simplify this complex rational expression. Find the LCD of $x + 2$, 1, $\frac{5}{x}$, and $\frac{6}{x^2}$, which is x^2. Multiply each term in the numerator and denominator by x^2, and simplify.

$$\frac{x+2}{1+\dfrac{5}{x}+\dfrac{6}{x^2}}=\frac{x+2}{1+\dfrac{5}{x}+\dfrac{6}{x^2}}\cdot\frac{x^2}{x^2}$$

$$=\frac{x^2(x+2)}{x^2(1)+\cancel{x^2}\left(\dfrac{5}{\cancel{x}}\right)+\cancel{x^2}\left(\dfrac{6}{\cancel{x^2}}\right)}$$

$$=\frac{x^2(x+2)}{x^2+5x+6}=\frac{x^2\cancel{(x+2)}}{\cancel{(x+2)}(x+3)}=\frac{x^2}{x+3}\qquad(x\neq0,\,-2,\,-3)$$

 **Practice**

In 1–18, express each complex fraction or rational expression in simplest form.

1. $\dfrac{\dfrac{4}{5}}{\dfrac{2}{5}}$

2. $\dfrac{\dfrac{5}{9x}}{\dfrac{2}{3x}}$

3. $\dfrac{\dfrac{6}{7}}{14}$

4. $\dfrac{\dfrac{3}{7}}{2\dfrac{1}{3}}$

5. $\dfrac{1+\dfrac{1}{a}}{3a}$

6. $\dfrac{\dfrac{2}{3}+\dfrac{5}{9a}}{\dfrac{7}{18a}}$

7. $\dfrac{2a+2b}{\dfrac{2}{a}+\dfrac{2}{b}}$

8. $\dfrac{\dfrac{1}{3}+\dfrac{3}{w}}{\dfrac{6}{w}}$

9. $\dfrac{\dfrac{1}{x}+\dfrac{1}{y}}{\dfrac{1}{x}-\dfrac{1}{y}}$

10. $\dfrac{\dfrac{2n}{3}+\dfrac{3}{2n}}{\dfrac{4n}{9}+\dfrac{1}{n}}$

11. $\dfrac{\dfrac{2}{a}+\dfrac{4}{b}}{\dfrac{4a}{b}-\dfrac{b}{a}}$

12. $\dfrac{1-\dfrac{3}{y}}{\dfrac{9}{y^2}-1}$

13. $\dfrac{\dfrac{s}{s-1}+\dfrac{s}{s+1}}{\dfrac{s}{s+1}}$

14. $\dfrac{1-\dfrac{2}{x}-\dfrac{24}{x^2}}{1-\dfrac{6}{x}}$

15. $\dfrac{1+\dfrac{5}{x}-\dfrac{14}{x^2}}{x-\dfrac{4}{x}}$

16. $\dfrac{y-\dfrac{28}{y+3}}{y-\dfrac{4}{y-3}}$

17. $\dfrac{\dfrac{5}{x}-\dfrac{x}{5}}{1+\dfrac{8}{x}+\dfrac{15}{x^2}}$

18. $\dfrac{1-\dfrac{2}{x}-\dfrac{48}{x^2}}{1+\dfrac{8}{x}+\dfrac{12}{x^2}}$

In 19–20, select the numeral preceding the expression that best completes the statement.

19. In electronics, when two resistors, R_1 and R_2, are connected in parallel, their combined resistance is given by the formula $\dfrac{1}{\dfrac{1}{R_1}+\dfrac{1}{R_2}}$.

When simplified, this complex rational expression is equivalent to

(1) R_1+R_2

(3) $\dfrac{R_1+R_2}{R_1R_2}$

(2) R_1R_2

(4) $\dfrac{R_1R_2}{R_1+R_2}$

20. In physics, the formula for the focal length of a mirror is $\dfrac{1}{\dfrac{1}{s}+\dfrac{1}{s'}}$. This complex rational expression can be simplified to

(1) $s\cdot s'$

(3) $\dfrac{s\cdot s'}{s+s'}$

(2) $s+s'$

(4) $\dfrac{s+s'}{s\cdot s'}$

5.7 Solving Fractional Equations

To solve an equation containing fractions or rational expressions, multiply both sides of the equation by the least common denominator of all fractions and rational expressions that appear in the equation. Then, solve the resulting equation.

 **MODEL PROBLEMS**

1. Solve for x and check.

   a. $\dfrac{2}{3} + \dfrac{4}{x} = \dfrac{5}{6}$

   b. $\dfrac{10}{x^2} + \dfrac{3}{x} = 1$

SOLUTION

a. $\dfrac{2}{3} + \dfrac{4}{x} = \dfrac{5}{6}$

First, find the LCD of $\dfrac{2}{3}$, $\dfrac{4}{x}$, and $\dfrac{5}{6}$, which is $6x$, and then multiply both sides of the equation by $6x$. Solve the resulting equation.

$$\frac{2}{3} + \frac{4}{x} = \frac{5}{6}$$

$$6x \cdot \left(\frac{2}{3} + \frac{4}{x}\right) = \left(\frac{5}{6}\right) \cdot 6x$$

$$\overset{2}{6x} \cdot \frac{2}{3} + 6x \cdot \frac{4}{x} = \frac{5}{6} \cdot 6x$$

$$4x + 24 = 5x$$

$$x = 24$$

Check:

To check the answer, substitute 24 for all values of x in the original equation.

$$\frac{2}{3} + \frac{4}{x} = \frac{5}{6}$$

$$\frac{2}{3} + \frac{4}{24} \overset{?}{=} \frac{5}{6}$$

$$\frac{2}{3} + \frac{1}{6} \overset{?}{=} \frac{5}{6}$$

$$\frac{4}{6} + \frac{1}{6} \overset{?}{=} \frac{5}{6}$$

$$\frac{5}{6} = \frac{5}{6} ✓$$

Remember: When you are checking your solution, ALWAYS go back and substitute the solution for the variable in the original equation.

b. $\dfrac{10}{x^2} + \dfrac{3}{x} = 1$

First, find the LCD of x^2, x, and 1, which is x^2. Multiply both sides of the equation by x^2 and then solve the resulting equation.

$$\frac{10}{x^2} + \frac{3}{x} = 1$$

$$x^2 \cdot \left(\frac{10}{x^2} + \frac{3}{x} \right) = x^2 \cdot (1)$$

$$\cancel{x^2} \cdot \frac{10}{\cancel{x^2}} + \overset{x}{\cancel{x^2}} \cdot \frac{3}{\cancel{x}} = x^2$$

$$10 + 3x = x^2$$

This is a quadratic equation, which can be set equal to zero, factored, and then solved.

$$x^2 - 3x - 10 = 0$$
$$(x - 5)(x + 2) = 0$$
$$x - 5 = 0 \qquad x + 2 = 0$$
$$x = 5 \qquad\qquad x = -2$$

Check:

We must check both solutions in the original equation.

$x = 5$	$x = -2$
$\dfrac{10}{x^2} + \dfrac{3}{x} = 1$	$\dfrac{10}{x^2} + \dfrac{3}{x} = 1$
$\dfrac{10}{5^2} + \dfrac{3}{5} \overset{?}{=} 1$	$\dfrac{10}{(-2)^2} + \dfrac{3}{-2} \overset{?}{=} 1$
$\dfrac{10}{25} + \dfrac{3}{5} \overset{?}{=} 1$	$\dfrac{10}{4} - \dfrac{3}{2} \overset{?}{=} 1$
$\dfrac{2}{5} + \dfrac{3}{5} \overset{?}{=} 1$	$\dfrac{5}{2} - \dfrac{3}{2} \overset{?}{=} 1$
$1 = 1 \checkmark$	$1 = 1 \checkmark$

Note: When you multiply both sides of the equation by the least common denominator, you do not *necessarily* get an equivalent equation. Just as when we solved radical equations and absolute value equations, in changing the original equation to enable us to solve it, we sometimes receive an extraneous root. Thus, it is essential that you *always* check your answers in the *original* equation. The following example will demonstrate this.

2. Solve for y.

$$\frac{2}{y + 5} + \frac{20}{y^2 - 25} = 1$$

$$\frac{2}{y+5} + \frac{20}{y^2-25} = 1$$

Factor the second denominator to determine the LCD, multiply both sides of the equation by the LCD, and then solve the resulting equation.

$$\frac{2}{y+5} + \frac{20}{(y+5)(y-5)} = 1 \qquad \text{The LCD is } (y+5)(y-5).$$

$$(y+5)(y-5) \cdot \left(\frac{2}{(y+5)} + \frac{20}{(y+5)(y-5)} \right) = 1 \cdot (y+5)(y-5)$$

$$\cancel{(y+5)}(y-5) \cdot \frac{2}{\cancel{y+5}} + \cancel{(y+5)(y-5)} \frac{20}{\cancel{(y+5)(y-5)}} = 1 \cdot (y+5)(y-5)$$

$$2(y-5) + 20 = (y+5)(y-5)$$
$$2y - 10 + 20 = y^2 - 25$$
$$2y + 10 = y^2 - 25$$
$$y^2 - 2y - 35 = 0$$
$$(y-7)(y+5) = 0$$
$$y - 7 = 0 \qquad y + 5 = 0$$
$$y = 7 \qquad\quad y = -5$$

Although the question did not specifically require a check, we MUST check our answers.

Check:

$y = 7$	$y = -5$
$\dfrac{2}{y+5} + \dfrac{20}{y^2-25} = 1$	$\dfrac{2}{y+5} + \dfrac{20}{y^2-25} = 1$
$\dfrac{2}{7+5} + \dfrac{20}{7^2-25} \overset{?}{=} 1$	$\dfrac{2}{-5+5} + \dfrac{20}{(-5)^2-25} \overset{?}{=} 1$
$\dfrac{2}{12} + \dfrac{20}{49-25} \overset{?}{=} 1$	$\dfrac{2}{0} + \dfrac{20}{0} \overset{?}{=} 1$
$\dfrac{1}{6} + \dfrac{20}{24} \overset{?}{=} 1$	Division by 0 is undefined.
$\dfrac{1}{6} + \dfrac{5}{6} \overset{?}{=} 1$	Thus, the statement here is meaningless, and $y = -5$ is an extraneous solution.
$1 = 1 \checkmark$	

Answer: $y = 7$

Remember: Always check your answers in the *original* equation. In this question, if we had checked our answer in any equation other than the original, both answers would have checked. However, $y = -5$ is not a root of the original equation, and is therefore not a solution.

In 1–15, solve each equation.

1. $\dfrac{3}{a} + \dfrac{5}{2a} = \dfrac{1}{2}$

2. $\dfrac{4}{r} + \dfrac{9 - 4r}{3r} = \dfrac{r}{3}$

3. $\dfrac{1}{6x} + \dfrac{8}{x} = \dfrac{x}{6}$

4. $4 + \dfrac{b}{b + 5} = \dfrac{30}{b + 5}$

5. $1 + \dfrac{2}{x} = \dfrac{3}{x^2}$

6. $3 + \dfrac{a}{a - 6} = \dfrac{6}{a - 6}$

7. $\dfrac{1}{4} + \dfrac{2}{a + 3} = \dfrac{3}{8}$

8. $\dfrac{2}{y + 3} + \dfrac{4}{y} = \dfrac{6}{2y + 6}$

9. $\dfrac{5}{a + 3} - \dfrac{3}{a + 4} = \dfrac{21}{a^2 + 7a + 12}$

10. $2 + \dfrac{4}{x + 2} = \dfrac{6x - 4}{x^2 - 4}$

11. $\dfrac{y}{y - 4} + \dfrac{2}{y + 1} = \dfrac{y - 5}{y^2 - 3y - 4}$

12. $\dfrac{x + 1}{x + 2} - \dfrac{2}{x} = \dfrac{-4}{x^2 + 2x}$

13. $\dfrac{a}{3a + 6} + \dfrac{2}{3a - 6} = \dfrac{1}{a^2 - 4}$

14. $\dfrac{4n + 3}{n - 6} + \dfrac{n - 4}{6 - n} = \dfrac{44}{2n - 12}$

15. $\dfrac{3}{x + 3} - \dfrac{2}{x - 2} = 1$

16. What fraction when added to its reciprocal is equal to $\dfrac{13}{6}$?

17. The denominator of a fraction is 1 more than the numerator. If 2 were added to both the numerator and the denominator, the new fraction would equal $\dfrac{4}{5}$. Find the original fraction.

18. Arif estimates that it will take him 8 hours to type his term paper. If he could convince his girlfriend Natisha to bring over her laptop computer and help him with the typing, the two of them could type the paper in 5 hours.
    a. What portion of the term paper could Arif type in 1 hour?
    b. What portion of the term paper could Arif type in 5 hours?
    c. If it takes Natisha n hours to type the paper alone, what portion of the paper could she type in 1 hour? In 5 hours?
    d. Arif and Natisha have decided to work together. Write an equation that could be used

to estimate the time it would take Natisha to type the paper if she worked alone.
    e. Solve the equation to find how long it would take Natisha to type the paper if she worked alone.

19. Janine has an old printer that took 10 minutes to print her assignment. She just bought a new printer that printed the same assignment in 5 minutes. She has decided to network the two printers so that they can work together and she can print even faster.
    a. If t represents the time it would take to print the assignment if the two printers were networked, what portion of the assignment would her old printer complete?
    b. What portion of the assignment would her new printer complete?
    c. Determine how long it would take to print the assignment if the two printers were working together.

20. Joey is thinking of changing his cellular phone company. When he spoke to his present phone company, they told him that the average cost per minute is $0.05 (after taking into account the monthly charge). CellsRUs has a plan for $25 per month plus $0.03 per minute.
    a. If n is the number of minutes Joey spends on the phone per month, what is the total cost for Joey per month if he switches to CellsRUs?
    b. Represent the average cost per minute if Joey signs on with CellsRUs.
    c. How many minutes does Joey have to use per month for CellsRUs to be the better deal?

21. Han Diman is opening a home repair business. He estimates that it will cost him $300 to buy his equipment, and $20 a week to rent storage space to store his equipment.
    a. If w represents the number of weeks that Han is in business, represent the total cost to Han when he is in business for w weeks.
    b. What is the average cost per week that Han is in business?
    c. Han wants to determine how many weeks he would have to stay in business for the average cost per week to equal $50. Write an equation to represent this and solve the equation.

In 22–25, select the numeral preceding the expression that best answers the question.

22. What is the solution set of the equation

$$\frac{x}{x + 3} + \frac{2}{x + 1} = \frac{6}{x^2 + 4x + 3}?$$

(1) $\{-3\}$ (3) $\{-3, 0\}$
(2) $\{0\}$ (4) $\{\ \}$

23. Which of the following is a solution, in simplest $a + bi$ form, of the equation

$$\frac{x + 1}{3} + \frac{x + 1}{x} = \frac{-5}{3x}?$$

(1) $-1 \pm i$ (3) $1 \pm i$
(2) $-2 \pm 2i$ (4) $2 \pm 2i$

24. Express the roots of the equation $x + \frac{3}{x} = \frac{5}{2}$ in simplest $a + bi$ form.

(1) $-\frac{5}{4} \pm \frac{\sqrt{13}}{4}i$ (3) $-\frac{5}{4} \pm \frac{\sqrt{23}}{4}i$
(2) $\frac{5}{4} \pm \frac{\sqrt{13}}{4}i$ (4) $\frac{5}{4} \pm \frac{\sqrt{23}}{4}i$

25. Wanda's Widget Company manufactures widgets. It costs Wanda $1,000 per month for her fixed costs, plus $10 to produce each widget. If Wanda produces w widgets each month, what is the average cost per widget?

(1) $\frac{1000 + 10w}{w}$ (3) $\frac{1000 + 10w}{10}$
(2) $\frac{1000w + 10}{w}$ (4) $\frac{1000w + 10}{1000}$

CHAPTER REVIEW

In 1–16, select the numeral preceding the expression or diagram that best completes the statement or answers the question.

1. What is the solution set for the equation $|2x - 4| + 3 = 5$?
(1) $\{1\}$ (3) $\{3\}$
(2) $\{1, 3\}$ (4) $\{\pm 3\}$

2. Which of the following is the graph of the solution to $|12 - 3x| \geq 30$?

(1)   −6 0   14
(2)   −6 0   14
(3)   −14   0 6
(4)   −6 0   14

3. Carmela's parents want her home within 30 minutes of midnight. Which equation represents her curfew?
(1) $|x - 12| = 30$ (3) $|x + 12| = \frac{1}{2}$
(2) $|12 - x| = 30$ (4) $|12 - x| = \frac{1}{2}$

4. Which of the following is *not* in the solution set of $\left|\frac{3x - 12}{4}\right| \leq 6$?
(1) -6 (3) 2
(2) -4 (4) 12

5. When Dr. Leroi Mathman, an eccentric scientist, was asked how long it takes him to get to work, he said, "Depending on traffic, $|30 - x| \leq 10$." How would a nonmathematician describe the length of the trip?
(1) from 10 to 30 minutes
(2) 10 minutes less than 30 minutes
(3) 40 minutes
(4) from 20 to 40 minutes

6. For what value(s) of x is the expression $\frac{2x + 3}{4x^3 - x}$ undefined?

(1) $\left\{-\frac{1}{2}, 0\right\}$ (3) $\{0\}$

(2) $\left\{-\frac{1}{2}, 0, \frac{1}{2}\right\}$ (4) $\{0, 1, 2\}$

7. When reduced to lowest terms, $\frac{4c^2 - c - 18}{8c - 18}$ equals

(1) $\frac{c}{2}$ (3) c

(2) $\frac{c + 2}{2}$ (4) $\frac{4c - 1}{2}$

8. The least common denominator for $\frac{5x + 3}{x^2 - 1} + \frac{4}{1 + x}$, given that $x \neq \pm 1$, is

(1) $1 + x$ (3) $(x^2 - 1)(1 + x)$
(2) $x^2 - 1$ (4) $x^2 + 1$

9. The expression $\frac{c^2d}{cd} - \frac{cd^2}{cd}$, where $c \neq 0$ and $d \neq 0$, is equivalent to which of the following?

(1) $c + d$ (3) $\frac{c}{d}$

(2) $c - d$ (4) $\frac{d}{c}$

10. In simplest form, $\frac{m^2 - m - 42}{2m + 12} \cdot$

$\frac{3m^2 - m}{3m^2 - 22m + 7}$ equals

(1) $\frac{3m}{2}$ (3) $\frac{m}{2}$

(2) m (4) $\frac{3m - 1}{(3m + 1)(m - 6)}$

11. For all values at which it is defined, the expression $\frac{6a^2 + a - 1}{4a^2 - 1} \div \frac{6a^2 + 13a - 5}{5 - 8a - 4a^2}$ is equivalent to

(1) 1 (3) $\frac{1 - 2a}{2a - 1}$

(2) -1 (4) $\frac{5 + 2a}{2a - 1}$

12. For all values at which it is defined, the expression $\frac{3x^2 - 6x}{9x^2} \div \frac{3x^2 - 4x - 4}{4 - 9x^2}$ is equivalent to

(1) $\frac{2 - 3x}{3x}$ (3) $\frac{x - 2}{3x^2}$

(2) $\frac{2 - 3x}{3x + 2}$ (4) $\frac{2 + 3x}{3x}$

13. When simplified, $\frac{\frac{b - a}{a}}{\frac{1}{a} - \frac{1}{b}}$, when $a \neq 0$ and $b \neq 0$, equals

(1) a   (3) $b - a$
(2) b   (4) $a - b$

14. The solution set to the equation $\frac{x}{2x + 8} + \frac{2}{2x - 8} = \frac{16}{x^2 - 16}$ is

(1) $\{-4, 6\}$ (3) $\{6\}$
(2) $\{-6, 4\}$ (4) $\{4\}$

15. The solution to $\frac{4}{x + 1} - \frac{x - 1}{2x - 1} = 1$ is

(1) $\{2\}$ (3) $\left\{\frac{1}{3}, 3\right\}$

(2) $\left\{\frac{1}{3}, 2\right\}$ (4) $\{\,\}$

16. The value(s) of x in the equation $\frac{x - 2}{4} = \frac{2x - 1}{x + 7}$, given $x \neq 7$, is

(1) $\{-2\}$ (3) $\{-5, 2\}$
(2) $\{5\}$ (4) $\{-2, 5\}$

17. The area of a parallelogram is represented by the expression $\frac{2c^2 - 5c - 3}{c^2 - 9}$. If the height of the parallelogram is represented by $\frac{6c^2 + c - 1}{4c + 12}$, find the length of the base of the parallelogram in terms of c.

18. The Student Civic Club raised $\frac{2x^2 + 5x - 12}{8 - 2x}$ for scholarships by running a children's fair, but their expenses totaled $\frac{-4x - 4}{4 - x}$. How much money, in terms of x, did they make after expenses for scholarships?

19. Savannah's art class designed a large pyramid for their display in the homecoming parade. The height of the pymid was $\frac{2x^2 + 5x + 2}{x^2 - 4}$ and its rectangular base was $\frac{x^2 - 5x + 6}{4x + 2}$ by $\frac{4x^2 + 8x + 4}{2x^2 - 4x - 6}$. Find the volume of the completed pyramid in terms of x.

20. The denominator of a fraction is three more than twice the numerator. If the denominator is increased by five and the numerator is unchanged, the new fraction equals $\frac{1}{4}$. Find original fraction.

You can use your calculator to solve many of the equations presented in this chapter, for example, the equation $|3x + 1| = 5$. To solve this equation graphically, we enter $|3x + 1|$ into Y_1 and 5 into Y_2 and see where the two graphs intersect. Press the (Y=) key and enter the information as shown below.

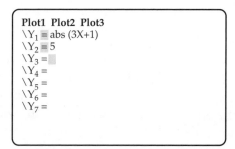

Note: To obtain the abs(, you can go into Catalog by pressing (2nd)(0) and selecting the first entry. Alternatively, you can go to the (MATH) menu, across to NUM, and select the first entry.

Once the information is entered, graph the equations in the standard viewing window. ((ZOOM)(6) was used to produce the window shown, which is $[-10, 10] \times [-10, 10]$.)

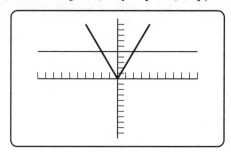

To find the two points of intersection (whose x-coordinates are the two solutions of our equation), we will use the CALC feature of the calculator. Select (2nd)(TRACE) to get the window shown in the screen below.

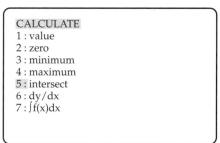

Select 5: intersect. Since there are only two curves, when you are asked for the First curve and the Second curve, simply press (ENTER). Next, you will be asked for a guess. Move your cursor closer to one of the intersection points, and then press (ENTER). If you move your cursor closer to the right point, you should get the screen shown below.

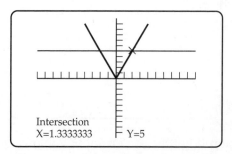

We can see that the left side of our equation, $|3x + 1|$, is equal to the right side of our equation when $x = 1.3333333$. You may recognize this as the fraction $\frac{4}{3}$. If you would like the calculator to convert the decimal to a fraction, press (2nd)(MODE), which will return you to the Home Screen. Press (X,T,Θ,n) and then (ENTER). The calculator will show you what value is stored as X, in this case 1.3333333. Now, press (MATH) and then select option 1 : (▶) Frac (ENTER), (ENTER). This will convert the decimal 1.3333333 to the fraction $\frac{4}{3}$. The screen shot below illustrates what was done.

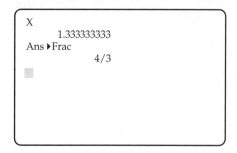

We can find the other solution to the equation by following the same procedure as outlined above, except selecting the left intersection point. This will give us the value of $x = -2$.

As a check, we can solve the same equation algebraically.

$$|3x + 1| = 5$$

$$3x + 1 = 5 \qquad 3x + 1 = -5$$
$$3x = 4 \qquad\quad 3x = -6$$
$$x = \frac{4}{3} \qquad\quad x = -2$$

The TI-83 also has a Solver feature that can be used to find the roots of the equation. As shown below, select $\boxed{\text{MATH}}$ $\boxed{0}$ to begin the process.

```
MATH NUM CPX PRB
4↑ ³√(
5 : ˣ√
6 : fMin(
7 : fMax(
8 : nDeriv(
9 : fnInt(
0 : Solver ...
```

You should get the screen shown below.

```
EQUATION SOLVER
eqn : 0=
```

If you do not get this screen, you already have an equation entered into your Solver. Press the $\boxed{\blacktriangle}$ to return to the Solver screen, and clear whatever equation is there. We have to transform our equation by moving all the terms to the right. Enter the information as shown below.

```
EQUATION SOLVER
eqn : 0=abs (3X+1)–
5
```

Once the information is entered, press $\boxed{\blacktriangledown}$ or $\boxed{\text{ENTER}}$ to get the screen as shown.

```
abs (3X+1) –5=0
   X=-1
   bound={-1 E99, 1...
```

Your X= may have a different value than the one shown above. The x-coordinate shown corresponds to the x-coordinate last used in your graph. You may change this by simply entering a value you would like to try. Enter -1 as a guess for the x-coordinate. Select $\boxed{\text{ALPHA}}$ $\boxed{\text{ENTER}}$ to solve the equation. You will then get the information shown below.

```
abs (3X+1) –5=0
• X=-2
   bound={-1 E99, 1...
• left–rt=0
```

We obtain only one answer, the answer closest to -1.

Note: Be aware that Solver can sometimes be unreliable, and will sometimes fail to find a solution that exists.

Practice

Go back to some of the equations in this chapter. Try solving them graphically, or by using the Solver feature of your calculator.

Remember: When you are entering equations involving fractions, be sure to use parentheses to group the whole numerator and the whole denominator.

For example, the fraction $\frac{x + 1}{x + 2}$ must be entered as $(x + 1) \div (x + 2)$.

CHAPTER 6

Relations & Functions

6.1 Basic Concepts

Relations

In mathematics, a **relation** is any set of ordered pairs. A relation can consist of numbers or other items, such as months or names, and may be presented as a list, a table, or a graph. The following are examples of relations.

Relation *A*: {(February, 2), (April, 4), (June, 6), (August, 8), (November, 11)}

Relation *B*: {(1991, 28), (1996, 29), (1997, 28), (2000, 29), (2003, 28)}

Relation *C*: {(Joachim, 64), (Israel, 67), (Tomei, 56), (Marsha, 68), (Davida, 63)}

Relation *D*: {(4, 13), (−2, 7), (5, 14), (−8, 1), (−4, 5)}

Relation *E*:

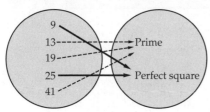

Relation *F*:

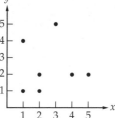

Relation *G*:

x	*y*
1	−5
2	−3
2	−1
−4	1
−4	3

Relation *H*:

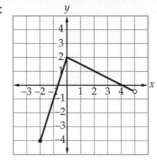

The **domain** of a relation is the set of first, or independent, elements. The **range** of a relation is the set of second, or dependent, elements. The domain and range of the relations above are listed in the table below. Notice that the number of elements in a domain and range are not necessarily equal since an element appearing twice in a domain or in a range is only listed once.

Relation	Domain	Range
A	{February, April, June, August, November}	{2, 4, 6, 8, 11}
B	{1991, 1996, 1997, 2000, 2003}	{28, 29}
C	{Joachim, Israel, Tomei, Marsha, Davida}	{64, 67, 56, 68, 63}
D	{4, −2, 5, −8, −4}	{13, 7, 14, 1, 5}
E	{9, 13, 19, 25, 41}	{prime, perfect square}
F	{1, 2, 3, 4, 5}	{1, 2, 4, 5}
G	{1, 2, −4}	{−5, −3, −1, 1, 3}
H	$\{x \mid -2 \leq x < 5\}$	$\{y \mid -4 \leq y \leq 2\}$

In some relations, there is a rule or method for the relationship that may be discovered and used to find other elements of the relation. For example, the rule in relation *A* is that each element of the range is the number of the month on the calendar. Another element of that relation might be {July, 7}. In relation *D*, each element in the range is 9 more than its corresponding element in the domain. In relation *H*, since the graph is continuous, all points, integer and noninteger, had to be included in the domain and range, a different notation was used.

Practice

In 1–6, state the domain and range of each relation. Find the rule that defines the relationship, if there is one.

1. {(Albany, New York), (Bismarck, North Dakota), (Juneau, Alaska)}

2. {(1, January), (4, July), (12, October), (11, November), (25, December)}

3. {(*Friends*, Thursday), (*ER*, Thursday), (*Dawson's Creek*, Wednesday), (*Sopranos*, Sunday), (*West Wing*, Wednesday), (*Malcolm in the Middle*, Sunday)}

4. $\{(3, 9), (-2, 4), (4, 16), (-1, 1),$
$(-3, 9), (5, 25)\}$

5. $\{(-10, 4), (-8, 3), (-4, 1),$
$(-2, 0), (0, -1)\}$

6. $\{(2, 1), (4, 5), (5, 7), (7, 11),$
$(9, 15)\}$

*In 7–10, state the relationship as a set
of ordered pairs and then state the domain and range for each relation.*

7.

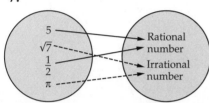

8.

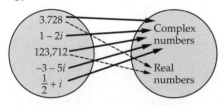

9.

1st element	2nd element
-6	-5
-1	5
4	15
9	25

10.

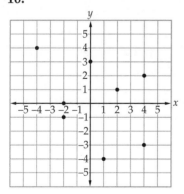

*In 11–15, the graphs show rela-
tions on the coordinate axes of
real numbers. State the domain
and range of each relation.*

11.

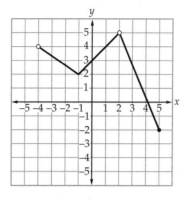

12.

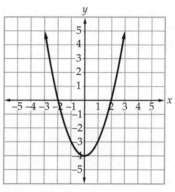

13.

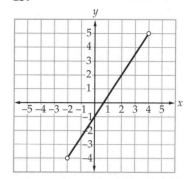

14.

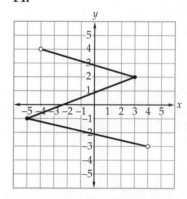

15.

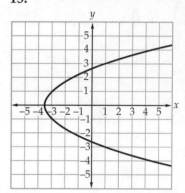

Functions

A **function** is a relation in which each element of the domain corresponds to a unique element in the range. That is, each independent variable is paired with only one dependent variable. In other words, each x has one and only one corresponding y-value. In the diagram below, relation A is not a function, but relation B is.

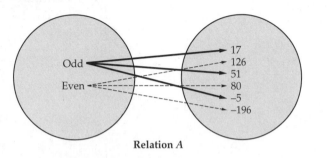

Relation A

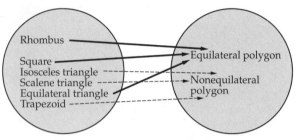

Relation B

In relation A, the domain entry of even number corresponds to more than one value in the range, so it cannot be a function. In relation B, each figure in the domain is either an equilateral polygon or it is not. None of the polygons can be in both elements of the range, so each input corresponds to one output.

MODEL PROBLEM

List the domain and range of each relation and explain why the relation is or is not a function.

a. A: {(purple, lilac), (yellow, daffodil), (pink, carnation), (purple, tulip)}
b. B: {(−7, 3), (−3, 8), (−1, 10), (4, 3)}
c. C: {(4, 2), (9, −3), (25, 5), (16, −4), (9, 3)}
d. D: {(1, 13), (5, 10), (9, −7), (13, −4), (17, −1)}

SOLUTION

a. Domain of A: {purple, yellow, pink}   Range of A: {lilac, daffodil, carnation, tulip}
   A is not a function because purple corresponds to both tulip and lilac. Each element of the domain does not have one and only one corresponding value in the range.
b. Domain of B: {−7, −3, −1, 4}   Range of B: {3, 8, 10}
   B is a function even though 3 repeats in the range, since each value of the domain corresponds to one and only one value in the range.
c. Domain of C: {4, 9, 25, 16}   Range of C: {2, −3, 5, −4, 3}
   C is not function because 9 in the domain corresponds to both 3 and −3 in the range.
d. Domain of D: {1, 5, 9, 13, 17}   Range of D: {13, 10, −7, −4, −1}
   D is a function because each value of the domain corresponds to one and only one value in the range.

Note: A relation with more elements in the range than in the domain is never a function. Also, all functions are relations, but not all relations are functions.

Vertical-Line Test In a graph, if a value in the domain repeats, it would present two or more values in a vertical line, so we can use the vertical-line test to determine if the graph represents a function. The **vertical-line test** says that if a vertical line drawn at any position over the domain of the graph crosses the graph more than once, the graph does not represent a function. In other words, if any x-value corresponds to more than one y-value, the graph does not represent a function.

Consider the following graphs.

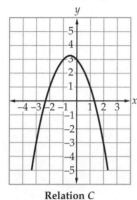

Relation C

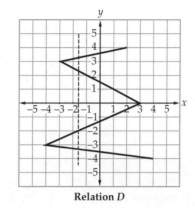

Relation D

For the graph of relation C, a vertical line drawn anywhere in the graph of the parabola will touch the graph only once, which means each x-value corresponds to only one y-value. Therefore, relation C is a function. On the other hand, a vertical line in the graph of relation D, at $x = -1.6$, hits the graph four times, which means that there are four different y-values that correspond to the x-value of -1.6. Therefore, relation D is not a function.

Applications There are many situations in everyday life that can be represented as graphs in which one variable is a function of the other. For example, distance may be a function of time, money earned may be a function of years of experience, or speed may be a function of time. You may not be able to write an algebraic equation of many such functions, but often it is possible to sketch a graph of the situation as long as you clearly identify the independent and dependent variables.

Remember: The independent variable is on the horizontal axis and the dependent variable is on the vertical axis.

A New York subway train slows down as it approaches the 42nd Street station, stops at the station for 2 minutes, and then continues on its route. Which graph below shows the speed of the train compared to the time elapsed?

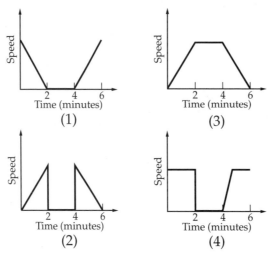

SOLUTION

In choice 1, the train's speed decreases gradually to zero from an unspecified rate, remains at zero for 2 minutes, and then increases again to its earlier rate. In choice 2, the train's speed increases from zero to an unspecified rate, decreases immediately to zero, remains at zero for 2 minutes, then accelerates immediately back to the earlier speed, and then gradually returns to zero. In choice 3, the train's speed increases from zero to an unspecified rate, remains there for 2 minutes, and then decreases back to zero. In choice 4, the train's speed begins at an unspecified rate, decreases immediately to zero, remains at zero for 2 minutes, accelerates slowly to its earlier speed, and remains at that speed. The answer is choice 1 since that most clearly represents the given situation.

Practice

In 1–15, determine if each relation is or is not a function. Explain your reasoning.

1.

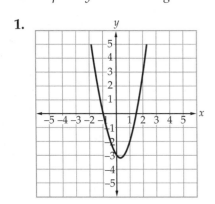

2.

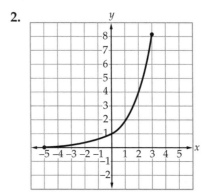

3.

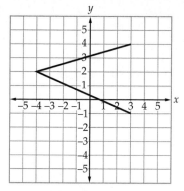

4.

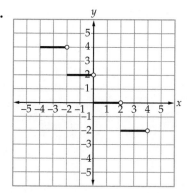

5.

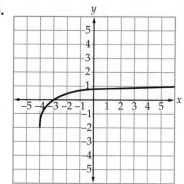

6.

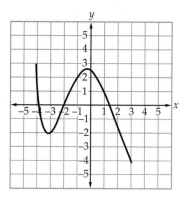

7.

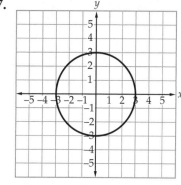

8.

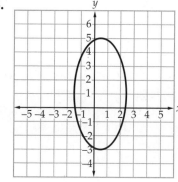

9.

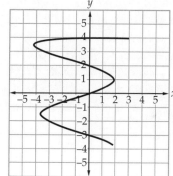

10. $y = 2x^2 - 3x + 1$

11. $y = \frac{3}{2}x - 4$

12. $y = -3x^4 + x^3 - 2x + 1$

13. Relation *A:* {(4, −1), (7, −3), (10, −5), (13, −7)}

14. Relation *B:* {(January, Aquarius), (April, Aries), (May, Gemini), (August, Leo)}

15. Relation *C:* {(−2, 8), (0, 5), (3, −1), (0, 7), (−2, 10)}

In 16–18, select the numeral under the graph that best answers the question.

16. Abdul left for school walking casually until he realized he'd forgotten his calculator. He turned and hurried home, got the calculator, and ran so he wouldn't be late for class. Which graph below depicts the situation in which distance from home is a function of time elapsed?

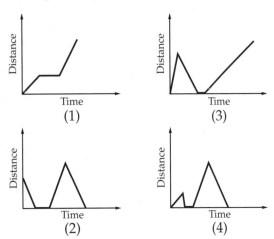

17. Josef is pushing his little brother Ivan on the swings and Ivan wants to go higher and higher. If Josef keeps pushing him higher, which of the following graphs represents a function in which Ivan's height above the ground is dependent on time elapsed?

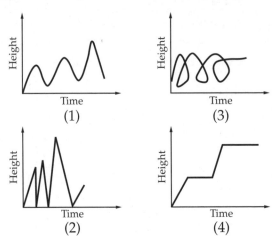

18. Hollis had money in her savings account. She spent some money on new clothes, then worked a part-time job and saved her salary until she had enough to pay her car insurance. Which of the following graphs shows how her savings changed as a function of time?

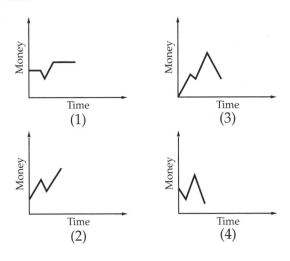

6.2 Function Notation

Function notation is shorthand to indicate that the rule or the equation being discussed is, indeed, a function. If the rule of a function states that "each element of the range is one greater than twice the corresponding element of the domain," the rule (or equation) could be written in a number of ways.

One form of notation is the one you have used throughout algebra, the equation. For example, $y = 2x + 1$ tells us that the y-value is one more than twice the x-value. Since x is often used to denote the domain and y the range, this expression clearly assigns one element in the range to each element in the domain.

Another type of function notation names the function, indicates the variable inside parentheses, and then, following an equal sign, defines the rule of the function. In this format, the rule might appear as: $f(x) = 2x + 1$. In this case, x represents the element in the domain and $f(x)$ represents the corresponding element in the range. An ordered pair belonging to the solution set of this function could be represented as $(x, f(x))$ rather than (x, y). It is very important to remember that $f(x) = y$.

Alternately, the function may be shown as: $x \xrightarrow{f} 2x + 1$. This states that under the function f, any element of the domain becomes twice itself, plus one.

 **MODEL PROBLEMS**

1. If $f(\psi) = 3(\psi) - 4$, evaluate $f(5)$.

SOLUTION

In this case, ψ represents the element in the domain and $f(\psi)$ represents the corresponding element in the range.

Note: The ψ symbol could be any variable or symbol you prefer, but the main idea is that whatever symbol appears in the parenthesis next to the function's name is then substituted on the right so that its corresponding range value may be determined.

Therefore, we are really evaluating the quantity "three times the domain element minus four." We substitute and find that $f(5) = 3(5) - 4$, which equals 11. Therefore, the point $(5, 11)$ is on the graph of the line $y = 3x - 4$ as shown below.

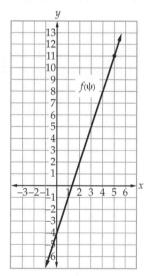

To test this idea, using the same function, $f(\psi) = 3(\psi) - 4$, evaluate $f(1)$.

$$f(\psi) = 3(\psi) - 4 \qquad \text{First, write the rule of the function.}$$

$$f(1) = 3(1) - 4 \qquad \text{Now, substitute for the variable and simplify.}$$
$$f(1) = 3 - 4$$
$$f(1) = -1 \qquad \text{This means, when } x = 1, y = -1.$$

Notice that the coordinate point $(1, -1)$ appears on the graph of this function.

2. If function $h(x)$ is represented by the mapping below, find:
   a. $h(3)$
   b. $h(-3)$
   c. $h(0)$
   d. the value of x if $h(x) = 5$

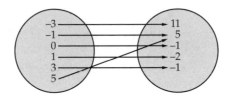

SOLUTION

a. Since the first circle represents the domain and the second the range, we look in the first circle to find the element 3 and then follow the arrow to find the corresponding value in the range. $h(3)$ maps to -1, so $h(3) = -1$.
b. As above, we look in the first circle for -3 and see that it maps to 11.
c. As above, we look in the domain for 0 and find that it maps to -1.
d. In this example, we are given the value of $h(x)$, which is an element in the range, so we look in the second circle to find 5 and work backward to find the element(s) in the domain that correspond to 5. There are two values in the domain, -1 and 5, for which the statement $h(x) = 5$ would be true. There are two solutions.

Practice

1. If a function $f(x)$ is defined as $f(x) = x^2 + x - 2$, evaluate
   a. $f(3)$
   b. $f\left(\frac{1}{2}\right)$
   c. $f(-1)$

2. A function $g(x)$ is defined as $g(x) = 3 - 5x - 2x^2$. Find the value of
   a. $g(-2)$
   b. $g(1.4)$
   c. $g(5)$

3. Given $f(x) = 4 - \frac{1}{2}x$, find x such that $f(x) = 1$.

4. Given $g(x) = x^2 - 3x - 1$, find x such that $g(x) = 3$.

5. If the function $h(x)$ is defined as $h(x) = x^3 - x^2 + 1$, find
   a. $h(-2)$
   b. $h(2.5)$
   c. $h\left(-\frac{1}{2}\right)$
   d. x such that $h(x) = 1$

In 6–11, use the graph of the function f(x) shown below.

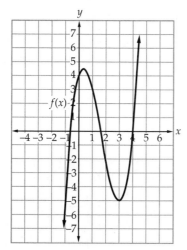

6. Find $f(2)$.

7. Find $f(-1)$.

8. Find $f\left(\frac{1}{2}\right)$.

9. Find $f(3.5)$.

10. For how many values of x does $f(x) = -2$?

11. If $f(x) = 4$, estimate the possible values of x.

In 12–17, the rule that defines the function g(x) is given. Find **a.** g(1) and **b.** g(−2).

12. $g(x) = 12 - 3x$

13. $g(x) = x^2 - 4$

14. $g(x) = \dfrac{2x + 1}{x}$

15. $g(x) = 5$

16. $g(x) = -\dfrac{3}{4}x + 7$

17. $g(x) = 2x^2 - 5x + 3$

In 18–22, select the numeral preceding the expression that best completes the sentence or answers the question.

18. Given the function, $f(x) = 2x^4 - 3x^3 + x - 7$, the point $(2, f(2))$ appears on the graph of $f(x)$. The value of $f(2)$ is
   (1) -13 (3) 3
   (2) 2   (4) 227

19. If $x \xrightarrow{g} 3 - 2x$, which coordinate point appears on the graph of this function?
   (1) $(1, -2)$ (3) $(-1, 2)$
   (2) $(2, -1)$ (4) $(-2, 1)$

In 20–22, use the diagram below.

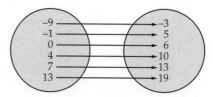

20. If $f(x) = 13$, what is the corresponding element in the domain?
   (1) 19   (3) 0
   (2) 7   (4) -3

21. The statement $f(-1) = 5$ implies which of the following to be true?
   (1) 5 is in the domain and -1 is in the range.
   (2) The coordinate point $(-1, 5)$ would appear on the graph of this function.
   (3) The coordinate point $(5, -1)$ would appear on the graph of this function.
   (4) Both -1 and 5 are elements in the range of this function.

22. Given the partial mapping of the domain and range of the function $f(x)$ in the figure above, which of the following might represent the rule of the function $f(x)$?
   (1) $f(x) = 3x - 9$ (3) $f(x) = x$
   (2) $f(x) = 1 - 2x$ (4) $f(x) = x + 6$

6.3 Domain and Range

In many cases, the domain and range of a function are the set of all real numbers *R*, such as in the case of a line, or linear function. The diagrams below represent a few functions whose domain and range are the set of all reals.

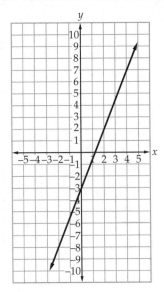 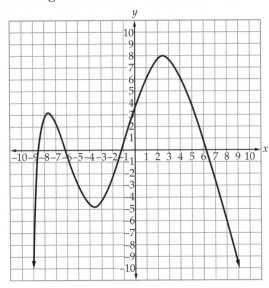 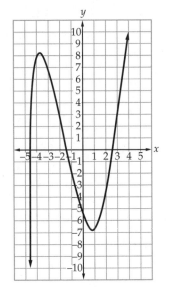

However, other functions can exist only if we limit the domain. For example, in the equation $y = \frac{x + 3}{x^2 - 4}$, the domain cannot include ±2 or the expression will be undefined. Therefore, we say the domain is all real numbers, except ±2, which is written as $R/\{\pm 2\}$.

A graph of this function is shown below.

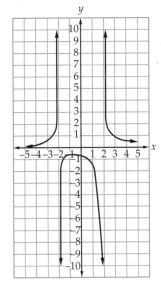

Notice that while the graph approaches the values of +2 and −2 from both the right and the left, it never actually reaches those values. Another type of function whose domain must be limited in order to avoid imaginary numbers is a radical equation, such as $y = \sqrt{x - 6}$. In this case, the domain is such that $x \geq 6$. Rules for finding the domain and range are summarized in the table on page 149.

Type of Function	Example of Function	Domain	Range	Comments
Linear function	$y = 2x - 1$	All real numbers	All real numbers	Lines in the form $y = mx + b$, where $m \neq 0$ and $b \neq 0$, are infinite; so are the domain and range.
Quadratic function	$y = x^2 - 4$	All real numbers	$y \geq -4$	If a parabola opens upward, its range has a minimum value but it grows without limit in a positive direction.
	$y = -2x^2 + 4x + 5$		$y \leq 5$	If a parabola opens downward, its range has a maximum value but it grows without limit in its negative direction.
Cubic function	$y = x^3 + 6$	All real numbers	All real numbers	
Absolute value function	$y = \lvert 2x - 3 \rvert$	All real numbers	$y \geq 0$	
Rational function	$y = \dfrac{3x - 1}{x + 5}$	All real numbers except $x = -5$, also written $R/\{-5\}$		
Functions with radicals	$y = \sqrt{10 - x}$	$x \leq 10$	$y \geq 0$	The domain cannot allow a negative number under the radical; set the radicand greater than or equal to zero and solve to find the domain.
	$f(x) = \dfrac{1}{\sqrt{x + 8}}$	$x > -8$	$y > 0$	Both the rules for fractions and radicals apply here! Therefore, set the radicand to be greater than zero (instead of equal to zero) and solve to find the domain.

In 1–3, find the largest possible domain for each function.

1. $f(x) = \dfrac{3x + 1}{x^2 + 3x - 4}$ **2.** $g(x) = \dfrac{7x}{\sqrt{5 - 2x}}$ **3.** $h(x) = \sqrt{2x - 4}$

SOLUTIONS

1. To find the domain, set the denominator equal to zero and solve. The domain is all real numbers except those values for which $x^2 + 3x - 4$ equals 0.

$$x^2 + 3x - 4 = 0$$
$$(x + 4)(x - 1) = 0$$
$$x = -4 \qquad x = 1$$

Answer: Domain: All real numbers except -4 and 1.

2. To find the domain, we set the radicand greater than zero and solve.

$$5 - 2x > 0$$
$$-2x > -5$$
$$x < \frac{5}{2}$$

Answer: The domain is $x < \frac{5}{2}$.

3. To find the domain, set the radicand greater than or equal to zero and solve.

$$2x - 4 \geq 0$$
$$2x \geq 4$$
$$x \geq 2$$

Answer: The domain is $x \geq 2$.

In 4–6, determine the largest possible domain and range for each function.

4. $g(x) = x^2 - 8x + 15$ **5.** $f(x) = \frac{2}{3}x + 10$ **6.** $h(x) = |3 - 4x|$

SOLUTIONS

4. The domain of a quadratic function is all real numbers. To find its range, find the vertex point. Use the equation $x = -\dfrac{b}{2a}$; so $x = \dfrac{-(-8)}{2(1)} = 4$. Substituting 4 into the equation, we find that $y = -1$. Since the parabola opens upward, the range of the function is $y \geq -1$.

5. Since this is a linear function, the domain and range are the set of all real numbers.

6. This problem gives us an absolute value function. Its domain is all real numbers and its range is $y \geq 0$.

7. If the a function $f(x)$ is defined as $f(x) = 4x - 7$ with a domain such that $-2 \leq x \leq 7$, find
   a. the range
   b. the smallest element in the range

SOLUTION

a. To find the range of a linear function, given a domain, substitute the smallest and largest elements of the domain in the function and find the boundaries of the range. $f(-2) = 4(-2) - 7 = -15$ and $f(7) = 4(7) - 7 = 21$. Therefore, the range for $f(x)$ is $-15 \leq y \leq 21$.

b. The smallest element in the range is -15.

Note: To determine the domain and range by looking at the graph of a continuous function, find the left and rightmost points to determine the domain and the highest and lowest-most points to identify the range.

In 8–10, approximate the domain and the range of each graph.

8.

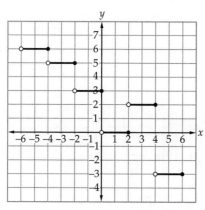

9.

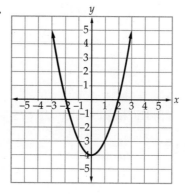

10.

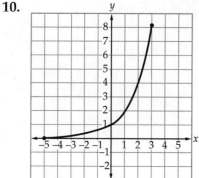

SOLUTIONS

8. This graph shows what is called a "step function." The y-values are not continuous, but appear to jump in steplike movements. The range, therefore, is not a continuous set of values, but a limited set of integers: $\{6, 5, 3, 2, 0, -3\}$. The domain, despite the open circles on the left ends of the line segments, is a continuous set of numbers between -6 and 6 because the closed circles include the omitted values on the next line segment.

Answer: The domain is $-6 < x \leq 6$.

9. Domain: All reals   Range: $y \geq -4$

10. Domain: $-5 \leq x \leq 3$ Range: $0 \leq y \leq 8$

In 1–8, select the numeral preceding the expression that best completes the statement or answers the question.

1. Given the function $f(x) = x^2 - 6x - 7$ with a domain of $-2 \le x \le 8$, the smallest value in the range is
   (1) 9 (3) −16
   (2) −7 (4) −31

2. Which of the following functions has a limited domain?
   (1) $y = 5x - 1$ (3) $y = \frac{2x + 5}{x - 6}$
   (2) $y = x^2 - 9$ (4) $y = 4$

3. If $g(x)$ is defined as $g(x) = -2x^3 + 5x^2 + 4x - 3$ and the domain is $-3 \le x \le 5$, the largest element in the range is
   (1) 189 (3) 25
   (2) 84 (4) 9

4. What is the domain of the function $h(x) = \frac{x + 4}{x^2 - 5x}$?
   (1) $R/\{-4\}$ (3) $R/\{-5, 0\}$
   (2) $R/\{0, 5\}$ (4) $R/\{-5, -4, 0\}$

5. What is the domain of the function $y = \sqrt{3x + 12}$?
   (1) $x \ge 4$ (3) $x \ge -12$
   (2) $x \ge -4$ (4) $x \ge 0$

6. What is the range of the relation $f(x) = 3x^2 - 5x$ if the domain is $\{0, 1, 2\}$?
   (1) $\{0, 1, 2\}$ (3) $\{-1, -2, 0\}$
   (2) $\{-2, 0, 2\}$ (4) $y \ge 0$

7. Which of the following values is not in the domain of the function $f(x) = \frac{5 - x}{\sqrt{2x^2 - 8}}$?
   (1) 5 (3) −2
   (2) 3 (4) −3

8. Which of the following functions does not have a domain of all real numbers?
   (1) $y = \frac{1}{2}x - 3$
   (2) $f(x) = x^3 - 4x^2 + 7$
   (3) $y = \left|\frac{4}{3}x - 2\right|$
   (4) $y = \frac{4}{x - 2}$

In 9–12, find the domain and range of the function shown in each graph.

9.
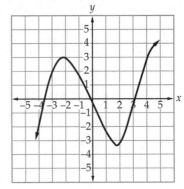

10.
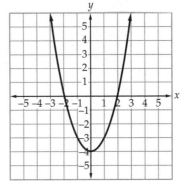

11.
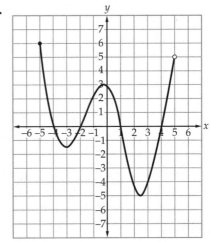

12.
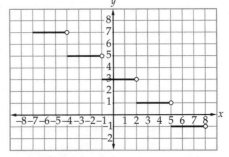

In 13–15, find the largest possible domain for each function.

13. $g(x) = \dfrac{x^2 + 2x + 1}{3x^2 - 12}$

14. $f(x) = \dfrac{2x - 4}{\sqrt{3x + 9}}$

15. $h(x) = \dfrac{x - 3}{\sqrt{x^2 + 1}}$

In 16–21, find the largest possible domain and range for each function.

16. $y = 16 - x^2$

17. $f(x) = \frac{2}{3}x + 1$

18. $y = x^2 + 6x + 9$

19. $g(x) = \sqrt{9 - x^2}$

20. $h(x) = |3x - 6|$

21. $y = x^3 - 2x^2 - 1$

6.4 Composition of Functions

Just as in arithmetic, we perform operations with numbers, we can also perform operations with functions. We can add, subtract, multiply, or divide functions.

MODEL PROBLEM

If $f(x)$ is defined as $f(x) = x + 2$ and $g(x)$ is defined as $g(x) = x^2 - 4$, find

a. $f(x) + g(x)$
b. $f(x) - g(x)$
c. $f(x)g(x)$
d. $\dfrac{g(x)}{f(x)}$

SOLUTION

These operations are performed just as in arithmetic or algebra.

a. To add functions, combine like terms.

$$f(x) + g(x) = x + 2 + x^2 - 4$$
$$= x^2 + x - 2$$

b. To subtract functions, add the inverse of the second function.

$$f(x) - g(x) = f(x) + (-g(x))$$
$$= x + 2 - (x^2 - 4)$$
$$= x + 2 - x^2 + 4$$
$$= -x^2 + x + 6$$

c. To multiply functions, use the distributive property to multiply the polynomials.

$$f(x)g(x) = (x + 2)(x^2 - 4)$$
$$= x^3 + 2x^2 - 4x - 8$$

d. To divide functions, factor each and reduce if possible.

$$\frac{g(x)}{f(x)} = \frac{x^2 - 4}{x + 2} \ (x \neq -2)$$

$$= \frac{(x + 2)(x - 2)}{x + 2}$$

$$= x - 2$$

In dealing with functions, however, we have a fifth operation called **composition**. In composition of functions, the result obtained from performing the operations of one function is then used as the domain value in a second function. Compositions may be indicated by one parentheses within another, such as $f(g(x))$, read "f of g of x" or "f following g of x." Using an open circle, as in this notation, may also show compositions: $(f \circ g)(x)$, also read "f following g of x" or "f composition g of x." To perform a composition, it is important to remember that just as we always begin operations inside the parentheses, we complete the function inside the innermost parentheses (or on the right) first. Using the functions $f(x)$ and $g(x)$ already defined, let us look at $f(g(x))$ and $(g \circ f)(x)$.

Remember: Always perform compositions from right to left.

 MODEL PROBLEM

If $f(x)$ is defined as $f(x) = x + 2$ and $g(x)$ is defined as $g(x) = x^2 - 4$ find

a. $f(g(3))$ **b.** $(g \circ f)(3)$ **c.** $(f \circ f)(5)$

SOLUTION

a. $f(g(3))$ means we must find $g(3)$ and use that answer in the $f(x)$ function. Since $g(x) = x^2 - 4$ we replace x with 3 and evaluate $3^2 - 4 = 5$. Next we evaluate $f(5)$. Since $f(x) = x + 2$, $f(5) = 5 + 2 = 7$. Therefore $f(g(3)) = 7$.

b. To evaluate $(g \circ f)(3)$, we first find $f(3)$ by substituting 3 in place of x in the $f(x)$ function. $f(x) = x + 2$ so $f(3) = 3 + 2 = 5$. Next we evaluate $g(5)$. Since $g(x) = x^2 - 4$, $g(5) = 5^2 - 4 = 21$. Therefore, $(g \circ f)(3) = 21$.

Note: Notice that composition is not a commutative operation. You usually do not get the same results performing $(g \circ f)(3)$ as you will performing $(f \circ g)(3)$.

c. To evaluate $(f \circ f)(5)$, we first find $f(5)$: $f(x) = x + 2$, so $f(5) = 5 + 2 = 7$. Next we evaluate $f(7)$. $f(7) = 7 + 2 = 9$. Therefore, $(f \circ f)(5) = 9$.

Sometimes we are asked to find the **rule of a (composite) function** that is defined as the single function that will perform the same operation as a composition, but in one step. To find the rule of a composite function, we replace the x in the outer function with the innermost function.

1. If $f(x)$ is defined as $f(x) = x + 2$ and $g(x)$ is defined as $g(x) = x^2 - 4$, find the rule of

   a. $g(f(x))$

   b. $f(g(x))$

SOLUTION

a. Finding $g(f(x))$ is equivalent to finding $g(x + 2)$ so we simply replace each x in the $g(x)$ function with $(x + 2)$.

$$g(x) = x^2 - 4, \text{ so } g(x + 2) = (x + 2)^2 - 4$$
$$g(x + 2) = x^2 + 4x + 4 - 4$$
$$g(x + 2) = x^2 + 4x$$

Answer: The rule of $g(f(x))$ is $x^2 + 4x$.

b. Finding $f(g(x))$ is equivalent to finding $f(x^2 - 4)$ so we simply replace each x in the $f(x)$ function with $x^2 - 4$.

$$f(x) = x + 2, \text{ so } f(x^2 - 4) = x^2 - 4 + 2.$$
$$f(x^2 - 4) = x^2 - 2$$

Answer: The rule of $f(g(x))$ is $x^2 - 2$.

2. If $h(x) = 3x + 2$ and $f(x) = \frac{x - 2}{3}$, find

   a. $(f \circ h)(x)$

   b. $(h \circ f)(x)$

What unusual results do you find?

SOLUTION

a. $(f \circ h)(x) = f(3x + 2)$

Since $f(x) = \frac{x - 2}{3}$, $f(3x + 2) = \frac{(3x + 2) - 2}{3}$.

$$f(3x + 2) = \frac{3x}{3}$$
$$f(3x + 2) = x$$

b. $(h \circ f)(x)$ means $h\left(\frac{x - 2}{3}\right)$.

Since $h(x) = 3x + 2$, $h\left(\frac{x - 2}{3}\right) = 3\left(\frac{x - 2}{3}\right) + 2$.

$$h\left(\frac{x - 2}{3}\right) = x - 2 + 2$$
$$h\left(\frac{x - 2}{3}\right) = x$$

It is unusual for the commutative property to apply to composition of functions, yet $(h \circ f)(x) = (f \circ h)(x)$. You will learn why this happened in the next section.

The graphs of functions can also be used to find compositions. Consider the graphs of $g(x)$ and $j(x)$ shown below.

📖 MODEL PROBLEM

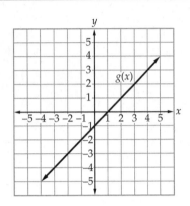
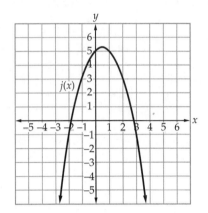

Using the functions graphed above, find

a. $j(g(4))$
b. $g(j(-1))$
c. $(j \circ g)(1)$
d. $(j \circ j)(-2)$
e. x if $j(g(x)) = 3$

SOLUTION
For parts a, b, c, and d, simply evaluate the innermost function on the pertinent graph and then use that answer in the outer function.

a. $j(g(4)) = -1$. On examining the $g(x)$ function, we find $g(4) = 3$. Next we find $j(3)$ on the graph of the $j(x)$ function and discover that when $x = 3$, the y-coordinate is -1.

b. $g(j(-1)) = 2$. On examining the $j(x)$ function, we find $j(-1) = 3$. Then we evaluate $g(3)$ on the $g(x)$ graph and find the y-coordinate that corresponds to an x of 3 is 2.

c. $(j \circ g)(1) = 5$. When we look at the $g(x)$ function, we find $g(1) = 0$. We then look at the graph of the $j(x)$ and learn that $j(0) = 5$.

d. $(j \circ j)(-2) = 3$. On the graph of the $j(x)$ function, $j(-2) = -1$; then $j(-1) = 3$.

e. Part e of the model problem gives us the y-coordinate after the composition, so we need to work backward to determine the original x-value(s).

First we find the x-values on the graph of the $j(x)$ function for which $y = 3$. The two x-values that correspond to a y-value of 3 are $x = -1$ and $x = 2$. Now we go to the graph of the function $g(x)$ and determine the x-values that make $g(x) = -1$ and $g(x) = 2$. We see that $g(x) = -1$ if $x = 0$ and $g(x) = 2$ if $x = 3$.

In 1–14, use the functions f(x), g(x), h(x), and j(x).

$f(x) = 2 - 5x$ $g(x) = x^2 - 16$

$h(x) = \sqrt{x + 16}$ $j(x) = x^2 - 3x - 4$

Find each of the following:

1. $g(x) + j(x)$

2. $f(x)g(x)$

3. $j(x) - g(x)$

4. $\dfrac{g(x)}{j(x)}$

5. $(h \circ j)(4)$

6. $g(f(2))$

7. $f(g(2))$

8. $f(j(-3))$

9. $j(f(-3))$

10. $(g \circ h)(-7)$

11. $(h \circ j)(-7)$

12. $g(h(x))$

13. $(h \circ j)(x)$

14. $(f \circ g)(x)$

In 15–20, consider the functions whose graphs are shown below. Then select the numeral preceding the expression that best completes the sentence or answers the question.

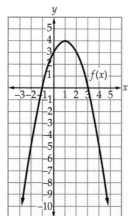
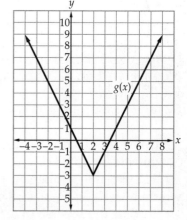

15. The composition $(g \circ f)(2)$ is
    (1) -3
    (2) -1
    (3) 3
    (4) not visible on graph

16. The composition $(f \circ g)(0)$ is equivalent to which of the following compositions?
    (1) $(g \circ f)(0)$ (3) $(f \circ f)(1)$
    (2) $(f \circ g)(3)$ (4) $(f \circ g)(4)$

17. The composition $(f \circ g)(-1)$ is
    (1) -1 (3) 1
    (2) 0   (4) 4

18. For which of the following values of x does $(f \circ g)(x) = 3$?
    (1) $\{0, 2\}$ (3) $\{0.5, 4.5\}$
    (2) $\{-1, 5\}$ (4) $\{-1.2, 3.2\}$

19. Which statement is invalid with respect to functions $f(x)$ and $g(x)$?
    (1) $(f \circ g)(1) = 0$ (3) $(f \circ g)\left(\dfrac{1}{2}\right) = 3$
    (2) $(g \circ f)(1) = 1$ (4) $(f \circ g)(5) = \{\ \}$

20. The composition $(f \circ g)(4.5)$ equals
    (1) 1   (3) 3
    (2) 2   (4) $\{\ \}$

6.5 Inverse Functions

Finding Inverses Algebraically

In section 6.1, we defined a function as a relationship in which each element of the domain corresponds to a unique element in the range. Functions are said to be **one-to-one** when each element of the domain has a unique value in the range and vice versa.

For every one-to-one function $f(x)$, if we interchange the domain and range of the original function, we obtain a new function called $f^{-1}(x)$, read "f-inverse." Hence, the **inverse** of a function is a relation in which the domain and range of the original function have been exchanged.

Note: Be careful, $f^{-1}(x)$ is not the reciprocal of $f(x)$.

Consider function A: $\{(3, 11), (2, 7), (1, 3), (0, -1)\}$. The domain of A is $\{3, 2, 1, 0\}$ while its range is $\{11, 7, 3, -1\}$. The inverse of A, written as A^{-1}, has a domain of $\{11, 7, 3, -1\}$ and a range of $\{3, 2, 1, 0\}$. The coordinate points of the function $A^{-1}(x)$ would be $\{(11, 3), (7, 2), (3, 1), (-1, 0)\}$.

To find the inverse of a function algebraically, we use the same approach as with sets. We interchange the domain and range. In working with a function defined by an equation, we interchange the symbols for the domain and range, the x and y, and then isolate the new y.

 MODEL PROBLEMS

---

1. Find the inverse of $f(x)$ if $f(x) = \frac{2}{3}x + 4$.

SOLUTION

Since $f(x) = y$, the given equation can be written as
$$y = \frac{2}{3}x + 4.$$

Rewrite the equation, interchanging x and y.
$$x = \frac{2}{3}y + 4.$$

Isolate the y.
$$x - 4 = \frac{2}{3}y$$

$$\frac{3}{2}(x - 4) = y$$

Simplify and substitute the $f^{-1}(x)$ notation for y.
$$\frac{3}{2}x - 6 = f^{-1}(x)$$

Answer: The inverse of the original function is $f^{-1}(x) = \frac{3}{2}x - 6$.

---

2. Find $g^{-1}(x)$ if $g(x) = \sqrt[3]{2x - 1}$.

Interchange the domain and range.

$$x = \sqrt[3]{2y - 1}$$

Cube both sides.

$$x^3 = 2y - 1$$

Perform inverse operations to isolate y.

$$x^3 + 1 = 2y$$

$$\frac{x^3 + 1}{2} = y$$

Rewrite in function notation.

$$g^{-1}(x) = \frac{x^3 + 1}{2}$$

3. Given the function $g(x) = 2x^2 - 1$ with $x \geq 0$. Find each of the following:
   a. $g^{-1}(x)$
   b. $(g \circ g^{-1})(x)$
   c. $(g^{-1} \circ g)(x)$
   d. What is unusual about the answers in parts b and c? What could they suggest? (Hint: Remember Model Problem 2 in section 6.4.)

SOLUTION

a.

$$y = 2x^2 - 1$$
$$x = 2y^2 - 1$$
$$x + 1 = 2y^2$$
$$\frac{x + 1}{2} = y^2$$
$$\sqrt{\frac{x + 1}{2}} = y$$
$$\sqrt{\frac{x + 1}{2}} = g^{-1}(x)$$

b. $(g \circ g^{-1})(x) = g\left(\sqrt{\frac{x + 1}{2}}\right)$

$$= 2\left(\sqrt{\frac{x + 1}{2}}\right)^2 - 1$$

$$= 2 \cdot \frac{x + 1}{2} - 1$$

$$= x + 1 - 1$$

$$(g \circ g^{-1})(x) = x$$

c. $(g^{-1} \circ g)(x) = g^{-1}(2x^2 - 1)$

$$= \sqrt{\frac{(2x^2 - 1) + 1}{2}}$$

$$= \sqrt{\frac{2x^2}{2}}$$

$$= \sqrt{x^2}$$

$$(g^{-1} \circ g)(x) = x$$

> **Note:** While it is true that $\sqrt{x^2} = |x|$, in this case $x \geq 0$, so only the positive x is valid.
>
> **d.** The composition of the function of the inverse and the composition of the inverse of the function both yielded answers of x. For any functions $f(x)$ and $g(x)$, if $(f \circ g)(x) = (g \circ f)(x) = x$, then $f(x)$ and $g(x)$ are inverses of one another. This means that $(f \circ f^{-1})(x) = (f^{-1} \circ f)(x) = x$.

Practice

In 1–5, find the inverse of each function.

1. A: $\{(8, 5), (6, 8), (4, 11), (2, 14)\}$

2. B: $\{(-2, 3), (-5, 5), (-8, 7), (-11, 9)\}$

3. C: $\{(*, \&), (\$, \%), (@, +), (\#, !)\}$

4. D: $\{(\Delta, \Phi), (\Gamma, \Sigma), (\Upsilon, \Psi), (\Lambda, P)\}$

5. E: $\{(2, 9), (4, -5), (13, 8), (-1, -10)\}$

In 6–11, find the inverse of each function and write it in simplified form.

6. $y = 4x + 7$

7. $y + 3x = -1$

8. $f(x) = \frac{2}{5}x - 6$

9. $f(x) = \sqrt[3]{x - 4}$

10. $g(x) = 3x^3 - 6$

11. $y - \frac{2}{3} = 4x$

In 12–20, select the numeral preceding the expression that best completes the statement or answers the question.

12. If $g(x) = 3x + 1$, then $g^{-1}(4)$ equals
(1) $\frac{1}{13}$ (3) 1
(2) $\frac{1}{4}$ (4) 12

13. For which pair of functions does $(f \circ g)(x) = (g \circ f)(x)$?
(1) $f(x) = 2x; g(x) = 2 - x$
(2) $f(x) = x^3; g(x) = \sqrt[3]{x}$
(3) $f(x) = 1 - x; g(x) = x - 1$
(4) $f(x) = 4x + 1; g(x) = x - 4$

14. If the function $j(x)$ is defined by $j(x) = \sqrt{x - 4}$, for $x \geq 4$, which of the following represents $j^{-1}(x)$, when $x \geq 0$?
(1) $\sqrt{4 + x}$ (3) $x^2 + 4$
(2) $\frac{1}{\sqrt{x - 4}}$ (4) $4 - x^2$

15. If $h(x) = \frac{1}{2}x - 3$ and $j(x) = 2x - 1$, the solution to $j(h^{-1}(-3))$ is
(1) 0 (3) -1
(2) $-\frac{1}{3}$ (4) -10

16. If $f(x) = \sqrt{\frac{2}{3}x - 1}$, then $f^{-1}(-5)$ is
(1) an imaginary number
(2) 39
(3) 36
(4) $\frac{52}{3}$

17. If $h(x) = 2 - \frac{x}{2}$, find $(h \circ h^{-1})(2)$.
(1) x (3) $\frac{1}{2}$
(2) 2 (4) 0

18. Which relation is a one-to-one function?
(1) $\{(x, y), (x, z), (x, a)\}$ (3) $\{(x, z), (y, z), (a, y)\}$
(2) $\{(x, y), (y, z), (z, y)\}$ (4) $\{(x, y), (y, z), (z, a)\}$

19. If $f(x) = 10 - 2x$, which of the following represents $f^{-1}(x)$?
(1) $f^{-1}(x) = 2x - 10$ (3) $f^{-1}(x) = 2x - 10$
(2) $f^{-1}(x) = \frac{1}{2}x - 5$ (4) $f^{-1}(x) = -\frac{1}{2}x + 5$

20. If $g(x) = \sqrt[3]{2x + 3}$, $g^{-1}(2)$ equals
(1) $-\frac{1}{2}$ (3) $\frac{5}{2}$
(2) $\sqrt[3]{7}$ (4) $\frac{11}{2}$

Finding Inverses Graphically

To find the inverse of a function algebraically, we interchanged the domain and the range. The same concept is used when graphing, but here, the range and domain are interchanged by a reflection in the line $y = x$. You'll recall from Math A, that the point (x, y) maps to (y, x) under such a reflection so the domain and range are effectively switched.

 **MODEL PROBLEM**

Sketch the function $f(x) = 2x + 4$ and, on the same axes, its inverse.

SOLUTION

The function $f(x) = 2x + 4$ has a y-intercept of $(0, 4)$ and a slope of 2. Therefore, we begin at the point $(0, 4)$ and move up 2 and to the right 1 to find each successive point. Then begin at $(0, 4)$ and move down 2 and left 1 to sketch the original function. To sketch the inverse, reflect each integral point in the line $y = x$. For example,

$$(-4, -4) \longrightarrow (-4, -4)$$
$$(-3, -2) \longrightarrow (-2, -3)$$
$$(-2, 0) \longrightarrow (0, -2)$$
$$(-1, 2) \longrightarrow (2, -1)$$
$$(0, 4) \longrightarrow (4, 0)$$
$$(1, 6) \longrightarrow (6, 1)$$

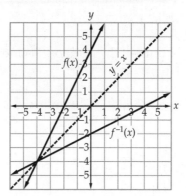

We know from section 6.1 that in order to determine if a graph represents a function, we can use the vertical-line test. The vertical-line test says that if a vertical line drawn at any position over the domain of the graph crosses the graph more than once, the graph does not represent a function.

To determine if the function has an inverse, we can use the horizontal-line test. A function passes the **horizontal-line test** when any horizontal line drawn intersects the graph of the function at most once. In an inverse, the domain of the original figure becomes the range, so no y-value can be repeated if a function is to have an inverse.

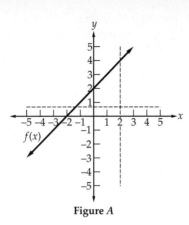

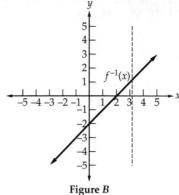

Figure A   Figure B

Notice that the graph of $f(x)$, defined as $f(x) = x + 2$, and its inverse, $f^{-1}(x)$, are functions. We can be certain of this because $f(x)$ passes both the vertical- and horizontal-line tests (Figure A). When we graph $f^{-1}(x) = x - 2$, as shown in Figure B, it passes the vertical-line test.

Now consider this graph.

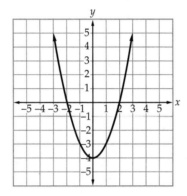

This graph will pass the vertical-line test but fail the horizontal-line test so it is not a one-to-one function. It does not have an inverse.

Note: When graphing, you may check your equation of an inverse by using your TI-83 Plus.

 MODEL PROBLEM

If $f(x) = 3x + 9$, find the equation of its inverse.

SOLUTION
Find the inverse algebraically as we've done before.
Interchange the domain and range. $x = 3y + 9$

Isolate y. $x - 9 = 3y$

$$\frac{x}{3} - 3 = y$$

Answer: The inverse is $f^{-1}(x) = \frac{x}{3} - 3$.

To check this, enter your original function in Y_1 and what you consider to be the inverse in Y_2. Now, go to the DRAW Menu (2nd, PGRM)) and scroll down to 8:Draw Inv.

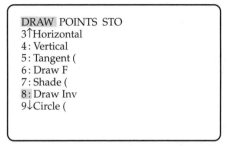

Hit ENTER. This transfers the command to the home screen where the calculator waits for you to tell it which function you want the inverse of. Use the sequence of keys VARS, ▶, (Y-VARS, 1: Function) ENTER, (1: Y_1) to tell the calculator you want the inverse of Y_1. Then hit ENTER, ENTER. The calculator will graph $f(x)$, your answer for $f^{-1}(x)$, and the calculator's drawing of $f^{-1}(x)$.

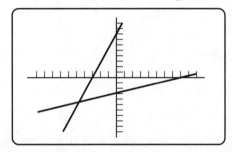

If you see only two graphs on the screen, you know your answer is correct. If a third graph appears, then your definition of the inverse is incorrect.

Note: The Draw menu produces a "drawing," not a graph. Neither the trace function nor any of the CALCULATE operations will work on a drawing. To erase the drawing, you must go to the DRAW menu and ENTER 1: ClrDraw. Be careful: since this is a DRAW command, the calculator will draw the inverse of functions that are not one-to-one.

To practice this approach, go back to Practice exercises 6–11 on page 160 and check your answers using the calculator.

As stated earlier, a function has an inverse only if it is a one-to-one function, that is, if each element of the domain has one and only one corresponding element in the range. Therefore, it is necessary with some functions to restrict the domain in order to eliminate double values in the range.

For example, consider the function $y = x^2$. If the domain were unrestricted, the function would not have an inverse because the function fails the horizontal-line test and the new relation fails the vertical-line test as shown on page 164.

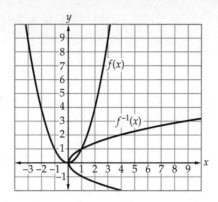

If we restrict the domain of $y = x^2$ to $x \geq 0$ to limit the elements in the domain, the function does have an inverse, as shown below.

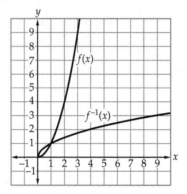

Restricting the domain is most often necessary with quadratic and trigonometric functions, as you will see later in this course.

CHAPTER REVIEW

In 1–10, determine if each of the following relations is a function or not. Explain your answer. If the relation is a function, state its domain and range.

1. $\{(6, 3), (5, 8), (2, 7)\}$

2. $\{(5, 4), (5, 5), (5, 6)\}$

3. $\{(1, 2), (2, 2), (3, 2)\}$

4.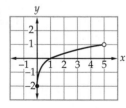

5.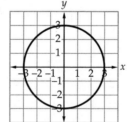

6.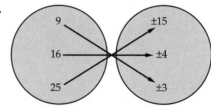

7. $y = 2x - 6$

8. $y = (x + 2)^2 - 1$

9. $y = x^3 + 3x - 4$

10. $y = \sqrt{x - 4}$

11. Roger has just passed his road test and would like to buy a car. He has taken a part-time job, and saves $10 each week toward the purchase of his car. After ten weeks, Roger realizes that he will be in college by the time he has enough money to buy the car. So Roger quits his job and takes another job, which pays more money. This enables him to save $50 each week. Which of the following graphs could be used to represent the amount of money Roger has saved as a function of the number of weeks he has worked?

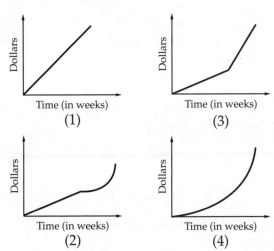

12. Felicia left home at 7:30 A.M. to walk to school. On the way, she stopped at her friend's house and had a glass of orange juice. Five minutes after she arrived, Felicia and her friend continued on to school, arriving at 8:00 A.M. As soon as she got to her locker, Felicia realized that she left her book bag at her friend's house, and ran all the way back to pick it up, and then ran back to school. She got to school at 8:19 A.M., just in time for the bell, which rang at 8:20 A.M. Sketch a graph which would represent the distance, $d(t)$, Felicia traveled from her home as a function of time, t. (Let $t = 0$ represent the time Felicia left her house.)

13. If $g(n) = 5n + 6$, find
   a. $g(5)$
   b. n if $g(n) = 21$
   c. the domain and range of $g(n)$
   d. $g^{-1}(n)$

14. Given: $f(x)$ as shown in the accompanying diagram.

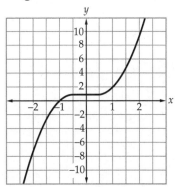

Find:
   a. $f(2)$
   b. x such that $f(x) = 2$
   c. $f^{-1}(2)$
   d. the element in the domain that corresponds to 0 in the range

15. What are the domain and range of the function pictured below?

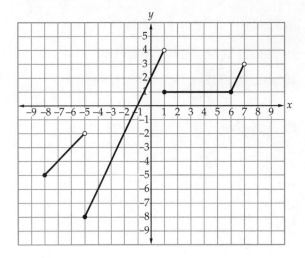

16. Given: $h(x) = \sqrt{x - 5}$.
   a. Find the domain and range of $h(x)$.
   b. Is $h(x)$ a one-to-one function? Why?

17. Given: $f(x) = 2x + 3$ and $g(x) = x^2 - 4$, find
   a. $f(g(5))$
   b. $(g \circ f)(x)$
   c. $f^{-1}(x)$

18. Given $f(x)$ and $g(x)$ as pictured in the accompanying diagrams.

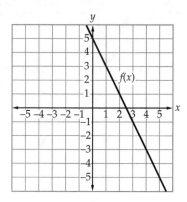

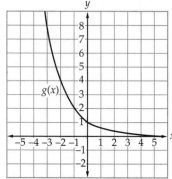

a. Find $f(g(-2))$.
b. Find $(g \circ f)(3)$.
c. Find $f^{-1}(-3)$.

In 19–22, find the inverse of each function.

19. $\{(a, b), (c, d), (e, f), (g, h)\}$

20. $\{(2, 8), (3, 27), (4, 64), (5, 125)\}$

21. $h(x) = \sqrt[3]{2x + 1}$

22. $r(t) = \frac{3}{4}t - 5$

In 23–28, select the numeral preceding the word or expression that best completes the statement or answers the question.

23. The function $g(t)$ is defined as $g(t) = t^2 - 4$ with the domain $-6 \le t \le 2$. What is the smallest element in the range?
(1) -6 (3) 0
(2) -4 (4) 32

24. Which of the following values is not in the domain of $y = \sqrt{x^2 - 2x - 24}$?
(1) -5 (3) 6
(2) 2 (4) 8

25. If $s(x) = |3x - 4|$, then $s(0) =$
(1) -4 (3) 2
(2) 0 (4) 4

26. What is the maximum value of the function $y = -x^2 + 3$?
(1) 0
(2) 2
(3) 3
(4) It has no maximum value.

27. For what values of x will the function $f(x) = \sqrt{x + 4}$ be real?
(1) $\{x \mid x \ge 0\}$ (3) $\{x \mid x \le 4\}$
(2) $\{x \mid x \ge 4\}$ (4) $\{x \mid x \ge -4\}$

28. For which value of x is the function $g(x) = \frac{x + 1}{x - 5}$ undefined?
(1) -5 (3) 0
(2) -1 (4) 5

Your TI-83 can be of great use in your study of functions.

Function Notation

First, when you evaluate a function for a specific value, you have several possible approaches to verify (or obtain) your answer.

If $g(x) = 2x^2 + 7x - 3$, evaluate $g(-5)$ and $g(7)$.

CALCULATOR SOLUTIONS

Method 1

Enter the function in Y_1 and then go to the Home Screen, (2nd) QUIT. Type $Y_1(-5)$. Use the Y-VARS menu 1, (ENTER) (ENTER) (−5) (ENTER). The calculator will reveal the answer. Then hit (2nd) (ENTER), and the calculator will return the problem you just did. Edit that problem by replacing the −5 with a 7, hit (ENTER), and that answer appears as well.

$Y_1 (-5)$

  12

$Y_1 (7)$

  144

Method 2

Enter the function in Y_1 and then go to (2nd) CALC, 1:value (ENTER). The calculator will return to the graph of the function with an X= blinking in the lower left of the screen. Enter the value of x you want and (ENTER) and the corresponding y-value will pop up on the screen.

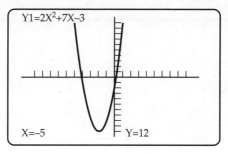

Y1=2X²+7X−3

X=−5   Y=12

Method 3

Enter the function in Y_1 and graph. Press TRACE and then type the x-value you are looking for, −5, and (ENTER). The calculator will TRACE that point and the corresponding Y will pop up on the screen. Repeat the procedure for 7.

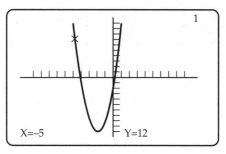

                                              1

X=−5   Y=12

Method 4

Enter the function in Y_1 and go to TABLE ((2nd) GRAPH) and get the values needed.

Domain and Range

When you are trying to find the domain and range of a function, the calculator can give you a strong idea of the solution if you examine the graph for empty spots or the table for ERROR messages.

MODEL PROBLEM

Find the domain and range for the function $f(x) = \frac{4x - 1}{x}$.

CALCULATOR SOLUTIONS

Method 1

Enter the function in Y_1 and graph. Notice the graph does not cross the y-axis. Reset your window to view x from -2 to 2 and y from -20 to 20 to enlarge the picture and verify this.

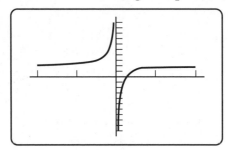

The domain would appear to be $R/\{0\}$ while the range seems to be $R/\{4\}$. To solve the problem algebraically, we would set the denominator equal to 0, which means $x = 0$ is the "forbidden" value in the domain.

Method 2

Enter the function in Y_1 and go to TABLE.

X	Y_1	
-2	4.5	
-1	5	
0	ERROR	
1	3	
2	3.5	
3	3.6667	
4	3.75	
X=-2		

Notice the ERROR message at $x = 0$. (Scroll up or down, if needed, to see $x = 0$.) This tells you that the function is undefined at that value of x. If you scroll up or down on the table of values, however, there are no other values for which that occurs, so you can say the domain is $R/\{0\}$.

Composition

The TI-83 is also capable of performing composition of functions.

If $f(x) = 3x + 4$ and $g(x) = x^2 - 2$, evaluate
a. $f(g(3))$
b. $g(f(3))$

CALCULATOR SOLUTION

a. Enter the $f(x)$ function in Y_1 and the $g(x)$ function in Y_2. Go to the Home Screen and enter $Y_1(Y_2(3))$. Hit (ENTER). The value of $f(g(3))$ is 25.
b. Now enter $Y_2(Y_1(3))$ using the same procedure and hit (ENTER). The value of $g(f(3))$ is 167.

```
Y₁ (Y₂ (3))
                25
Y₂ (Y₁ (3))
              167
```

Inverses

The calculator cannot give you the equation of the function's inverse, but using the DRAW menu, as stated in section 6.5, will show you the graph of the inverse.

Remember: The calculator will draw an inverse even if one doesn't exist, since this is only a drawing, not a graph of a function.

Practice

Try some of the problems in this chapter's Practice sections to test your understanding of and comfort with these calculator approaches.

CHAPTER 7

Conic Sections

7.1 Circles and Parabolas

As far back as Aristotle, mathematicians studied three-dimensional figures such as cones and were fascinated by the various two-dimensional figures that could be obtained by slicing a cone at various angles. A Greek mathematician by the name of Apollonius studied cones and discovered the various conic sections we have today. For example, he proved that a right cylindrical cone sliced horizontally to its base produces a circle.

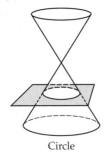
Circle

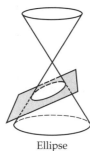
Ellipse

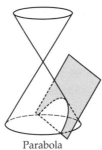
Parabola

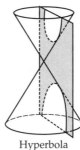
Hyperbola

Circles

As you know from Chapter 2, a circle is the locus of points that are equidistant from a given point, known as the center. The equation of a circle whose center is at the origin is simply $x^2 + y^2 = r^2$ where r represents the length of the radius of the circle. The standard equation of a circle whose center is not the origin, but a point (h, k), is $(x - h)^2 + (y - k)^2 = r^2$, where r again represents the length of the radius.

The equation $x^2 + y^2 = 4$ represents a circle with its center at $(0, 0)$ and a radius of length 2. Every point on the circle is 2 units away from the origin, the center of this circle. The equation $(x - 4)^2 + (y + 3)^2 = 4$ represents a circle with a center at $(4, -3)$ and a radius of length 2. Every point on the circle is

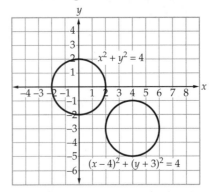

2 units away from the center $(4, -3)$. In other words, the circle is the same size as $x^2 + y^2 = 4$ but moved so its center is at $(4, -3)$.

Notice that neither of the circles drawn above could be a function because each x-value corresponds to two y-values. (Circles fail the vertical-line test.) Since the TI-83 only graphs functions, graphing circles is a bit tricky. It can be done, however, with a little algebraic manipulation.

MODEL PROBLEM

Use your graphing calculator to graph the circles $x^2 + y^2 = 4$ and $(x - 4)^2 + (y + 3)^2 = 4$.

SOLUTION

First, solve the equations for y by isolating the y in each expression.

$$y^2 = 4 - x^2 \qquad (y + 3)^2 = 4 - (x - 4)^2$$

Now, take the square root of each side of the equations.

$$y = \pm\sqrt{4 - x^2} \qquad y + 3 = \pm\sqrt{4 - (x - 4)^2}$$

Once again, isolate the y if necessary. $\qquad y = -3 \pm \sqrt{4 - (x - 4)^2}$

We now have two different functions for each equation to enter into Y_1, Y_2, Y_3, and Y_4 on the calculator. Each of the equations is a semicircle that will appear to be a circle when joined with its partner if your window is properly set.

Remember: Use the decimal window (ZOOM 4) or the square window (ZOOM 5) to see your circles. In this case, the ZOOM 4 window was enlarged to be -4.7 to 9.4 for x and -6.2 to 3.1 for y since the second circle was outside of the standard decimal window.

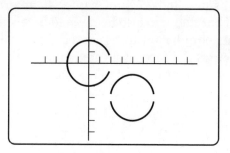

MODEL PROBLEMS

In 1–3, determine the center and the length of the radius of each circle.

Problem	Solution
1. $x^2 + y^2 = 10$	center: $(0, 0)$; radius $= \sqrt{10}$
2. $(x + 3)^2 + y^2 = 9$	center: $(-3, 0)$; $r = 3$
3. $(x - 1)^2 + (y + 4)^2 = 16$	center: $(1, -4)$; $r = 4$

4. Which of the following points is not on the circle $x^2 + y^2 = 25$?
    (1) $(5, 0)$
    (2) $(3, 4)$
    (3) $(-5, 5)$
    (4) $(-3, 4)$

SOLUTION
Choice 3, $(-5, 5)$, is not on the circle because if you substitute the coordinates into the equation, you find that $x^2 + y^2 = 50$ not 25.

Parabolas

Another conic section we have already studied is the parabola. The figure shows that to obtain a parabola from a cone, we cut diagonally through just one cone.

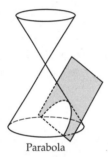

Parabola

    Parabolas, as you know from Chapter 4, are graphic representations of quadratic functions, but they can also be defined in terms of locus. A **parabola** is the locus of all points equidistant from a fixed point called the **focus** and a fixed line called the **directrix.** The focus is located on the axis of symmetry of the parabola at the same distance from the parabola as the directrix.

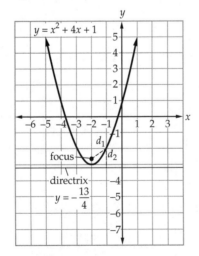

    Clearly this parabola is a function. In this case, the equation of the parabola is $y = x^2 + 4x + 1$ in standard quadratic form or $y = (x + 2)^2 - 3$ in vertex form. The **vertex form** of a parabola is $y = a(x - h)^2 + k$ where (h, k) are the coordinates of the vertex. In this case the vertex (or turning point) is $(-2, -3)$, the focus is

$\left(-2, -\frac{11}{4}\right)$, and the directrix is $y = -\frac{13}{4}$. As stated above, the distance from the focus to any point of the parabola must equal the distance from that point on the parabola to the directrix. To demonstrate this, we will use the point $(-1, -2)$ and calculate d_1, the distance from the focus to the point, and d_2, the distance from the directrix to the same point.

$$d_1 = \sqrt{(-1 - (-2))^2 + \left(-2 - \left(-\frac{11}{4}\right)\right)^2} \qquad d_2 = \sqrt{(-1 - (-1))^2 + \left(-2 - \left(-\frac{13}{4}\right)\right)^2}$$

$$d_1 = \sqrt{1^2 + \left(\frac{3}{4}\right)^2} \qquad d_2 = \sqrt{0^2 + \left(\frac{5}{4}\right)^2}$$

$$d_1 = \sqrt{\frac{16}{16} + \frac{9}{16}} \qquad d_2 = \sqrt{\frac{25}{16}}$$

$$d_1 = \sqrt{\frac{25}{16}} \qquad d_2 = \frac{5}{4}$$

$$d_1 = \frac{5}{4}$$

Hence, the distance between the focus and any point equals the distance between the directrix and the same point.

MODEL PROBLEMS

1. Find the vertex and the axis of symmetry of the parabola $y = 2x^2 - 8x + 1$.

SOLUTION
First, find the axis of symmetry, using the formula $x = -\frac{b}{2a}$.

$x = -\frac{(-8)}{2(2)}$, so $x = 2$. The vertex is the point $\left(-\frac{b}{2a}, f\left(-\frac{b}{2a}\right)\right)$.

Therefore, $y = 2(2)^2 - 8(2) + 1$ and $y = -7$.

Answer: The vertex is $(2, -7)$.

2. Write the equation of the parabola whose vertex is $(-4, 2)$ and whose focus is $\left(-4, \frac{5}{2}\right)$.

SOLUTION
Substitute the values of the vertex into the vertex formula, $y = a(x - h)^2 + k$. $y = a(x + 4)^2 + 2$. The y-coordinate of the focus reveals the distance, d, from the focus to the vertex. In this case, $d = \frac{1}{2}$ and $a = \frac{1}{4d}$. By substitution, $a = \dfrac{1}{4\left(\frac{1}{2}\right)} = \frac{1}{2}$.

Answer: The equation of the parabola is $y = \frac{1}{2}(x + 4)^2 + 2$.

3. Given the parabola $y + 4 = 4(x - 3)^2$, state the coordinates of the vertex, the focus, and the equation of the directrix.

SOLUTION

Isolate the y. $y = 4(x - 3)^2 - 4$, so the vertex is $(3, -4)$. To find the focus, use the rule that says $a = \dfrac{1}{4d}$ where d is the distance between the focal point and the vertex.

$$4 = \frac{1}{4d}$$

$$16d = 1$$

$$d = \frac{1}{16}$$

The focal point is $\dfrac{1}{16}$ above k, the y-coordinate of the vertex, and the directix is $\dfrac{1}{16}$ below k.

Answer: The focal point is $\left(3, -\dfrac{15}{16}\right)$, while the directrix is $y = -4\dfrac{1}{16}$.

4. Find the distance from the point $(2, -5)$ to the focal point and to the directrix of the parabola $y = 2(x - 3)^2 - 7$.

SOLUTION

First we must find the focal point of the equation $y = 2(x - 3)^2 - 7$. The x-value of the focal point is 3, and the y-value will be d units greater than the y-coordinate of the vertex.

$$a = \frac{1}{4d}$$

$$2 = \frac{1}{4d}$$

$$d = \frac{1}{8}$$

The focal point is therefore $\left(3, -\dfrac{55}{8}\right)$. The directrix is $y = -\dfrac{57}{8}$. Let d_1 equal the distance from the focal point to $(2, -5)$ and d_2 equal the distance from the directrix to $(2, -5)$.

$$d_1 = \sqrt{(3 - 2)^2 + \left(\frac{-55}{8} - (-5)\right)^2} \qquad d_2 = \sqrt{(2 - 2)^2 + \left(-5 - \left(\frac{-57}{8}\right)\right)^2}$$

$$d_1 = \sqrt{1^2 + \left(\frac{-15}{8}\right)^2} \qquad d_2 = \sqrt{0 + \left(\frac{17}{8}\right)^2}$$

$$d_1 = \sqrt{\frac{64}{64} + \frac{225}{64}} \qquad d_2 = \sqrt{\frac{289}{64}} = \frac{17}{8}$$

$$d_1 = \sqrt{\frac{289}{64}} = \frac{17}{8}$$

Answer: The distance d_1 is equal to the distance $d_2 = \dfrac{17}{8}$.

The table below summarizes the formulas involving a parabola.

Equation	$y = a(x - h)^2 + k$ / $(a > 0)$
Axis of symmetry	$x = h$
Vertex	(h, k)
Focus	$\left(h, k + \dfrac{1}{4a} \right)$
Directrix	$y = k - \dfrac{1}{4a}$

Practice

In 1–10, select the numeral preceding the word or expression that best completes the sentence or answers the question.

1. The center of the circle $(x - 4)^2 + (y + 2)^2 = 9$ is
   (1) $(4, -3)$ (3) $(-4, 2)$
   (2) $(4, 2)$ (4) $(4, -2)$

2. Which of the following circles has a center of $(1, 0)$ and a radius of length 4?
   (1) $x^2 + y^2 = 4^2$
   (2) $(x + 1)^2 + y^2 = 4^2$
   (3) $(x - 1)^2 + y^2 = 4^2$
   (4) $x^2 + y^2 = 4$

3. Which of the following points is *not* on the circle $(x - 4)^2 + (y - 3)^2 = 25$?
   (1) $(8, 6)$ (3) $(0, 0)$
   (2) $(-1, 3)$ (4) $(-4, -3)$

4. Jenfryda is playing with a Frisbee whose diameter is 12 inches. If she tosses it onto a coordinate plane, and its center falls on the point $(-2, 1)$, what is the equation of the Frisbee?
   (1) $x^2 + y^2 = 36$
   (2) $(x - 2)^2 + (y - 1)^2 = 36$
   (3) $(x + 2)^2 + (y - 1)^2 = 36$
   (4) $(x - 2)^2 + (y + 1)^2 = 36$

5. If $f(x) = 3x^2 - 6x + 2$, what is the vertex point of the parabola?
   (1) $(1, -1)$ (3) $(-1, 11)$
   (2) $(1, 2)$ (4) $(0, 2)$

6. If $g(x) = -x^2 + 4x + 5$, the directrix is the line whose equation is
   (1) $y = -\dfrac{1}{4}$ (3) $x = 2$
   (2) $y = \dfrac{37}{4}$ (4) $y = \dfrac{35}{4}$

7. Which of the following equations has a vertex of $(3, -1)$ and a focal point of $\left(3, \dfrac{1}{2} \right)$?
   (1) $y = (x - 3)^2 + 1$
   (2) $y = (x + 3)^2 - 1$
   (3) $y = \dfrac{1}{6}(x - 3)^2 - 1$
   (4) $y = \dfrac{1}{2}(x - 3)^2 + 1$

8. Which statement is *not* true of the parabola $y = x^2 - 5x - 14$?
   (1) The parabola is a function.
   (2) It has a minimum point at $(2.5, -20.25)$.
   (3) It has a directrix of $y = -20.5$.
   (4) The axis of symmetry is $y = 2.5$.

9. Harmony and Melodie were blowing bubbles when one of them landed on Derek's math homework and burst on the graph paper. The bubble formed a perfect circle on the coordinate grid with a center at $(6, -5)$ and a radius of 4.5. Which of the following represents the equation of the bubble's circle?
   (1) $4.5^2 = (x - 6)^2 + (y + 5)^2$
   (2) $x^2 + y^2 = (4.5)^2$
   (3) $(x + 6)^2 + (y - 5)^2 = 20.25$
   (4) $(x - 6)^2 - (y + 5)^2 = 20.25$

10. Someone left a hot coffee mug on Mrs. Hilton's coffee table and it stained the table. Unfortunately, no one will admit guilt. Mrs. Hilton decides to find the diameter of the mug so she can determine whose mug created the stain. If the equation of the circle left by the coffee mug is $(x - 1)^2 + (y + 4)^2 = 7.84$, what is the diameter of the mug?

(1) 7.84   (3) 2.8
(2) 5.6   (4) 1.4

In 11–15, find the center and the length of the radius of each circle.

11. $(x + 7)^2 + y^2 = 29.16$

12. $x^2 + (y - 3)^2 = 13.69$

13. $(x + 2)^2 + \left(y + \frac{1}{2}\right)^2 = 16$

14. $(x - 5)^2 + (y + 2)^2 = 23.04$

15. $(x + 1.5)^2 + (y - 3.6)^2 = 10$

In 16–20, find the axis of symmetry, vertex, focus, and directrix of each parabola.

16. $y = x^2 - 6x + 4$

17. $y + 5 = x^2 - 6x$

18. $y = 2(x - 4)^2 - 8$

19. $y = -1(x - 3)^2 + 7$

20. $y = 4x^2 - 8x - 12$

7.2 Ellipses and Hyperbolas

Ellipses

An ellipse is obtained by slicing a right cylindrical cone on the diagonal as shown below.

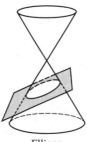

Ellipse

Unlike a circle, the distance from the ellipse to its center is not a constant value, so there are no equal radii. However, the sum of the distances from the two fixed points to any point on the ellipse is a constant value. That is, the distance from any point on the ellipse to F_1 plus the distance from F_2 to the same point on the ellipse must equal the sum of the distances from any other point on the ellipse to F_1 and F_2. Each of the fixed points is a focus (plural, foci) of the ellipse.

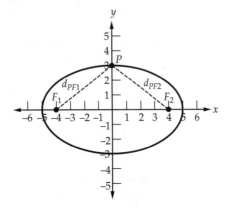

In this case, $d_{PF1} + d_{PF2}$, the distance from a point P to focal point 1 plus the distance from the same point P to focal point 2, equals 10 units. Therefore, for every point on the ellipse, the sum of the distances from that point to the two foci must total 10. The standard formula of an ellipse whose center is at the origin is $\frac{x^2}{a^2} + \frac{y^2}{b^2} = 1$ where $2a$ is the length of the horizontal axis, $2b$ is the length of the vertical axis and $2c$ is the distance between the foci, given that $c^2 = a^2 - b^2$.

The longer axis of an ellipse is called the **major axis** while the shorter axis is the **minor axis.** For $a^2 > b^2$, $\frac{x^2}{a^2} + \frac{y^2}{b^2} = 1$ is an ellipse with a horizontal major axis. $\frac{x^2}{b^2} + \frac{y^2}{a^2} = 1$ is an ellipse with a vertical major axis.

The equation of the ellipse shown in the figure above is $\frac{x^2}{25} + \frac{y^2}{9} = 1$. The length of the major axis is $2\sqrt{25}$ or 10 and the length of the minor axis is $2\sqrt{9}$ or 6. The distance between the foci is $2\sqrt{25 - 9} = 2\sqrt{16} = 2 \cdot 4 = 8$.

An ellipse whose center is not the origin, but the point (h, k), has a standard equation of $\frac{(x - h)^2}{a^2} + \frac{(y - k)^2}{b^2} = 1$ where $2a$ is equal to the length of the major axis, $2b$ is equal to the length of the minor axis, and $2c$ is equal to the distance between the foci. The ellipse $\frac{(x - 4)^2}{25} + \frac{(y + 6)^2}{9} = 1$ is the same as the ellipse $\frac{x^2}{25} + \frac{y^2}{9} = 1$ if it is shifted so the center is $(4, -6)$ instead of $(0, 0)$.

Note: The center of the ellipse is the midpoint of the line segment connecting the foci, so if you know the foci but not the center, or the center and the distance between the foci but not their coordinates, it is easy to do the calculations.

MODEL PROBLEMS

1. Consider the ellipse whose equation is $\frac{(x - 3)^2}{25} + \frac{(y + 2)^2}{169} = 1$.

   a. What is its center? b. What are the lengths of the major and minor axes and the distance between the foci? c. Find the coordinates of the focal points. d. Sketch the ellipse.

SOLUTION
a. The center is the point (h, k) which for this equation is $(3, -2)$.
b. The minor axis is 10 units long $(2\sqrt{25})$, while the major axis is 26 units long $(2\sqrt{169})$.

To find the distance between the foci, use the formula $c^2 = |a^2 - b^2|$.

$$c = \sqrt{169 - 25} = \sqrt{144}, \text{ so } c = 12$$

Therefore, $2c = 24$, the distance between the foci.

c. The foci always appear on the major axis, in this case, the vertical one. To find them add ± 12 to the y-coordinate of the center and keep the x the same. Therefore, the focal points are $(3, -2 + 12)$ or $(3, 10)$ and $(3, -2 - 12)$ or $(3, -14)$.

d. To start the sketch by hand, first identify the center. Then go 5 units to the left and right of the center to find the endpoints of the minor axis and 13 units above and below the center to find the endpoints of the major axis.

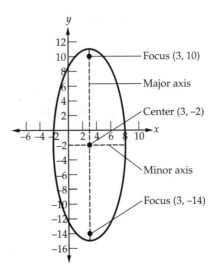

To graph the ellipse on some calculators, you must first solve for y and then use two separate equations, as we did with the circle, so that the calculator will graph a nonfunction.

Note: The newer TI-83 Plus, however, may contain a Conics Application that will be discussed in section 7.6.

$$\frac{(x - 3)^2}{25} + \frac{(y + 2)^2}{169} = 1$$

First multiply through by 169.

$$\frac{169(x - 3)^2}{25} + (y + 2)^2 = 169$$

Now, isolate y by subtracting the x term.

$$(y + 2)^2 = 169 - \frac{169(x - 3)^2}{25}$$

Take the square root of each side.

$$y + 2 = \pm\sqrt{169 - \frac{169(x - 3)^2}{25}}$$

Finally, isolate y.

$$y = -2 \pm\sqrt{169 - \frac{169(x - 3)^2}{25}}$$

In the $\boxed{Y=}$ screen, let Y_1 equal the positive value of the equation and Y_2 equal the negative value of the equation.

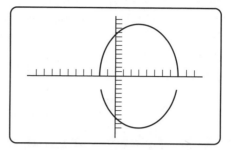

```
Plot1  Plot2  Plot3
\Y₁ = ⁻2+√(169−169
/25 (X–3)²)
\Y₂ = ⁻2–√(169−169
/25 (X–3)²)
\Y₃ =
\Y₄ =
\Y₅ =
```

Sometimes an equation is not in standard elliptical form, and you must complete the square to get it in that format.

2. Rewrite the equation $2x^2 + y^2 + 4x - 10y = 21$ in standard form and identify the center and the lengths of the major and minor axes.

SOLUTION

First group the x and y terms separately.

$$2(x^2 + 2x) + (y^2 - 10y) = 21$$

Now, complete the square for x and for y.

$$2(x^2 + 2x + 1) + (y^2 - 10y + 25) = 21 + 2 + 25$$

$$2(x + 1)^2 + (y - 5)^2 = 48$$

Divide through by 48 so the equation will be equal to 1.

$$\frac{(x + 1)^2}{24} + \frac{(y - 5)^2}{48} = 1$$

Answer: The center of the ellipse is $(-1, 5)$; the length of the major axis is $2\sqrt{48} = 8\sqrt{3}$. The length of the minor axis is $2\sqrt{24} = 4\sqrt{6}$.

3. Determine the type of conic section each equation represents and give as much information as you can about each figure.
   a. $(x + 6)^2 + y^2 = 25$

   b. $\dfrac{(x + 3)^2}{4} + \dfrac{\left(y - \frac{1}{2}\right)^2}{36} = 1$

   c. $y = (x + 3)^2 - 4$

SOLUTION

a. This equation represents a circle with a center at $(-6, 0)$ and a radius of 5 units. It is not a function.

b. This equation represents an ellipse with a center at $\left(-3, \frac{1}{2}\right)$. The vertical axis is the major axis with a length of 12 and the horizontal or minor axis has a length of 4. The distance between the foci is $2\sqrt{32} = 8\sqrt{2}$, so the foci are $\left(-3, \frac{1}{2} \pm 8\sqrt{2}\right)$. The endpoints of the minor axis are $\left(-1, \frac{1}{2}\right)$ and $\left(-5, \frac{1}{2}\right)$, while the endpoints of the major axis are $\left(-3, \frac{13}{2}\right)$ and $\left(-3, \frac{-11}{2}\right)$. This equation does not represent a function.

c. This equation represents a quadratic function whose graph is an upward parabola with a vertex at $(-3, -4)$. The directrix is $y = -4.25$ and the focus is at $(-3, -3.75)$.

Hyperbolas

Slicing vertically downward through both sections of the right circular cone creates another conic section, the **hyperbola.**

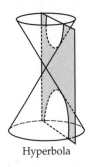

Hyperbola

In an ellipse, the sum of the distance from the two focal points is a constant value. In a hyperbola, the difference between the distances from the two fixed points is a constant value. In other words, the distance from any point P on the hyperbola to F_1 minus the distance from F_2 to the same point on the hyperbola must be equal to the distances from any other point on the hyperbola to F_1 and F_2. In other words, $P_1F_1 - P_1F_2 = P_2F_1 - P_2F_2$ for a hyperbola.

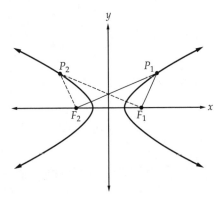

This form of hyperbola is called a **nonrectangular hyperbola.** Like the ellipse, the hyperbola is not a function. The hyperbola also has two "branches" or "arms," but rather than turning in on each other to form a closed curve, the two parts of the relation turn away from each other and move outward away from their foci and center. The **transverse axis** is the segment that connects the vertices. The foci lie on the line that contains the transverse axis. The **conjugate axis** passes through the center, which is the midpoint of the segment connecting the foci.

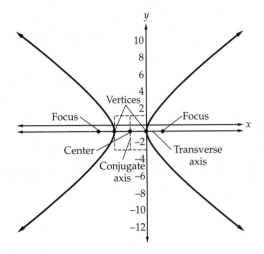

The standard equation of a nonrectangular hyperbola is much the same as that for the ellipse, except the hyperbola's equation contains a subtraction sign rather than an addition sign. The standard form of a nonrectangular hyperbola is $\frac{(x-h)^2}{a^2} - \frac{(y-k)^2}{b^2} = 1$ where (h, k) is the center of the hyperbola, $2a$ is the length of the transverse axis, $2b$ is the length of the conjugate axis, and $2c$ is the distance between the foci where $c^2 = a^2 - b^2$. The coordinates of the vertices, points on each branch nearest the center, are $(a + h, k)$ and $(-a + h, k)$ and the coordinates of the foci are $(c + h, k)$ and $(-c + h, k)$. A hyperbola whose foci are on the y-axis has an equation of the form $\frac{y^2}{a^2} - \frac{x^2}{b^2} = 1$.

Note: The lengths of a, b, and c are related differently for a hyperbola than they are for an ellipse.

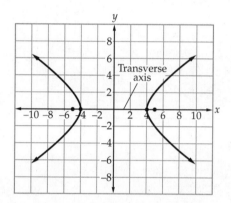

The equation of the graph shown in the figure above is $\frac{x^2}{16} - \frac{y^2}{9} = 1$; therefore, the center is the origin. In this case, the transverse axis is the horizontal one and measures $2 \cdot 4$ or 8, which is the distance between the vertices or turning points of the hyperbola. The vertices are $(-4, 0)$ and $(4, 0)$, while the foci are $(-5, 0)$ and $(5, 0)$. Notice how the hyperbola coexists with the ellipse of similar terms, $\frac{x^2}{16} + \frac{y^2}{9} = 1$, in the graph below.

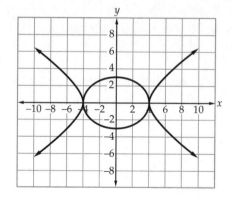

The hyperbola and ellipse share the same center, $(0, 0)$, and the vertices $(-4, 0)$ and $(4, 0)$ but otherwise move in opposite directions, forming two very different conic sections.

Sketch the graph of the equation $\dfrac{x^2}{25} - \dfrac{(y-2)^2}{16} = 1$.

SOLUTION

To graph a nonrectangular hyperbola, we make use of a specific attribute of these figures. Between the parts of the hyperbola, there is a rectangle whose diagonals form the **asymptotes** that approach the hyperbola. These asymptotes have equations of $y = k \pm \dfrac{b}{a}(x - h)$ if the transverse axis is horizontal, and $y = k \pm \dfrac{a}{b}(x - h)$ if the transverse axis is vertical. In this hyperbola, the transverse axis is horizontal, so the asymptotes are $y = 2 \pm \dfrac{4}{5}(x - 0)$, which simplifies to $y = 2 \pm \dfrac{4}{5}x$. To graph this hyperbola, first sketch the asymptotes.

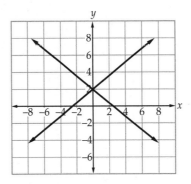

We know the center of the hyperbola is $(0, 2)$, the intersection of these asymptotes, and the vertices are at $(5, 2)$ and $(-5, 2)$. Draw a rectangle using the vertices as location points for the vertical sides.

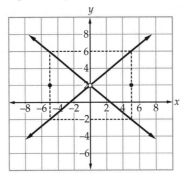

Now, using the asymptotes and the vertices on the rectangle as your guide, sketch the two branches of the hyperbola.

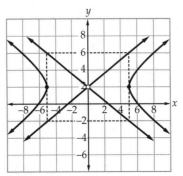

The table contains a summary of formulas and facts about hyperbolas and ellipses with center at the origin.

	Hyperbola			Ellipse	
Equation	$\dfrac{x^2}{a^2} - \dfrac{y^2}{b^2} = 1$	$\dfrac{y^2}{a^2} - \dfrac{x^2}{b^2} = 1$	Equation	$\dfrac{x^2}{a^2} + \dfrac{y^2}{b^2} = 1$ $(a > b)$	$\dfrac{x^2}{b^2} + \dfrac{y^2}{a^2} = 1$ $(b > a)$
Transverse axis	Horizontal on x-axis; length $= 2a$	Vertical on y-axis; length $= 2a$	Major axis	Horizontal on x-axis; length $= 2a$	Vertical on y-axis; length $= 2a$
Conjugate axis	Vertical on y-axis; length $= 2b$	Horizontal on x-axis; length $= 2b$	Minor axis	Vertical on y-axis; length $= 2b$	Horizontal on x-axis; length $= 2b$
Foci	$(\pm c, 0)$ where $c^2 = a^2 + b^2$	$(0, \pm c)$ where $c^2 = a^2 + b^2$	Foci	$(\pm c, 0)$ where $c^2 = a^2 - b^2$	$(0, \pm c)$ where $c^2 = a^2 - b^2$
Asymptotes	$y = \pm\dfrac{b}{a}x$	$y = \pm\dfrac{a}{b}x$			

Eccentricity

The **eccentricity**, e, of a conic section is a ratio comparing the distance from the point P on the conic to the focus and the distance from point P to the directrix (D) in the case of a parabola, or the vertex in the case of an ellipse or hyperbola.

In a parabola, $e = \dfrac{PF}{PD} = 1$ where PF is the distance from point P to the focus (F)

and PD is the distance from point P to the directrix. If the eccentricity, (e), is zero, the figure is a circle. If e is between zero and 1, the figure is an ellipse.

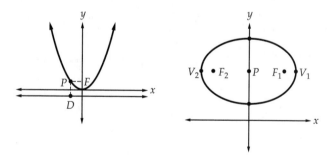

Note: The closer the eccentricity is to 1, the more eccentric or flatter the ellipse becomes.

$e = 0 \qquad e = 0.4 \qquad e = 0.7$

In the case of a hyperbola, the distance from the focal point F to point P is greater than the distance from the vertex to the same point P, so the eccentricity of a hyperbola is greater than 1.

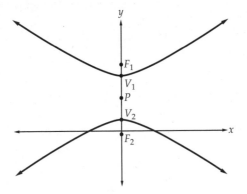

Practice

In 1–9, identify each conic section as a circle, a parabola, an ellipse, or a nonrectangular hyperbola. What information can you provide about the graph of this equation?

1. $4x^2 + (y - 5)^2 = 36$

2. $\dfrac{(x + 1)^2}{25} + \dfrac{(y + 4)^2}{49} = 1$

3. $y = (x + 5)^2 - 6$

4. $(x - 2)^2 + (y - 3)^2 = 16$

5. $9x^2 - 25(y - 1)^2 = 225$

6. $y = 3x^2 - 5x + 2$

7. $\dfrac{(x - 4)^2}{25} - \dfrac{(y + 2)^2}{9} = 1$

8. $(x + 5)^2 + (y - 1)^2 = 4$

9. $x^2 + y^2 - 4x + 6y = 7$

In 10–19, choose the numeral preceding the word or expression that best completes the sentence or answers the question.

10. Which of the following equations represents a function?
    (1) $x^2 + (y - 3)^2 = 16$
    (2) $(x - 8)^2 + y^2 = 10$
    (3) $y - 1 = (x + 9)^2$
    (4) $\dfrac{(x + 4)^2}{9} + \dfrac{y^2}{4} = 1$

11. The x-intercepts of the relation $2x^2 + y^2 = 32$ are
    (1) $\{(4, 0), (-4, 0)\}$ (3) $\{(2, 0), (32, 0)\}$
    (2) $\{(16, 0) (-16, 0)\}$ (4) $\{(2, 0), (-2, 0)\}$

12. The length of the minor axis in the ellipse $4x^2 + (y - 7)^2 = 64$ is
    (1) 64   (3) 8
    (2) 16   (4) 4

13. Which of the following is *not* true about $3(x - 1)^2 + (y + 6)^2 = 12$?
    (1) The graph represents an ellipse with a center of $(1, -6)$.
    (2) This graph has a directrix of $y = 3$.
    (3) This figure, when graphed, has two foci.
    (4) This figure is not a function.

14. Which equation represents the graph shown below?

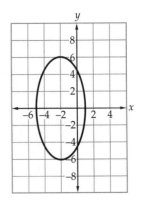

(1) $\dfrac{(x + 2)^2}{9} + \dfrac{y^2}{36} = 1$

(2) $\dfrac{(x - 4)^2}{16} + \dfrac{(y + 2)^2}{16} = 1$

(3) $(x - 4)^2 + 3(y + 4)^2 = 27$

(4) $(x + 2)^2 + y^2 = 36$

15. If a, b, and c are positive, unequal numbers, the graph of $ax^2 + bx + c = y$ is
(1) a circle
(2) an ellipse
(3) a nonrectangular hyperbola
(4) a parabola

16. Which of the following does *not* lie on the ellipse $\dfrac{(x - 1)^2}{16} + \dfrac{(y + 4)^2}{49} = 1$?

(1) $(1, -4)$ (3) $(-3, -4)$
(2) $(5, -4)$ (4) $(1, 3)$

17. Gagneet's flashlight beam throws an elliptical shape on the coordinate grid. If the major axis is vertical and 10 units in length while the minor axis is 6 units, and the center of the ellipse falls at $(-5, 2)$, what is the equation of the flashlight's reflection?
(1) $9(x - 5)^2 + 25(y + 2)^2 = 1$
(2) $25(x - 5)^2 + 9(y - 2)^2 = 1$
(3) $9(x + 5)^2 + 25(y + 2)^2 = 225$
(4) $25(x + 5)^2 + 9(y - 2)^2 = 225$

18. Jared's neighbors just put in an elliptical swimming pool. If the equation of the pool is $324(x - 3)^2 + 576(y + 6)^2 = 186{,}624$, what are the lengths of the major and minor axes of the pool in feet?
(1) 324 by 576   (3) 36 by 48
(2) 18 by 24   (4) 432 by 432

19. If the eccentricity of a conic is 1.3, the conic is
(1) a circle   (3) a hyperbola
(2) an ellipse   (4) a parabola

20. Sketch the graph of $\dfrac{(x + 2)^2}{9} + \dfrac{(y - 4)^2}{25} = 1$.

21. Sketch the graph of $\dfrac{(x - 3)^2}{36} - \dfrac{(y + 1)^2}{16} = 1$.

7.3 Inverse Variation and Rectangular Hyperbolas

Inverse variation is a relationship between two variables in which one value increases as the other decreases. For example, if the number of slices of pizza you eat varies inversely with the number of people sharing the pie, this means the more people eating the pizza, the fewer slices for you.

Mathematically, the equation of an inverse variation is in the form:

$$xy = k \qquad \text{or} \qquad x = \dfrac{k}{y} \qquad \text{or} \qquad y = \dfrac{k}{x}$$

where x and y are variables and k is the **constant of proportionality.**

For example, $xy = 12$ means that the product of these two variables, k, must equal 12. If x is 3, y must be 4; if x doubles to 6, y is halved to be 2. (The operations performed on the variables are inverse operations.)

Graphically, an inverse variation is always a **rectangular hyperbola.** This function has two branches, appearing in the first and third quadrants when k is positive and in the second and fourth quadrants when k is negative. The graph can never cross either axis because the product of x and y must equal k, and if either x or y equals zero, the product must be zero.

Consider the graph of $xy = 12$, shown below.

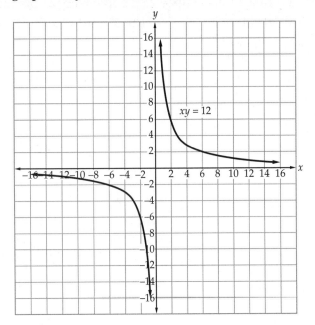

Notice the graph gets closer and closer to the x- and y-axes, but it can never reach them since a product of zero is unattainable. When a graph gets closer and closer to a value, but never reaches it, it is said to be **asymptotic** to that value. Rectangular hyperbolas are asymptotic to both the x- and y-axes.

---

1. If x varies inversely as y and $x = 24$ when $y = 6$, what is the value of y when x is 12?
(1) 144
(2) 48
(3) 16
(4) 12

SOLUTION

Note: You may solve for k and then create a second equation equal to k.

$$xy = k$$
$$6 \cdot 24 = 144$$
$$12 \cdot y = 144$$
$$y = 12$$

As an alternative, you may set the two pairs of elements, which vary inversely, equal to each other and solve. $6 \cdot 24 = 12 \cdot y$.
In either case, $y = 12$.

Answer: (4)

Remember: When x is halved, y is doubled.

---

2. The rate at which Ishmir travels from home to his college varies inversely as the time it takes to make the trip. If Ishmir can make the trip in 4 hours at 45 miles per hours, how many miles per hour must he travel to make the trip in 3 hours?
   (1) 65
   (2) 60
   (3) 55
   (4) 50

SOLUTION
Use the equation: rate · time = constant.

$$45 \cdot 4 = 180, \text{ so } r \cdot 3 = 180 \text{ and } r = 60.$$

Answer: (2)

3. The amount of the tip each waiter receives after a wedding is inversely proportional to the number of waiters serving the event. If the total amount for tips at the Klaiwith-Sims wedding was $1,200 and n represents the number of waiters and t represents the tip received, which of these represents the relationship between n and t?

   (1) $n = \dfrac{t}{1{,}200}$

   (2) $1{,}200 = \dfrac{n}{t}$

   (3) $1{,}200 = \dfrac{t}{n}$

   (4) $n = \dfrac{1{,}200}{t}$

SOLUTION

$$n \cdot t = \text{total tip}$$
$$nt = 1{,}200$$
$$n = \frac{1{,}200}{t}$$

Answer: (4)

4. If a varies inversely as b, the missing value in the table is

a	36	24	18
b	6	9	?

   (1) 3
   (2) 12
   (3) 15
   (4) 216

SOLUTION

$$a \cdot b = \text{constant}$$
$$36 \cdot 6 = 216 \text{ or } 36 \cdot 6 = 18 \cdot b, \text{ so } b = 12.$$

Answer: (2)

In 1–10, write the numeral preceding the expression that best answers the question.

1. Grandma Krieg has discovered that her enjoyment of Kathleen and Maria's Barney video varies inversely to the number of times she has watched it. If her third viewing of the video offered only 84% enjoyment, how much did she enjoy the twelfth showing?
   (1) 73%   (3) 36%
   (2) 50%   (4) 21%

2. TJ's Brick Works found that within reason, the number of workers on a job varies inversely to the time needed to finish a project. If 4 workers can complete a brick patio in 20 hours, how many workers are needed to finish the job in 5 hours?
   (1) 20   (3) 12
   (2) 16   (4) 8

3. If x varies inversely as y and x measures 14 when y is 6, find x when y is 4.
   (1) 84   (3) 21
   (2) 56   (4) $\frac{28}{3}$

4. The efficiency department of a mail and phone order company discovered the accuracy of phone orders varied inversely as the number of hours in the operator's shift. If employees who worked two-hour shifts were 98% accurate, how many hours were worked by those with 24.5% accuracy?
   (1) 8   (3) 4
   (2) 6   (4) 3

5. Given the area of a rectangle to be 360 square inches, the length of the rectangle varies inversely as the width. If the length of the rectangle is 20 square inches, what is the width?
   (1) 7,200   (3) 72
   (2) 180   (4) 18

6. If m varies inversely as n and m is 48 when n is 12, what is m when n is 18?
   (1) 36   (3) 30
   (2) 32   (4) 24

7. If p varies inversely as q, find the missing value in the table.

p	40	30	20
q	9	?	18

   (1) 4.5   (3) 15
   (2) 12   (4) 16

8. Because Kelly's coach believes every player should get an equal opportunity to play, she varies the playing time so that it is inversely proportional to the number of players who show up for a game. When the whole team of 16 players attends, each player has 18 minutes of playing time. How many players must be absent for Kelly to play 24 minutes?
   (1) 12   (3) 6
   (2) 8   (4) 4

9. When David drives to Melissa's college to visit her, his travel time varies inversely as his speed. If he drives at 56 miles per hour, he arrives in 3 hours. How many minutes would he save if he traveled at 60 miles per hour?
   (1) 80   (3) 28
   (2) 40   (4) 12

10. If a varies inversely as b and $a = 15$ when $b = 8$, what is a when $b = 12$?
    (1) 10   (3) 30
    (2) 16   (4) 120

11. Sketch the graph of the function $y = -\frac{8}{x}$.

12. Sketch the graph of the function $xy = 16$.

Determine the equation of each graph.

13.

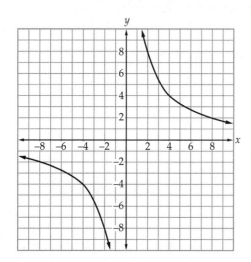

14.

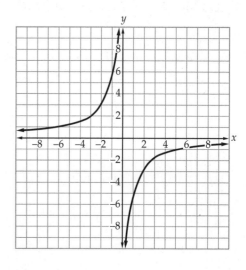

7.4 Systems of Equations with Conics

A **system of equations** is two or more equations with at least one common solution. Just as with quadratic systems, systems that contain conics can be solved algebraically or graphically on the same coordinate plane.

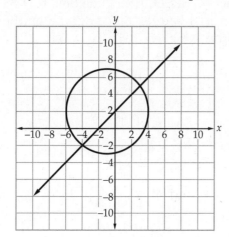

The conic shown is the circle whose equation is $(x + 1)^2 + (y - 2)^2 = 25$ while the equation of the line is $y = x + 2$. To identify the common solutions, we may either examine the graph or solve the system algebraically by substitution.

$$(x + 1)^2 + (y - 2)^2 = 25$$
$$(x + 1)^2 + (x + 2 - 2)^2 = 25 \qquad \text{Since } y = x + 2 \text{, we replace } y \text{ with } (x + 2).$$
$$(x + 1)^2 + x^2 = 25$$
$$x^2 + 2x + 1 + x^2 = 25$$
$$2x^2 + 2x - 24 = 0$$
$$x^2 + x - 12 = 0$$
$$(x + 4)(x - 3) = 0$$
$$x + 4 = 0 \qquad x - 3 = 0$$
$$x = -4 \qquad x = 3$$

By substituting the values of x in one of the original equations, we find the corresponding values of y. Then we can identify the intersection points as $(-4, -2)$ and $(3, 5)$.

Consider the graphs of the two conics below.

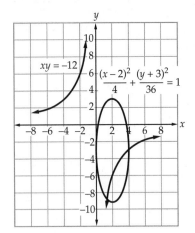

The conics shown here are the rectangular hyperbola whose equation is $xy = -12$ and the ellipse whose equation is $\dfrac{(x-2)^2}{4} + \dfrac{(y+3)^2}{36} = 1$. To find their common solutions, we have a choice of an algebraic solution or using the INTERSECT function on the TI-83 Plus. In this case, however, solving by substitution brings us to the equation $x^4 - 4x^3 + x^2 - 8x + 16 = 0$, which cannot be solved by factoring or the quadratic formula. In this case, using the INTERSECT function on the TI-83 Plus is a better method of solution. Remember that before you can graph on the TI-83 Plus, your equation must be in function format.

Solve for y.

$$\frac{(x-2)^2}{4} + \frac{(y+3)^2}{36} - 1$$

$$9(x-2)^2 + (y+3)^2 = 36$$

$$(y+3)^2 = 36 - 9(x-2)^2$$

$$y + 3 = \pm\sqrt{36 - 9(x-2)^2}$$

$$y = -3 \pm\sqrt{36 - 9(x-2)^2}$$

Enter one of the equations in Y_1 and the other in Y_2 and enter $y = \dfrac{-12}{x}$ in Y_3.

```
Plot1  Plot2  Plot3
\Y₁ =-3+√(36-9(X-
2)²)
\Y₂ =-3-√(36-9(X-
2)²)
\Y₃ =-12/X
\Y₄ =
\Y₅ =
```

Press (ZOOM) 6 and examine the graph that presents itself.

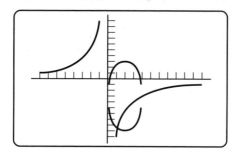

Notice that the ellipse is not shown fully closed, but if you go to the table of values as shown below, the graph is defined for all values $0 \le x \le 4$.

X	Y_1	Y_2
0	–3	–3
1	2.1962	–8.196
2	3	–9
3	2.1962	–8.196
4	–3	–3
5	ERROR	ERROR
6	ERROR	ERROR

X=0

Use (2nd) (TRACE) (CALCULATE) 5: intersect to find the intersection of the graphs. Be careful to clearly identify the equations that are intersecting. One solution is $(1.378, -8.703)$ and the other is $(4, -3)$.

Note: A system of two conic sections may have from zero to four solutions.

Practice

Use an algebraic or calculator method to solve each system.

1. $x^2 - y^2 = 9$
   $y = x^2 - 5x - 4$

2. $x^2 + 5y^2 = 25$
   $x^2 + y^2 = 25$

3. $\dfrac{(x + 3)^2}{4} + \dfrac{(y - 4)^2}{16} = 1$
   $y = 3x + 7$

4. $xy = 10$
   $y = 2x^2 - 3x + 3$

5. $(x + 2)^2 - 4 = y$
   $y = -x^2 + 2x + 4$

6. $y = -(x + 1)^2 + 3$
   $\dfrac{(x + 1)^2}{4} + \dfrac{y^2}{9} = 1$

7. Mrs. Hoity-Toity is outrageously proud of her private gardens. Her groundskeeper recently installed an elliptical pool whose equation is $\dfrac{(x - 8)^2}{64} + \dfrac{(y - 7)^2}{16} = 1$. Now Mrs. Hoity-Toity wants a parabolic bridge to span the pool but she can't decide which equation will make a better appearance over the water. The first design is represented by the equation $y = -x^2 + 7x + 1$ and the second by $y = -0.3x^2 + 4x + 4$. Graph both parabolic equations with the ellipse and advise her which is preferable. Explain your reasoning.

8. Sketch the graphs on the same axes and find their intersections.

   $\dfrac{(x + 4)^2}{16} + \dfrac{(y - 1)^2}{9} = 1$

   $\dfrac{x^2}{16} + \dfrac{(y - 1)^2}{36} = 1$

1. If x varies inversely as y and $x = 6$ when $y = 8$, find x when $y = 3$.

2. Write an equation for a circle whose center is $(4, 5)$ and whose radius is 7.

3. Write an equation for an ellipse whose center is $(1, -1)$, with a horizontal major axis of length 6 and a vertical minor axis of length 4.

4. What is the vertex of the parabola $y = -2x^2 - 4x + 3$?

5. Write an equation for the conic section whose graph is shown below.

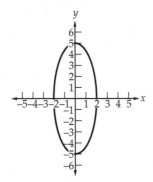

6. What are the lengths of the major and minor axes of $\dfrac{(x+3)^2}{49} + \dfrac{(y-5)^2}{81} = 1$?

7. What number is *not* in the domain of $xy = 4$?

8. Two marbles are going around two different tracks at the same time. The red marble travels around a track whose equation is $\dfrac{x^2}{25} + \dfrac{y^2}{16} = 1$. The blue marble travels around a track whose equation is $x^2 + y^2 = 25$. Do the two tracks have any points in common? If so, what are the coordinates of the point(s) of intersection?

9. What are the y-intercepts of the ellipse $4x^2 + y^2 - 8x + 6y - 3 = 0$?

10. Write an equation for the line tangent to the circle $x^2 + y^2 = 25$ at the point whose x-coordinate is 3.

11. What are the x-intercepts of the hyperbola $x^2 - 6x = 4y^2 + 55$?

In 12–21, write the numeral preceding the word or expression that best completes the statement or answers the question.

12. What conic section has an equation $xy = 18$?
    (1) circle
    (2) ellipse
    (3) hyperbola
    (4) parabola

13. Which of the following is the equation for the graph shown below?

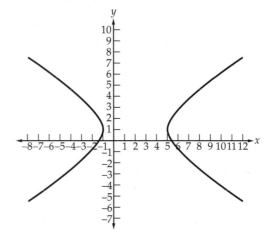

(1) $\dfrac{(x-2)^2}{9} + \dfrac{(y-1)^2}{4} = 1$

(2) $\dfrac{(x-2)^2}{9} - \dfrac{(y-1)^2}{4} = 1$

(3) $\dfrac{(x-2)^2}{4} + \dfrac{(y-1)^2}{9} = 1$

(4) $\dfrac{(x-2)^2}{4} - \dfrac{(y-1)^2}{9} = 1$

14. Identify the conic section whose equation is $x^2 - y^2 - 3x - 4y = 2$.
    (1) circle
    (2) ellipse
    (3) hyperbola
    (4) parabola

15. If x varies inversely as y and $x = 2$ when $y = 12$, when $y = 3$, $x =$
    (1) $\dfrac{1}{2}$
    (2) 2
    (3) 6
    (4) 8

16. An equation of an ellipse is
    (1) $x + y = 3$
    (2) $x^2 + y^2 = 3$
    (3) $2x^2 + y^2 = 3$
    (4) $x^2 - y^2 = 3$

17. If the eccentricity of a conic is zero, the conic is
    (1) a circle
    (2) an ellipse
    (3) a hyperbola
    (4) a parabola

18. Given: a varies inversely as b. If a is multiplied by $\frac{3}{2}$, then b is

    (1) doubled   (3) halved

    (2) multiplied by $\frac{2}{3}$ (4) tripled

19. In which quadrants does the graph of the equation $xy = 20$ lie?
    (1) I and II   (3) I and III
    (2) II and III   (4) all four quadrants

20. In how many places do the graphs of $y = x^2 - 9$ and $x^2 + y^2 = 1$ intersect?
    (1) 1   (3) 3
    (2) 2   (4) 0

21. What is the area of a circle whose equation is $(x + 7)^2 + (y - 2)^2 = 36$?
    (1) 4π (3) 36π
    (2) 36 (4) 49π

22. Given the equation $x^2 + y^2 - 2x + 4y + 1 = 0$,
    a. identify the conic section
    b. complete the square to find the center and other pertinent information
    c. sketch the graph

23. Juan Carlos and his friends are renting a limousine to take them to the Junior Prom. If they can get a total of 10 people to ride in the limousine, it will cost them only $40 each. However, at this point Juan Carlos has only four friends who are interested in riding together. If they can't find anyone else to go with them, how much will the limousine cost each person?

24. A fireplace arch is to be constructed in the shape of the top half of an ellipse whose equation is $\frac{x^2}{16} + \frac{y^2}{25} = 1$. When a chimney sweep comes to clean the chimney, she will need to be able to have enough room to manipulate. The chimney sweep needs to have a work area inside the fireplace 4 feet high and 3 feet wide. Does she have enough room? Explain your reasoning.

25. The track team at ConicsRUs High School is planning some construction. They are going to draw up plans using graph paper. However, it quickly becomes apparent that there are problems with the plans and that the team needs expert help.
    a. The team wants to build a circular track with its center at the point $(-20, 30)$ and a radius of 20 meters. Write an equation for the circle and make a sketch of it.
    b. They also plan to build an elliptical track that has a center at $(10, 10)$, a vertical major axis with a length of 60 meters, and a horizontal minor axis with a length of 50 meters. Write an equation for the ellipse and make a sketch of it on the same axes you used in part a.
    c. Can the track team use both tracks at the same time? If not, rewrite one or both equations to enable them to do so.

26. The Horticulture Club at Weluvmath High School is going to plant a garden. The members have decided to incorporate their knowledge of conic sections with their knowledge of gardening. They are going to plant marigolds and petunias and they need to see if there is any overlap in the two areas they have planned.
    a. The marigolds will be planted in the shape of a hyperbola whose vertices are $(5, 0)$ and $(-5, 0)$ such that $b = 4$. Write the equation of this hyperbola.
    b. The petunias will be planted in the shape of an ellipse whose center is at the origin, and has a horizontal major axis with a length of 8 feet and a vertical minor axis with a length of 6 feet. Write the equation of this ellipse.
    c. Does the area formed by the marigolds intersect the area formed by the petunias? Explain your reasoning.

Calculators and Conics

Some of the newer TI-83 Plus calculators contain **Applications** that are special programs for various situations. To view the applications on your calculator, hit the blue APPS key. The following menu, or one similar, will appear.

```
APPLICATIONS
1 : Finance...
2 : CBL/CBR
3 : Conics
4 : CtlgHelp
5 : Prob Sim
6 : Start–up
7 : StudyCrd
```

Note: If your TI-83 Plus calculator does not have this application, go to the Texas Instruments' web site (http://education.ti.com) and download the Conic Graphing App.

When you highlight the Conic App and hit (ENTER), or just type (3), the number before the Conics application, the following screen appears.

```
CONICS
1 : CIRCLE
2 : ELLIPSE
3 : HYPERBOLA
4 : PARABOLA

INFO       QUIT
```

Note: There is a choice of different conics we have already discussed. When you choose one of these conics, the application gives you a choice of two versions of the equation for that particular conic, allowing you to select a vertical or horizontal orientation when considering the ellipse and hyperbola.

```
CIRCLE
1 : (X–H)² + (Y–K)² = R²      ⊕
2 : AX² + AY² + BX + CY + D=0  ⊕

ESC
```

```
ELLIPSE
1 :  (X–H)²/A² + (Y–K)²/B² =1      ⊕
2 :  (X–H)²/B² + (Y–K)²/A² =1      ⊖

ESC
```

```
HYPERBOLA
1 :  (X–H)²/A² − (Y–K)²/B² =1      )(
2 :  (Y–K)²/A² − (X–H)²/B² =1      ⋇

ESC
```

```
PARABOLA
1 : (Y–K)² = 4P(X–H)      ⊬
2 : (X–H)² = 4P(Y–K)      ⊻

ESC
```

Circles

Choose CIRCLE in the CONICS menu by entering (1). In this case, the two options are different ways of writing the same equation. The second option, $ax^2 + ay^2 + bx + cy + d = 0$, is simply equation 1, $(x - h)^2 + (y - k)^2 = r^2$, in non-factored form. Choose option 1. You will see the screen below, without the values for h, k, and r.

```
CIRCLE
(X–H)² + (Y–K)² = R²

H=3
K=–2
R=4

ESC
```

Enter these values: $h = 3$, $k = -2$, and $r = 4$. Then press (GRAPH).

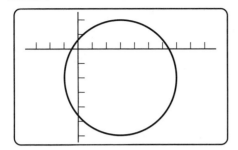

The calculator has graphed a circle with a center at $(3, -2)$ and a radius equal to 4. To go back to the previous screen, use the ESC command the program has set up as the (Y =) key. Rewrite the equation $(x - 3)^2 + (y + 2)^2 = 4^2$ in simplest form. Enter the A, B, C, and D values and graph using option 2.

Ellipses

Go to the ellipse screen and graph the ellipse in which $A = 4$, $B = 3$, $H = -1$, and $K = 2$. The resulting ellipse should look like the screen below.

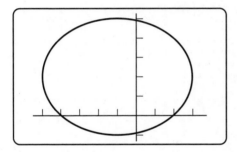

Now interchange the A and B values so $A = 3$ and $B = 4$. The resulting ellipse has a vertical rather than a horizontal orientation as shown below.

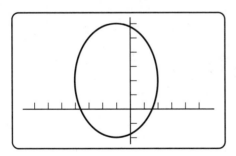

Hyperbolas

Explore the hyperbola graphing option using the same values for A, B, H, and K as we used to graph the ellipses. Again, the vertical and horizontal direction of the hyperbola is altered when we choose option 2 rather than option 1.

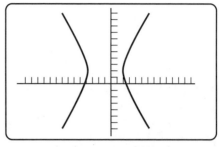

$A = 3$, $B = 4$, $H = -1$, and $K = 2$

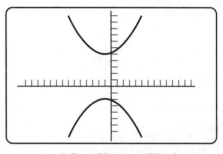

$A = 3$, $B = 4$, $H = -1$, and $K = 2$

Practice

You may now want to return to the exercises earlier in the chapter and practice some of the problems using the Conic Applications on your calculator.

CHAPTER 8

Transformations

8.1 Review of Transformations

Line Reflections and Line Symmetry

Perhaps when you were younger, you made a valentine. You may have taken a piece of paper, folded it in half, drawn half of a heart, and cut along the curve you drew. After you opened it up, you had the whole heart.

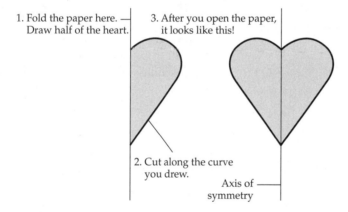

1. Fold the paper here. Draw half of the heart.

3. After you open the paper, it looks like this!

2. Cut along the curve you drew.

Axis of symmetry

The fold in the paper is the **axis of symmetry,** and the half heart you drew is reflected in the axis of symmetry as shown in the figure above. Thus, the heart drawn has **line symmetry,** since the heart is identical on both sides of the axis of symmetry. Note that a figure and its reflection are mirror images. The line in which the figure is reflected is a line of symmetry for the figure and its image. A **reflection** does not change the size or the shape of the figure, just the way it faces.

There are numerous examples of line symmetry in the real world and also in the world of coordinate geometry.

Triangle *ABC* has coordinates *A*(1, 2), *B*(2, 7), *C*(5, 4).

a. Draw and label triangle *ABC*.

b. Reflect the graph drawn in part **a** in the *x*-axis, and state the coordinates of *A'B'C'*, the image of triangle *ABC*.

c. Reflect the graph drawn in part **a** in the line *y* = *x*, and state the coordinates of *A"B"C"*, the image of triangle *ABC*.

SOLUTION

We are given *A*(1, 2), *B*(2, 7), *C*(5, 4).

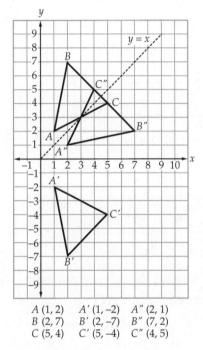

A (1, 2)	*A'* (1, −2)	*A"* (2, 1)
B (2, 7)	*B'* (2, −7)	*B"* (7, 2)
C (5, 4)	*C'* (5, −4)	*C"* (4, 5)

a. We sketch triangle *ABC* as shown. It is often clearer to put the labels on the figure, but write the coordinates on the side or below, as shown in the figure.

b. When we reflect triangle *ABC* in the *x*-axis, the *x*-coordinates stay the same. However, all of the *y*-coordinates are opposites.

c. When we reflect triangle *ABC* in the line *y* = *x*, the *x*- and *y*-coordinates are switched.

If you have trouble determining the image of a figure after a line reflection, try this method.

1. Sketch the figure and the line that will be used for reflection.
2. Use a pencil to darken the line enough so that it is easy to fold the paper over the line.
3. Also darken the vertices of the figure that is being reflected. Darken the vertices enough so that you can see each vertex from the other side of the paper.
4. Fold the paper on the "fold line." From the backside of the paper, darken each vertex.
5. Open the paper and see where the new vertices are.
6. Connect the vertices to form the new figure.

Point Reflections and Point Symmetry

Look at the figure below.

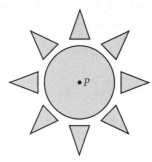

Now, turn your book upside down, and look at the figure again.
Every point on the figure reflects to an image of itself through the center of the figure, point *P*, which is the point of reflection.

The **point of reflection** is the midpoint of the line segment joining the given point and its image.

 MODEL PROBLEM

Draw the image of parallelogram *WXYZ* reflected in point *Z*. Call the image *W'X'Y'Z'*.

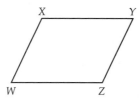

SOLUTION

1. Draw a segment from vertex *W* through *Z* so that *WZ* = *ZW'*. Draw a segment from *Y* through *Z* so that *YZ* = *ZY'*. Draw a segment from *X* through *Z* so that *XZ* = *ZX'*. Point *Z* is an image of itself.

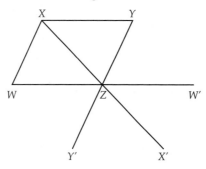

2. Connect *W'*, *X'*, *Y'* and *Z'*.

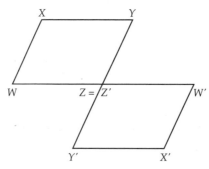

W'X'Y'Z' is the image of *WXYZ* reflected in point *Z*.

Point symmetry occurs in a figure when the figure is its own image under a reflection in a point. Figures that have point symmetry look the same when they are turned upside down. Once again, look at the figure below.

This figure is its own image under a reflection in point *P*.

MODEL PROBLEM

Determine whether each of the figures has point symmetry, line symmetry, or neither. If the figure has line symmetry, draw the axis of symmetry.

a.

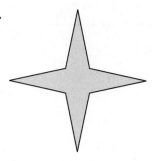

b.

SOLUTION

a. This figure has both point and line symmetry. We can see that it has point symmetry by turning the figure upside down and seeing that the upside-down figure is identical to the right-side-up figure. (The point of reflection and lines of symmetry are shown below.)

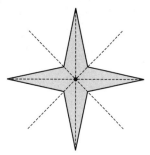

We can demonstrate that the figure has line symmetry by tracing the figure and folding the paper along any of the dotted lines shown so that the two halves match exactly.

b. This figure does not have point symmetry. If we turn the figure upside down, it does not look the same as the given figure. The figure does, however, have line symmetry. If you trace the figure and fold the paper along one of the dotted lines shown, you will see that both sides of the figure are identical.

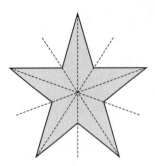

We can also examine examples of point symmetry in the coordinate plane.

 MODEL PROBLEM

Find the image of each of the following points under a reflection in the origin.

a. $(2, 6)$
b. $(-5, 3)$

SOLUTION
a. Plot the point $(2, 6)$ on a coordinate plane. Draw a line segment connecting $(2, 6)$ to the origin, and an equal and opposite line segment connecting the origin to the image of $(2, 6)$, $(-2, -6)$

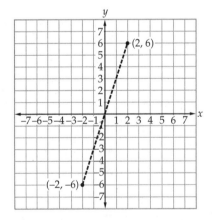

Note: The coordinates of the image are the opposites of the coordinates of the given point.

b. Plot $(-5, 3)$ on a coordinate plane. Draw a line segment from the point to the origin. Then draw an equal and opposite line segment to the image of $(-5, 3)$, which is $(5, -3)$.

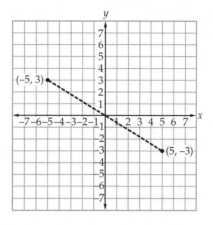

Rotations

A **rotation** is a transformation that turns a figure about a fixed point called the center of rotation. A rotation of 90° is denoted $R_{90°}$. A rotation does not change the size or shape of the figure.

Note: With rotations, it is assumed the direction of the rotation is counterclockwise unless it is otherwise specified.

1. Plot the point $(3, 6)$ and find its image under the rotation $R_{90°}$ about the origin.

SOLUTION
First, plot the point $(3, 6)$ on a coordinate plane.

You want to rotate this point 90° in a counterclockwise direction. The figure below illustrates the rotation and shows that the image of $(3, 6)$ after a 90° rotation is the point $(-6, 3)$

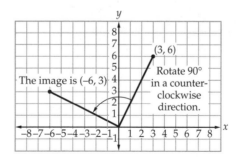

Here's another way to find the image of (3, 6) after a 90° rotation.

1. Plot the point (3, 6) on a coordinate plane.

2. Place your pencil point on the center of rotation, in this case the origin, and turn your paper 90° (a quarter turn) in a counterclockwise direction.

3. Notice that the point is now at (−6, 3).

4. Turn the paper right side up and plot the point (−6, 3).

Answer: The point (−6, 3) is the image of the point (3, 6) under a 90° rotation.

2. Plot the point (2, 5) and find its image under the rotation $R_{180°}$ about the origin.

SOLUTION
Plot the point (2, 5).

You need to determine where the image of (2, 5) will be after a 180° rotation. An easy way to determine this would be to rotate your paper 180° (a half turn) in a counterclockwise direction. The paper is upside down and the image of (2, 5) is (−2, −5). Thus, a 180° rotation about the origin is the same as a point reflection in the origin.

3. Plot the point (3, −4) and find its image under the rotation $R_{270°}$ about the origin.

SOLUTION
Plot the point (3, −4). To determine where the image of (3, 4) will be after a 270° rotation, rotate your paper 270° (a three-quarter turn) in a counterclockwise direction. The image is at (−4, −3).

Note: You could have reached the same location by rotating your paper 90° in a *clockwise* direction.

Thus, a 270° rotation in a *counterclockwise* direction is the same as a 90° rotation in a *clockwise* direction. This can be shown as $R_{270°} = R_{−90°}$. The negative sign in front of the 90° indicates the rotation is in the direction opposite to that normally used, that is, a *clockwise* direction.

To determine equivalent rotations in a positive (counterclockwise) and negative (clockwise) direction, subtract the angle measure you are given from 360°.

4. a. Sketch the triangle formed by the points $A(1, 2)$, $B(6, 2)$, and $C(3, 6)$.

   b. On the same set of axes, graph and state the coordinates of $\triangle A'B'C'$, the image of $\triangle ABC$ after $R_{-90°}$.

SOLUTION

a. Sketch triangle ABC, as shown in the figure below.

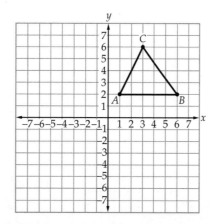

b. Since we are rotating $-90°$, turn your paper 90° (a quarter turn) in a *clockwise* direction. Record the coordinates. Turn your paper back to where you started, and plot the new points. The coordinates are $A'(2, -1)$, $B'(2, -6)$, and $C'(6, -3)$. The diagram below shows triangle ABC and its image triangle $A'B'C'$.

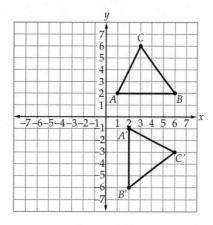

5. What positive rotation would be equivalent to $R_{-60°}$?

SOLUTION

Subtract 60° from 360°, giving a result of 300°.

Thus, $R_{-60°} = R_{300°}$.

The table below summarizes the rules for some common transformations.

Type of Transformation	Symbolically	Helpful Hint	Image of (2, 7)
Reflection in the x-axis	$r_{x\text{-axis}}(x, y) = (x, -y)$	Negate the y-coordinate.	$(2, -7)$
Reflection in the y-axis	$r_{y\text{-axis}}(x, y) = (-x, y)$	Negate the x-coordinate.	$(-2, 7)$
Reflection in the line $y = x$	$r_{y=x}(x, y) = (y, x)$	Switch the x- and y-coordinates.	$(7, 2)$
Reflection in the line $y = -x$	$r_{y=-x}(x, y) = (-y, -x)$	Switch and negate the x- and y-coordinates.	$(-7, -2)$
Reflection in the origin	$R_O(x, y) = (-x, -y)$	Negate both the x- and y-coordinates.	$(-2, -7)$
Rotation of 90°	$R_{90°}(x, y) = (-y, x)$	Negate the y-coordinate, *then* switch the coordinates.	$(-7, 2)$
Rotation of 180°	$R_{180°}(x, y) = (-x, -y)$	Negate both coordinates. (Same as point reflection in the origin.)	$(-2, -7)$
Rotation of 270°	$R_{270°}(x, y) = (y, -x)$	Negate the x-coordinate, *then* switch the coordinates.	$(7, -2)$

Translations

Look at the coordinate plane pictured below.

Take a coin, and center it on the origin. Now move the coin 3 spaces to the right and up 2 spaces. Where is the coin now? It should be centered on the point (3, 2) as pictured below.

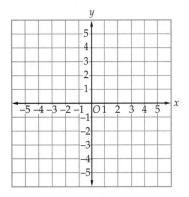

The movement you performed is a translation (or slide). All points in the coin were moved 3 units right and 2 units up. The notation for this translation is $T_{3,2}(x, y) = (x + 3, y + 2)$. A translation does not change the size, shape, or orientation of a figure.

MODEL PROBLEM

Given the equation of circle O: $(x + 1)^2 + (y - 4)^2 = 9$.

a. Find the coordinates of the center and the length of the radius of circle O.
b. Sketch a graph of circle O.
c. Find the coordinates of the center of circle O', the image of circle O after a translation of $T_{-3,-4}$.
d. On the same set of axes, sketch a graph of circle O'.

SOLUTION

a. The equation of a circle with center at (h, k) and a radius of length r is $(x - h)^2 + (y - k)^2 = r^2$. Our circle has a center at $(-1, 4)$ and a radius of 3 units.
b. The graph of circle O is shown below.
c. After a translation of $T_{-3,-4}$, the new center (as well as the other points on the circle) is moved 3 units to the left and 4 units down. Thus, the new center is $(-1 - 3, 4 - 4) = (-4, 0)$.
d. The new circle, O', has a center at $(-4, 0)$ and a radius of 3 units and is shown below.

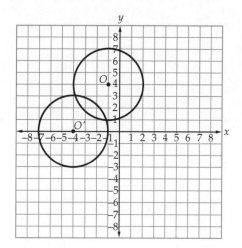

Dilations

The pupils of your eyes dilate when you go into a dark room to allow more light to enter your eyes. According to Webster's Dictionary, the word *dilate* means "to become wider or larger." In mathematics, we use the word *dilation* to indicate a change in the size of an object, regardless of whether the object gets larger or smaller. The **constant of dilation** is the factor by which the size of the figure is changed. A dilation that doubles the size of the figure has a constant of 2 and is written D_2. Under a dilation of factor k, the image of $P(x, y)$ is $P'(kx, ky)$.

Triangle *YES* has coordinates $Y(-6, 1)$, $E(-2, 3)$, and $S(-4, 7)$.

a. On a coordinate plane, draw and label triangle *YES*.
b. Graph and state the coordinates of triangle $Y'E'S'$, the image of triangle *YES* after $R_{90°}$ about the origin.
c. Graph and state the coordinates of triangle $Y''E''S''$, the image of triangle $Y'E'S'$, after $T_{4,5}$.
d. Graph and state the coordinates of triangle $Y'''E'''S'''$, the image of triangle $Y''E''S''$, after D_2.

SOLUTION

a. $\triangle YES$ is shown on the graph below.
b. After a 90° counterclockwise rotation, the new coordinates will be $Y'(-1, -6)$, $E'(-3, -2)$, $S'(-7, -4)$. (This can be obtained by turning your paper a quarter turn in a counterclockwise direction.)
c. $T_{4,5}$ means to move the entire triangle $Y'E'S'$ 4 units to the right and 5 units up. The new coordinates are $Y'' = (-1 + 4, -6 + 5) = (3, -1)$, $E'' = (-3 + 4, -2 + 5) = (1, 3)$, $S'' = (-7 + 4, -4 + 5) = (-3, 1)$.
d. D_2 indicates a dilation of 2. The coordinates of each vertex are multiplied by 2. The new coordinates are $Y'''(6, -2)$, $E'''(2, 6)$, $S'''(-6, 2)$. These coordinates are also shown on the graph below.

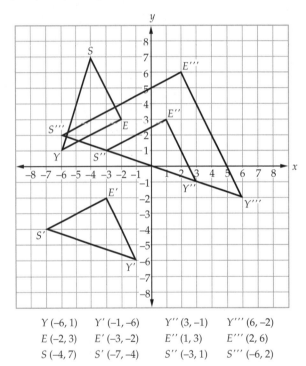

Y (–6, 1)	Y' (–1, –6)	Y'' (3, –1)	Y''' (6, –2)
E (–2, 3)	E' (–3, –2)	E'' (1, 3)	E''' (2, 6)
S (–4, 7)	S' (–7, –4)	S'' (–3, 1)	S''' (–6, 2)

Notice how crowded the four figures are. Thus, we recommend that you label only the vertices on the graph, and write the coordinates on the side.

1. **a.** If possible, name two letters of the alphabet that have horizontal line symmetry only.
   b. If possible, name two letters of the alphabet that have vertical line symmetry only.
   c. Are there any letters of the alphabet that have both vertical and horizontal line symmetry? If so, what are they?
   d. If possible, name two letters of the alphabet that have point symmetry only.
   e. If possible, name two letters of the alphabet that have point and line symmetry.

2. A translation maps $(-6, 2)$ onto $(-4, -2)$. Find the image of $(3, 5)$ under the same translation.

3. What is the image of $(3, 9)$ under a clockwise rotation of $90°$?

4. If $P'(2, -6)$ is the image of point P after the dilation D_2, what are the coordinates of point P?

5. A transformation maps (x, y) onto $(x + 2, y - 1)$. Find the coordinates of A', the image of point $A(-2, 6)$ under the same transformation.

6. What is the image of the letter H after $R_{180°}$?

7. What is the image of $(-6, 8)$ after R_O?

8. Find the coordinates of the point $(-1, 3)$ after the transformation $T_{-3,2}$.

9. Find the image of the point $(5, 7)$ after a reflection in the line $y = x$.

10. The domain of $f(x)$ is $-5 < x < 7$. What is the smallest value of the domain after $T_{1,2}$?

In 11–20, write the numeral preceding the word or expression that best completes the statement or answers the question.

11. Which of the following is equivalent to $R_{40°}$?
    (1) $R_{-320°}$ (3) $R_{140°}$
    (2) $R_{-40°}$ (4) $R_{320°}$

12. How many lines of symmetry does the letter E have?
    (1) 1   (3) 3
    (2) 2   (4) 0

13. Reflecting $(3, -5)$ in the line $y = -x$ yields an image of
    (1) $(-3, -5)$ (3) $(-5, -3)$
    (2) $(-5, 3)$ (4) $(5, -3)$

14. What are the coordinates of the point $(-3, 4)$ under D_3?
    (1) $(0, 7)$ (3) $(-9, 12)$
    (2) $(0, -7)$ (4) $(9, 12)$

15. The coordinates of B are $(-4, 3)$. What are the coordinates of B', the image of B after $r_{x\text{-axis}}$?
    (1) $(4, 3)$ (3) $(3, -4)$
    (2) $(-4, -3)$ (4) $(-3, 4)$

16. Which of the following words has point symmetry?
    (1) pop   (3) mom
    (2) pod   (4) oz

17. The domain of $f(x)$ is $-2 < x < 6$. What is the domain of $g(x)$, the image of $f(x)$ after $D_{\frac{1}{2}}$?
    (1) $-2.5 < x < 5.5$ (3) $-4 < x < 12$
    (2) $-1.5 < x < 6.5$ (4) $-1 < x < 3$

18. Which of the following transformations could map the point $(1, 2)$ onto the point $(3, 6)$?
    (1) $T_{2,3}$ (3) D_3
    (2) $T_{3,2}$ (4) $r_{y=x}$

19. If the coordinates of D' are $(-5, 6)$ and D' is the image of D after a reflection in the y-axis, which of the following are the coordinates of point D?
    (1) $(-5, 6)$ (3) $(-5, -6)$
    (2) $(5, -6)$ (4) $(5, 6)$

20. Which symbol has both point and line symmetry?
    (1) ♣   (3) ♥
    (2) ♦   (4) ♠

21. Circle O is centered at the origin and has a radius of 5.
    a. Write the equation for circle O.
    b. Circle O' is the image of circle O after a translation of $T_{2,-3}$. What is the center of circle O'? What is the radius of O'?
    c. Write the equation for circle O'.

22. Given the parabola $f(x) = x^2$.
   a. Graph $f(x)$.
   b. What is the vertex of $f(x)$?
   c. Reflect $f(x)$ in the x-axis and sketch it on the same set of axes.
   d. Write an equation for the graph drawn in part **c**.
   e. What is the range of the function drawn in part **c**?
   f. Given the translation $T_{-3,-2}$. What would the vertex of $f(x)$ be under such a translation?

23. Given $g(x)$ as drawn in the figure below.

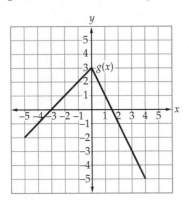

a. Sketch $h(x)$, the image of $g(x)$ after $T_{1,-2}$.
b. Sketch $j(x)$, the image of $g(x)$ after R_O.
c. Sketch $k(x)$, the image of $g(x)$ after $r_{y\text{-axis}}$.

24. Triangle AMY has coordinates $A(2, 5)$, $M(7, 3)$, and $Y(4, 6)$.
   a. On a coordinate plane, draw and label triangle AMY.
   b. Graph and state the coordinates of triangle $A'M'Y'$, the image of triangle AMY after a reflection in the line $y = -x$.
   c. Graph and state the coordinates of triangle $A''M''Y''$, the image of triangle AMY after a reflection in the origin.
   d. Graph and state the coordinates of triangle $A'''M'''Y'''$, the image of triangle AMY after the translation $T_{-3,-4}$.

8.2 Isometries, Orientation, and Other Properties

A line reflection can be thought of as a flip, a rotation as a turn, and a translation as a slide. The image of a figure is congruent to the original figure that was flipped, turned, or slid. Thus, we can say that distance is *preserved*. Angle measure, parallelism, midpoint, area, and collinearity are all also preserved. A transformation that preserves distance is called an **isometry.**

A dilation, however, changes the size of the image. Thus, we can say that a dilation is not an isometry; neither distance nor area is preserved. A dilation image is similar to the original figure. On the other hand, line reflection, point reflection, rotation, and translation are all examples of isometries.

The order in which the vertices of a figure appear is called the orientation of the figure. A transformation may or may not preserve this orientation. A **direct isometry** is an isometry that preserves orientation (the order of the vertices). An **opposite isometry** is an isometry that changes the order of the vertices from counterclockwise to clockwise or vice versa.

1. Triangle *JAN* has vertices *J*(−2, 6), *A*(4, 2), and *N*(8, 2)
   a. On a coordinate plane, graph and label triangle *JAN*.
   b. Graph and state the coordinates of triangle *J′A′N′*, the image of triangle *JAN* after $D_{\frac{1}{2}}$.
   c. Graph and state the coordinates of triangle *J″A″N″*, the image of triangle *JAN* after $r_{x\text{-axis}}$.
   d. Which of the transformations is not an isometry? Explain your answer.
   e. In which of the transformations is the orientation (order) changed?

SOLUTION

a. △*JAN* is shown in the graph below.
b. A dilation changes the size of the figure, since we multiply each of the coordinates by the constant of dilation, which in this case is $\frac{1}{2}$. Therefore, the new coordinates are *J′*(−1, 3), *A′*(2, 1), and *N′*(4, 1).
c. When we reflect in the *x*-axis, we negate all of the *y*-values. Thus, the new coordinates are *J″*(−2, −6), *A″*(4, −2), and *N″*(8, −2).
d. Looking at △*JAN*, △*J′A′N′*, and △*J″A″N″*, notice that △*JAN* and its image △*J″A″N″* are the same size, while △*JAN* and its image △*J′A′N′* are different sizes. Therefore, the dilation is not an isometry, since it changed the size of the original triangle.
e. In △*JAN* and its image △*J′A′N′*, when we start from *J* and proceed in a counterclockwise order, we obtain the letters *J*, *A*, and *N*. On the other hand, in △*J″A″N″*, when we start with *J* and proceed in a counterclockwise order, we obtain the letters *J*, *N*, and *A*. Thus, in the reflection in the *x*-axis, the orientation (order) is changed.

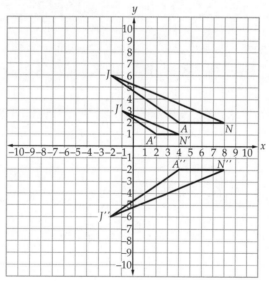

J (−2, 6)	J′ (−1, 3)	J″ (−2, −6)
A (4, 2)	A′ (2, 1)	A″ (4, −2)
N (8, 2)	N′ (4, 1)	N″ (8, −2)

This reflection in the *x*-axis is an example of an opposite isometry. In fact, every line reflection is an opposite isometry. Try a few examples to prove this to yourself.

2. The coordinates of triangle *ABC* are *A*(3, 2), *B*(7, 6), and *C*(7, 1)
   a. On a coordinate plane, draw and label triangle *ABC*.
   b. Graph and state the coordinates of triangle *A′B′C′*, the image of triangle *ABC* after $r_{y\text{-axis}}$.
   c. Graph and state the coordinates of triangle *A″B″C″*, the image of triangle *A′B′C′* after a translation of $T_{0,-7}$.
   d. Which of the above transformations is an example of a direct isometry?

SOLUTION

a. △*ABC* is shown in the graph below.

b. When we reflect in the *y*-axis, we negate all the *x*-values. Thus, the coordinates for triangle *A′B′C′* are *A′*(−3, 2), *B′*(−7, 6), and *C′*(−7, 1).

c. Remember to use △*A′B′C′* to form △*A″B″C″*. Based on the rule of the translation, we leave the *x*-values the same, and subtract 7 from each of the *y*-values. The coordinates for △*A″B″C″* are *A″*(−3, −5), *B″*(−7, −1), and *C″*(−7, −6).

d. The translation is an example of a direct isometry. It preserves both distance and orientation.

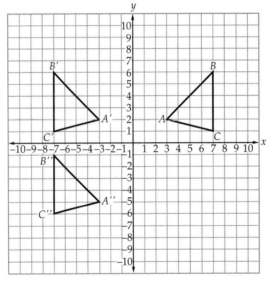

A (3, 2)	*A′* (−3, 2)	*A″* (−3, −5)
B (7, 6)	*B′* (−7, 6)	*B″* (−7, −1)
C (7, 1)	*C′* (−7, 1)	*C″* (−7, −6)

In 1–10, write the numeral preceding the word or expression that best completes the statement or answers the question.

1. Which of the following is not an isometry?
   (1) line reflection   (3) dilation
   (2) point reflection   (4) glide reflection

2. Which of the following is an opposite isometry?
   (1) rotation   (3) dilation
   (2) point reflection   (4) line reflection

3. Which property is not preserved under $r_{y=x}$?
   (1) distance   (3) orientation
   (2) angle measure   (4) parallelism

4. Which property is not preserved under a dilation?
   (1) distance   (3) orientation
   (2) angle measure   (4) parallelism

5. Which of the following illustrates a direct isometry?

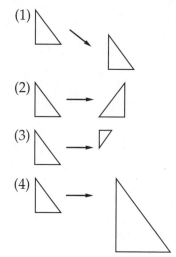

6. A function, $f(x)$, is graphed on a coordinate plane. After a rotation, the image of $f(x)$
   (1) must also be a function
   (2) cannot be a function
   (3) could be a function, but doesn't have to be one
   (4) There's not enough information to make a conclusion.

7. Which of the following transformations does not preserve orientation?
   (1) $(x, y) \rightarrow (-x, -y)$
   (2) $(x, y) \rightarrow (x + 3, y + 2)$

   (3) $(x, y) \rightarrow (2x, 2y)$
   (4) $(x, y) \rightarrow (y, x)$

8. Which transformation is not an isometry?
   (1) $(x, y) \rightarrow (-x, -y)$
   (2) $(x, y) \rightarrow (x + 3, y + 2)$
   (3) $(x, y) \rightarrow (2x, 2y)$
   (4) $(x, y) \rightarrow (y, x)$

9. Which transformation is a direct isometry?
   (1) $(x, y) \rightarrow (-x, -y)$
   (2) $(x, y) \rightarrow (-x, y)$
   (3) $(x, y) \rightarrow (2x, 2y)$
   (4) $(x, y) \rightarrow (y, x)$

10. Which transformation is an opposite isometry?
    (1) $(x, y) \rightarrow (-x, -y)$
    (2) $(x, y) \rightarrow (-x, y)$
    (3) $(x, y) \rightarrow (2x, 2y)$
    (4) $(x, y) \rightarrow (x - 5, y - 2)$

11. The vertices of triangle DOG are $D(2, -1)$, $O(6, -4)$, and $G(4, -8)$. Under transformation A, $(x, y) \rightarrow (2x + 2, 2y + 1)$.
    a. Sketch $\triangle DOG$, and its image $\triangle D'O'G'$, after transformation A.
    b. Is transformation A a direct isometry, an opposite isometry, or not an isometry at all? Explain.

12. The vertices of triangle CAT are $C(-2, 3)$, $A(3, 3)$, and $T(0, -2)$. Given the transformations B, D, and F defined as follows
    $B(x, y) \rightarrow (y, x)$
    $D(x, y) \rightarrow (-x, -y)$
    $F(x, y) \rightarrow (x + 4, y - 3)$.
    a. Graph $\triangle CAT$ and its image $\triangle C'A'T'$, after transformation B.
    b. Graph $\triangle C''A''T''$, the image of $\triangle CAT$ after transformation D.
    c. Graph $\triangle C'''A'''T'''$, the image of $\triangle CAT$ after transformation F.
    d. Which of the above transformations are isometries? Explain.
    e. Which of the above transformations are direct isometries? Explain.
    f. Which of the above transformations are opposite isometries? Explain.

8.3 Composition of Transformations

Just as we can have a composition of functions, so too can we have a composition of transformations. The first transformation produces an image, then the second transformation is performed on that image. The symbol for a composition of transformations is the same as for a composition of functions. For example, a rotation of 90° followed by a rotation of 180° would be indicated by $R_{180°} \circ R_{90°}$. Just as with functions, it is important to realize which transformation is performed first. $R_{180°} \circ R_{90°}$ is read as "a rotation of 180° following a rotation of 90°." In this particular case, you would get the same result regardless of which rotation was performed first, but this is not always the case.

Note: To remember which transformation to perform first, replace the composition symbol and what follows it inside parentheses. Then work from the inside out. For example, when you are given $R_{180°} \circ R_{90°}$, replace the $\circ$ with parentheses around $R_{90°}$ as shown.

$$R_{180°} \circ R_{90°} \rightarrow R_{180°}(R_{90°})$$

Now it is clear that the 90° rotation must be done first.

MODEL PROBLEM

The coordinates of triangle *FUN* are $F(-5, 1)$, $U(-1, 1)$, and $N(-1, 7)$.

a. On a coordinate plane, draw and label $\triangle FUN$.
b. Draw and label $\triangle F'U'N'$, the image of $\triangle FUN$ after $r_{x\text{-axis}}$.
c. Draw and label $\triangle F''U''N''$, the image of $\triangle F'U'N'$ after $r_{y\text{-axis}}$.
d. What single transformation is equivalent to $r_{y\text{-axis}} \circ r_{x\text{-axis}}$?

SOLUTION

a. $\triangle FUN$ is shown on the graph.
b. When we reflect in the x-axis, we negate all of the y-values. Thus, the coordinates of $\triangle F'U'N'$ are $F'(-5, -1)$, $U'(-1, -1)$, and $N'(-1, -7)$, as shown in the graph.
c. Be sure to use $\triangle F'U'N'$ to obtain $\triangle F''U''N''$. Since we are reflecting in the y-axis, we negate all of the x-values. The coordinates of $\triangle F''U''N''$ are $F''(5, -1)$, $U''(1, -1)$, and $N''(1, -7)$, as shown in the figure.
d. To decide what single transformation is equivalent to $r_{y\text{-axis}} \circ r_{x\text{-axis}}$, look at $\triangle FUN$ and at $\triangle F''U''N''$. Ask yourself the question, "How can I get from $\triangle FUN$ to $\triangle F''U''N''$ in only one step?" Since $\triangle F''U''N''$ is $\triangle FUN$ turned upside down, it is a point reflection of $\triangle FUN$ through the origin (O). Thus, our answer is R_O. Since a 180° rotation is equivalent to R_O, an alternative answer would be $R_{180°}$.

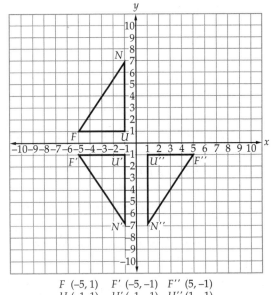

F $(-5, 1)$	F' $(-5, -1)$	F'' $(5, -1)$
U $(-1, 1)$	U' $(-1, -1)$	U'' $(1, -1)$
N $(-1, 7)$	N' $(-1, -7)$	N'' $(1, -7)$

A **glide reflection** is a composition of a line reflection and a translation that is parallel to the line of reflection or vice versa.

MODEL PROBLEM

The coordinates of triangle GLD are $G(1, -5)$, $L(6, -4)$, and $D(3, -1)$.

a. Draw and label $\triangle GLD$.
b. Draw and label $\triangle G'L'D'$, the image of $\triangle GLD$ after $T_{-8,0}$.
c. Draw and label $\triangle G''L''D''$, the image of $\triangle G'L'D'$ after $r_{x\text{-axis}}$.
d. What single transformation maps $\triangle GLD$ onto $\triangle G''L''D''$?
e. Draw and label $\triangle G'''L'''D'''$, the image of $\triangle GLD$ after $T_{-8,0} \circ r_{x\text{-axis}}$. How does this image compare to $\triangle G''L''D''$?

SOLUTION

a. $\triangle GLD$ is drawn below.
b. The translation slides the triangle 8 units to the left. The new coordinates are $G'(-7, -5)$, $L'(-2, -4)$, and $D'(-5, -1)$.
c. A reflection over the x-axis produces the triangle as shown. The new coordinates are $G''(-7, 5)$, $L''(-2, 4)$, and $D''(-5, 1)$.
d. The translation $T_{-8,0}$ is parallel to the x-axis, which is the line of reflection. This composition is a glide reflection.
e. The new coordinates are $G'''(-7, 5)$, $L'''(-2, 4)$, and $D'''(-5, 1)$.
   The two images are the same.

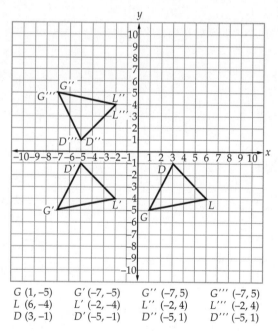

G (1, –5)	G' (–7, –5)	G'' (–7, 5)	G''' (–7, 5)
L (6, –4)	L' (–2, –4)	L'' (–2, 4)	L''' (–2, 4)
D (3, –1)	D' (–5, –1)	D'' (–5, 1)	D''' (–5, 1)

Note: A glide reflection is a special composition since it is commutative.

Remember: Since a line reflection can be thought of as "flip," and a translation can be thought of as a "slide," "a flip and a slide make a glide."

The example below illustrates how we can combine symmetry with our study of composition of transformations.

MODEL PROBLEMS

1. In the accompanying figure, l and m are lines of symmetry for pentagon $ABCDE$. Find $r_l \circ r_m(E)$.

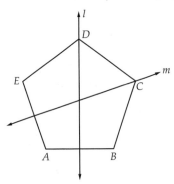

SOLUTION

First, determine which transformation to perform first.

$$r_l \circ r_m(E) \rightarrow r_l(r_m(E))$$

Imagine folding the paper on line m to see that $r_m(E) = A$.
Now, imagine folding the paper on line l to see that $r_l(A) = B$.
Thus, $r_l \circ r_m(E) = B$.

2. In the figure below, line n is a line of symmetry in square $MATH$. Find $R_{90°} \circ r_n(A)$.

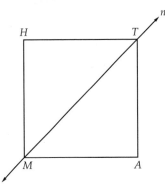

SOLUTION

First, determine which transformation to perform first.

$$R_{90°} \circ r_n(A) \rightarrow R_{90°}(r_n(A))$$

Imagine folding the paper on line n to see that $r_n(A) = H$. Now, turn your paper 90° in a counter-clockwise direction. Point H is now in the bottom left-hand corner of the figure. Remember that position. Turn your paper right side up to see that M is now in the bottom left-hand corner. Thus, $R_{90°}(H) = M$.

Putting this together, we get $R_{90°} \circ r_n(A) = M$.

3. Given triangle *TRY*, with coordinates $T(-2, 3)$, $R(3, 6)$, and $Y(1, -1)$.
  a. Find the coordinates of $\triangle T'R'Y'$, the image of $\triangle TRY$ after $R_{90°}$.
  b. Find the coordinates of $\triangle T''R''Y''$, the image of $\triangle T'R'Y'$ after $r_{x\text{-axis}}$.
  c. What kind of isometry is $R_{90°}$?
  d. What kind of isometry is $r_{x\text{-axis}}$?
  e. What kind of isometry is $r_{x\text{-axis}} \circ R_{90°}$?

SOLUTION

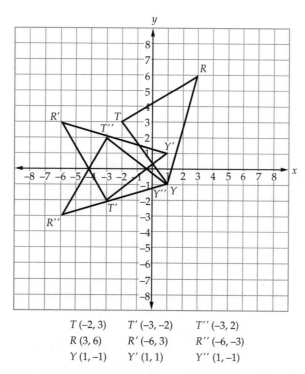

$T(-2, 3)$	$T'(-3, -2)$	$T''(-3, 2)$
$R(3, 6)$	$R'(-6, 3)$	$R''(-6, -3)$
$Y(1, -1)$	$Y'(1, 1)$	$Y''(1, -1)$

a. As shown in the figure, the coordinates are $T'(-3, -2)$, $R'(-6, 3)$, and $Y'(1, 1)$.
b. The coordinates are $T''(-3, 2)$, $R''(-6, -3)$, and $Y''(1, -1)$.
c. Since the orientation of the points is the same, $R_{90°}$ is a direct isometry.
d. Since the orientation of the points is different, $r_{x\text{-axis}}$ is an opposite isometry.
e. The composition produces an opposite isometry.

Note: The composition of a direct isometry and an opposite isometry is always an opposite isometry.

1. In the accompanying figure, lines p and q are symmetry lines for regular hexagon HEXAGN. Find $r_q \circ r_p(X)$.

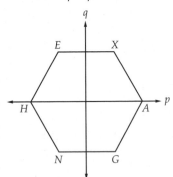

2. In the accompanying figure, lines r and s are symmetry lines for regular octagon, REOCTAGN. Find $r_s \circ r_r(O)$.

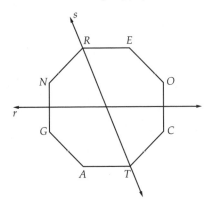

3. What single rotation is equivalent to $R_{40°} \circ R_{60°} \circ R_{-10°}$?

4. Write a composition of three rotations that will produce a rotation equivalent to $R_{100°}$.

5. Write a composition of two rotations that will produce a rotation equivalent to R_O.

6. What single transformation is equivalent to the composition of a line reflection and a translation that is parallel to the line of reflection?

7. What are the coordinates of $r_{x=4} \circ r_{y=3}(2, 5)$?

8. Given circle O, whose equation is $x^2 + y^2 = 25$. Find the center of circle O', the image of circle O after the composition, $r_{x\text{-axis}} \circ T_{2,3}(O)$.

9. Given $f(x) = x^2$ and $g(x) = r_{y\text{-axis}} \circ r_{x\text{-axis}} f(x)$. Is $g(x)$ also a function? Explain.

10. Find $r_{y=x} \circ r_{y=x}(2, 7)$

In 11–21, write the numeral preceding the word or expression that best completes the statement or answers the question.

11. $R_{240°} \circ R_{-40°}$ is equivalent to which of the following?
    (1) $R_{360°}$ (3) $R_{200°}$
    (2) $R_{280°}$ (4) $R_{40°}$

12. In the accompany figure, l and m are symmetry lines. What is $r_l \circ r_m (\overline{MA})$?

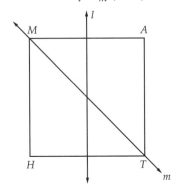

    (1) $\overline{MA}$ (3) $\overline{TH}$
    (2) $\overline{AT}$ (4) $\overline{HM}$

13. $R_O \circ R_O(x, y)$ would result in a point whose coordinates are
    (1) (x, y) (3) $(x, -y)$
    (2) $(-x, y)$ (4) (y, x)

14. Which composition would produce an image triangle whose area is not equal to the area of the original triangle?
    (1) $r_{y\text{-axis}} \circ r_{x\text{-axis}}$ (3) $r_{y=-x} \circ D_3$
    (2) $T_{2,-3} \circ r_{y=x}$ (4) $R_O \circ R_O$

15. $r_{y=x} \circ r_{x\text{-axis}}$ produces a transformation that is
    (1) a direct isometry
    (2) an opposite isometry
    (3) an isometry that is both direct and opposite
    (4) not an isometry

16. $D_2 \circ D_{\frac{1}{2}}(x, y) =$
    (1) $(2x, 2y)$
    (2) (x, y)
    (3) $\left(\frac{1}{2}x, \frac{1}{2}y\right)$
    (4) $\left(\frac{1}{4}x, \frac{1}{4}y\right)$

17. What is $r_{y=2} \circ r_{x\text{-axis}}(-3, 4)$?
    (1) $(-3, 0)$ (3) $(-3, 4)$
    (2) $(-3, 2)$ (4) $(-3, 8)$

18. Given square $ABCD$. What is $R_{90°} \circ R_{180°}(A)$?
    (1) A (3) C
    (2) B (4) D

19. Which of the following is equivalent to $T_{2,4} \circ T_{2,-4}$?
    (1) $T_{4,8}$ (3) $T_{4,0}$
    (2) $T_{4,-16}$ (4) $T_{0,-8}$

20. $r_{y=x} \circ r_{y=x}(x, y) =$
    (1) (x, y) (3) $(x, -y)$
    (2) $(-x, y)$ (4) (y, x)

21. Which property is not preserved under a glide reflection?
    (1) distance   (3) orientation
    (2) angle measure   (4) parallelism

22. Triangle CMP has vertices $C(1, 2)$, $M(5, 7)$, and $P(8, 4)$.
    a. On a coordinate plane, draw and label triangle CMP.

b. On the same set of axes, draw and label two images leading to $R_O \circ r_{y=x}(\triangle CMP)$. Label the first image $\triangle C'M'P'$, and the second image $\triangle C''M''P''$.

c. Find the coordinates of $\triangle C''M''P''$, the image of $\triangle CMP$ after $R_O \circ r_{y=x}(\triangle CMP)$.

d. What single transformation would produce the same result as $R_O \circ r_{y=x}(\triangle CMP)$?

23. a. On a coordinate plane, graph and label triangle XYZ whose coordinates are $X(-5, 3)$, $Y(2, 6)$, and $Z(7, 1)$.

b. Graph and label triangle $X'Y'Z'$, the image of triangle XYZ after $r_{y\text{-axis}}$.

c. Graph and label triangle $X''Y''Z''$, the image of triangle $X'Y'Z'$ after $r_{y=x}$.

d. The composition $r_{y=x} \circ r_{y\text{-axis}}(\triangle XYZ) = \triangle X''Y''Z''$ is a
    (1) rotation   (3) translation
    (2) dilation   (4) glide reflection

24. a. Find $r_{y=x} \circ r_{y=x}(P)$ for any point P.
    b. What concept did we study in functions that produces the same result?
    c. What does that tell us about $r_{y=x}$?

CHAPTER REVIEW

In 1–17, write the numeral preceding the word or expression that best completes the statement or answers the question.

1. If the coordinates of Q are $(-2, 5)$ what are the coordinates of $(r_{y\text{-axis}} \circ R_{90°})(Q)$?
    (1) $(-2, -5)$ (3) $(5, -2)$
    (2) $(-5, 2)$ (4) $(2, -5)$

2. Which of the following is not an isometry?
    (1) $(x, y) \rightarrow (-y, x)$
    (2) $(x, y) \rightarrow (-4 + x, y + 3)$
    (3) $(x, y) \rightarrow (x, 2y)$
    (4) $(x, y) \rightarrow (-x, y)$

3. If line a is parallel to line b, then $r_a \circ r_b(\triangle CTH)$ is equivalent to a
    (1) translation
    (2) rotation
    (3) dilation
    (4) reflection in $y = x$

4. The transformation that moves every point in the plane under the rule $(x, y) \rightarrow (y, -x)$ is a
    (1) rotation
    (2) reflection in the x-axis
    (3) dilation
    (4) point reflection

5. Using the diagram of a regular polygon below, find $R_{-120°} \circ R_{180°} \circ R_{240°}(B)$.

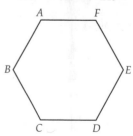

    (1) A (3) E
    (2) B (4) F

6. In this figure, p, m, and n are lines of symmetry. Find $r_p \circ r_n \circ r_m(D)$.

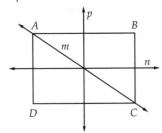

(1) A (3) C
(2) B (4) D

7. If point $M(-5, 8)$ is reflected in the line $y = 2$, what are the coordinates of M'?
(1) $(-5, 10)$ (3) $(9, -4)$
(2) $(-5, -4)$ (4) $(-3, 10)$

8. A transformation maps $(1, 3)$ onto $(-3, -1)$. This transformation is equivalent to a
(1) rotation of $90°$
(2) reflection in the origin
(3) reflection in the line $y = -x$
(4) translation of $-3, -1$

9. By which transformation can the inverse of a function be found?
(1) a reflection in the line $y = x$
(2) a reflection in the line $y = -x$
(3) a rotation of $90°$ counterclockwise
(4) a reflection in the origin

10. Which of these transformations would alter the perimeter of a triangle?
(1) $(x, y) \rightarrow (x + 2, y - 3)$
(2) $(x, y) \rightarrow (4x, 2y)$
(3) $(x, y) \rightarrow (x, -y)$
(4) $(x, y) \rightarrow (y, -x)$

11. If the point $(0, -4)$ is rotated $90°$ *clockwise* about the origin, its image is on the line
(1) $y = x$ (3) $x = 0$
(2) $y = -x$ (4) $y = 0$

12. Which of the following compositions is a direct isometry?
(1) $R_{90°} \circ r_{x\text{-axis}}$ (3) $r_{x=1} \circ r_{y\text{-axis}}$
(2) $r_{y=x} \circ T_{-3,4}$ (4) $D_2 \circ r_{y=x}$

13. If the dilation D_k of point $A(4, -8)$ is $A'(-2, 4)$, the dilation factor k equals
(1) $-\dfrac{1}{2}$ (3) 2

(2) $\dfrac{1}{2}$ (4) 4

14. If a parabola $y = ax^2 + bx + c$ is reflected in the x-axis, its new equation could be written as
(1) $ax^2 - bx - c = y$
(2) $-ax^2 + bx + c = y$
(3) $-ax^2 - bx - c = y$
(4) $ax^2 + bx - c = y$

15. Look at the accompanying figure.

If the figure is rotated $90°$ counterclockwise and then reflected in the y-axis, its image would be which of the following?

(1)   (2)   (3)   (4)

16. Use the diagram provided to evaluate $(r_c \circ r_d)(K)$.

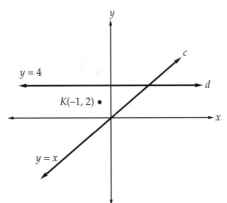

(1) $(1, 2)$ (3) $(6, -1)$
(2) $(2, 9)$ (4) $(-1, 6)$

17. If $F(x, y) = (x + 3, y - 2)$ and $G(x, y) = (2x, -y)$, what is the rule of the composition of $(F \circ G)(x, y)$?
(1) $(2x + 6, -y + 2)$
(2) $(2x + 3, -y - 2)$
(3) $(2x + 6, -y - 2)$
(4) $(2x + 3, -2y + 2)$

18. a. Draw and label the graph of the equation $xy = 8$ in the interval $-8 \le x \le 8$.
    b. On the same axes, draw and label the graph of the image of $xy = 8$ after a rotation of $90°$ counterclockwise.
    c. Write the equation of the graph drawn in part b.

d. On the same axes, draw and label the graph of the image of $xy = 8$ after a dilation of -2.

e. Write the equation of the graph drawn in part **d**.

19. Triangle CTH has coordinates $C(-3, 4)$, $T(1, 9)$, and $H(-3, 10)$.

   a. Graph and state the coordinates of $\triangle C'T'H'$, the image of $\triangle CTH$ under the composition $R_{90°} \circ r_{x\text{-axis}}$.

   b. State the single transformation equivalent to $R_{90°} \circ r_{x\text{-axis}}$.

   c. Graph and state the coordinates of $\triangle C''T''H''$, the image of $\triangle C'T'H'$ after $D_2 \circ T_{-5,-2}$.

20. a. Sketch the graph of $f(x) = 2x^2 - 8$ in the interval $-4 \le x \le 4$.

   b. Graph $f'(x)$, the image of $f(x)$ after $r_{y=x}$, and write its equation.

   c. Graph $f''(x)$, the image of $f'(x)$ after D_2.

21. a. Sketch the graph of $\dfrac{(x-3)^2}{81} + \dfrac{(y+2)^2}{144} = 1$.

   b. Reflect the given graph in the x-axis and write its new equation.

   c. Translate the given graph by $T_{-4,6}$ and state the new equation.

22. Mrs. Magnificent's art class is going to do a mural on the cafeteria wall. The original painting they are copying is 18 inches by 24 inches, and they plan to enlarge the painting by a factor of 8.

   a. What is the area of the original painting in square feet?

   b. What is the area of the mural in square feet?

   c. If the principal wants an undecorated border of at least 2 feet around the mural on the cafeteria wall, how should the mural be placed on a wall that is 20 feet by 24 feet?

You can use your graphing calculator to illustrate some line reflections of functions. Consider the function $f(x) = (x + 5)^2 - 3$. Enter this function as Y_1. This is a parabola whose graph is shown below. The window shown is a standard viewing window, $[-10, 10] \times [-10, 10]$, which can be obtained by pressing (ZOOM) (6).

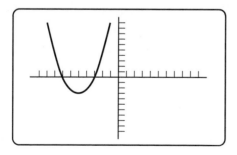

Notice the vertex is $(-5, -3)$.

Let us show the image of $f(x)$ after $r_{y\text{-axis}}$, a reflection in the y-axis. When you reflect a function in the y-axis, you negate the x-values. Go to your (Y =) screen and enter into Y_2, $Y_2 = Y_1(-X)$. Use the following keystrokes to enter the equations.

Press (VARS) and select Y-VARS as shown.

```
VARS  Y-VARS
1: Function...
2: Parametric...
3: Polar...
4: On/Off...
```

Press (ENTER) to get

```
FUNCTION
1: Y₁
2: Y₂
3: Y₃
4: Y₄
5: Y₅
6: Y₆
7↓Y₇
```

Again, press (ENTER) to get

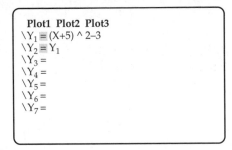

We want to graph $Y_1(-X)$, so enter the information shown.

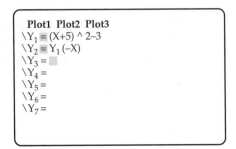

To obtain the graph of the reflection shown below, press (ZOOM) (6).

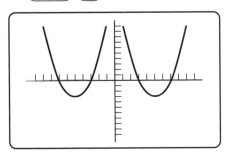

To reflect $f(x)$ in the x-axis, we negate the y-values. Go to the (Y =) screen and enter into Y_2, $Y_2 = -Y_1(X)$ as shown.

Plot1 Plot2 Plot3
\Y_1 = (X+5) ^ 2–3
\Y_2 = –Y_1 (X)
\Y_3 = ■
\Y_4 =
\Y_5 =
\Y_6 =
\Y_7 =

When you graph the two functions, you obtain the graph shown below.

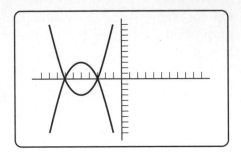

To reflect figure in the line $y = x$, we use the Draw capability of the calculator, as explained in section 6.7. To illustrate the reflection of the original equation in the line $y = x$, go back to your (Y =) menu, and enter $y = x$ as the equation for Y_2. From the Draw menu, select DrawInv (8). We want DrawInv Y_1, so follow the procedure above for entering Y_1 and press (ENTER). You should get the screen shown below.

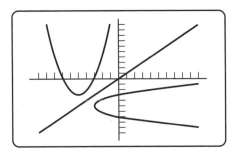

Since we are in a standard viewing window, the spacing for the x- and y-coordinates is not the same, so our graph is a bit distorted. You can enter (ZOOM) (5) for a graph that is more in proportion, as shown below.

Note: You have to redraw the image.

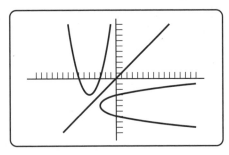

Practice

Go back to some of the examples and exercises in Sections 8.1 through 8.4 and try to graph line reflections using your calculator.

CHAPTER 9
Exponential Functions

9.1 Review of Exponents and Scientific Notation

Exponents

In a term such as x^4, x is the **base** and 4 is the **exponent** that tells how many times the base is used as a factor. An exponent is a short-cut way of writing multiplication. For example, instead of writing $x \cdot x \cdot x \cdot x$, we can write x^4. Therefore, if we multiply $x^4 \cdot x^3$, it is the same as multiplying $x \cdot x \cdot x \cdot x \cdot x \cdot x \cdot x = xxxxxxx = x^7$. It is much more convenient to remember the rule for multiplication: keep the base the same, and add the exponents.

When we divide $x^4 \div x^3$, we can rewrite this expression as $\frac{x \cdot x \cdot x \cdot x}{x \cdot x \cdot x}$ and "cancel." $\frac{x \cdot x \cdot x \cdot x}{x \cdot x \cdot x} = \frac{\cancel{x} \cdot \cancel{x} \cdot \cancel{x} \cdot x}{\cancel{x} \cdot \cancel{x} \cdot \cancel{x}} = x = x^{4-3}$. We can remember the rule for division: keep the base the same and subtract the exponents.

To raise x^3 to the second power, we have $(x^3)^2$. We can rewrite this and follow our rules for multiplication: $(x^3)^2 = (x^3)(x^3) = x^6$. However, it is easier to remember that we keep the bases the same and multiply the exponents.

Make sure that you know these rules.

$$x^a \cdot x^b = x^{a+b} \qquad \text{Multiplication Rule}$$
$$x^a \div x^b = x^{a-b} \qquad \text{Division Rule}$$
$$(x^a)^b = x^{ab} \qquad \text{Power Rule}$$

These rules can be used to verify two other rules.

$$(xy)^a = x^a y^a \qquad \text{Power of a Product Rule}$$
$$\left(\frac{x}{y}\right)^a = \frac{x^a}{y^a} \qquad \text{Power of a Quotient Rule}$$

We can apply our division rule to the following problem: $x^a \div x^a = x^{a-a} = x^0$. We know that if we divide any nonzero number by itself, we always get 1. Therefore $x^a \div x^a = 1$. Since $x^a \div x^a = x^0$ and $x^a \div x^a = 1$, we can conclude that $x^0 = 1$.

Note: Any nonzero number raised to the zero power is 1.

Negative Exponents

We know that $x^4 \div x^3 = x$. What happens if we have $x^3 \div x^4$? $x^3 \div x^4 = x^{3-4} = x^{-1}$.

We also know that $x^3 \div x^4 = \frac{x \cdot x \cdot x}{x \cdot x \cdot x \cdot x} = \frac{1}{x}$. Therefore, we can conclude that $x^{-1} = \frac{1}{x}$. Similarly, $x^{-2} = \frac{1}{x^2}$ and $\frac{1}{x^{-1}} = \frac{1}{\frac{1}{x}} = \frac{1}{1} \cdot \frac{x}{1} = x$. A negative exponent means to "flip": $x^{-1} = \frac{1}{x}$ and $\frac{1}{x^{-1}} = x$ ($x \neq 0$). The rules for operations with positive exponents can also be applied to negative exponents.

 MODEL PROBLEM

Simplify each expression.

a. $3a^2b^3c^4 \cdot 5ab^2c^6$

b. $\dfrac{35x^4y^5z^{10}}{7xy^7z^{10}}$

c. $\left(\dfrac{1}{2}\right)^{-2} \cdot 3^0 \cdot 4^{-3}$

d. $-2^{-4} \cdot (-2)^{-4}$

SOLUTION

a. $3a^2b^3c^4 \cdot 5ab^2c^6$
We multiply the 3 by 5, leave the bases the same for a, b, and c, and add the exponents.
$3a^2b^3c^4 \cdot 5ab^2c^6 = 3 \cdot 5a^{2+1}b^{3+2}c^{4+6} = 15a^3b^5c^{10}$.

b. $\dfrac{35x^4y^5z^{10}}{7xy^7z^{10}}$
We divide the 35 by 7, leave the bases the same for x, y, and z, and subtract the exponents.
$\dfrac{35x^4y^5z^{10}}{7xy^7z^{10}} = 5x^{4-1}y^{5-7}z^{10-10} = 5x^3y^{-2}z^0 = 5x^3y^{-2}$.

Remember: $z^0 = 1$.

c. $\left(\dfrac{1}{2}\right)^{-2} \cdot 3^0 \cdot 4^{-3}$

Remember: A negative exponent means to "flip," and any number (except 0) to the 0 power is 1.

So we can rewrite the expression as follows:

$$\left(\frac{1}{2}\right)^{-2} \cdot 3^0 \cdot 4^{-3} = \left(\frac{2}{1}\right)^2 \cdot 1 \cdot \frac{1}{4^3}$$

$$= \frac{4}{1} \cdot \frac{1}{\underset{16}{64}}$$

$$= \frac{1}{16}$$

d. $-2^{-4} \cdot (-2)^{-4}$

Notice the difference between the two numbers in the expression, and remember your order of operations. When we see -2^{-4}, we follow the order of operations, which tells us to raise the 2 to the -4 power, and then negate the answer.

$(-2)^{-4}$ tells us to take the number -2 and raise it to the -4 power.

Thus, $-2^{-4} \cdot (-2)^{-4} = -\dfrac{1}{2^4} \cdot \dfrac{1}{(-2)^4}$

$$= -\dfrac{1}{16} \cdot \dfrac{1}{16}$$

$$= -\dfrac{1}{256}$$

Fractional Exponents

How can we rewrite $\sqrt{x}$ as x to some power?
We know that $\sqrt{x} \cdot \sqrt{x} = x$. Thus, $x^{\text{power}} \cdot x^{\text{power}} = x^1$.
When we multiply, we add the exponents.

$$x^{\text{power}} \cdot x^{\text{power}} = x^1$$
$$x^{\text{power} + \text{power}} = x^1$$
$$x^{2 \cdot \text{power}} = x^1$$
$$2 \cdot \text{power} = 1$$
$$\text{power} = \frac{1}{2}$$

Thus, $\sqrt{x} = x^{\frac{1}{2}}$

Note: Fractional powers are roots.

$$x^{\frac{1}{2}} = \sqrt{x} \qquad x^{\frac{1}{3}} = \sqrt[3]{x} \qquad x^{\frac{1}{4}} = \sqrt[4]{x}$$

 **MODEL PROBLEM**

Simplify each expression.

a. $16^{\frac{3}{4}}$

b. $16^{-\frac{3}{4}}$

c. $-8^{\frac{2}{3}}$

d. $(-8)^{\frac{2}{3}}$

e. $(-8)^{-\frac{2}{3}}$

SOLUTION

a. $16^{\frac{3}{4}}$

We find the 4th root of 16 and then raise it to the 3rd power. (Alternatively, you could raise 16 to the 3rd power and then find the 4th root of that number, but it is usually easier to find the root first.)

$$16^{\frac{3}{4}} = \left(\sqrt[4]{16} \right)^3 = 2^3 = 8$$

b. $16^{-\frac{3}{4}}$

This is the same question as above except the exponent is negative. We need to find the reciprocal of our answer to part **a.**

Thus, $16^{-\frac{3}{4}} = \frac{1}{8}$.

c. $-8^{\frac{2}{3}}$

We must find the cube root of 8, raise that to the 2nd power, and then negate our answer.

$$-8^{\frac{2}{3}} = -\left(\sqrt[3]{8}\right)^2$$
$$= -2^2$$
$$= -4$$

d. $(-8)^{\frac{2}{3}}$

This time we are finding the cube root of -8, and raising that to the 2nd power.

$$(-8)^{\frac{2}{3}} = \left(\sqrt[3]{-8}\right)^2$$
$$= (-2)^2$$
$$= 4$$

e. $(-8)^{-\frac{2}{3}}$

This is the same question as part **d** except the exponent is negative. We need to find the reciprocal of our previous answer.

$$(-8)^{-\frac{2}{3}} = \frac{1}{4}$$

Scientific Notation

Scientific notation is useful for working with very large or very small numbers. For example, the mass of the earth is about 5,980,000,000,000,000,000,000,000 kilograms. In order to calculate this, scientists used Newton's law of universal gravitation that says that the force between the earth and another object is directly proportional to the product of the masses of the particles and inversely proportional to the square of the distances between them. In symbols, $F = G\,\dfrac{m_1 \cdot m_2}{r_2}$, where m_1 and m_2 are the masses of the two objects, r is the distance separating the two objects, and G is the constant 0.0000000000667259.

When we read the very large and the very small numbers in the preceding paragraph, we must stop to calculate what they represent. It would be much easier if we represented these numbers in scientific notation. A number written in **scientific notation** contains a number between 1 and 10 multiplied by a power of 10. For example, 3.42×10^5 and 7.16×10^{-2} are written in scientific notation.

$3.42 \times 10^5 = 3.42 \times 100{,}000 = 342{,}000$ (Move the decimal point 5 places to the right.)

$7.16 \times 10^{-2} = 7.16 \times \dfrac{1}{100} = 7.16 \times 0.01 = 0.0716$ (Move the decimal point 2 places to the left.)

To convert a number to scientific notation, rewrite the number with a single digit in front of the decimal point. Count the number of places you moved the decimal point to obtain this number. That is the power of 10 you will multiply by.

For example, we said that the mass of the earth is about 5,980,000,000,000,000, 000,000,000 kilograms. To convert this huge number to scientific notation, we move the decimal point to between the 5 and the 9. Since the decimal point was originally at the end of the number, this would move the decimal point 24 places to the left. Thus $5,980,000,000,000,000,000,000,000 = 5.98 \times 10^{24}$.

We follow the same procedure when we have very small numbers. The constant 0.0000000000667259 mentioned above can also be written in scientific notation. Move the decimal point to between the two 6s. This would move the decimal point 11 places to the right. Since we have a number less than 1, our exponent must be negative. Thus $0.0000000000667259 = 6.67259 \times 10^{-11}$.

 MODEL PROBLEM

Complete each calculation and express the result in scientific notation and ordinary decimal notation.

a. $(4.5 \times 10^3)(5.32 \times 10^4)$

b. $\dfrac{2.716 \times 10^6}{6.79 \times 10^2}$

SOLUTION

a. $(4.5 \times 10^3)(5.32 \times 10^4)$

Multiply 4.5 by 5.32 and 10^3 by 10^4.

Remember: When we multiply numbers with exponents, we leave the base the same and add the exponents.

$$(4.5 \times 10^3)(5.32 \times 10^4) = 23.94 \times 10^7$$

Now, we need to write 23.94×10^7 in scientific notation. Move the decimal point one place to the left: $23.94 = 2.394 \times 10$. Thus, $23.94 \times 10^7 = (2.394 \times 10) \times 10^7 = 2.394 \times 10^8$.

To convert 2.394×10^8 to decimal notation, we move the decimal point 8 places to the right: $2.394 \times 10^8 = 239,400,000.$

b. $\dfrac{2.716 \times 10^6}{6.79 \times 10^2}$

Divide 2.716 by 6.79 and 10^6 by 10^2.

Remember: When we divide numbers with exponents, we leave the base the same and subtract the exponents.

$$\frac{2.716 \times 10^6}{6.79 \times 10^2} = 0.4 \times 10^4$$

We need to write 0.4×10^4 in scientific notation. Move the decimal point one place to the right: $0.4 = 4 \times 10^{-1}$. Thus, $0.4 \times 10^4 = 4 \times 10^{-1} \times 10^4 = 4 \times 10^3$.

To convert 4×10^3 to decimal notation, we move the decimal point 3 places to the right. $4 \times 10^3 = 4,000$

In 1–15, simplify each expression.

1. $5x^0$

2. $(5x)^0$

3. $(3a^2b^4c)(2.5a^{-4}bc)$

4. $3^{-2} \cdot -2^3$

5. $32^{\frac{3}{5}}$

6. $\dfrac{16r^3s^{10}t^{-2}}{24r^3s^{-3}t^2}$

7. $-3y^0$

8. $(-3y)^0$

9. $(-2)^{-2}$

10. -2^{-2}

11. $(5c^{-3}d^{-6}e^2)(2c^{-4}d^{-2}e^{-2})$

12. $-81^{-\frac{3}{4}}$

13. $(-81)^{-\frac{3}{4}}$

14. $\dfrac{2.25s^{-4}r^5}{0.5s^{-4}r^{-2}}$

15. $(-0.35x^4y^{-4}z^8)(0.2xy^4z^{-6})$

16. If $f(x) = 18x^{-3}$, find $f(3)$.

17. Evaluate $g(4)$ if $g(x) = 12x^0$.

18. If $h(x) = 16x^{-\frac{2}{5}}$, find $h(32)$.

19. Write 67,200,000,000,000 in scientific notation.

20. Write 0.00000000048 in scientific notation.

In 21–30, select the numeral preceding the expression that best completes the sentence or answers the question.

21. Write 234,000,000,000 in scientific notation.
    (1) 23.4×10^{11} (3) 2.34×10^{10}
    (2) 2.34×10^{11} (4) 0.234×10^{10}

22. If $f(x) = 4^x$, then $f(-2)$ equals
    (1) -16 (3) $\dfrac{1}{16}$
    (2) -8 (4) $\dfrac{1}{8}$

23. For what value of x is the expression $(x + 1)^{-2}$ undefined?
    (1) 1
    (2) 0
    (3) -1
    (4) It's never undefined.

24. If $f(x) = x^{\frac{2}{3}}$ and $g(x) = x^{\frac{1}{2}}$, what is $(f \circ g)(64)$?
    (1) 8   (3) 2
    (2) 4   (4) -2

25. Write 0.000394 in scientific notation.
    (1) -3.94×10^3 (3) 3.94×10^{-3}
    (2) 3.94×10^{-4} (4) 394×10^4

26. If $h(x) = x^0 + x^{\frac{2}{3}} + x^{-\frac{2}{3}}$, evaluate $h(27)$.
    (1) 1   (3) $9\dfrac{8}{9}$
    (2) 9   (4) $10\dfrac{1}{9}$

27. What is the product of 4^2 and 4^4?
    (1) 16^8 (3) 4^8
    (2) 16^6 (4) 4^6

28. Expressed in $a + bi$ form, $(2 + 3i)^{-1}$ is equivalent to
    (1) $\dfrac{2}{13} - \dfrac{3}{13}i$ (3) $-\dfrac{2}{5} - \dfrac{3}{5}i$
    (2) $-\dfrac{2}{5} + \dfrac{3}{5}i$ (4) $-2 - 3i$

29. Express the product of 2.56×10^5 and 6.498×10^{-5} in scientific notation.
    (1) 1.663488×10^{-25} (3) 3.9397×10^{-1}
    (2) 1.663488×10^{-1} (4) 1.663488×10

30. If $f(x) = (10x)^0 + x^{-2} + x^{\frac{1}{2}}$, evaluate $f(9)$.
    (1) -5 (3) $3\dfrac{1}{81}$
    (2) -3.5 (4) $4\dfrac{1}{81}$

31. According to *Forbes* magazine, the two richest people in the world for the year 2001 were Bill Gates, worth $58.7 billion, and Warren Buffett, worth $32.3 billion. What is the difference in the net worth of the two men? Express your answer in scientific notation.

32. According to the United States Treasury, the national debt as of July 23, 2001, was $5,721,846,564,456.14. Express this number in words, and in scientific notation.

9.2 Exponential Functions

If you won a contest and were given the choice of the following prizes, which one would you choose?

1. $1,000 if you collected the money on day 1, $2,000 if you waited until day 2 to collect your money, $3,000 if you waited until day 3 to collect your money, $4,000 if you waited until day 4 to collect your money, and so on. You could collect your money at any time, or wait until the end of 20 days and collect the money at that time.

2. $1 if you collected the money on day 1, $2 if you waited until day 2 to collect your money, $4 if you waited until day 3 to collect your money, $8 if you waited until day 4 to collect your money, and so on. You could collect your money at any time, or wait until the end of 20 days and collect the money at that time.

At first glance, it appears that the first choice is a much better offer. If you collected your money on day 5, you would receive $5,000 from the first option, while only receiving $16 from the second one. However, how much would you collect from each offer if you waited 20 days?

Option 1 pays $1,000 times the number of days you wait to collect the money. For example, the money paid on day 3 is $1,000(3) = $3,000. So, if you left your money for 20 days, it would pay $1,000(20) or $20,000.

The numbers in Option 2 are all powers of 2. For example, if you collected your money on day 1, you would receive $$2^0 = $1$$. The money paid on day 2 is $$2^1$$, the money paid on the day 3 is $$2^2$$, and the money paid on the day 4 is $$2^3$$. So, the money paid on day 20 would be $$2^{19}$$. Enter this number in your calculator. Are you surprised by the result?

If you chose the second option and waited 20 days to collect your money, you would receive $$2^{19}$$ or $524,288. This is certainly quite amazing!

Let us look at the equations for the two options.

Option 1: $1,000(number of days)

If we let x represent the number of days, the equation for this option would be $y = 1,000x$.

Option 2: $2^{\text{number of days}-1}$

If we let x represent the number of days, the equation for this option would be $y = 2^{x-1}$.

We can make a table of values for each of the equations.

x	1	2	3	4	5	6	7	8	9	10
$1{,}000x$	1,000	2,000	3,000	4,000	5,000	6,000	7,000	8,000	9,000	10,000
2^{x-1}	1	2	4	8	16	32	64	128	256	512

Notice that, although Option 1 still pays more money, Option 2 seems to be "catching up." We could continue our table to see when Option 2 would pay more money than Option 1.

x	11	12	13	14	15	16	17	18	19	20
$1{,}000x$	11,000	12,000	13,000	14,000	15,000	16,000	17,000	18,000	19,000	20,000
2^{x-1}	1,024	2,048	4,096	8,192	16,384	32,768	65,536	131,072	262,144	524,288

How do we know that Option 1 will not again become a better choice? Let's graph the two equations to see. Enter the functions as follows, being sure to put the $x - 1$ into parentheses.

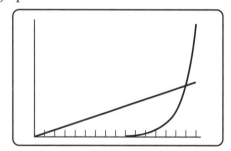

Be aware that our equations are valid only for integer values of x from 1 to 20. We could enter the values as *discrete data*, that is, just the 20 points. However, it is easier for us to enter the two equations and just focus on the values we need. Let's look at the first 16 days. So, set your window to [0, 16] and press (ZOOM) (0). This will adjust the y-values to correspond with values of x from 0 to 16. You should obtain the following graph.

The first equation is a linear function. The dollar amounts increase at a constant rate of \$1,000 per day. The second equation is an exponential function. Although each day's prize money doubles the previous day's money, the dollar amount of the increase is constantly increasing. The linear function will never "catch up" to the exponential function.

Let us now focus on the concept of exponential functions in general. An **exponential function** has the form $y = b^x$ where $b > 0$, $b \neq 1$, and x is a variable. $y = 2^x$, $y = 2^{x-1}$, $y = 3^x$, and $y = 3^{x+1}$ are examples of exponential functions. If $b > 1$, then as the x-values increase, the y-values also increase. What happens as the x-values decrease? Look at the function $y = 3^x$, and its table of values.

x	-3	-2	-1	0	1	2	3
3^x	$\frac{1}{27}$	$\frac{1}{9}$	$\frac{1}{3}$	1	3	9	27

Since 3 raised to any power is always a positive number, as the x-values become more and more negative, the y-values get smaller and smaller, but remain positive, never actually reaching 0. Since $y = 3^x$ is defined for all real values of x, our domain is the set of real numbers; our range is the set of positive real numbers, that is, $\{y \mid y > 0\}$. We can view the graph in the window $[-3, 3] \times [0, 30]$.

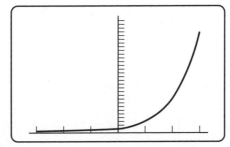

The curve is very similar to the graph of $y = 2^{x-1}$.

Next, consider the function $y = \left(\frac{1}{2}\right)^x$. In this case, the value of the base is positive but less than 1. A table of values will help us to determine what we expect to see in the graph.

x	-3	-2	-1	0	1	2	3
$\left(\frac{1}{2}\right)^x$	8	4	2	1	$\frac{1}{2}$	$\frac{1}{4}$	$\frac{1}{8}$

The pattern is the opposite of the two previous exponential functions we studied. In this case, as the x-values increase the y-values decrease, and as the x-values decrease the y-values increase. The domain and range remain the same. The domain is the set of real numbers; the range is the set of positive real numbers, that is, $\{y \mid y > 0\}$.

Examine the graph of this exponential function.

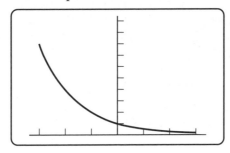

The graph of $y = \left(\frac{1}{2}\right)^x$ is the reflection in the y-axis of $y = 2^x$. The line $y = 0$ (the x-axis) is a horizontal asymptote for both functions. Each graph intersects the y-axis at the point $(0, 1)$. Recall that when we reflect in the y-axis, we negate the x-values. Therefore, for each point (x, y) on the graph of $y = 2^x$, there is a corresponding point $(-x, y)$ on the graph of $y = 2^{-x} = \dfrac{1}{2^x} = \left(\dfrac{1}{2}\right)^x$. We can say that the graph is **asymptotic** to the x-axis, or that the x-axis (whose equation is $y = 0$) is an **asymptote.**

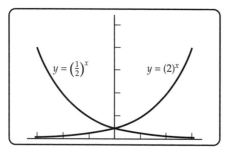

MODEL PROBLEMS

1. **a.** On a coordinate plane, sketch the graph of $f(x) = 2^x$ in the interval $-3 \le x \le 3$.
   b Evaluate $f(2)$.
   c. Evaluate $f(2.5)$, to the nearest thousandth.
   d. Solve for x: $f(x) = 2$.
   e. Solve for x: $f(x) = 2.5$, to the nearest thousandth.

SOLUTION

a.

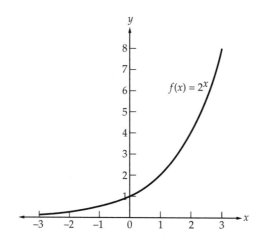

b. We can substitute 2 for the value of x in the function $f(x) = 2^x$ and obtain $f(2) = 2^2 = 4$.
c. We can substitute 2.5 for the value of x in the function $f(x) = 2^x$ and obtain $f(2.5) = 2^{2.5}$. We need the calculator to evaluate this. $f(2.5) = 2^{2.5} = 5.657$.

Note: We could also utilize the tracing feature of the calculator. Press (TRACE) and enter 2.5 as the value of x.

d. $f(x) = 2$ is asking us to find a value of x such that $2^x = 2$. We know that $2^1 = 2$. Therefore, $x = 1$.
e. $f(x) = 2.5$ is asking us to find a value of x such that $2^x = 2.5$. We know that $2^1 = 2$ and $2^2 = 4$. Therefore our answer is between 1 and 2. We must use a calculator to solve this equation.

   Since we are being asked to find an x-value that will produce a y-value of 2.5, graph $y = 2^x$ and also $y = 2.5$. Find the intersection of the two graphs. (After both equations are graphed, press (2nd) CALC (5) (intersect).) We see that $x = 1.322$.

We can generalize what we have noticed through our exploration of exponential functions.

The equation $y = b^x$, where $b > 0$ and $b \neq 1$, is an exponential function.
Domain: $\{x \mid x \in \mathbb{R}\}$
Range: $\{y \mid y > 0\}$
If $b > 1$, as the x-values increase, the y-values increase.
If $0 < b < 1$, as the x-values increase, the y-values decrease.

The function $y = b^x$ is a one-to-one function, which is asymptotic to the x-axis and has a y-intercept of 1.

2. Graph $y = 2^x$, $y = 3^x$, and $y = 4^x$ on the same set of axes. Comment on their similarities and differences.

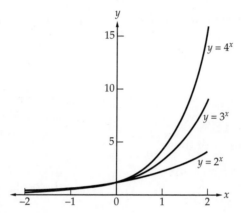

SOLUTION

Notice that the graphs are quite similar and that the domain and range for each function are the same.

Domain: $\{x \mid x \in \mathbb{R}\}$

Range: $\{y \mid y > 0\}$

For each graph, as the x-values increase, the y-values also increase. The y-intercept for each function is the same point, $(0, 1)$. When $x > 0$, the function $y = 4^x$ increases more quickly than the other two. When $x < 0$, the function $y = 4^x$ decreases more quickly.

In 1–10, write the numeral preceding the word or expression that best completes the statement or answers the question.

1. The graph of the equation $y = b^x$, where $b > 0$, lies in quadrants
   (1) I and II
   (3) III and IV
   (2) II and III
   (4) I and IV

2. If the graphs of $y = x$ and $y = 2^x$ are drawn on the same set of axes, they will intersect when x is equal to
   (1) 1
   (3) 0
   (2) 2
   (4) They will never intersect.

3. If the graphs of $y = 2x$ and $y = 2^x$ are drawn on the same set of axes, they will intersect when x is equal to
   (1) 1
   (3) 1 and 2
   (2) 2
   (4) They will never intersect.

4. Which of the equations is an exponential function?
   I. $y = x^2$ II. $y = 0.6^x$
   (1) I
   (3) I and II
   (2) II
   (4) neither of these

5. Which of the following is *not* a function?
   (1) $y = \left(\frac{1}{3}\right)^x$
   (3) $y = (x - 3)^2$
   (2) $xy = 16$
   (4) $x^2 + y^2 = 5$

6. Which of the following is *not* in the domain of $y = 2^x$?
   (1) -2
   (3) 3
   (2) 0
   (4) They are all in the domain.

7. Which of the following is *not* in the range of $y = 2^x$?
   (1) -2
   (3) 3
   (2) 1
   (4) They are all in the range.

8. If $f(x) = 5^x$, find $f(-2)$.
   (1) -25
   (3) $\frac{1}{25}$
   (2) -10
   (4) $\frac{1}{10}$

9. If $f(x) = 4^x$, what x-value would satisfy the equation $f(x) = 64$?
   (1) 16
   (3) 3
   (2) 8
   (4) 4

10. The graph of $y = \left(\frac{1}{b}\right)^x$ for $b > 0$ is a reflection of the graph of $y = b^x$ in the
    (1) x-axis
    (3) line $y = x$
    (2) y-axis
    (4) line $y = -x$

11. a. Complete the table for the y-values of the equation $y = 4^x$.

x	-2	-1	0	1	2
y					

    b. Use the completed table to graph the equation $y = 4^x$ on a coordinate plane, for the interval $-2 \le x \le 2$. Label the graph A.
    c. Reflect the graph in the y-axis. Label the graph B.
    d. Write an equation for the function whose graph is B.

12. a. On a coordinate plane, sketch the graph of $f(x) = 3^x$ in the interval $-3 \le x \le 2$.
    b. Use your calculator to find $f(-1.6)$.
    c. Use your calculator to graph the function and find the value of x that would satisfy the equation $f(x) = 1.6$.

13. a. On a coordinate plane, sketch the graph of $y = \left(\frac{1}{4}\right)^x$ in the interval $-2 \le x \le 2$.
    b. On the same set of axes, sketch the graph of $y = x + 5$.
    c. Use your calculator to graph the functions and find the value of x that would satisfy the equation $\left(\frac{1}{4}\right)^x = x + 5$.

14. a. Graph and label the function $y = 2^x$ in the interval $-3 \le x \le 3$.
    b. On the same set of axes, sketch the reflection of $y = 2^x$ in the x-axis and label the image B.
    c. Write an equation for the function whose graph is B.

15. a. Graph and label the function $y = \left(\frac{1}{2}\right)^x$ in the interval $-3 \le x \le 3$.

b. On the same set of axes, sketch the translation of $y = \left(\frac{1}{2}\right)^x$ under $T_{0, -3}$.

c. What are the x- and y-intercepts of the graph drawn in part **a**?

d. What are the x- and y-intercepts of the graph drawn in part **b**?

16. One of the graphs shown below is the graph of $y = \left(\frac{2}{3}\right)^x$, the other is the graph of $y = \left(\frac{3}{2}\right)^x$. Identify each of the graphs and explain your reasoning.

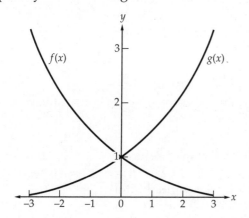

17. Graph $y = \left(\frac{1}{2}\right)^x$, $y = \left(\frac{1}{3}\right)^x$, and $y = \left(\frac{1}{4}\right)^x$.

Discuss the similarities and differences of the three graphs.

18. a. Graph $y = 3^x$.

b. On the same set of axes, sketch the transformation of the graph drawn in part **a** under $r_{x\text{-axis}}$.

c. Write an equation for the graph drawn in part **b**.

19. a. Graph $y = \left(\frac{3}{4}\right)^x$.

b. On the same set of axes, sketch the transformation of the graph drawn in part **a** under $r_{y\text{-axis}}$.

c. Write an equation for the graph drawn in part **b**.

20. a. Graph $y = 2^x$.

b. On the same set of axes, sketch the transformation of the graph drawn in part **a** under $T_{0, 3}$.

c. Write an equation for the graph drawn in part **b**.

21. Match each graph drawn below with one of the following equations.

$$y = 2^x \quad y = 2^{-x} \quad y = 3^x \quad y = 3^{-x} \quad y = -3^x$$

Explain the criteria you used to match each graph with an equation without using your calculator.

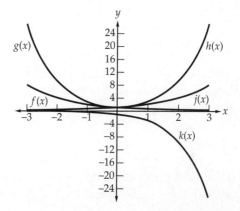

22. Given the functions $f(x) = 2^x$ and $g(x) = 4^x$. Answer the following questions without using your calculator.

a. For what value(s) of x are the two functions equal?

b. Which function has greater values when $x > 0$? Explain.

c. Which function has greater values when $x < 0$? Explain.

23. Given the functions $h(x) = 2^x$ and $j(x) = \left(\frac{1}{2}\right)^x$, answer each question without using your calculator.

a. For what value(s) of x are the two functions equal?

b. Which function has greater values when $x > 0$? Explain.

c. Which function has greater values when $x < 0$? Explain.

d. Rewrite $j(x)$ using a negative exponent.

e. What transformation would map $h(x)$ onto $j(x)$?

9.3 Real-World Applications

There are numerous applications of exponential functions in the real world. One of the most familiar examples of exponential growth is the concept of compound interest. If you invested $1 in the bank at 4% annual interest and you earned *simple interest* on your money, you would receive 4% of $1 or $0.04 each year. If you left your money in the bank for 10 years you would have gained $0.04 each year for the 10 years, giving you a total of $0.40 interest. The amount you would have in the bank would be $1.40. However, if you earned interest that was *compounded* each year, you would earn interest not only on the original $1 but also on the interest you gained each year.

In the first year, you earn 4% interest on $1. This is a 4% increase on your $1 investment, so you would receive 104% of your $1 or 1(1.04). In the second year, you receive a 4% increase on the previous year's money. So, you would have 1(1.04)(1.04) or 1.04^2. This would continue in the third year, where you would have 1(1.04)(1.04)(1.04) or 1.04^3. Thus, in 10 years, you would have 1.04^{10} or $1.48. You would receive $0.48 interest over the 10-year period if the interest were compounded annually. Of course, if you had more than $1 in the bank, this could make a significant difference in the amount of interest you received.

In general, exponential functions are in the form $f(x) = ab^x$, where $a \neq 0, b > 0$, and $b \neq 1$. In an exponential function, since $f(0) = ab^0 = a(1) = a$, a is called the *initial value* and b is called the *growth factor*. If $b > 1$, the model is increasing or growing; if $0 < b < 1$, the model is decreasing or decaying.

Note: Given an exponential function in the form $y = ab^x$, the y-intercept is $(0, a)$.

In our interest example, if you had $100 in the bank gaining 4% annual interest, compounded annually, the equation $f(x) = 100(1.04)^x$ would model the amount of money you would have in the bank after x years. To find the amount of money you would have after 10 years, substitute 10 for x. Thus, $f(10) = 100(1.04)^{10} = 148.02$. You would have $148.02 in 10 years.

 MODEL PROBLEMS

1. In the 2000–2001 school year, the average cost for one year at a four-year private college was $16,332, which was an increase of 5.2% from the previous year. If this trend were to continue, the equation $C(x) = 16{,}332(1.052)^x$ could be used to model the cost, $C(x)$, of a college education x years from 2000.

   a. Find $C(4)$.
   b. If this trend continues, how much would parents expect to pay for their newborn baby's first year of college? (Assume the child would enter college in 18 years.)
   c. If this trend continues, when will one year of a private college cost $50,000?

a. To find $C(4)$, substitute 4 for x in the formula $C(x) = 16{,}332(1.052)^x$. Thus, $C(4) = 16{,}332(1.052)^4 = 20{,}003.33$. This means that the cost would be \$20,003.33 in 2004.

b. To find the cost of a year of college 18 years from now, substitute 18 for x in the formula $C(x) = 16{,}332(1.052)^x$ to get $C(18) = 16{,}332(1.052)^{18} = 40{,}674.54$. Thus, it would cost the parents \$40,674 for their child's first year of college. Alternatively, you could obtain an answer by graphing the function and evaluating the function for $x = 18$, as shown below.

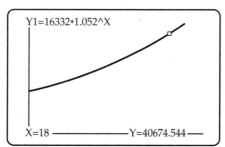

c. To find when the cost will be \$50,000, set $C(x) = 50{,}000$ and solve for x. Graph $y = 16{,}332(1.052)^x$ and also graph $y = 50{,}000$. Use the calculator to determine when the two graphs intersect, as shown below.

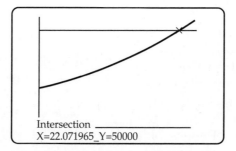

According to the graph, one year of a private college will cost \$50,000 in approximately 22 years from 2000, which will be the year 2022.

Note: We can gain quite a bit of information from reading graphs, including determining a possible equation for a function.

2. Tanisha is a talented artist who has begun her own business designing and printing custom greeting cards. The number of customers has grown steadily, as illustrated in the graph below.

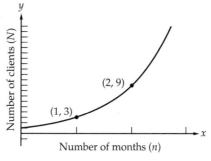

a. How many customers did Tanisha have initially?

b. Write an exponential equation for $N(t)$, the number of customers Tanisha has t months after she began her business.

c. Based on your formula from part **b**, evaluate $N(3)$. Interpret what this means in terms of the number of clients Tanisha has.

SOLUTION

a. By looking at the graph, at time 0, we see that Tanisha has 1 client.

b. We now have three points on the graph: (0, 1), (1, 3), and (2, 9). We can see that the graph is an exponential function. The second coordinate is always a power of 3. For example, $1 = 3^0$, $3 = 3^1$, and $9 = 3^2$. So, our equation is $N(t) = 3^t$.

  We can also determine the formula algebraically. First, the formula for an exponential function is $N(t) = ab^t$, where a is the initial value. Since our initial value is 1, we know that our formula is $N(t) = 1 \cdot b^t = b^t$.

  Now, we can substitute values for t and $N(t)$, giving us $3 = b^1$. Thus $b = 3$ and our equation is $N(t) = 3^t$.

c. Substitute 3 for the t in the above formula: $N(3) = 3^3 = 27$. Thus, Tanisha has 27 customers 3 months after she began her business.

Practice

In 1–5, select the numeral preceding the expression that best answers the question.

1. According to the U.S. Census Bureau, there were approximately 7 million households with access to computers in 1984. Computer usage in the United States from 1984 through 1997 grew at a rate of approximately 14% per year. Which of the following equations could be used to model the number of households (in millions) with computers, beginning in the year 1984?
   (1) $N(t) = 7(0.14)^t$ (3) $N(t) = 7.14^t$
   (2) $N(t) = 7(1.14)^t$ (4) $N(t) = 14(0.07)^t$

2. José took a piece of paper and cut it in half. He put the two pieces together and then cut them in half again. He then put the four pieces of paper together and cut them in half again. If he continued to do this over and over again, the number of pieces obtained after each cut could be represented by the graph shown.

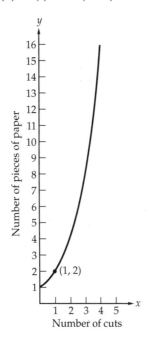

Number of pieces of paper

(1, 2)

1 2 3 4 5
Number of cuts

Which of the following equations could be used to represent the graph?
   (1) $y = 2x$ (3) $y = 2^x$
   (2) $y = 2x + 1$ (4) $y = 2^{x-1}$

3. The population of Lonely Town, NY, can be modeled by the equation $P(t) = 2,300(0.85)^t$, where $t = 0$ represents the year 2000. In what year will the population of Lonely Town be approximately half the size it was in the year 2000?
   (1) 2002   (3) 2006
   (2) 2004   (4) 2008

4. The table below represents the number of people who are living in Fun Town, NY.

Time (in years since 2000)	0	1	2	3	4
Population (in thousands)	1	3	9	27	81

Which of the following equations can be used to represent the number of people living in Fun Town, NY?
   (1) $P(t) = 3t$ (3) $P(t) = 3^t$
   (2) $P(t) = 3t^2$ (4) $P(t) = 3(3)^t$

5. Sumil has invested \$1,000 in a toy company. The value of his investment can be modeled by the function $V(t) = 1,000(0.70)^t$, where t is the time, in years, since Sumil made his investment. If the trend continues, how much will Sumil's investment be worth after 5 years?

    (1) \$3,500   (3) \$437.28
    (2) \$700   (4) \$168.07

6. Suppose you received an inheritance of \$5,000 and decided to invest it at 5% interest, compounded annually. The equation $A(x) = 5,000(1.05)^x$ can be used to model this function, where x is the number of years your money is invested and $A(x)$ represents the amount of money you have.
    a. How much will you have in 5 years?
    b. At this rate, about how long will it take for your money to double?

7. Good news! Your parents have decided to give you an allowance to help with your school expenses. You have two options. Option 1: \$1 per day. Option 2: 1¢ on day 1, 2¢ on day two, 4¢ on day 3, and so forth. Use the equation $y = x$ to model the amount earned each day by using the first option and $y = 0.01(2^x)$ to model the amount earned each day by using the second option.
    a. For how many days will the first option be a better choice?
    b. When will the two options be worth the same amount? What happens after that?

8. MacArthur High School is holding a math contest. Each week, students are given math problems to solve. At the end of the week, only the top half of participants is invited to continue with the contest. If 200 students initially enroll to participate in the contest, the equation $N(t) = 200(0.5)^t$ can be used to determine the number of students, $N(t)$, participating in the contest after t weeks. This will continue until there is only one student left, who will be declared the winner.
    a. When will there be only 25% of the original 200 students remaining?
    b. How many participants will be left after 3 weeks?

9. Given the function $F(x) = 20(0.90)^x$, where $F(x)$ is the number of fish in Jason's fish tank and x is the number of days since Jason set up the tank.
    a. How many fish did Jason have to start?
    b. What is happening to Jason's fish? Explain.

10. Match each situation to a possible graph, without using a calculator. Explain how you arrived at your conclusion.

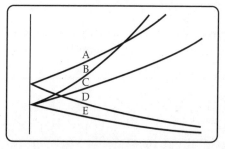

    i. Melissa deposited \$200 in the bank. She received 4% interest, compounded annually.
    ii. Tom deposited \$300 in the bank. He received 4% interest, compounded annually.
    iii. Sara deposited \$200 in the bank. She received 7% interest, compounded annually.
    iv. Jeff invested \$300 in the stock market. Unfortunately, he lost approximately 5% of his investment each year.
    v. Jennifer invested \$200 in the stock market. Unfortunately, she lost approximately 5% of her investment each year.

11. As cars get older they are worth less than when they were new. This is called *depreciation*. Assume that you bought a new 2001 car for \$13,700 and that it depreciates at approximately 20% per year. An equation that will model the value of your car, $V(t)$, where t is the number of years since 2001, is $V(t) = 13,700(0.8)^t$.
    a. Find $V(1)$. Explain what this means in terms of the value of your car.
    b. In how many years will the car be worth only half of what you paid for it?

12. Given the function $P(t) = 20(1.15)^t$, where $P(t)$ is the population, in thousands, of people in a town, t years after 1990.
    a. What was the initial population of the town?
    b. At what rate is the population growing?

13. Give an example of an exponential function that would occur in the real world. How do you know your function is exponential?

14. Carbon-14 is a radioactive isotope that scientists use to help them determine the age of various objects. It decays according the function $A(t) = A_0(0.999879)^t$, where $A(t)$ is the amount of carbon-14 present in an object. A_0 is the initial amount of carbon-14 and t is the time in years. If scientists found an object containing 30 grams of carbon-14, and they knew that the object originally contained 100 grams, how old is the object? (Give your answer to the nearest number of years.)

9.4 Equations with Fractional or Negative Exponents

Let's recall the process used in solving equations containing radicals.

 MODEL PROBLEM

Solve for x: $\sqrt{2x - 4} + 3 = 5$.

SOLUTION

$$\sqrt{2x - 4} + 3 = 5$$
$$\sqrt{2x + 4} = 2 \qquad \text{Isolate the radical.}$$
$$\left(\sqrt{2x - 4}\right)^2 = 2^2 \qquad \text{Square both sides.}$$
$$2x - 4 = 4 \qquad \text{Simplify.}$$
$$2x = 8 \qquad \text{Solve.}$$
$$x = 4$$

Check for extraneous roots.

$$\sqrt{2x - 4} + 3 = 5$$
$$\sqrt{2(4) - 4} + 3 \overset{?}{=} 5$$
$$\sqrt{4} + 3 \overset{?}{=} 5$$
$$5 = 5 \checkmark$$

We know that radicals can be written as fractional exponents. Thus, we can rewrite $\sqrt{2x - 4}$ as $(2x - 4)^{\frac{1}{2}}$ and we can rewrite the equation above as $(2x - 4)^{\frac{1}{2}} + 3 = 5$. To solve this equation, we first isolate the expression with the exponent. Then, we raise both sides of the equation to the second power and continue as we did in the Model Problem above. If the exponent had been $\frac{1}{3}$ instead of $\frac{1}{2}$, we would have raised both sides of the equation to the third power.

What do we do if we have an exponent of $\frac{3}{4}$? Look at the following example.

Solve for x: $x^{\frac{3}{4}} = 8$.

We want to eliminate the exponent to leave us with $x^1 = x$. Recall that when raising a power to a power, we multiply the exponents. What number when multiplied with $\frac{3}{4}$ will give 1? The answer is $\frac{4}{3}$, which is the reciprocal of $\frac{3}{4}$.

Let's try it.

Solve for x: $x^{\frac{3}{4}} = 8$.

$$\left(x^{\frac{3}{4}}\right)^{\frac{4}{3}} = 8^{\frac{4}{3}} \quad \text{Raise both sides to the } \frac{4}{3} \text{ power.}$$

Note: $\left(x^{\frac{3}{4}}\right)^{\frac{4}{3}} = x^{\frac{3}{4}\cdot\frac{4}{3}} = x^1 = x$

$$x = 16 \quad \text{Simplify.}$$

Check the solution in the original equation.

$$x^{\frac{3}{4}} = 8$$
$$16^{\frac{3}{4}} \overset{?}{=} 8$$
$$8 = 8 \checkmark$$

To solve equations with fractional or negative exponents

1. Isolate the expression containing the exponent.
2. Raise both sides to the reciprocal of the power.
3. Solve the resulting equation.
4. Check your answer in the original equation.

MODEL PROBLEM

Solve for y.

a. $3y^{\frac{3}{2}} = 192$

b. $(y + 3)^{\frac{5}{2}} = 32$

c. $2(3y - 4)^{\frac{3}{5}} - 4 = 50$

d. $\left(2y - \dfrac{5}{16}\right)^{-\frac{3}{4}} - 1 = 7$

e. $(y - 6)^{-\frac{1}{2}} + 5 = 3$

SOLUTION

a. $\quad 3y^{\frac{3}{2}} = 192$

$\quad\quad\quad y^{\frac{3}{2}} = 64 \quad\quad \text{Isolate the } y\text{-value.}$

$\quad\quad \left(y^{\frac{3}{2}}\right)^{\frac{2}{3}} = 64^{\frac{2}{3}} \quad\quad \text{Raise both sides to the } \frac{2}{3} \text{ power.}$

$\quad\quad\quad\quad y = 16 \quad\quad \text{Simplify.}$

Check the solution in the original equation.

$$3y^{\frac{3}{2}} = 192$$

$$3(16)^{\frac{3}{2}} \stackrel{?}{=} 192$$

$$3(64) \stackrel{?}{=} 192$$

$$192 = 192 \checkmark$$

b. $(y + 3)^{\frac{5}{2}} = 32$

$\left((y + 3)^{\frac{5}{2}}\right)^{\frac{2}{5}} = 32^{\frac{2}{5}}$ Raise both sides to the $\frac{2}{5}$ power.

$y + 3 = 4$

$y = 1$ Simplify.

Check the solution in the original equation:

$$(y + 3)^{\frac{5}{2}} = 32$$

$$(1 + 3)^{\frac{5}{2}} \stackrel{?}{=} 32$$

$$4^{\frac{5}{2}} \stackrel{?}{=} 32$$

$$32 = 32 \checkmark$$

c. $2(3y - 4)^{\frac{3}{5}} - 4 = 50$

$2(3y - 4)^{\frac{3}{5}} = 54$ Isolate the expression containing the exponent.

$(3y - 4)^{\frac{3}{5}} = 27$

$\left((3y - 4)^{\frac{3}{5}}\right)^{\frac{5}{3}} = 27^{\frac{5}{3}}$ Raise both sides to the $\frac{5}{3}$ power.

$3y - 4 = 243$

$3y = 247$ Simplify.

$y = \dfrac{247}{3}$

Check:

$$2(3y - 4)^{\frac{3}{5}} - 4 = 50$$

$$2\left(3\left(\frac{247}{3}\right) - 4\right)^{\frac{3}{5}} - 4 \stackrel{?}{=} 50$$

$$2(247 - 4)^{\frac{3}{5}} - 4 \stackrel{?}{=} 50$$

$$2(243)^{\frac{3}{5}} - 4 \stackrel{?}{=} 50$$

$$2(27) - 4 \stackrel{?}{=} 50$$

$$50 = 50 \checkmark$$

d. $\left(2y - \dfrac{5}{16}\right)^{-\frac{3}{4}} - 1 = 7$

$$\left(2y - \dfrac{5}{16}\right)^{-\frac{3}{4}} = 8 \qquad \text{Isolate the expression containing the exponent.}$$

$$\left(\left(2y - \dfrac{5}{16}\right)^{-\frac{3}{4}}\right)^{-\frac{4}{3}} = 8^{-\frac{4}{3}} \qquad \text{Raise both sides to the } -\dfrac{4}{3} \text{ power.}$$

$$2y - \dfrac{5}{16} = \dfrac{1}{16} \qquad \text{Simplify.}$$

$$2y = \dfrac{6}{16}$$

$$y = \dfrac{3}{16}$$

Check:

$$\left(2y - \dfrac{5}{16}\right)^{-\frac{3}{4}} - 1 = 7$$

$$\left(2\left(\dfrac{3}{16}\right) - \dfrac{5}{16}\right)^{-\frac{3}{4}} - 1 \overset{?}{=} 7$$

$$\left(\dfrac{6}{16} - \dfrac{5}{16}\right)^{-\frac{3}{4}} - 1 \overset{?}{=} 7$$

$$\left(\dfrac{1}{16}\right)^{-\frac{3}{4}} - 1 \overset{?}{=} 7$$

$$8 - 1 \overset{?}{=} 7$$

$$7 = 7 \checkmark$$

e. $(y - 6)^{-\frac{1}{2}} + 5 = 3$

$$(y - 6)^{-\frac{1}{2}} = -2 \qquad \text{Isolate the } y\text{-value.}$$

$$\left((y - 6)^{-\frac{1}{2}}\right)^{-2} = (-2)^{-2} \qquad \text{Raise both sides to the } -2 \text{ power.}$$

$$y - 6 = \dfrac{1}{4} \qquad \text{Simplify.}$$

$$y = 6\dfrac{1}{4}$$

Check the solution in the original equation.

$$(y - 6)^{-\frac{1}{2}} + 5 = 3$$

$$\left(6\dfrac{1}{4} - 6\right)^{-\frac{1}{2}} + 5 \overset{?}{=} 3$$

$$\left(\dfrac{1}{4}\right)^{-\frac{1}{2}} + 5 \overset{?}{=} 3$$

$$2 + 5 \overset{?}{=} 3$$

$$7 \neq 3$$

Our solution does not check in the original equation. We could have determined this as we were solving the equation when we obtained $(y - 6)^{-\frac{1}{2}} = -2$, because no real number has a square root of -2. Since our equation does not have a solution, we indicate the solution set with the symbol for empty set, ø.

In 1–16, solve and check. All variables represent positive numbers.

1. $x^{\frac{2}{3}} = 25$

2. $y^{\frac{3}{4}} = 125$

3. $z^{-\frac{5}{3}} = 243$

4. $2a^{-\frac{1}{4}} = 12$ $a = 1296$

5. $a^{\frac{3}{5}} - 2 = 25$ $a = 243$

6. $2b^{-\frac{1}{3}} + 5 = 15$ $b = 500$

7. $3r^{-\frac{3}{4}} = 81$ $r = 117$

8. $-4s^{-\frac{3}{5}} - 1 = 31$ $s = -72$

9. $(g - 1)^{\frac{1}{2}} = 5$ $g = 26$

10. $(w + 1)^{-\frac{1}{3}} = 2$ $w = 7$

11. $(r - 4)^{-\frac{1}{2}} - 1 = 5$ $r = 40$

12. $2(v - 1)^{\frac{4}{3}} = 32$ $v = 9$

13. $(3x - 1)^{\frac{3}{5}} = 125$

14. $(5z - 2)^{\frac{5}{3}} - 1 = 31$

15. $3(2m + 3)^{\frac{2}{3}} + 2 = 77$

16. $2(3y + 2)^{-\frac{5}{2}} = \dfrac{1}{16}$

In 17–20, select the numeral preceding the expression that best completes the statement or answers the question.

17. Which of the following equations does not have a solution in the set of real numbers?

   (①) $y^{\frac{2}{3}} = -4$ (3) $y^{-\frac{2}{3}} - 8$

   (2) $y^{\frac{1}{3}} = -8$ (4) $y^{-\frac{1}{2}} = 5$

18. A root of $(z - 2)^{-\frac{3}{4}} = 8$ is

   (1) -2 (3) $\dfrac{31}{16}$

   (2) $-\dfrac{31}{16}$ (④) $\dfrac{33}{16}$

19. To solve the equation $\sqrt{(x + 1)^3} = 4$, we can rewrite the equation as

   (1) $\dfrac{2}{3}(x + 1) = 4$ (3) $(x + 1)^{\frac{2}{3}} = 4$

   (2) $\dfrac{3}{2}(x + 1) = 4$ (④) $(x + 1)^{\frac{3}{2}} = 4$

20. The solution of the equation $y^{\frac{2}{3}} = 8$ is

   (1) rational   (3) imaginary

   (②) irrational   (4) nonexistent

9.5 Exponential Equations

Just as an exponential function is a function in which the variable is in the exponent, an **exponential equation** is an equation in which the variable appears in an exponent. Let us look at an example.

Solve for x.

    $3^x = 9$

We know that $9 = 3^2$, so we know that x must be equal to 2. What if we had to solve the equation $3^{x-1} = 9$? We know that $9 = 3^2$, so $x - 1 = 2$ and $x = 3$. What if we had $3^{2x-3} = 9$? Again, since $9 = 3^2$, we have $2x - 3 = 2$ and $x = \dfrac{5}{2}$.

    Think about how we are solving these equations. We are rewriting both sides of the equations with the same base, setting the exponents equal to each other, and solving the resulting equation.

Remember: If $b^x = b^y$, when $b \neq 0, 1$, then $x = y$.

1. Solve for y: $2^{3y-6} = 8$.

SOLUTION

$$2^{3y-6} = 8$$
$$2^{3y-6} = 2^3 \qquad \text{Rewrite 8 as a power of 2 since } 8 = 2^3.$$
$$3y - 6 = 3 \qquad \text{The bases are the same, so we can now equate the exponents.}$$
$$3y = 9 \qquad \text{Solve the equation.}$$
$$y = 3$$

Check the solution.

$$2^{3y-6} = 8$$
$$2^{3(3)-6} \overset{?}{=} 8$$
$$2^3 \overset{?}{=} 8$$
$$8 = 8 \checkmark$$

Sometimes we have to rewrite both sides of the equation, as shown in the examples below.

2. Solve.

    a. $9^x = 27$

    b. $4^{x+1} = 8^x$

    c. $\left(\dfrac{1}{9}\right)^x = 27^{1-x}$

SOLUTION

a.
$$9^x = 27$$
$$(3^2)^x = 3^3 \qquad \text{Rewrite both sides of the equation as powers of 3.}$$
$$3^{2x} = 3^3 \qquad \text{Simplify the left side by multiplying the exponents.}$$
$$2x = 3 \qquad \text{Since the bases are the same, equate the exponents.}$$
$$x = \frac{3}{2} \qquad \text{Solve the resulting equation.}$$

Check:

$$9^x = 27$$
$$9^{\frac{3}{2}} \overset{?}{=} 27$$
$$27 = 27 \checkmark$$

b.
$$4^{x+1} = 8^x$$
$$(2^2)^{x+1} = 2^{3x} \qquad \text{Rewrite both sides of the equation as powers of 2.}$$
$$2(x + 1) = 3x \qquad \text{Since the bases are the same, equate the exponents.}$$
$$\qquad\qquad\qquad\quad \text{Note: Be sure to multiply the entire } x + 1 \text{ by the 2.}$$
$$2x + 2 = 3x \qquad \text{Solve the resulting equation.}$$
$$x = 2$$

Check:

$$4^{x+1} = 8^x$$
$$4^{2+1} \stackrel{?}{=} 8^2$$
$$4^3 \stackrel{?}{=} 8^2$$
$$64 = 64 \checkmark$$

c. $\left(\dfrac{1}{9}\right)^x = 27^{1-x}$

$(3^{-2})^x = (3^3)^{1-x}$ Rewrite both sides of the equation as powers of 3.

$-2x = 3(1-x)$ Since the bases are the same, equate the exponents.

$-2x = 3 - 3x$ Solve the resulting equation.

$x = 3$

Check:

$$\left(\dfrac{1}{9}\right)^x = 27^{1-x}$$

$$\left(\dfrac{1}{9}\right)^3 \stackrel{?}{=} 27^{1-3}$$

$$\left(\dfrac{1}{9}\right)^3 \stackrel{?}{=} 27^{-2}$$

$$\dfrac{1}{729} = \dfrac{1}{729} \checkmark$$

Note: In solving exponential equations, it is not always possible to rewrite both sides of the equation in terms of the same base. The method for solving such equations algebraically will be discussed in Chapter 10. At this point, you could use your graphing calculator as illustrated in the Model Problem below.

3. Solve for x: $2^{-2x} = 3^{x+1}$.

SOLUTION

We cannot change both sides of the equation to the same base. At this point, we have no algebraic means of solving this equation. We can, however, use a graphing calculator to solve the equation. First, enter both equations into the $\boxed{\text{Y} =}$ editor of the calculator. Be sure to put the $-2x$ and the $x + 1$ into parentheses.

```
Plot1  Plot2  Plot3
\Y₁ = 2^(–2X)
\Y₂ = 3^(X+1)
\Y₃ =
\Y₄ =
\Y₅ =
\Y₆ =
\Y₇ =
```

When the two equations are graphed in the window $[-2, 2] \times [-3, 16]$, we obtain the graph shown below.

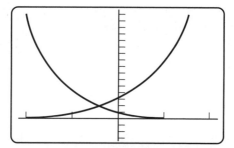

We can see that the two graphs intersect. Enter (2nd) CALC, Option 5 (intersect), and obtain the point of intersection.

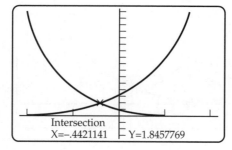

Intersection
X=-.4421141   Y=1.8457769

Thus, our solution is $x = -0.4421141$.

We could also use the calculator to solve exponential equations that can be expressed as integral powers of the same base.

---

4. Solve for x: $2^{-2x} = 4^{x+1}$.

SOLUTION

We could solve this problem algebraically by rewriting the right side of the equation as a power of 2, and then proceeding as explained above.

$$2^{-2x} = 4^{x+1}$$
$$2^{-2x} = (2^2)^{x+1} \qquad \text{Since the bases are the same, equate the exponents.}$$
$$-2x = 2x + 2 \qquad \text{Solve.}$$
$$-4x = 2$$
$$x = -\frac{1}{2}$$

Check:

$$2^{-2x} = 4^{x+1}$$
$$(2)^{-2 \cdot -\frac{1}{2}} \overset{?}{=} (4)^{-\frac{1}{2}+1}$$
$$2^1 \overset{?}{=} 4^{\frac{1}{2}}$$
$$2 = 2 \checkmark$$

However, we could also solve the equation graphically.
First enter the two equations in the (Y =) editor as shown.

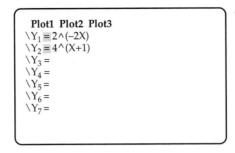

Plot1 Plot2 Plot3
$\backslash Y_1 = 2\wedge(-2X)$
$\backslash Y_2 = 4\wedge(X+1)$
$\backslash Y_3 =$
$\backslash Y_4 =$
$\backslash Y_5 =$
$\backslash Y_6 =$
$\backslash Y_7 =$

Graph both equations, and use your calculator to find the point of intersection.

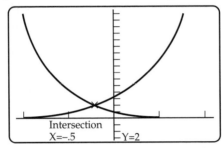

Intersection
X=−.5   Y=2

Notice the point of intersection occurs at $x = 0.5$.

Practice

In 1–15, solve and check.

1. $5^x = 125$

2. $6^{z-2} = 216$

3. $2^{r+1} = 4^r$

4. $3^{2x} = 27^{x+1}$

5. $5^{x-1} = \dfrac{1}{125}$

6. $\dfrac{1}{36} = 6^{2x}$

7. $4^s = 8^{s-2}$

8. $25^{x-1} = 125^x$

9. $\dfrac{1}{8} = 16^x$

10. $9^{x-1} = 27^{x+1}$ $x = -5$

11. $216 = 36^n$

12. $100^p = 1,000^{p+1}$ $p = -3$

13. $16^{x-2} = 64^{x-3}$ $x = 5$

14. $2^{x^2-x} = 4$ $x = 2$ $x = -1$

15. $\left(\dfrac{1}{49}\right)^{x+1} = 343^x$ $x = -\dfrac{2}{5}$

In 16–20, select the numeral preceding the word or expression that best completes the statement or answers the question.

16. Solve for y: $4^y = 8^{y-1}$.
    (1) 1   (3) 3
    (2) 2   (4) 4

17. The solution set of $3^{x^2-x} = 9^x$ is
    (1) {0}   (3) 3
    (2) {0, 2}   (4) {0, 3}

18. Solve for z: $16^{z-2} = \left(\dfrac{1}{8}\right)^z$.

    (1) −2   (3) $\dfrac{7}{8}$

    (2) −1   (4) $\dfrac{8}{7}$

19. Solve for x: $\left(\dfrac{9}{16}\right)^x = \dfrac{27}{64}$.

(1) $\dfrac{2}{3}$

(3) 3

(2) $\dfrac{3}{2}$

(4) 4

20. Solve for y: $125^{-2x} = 25^{x+1}$.

(1) $-\dfrac{1}{4}$

(3) $\dfrac{5}{2}$

(2) $\dfrac{1}{4}$

(4) 4

In 21–30, solve each equation using your graphing calculator. Indicate which problems could be solved algebraically, and solve them algebraically as well as graphically.

21. $9^{r+1} = 27$

22. $4^{w-1} = 5$

23. $36^p = 216^{p-1}$

24. $12^x = 24^{x-2}$

25. $0.25^v = 16$

26. $0.35^w = 12$

27. $25^{x+1} = 5^x$

28. $6^{2r} = 4^{r+3}$

29. $2^{x-2} = 6^x$

30. $3^m = 6^{m-2}$

CHAPTER REVIEW

In 1–20, choose the numeral preceding the expression that best answers the question.

1. In which quadrants does the graph of $y = 4^x$ appear?
   (1) I and II   (3) III and IV
   (2) II and III   (4) I and IV

2. $(9)^3(9)^1$ is *not* equal to which of the following?
   (1) 9^4 (3) 6,561
   (2) 3^8 (4) 81^4

3. Evaluate $6^0 - 9^{\frac{1}{2}}$.

   (1) -1.5 (3) 3
   (2) -2 (4) 4.5

4. Expressed without negative exponents, the expression $\dfrac{(2a^2b^4)^2}{2a^3b^{-5}}$ is equivalent to which of the following?

   (1) $1ab^3$ (3) $\dfrac{2a}{b}$

   (2) $2ab^{13}$ (4) $\dfrac{2b^3}{a}$

5. If $4^x = 64$, what is the value of x?
   (1) 1   (3) 3
   (2) 2   (4) 16

6. Find the exact value of $\left(\dfrac{9}{16}\right)^{-\frac{3}{2}}$.

   (1) $-\dfrac{64}{27}$ (3) $\dfrac{27}{64}$

   (2) $-\dfrac{3}{4}$ (4) $\dfrac{64}{27}$

7. Simplify: $\dfrac{4^x}{4^2}$.

   (1) $\dfrac{x}{2}$ (3) $x - 2$

   (2) 4^{x-2} (4) 16^{x-2}

8. Solve for x: $5^{x+1} = 125^x$.

   (1) $\dfrac{1}{2}$ (3) 3

   (2) 2   (4) 4

9. Evaluate $(4x^3y^2)(-3x^4y^{-2})$.
   (1) $-12x^7y$ (3) $-12x^{12}$
   (2) $-12x^7$ (4) $-12x^{12}y^4$

10. Solve for x: $3x^{\frac{3}{2}} - 6 = 75$.
   (1) $\left(\sqrt[2]{23}\right)^3$ (3) 9

   (2) 27   (4) $\left(\sqrt[3]{23}\right)^2$

11. If $k = 4$, evaluate $3(k^0)^{\frac{3}{2}}$.

(1) 1

(2) $\frac{9}{6}$

(3) 3

(4) 24

12. What coordinate point do the functions $y = 5^x$ and $y = \left(\frac{1}{5}\right)^x$ share?

(1) $(0, -1)$

(2) $(0, 1)$

(3) $(-1, 0)$

(4) $(1, 0)$

13. In the diagram below, the graph of $y = 2^x$ is drawn. The graph obtained by reflecting this graph in the y-axis would have which equation?

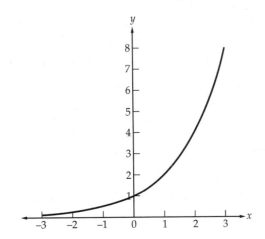

(1) $x = 2^y$

(2) $y = -2^x$

(3) $y = 2^{-x}$

(4) $-y = 2^x$

14. Solve for x: $2^{x+2} = 4^{x-1}$.

(1) 1

(2) 2

(3) 3

(4) 4

15. Solve for x: $8^x = 2^{x+6}$.

(1) $\frac{1}{2}$

(2) 2

(3) 3

(4) 4

16. In the set of complex numbers, if $f(x) = 3x^2 + 3x^{\frac{1}{2}} + 3x$, what is the value of $f(-4)$?

(1) 24

(2) $24 + 6i$

(3) 36

(4) $36 + 6i$

17. If the holiday lights in your neighborhood can be measured by the exponential formula $L(t) = 143(1.093)^t$ where t = number of days after December 12th, find the rate at which the number of lights is increasing.

(1) 143%

(2) 109.3%

(3) 93%

(4) 9.3%

18. If the number 0.38467 is written in scientific notation, it is 3.8467×10^x. What is the value of x?

(1) -3

(2) -1

(3) 1

(4) 4

19. Each time Juanita bowls, her score increases by 5% of her previous score. If her initial score is represented by a, which equation shows this relationship?

(1) $y = a(1.5)^x$

(2) $y = a(1.05)^x$

(3) $y = 0.05^x$

(4) $y = a(0.5)^x$

20. Minerva did a study of babysitting rates in her neighborhood over the last three years and discovered that the function $b(t) = 6.25(1.2)^t$ represents the change in pricing, where t is the number of years since 2000. What was the babysitting cost per hour in Minerva's neighborhood in 2000?

(1) $7.50

(2) $6.25

(3) $5.00

(4) $1.20

21. The following formulas represent salaries promised to new employees at five different software companies, where t represents years.

   i. $P(t) = 38,500 + 1,000t$

  ii. $P(t) = 35,000(1.062)^t$

 iii. $P(t) = 32,000(1.5)^t$

  iv. $P(t) = 41,000$

  v. $P(t) = 47,500 - 1,500t$

Match the four following statements with the salaries shown above.

a. This company promises a constant salary, no raises.

b. The company offers a $1000 bonus for each year of service.

c. An employee who stayed with this company for 2 years would more than double her salary.

d. If an employee stayed with this company long enough, she would end up paying the company to work there.

Now, write a description of the salary function you did not use in the matching.

22. The population of the village of Elfdom in the North Pole suburbs has a steady population represented by the exponential function $P(t) = 11{,}493(1.029587)^t$, where t represents the number of years since 1985 when the village was incorporated.
    a. What is the annual rate of growth?
    b. In what calendar year will the population be 17,500?
    c. About how many years will it take for the elves to double their 1985 population?

23. Americans have been steadily increasing their usage of bottled water. In fact, between 1987 and 1996, our use of bottle water actually doubled. If the yearly usage of water, in billions of gallons sold, can be represented by the function $y = 1.55(1.072)^t$, where t represents the number of years since 1987,
    a. how many billions of gallons of water were sold in 1987?
    b. how many gallons were sold in 2000, if this trend continued?

c. what is the yearly rate of growth in sales of bottled water?
d. If Americans continue to prefer bottled water at a similar rate, in what year will sales top 100 billion gallons of bottled water?

24. Hiram and Elsbeth graduate from college in the same year and start working at different firms. Hiram's salary, in thousands of dollars, is represented by the exponential function $H(t) = 39.5(1.045)^t$, while Elsbeth's salary, in thousands of dollars, is represented by the exponential formula $E(t) = 34.6(1.054)^t$.
    a. Whose salary is higher when the pair start working? What is each salary?
    b. Describe the behavior of the two formulas and interpret their meaning.
    c. If they started working in 2000, in what year will their salaries be equal? What will that salary be?

CHAPTER 10

Logarithms

10.1 Inverse of an Exponential Function

A **logarithmic** function can be defined as the inverse of an exponential function. Given the exponential function $f(x) = 4^x$, to find its inverse, we interchange the domain and range.

$y = 4^x$
$x = 4^y$

Graphically, the function $f(x) = 4^x$, as shown below, lies in Quadrants I and II while its inverse $f^{-1}(x) = 4^y$ appears in Quadrants I and IV.

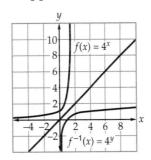

Remember: To find an inverse graphically, simply reflect the function in the identity line, $y = x$.

The values of the domain and range are interchanged in any inverse as demonstrated by this table of values of these two functions.

$y = 4^x$		$x = 4^y$	
x	y	x	y
$-\dfrac{3}{2}$	$\dfrac{1}{8}$	$\dfrac{1}{8}$	$-\dfrac{3}{2}$
-1	$\dfrac{1}{4}$	$\dfrac{1}{4}$	-1
$-\dfrac{1}{2}$	$\dfrac{1}{2}$	$\dfrac{1}{2}$	$-\dfrac{1}{2}$
0	1	1	0
$\dfrac{1}{2}$	2	2	$\dfrac{1}{2}$
1	4	4	1
$\dfrac{3}{2}$	8	8	$\dfrac{3}{2}$

Traditionally, however, we prefer to write equations that define functions in terms of x. The expression $x = 4^y$ can be translated as

y is the exponent to base 4 which produces the result x.

Since a logarithm is an exponent, this can be rewritten as

y is the logarithm to base 4 of x.

In mathematical notation we write: $y = \log_4 x$. $y = \log_4 x$ is the inverse of $y = 4^x$. We can summarize this rule as follows:

For $b > 0$ and $b \neq 1$, $x = b^y \leftrightarrow y = \log_b x$.

 **MODEL PROBLEMS**

1. For the function $y = 2^x$
   a. find the inverse of the function and express it in exponential and logarithmic form.
   b. sketch the graph of $y = 2^x$ such that $-3 \leq x \leq 3$. Then, on the same axes, sketch its inverse.

   SOLUTION
   a. $x = 2^y$ and $y = \log_2 x$ both represent the inverse of $y = 2^x$. They are equivalent expressions.
   b.
   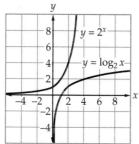

Notice that once again, the values of the domain and range are interchanged in this list of values, indicating that the functions are inverses.

$y = 2^x$		$y = \log_2 x$	
x	y	x	y
-3	$\dfrac{1}{8}$	$\dfrac{1}{8}$	-3
-2	$\dfrac{1}{4}$	$\dfrac{1}{4}$	-2
-1	$\dfrac{1}{2}$	$\dfrac{1}{2}$	-1
0	1	1	0
1	2	2	1
2	4	4	2
3	8	8	3

A way of checking a logarithmic graph is to examine its inverse, the exponential function, verifying that the values of the x and y coordinates are properly interchanged.

Remember: Since an exponential function has a range of $y > 0$, remember that, as the inverse of an exponential function, a logarithmic function will have a domain of $x > 0$. The line $x = 0$ (the y-axis) is a vertical asymptote for the graph of a logarithmic function.

2. Determine the equation of the function shown in the graph below.

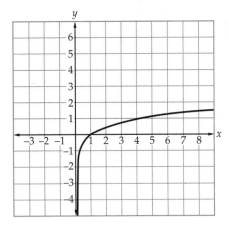

(1) $y = \log_2 x$
(2) $y = 3^x$
(3) $y = \log_4 x$
(4) $y = \log_6 x$

Practice

In 1–10, select the numeral preceding the word or expression that best completes the sentence or answers the question.

1. Which of the following equations represents the inverse of $y = 3^x$?
   (1) $y = x^3$ (3) $x = \log_3 y$
   (2) $y = 3^x$ (4) $y = \log_3 x$ ✓

2. The graph of the function $y = \log_5 x$ appears in which quadrants?
   (1) I and II   (3) II and III
   (2) I and IV ✓   (4) III and IV

3. The point $(1, 0)$ is always present on the graph of which type of function?
   (1) $y = ax^2 + bx + c$ (3) $y = \log_b x$ ✓
   (2) $f(x) = b^x$ (4) $f(x) = mx + b$

4. Which number is not in the domain of the function $f(x) = \log_5 x$?
   (1) 1   (3) 3
   (2) 2   (4) 0 ✓

5. The inverse of the function $y = \log_2 x$ is
   (1) $y^2 = x$ (3) $x = 2^y$
   (2) $y = 2^x$ ✓   (4) $y = \log_x 2$

6. If $y = 2^x$ and $y = \left(\frac{1}{2}\right)^x$ are graphed on the same set of axes, which transformation would map them onto one another?
   (1) reflection in the y-axis ✓
   (2) rotation 180°
   (3) reflection in the origin
   (4) reflection in the line $y = x$

7. If $y = \log_{10} x$ and $1 < y < 2$, then which of the following is a true statement?
   (1) $x < 0$ (3) $0 < x < 10$
   (2) $x = 0$ (4) $10 < x < 100$ ✓

8. Which of the following equations represents the graph shown below?

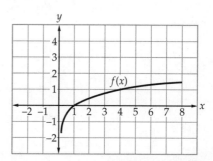

   (1) $y = 4^x$ (3) $f(x) = \log_4 x$ ✓
   (2) $f(x) = \log_2 x$ (4) $f(x) = \log_{10} x$

9. At what coordinate point will the graphs of $f(x) = \log_3 x$ intersect the y-axis?
   (1) $(0, 1)$
   (2) $(1, 0)$
   (3) $(0, 3)$
   (4) It will not intersect the y-axis. ✓

10. Which of the following equations is *not* equivalent to $y = \log_2 x$?
    (1) $y = 2^x$ ✓   (3) $x = \left(\frac{1}{2}\right)^{-y}$
    (2) $x = 2^y$ (4) All are equivalent.

In 11–16, write the inverse of each function.

11. $y = 6^x$ $\log_6 x = y$

12. $f(x) = \log_4 x$ $4^x = y$

13. $y = \left(\frac{2}{3}\right)^x$ $\log_{2/3} x = y$

14. $f(x) = \log_{10} x$ $10^x = y$

15. $y = \log_x 2$ $y^x = 2$

16. $f(x) = 10^x$ $\log_{10} x = y$

In 17–20, use graph paper or a graphing calculator.

17. a. Sketch the graph of the function $f(x) = 3^x$ in the interval $-2 \le x \le 2$.
   b. On the same set of axes, sketch the inverse of the function in part **a** and label it B.
   c. What is the equation of the graph sketched in part **b**?

18. a. Sketch the graph of the function $f(x) = \left(\dfrac{1}{2}\right)^x$ in the interval $-3 \le x \le 3$.
   b. On the same set of axes, sketch the inverse of $f(x) = \left(\dfrac{1}{2}\right)^x$ and label it B.
   c. What is the equation of the graph sketched in part **b**?

19. a. Complete the table below for the function $f(x) = \log_{\frac{1}{2}} x$.

x	8	4	2	1	0	$\frac{1}{4}$	$\frac{1}{8}$
y	-3	-2	-1	0	1	2	3

   b. Sketch the graph whose values are shown above and label it B.
   c. Rotate $f(x) = \log_{\frac{1}{2}} x$ 180° counterclockwise and label it C. Complete the new table of values.
   d. Reflect $f(x) = \log_{\frac{1}{2}} x$ in the line $y = x$ and label it D. Complete the new table of values.
   e. What is the equation of the graph shown in part **d**?

20. a. Sketch the graph of $y = \log_5 x$ in the interval $-2 \le y \le 2$.
   b. Find the intersection of $y = \log_5 x$ and the line $x = 1$.

10.2 Logarithmic Form of an Equation

Both logarithmic and exponential functions give information about a power. The statement $y = \log_2 16$ can be translated into the exponential form $2^y = 16$ (in this case, $y = 4$).

Any logarithmic equation can be rewritten in exponential form.

Logarithmic Form	Exponential Form
$2 = \log_5 25$	$5^2 = 25$
$3 = \log_4 64$	$4^3 = 64$
$\dfrac{1}{2} = \log_9 3$	$9^{\frac{1}{2}} = 3$
$-1 = \log_{10} \dfrac{1}{10}$	$10^{-1} = \dfrac{1}{10}$

The general rule for logs and exponents says:

$$\log_b c = a \quad \leftrightarrow \quad b^a = c \quad \text{(such that } b > 0 \text{ and } b \ne 1\text{)}$$

1. Rewrite $y = \log_4 16$ in exponential form.

SOLUTION

Remember the equation $y = \log_4 16$ means "4 to the y power is equal to 16."
Therefore, the exponential equation is $4^y = 16$ (in this case, $y = 2$).

Remember: The number to the right and below the word *log* will be the base of the exponential equation.

2. Rewrite $81 = 3^4$ as a logarithmic statement.

SOLUTION

Since 4 is the exponent in the expression $81 = 3^4$, the logarithmic equation would be $4 = \log_3 81$.

3. Solve for x: $2 = \log_{12} x$.

SOLUTION

To solve, first rewrite the equation in exponential form: $12^2 = x$. Then evaluate by performing the indicated operation: $12^2 = 144$, so $x = 144$.

4. Solve for x: $x = \log_4 8$.

SOLUTION

To solve, first rewrite the equation in exponential form: $4^x = 8$. In this case, we need to solve for the exponent x, so we need to rewrite the equation to make the bases equal. As you learned in the last chapter, when the bases are equal, the exponents will also be equal.

$$4^x = 8$$
$$2^{2x} = 2^3$$
$$2x = 3$$
$$x = \frac{3}{2}$$

5. Solve for x: $\frac{1}{2} = \log_x 16$.

SOLUTION

To solve, first we rewrite as an exponential equation: $x^{\frac{1}{2}} = 16$. To solve for x, we raise each side of the equation to the inverse of the given power to reduce it to 1.

$$\left(x^{\frac{1}{2}}\right)^2 = 16^2$$
$$x = 256$$

6. If $f(x) = \log_8 x$, evaluate $f(4)$.

SOLUTION

First we replace the x with a 4: $f(4) = \log_8 4$ or $y = \log_8 4$. Then we rewrite it as an exponential equation and solve for y.
$$8^y = 4$$

Again, we need to make the bases the same.
$$2^{3y} = 2^2$$
$$3y = 2$$
$$y = \frac{2}{3}$$

In 1–8, write the exponential equation in logarithmic form.

1. $3^5 = 243$ $\log_3 243 = 5$

2. $16^{\frac{1}{2}} = 4$ $\log_{16} 4 = \frac{1}{2}$

3. $36 = 6^2$ $\log_6 36 = 2$

4. $\frac{1}{4} = 2^{-2}$ $\log_2 \frac{1}{4} = -2$

5. $\left(\frac{5}{6}\right)^2 = \frac{25}{36}$ $\log_{5/6} \frac{25}{36} = 2$

6. $10^{-2} = 0.01$ $\log_{10} 0.01 = -2$

7. $7 = 49^{\frac{1}{2}}$ $\log_{49} 7 = \frac{1}{2}$

8. $b^a = c$ $\log_b c = a$

In 9–14, write the logarithmic equation in exponential form.

9. $6 = \log_2 64$ $2^6 = 64$

10. $3 = \log_5 125$ $5^3 = 125$

11. $-3 = \log_{10} 0.001$ $10^{-3} = 0.001$

12. $\frac{1}{2} = \log_4 2$ $4^{1/2} = 2$

13. $2 = \log_{11} 121$ $11^2 = 121$

14. $-2 = \log_2 \frac{1}{4}$ $2^{-2} = \frac{1}{4}$

In 15–20, solve for x.

15. $x = \log_3 81$ $3^x = 81$ $x = 4$

16. $x = \log_4 \frac{1}{2}$ $4^x = \frac{1}{2}$ $x = -2$

17. $x = \log_9 27$ $9^x = 27$ $x = \frac{3}{2}$

18. $x = \log_{10} 10,000$ $10^x = 10,000$ $x = 4$

19. $x = \log_5 \frac{1}{25}$ $5^x = \frac{1}{25}$ $x = -2$

20. $x = \log_2 8$ $2^x = 8$ $x = 3$

In 21–26, solve for x.

21. $\log_4 x = 3$ $4^3 = x$ $x = 64$

22. $\log_9 x = -2$ $9^{-2} = x$ $x = \frac{1}{81}$

23. $\log_{25} x = \frac{1}{2}$ $25^{1/2} = x$ $x = 5$

24. $\log_{10} x = -3$ $10^{-3} = x$ $x = .001$

25. $\log_{\sqrt{3}} x = 6$ $\sqrt{3}^6 = x$ $x = 27$

26. $\log_7 x = -1$ $7^{-1} = x$ $x = \frac{1}{7}$

In 27–32, solve for x.

27. $\log_x 32 = 5$ $x^5 = 32$ $x = 2$

28. $\log_x 27 = \frac{3}{2}$ $x^{3/2} = 27$ $x = 9$

29. $\log_x 100 = 2$ $x^2 = 100$ $x = 10$

30. $\log_x \frac{1}{2} = -1$ $x^{-1} = \frac{1}{2}$ $x = 2$

31. $\log_x 216 = 3$ $x^3 = 216$ $x = 6$

32. $\log_x \sqrt{2} = \frac{1}{2}$ $x^{1/2} = \sqrt{2}$ $x = 2$

In 33–40, select the numeral preceding the expression that best completes the sentence or answers the question.

33. If $f(x) = \log_{10} x$, the value of $f(10,000)$ is
(1) 1,000   (3) 10
(2) 100   (4) 4 ✓

34. The value of x in the equation $\log_8 x = -\frac{2}{3}$ is
(1) 64   (3) 4
(2) 16   (4) $\frac{1}{4}$ ✓

35. The value of x in the equation $x = \log_{10} 0.001$ is
(1) 1   (3) -3 ✓
(2) -2 (4) -4

36. If $\log_{(x + 1)} 64 = 2$, find the value of x.
(1) 8   (3) 3
(2) 7 ✓   (4) 2

37. If $x = \log_2 6$, then 4^x equals
(1) 1   (3) 36 ✓
(2) 16   (4) 256

38. If $\log_a \frac{2}{b} = -1$, then a equals
(1) b (3) $\frac{b}{2}$ ✓
(2) $\frac{2}{b}$ (4) $\frac{-2}{b}$

39. If $\log_b n = y$, then n equals
   (1) yb (3) y^b
   (2) $\dfrac{y}{b}$ (4) b^y

40. If $\log_{25} x = -\dfrac{3}{2}$, the value of x is
   (1) -125 (3) $\dfrac{1}{125}$
   (2) $-\dfrac{1}{125}$ (4) 125

10.3 Logarithmic Rules

Since logarithms are exponents, all of the rules of exponents apply to logarithms as well, for all positive numbers m, n, and b where $b \neq 1$.

	Exponential Rule	Logarithmic Rule	Example of Log Rule
Product	$(x^m)(x^n) = x^{m+n}$	$\log_b mn = \log_b m + \log_b n$	$\log_b 50 = \log_b 5 + \log_b 10$
Quotient	$\dfrac{x^m}{x^n} = x^{m-n}$	$\log_b \dfrac{m}{n} = \log_b m - \log_b n$	$\log_b \dfrac{145}{12} = \log_b 145 - \log_b 12$
Power	$(x^m)^n = x^{mn}$	$\log_b m^n = n\log_b m$	$\log_b 10^2 = 2\log_b 10$

In words, the product rule of logarithms says that if two numbers are being multiplied, we add their logarithms together. For example,

$$\log_b (793 \cdot 915) = \log_b 793 + \log_b 915$$
$$\log_2 (16 \cdot 64) = \log_2 (2^4 \cdot 2^6) = \log_2 (2^{4+6}) = \log_2 (2^{10}) = 10 \log_2 2 = 10$$

In today's world of calculators, it does not seem to make much difference whether we multiply and then take the logarithm of the result or find the two logarithms and then add, but logarithms were first used in the 17th century before mechanical math machines existed to facilitate math operations. As recently as the latter half of the 20th century, logarithms were invaluable to engineers in forming the basis of operations for the slide rule.

The quotient rule of logarithms says that if two numbers are being divided, we subtract the logarithm of the denominator from the logarithm of the numerator.

$$\log_b \frac{57}{8} = \log_b 57 - \log_b 8$$

Lastly, the power rule of logarithms says that if one number is being raised to a power, the logarithm is the product of the power and the logarithm of the number.

$$\log_b 1{,}324^{\frac{1}{2}} = \frac{1}{2} \log_b 1{,}324$$

Note: Since an exponent of $\frac{1}{2}$ means square root, this is the method some calculators use to find the square root of numbers.

1. If $\log_b 3 = g$ and $\log_b 2 = h$, express each of the following in terms of g and h.
   a. $\log_b 6$
   b. $\log_b 12$

   c. $\log_b \dfrac{3}{2}$

   d. $\log_b 36$

SOLUTION

We need to rewrite each expression in terms of $\log_b 3$ and $\log_b 2$ and then substitute the values we know.

a. $\begin{aligned} \log_b 6 &= \log_b (2 \cdot 3) \\ &= \log_b 2 + \log_b 3 \\ &= h + g \end{aligned}$

b. $\begin{aligned} \log_b 12 &= \log_b (2 \cdot 2 \cdot 3) \\ &= \log_b 2 + \log_b 2 + \log_b 3 \\ &= h + h + g = 2h + g \end{aligned}$

c. $\begin{aligned} \log_b \frac{3}{2} &= \log_b 3 - \log_b 2 \\[4pt] &= g - h \end{aligned}$

d. $\begin{aligned} \log_b 36 &= \log_b (4 \cdot 9) \\ &= \log_b (2^2 \cdot 3^2) \\ &= \log_b 2^2 + \log_b 3^2 \\ &= 2 \log_b 2 + 2 \log_b 3 \\ &= 2h + 2g \end{aligned}$ or $\begin{aligned} \log_b 36 &= \log_b 6 + \log_b 6 \\ \text{Using results above} \\ &= h + g + h + g \\ &= 2h + 2g \end{aligned}$

2. If $\log_b 5 = 1.367$, which of the following represents $\log_b 25$?
   (1) 26.367
   (2) 2.734
   (3) 1.868689
   (4) 0.6835

SOLUTION

Again, we simplify the log expression given and then substitute.

$$\begin{aligned} \log_b 25 &= \log_b 5^2 \\ &= 2 \log_b 5 \\ &= 2(1.367) = 2.734 \end{aligned}$$

Answer: (2)

3. If $\log_b x = \log_b p + \log_b t - \dfrac{1}{2} \log_b q$, which expression represents x?

   (1) $pt \sqrt{q}$
   (2) $p + t - q^2$

   (3) $\dfrac{pt}{\sqrt{q}}$

   (4) $\dfrac{p}{tq}$

Now we have to "undo" the logarithmic rules in this expression. In this case we know the logarithm and are finding the number that has that logarithm. This number is called the **antilogarithm** or antilog.

$$\log_b x = \log_b p + \log_b t - \frac{1}{2}\log_b q \qquad \text{Addition of logs indicates multiplication of terms.}$$

$$\log_b x = \log_b pt - \frac{1}{2}\log_b q \qquad \text{Multiplication of logs indicates raising to a power.}$$

$$\log_b x = \log_b pt - \log_b q^{\frac{1}{2}} \qquad \text{Subtraction of logs indicates division of terms.}$$

$$\log_b x = \log_b \frac{pt}{q^{\frac{1}{2}}} \qquad \text{An exponent of } \frac{1}{2} \text{ indicates square root.}$$

$$\log_b x = \log_b \frac{pt}{\sqrt{q}} \qquad \text{Take the antilog of each side.}$$

$$x = \frac{pt}{\sqrt{q}}$$

Answer: (3)

4. If $x = \dfrac{m^2 n}{p\sqrt{s}}$, which expression represents $\log_b x$?

(1) $2\log_b m + \log_b n - \dfrac{1}{2}p\log_b s$

(2) $2\log_b m + \log_b n - \log_b p + \dfrac{1}{2}\log_b s$

(3) $2\log_b mn - \left(\log_b p + \dfrac{1}{2}\log_b s\right)$

(4) $2\log_b m + \log_b n - \left(\log_b p + \dfrac{1}{2}\log_b s\right)$

SOLUTION

Here we need to take the logarithm of each side of the equation and apply the appropriate logarithmic rules to the right-hand side.

$$\log_b x = \log \frac{m^2 n}{p\sqrt{s}}$$

$$\log_b x = \log m^2 n - \log_b p\sqrt{s} \qquad \text{Division of terms uses subtraction of logarithms.}$$

$$\log_b x = \log_b m^2 + \log_b n - \left(\log_b p + \log_b \sqrt{s}\right) \qquad \text{Multiplication of terms uses addition of logarithms.}$$

$$\log x = 2\log m + \log n - \left(\log p + \frac{1}{2}\log s\right) \qquad \text{Powers become products of logarithms.}$$

Answer: (4)

5. If $\log_4 (4x) + \log_4 (x) = \log_4 (64)$, find the value of x.

SOLUTION

$$\log_4 (4x) + \log_4 (x) = \log_4 (64)$$
$$\log_4 (4x \cdot x) = \log_4 (64) \qquad \text{Simplify the left-hand side of the equation.}$$
$$\log_4 (4x^2) = \log_4 (64)$$
$$(4x^2) = 64$$
$$x^2 = 16 \qquad \text{Since the domain of logarithms is } x > 0.$$
$$x = 4$$

6. Evaluate $\log_2 32 - \log_2 1$.

SOLUTION

$\log_2 32 - \log_2 1$ can be rewritten as $\log_2 \dfrac{32}{1}$ or $2^x = 32$, which equals 5.

7. Solve for x: $\log_2 x + \log_2 (x - 4) = 5$.

SOLUTION

$$\log_2 x(x - 4) = 5 \qquad \text{First undo the logarithmic operations.}$$
$$x(x - 4) = 2^5 \qquad \text{Now, rewrite as an exponential equation.}$$
$$x^2 - 4x - 32 = 0 \qquad \text{Solve the resulting quadratic equation.}$$
$$(x - 8)(x + 4) = 0$$
$$x = 8 \quad x \neq -4 \qquad \text{Remember, you cannot take the log of a negative number.}$$

![Practice]

In 1–16, select the numeral preceding the word or expression that best completes the sentence or answers the question.

1. If $\log_b 5 = m$ and $\log_b 2 = n$, then $\log_b 20$ can be represented as which of the following?
(1) $m + n^2$ (3) $2mn$
(2) $m + 2n$ (4) $2m + n$

2. If $x = \dfrac{a\sqrt{b}}{c}$, then $\log_{10} x$ equals

(1) $\dfrac{\log_{10} a \cdot \log_{10} \sqrt{b}}{\log_{10} c}$

(2) $\log_{10} a + \frac{1}{2} \log_{10} b + \log_{10} c$

(3) $\dfrac{\log_{10} a + \frac{1}{2}\log_{10} b}{\log_{10} c}$

(4) $\log_{10} a + \frac{1}{2} \log_{10} b - \log_{10} c$

In 3–5, use the following:

$$\log_a 7 = 4.61 \quad \log_a 2 = 1.73 \quad \log_a 3 = 2.14$$

3. Which of the following represents $\log_a 12$?
(1) 3.87   (3) 6.404806
(2) 5.6   (4) 14.9769

4. Which represents $\log_a 42$?
(1) 3.87   (3) 17.0312
(2) 8.48   (4) 27.66

5. Which expression represents $\log_a \sqrt{6}$?
(1) 1.935   (3) 2.4495
(2) 1.967   (4) 3.87

6. Evaluate $\log_4 1 - 3 \log_4 2 + \frac{1}{2} \log_4 16$.

(1) $-\dfrac{3}{2}$ (3) $\dfrac{1}{2}$

(2) $-\dfrac{1}{2}$ (4) $\dfrac{3}{2}$

7. If $2 \log_{10} x = \log_{10} 2x$, then x equals
   (1) 1   (3) 3
   (2) 2   (4) 4

8. If $x = \dfrac{8^2 \sqrt[3]{5}}{21}$, which of the following represents $\log_b x$?

   (1) $2 \log_b 8 + \dfrac{1}{3} \log_b 5 - 2 \log_b 21$

   (2) $\dfrac{\log_b 8^2 \cdot \dfrac{1}{3} \log_b \sqrt{5}}{\log_b 21}$

   (3) $2 \log_b 8 - 2 \log_b 5 - \log_b 21$

   (4) $2 \log_b 8 + \dfrac{1}{3} \log_b 5 - \log_b 21$

9. If $\log_b x = 2 \log_b a - \left(3 \log_b b + \dfrac{1}{2} \log_b d \right)$, which expression is equivalent to x?

   (1) $a^2 b^3 c^{\frac{1}{2}}$ (3) $\dfrac{a^2}{b^3 \sqrt{d}}$

   (2) $\dfrac{a^2}{\sqrt{b^3 d}}$ (4) $\dfrac{a^2 b^3}{\sqrt{d}}$

10. The value of $\log_2 16 - \log_2 4$ is
    (1) 1   (3) 3
    (2) 2   (4) 4

11. If $\log_b 3 = p$ and $\log_b 6 = q$, express $\log_b \sqrt{\dfrac{1}{2}}$ in terms of p and q.

    (1) $p - q$ (3) $\dfrac{1}{2} p - q$

    (2) $\dfrac{1}{2} pq$ (4) $\dfrac{1}{2}(p - q)$

12. To simplify the expression $\log_z 45^2 \cdot \sqrt{873}$, which log rule(s) would you use?
    (1) quotient and power rules
    (2) product and power rules
    (3) quotient and product rules
    (4) product, quotient, and power rules

13. Solve for x: $\log_6 (x) = \log_6 (36) - \log_6 \left(\dfrac{1}{6} \right)$.
    (1) 216   (3) 3
    (2) 36   (4) 0

14. Solve for x: $\log_5 (125x) = \log_5 (25x) + \log_5 x$.
    (1) 625   (3) 25
    (2) 125   (4) 5

15. Solve for x: $2 \log_4 x - \log_4 (x + 3) = 1$.
    (1) $\{-2, 6\}$ (3) $\{6\}$
    (2) $\{-2\}$ (4) $\{ \}$

16. Solve for a: $2 \log_3 a - \log_3 (a + 4) = 2$.
    (1) $\{3, -12\}$ (3) $\{12\}$
    (2) $\{-3\}$ (4) $\{ \}$

In 17 and 18, express x in terms of p, q, and r.

17. $\log_z x = 3 \log_z p + \dfrac{1}{2} \log_z r - \log_z q$

18. $\log_z x = \dfrac{1}{3}(\log_z q + \log_z r) - 2 \log_z p$

In 19 and 20, rewrite each equation as an equivalent logarithmic expression.

19. $x = p^2 q^3 r$

20. $x = \dfrac{\sqrt{pr}}{q^3}$ $\log x = \dfrac{1}{2} \log p + \dfrac{1}{2} \log r - 3 \log q$

10.4 Common Logarithms

Since there are many different exponents and bases available in the world of real numbers, there are also many different logarithms. One of the most often used is the **common logarithm,** in which the base is 10. Since our numeric system is base 10, it makes sense that 10 is frequently seen. In fact, the absence of a base in a logarithmic expression or equation signals that the log is in base 10.

    $\log x = 4$ has the same meaning as $\log_{10} x = 4$ or $10^4 = x$.
    $\log 532 = 2.725911632$ makes the same statement as $10^{2.725911632} = 532$.

    Unless the number we are dealing with is an integral power of 10, its logarithm will be shown in two parts: an integer called the **characteristic** and a decimal known as the **mantissa.** The characteristic gives us a rough idea of the number while the mantissa narrows it down to a specific value.

A characteristic of 1, for example, tells us the number is between 10^1 and 10^2 or between 10 and 100, while a characteristic of 3 tells us the number is between 10^3 and 10^4 or between 1,000 and 10,000.

 **MODEL PROBLEMS**

---

1. If log x = 2.2581927, analyze the information provided by the characteristic and then use your calculator to find the value of x to the nearest hundredth.

SOLUTION
Since the characteristic is 2, the number is between 10^2 and 10^3 or between 100 and 1,000. To find the exact value of the number whose logarithm is 2.2581927, use (2nd) (LOG), which will produce 10^(on the home screen. Type in the logarithm, press (ENTER), and you learn that x = 181.2143977.

2. Which of the following numbers would have the same characteristic as 78.21?
   (1) 216
   (2) 7,821
   (3) 12.87
   (4) 782.1

SOLUTION
Since 78.21 is a number between 10 and 100, its characteristic is 1. The only number present between 10 and 100 is choice (3) 12.87, so its characteristic is also 1.

Note: To find the characteristic of a number, we rewrite the number in scientific notation. The number of decimal places the decimal point is moved to put the number in scientific notation is another way of finding the characteristic.

3. Use your calculator to solve for N: log N = 2.57863921.

SOLUTION
To solve log N = 2.57863921 we want to rewrite the expression in exponential form:
$10^{2.57863921}$ = N.
On your calculator, use (2nd) (LOG), which gives you the 10^x. Enter the value of N and press (ENTER) and you find the answer is 379.

4. If log 4.389 = a, which of these would represent log 43.89?
   (1) $10a + 10$
   (2) $1 + a$
   (3) $a - 1$

SOLUTION

$$\log 43.89 = \log (10 \cdot 4.389)$$
$$= \log 10 + \log 4.389$$
$$= 1 + a$$

Answer: (3)

---

5. Which log could not have the same mantissa as log 3.14?
    (1) 0.0314
    (2) 30.14
    (3) 314
    (4) 3,140

SOLUTION

Any number that has the same mantissa as log 3.14 must contain the same digits, in the same exact order. Each log would be evaluated as log 3.14 + log (10^x).

    (1) log 0.0314 = log (3.14 · 0.01) = log 3.14 + log 0.01
    (2) log 30.14 = log (3.014 · 10) = log 3.014 + log 10
    (3) log 314 = log (3.14 · 100) = log 3.14 + log 100
    (4) log 3,140 = log (3.14 · 1,000) = log 3.14 + log 1,000

Answer: (2). It does not share the same mantissa (0.4969296481) as log 3.14.

Practice

In 1–10, select the numeral preceding the expression that best completes the sentence or answers the question.

1. If log N = 3.5777, find N to the nearest ten-thousandth.
    (1) 3481.8722   (3) 5724.0049
    (2) 3781.8126   (4) 6781.9292

2. If log 3.87 = a, then log 3,870 equals
    (1) 1,000a (3) 3 + a
    (2) 1,000 + a (4) 3a

3. If $f(x)$ = log x, then $f(100,000)$ is equal to
    (1) 7   (3) 5
    (2) 6   (4) 4

4. If log 8 = w, then log 640 equals
    (1) 4w + 1   (3) w + 80
    (2) 10w^2 (4) 2w + 1

5. If 10^x = k, which expression is equivalent to 10^{x-1}?
    (1) $k - 10$ (3) $\dfrac{10}{k}$
    (2) $k - 1$ (4) $\dfrac{k}{10}$

6. If log 8.73 = a, then log 873 equals which of the following?
    (1) 10(a + 1)   (3) a + 11
    (2) a + 2   (4) $\dfrac{a+1}{10}$

7. log $\sqrt{\dfrac{100}{n}}$ equals
    (1) $1 - \dfrac{\log n}{2}$ (3) $2 - \log n$
    (2) $10 - \dfrac{\log n}{2}$ (4) $\dfrac{2}{\log n}$

8. If $10^{2.468}$ = 293.765, which of the following is $10^{0.468}$?
    (1) 0.293765   (3) 29.3765
    (2) 2.93765   (4) 29,376.5

9. If log 5 = a, then log 0.05 equals
    (1) $a - 2$ (3) $\dfrac{5}{0.05}$
    (2) $\dfrac{a}{100}$ (4) $a - 100$

10. If log N = 0.730812, what is the value of N to the nearest ten thousandth?
    (1) 0.7308   (3) 538.04
    (2) 5.3804   (4) 53.804

10.5 Exponential and Logarithmic Equations

In Chapter 9, you learned how to solve exponential equations by rewriting the expressions so they shared the same base. For example, in the equation $9^x = 27$, we could rewrite both members of the equation as powers of 3: $3^{2x} = 3^3$. Then, since the bases were the same, we set the exponents equal to one another: $2x = 3$, so $x = \frac{3}{2}$. In other words, $9^{\frac{3}{2}} = 27$.

However, for equations like $7^x = 83$, the bases cannot be made equal. Neither 7 nor 83 can be written as a power of the same base. In cases like this, we could solve by graphing as we did in the last chapter, or we could use logarithms to solve for x.

 **MODEL PROBLEMS**

---

1. Solve $7^x = 83$ for x to the nearest ten thousandth.

SOLUTION

Since $7^2 = 49$ and $7^3 = 343$, we can estimate that the value of x is between 2 and 3, and much closer to 2.

$$7^x = 83$$
$$\log 7^x = \log 83 \qquad \text{First, take the logarithm of each side.}$$
$$x \log 7 = \log 83 \qquad \text{Second, apply the power rule of logarithms.}$$
$$x = \frac{\log 83}{\log 7} \qquad \text{Isolate the } x \text{ by dividing by } \log 7.$$
$$x = 2.270834864 \qquad \text{Use your calculator to solve for } x.$$
$$x = 2.2708 \qquad \text{Round the answer as specified.}$$

The solution agrees with the estimate.

Note: It is possible to change from one base to another with the **change of base formula**:

$$\log_a n = \frac{\log_{10} n}{\log_{10} a} \, (a \neq 0 \text{ or } 1)$$

Sometimes an equation to be solved is written in logarithmic form. As in the last chapter, our first step is to rewrite the equation in exponential form to explore a means of solution.

2. Solve $\log_6 239 = x$ for x to the nearest thousandth.

SOLUTION

$$\log_6 239 = x$$

$6^x = 239$	First, rewrite the equation in exponential form.
$\log 6^x = \log 239$	Second, take the log of each side.
$x\log 6 = \log 239$	Apply the power rule of logarithms.
$x = \dfrac{\log 239}{\log 6}$	Divide to isolate the variable.
$x = 3.056472504$	Use your calculator to evaluate x.
$x = 3.056$	Round off as specified.

At times, you may be solving an equation to determine the base of a power. In this type of problem, you will need to find the antilogarithm.

3. Using logarithms, solve for x to the nearest tenth: $x^{5.2} = 112$.

SOLUTION

$x^{5.2} = 112$	
$\log x^{5.2} = \log 112$	First, take the logarithm of each side.
$5.2 \log x = \log 112$	Apply the power rule of logarithms.
$\log x = \dfrac{\log 112}{5.2}$	Divide by 5.2 to isolate the variable.
$\log x = 0.394080389$	Use your calculator to simplify the right side.
$x = 2.477880677$	Find the antilogarithm by using the 10^x key on your calculator.
$x = 2.5$	Round to the nearest tenth.

Logarithmic equations are solved by "undoing" the logarithmic operations and replacing the given equation with its equivalent algebraic format.

4. Solve for all values of x: $\log (x - 1) + \log (2x - 3) = 1$.

Remember: When no other base is shown, the base is assumed to be 10.

SOLUTION

$$\log (x - 1) + \log (2x - 3) = 1$$
$$\log (x - 1)(2x - 3) = 1 \qquad \text{Undo the product rule of logarithms.}$$
$$(x - 1)(2x - 3) = 10^1 \qquad \text{Rewrite as an exponential equation.}$$
$$2x^2 - 5x + 3 = 10 \qquad \text{Perform indicated operations to find the quadratic.}$$

$$2x^2 - 5x - 7 = 0 \qquad \text{Set equal to zero and solve.}$$
$$(2x - 7)(x + 1) = 0$$
$$2x - 7 = 0 \qquad x + 1 = 0$$
$$2x = 7 \qquad x = -1 \qquad \text{We must reject this answer since we cannot take the logarithm of a negative number.}$$

$$x = \frac{7}{2}$$

Since the domain of logarithmic equations is $x > 0$, the log of a negative number does not exist.

The solution to the original equation is only $x = \frac{7}{2}$.

Note: Logarithmic equations in base 10 can also be solved by using your graphing calculator. Insert the left side of the equation in Y_1 and the right side in Y_2 and then use (2nd) (TRACE) (CALCULATE, 5: intersect) to find the solution(s).

Practice

In 1–8, solve each equation for x. Round to the nearest hundredth.

1. $5^x = 38$

2. $3^{2x} = 108$

3. $x = \log_3 152$

4. $4.83^x = 29.1$

5. $x^{3.2} = 87$

6. $x = \log_7 513$

7. $13.2^x = 4{,}719$

8. $x^{2.8} = 31$

9. Using logarithms, solve for x to the nearest thousandth: $2^x = \frac{3}{2}$.

10. Using logarithms, solve for x to the nearest thousandth: $x = \log_5 1{,}692$.

11. Using logarithms, solve for x to the nearest ten thousandth: $4.5^x = 78$.

12. Using logarithms, solve for x to the nearest thousandth: $x = \left(\sqrt[3]{0.592} \right)^2$.

In 13–20, solve each equation for all values of x. Be certain to check that your answers are valid.

13. $2 \log_2 x - \log_2 (x - 1) = 3$

14. $\log (x - 2) + \log (2x - 3) = 2 \log x$

15. $\log_2 (4x + 10) - \log_2 (x + 1) = 3$

16. $\log_3 (2x - 1) + \log_3 (x + 7) = 3$

17. $\log_2 (x + 5) - \log_2 (x - 2) = 3$

18. $\log (3x - 2) + \log (x - 1) = \log 2x$

19. $\log_4 (x^2 + 3x) - \log_4 (x + 5) = 1$

20. $2 \log_3 x - \log_3 (x - 2) = 2$

10.6 Applications of Exponents and Logarithms

Exponential and logarithmic functions are often found in real-life problems. These can be solved algebraically or graphically as demonstrated in the problem below.

 **MODEL PROBLEM**

Jack and Jill were sightseeing in the desert when their camper ran out of gas along a level stretch of interstate highway. The speed of their camper decreased exponentially over time. The camper's speed function is represented by $P(t)$ where the speed P is measured in miles per minute, and t is expressed in minutes:

$$P(t) = 1.2(0.58697)^t$$

To the nearest minute, how long did it take until their speed was 0.01 mile per minute?

SOLUTION

First we will examine the problem using logarithms.

$0.01 = 1.2(0.58697)^t$	Set the desired speed equal to $P(t)$.
$\dfrac{0.01}{1.2} = (0.58697)^t$	Isolate the base of the exponent.
$\log \dfrac{0.01}{1.2} = \log (0.58697)^t$	Take the logarithm of each side.
$\log 0.01 - \log 1.2 = t\log 0.58697$	Use logarithm rules to simplify equation.
$\dfrac{\log 0.01 - \log 1.2}{\log 0.58697} = t$	Isolate t.
$8.985843415 = t$	Use your calculator to find t.
$9 \text{ minutes} \approx t$	

To solve the problem graphically, first, enter function $P(t)$ in Y_1 and the desired value in Y_2.

```
Plot1  Plot2  Plot3
\Y1 = 1.2 (.58697)^
X
\Y2 = .01
\Y3 =
\Y4 =
\Y5 =
\Y6 =
```

Set the window for $0 \leq x \leq 10$ and $-0.25 \leq y \leq 1.2$ and graph.

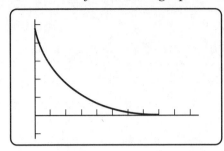

Notice that the line $y = 0.01$ is not visible because its distance from the y-axis is so small. The TI-83 will, however, find the intersection of the two functions. Use (2nd) and (TRACE) (CALCULATE) and 5: intersect.

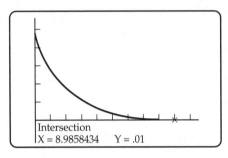

Notice that the solution is the same as the one we found earlier using logarithms.

Practice

Solve the following problems using logarithms. Round as indicated.

1. A dastardly criminal planted 37 ounces of radioactive krypton-85 in a safety-deposit box near *The Daily Planet* on January 1, 1979. The function showing the strength of the remaining krypton-85 is $K(t) = 37(0.9376)^t$ where t represents the years since 1979. If any amount over 8 ounces will immobilize Superman,
   a. what is the first year in which there will be fewer than 8 ounces of krypton in the bank vault?
   b. will it be safe for Superman to enter the bank vault to prevent a planned jewel heist on New Year's Eve, 2004?
   c. how much krypton-85, to the nearest tenth of an ounce, remains on January 1, 2004?

2. Bacteria being grown for research programs at a university have a population modeled by the function $B(t) = 1.25(2)^t$ where $B(t)$ is in tens of thousands of bacteria and t represents the time in hours. After how many hours will the bacteria population reach 1,000,000? (Round to the nearest hundredth of an hour.)

3. The number of Canadian geese roaming the sports fields in one school district grows every year according to the function $G(t) = 24(1.2314)^t$ where t is years since 1998. The Parent-Teacher Association has suggested hiring dogs to chase the geese, but the dog squads will not work with geese populations fewer than 70. In what year can the county hire the geese chasers?

4. The percentage of the United States population that is foreign-born is growing at an exponential rate. The function is represented by the equation $P(t) = 4.5907(1.027)^t$ where P is in millions and t is the number of years since 1970. In what year did the number of people born outside the United States double their population of 1970?

5. The population of Ghostton, Nevada, is modeled by the function $G(t) = 1,824(0.896)^t$ where t is the number of years since 1980. In what year will the population be fewer than 50 people?

6. Environmentalists in Ireland are concerned about the growth of the leprechaun population, represented by the function $L(t) = 1,208(1.265)^t$ where t is the number of years since 1990. Since leprechauns live at the base of rainbows, an increase in leprechauns without a corresponding increase in rainbows will be detrimental to the survival of the leprechauns. If there are only enough rainbows for 10,000 leprechauns, how many years does the government have to solve this problem?

7. Deirdre and Alan graduated with master's degrees in business in May 2000 and accepted jobs at competing firms. Deirdre's contracted salary is represented by the function $D(t) = 46,500(1.082)^t$ while Alan's salary is $A(t) = 51,000(1.065)^t$.
   a. In what year will Deirdre and Alan earn the same salary?
   b. What will that salary be?
   c. When will each of these employees first earn $100,000?

CHAPTER REVIEW

1. Solve for x: $\log_x 16 = 4$.

2. If $f(x) = \log x$, evaluate $f(1,000)$.

3. Evaluate $\log_a a$.

4. Write as a single logarithm: $\log 2 + 3\log x - \frac{1}{2} \log b$.

5. If $x = \log_2 6$, find the value of x, to the nearest thousandth.

6. If $f(x) = \log_3 x$, what are the domain and range of $f(x)$?

7. Solve for x: $\log x + \log (x + 3) = 1$.

8. If $\log_{x-2} 125 = 3$, find x.

9. Solve for x: $\log (x - 2) + \log (2x - 3) = 2 \log x$.

10. Evaluate $\log_b 1$.

In 11–20, select the numeral preceding the word or expression that best completes the statement or answers the question.

11. If $x = \dfrac{a\sqrt{b}}{cd}$, which expression is equivalent to $\log x$?

   (1) $\log a + \frac{1}{2} \log b - \log c + \log d$

   (2) $\log a - \frac{1}{2} \log b - \log c + \log d$

   (3) $\frac{1}{2} \log a + \frac{1}{2} \log b - \log c + \log d$

   (4) $\log a + \frac{1}{2} \log b - \log c - \log d$

12. The inverse of $y = 10^x$ is obtained by reflecting $y = 10^x$ in the line
   (1) $y = x$ (3) $y = 0$
   (2) $y = -x$ (4) $x = 0$

13. The graph of $y = \log_4 x$ lies entirely in quadrants
    (1) I and II   (3) III and IV
    (2) II and III   (4) IV and I

14. If $\log a = x$ and $\log b = y$, then $\log \sqrt{ab}$ is equal to
    (1) $\frac{1}{2}xy$ (3) $\frac{1}{2}x + \frac{1}{2}y$
    (2) $\frac{1}{2}x + y$ (4) $\frac{1}{2}x - \frac{1}{2}y$

15. If $\log_x 3 = \frac{1}{4}$, what is the value of x?
    (1) 81   (3) $3\frac{1}{4}$
    (2) 27   (4) $\sqrt[4]{3}$

16. The equation $y = a^x$ expressed in logarithmic form is
    (1) $y = \log_a x$ (3) $x = \log_y a$
    (2) $x = \log_a y$ (4) $a = \log_y x$

17. If $\log 6 = a$, then $\log 600 =$
    (1) $100a$ (3) $a - 2$
    (2) $a + 2$ (4) $2a$

18. If the graphs of $y = \log_4 x$ and $y = 3$ are drawn on the same set of axes, they will intersect when $x =$
    (1) 64   (3) 3
    (2) 12   (4) $3^{\frac{1}{4}}$

19. Which value is *not* in the range of the function $y = \log_5 x$?
    (1) -2
    (2) 0
    (3) 3
    (4) The range is $\{y \mid y \in \mathbb{R}\}$.

20. What is the inverse of $y = \log_4 x$?
    (1) $x = 4^y$ (3) $x = y^4$
    (2) $y = 4^x$ (4) $y = x^4$

21. a. Graph $y = 2^x$.
    b. On the same set of axes, sketch and label the reflection of the graph $y = 2^x$ in the line $y = x$.
    c. Write an equation for the graph drawn in part b.
    d. What are the domain and range of the graph drawn in part b?
    e. Using the graph drawn in part b, describe what happens to the y-values as x approaches 0.

22. Frank Logman has been trying to build up his muscles by doing some chin-ups. Although Frank is not physically fit, he is an excellent mathematics student. So, Frank has discovered that he can model the number of chin-ups he can complete by the equation $F(t) = \log t$, where t is the time in days since he started working out.
    a. Graph $F(t)$ in the interval $1 \le t \le 120$.
    b. Find $F(100)$ and explain what is meant by this.
    c. Find t such that $F(t) = 3$. Explain your answer. (Hint: You may have to adjust your window to answer this question.)

23. Mike Lockman has also been trying to build up his muscles by doing some chin-ups. Mike is physically fit, but is not such a good mathematics student. However, Frank has assured Mike that he too can use a mathematical equation to model the number of chin-ups completed. The number of chin-ups Mike can complete, $M(t)$, can be represented by the equation $M(t) = 1.035^t$, where t is the time in days since he first started working out.
    a. Graph $M(t)$ in the interval $1 \le t \le 120$.
    b. Find $M(100)$ and explain what is meant by this.
    c. Find t such that $M(t) = 3$. Explain your answer. (Hint: You may have to adjust your window to answer this question.)
    d. Who do you think is more likely to make the bodybuilding team, Frank or Mike? Explain your answer.

24. Given $\log 2 = a$ and $\log 3 = b$. Express each of the following in terms of a and b.
    a. $\log 18$
    b. $\log \frac{2}{3}$
    c. $\log 24$
    d. $\log 54$
    e. $\log 1.5$

25. a. Complete the table for the values of y for the equation $y = \log_3 x$.

x	$\frac{1}{9}$	$\frac{1}{3}$	1	3	9
y					

    b. Using the completed table, draw the graph of the equation $y = \log_3 x$ in the interval $\frac{1}{9} \le x \le 9$.

CHAPTER 11

Regressions

11.1 Line of Best Fit

If you are given two points on a coordinate graph and asked what line connects those two points, it's not a difficult job to determine the equation of the line. You know from geometry that any two points can form one and only line so you could simply draw a line on the graph connecting the two points, then use the point-slope or slope-intercept method to determine the equation. But, whichever method you choose, there is only one line possible to connect two points.

MODEL PROBLEM

Determine the equation of the line connecting the points $(-1, -2)$ and $(5, 6)$.

GRAPHIC SOLUTION

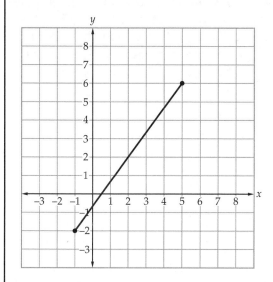

Connect the two points $(-1, -2)$ and $(5, 6)$ and find the slope. Unfortunately, the graph shows that the y-intercept is not an integer, so you must estimate the value of the y-intercept. In this situation, the algebraic method of solution is a better one.

The line on which these two points occur is therefore $y = \frac{4}{3}x - \frac{2}{3}$.

In some cases, however, it is not as easy to determine a specific line through a set of points because the points do not all lie on a unique line.

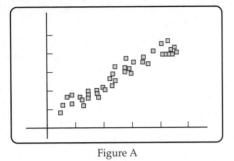

Figure A

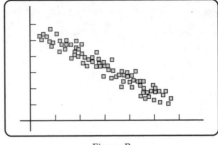

Figure B

The figures above represent graphs called **scatterplots**, which are basically sets of points scattered on the coordinate plane. In these graphs, no one line can be drawn to pass through all the points shown. Instead, we look for the **line of best fit.** Various lines are drawn through as many points as possible in the set and then the distance between each point and the arbitrary lines are calculated. Each distance is then squared and the line of best fit is the line that has the smallest sum for all the squares of the distances. This procedure for finding the line of best fit is called the **method of least squares** or **linear regression.** Formulas to find the line of best fit were developed by mathematician Adrien Legendre in 1805. Today it is possible to use software or calculators to quickly find the line of best fit for our problems. Below, you can see the lines of best fit the TI-83 created for each scatterplot. Some of the data points lie on the line, while others fall above or below it.

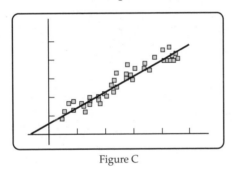

Figure C

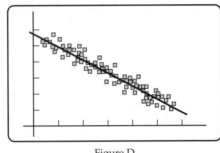

Figure D

To measure how well the data matches the line of best fit, mathematicians use a **correlation coefficient** (denoted as r). If the y-coordinate of points is increasing as the x-coordinate increases, the correlation coefficient is positive, as in Figures A and C above. If the y-coordinate of the points is decreasing as the x-coordinate increases, the correlation coefficient is negative, as in Figures B and D above. The sign of the correlation coefficient is the same as the sign of the slope of the line of best fit through the points. An ideal linear correlation coefficient is $+1$ for an increasing linear function and -1 for a decreasing linear function. In Figure E below, the scatterplot has a correlation coefficient of $+1$ while in Figure F, the correlation coefficient is -1.

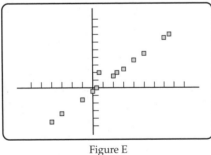

Figure E

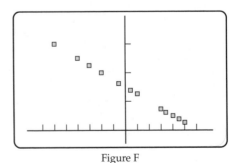

Figure F

Figure G has a correlation coefficient of approximately 0.75, meaning that the linear relationship of the data is somewhat weaker than for an exact linear relationship that would have a correlation coefficient of +1 or −1. Since the points in Figure H do not show any linear relationship, that graph has a very low correlation coefficient of −0.05.

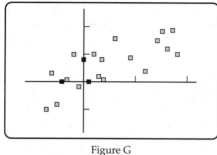

Figure G   Figure H

Hence, a correlation coefficient close to 0 signifies no correlation while a correlation coefficient close to +1 or −1 indicates that the points in the scatterplot cluster near the calculated line of best fit.

Note: A data set with a correlation coefficient of $r = \pm 1$ is an example of **direct variation.** That is, as x increases, y increases and vice versa.

It is important, however, to realize that even if there is a strong correlation between dependent and independent data, there is not necessarily a cause and effect relationship. If you compare reading ability and age, it is probable that in most cases, reading ability will increase as an individual's age does, but only because as people grow older, they also gain more education and a higher reading level. To say that a person age 16 reads better than a child 3 years old is accurate, but it is not valid to credit age as the cause of better reading.

MODEL PROBLEMS

1. The scatterplot below would most likely have which of the following correlation coefficients?

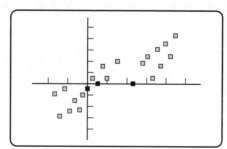

(1) −1
(2) −0.54
(3) 0.875
(4) 1

The figure shows a scatterplot with a positive upward movement, so the correlation coefficient must be positive. This eliminates choices 1 and 2. The majority of points appear to be almost collinear, but there are some points outside the main cluster, so it is not an ideal line of best fit. The correct answer is choice 3, 0.875.

2. Which of the following scatterplots would have a correlation coefficient of +1?

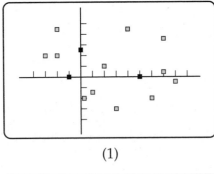

(1)

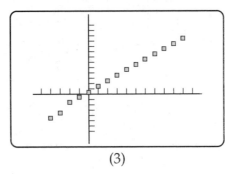

(3)

(4) None of these

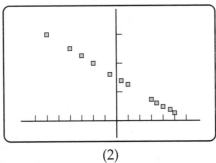

(2)

SOLUTION

In choice 1, few of the points are collinear so this would have a very low correlation coefficient. Choice 2 has a negative correlation coefficient, but choice 3 clearly has a positive correlation. Since all points appear collinear, it would have a correlation coefficient of +1, indicating an ideal line of best fit.

3. Determine whether the correlation between the following elements would have a positive, negative, or almost zero correlation.
   (1) the size of a backyard pool and the amount of water it holds
   (2) the weight of a steak and the price it costs
   (3) the number of people in the audience and the cost of a movie ticket
   (4) the number of partners in a law firm and the percent of the total each receives

SOLUTION
(1) Positive correlation; the bigger the pool, the more water needed to fill it.
(2) Positive correlation; meat is sold by weight, so the larger the steak, the more expensive it is.
(3) A correlation of almost zero; movie prices are standard, no matter how many people are in the theater.
(4) Negative correlation; the greater the number of partners, the less money each will receive.

Remember: Correlation coefficients of +1 or −1 indicate an excellent point alignment with the theoretical line of best fit. The negative is not a value judgment, but an indication of slope of the line of best fit.

In 1–6, match each scatterplot with the appropriate correlation coefficient.

1.

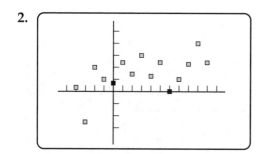

a. +1
b. +0.8
c. +0.3
d. 0
e. −0.6
f. −0.9

2.

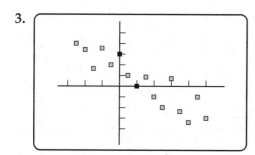

3.

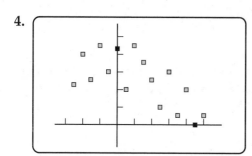

4.

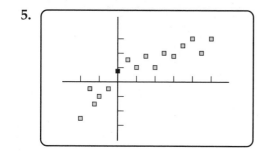

5.

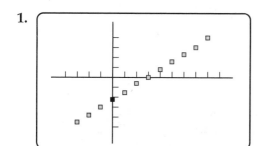

6.

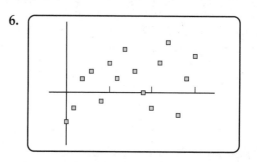

In 7–10, select the numeral preceding the word or expression that best answers the question.

7. The accompanying diagram shows a scatterplot.

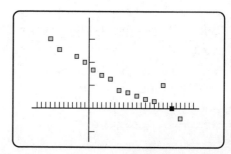

Which correlation coefficient could match the graph?
(1) −0.9   (3) 0.6
(2) −0.3   (4) 1

8. Which of the following is a true statement?
(1) The line of best fit always passes through each of the given data points.
(2) The line of best fit must have a correlation coefficient of +1 or −1.
(3) A correlation coefficient of −1 means that there is no correlation.
(4) If the correlation coefficient is negative, the line of best fit has a negative slope.

9. Which of the following correlation coefficients most clearly represents a linear relationship for a given set of data points?
(1) −0.89   (3) 0.58
(2) −0.52   (4) 0.76

10. Which of the following correlation coefficients would indicate no significant linear relationship for the independent and dependent variables in a data set?
(1) −1   (3) 0.15
(2) −0.52   (4) 0.90

For 11–17, consider the paired variables and decide whether they have a positive correlation, a negative correlation, or almost zero correlation. Be prepared to explain your reasoning.

11. The number of bedrooms in a family home and the number of years the family has lived there

12. The age of a child and the number of years of school that child has attended

13. The speed at which a car is driven and the distance traveled in a six-hour period

14. The age of a nonclassic car and its value for trade-in

15. The waiting time at a restaurant and the number of entrees offered

16. The number of college applicants to a university and the tuition charged

17. The number of cigarettes smoked a day and the smoker's lung capacity

In 18–20, match each graph with a description of its correlation coefficient: positive, negative, or almost zero.

18.

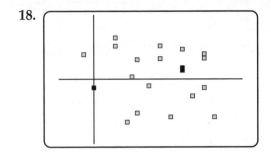

19.

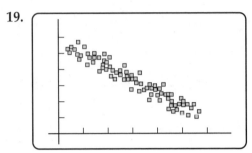

20.

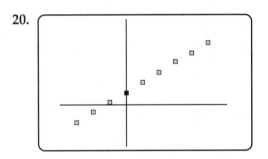

11.2 Linear Regression

If you have a set of points, you can use the calculator to find a graph or equation that represents that data. Once you have developed a graph, the calculator can find the linear regression line, or line of best fit.

MODEL PROBLEM

The table below gives the length of the right foot and the height of 10 males, all in centimeters.

Right foot (cm)	25.4	26.4	27.1	27.9	28	28.4	28.5	29.2	29.5	30
Height (cm)	165.1	170.2	175.3	179	181.2	182.9	183	184.2	185	186.9

a. Create the scatterplot that represents these data.
b. Determine the line of best fit for the given data.

c. What is the correlation coefficient for the size of right feet vs. height?

d. Is it a logical premise that foot size and height are dependent measures? Why?

e. Predict the approximate height of a person whose right foot measures   **1.** 24.8 cm   **2.** 31 cm.

SOLUTION

a. First, you need to enter the data. Use the (STAT) key. You will see the screen shown below.

```
EDIT CALC TESTS
1 : Edit...
2 : SortA(
3 : SortD(
4 : ClrList
5 : SetUpEditor
```

Press (1) or (ENTER) for Edit. Then you will see the following screen:

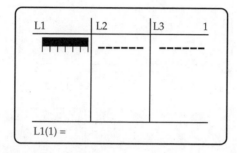

Note: If you see data on the screen, use the up arrow to go up to the top where the list names occur, hit the CLEAR button and go back down to the list.

Now enter the values given in L_1 and L_2 (lists 1 and 2).
The resulting data will appear as below.

L1	L2	L3	1
25.4	165.1	------	
26.4	170.2		
27.1	175.3		
27.9	179		
28	181.2		
28.4	182.9		
28.5	183		

L1(1) = 25.4

Next, use the (2nd) calculator key and the (Y =) key. The resulting screen is below.

```
STAT PLOTS
1 : Plot1...Off
    L1 L4    □
2 : Plot2...Off
    L3 L4    □
3 : Plot3...Off
    L4 L6    □
4↓PlotsOff
```

Press (ENTER) to get the following screen:

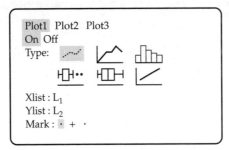

Use your calculator to highlight the items as shown and then press (ZOOM) (9), which will graph the points you have as shown below.

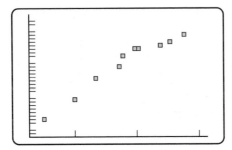

This is the scatterplot requested in part **a** of the Model Problem.

b. Now the calculator can find the equation. Press the (STAT) key again, but this time use the right arrow to move over to CALC.

EDIT CALC TESTS
1 : Edit...
2 : SortA(
3 : SortD(
4 : ClrList
5 : SetUpEditor

EDIT CALC TESTS
1 : 1–Var Stats
2 : 2–Var Stats
3 : Med–Med
4 : LinReg (ax+b)
5 : QuadReg
6 : CubicReg
7↓QuartReg

Since we want a linear regression, we press (4) or scroll down to 4: LinReg (ax + b) and press (ENTER). The calculator now prints that statement on the home screen. After the statement LinReg (ax + b), enter L_1, L_2, Y_1, which tells the calculator to use List 1 and List 2 and put the regression equation in the (Y =) screen, spot Y_1.

Note: If your data is in lists 3 and 4, be certain to inform the calculator to use L_3 and L_4. The calculator's default lists are L_1 and L_2.

LinReg (ax+b) L_1, L_2, Y_1

Press (ENTER) and the following screen appears.

```
LinReg
  y=ax+b
  a=4.830882353
  b=43.82205882
  r²= .9556128231
  r= .9775545116
■
```

If you round your a and b values to the nearest hundredth and substitute them into the standard linear equation, your answer to part **b** is $y = 4.83x + 43.82$.

c. The r indicates the correlation coefficient. Notice that $r = .9775545116$, so this line does not have a perfect correlation, but is a line of best fit for these data. An r of .978 indicates a strong linear relationship between the data sets.

d. It would seem likely that a person's height and foot size have a strong correlation since it would be physically difficult for a very tall individual to support his or her weight on very small feet and vice versa.

e. Plugging 24.8 into the linear regression model we get a height of 163.6 cm. When we use a foot length of 31 cm, we get a height predicted to be 193.6 cm. These are, however, predictions, not necessarily guaranteed data results. It should be noted that the farther from the original data the new values are, the less likely they will be accurate.

Note: If r, the correlation coefficient, does not appear on your screen, press the catalog button on your calculator, (2nd) (0). Scroll down to the D's and press (ENTER) next to Diagnostic On. The calculator will print DiagnosticOn on the home screen; hit (ENTER) again and the calculator will print Done. Then re-enter the linear regression command and now you will see the correlation coefficient.

Now hit (GRAPH) and you will see the graph below.

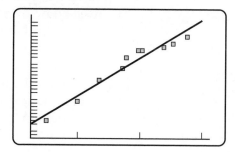

Notice the line $y = 4.83x + 43.82$ passes through the majority of points given.

In 1–5, select the numeral preceding the expression that best completes the statement or answers the question.

1. Janice has decided she wants to enter the New York Marathon next year, but she realizes she has a lot of training to do. She decides to start a regimen in which she runs 1 mile for a week and then increases her distance by $\frac{1}{2}$ mile, runs that distance for a week and increases her distance by $\frac{1}{2}$ mile again. Which of the following functions might be used to represent the number of miles run in week x?

   (1) $y = 4\left(\frac{1}{2}\right)x$ (3) $y = 1 + \frac{1}{2}x$

   (2) $y = \frac{1}{2} + 4x$ (4) $y = 1 + 4x$

2. Mr. Jackson records the number of miles traveled each time he fills up his gas tank and has recently noticed that his car has been getting lower gas mileage. He has calculated that the mileage he gets per gallon is changing according to the function $y = 28 - 0.65x$. On his twelfth fill-up, how many miles per gallon did he get?

   (1) 27.35   (3) 16
   (2) 20.2   (4) 7.8

In 3 and 4, use the following data from a survey of eight female high school juniors comparing right foot size and height.

Right foot (cm)	Height (cm)
22.1	157.1
22.9	160.8
23.1	161.4
23.4	161
24.1	162.8
24.6	164
25.4	164.7
26.1	164

3. The correlation coefficient of these data is
   (1) 1
   (2) 0.9017
   (3) 0.96711
   (4) 0.9237

4. The linear regression equation for these data is approximately
   (1) $y = 2.06x - 113$
   (2) $y = 2.06x + 113$
   (3) $y = 1.65x + 122.4$
   (4) $y = 1.65x - 122.4$

5. The number of sets of twins born in the United States has been increasing as shown in the table below.

Year	Number of Sets of Twins
1990	93,865
1991	94,779
1992	95,372
1993	96,445
1994	97,064

   Note: When years are given as part of the data, in order to make the calculations easier, we usually set the first year as 0, so in this problem, enter 0, 1, 2, 3, and 4 as the independent variable year in L_1.

   a. Find the line of best fit for these data.
   b. What is the correlation coefficient for these data to the nearest hundredth?
   c. Based on these data what might the number of twin births be expected to be in 1997?
   d. Actually in 1997, there were 104,137 sets of twins born. What does this mean about the line of best fit? What might explain this discrepancy?

6. Personal expenditures for clothing in the United States since 1992 are listed below. The expenditures are reported in billions of dollars.

Year	Clothing Expenditures
1992	283.5
1993	298.1
1994	312.7
1995	323.4
1996	338
1997	353.3
1998	367.9

a. Use the data to form a scatterplot.
b. Use linear regression to find the equation of the line of best fit for annual expenditures on clothes since 1992.
c. What is the correlation coefficient of your equation?
d. If there were approximately 270 million people in the U.S. in 1998, how much did each spend on personal clothing that year?
e. According to this model, how much will be spent in the U.S. on clothes in 2005? Do you think this is a reliable estimate? Why or why not?

7. George and Martha begin a woodworking business creating early American house signs. Suppose the cost of making 2 placards is $548.50, the cost of 5 placards is $561.25, the cost of 10 is $582.50, the cost of 25 placards is $646.25, the cost of 50 placards is $752.50, and the cost of 100 placards is $965.00.
   a. Find the linear function to represent the cost function of x placards.
   b. The placards are sold for $15.00 each, so the function which represents revenue is $R(x) = 15x$. If Profit = Revenue − Cost, what equation would represent the profit function?
   c. Find the profit on 100 house signs and 250 house signs.
   d. If George promises to take Martha to Hawaii when they make $7,500, how many units must be sold before they pack their suntan lotion?

8. Foreign adoptions have been growing in the United States. The data in the table shows the number of adoptions from Russia in the period 1992−1996.

Year	Number of Adoptions from Russia
1992	324
1993	746
1994	1,530
1995	1,896
1996	2,454

a. Find the equation that best suits these data such that the number of Russian adoptions is dependent on the year of the adoption proceedings.
b. What is the correlation coefficient? Do you find this acceptable? Why?
c. Approximately how many more Russian children were adopted each year during this period? (What is the slope of the function?)
d. Based on this mathematical model, how many Russian children would you expect to have been adopted in 1997?

9. The following table represents the number of United States radio stations on the air since 1950.

Year	Number of Radio Stations
1950	2,773
1955	3,211
1960	4,133
1965	5,249
1970	6,760
1975	8,844
1980	8,566
1985	10,359
1990	10,788
1995	11,834
1996	12,295
1997	12,482
1998	12,642

a. Create a scatterplot using these data.
b. Use linear regression to find the line of best fit for the number of radio stations on the air as a function of the year since 1950.
c. What is the correlation coefficient for the line of best fit?
d. According to this model, how many radio stations were present in the United States in 1982? In 2000?

10. Maria Elena's parents are planning her quince-anocera. They are considering two different restaurants whose costs are shown below.

Number of Guests	Restaurant A	Restaurant B
5	800	1,000
15	1,100	1,250
20	1,700	1,750
23	1,880	1,900
25	2,000	2,000

a. Create the scatterplots for each of the restaurants.
b. If $R(x)$ is defined as the cost of the meal dependent on the number of guests, find the lines of best fit for each restaurant.
c. What are the correlation coefficients for each?
d. If the family decides to invite 40 guests, what is the cost for each restaurant?
e. If the family has only 24 guests, which restaurant is less expensive?

11. The following table lists the average sale price of new one-family homes in the United States since 1975.

Year	Average Sale Price of Houses
1975	$42,600
1980	$76,400
1985	$100,822
1990	$149,800
1995	$158,700
1996	$166,400
1997	$176,200
1998	$181,900
1999	$195,800

a. Create a scatterplot using these data.
b. If $H(x)$ represents the average cost of a home in the United States as a function of the year of purchase, find the line of best fit for the data.
c. What is the correlation coefficient? Does this indicate a strong correlation?
d. If Doug and Marissa want to buy a one-family house in 2005 and are able to get one for the national average price, what should they expect to pay for it? Based on the behavior of the latter data points, is this a reasonable estimate? Why or why not?
e. Doug's parents bought their home in 1971. What price might they have paid for their home, based on the national average? Is this reasonable? Why or why not?

11.3 Exponential Regression Models

Since not all relationships between sets of data in the real world form linear patterns, other possibilities must be considered. Look at the data shown below.

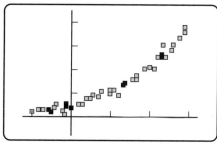

Window: [–1, 3] × [–1, 8]

The points on this scatterplot clearly do not form a linear relationship. Based on the shape of the curve, it looks as if this may be an exponential relationship. The figure below shows the scatterplot with the curve $y = 2^x$ sketched in the same viewing window. It appears as if the curve $y = 2^x$ might be a good model for the given data points.

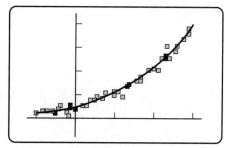

Window: [–1, 3] × [–1, 8]

Although the equation $y = 2^x$ was obtained by "eyeballing" the graph, your calculator has the ability to perform exponential regression. The process used to find an exponential regression model on the calculator is the same as that used for linear regression.

Exponential functions are in the form $y = ab^x$. They grow (or decay) at a constant percent rate.

MODEL PROBLEMS

1. If a cup of coffee is left on a countertop, it will cool off slowly. The following table shows the temperature of a cup of coffee sitting for 50 minutes.

Time	0	5	10	15	20	25	30	35	40	45	50
Temp °F	176.81	162.91	146.34	135.18	126.28	118.8	112.53	107.11	102.72	99.1	96.44

a. What type of equation does this appear to be?
b. Use the regression capability of your calculator to obtain an equation for an exponential function that could model the data.
c. Based on the *data*, what was the initial temperature of the coffee?

d. Based on the *equation*, what was the initial temperature of the coffee? Why is it different from your answer to part **c**?
e. Use your equation to find $f(18)$ and explain its meaning.
f. Use your equation to find x such that $f(x) = 118$ and explain its meaning.
g. Use your equation to find x such that $f(x) = 18$. Does this make sense? Why?

SOLUTION

1. a. If we graphed the information, it would look like this

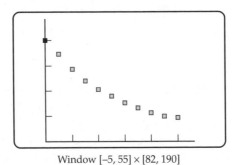

Window [–5, 55] × [82, 190]

The graph looks like a decreasing exponential function.
b. Use your calculator to perform the exponential regression. Press (STAT) (▶) CALC (0) (2nd) (1) (,) (2nd) (2) (,) (VARS) (▶) Y-VARS (1) (1) (ENTER) and obtain the equation $y = 167.05712815846 \times 0.9879610402685 \wedge x$.
c. Look at the data to see at time 0 minutes, the temperature of the coffee was 176.81°.
d. According to the equation, the initial temperature, $f(0)$, was approximately 167.06°. The regression model attempts to fit as much of the data as possible to the model and some points do not fit exactly.
e. Press (2nd) (TRACE) (CALCULATE) (1) and enter in 18 as the x-value. The result is $f(18) = 134.3327$. Eighteen minutes after being left on the counter, the temperature of the coffee is approximately 134.3327°.
f. You must find the time when the temperature is 118°. In Y_2 enter 118 and see where the two graphs intersect. The graphs show that approximately 28.703 minutes after the coffee is left on the countertop, its temperature is 118°.
g. You must find the time when the temperature is 18°. In Y_2 enter 18 and see where the two graphs intersect. (You will have to extend your graphing window to do so.) According to the equation, approximately 183.94661 minutes after the coffee is left on the countertop, its temperature is 18°. Unless the temperature of the room is 18° or less, this would be impossible. The lowest temperature the coffee could reach would be room temperature. Thus, the model will only work until that point.

2. The table below shows the population of New York State from 1810 to 1910.

Year	1810	1820	1830	1840	1850	1860
Population	959,049	1,372,812	1,918,608	2,428,921	3,097,394	3,880,735
Year	1870	1880	1890	1900	1910	
Population	4,382,759	5,082,871	5,997,853	7,268,894	9,113,614	

a. Use the information given in the table above to make a scatterplot of the population, $P(t)$, as a function of time, t, the number of years since 1800. Thus, $1810 = 10$, $1820 = 20$, etc.

b. Write an equation for an exponential function that could be used to model the data in the scatterplot.

c. Based on your equation, how fast was the population of New York State increasing?

d. Use your equation to predict the population in New York State in 1940.

e. The table below shows the population of New York State from 1920 to 1970. Add this information to that from part **a** to make a new scatterplot with the population of New York State from 1810–1970.

Year	1920	1930	1940	1950	1960	1970
Population	10,385,227	12,588,066	13,479,142	14,830,192	16,482,304	17,558,165

f. Write an equation for an exponential function that could be used to model the data in the scatterplot. Let t continue to represent the number of years since 1800.

g. Based on your equation, how fast was the population of New York State increasing?

h. Use your equation to find the population in New York State in 1940. How does this answer compare to the data above? How does it compare to your answer from part **d**? Why are the answers so different?

i. Use your equation to predict the population in New York State in 2000.

j. The actual population of New York State in 2000 was 18,146,185. How does this compare to your prediction? What could be the reason for your estimate being so far off?

SOLUTION

a. When you enter the information into L1 and L2 you get the following screen:

L1	L2	L3	3
10	959049	▮▮▮▮▮▮	
20	1.37E6		
30	1.92E6		
40	2.43E6		
50	3.1E6		
60	3.88E6		
70	4.38E6		

L3(1) =

Note: Although all of the information from the table was entered, some of the data appears in scientific notation. However, if you highlight a particular value, you can see the entire number.

L1	L2	L3	2
10	959049	- - - - -	
20	1.37E6		
30	1.92E6		
40	2.43E6		
50	3.1E6		
60	3.88E6		
70	4.38E6		

L2(5) = 3097394

b. Use your calculator to perform the exponential regression, and obtain the equation $P(t) = 954525.6668721 * 1.0212854293573^t$.

c. Based on the equation, the population in New York State is increasing at approximately 2.1285% per year.

d. To predict the population in 1940, go to 2nd CALC Value and enter 140 as the x-value. (You may have to extend your window.) The equation predicts that, in 1940, New York State would have approximately 18,213,216 people.

e. Enter the information in the lists.

f. Use your calculator to perform the exponential regression, and obtain the equation
$P(t) = 1143059.1728083 * 1.0177735672419^t$.

g. The population is increasing at approximately 1.777% per year.

h. This time when you enter 140 in for x you get a prediction of 13,465,800 people in 1940, which is 4,747,416 less than the prediction from part **d**. The predictions in part **d** are the results of extrapolating information. That is generally less reliable than interpolating information, as is being done here.

i. To obtain a prediction for 2000, you must find $P(200)$ and again extrapolate. The population predicted is 38,752,723 people.

j. The prediction is way off. We certainly know that the population of New York State did not continue to increase at a rate of 1.777% per year. Perhaps the population did not grow exponentially at all.

Practice

In 1–4, select the numeral preceding the word or expression that best answers the question.

1. Given the scatterplot below, which of the following equations could model the data?

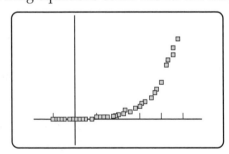

(1) $y = 1 + 1.7x$ (3) $y = 2(0.7)^x$
(2) $y = 2 + 0.7x$ (4) $y = 2(1.7)^x$

2. Given the scatterplot shown below, which of the following equations could model the data?

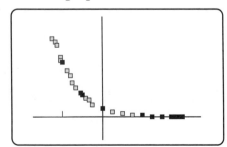

(1) $y = 5(0.4)^x$ (3) $y = -5(1.4)^x$
(2) $y = 5(1.4)^x$ (4) $y = 5 - 1.4^x$

In 3–4, use the following situation.

Although Charlie is only a junior in high school, he is quite a scientist already. He has been studying a colony of ants and has obtained the regression equation $A(t) = 23.12843(1.36840)^t$ to model the number of ants in the colony, $A(t)$, as a function of time, t, in weeks since Charlie began studying the colony.

3. Approximately, how many ants were there when Charlie first began to study them?
(1) 0   (3) 23
(2) 1.368   (4) 37

4. Approximately how many weeks did it take the ant colony to triple in size?
(1) 1.3   (3) 3
(2) 2.9   (4) 3.5

5. When she was born, Janine's grandparents invested $1,000 in a stock market fund for her. Now that she is 16 years old, Janine would like to decide whether to keep the money invested where it is, or transfer it to a bank account where she can receive 4% interest, compounded annually.

The following table shows how Janine's money has grown with her grandparents' investment.

Year	Amount
0	1,000
2	1,200
4	1,300
6	1,555
8	1,660
10	2,000
12	2,100
14	2,600
16	3,000

a. Enter the information in your calculator and make a scatterplot.
b. Write an exponential equation to model the data.
c. At what rate does the investment appear to be growing?
d. Assuming that the investment continues to grow at the same rate, use your equation to determine the amount of money Janine will have in 10 more years.
e. If Janine takes the $3,000 out now, and puts it in the bank to grow at 4%, the equation $y = 3,000 \cdot 1.04^x$ will model the amount of money she would have x years from now. How much money would Janine have 10 years from now if she chooses this option?
f. What advice would you give Janine about her investment? Explain your answer.

In 6–7, use the table below, which contains some information on the cellular telephone industry.

	Subscribers (1,000's)	Average Monthly Bill (dollars)
1990	5,283	80.90
1993	16,009	61.48
1994	24,134	56.21
1995	33,786	51.00

	Subscribers (1,000's)	Average Monthly Bill (dollars)
1996	44,043	47.70
1997	55,312	42.78
1998	69,209	39.43

6. a. Make a scatterplot of the number of subscribers as a function of the time in years since 1990.
   b. Write an exponential equation $S(t)$, where $S(t)$ is the number of subscribers as a function of time, t, since 1990.
   c. Based on your equation, determine the number of subscribers in 1997. Why is this number different from the data in the table?
   d. Based on your equation, how many subscribers would you expect in 1992?
   e. Based on your equation, when would you expect the number of subscribers to reach 10,000,000? 100,000,000?

7. a. Make a scatterplot of the average monthly bill as a function of the time in years since 1990.
   b. Write an exponential equation $B(t)$, where $B(t)$ is the average monthly bill as a function of time, t, since 1990.
   c. Your equation for $B(t)$ is in the form: $B(t) = ab^t$. What are the values for a and b in your equation for $B(t)$? What do they represent?
   d. Evaluate $B(5)$ and explain its meaning. How does this compare to the actual data?
   e. Based on your equation, what do you predict would be the average monthly bill in 1999? According to the data, it was $41.24. How do you explain the difference?

8. Kaitlyn is a scientist who is studying the decay of a radioactive substance. She has prepared the table below.

Time (days)	0	2	4	5	8	10	14
Amount (grams)	10	7.01	5.29	4.50	2.70	1.99	0.92

a. Make a scatterplot from the information above.

b. Write an equation for an exponential function to fit the data.

c According to your equation, what was the initial amount of radioactive substance? Why is it not exactly 10 grams?

d. How much of the radioactive substance remained after 6 days?

e. When will the substance disappear entirely?

9. Tommy has been collecting baseball cards since he was five years old. Now that he is starting to plan for college, Tommy is thinking of selling some of the cards. He has kept careful records of the number of baseball cards he has collected, and has prepared a table with this information.

Age	Number of Years Collecting	Number of Baseball Cards
5	0	5
8	3	20
10		50
12		130
14		340
15		550
17		1,400

a. Fill in the missing information in the table above.

b. Use the information from the table to make a scatterplot of the number of baseball cards Tommy has as a function of the number of years he has been collecting them.

c. Use the information to write an exponential equation to model the data.

d. Based on your equation, how many baseball cards did Tommy have when he was 13 years old?

e. At what rate is Tommy's baseball card collection increasing?

f. If Tommy's collection continued to increase at the same rate, how many cards would he have by the time he graduated from college at the age of 22?

g. If Tommy sold 400 of his cards at age 17, how many cards would he have left? Assuming his collection continued to increase at the same rate, write an equation to model the number of baseball cards he would have.

h. Based on your equation from part **g**, how many baseball cards would Tommy have in 5 years when he graduates from college?

10. The table below shows the numbers of students per computer in public school in the United States from 1985 to 1999.

Year	Years Since 1985	Number of Students
85–86	0	50
86–87	1	37
87–88		32
88–89		25
89–90		22
90–91		20
91–92		18
92–93		16
93–94		14
94–95		10.5
95–96		10
96–97		7.8
97–98		6.1
98–99		5.7

a. To make a scatterplot of the given points, complete the column to indicate the number of years since 1985.

b. Make a scatterplot of the given points, with the independent variable as the number of years since 1985 and the dependent variable as the number of students per computer.

c. Use your calculator to obtain the equation of an exponential function $N(t)$, the number of students per computer, where t is the time since 1985.

d. Find $N(5)$ and explain what this means in terms of the number of students per com-

puter. How does this compare to the actual data?

e. Find t such that $N(t) = 8$, and explain what this means in terms of the number of students per computer. How does this compare to the actual data?

11.4 Other Types of Regression

If you look at the Statistics menu of your calculator, you will see that there are many possible types of regression equations. Although many of them are beyond the scope of this course, a few will be explained in this section.

Consider the exponential equation $y = b^x$, $b > 1$. Its inverse is the logarithmic equation $y = \log_b x$. The graph of an exponential function takes a shape similar to the curve shown in the figure below on the left. The graph of a logarithmic function takes a shape similar to the one shown in the figure to the right below.

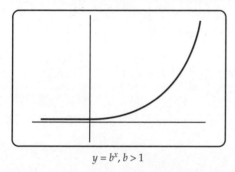

$y = b^x, b > 1$

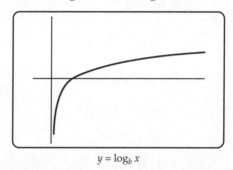

$y = \log_b x$

Just as every exponential equation in the form $y = b^x$ passes through the point $(0, 1)$, every logarithmic equation in the form $y = \log_b x$ passes through the point $(1, 0)$. An exponential equation in the form $y = ab^x$ passes through the point $(0, a)$. A logarithmic equation in the form $y = c \log_b x$ passes through the point $(1, 0)$. Although your calculator has the capability of performing logarithmic regression, it uses a special base that is not studied in this course. However, you should be able to recognize when a logarithmic equation would be a good model for a given function.

For example, the Richter Scale is a measure that was developed in 1935 by Charles F. Richter to compare the size of earthquakes. If you graphed the Richter magnitude of an earthquake as a function of the amplitude of its seismic waves, you would obtain a graph similar to the one shown below. You can see that a logarithmic function would be a good model for this data.

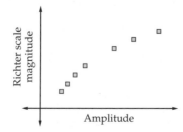

Other functions to consider are power functions. Exponential functions are in the form $y = ab^x$, where the variable is in the exponent. Power functions are in the form $y = ax^n$, where a and n are constants. In a power function such as the familiar quadratic $y = x^2$, the variable is in the base. Graphs of some power functions are shown below. (All graphs are in the standard viewing window.)

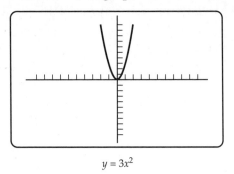

$y = 3x^2$

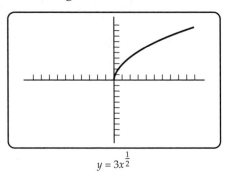

$y = 3x^{\frac{1}{2}}$

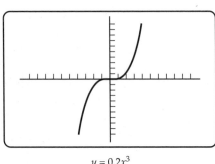

$y = 0.2x^3$

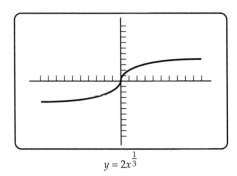

$y = 2x^{\frac{1}{3}}$

The example below illustrates the capability of your calculator to perform a power regression.

MODEL PROBLEM

If $f(x)$ is a power function with $f(1) = 0.2$, and $f(2) = 3.2$, $f(3) = 16.2$, $f(4) = 51.2$, and $f(5) = 125$, find $f(6)$.

SOLUTION
Make a scatterplot of the information, as shown in the graph below.

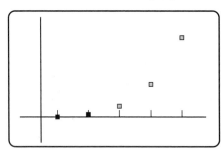

To generate an equation for $f(x)$, press (STAT) (▶) CALC (A:PwrReg) (ENTER) (VARS) (▶) Y-VARS (1) (1) (ENTER).
The equation is $y = 0.2x^4$. To find $f(6)$, extend your window to include x-values that are greater than 6, then press (2nd) (TRACE) (CALCULATE) (1) (6) (ENTER), and get $f(6) = 259.2$.

In 1–4, select the numeral preceding the word or expression that best answers the question.

1. Given the scatterplot below, which of the following equations could best model the data?

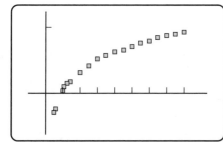

   (1) $y = 20 \log x$ (3) $y = 20(1.5)^x$
   (2) $y = 20(0.5)^x$ (4) $y = 20 + x$

In 2–3, use the data: $f(-1) = -8, f(0) = 6, f(0.8) = -4.4, f(1.5) = -3, f(2.7) = -0.6$.

2. What type of function would best model the given data?
   (1) linear   (3) logarithmic
   (2) exponential   (4) power

3. Find $f(3)$.
   (1) -0.5 (3) 0.6
   (2) 0   (4) 1.6

4. Given the scatterplot below, which of the following equations could best model the data?

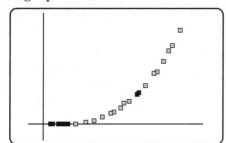

   (1) $y = 2.969x^{0.73}$ (3) $y = 0.73(2.969)^{-x}$
   (2) $y = 0.73x^{2.969}$ (4) $y = 0.73 + 2.929x$

5. Write an equation for a power function that will model the data below.

x	1	1.1	1.7	2	2.5	3	4
y	4	5	15	30	50	90	165

6. Darren would like to be valedictorian of his graduating class. Each night he spends more and more time studying. Darren also wants to win the Math Award at graduation, and often models events in his life by generating regression equations. Darren has modeled the number of hours spent studying as a function of the number of weeks since school began. The equation that Darren uses is $S(t) = 3.6 \log t$, where $S(t)$ is the number of hours spent studying each day, and t is the number of weeks since school began.
  a. According to Darren's equation, how many hours will he spend studying right before midterms (approximately 20 weeks after school began)?
  b. How many hours will he spend studying for his final exams (approximately 40 weeks after school began)?
  c. At what time of the year will Darren study for 5 hours a day?

7. One of the graphs below is the function $j(x) = 3x^4$ and the other is $k(x) = 3x^{\frac{1}{4}}$. Without using a calculator, how can you tell which function matches each graph?

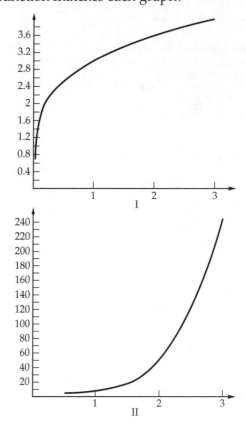

8. Match each of the scatterplots with one of the following equations that could be used to model it. Explain how you could do this without a calculator.

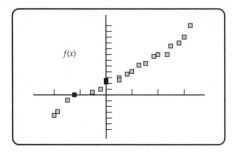

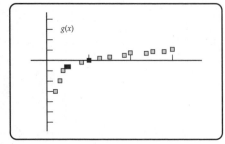

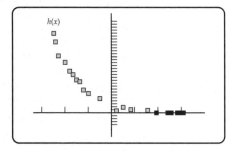

i. $y = 2.731154 \log x$

ii. $y = -2.731154 \log x$

iii. $y = 2.731154 \log (-x)$

iv. $y = 2.76522(0.40359)^x$

v. $y = 2.76522(1.40359)^x$

vi. $y = -2.76522(0.40359)^x$

vii. $y = 2.731154x + 2.214464$

viii. $y = -2.731154x + 2.214464$

ix. $y = 2.731154x - 2.214464$

9. Donnie wanted to determine if the length of a pendulum has any relationship to the time required for the pendulum to complete one oscillation. He has placed the information in a table as shown below.

Length (in ft)	0.5	1	1.5	2	2.5	3	3.5	4
Time (in sec)	0.9	1.2	1.3	1.6	1.8	1.9	2	2.1

a. Make a scatterplot of the information shown in the table, with time (in seconds) as a function of length (in feet).
b. Write an equation for a power function to model the data.
c. Use your formula to find the time required for a 5-foot pendulum to complete one oscillation.

d. According to a physics formula, $T = 2\pi\sqrt{\dfrac{l}{32}}$, where T is the time (in seconds) for one complete oscillation and l is the length (in feet) of a pendulum. Use this formula to find the time for a 5-foot-long pendulum to complete one oscillation. How does that compare to the data given in the table above and the number obtained using the formula from part c?

10. Elyssa wants to buy a digital camera, and needs $100 to make a deposit on the model she wants. She has been working after school, and saves as much as she can. However, Elyssa has a lot of other expenses, and she feels that she is not saving enough money. Each week Elyssa records the total amount of money she has saved. The information appears in the table below.

Week	2	3	4	5	6	7	8	9
Money	21	30	40	48	54	59	63	66

a. Make a scatterplot using the information from the table above.
b. By looking at your scatterplot, do you think a linear, exponential, or logarithmic function would best model the data? Why?
c. Which of the three types of functions would produce the fastest rate of growth? Why?
d. On the same set of axes, graph the function $y = 70 \log x$. Use this equation to determine how long it would take Elyssa to save the $100 deposit she needs.

In 1–4, match each scatterplot with one of the descriptions.

1.

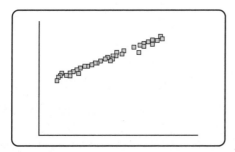

2.

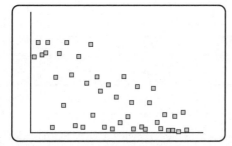

3.

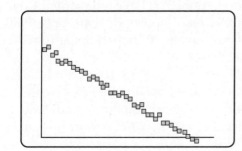

4.

    a. strong positive linear correlation
    b. strong negative linear correlation
    c. weak positive linear correlation
    d. weak negative linear correlation
    e. linear correlation close to zero

5. Sketch a scatterplot for data showing a correlation coefficient close to 1.

6. Sketch a scatterplot for data showing a correlation coefficient close to -1.

In 7–12, select the numeral preceding the word or expression that best answers the question.

7. Kelly Ann is on a traveling basketball team and has been working really hard on improving her shooting average before the season starts. At the last nine practices she scored the following number of points: 2, 10, 17, 23, 28, 32, 35, 37, 38. Plot the points as a function of the number of games and decide which of the following functions best describes her improvement.
    (1) linear
    (2) exponential
    (3) logarithmic
    (4) no functional relationship

In 8–10, use the following situation to answer the questions.

When he graduates from college, Rollo is interviewed at two different software companies, WARES R US and TOMORROW'S WARES.

8. The first firm, WARES R US, offers him an annual raise of $2,500 and a starting salary of $47,000. Which of the following is *false* with regard to his future financial status?
    (1) His salary will increase yearly by the exact same amount.
    (2) His salary is a linear function with the $2,500 being the rate of change in income.
    (3) His salary is a linear function with the $47,000 as the y-intercept.
    (4) Because his salary will increase each year, it is an exponential function.

9. The second company where Rollo interviewed, TOMORROW'S WARES, offers him a starting salary of $45,000 with an annual raise of 6%. Which of the following is a *false* statement with regard to this offer?
    (1) His salary will increase by a different dollar amount each year.
    (2) His salary is an exponential function with a yearly raise of $2,700.
    (3) His salary is an exponential function with a y-intercept of $45,000.
    (4) Because his salary increases each year, this is an increasing function.

10. Given the fact that the companies offer equivalent benefit packages and are equally close to his home, which of the following statements is mathematically accurate to describe Rollo's dilemma?
   (1) If Rollo plans to change jobs within five years, he would make more money working for WARES R US.
   (2) If Rollo wants to stay with the company for life, he should choose WARES R US and get to work.
   (3) If Rollo plans to change jobs within five years, he would make more money working for TOMORROW'S WARES.
   (4) The job offers are equivalent and he should just flip a coin.

11. Which of the following accurately describes a correlation coefficient?
   (1) A negative correlation factor *always* means there is no correlation between the dependent and independent variables.
   (2) A correlation coefficient of +1 means there is *always* a strong positive correlation between the dependent and independent variables.
   (3) No matter how good the correlation factor may be, *sometimes* there is no significance to the correlation between the dependent and independent variables.
   (4) *Sometimes* linear functions are found to have correlation coefficients of almost zero.

12. From the time Tiffany was 5 years old, her weeknight bedtime was a linear function that grew by $\frac{1}{4}$ hour each year. If, at age 18, her weeknight curfew is 11 P.M., what was her bedtime when she was 5?
   (1) 7:15 P.M.   (3) 7:45 P.M.
   (2) 7:30 P.M.   (4) 8:00 P.M.

13. The table below shows the average cost for annual tuition and fees in a public college.

Year	Cost	Year	Cost
1980	804	1990	1,908
1981	909	1991	2,137
1982	1,031	1992	2,334
1983	1,148	1993	2,527
1984	1,228	1994	2,820
1985	1,318	1995	2,977
1986	1,414	1996	3,151
1987	1,537	1997	3,323
1988	1,646	1998	3,486
1989	1,781	1999	3,644

   a. Make a scatterplot of average yearly cost of a public college education $C(t)$, as a function of time, t, in years since 1980.
   b. Write an equation for a linear function that will best fit the data.
   c. Based on your equation, find $C(0)$, $C(8)$, $C(18)$, and explain what this means.
   d. Based on your equation, predict the cost of a college education for your freshman year.
   e. Write an equation for an exponential function that will best fit the data.
   f. Based on your equation, find $C(0)$, $C(8)$, $C(18)$, and explain what this means.
   g. Based on your equation, predict the cost of a college education for your freshman year.
   h. Which function would you think fits the data better? Why?
   i. Which function do you prefer to be correct? Why?

14. The following table contains the average height (in inches) for girls and boys from ages 2 years to 13 years.

Age	Girls	Boys
2	35	36
3	38.5	39
4	41.75	42
5	44	44
6	46	46.75
7	48	49
8	50.75	51
9	53.25	53.25
10	55.5	55.25
11	58.5	57.25
12	60.5	59
13	61.25	61

a. Make a scatterplot of the average girl's height (in inches) as a function of her age.

b. Make a scatterplot of the average boy's height (in inches) as a function of his age.

c. Write a linear equation for the average girl's height as a function of her age.

d. Based on your equation, about how tall is the average 10-year-old girl? How does this compare to the actual data?

e. Based on your equation, how tall would you expect the average 14-year-old girl to be?

f. Write a linear equation for the average boy's height as a function of his age.

g. Based on your equations, who grows at a faster rate, boys or girls? Explain.

h. Based on your equation, how tall is the average 7-year-old boy? How does this compare to the actual data?

i. Based on your equation, how tall would you expect the average 21-year-old man to be? Does this make sense? Why?

15. You can graph the distance around the outside of a can as a function of the distance across a can.

Step 1: You will need 5 cans of various shapes and sizes (soup, tuna, paint, etc.), a ruler, and a piece of string

Step 2: Use the string to measure across the center of each of the cans.

Step 3: Use the ruler to determine this distance and record it in the table below.

Step 4: Use the string to measure the distance around the top of each of the cans.

Step 5: Use the ruler to determine this distance and record it in the table below.

Kind of Can					
Distance Across the Can					
Distance Around the Top					

a. Make a scatterplot of the distance around the top of the can as a function of the distance across the top of the can.

b. Write a linear equation that can be used to model this function.

c. What is the slope of the line?

d. You should have determined an approximate formula for the circumference of a circle. Since $C = \pi d$, the slope you found should have been approximately equal to π. How far off was your estimate?

16. This table shows the time required to cook a turkey of various weights.

Weight (pounds)	8	11	15.5	19.5	23
Cooking Time (hours)	2.5	3	4	5	6

    a. Make a scatterplot of the data, showing cooking time, $C(w)$, in hours, as a function of weight, w, in pounds.

    b. Write an equation for a linear function to model this data.

    c. Use your equation to determine the cooking time of a 17-pound turkey.

    d. What size turkey would take $3\frac{1}{2}$ hours to cook?

    e. Find $C(20)$ and explain what this means.

    f. Find w such that $C(w) = 20$ and explain what is meant by this.

    g. Are your answers to parts **e** and **f** useful? Explain.

17. The following table gives statistics for the growing number of Americans age 85 and over, in thousands, according to the Bureau of the Census.

Year	Pop.	Year	Pop.
1900	122	1960	929
1910	167	1970	1,409
1920	210	1980	2,240
1930	272	1990	3,021
1940	365	1995	3,685
1950	577		

    a. Create a scatterplot for the data.

    b. Would a linear, exponential, or logarithmic function best model this data in which the number of persons age 85 and over is dependent on the year since 1900?

    c. Use your calculator to find the regression function for the function you think most appropriate.

    d. Given your equation, what prediction does the function make for the population over 85 years of age in the year 2000?

    e. According to the predictions made by the Bureau of the Census, based on the 1990 statistics, they anticipated 4,312 thousand (or 4,312,000) people over the age of 85 in 2000. How does this answer compare to the one from your equation? Why?

    f. What explanation might there be for the increased longevity of seniors?

18. Because of environmental issues, the United States government has stepped in to monitor the fuel efficiency of new passenger cars. Since 1980, the U.S. Corporate Average Fuel Efficiency (CAFE) is 27.5 miles per gallon. Statistics for passenger cars' efficiency since 1975 are presented below.

Year of Car	Fuel Efficiency (miles per gallon)
1975	15.1
1980	22.6
1985	26.3
1990	26.9
1995	27.7
1996	28.3
1997	27.9

    a. In what year did passenger cars first surpass the CAFE of 27.5 miles per gallon?

    b. Create a scatterplot for this data.

    c. Consider which type of function might best represent this data. Justify your answer. The data can actually be modeled by the logarithmic function:
$f(x) = 15.2606 + 9.641844818 \log x$ where $f(x)$ is the miles per gallon and x is the number of years since 1975.

    d. What might the average fuel efficiency of a passenger car have been in 1983?

    e. If the function holds true, what might you expect the average fuel efficiency of a passenger car to be in 2005?

19. The issue of equal pay for equal work has been debated often in the United States. Below are the median incomes of men and women employed full-time, year-round, in the United States.

Year	Men's Median Income	Women's Median Income
1970	$9,184	$5,440
1975	$12,934	$7,719
1980	$19,173	$11,591
1985	$24,999	$16,252
1990	$28,979	$20,591
1995	$32,199	$23,777
1998	$36,252	$26,855

a. Create a scatterplot for the men's salaries and for the women's salaries.

Note: When using the same independent variable for both sets of data, enter the data in L_1, L_2, and L_3. Use L_1 and L_2 for Plot 1 and L_1 and L_3 for Plot 2.

b. What type of function do you think would best model the men's and women's median salaries as a function of the year since 1970?
c. Find the lines of best fit for the men's median salaries and the women's.
d. What are the correlation coefficients for each regression equation?
e. Based on these statistics, will women's salaries ever match men's? Why?
f. What is happening to the difference between the men's and women's median salaries? Mathematically, why is this occurring?
g. In the year 2010, if these models hold true, what will the difference in median salaries be?

20. The percentage of American homes using central air conditioning has been increasing since first commercially available as per the data below.

Year	% Using Central Air Conditioning
1978 (0)	23
1980 (2)	27
1982 (4)	28
1984 (6)	30
1987 (9)	36
1990 (12)	39
1993 (15)	44
1997 (19)	47

a. Create a scatterplot for the given data and determine what type of function might best suit this data (linear, exponential, or logarithmic) in which the percent of the population using central air conditioning is dependent on the year since 1978.
b. Use regression to find the line of best fit.
c. What is the linear correlation coefficient?
d. Based on this mathematical model, what is the annual rate of change in usage of central air conditioning?
e. Using the equation of the line of best fit, determine the percentage of American homes that used central air conditioning in 1995 and in 2001.
f. In what year will 95% of American homes have central air conditioning? Is this a reasonable possibility? Explain your reasoning.

There are a number of other types of regression that your TI-83 calculator is able to handle, but these are beyond the Math B curriculum: quadratic, cubic, quartic, natural log, and logistic regressions. Still, the procedures to explore these regressions are the same as those you have already studied and, sometimes, data appears that can produce interesting explorations and discussion.

1. Although the first Olympics in 1896 did not permit women to participate, in recent years, the percent of athletes in the Summer Olympics who are female is increasing steadily as shown by the data below.

Year	% Female Participants
1976	20.7
1980	21.5
1984	23.0
1988	25.8
1992	28.8
1996	34.2
2000	42.0

   a. Create a scatterplot for this data.
   b. Do you think an exponential or a linear function might better model this data?
   c. Find the equation you think best fits this information. What is its correlation coefficient?
   d. Now, calculate the quadratic regression equation. What is its correlation coefficient?
   e. Historically, we know the number of female participants did not start high and then fall to a minimum point before rising again, but sometimes a mathematical model does not mirror the cultural or historic issues surrounding the problem. Based on the two equations you have, what percent of the participants in 2004 might be female?
   f. Which estimate do you think is a better one? Justify your answer.

2. Consider the following data reporting cigarette consumption (in billions of cigarettes) in the United States from 1920 through 1999.

Year	Billions of Cigarettes
1900	2.5
1910	8.6
1920	44.6
1930	119.3
1940	181.9
1950	369.8
1960	484.4
1970	536.5
1980	631.5
1990	525
1997	480
1998	470
1999	435

   a. Create the scatterplot for this data. Notice how the plot seems to grow rapidly and then slow down before cigarette consumption begins to fall off.
   b. When did cigarette consumption grow the most rapidly? What events in history might account for this steep increase?
   c. When does the consumption drop? Why?
   d. Explore the various types of regression equations available on the calculator and find the best-fitting function.

CHAPTER 12

Trigonometric Functions

12.1 Unit Circle

A **unit circle** is a circle whose center is at the origin and whose radius is 1 unit. Point P starts at the point (1, 0). As P moves in a counterclockwise direction, the measure of the angle formed starts at 0° and increases until it reaches 360°. We use the Greek letter θ (theta) to represent the angle formed. (If P moved in a clockwise direction, the measure of the angle formed would start at 0° and *decrease* until it reached −360° after one complete revolution.)

As P moves around the circle, not only does the angle θ change, but the coordinates of point P also change. We will call the coordinates of point P (a, b). Since the distance from P to the origin remains at 1 unit, we can see that $\sqrt{a^2 + b^2} = 1$.

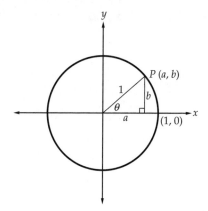

From your previous mathematics courses you may recall the following trigonometric ratios:

$$\sin \theta = \frac{\text{opposite}}{\text{hypotenuse}} \qquad \cos \theta = \frac{\text{adjacent}}{\text{hypotenuse}} \qquad \tan \theta = \frac{\text{opposite}}{\text{adjacent}}$$

Remember: You may have learned the acronym SOH CAH TOA to help you remember the above information.

Read down each of the following columns.

S	O	H	C	A	H	T	O	A
I	p	y	O	d	y	A	p	d
N	p	p	S	j	p	N	p	j
	o	o		a	o		o	a
	s	t		c	t		s	c
	i	e		e	e		i	e
	t	n		n	n		t	n
	e	u		t	u		e	t
		s			s			
		e			e			

Using the unit circle, we can see that the length of the hypotenuse remains at a constant value of 1. Therefore,

$$\sin\theta = \frac{\text{opposite}}{\text{hypotenuse}} = \frac{b}{1} = b \quad \cos\theta = \frac{\text{adjacent}}{\text{hypotenuse}} = \frac{a}{1} = a \quad \tan\theta = \frac{\text{opposite}}{\text{adjacent}} = \frac{b}{a}$$

Note: In a unit circle, $\cos\theta$ is the *x*-coordinate and $\sin\theta$ is the *y*-coordinate. You can write (x, y) in alphabetical order and $(\cos\theta, \sin\theta)$ in alphabetical order and match them up.

MODEL PROBLEMS

1. *P* is a point on a unit circle with coordinates (0.6, 0.8) as shown below.

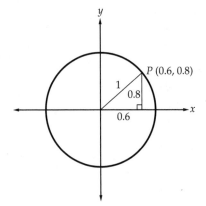

Find
a. $\cos\theta$ 0.6
b. $\sin\theta$ 0.8
c. $\tan\theta$ $0.8\big/0.6 = \frac{4}{3}$

SOLUTION

In a unit circle, the radius measures 1 unit.

a. $\cos \theta = \dfrac{\text{adjacent}}{\text{hypotenuse}} = \dfrac{0.6}{1} = 0.6$ ($\cos \theta$ is the x-coordinate)

b. $\sin \theta = \dfrac{\text{opposite}}{\text{hypotenuse}} = \dfrac{0.8}{1} = 0.8$ ($\sin \theta$ is the y-coordinate)

Since P is a point on the unit circle, when we see the coordinates of $(0.6, 0.8)$, we know that we have $(\cos \theta, \sin \theta)$. Thus $\cos \theta = 0.6$ and $\sin \theta = 0.8$.

CAUTION: You *must* be working on a unit circle for the x- and y-coordinates to be $\cos \theta$ and $\sin \theta$.

c. $\tan \theta = \dfrac{\text{opposite}}{\text{adjacent}} = \dfrac{0.8}{0.6} = \dfrac{4}{3}$ $\quad \left(\tan \theta = \dfrac{y\text{-coordinate}}{x\text{-coordinate}} = \dfrac{\sin \theta}{\cos \theta} \right)$

2. In the accompanying diagram of a unit circle, $\overline{BD}$ is tangent to circle O at D, $\overline{AC}$ is perpendicular to the x-axis, and $\overline{OA}$ is a radius.

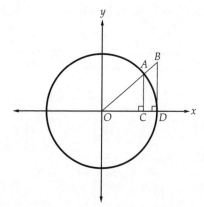

Note: A line segment is positive when it is above the x-axis or to the right of the y-axis. It is negative when it is below the x-axis or left of the y-axis.

Name a line segment whose directed distance is the value of
a. $\sin \theta$ AC
b. $\cos \theta$ OC
c. $\tan \theta$ BD

SOLUTION
a. Since $\sin \theta = \dfrac{\text{opposite}}{\text{hypotenuse}}$, we need to find a triangle whose hypotenuse measures 1. In triangle OAC, $OA = 1$. Thus, $\sin \theta = \dfrac{AC}{OA} = \dfrac{AC}{1} = AC$.

Answer: $\overline{AC}$

b. Since $\cos \theta = \dfrac{\text{adjacent}}{\text{hypotenuse}}$, we need to find a triangle whose hypotenuse measures 1. In triangle OAC, $OA = 1$. Thus, $\cos \theta = \dfrac{OC}{OA} = \dfrac{OC}{1} = OC$.

Answer: $\overline{OC}$

c. Since $\tan \theta = \dfrac{\text{opposite}}{\text{adjacent}}$, we need to find a triangle whose adjacent side measures 1. In triangle OBD, $OD = 1$. Thus, $\tan \theta = \dfrac{\text{opposite}}{\text{adjacent}} = \dfrac{BD}{OD} = \dfrac{BD}{1} = BD$.

Answer: $\overline{BD}$

As point P moves around the unit circle, and θ increases from $0°$ to $360°$, a and b change signs, and thus the signs of $\sin \theta$, $\cos \theta$, and $\tan \theta$ also change.

- In Quadrant I, a and b are both positive numbers, so $\sin \theta$ is positive, $\cos \theta$ is positive, and $\tan \theta$ is also positive.

- In Quadrant II, a is a negative number, and b is a positive number, so $\sin \theta$ is positive, $\cos \theta$ is negative, and $\tan \theta$ is also negative.

- In Quadrant III, a and b are both negative numbers, so $\sin \theta$ is negative, $\cos \theta$ is negative, and $\tan \theta$ is positive.

- In Quadrant IV, a is a positive number, and b is a negative number, so $\sin \theta$ is negative, $\cos \theta$ is positive, and $\tan \theta$ is negative.

This information can be summed up in the following diagram.

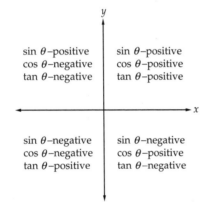

The following diagram lists the function that is positive in each quadrant.

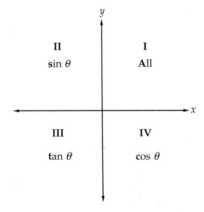

To help you recall which function is positive in each quadrant, remember that "**A**ll **s**tudents **t**ake **c**alculus," and write the first letter from each word in the quadrants from I to IV as shown above.

Name the quadrant in which θ lies if
a. $\sin \theta > 0$ and $\cos \theta < 0$ II
b. $\cos \theta > 0$ and $\tan \theta > 0$ I
c. $\sin \theta < 0$ and $\tan \theta > 0$ III
d. $\tan \theta < 0$ and $\cos \theta > 0$ IV

SOLUTION

a. $\sin \theta > 0$ and $\cos \theta < 0$

We are looking for a quadrant in which $\sin \theta$ is positive ($\sin \theta > 0$). This could occur in Quadrants I or II. We also need $\cos \theta$ to be negative ($\cos \theta < 0$). This could occur in Quadrants II or III. Both requirements are fulfilled in Quadrant II. Recording the information in a chart will make this much easier to analyze.

Step 1: Make a sketch of a Cartesian plane with the x- and y-axes and label the quadrants.

Step 2: Determine which quadrants have positive values for $\sin \theta$. Put a check mark in Quadrants I and II.

Step 3: Determine which quadrants have negative values for $\cos \theta$. Put a check mark in Quadrants II and III.

Step 4: Look to see which quadrant fulfills both conditions (has two check marks).

Answer: Quadrant II

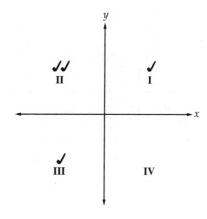

b. $\cos \theta > 0$ and $\tan \theta > 0$

Step 1: $\cos \theta > 0$ (positive $\cos \theta$): Quadrants I and IV

Step 2: $\tan \theta > 0$ (positive $\tan \theta$): Quadrants I and III

Step 3: Both requirements are fulfilled in the quadrant with two check marks (Quadrant I).

Answer: Quadrant I

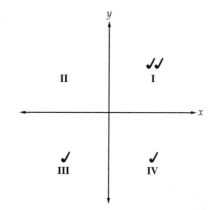

c. $\sin \theta < 0$ and $\tan \theta > 0$
Step 1: $\sin \theta < 0$: Quadrants III and IV
Step 2: $\tan \theta > 0$: Quadrants I and III

Answer: Quadrant III

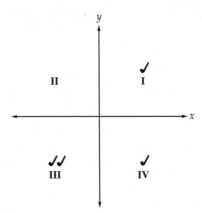

d. $\tan \theta < 0$ and $\cos \theta > 0$
Step 1: $\tan \theta < 0$: Quadrants II and IV
Step 2: $\cos \theta > 0$: Quadrants I and IV

Answer: Quadrant IV

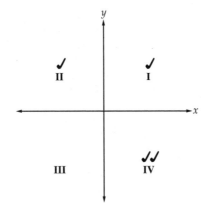

![Practice]

1. Fill in the table with the sign of the function in each quadrant.

Quadrant	$\sin \theta$	$\cos \theta$	$\tan \theta$
I	+	+	+
II	+	−	−
III	−	−	+
IV	−	+	−

In 2–3, use the diagram below where P is a point on a unit circle.

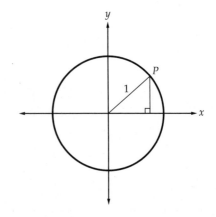

2. If the coordinates of point P are $(0.5, 0.5\sqrt{3})$, find
   a. $\sin \theta$ $.5\sqrt{3}$
   b. $\cos \theta$ $.5$
   c. $\tan \theta$ $\sqrt{3}$

3. If the coordinates of point P are $\left(\dfrac{\sqrt{2}}{2}, \dfrac{\sqrt{2}}{2}\right)$, find
   a. $\sin \theta$ $\sqrt{2}/2$
   b. $\cos \theta$ $\sqrt{2}/2$
   c. $\tan \theta$ 1

4. Given $m\angle A = 250$.
   a. In what quadrant does the terminal side of $\angle A$ lie? 3
   b. Is $\sin A$ positive or negative? Why? Yes, b/c the value is below the x-axis

In 5–11, select the numeral preceding the word or expression that best answers the question.

5. If $\sin \theta > 0$ and $\cos \theta < 0$, in which quadrant does θ lie?
   (1) I
   (2) II ✓
   (3) III
   (4) IV

6. If $\tan \theta$ is positive and $\cos \theta$ is negative, in what quadrant does θ terminate?
   (1) I
   (2) II
   (3) III ✓
   (4) IV

7. If $\sin B = -\dfrac{3}{5}$ and $\cos B > 0$, in what quadrant does $\angle B$ lie?
   (1) I
   (2) II
   (3) III
   (4) IV ✓

8. If $\tan A > 0$ and $(\tan A)(\sin A) > 0$, in what quadrant does $\angle A$ lie?
   (1) I ✓
   (2) II
   (3) III
   (4) IV

9. If $\tan x = -1$ and $\cos x = -\dfrac{\sqrt{2}}{2}$, in what quadrant could angle x terminate?
   (1) I
   (2) II ✓
   (3) III
   (4) IV

10. If $\sin \theta = -\dfrac{1}{2}$ and $\cos \theta = -\dfrac{\sqrt{3}}{2}$, which of the following could be the measure of θ?
   (1) 30°
   (2) 150°
   (3) 210° ✓
   (4) 330°

11. Which of the following could be true?
   (1) $\sin 300° = \dfrac{\sqrt{3}}{2}$
   (2) $\sin 240° = \dfrac{\sqrt{3}}{2}$
   (3) $\sin 120° = \dfrac{\sqrt{3}}{2}$ ✓
   (4) $\sin 60° = -\dfrac{\sqrt{3}}{2}$

In 12–15, use the figure below, where $OA = 1$, and $m\angle AOB = \theta$.

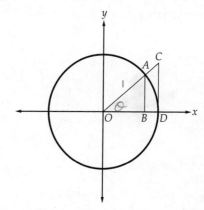

12. If the coordinates of point A are $\left(\dfrac{2}{3}, \dfrac{\sqrt{5}}{3}\right)$, find
   a. $\sin \theta$ $\sqrt{5}/3$
   b. $\cos \theta$ $\sqrt{2}/3$
   c. $\tan \theta$ $\sqrt{5}/2$

13. Name a line segment whose directed distance is the value of
   a. $\sin \theta$ AB
   b. $\cos \theta$ OB
   c. $\tan \theta$ CD

14. If the coordinates of point A are $\left(\dfrac{1}{2}, \dfrac{\sqrt{3}}{2}\right)$ and $\theta = 30°$, find $\cos 30°$.
   $1/2$

15. If the coordinates of point A are $\left(\dfrac{\sqrt{2}}{2}, \dfrac{\sqrt{2}}{2}\right)$ and $\theta = 45°$, find $\sin 45°$.
   $\sqrt{2}/2$

12.2 Degrees and Radians

The two most common units used to measure angles are degrees and radians. The Babylonians were responsible for dividing the circle into 360°. The radian is more commonly used in advanced mathematics. A **radian** is the measure of a central angle that intercepts an arc that is equal in length to the radius of the circle.

To help you understand the concept of radian measure, try this activity.

Given the following circle.

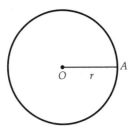

Step 1: Take a piece of string and place one end at point O, and cut it so the other end is at point A. Your string is now the length of the radius of the circle.

Step 2: Place one end of the string at A, and extend your string so that it lies along the circumference of the circle (the distance along the outside of the circle). Locate the point where the string ends, and label the point B. Connect B to O. Your angle should look like the one in the figure below.

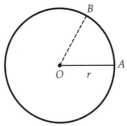

Angle BOA measures 1 radian.

Step 3: Now mark off the length of another radius along the circumference of your circle. Label the point C. m$\angle COA$ = 2 radians, since its length is twice the radius of the circle.

We could continue on in the same manner marking off the length of the radius around the circumference of the circle. Therefore, the measure of the central angle, θ, in radians, is the length of the intercepted arc, s, divided by the radius of the circle, r.

$$\theta = \frac{s}{r}$$

 MODEL PROBLEMS

1. Given: θ is the measure of the central angle in radians, s is the length of the intercepted arc, and r is the radius of the circle.
   a. If $s = 12$ and $r = 4$, find θ. 3
   b. If $r = 5$ and $\theta = 10$, find s. 50
   c. If $\theta = 3$ and $s = 15$, find r. 5

SOLUTION

a. Use the formula $\theta = \frac{s}{r}$.

$$\theta = \frac{12}{4}$$

$$\theta = 3$$

Answer: 3 radians

b. Use the formula $\theta = \frac{s}{r}$.

$$10 = \frac{s}{5}$$

$$s = 50$$

Answer: 50

c. Use the formula $\theta = \frac{s}{r}$.

$$3 = \frac{15}{r}$$

$$3r = 15$$

$$r = 5$$

Answer: 5

2. In a circle, a central angle of 2 radians intercepts an arc of 6 inches. Find the length of the radius of the circle.

SOLUTION

Use the formula $\theta = \frac{s}{r}$.

$$2 = \frac{6}{r}$$

$$2r = 6$$

$$r = 3$$

Answer: 3 inches

We know that the measure, in degrees, of the central angle formed by a complete rotation is 360°. To find the measure, in radians, of the central angle formed by a complete rotation we use our formula $\theta = \frac{s}{r}$.

The circumference of a circle (the length of the arc that is formed by one complete rotation) is equal to 2π times the radius of the circle ($C = 2\pi r$). Putting this in our formula, we get

$$\theta = \frac{2\pi r}{r} = 2\pi$$

- Since a complete rotation measures 360° in degrees and 2π radians in radians, 2π radians = 360°. Dividing both sides of the equation by 2, we obtain: π radians = 180°.

Note: It will be helpful for you to remember that π radians = 180°.

- To find the measure of 1 radian, divide both sides of the equation by π and obtain: 1 radian $= \frac{180°}{\pi} \approx 57°$.

We can convert from degrees to radians and from radians to degrees. Since $180° = \pi$ radians, we can see that $90° = \frac{\pi}{2}$ radians, $60° = \frac{\pi}{3}$ radians, and so on.

What do we do about an angle that measures $40°$? How can we convert $40°$ to radian measure? Since $1° = \frac{\pi \text{ radians}}{180}$, $40° = 40 \cdot \frac{\pi \text{ radians}}{180} = \frac{2}{9}$ radians.

When converting from degrees to radians, multiply the measure of the angle by $\frac{\pi \text{ radians}}{180°}$. The degrees in the numerator will "cancel" with the degrees in the denominator.

$$\frac{n \text{ \sout{degrees}}}{1} \cdot \frac{\pi \text{ radians}}{180 \text{ \sout{degrees}}} = \frac{n\pi}{180} \text{ radians}$$

Note: To convert from radians to degrees, we use the fact that 1 radian $= \frac{180°}{\pi \text{ radians}}$.

When converting from radians to degrees, multiply by $\frac{180°}{\pi \text{ radians}}$. The radians in the numerator will "cancel" with the radians in the denominator.

$$\frac{\theta \text{ \sout{radians}}}{1} \cdot \frac{180 \text{ degrees}}{\pi \text{ \sout{radians}}} = \frac{180\,\theta}{\pi} \text{ degrees}$$

MODEL PROBLEMS

1. Express $\frac{5\pi}{3}$ in degrees.

SOLUTION

Multiply by 1 in the form $\frac{180°}{\pi \text{ radians}}$.

$$\frac{5\pi}{3} \cdot \frac{\overset{60}{\cancel{180°}}}{\pi} = 300°$$

Answer: $300°$

2. Express $150°$ in radians.

Multiply by 1 in the form $\frac{\pi \text{ radians}}{180°}$.

$$\frac{\overset{5}{\cancel{150}}}{1} \cdot \frac{\pi}{\underset{6}{\cancel{180°}}} = \frac{5}{6}\pi$$

Answer: $\frac{5}{6}\pi$

 **Practice**

In 1–10, change each angle from degree measure to radian measure.

1. 120° $\cdot \frac{\pi}{180} = \frac{2\pi}{3}$

2. 270° $\cdot \frac{\pi}{180} = \frac{9\pi}{6}$

3. −50° $\cdot \frac{\pi}{180} = \frac{-50\pi}{180}$

4. 315° $\cdot \frac{\pi}{180} = \frac{7\pi}{4}$

5. −135° $\cdot \frac{\pi}{180} = \frac{-3\pi}{4}$

6. 80° $\cdot \frac{\pi}{180} = \frac{4\pi}{3}$

7. 330° $\cdot \frac{\pi}{180} = \frac{11\pi}{6}$

8. −180° $\cdot \frac{\pi}{180} = -\pi$

9. −45° $\cdot \frac{\pi}{180} = \frac{-\pi}{4}$

10. 240° $\cdot \frac{\pi}{180} = \frac{4\pi}{3}$

In 11–20, change each angle from radian measure to degree measure.

11. $\frac{3\pi}{2} \cdot \frac{180}{\pi} = 270$

12. $\frac{2\pi}{3} \cdot \frac{180}{\pi} = 120$

13. $\frac{5\pi}{4} \cdot \frac{180}{\pi} = 225$

14. $-\frac{\pi}{2} \cdot \frac{180}{\pi} = -90$

15. $\frac{5\pi}{6} \cdot \frac{180}{\pi} = 150$

16. $-\frac{7\pi}{4} \cdot \frac{180}{\pi} = -315$

17. $\frac{\pi}{5} \cdot \frac{180}{\pi} = 36$

18. $\frac{5\pi}{3} \cdot \frac{180}{\pi} = -300$

19. $-\frac{\pi}{6} \cdot \frac{180}{\pi} = -30$

20. $\pi \cdot \frac{180}{\pi} = 180$

21. Find the length of the radius of a circle in which a central angle of 4.5 radians intercepts an arc of 9 meters.

$x(4.5) = \left(\frac{9}{x}\right)x$

$\dfrac{4.5x}{4.5} = \dfrac{9}{4.5}$

$x = 2$

22. A pendulum makes an angle of 3 radians as its tip travels 18 feet. What is the length of the pendulum? $x(3) = \left(\frac{18}{x}\right)x \quad \frac{3x}{3} = \frac{18}{3} \quad x = 6$

23. Place in order from smallest to largest: 1 radian, 1 revolution, 1 degree, and 3 radians.
1 radian, 1 degree, 3 radians, 1 revolution

24. What is the measure of an angle formed by the hands of a clock at 2:30
    a. in degrees? 3
    b. in radians?

25. If the minute hand of a clock measures 6 inches, how long is the arc traced by this hand from 1:00 to 1:30? 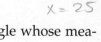 180

In 26–30, select the numeral preceding the word or expression that best completes the statement or answers the question.

26. An angle of $\frac{3\pi}{4}$ radians lies in quadrant
    (1) I
    (2) II
    (3) III
    (4) IV

27. Circle O has a radius of 10 inches. What is the length, in inches, of the arc subtended by a central angle measuring 2.5 radians?
    (1) 4
    (2) 25
    (3) 40 $10(2.5) = \left(\frac{x}{10}\right)10$
    (4) 250 $x = 25$

28. In what quadrant does an angle whose measure is $\frac{5\pi}{4}$ lie?
    (1) I
    (2) II
    (3) III
    (4) IV

29. In standard position, an angle of $\frac{5\pi}{3}$ has the same terminal side as an angle of
    (1) 60°
    (2) 120°
    (3) 240°
    (4) 300°

30. What is the image of (3, 2) under a counterclockwise rotation of π radians?
    (1) (2, 3)
    (2) (2, −3)
    (3) (−3, 2)
    (4) (−3, −2)

12.3 Special Angles and Reference and Coterminal Angles

You may recall the relationships between the legs and hypotenuse of the 30°-60° right triangle and the 45°-45° right triangle. For your reference, they are shown in the figures below.

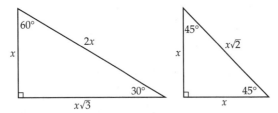

If we incorporate our knowledge of these special angles with our knowledge of the unit circle, we can extend our study of trigonometry to the other quadrants. In the accompanying diagram of a unit circle, $\overline{OA}$ is a radius, and $\overline{AC}$ is perpendicular to the x-axis. If $\theta = 30°$, we can determine that the coordinates of point A are

$\left(\dfrac{\sqrt{3}}{2}, \dfrac{1}{2} \right)$ and that $\sin 30° = \dfrac{1}{2}$, $\cos 30° = \dfrac{\sqrt{3}}{2}$, and $\tan 30° = \dfrac{\frac{1}{2}}{\frac{\sqrt{3}}{2}} = \dfrac{1}{2} \cdot \dfrac{2}{\sqrt{3}} = \dfrac{1}{\sqrt{3}} = \dfrac{1}{\sqrt{3}} \cdot \dfrac{\sqrt{3}}{\sqrt{3}} = \dfrac{\sqrt{3}}{3}$.

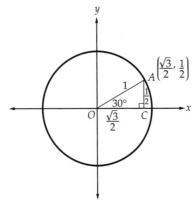

Now let's look at an angle in the second quadrant. Let $\theta = 150°$.

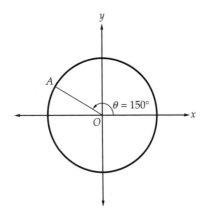

If we drop a perpendicular from A to a point C on the x-axis, $m\angle AOC = 30$.

We then know that the coordinates of point A are $\left(-\dfrac{\sqrt{3}}{2}, \dfrac{1}{2}\right)$.

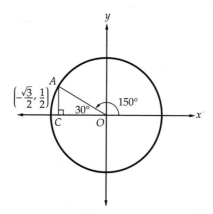

Since we are working in a unit circle, $\sin 150° = \dfrac{1}{2}$, $\cos 150° = -\dfrac{\sqrt{3}}{2}$, and $\tan 150° = -\dfrac{\sqrt{3}}{3}$.

Remember: When working in a unit circle, the x-coordinate is the cosine of the angle, and the y-coordinate is the sine of the angle. You can remember this by writing $(\cos \theta, \sin \theta)$ in alphabetical order, and (x, y) in alphabetical order and then matching them up.

The procedure is the same for angles in the other two quadrants. Let $\theta = 210°$. If we drop a perpendicular from A to a point C on the x-axis, $m\angle AOC = 30$.

We then know that the coordinates of point A are $\left(-\dfrac{\sqrt{3}}{2}, -\dfrac{1}{2}\right)$.

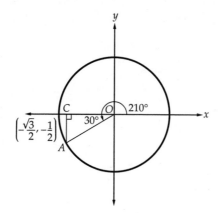

Thus, $\sin 210° = -\dfrac{1}{2}$, $\cos 210° = -\dfrac{\sqrt{3}}{2}$, and $\tan 210° = \dfrac{\sqrt{3}}{3}$.

Let $\theta = 330°$.

If we drop a perpendicular from A to a point C on the x-axis, $m\angle AOC = 30$. We then know that the coordinates of point A are $\left(\dfrac{\sqrt{3}}{2}, -\dfrac{1}{2}\right)$.

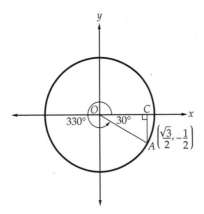

Thus, $\sin 330° = -\dfrac{1}{2}$, $\cos 330° = \dfrac{\sqrt{3}}{2}$, and $\tan 330° = -\dfrac{\sqrt{3}}{3}$.

In each of these cases, we referred back to a 30° angle. Thus, the 30° angle is called the **reference angle** and is the basis for finding the trigonometric functions of the other angles. When a 30° angle is reflected in the y-axis, it produces an angle in the second quadrant that would measure 150° in standard position. When it is reflected through the origin, it forms an angle in the third quadrant that measures 210° when measured in standard position. When it is reflected in the x-axis, it forms an angle in the fourth quadrant that would measure 330° in standard position.

For an angle in the given quadrant whose degree measure is θ

- Quadrant II: reference angle is $180° - \theta$ ($90° < \theta < 180°$)

- Quadrant III: reference angle is $\theta - 180°$ ($180° < \theta < 270°$)

- Quadrant IV: reference angle is $360° - \theta$ ($270° < \theta < 360°$)

The following chart may help you to identify reference angles.

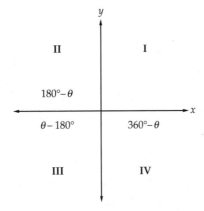

Angles that lie on the quadrant lines (0°, 90°, 180°, 270°, 360°) are called **quadrantal angles**. By looking at their x- and y-coordinates on a unit circle, we can determine the sine and cosine of each of these angles.

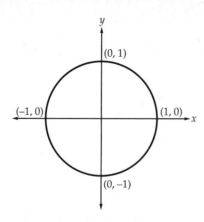

For example, cos 90° = 0 and sin 90° = 1, since the coordinates on the unit circle of the 90° quadrantal angle are (0, 1). Remember that the *x*-coordinate is the cosine of the angle and the *y*-coordinate is the sine of the angle. To determine the tangent of a quadrantal angle, use the formula $\tan \theta = \frac{\sin \theta}{\cos \theta}$. Thus tan 90° = $\frac{\sin 90°}{\cos 90°} = \frac{1}{0}$, which is undefined.

 MODEL PROBLEMS

1. Express each of the following as a function of a positive acute angle.
   a. sin 140° sin40
   b. cos 250° -cos70
   c. tan 300° -tan60

SOLUTION
a. Since 140° is in the second quadrant, we know that sin 140° is positive. Thus, sin 140° = sin (180° − 140°) = sin 40°.
b. Since 250° is in the third quadrant, we know that cos 250° is negative. Thus, cos 250° = −cos (250° − 180°) = −cos 70°.
c. Since 300° is in the fourth quadrant, we know that tan 300° is negative. Thus, tan 300° = −tan (360° − 300°) = −tan 60°.

2. Find the exact value for each expression.
   a. sin 300° -√3/2
   b. cos 135° -√2/2
   c. tan 240° √3
   d. sin 270° -1
   e. cos 180° -1

SOLUTION
Remember: The calculator cannot be used to obtain exact values of the trigonometric functions. The calculator will give only approximate values of these functions.

a. Since 300° is in the fourth quadrant, we know that sin 300° is negative. Thus, sin 300° = −sin (360° − 300°) = −sin 60°. (Refer back to your 30°-60° right triangle to finish the problem.)
   Sin 300° = −sin 60° = $-\frac{\sqrt{3}}{2}$.
b. Since 135° is in the second quadrant, we know that cos 135° is negative. Thus, cos 135° = −cos (180° − 135°) = −cos 45° = $-\frac{\sqrt{2}}{2}$.

c. Since 240° is in the third quadrant, we know that tan 240° is positive. Thus, tan 240° = tan (240° − 180°) = tan 60° = √3.

d. Since 270° lies on the y-axis, it is a quadrantal angle. The sine of the angle is its y-coordinate. Since the coordinates are $(0, -1)$, sin 270° = −1.

e. Since 180° lies on the x-axis, it is a quadrantal angle. The cosine of the angle is its x-coordinate. Since the coordinates are $(-1, 0)$, cos 180° = −1.

How do we find tan (−240°)? We know that proceeding 240° in a negative direction is the same as proceeding 120° in a positive direction. We can say that the −240° angle is **coterminal** with the 120° angle since they have the same *terminal* (ending) side. Since −240° is in the second quadrant, we know that tan (−240°) is negative. Thus, tan (−240°) = tan 120° = −tan (180° − 120°) = −tan 60° = −√3.

If two angles are **coterminal**, they share a common initial side and terminal side. The difference of their measures is 360° or a multiple of 360°.

How do we find cos 420°? We know that a 420° angle is more than one complete rotation. We can say that the 420° angle is coterminal with a 60° angle since they have the same *terminal* side. (420° − 360° = 60°) Since 420° is in the first quadrant, we know that cos 420° is positive. Thus, cos 420° = cos 60° = $\frac{1}{2}$.

 MODEL PROBLEM

Name the smallest positive angle coterminal with each of the following:
a. −330° ³⁰
b. 480° ¹²⁰
c. 750° ³⁰

SOLUTION
a. −330° is in the first quadrant and is coterminal with a 30° angle. Since −330° is measured in a clockwise direction, find the difference between 360° and 330°. (360° − 330° = 30°)
b. 480° is more than one complete rotation. Since 480° − 360° = 120°, we know that the 480° angle is coterminal with a 120° angle.
c. 750° is more than two complete rotations. (Two complete rotations are 720°.) Since 750° − 720° = 30°, we know that the 750° angle is coterminal with a 30° angle.

We can look at all of the same concepts using radian measure instead of degree measure. One way to find reference angles and function values is to convert the angle into degrees, and proceed from there as explained above. Alternatively, you could work in radian measure. We will illustrate that method in the Model Problems.

To find the reference angle for angles that are measured in radians, if θ is in

- Quadrant II the reference angle is $\pi - \theta$.

- Quadrant III the reference angle is $\theta - \pi$.

- Quadrant IV the reference angle is $2\pi - \theta$.

Refer to the following chart to help you identify reference angles.

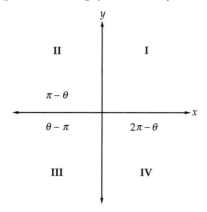

Note: To find the reference angle, ALWAYS use the horizontal axis (the angles of π and 2π or, in degrees, $180°$ and $360°$). NEVER use the vertical axis.

A graphical illustration of how to find reference angles is shown below.

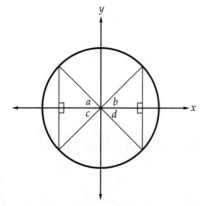

Notice how the four reference angles, *a*, *b*, *c*, and *d* all lie on the *x*-axis. When the four triangles are drawn together, they make a bow-tie shape. Keep this "bow-tie" in mind to help you find the reference angles. Always make sure that your reference angle is one of the four marked in the diagram.

MODEL PROBLEMS

1. Express each expression as a function of a positive acute angle.

   a. $\sin \dfrac{5\pi}{4}$ $-\sin\frac{\pi}{4}$

   b. $\tan \dfrac{7\pi}{6}$ $\tan\frac{\pi}{6}$

SOLUTION

a. Since $\dfrac{5\pi}{4}$ is in the third quadrant (it is larger than π and smaller than $\dfrac{3\pi}{2}$), we know that $\sin \dfrac{5\pi}{4}$ is negative. Thus, $\sin \dfrac{5\pi}{4} = -\sin \left(\dfrac{5\pi}{4} - \pi \right) = -\sin \dfrac{\pi}{4}$.

b. Since $\dfrac{7\pi}{6}$ is in the third quadrant (it is larger than π and smaller than $\dfrac{3\pi}{2}$), we know that $\tan \dfrac{7\pi}{6}$ is positive. Thus, $\tan \dfrac{7\pi}{6} = \tan \left(\dfrac{7\pi}{6} - \pi \right) = \tan \dfrac{\pi}{6}$.

2. Find the exact value for each function.

    a. $\cos \dfrac{2\pi}{3}$

    b. $\tan \dfrac{11\pi}{6}$

    c. $\sin 2\pi$

SOLUTION

a. Since $\dfrac{2\pi}{3}$ is in the second quadrant (it is larger than $\dfrac{\pi}{2}$ and smaller than π), we know that $\cos \dfrac{2\pi}{3}$ is negative. Thus, $\cos \dfrac{2\pi}{3} = -\cos\left(\pi - \dfrac{2\pi}{3}\right) = -\cos\dfrac{\pi}{3} = -\dfrac{1}{2}.$

b. Since $\dfrac{11\pi}{6}$ is in the fourth quadrant (it is larger than $\dfrac{3\pi}{2}$ and smaller than 2π), we know that $\tan$ $\dfrac{11\pi}{6}$ is negative. Thus, $\tan \dfrac{11\pi}{6} = -\tan\left(2\pi - \dfrac{11\pi}{6}\right) = -\tan\dfrac{\pi}{6} = -\sqrt{3}.$

c. Since 2π lies on the x-axis, it is a quadrantal angle. The sine of the angle is its y-coordinate. Since the coordinates are $(1, 0)$, $\sin 2\pi = 0$.

Practice

1. Copy and complete the table.

θ	0°	30°	45°	60°	90°	180°	270°	360°
Radians	0	$\frac{\pi}{6}$	$\frac{\pi}{4}$	$\frac{\pi}{3}$	$\frac{\pi}{2}$	π	$\frac{3\pi}{2}$	2π
Sin θ	0	$\frac{1}{2}$	$\frac{\sqrt{2}}{2}$	$\frac{\sqrt{3}}{2}$	1	0	-1	0
Cos θ	1	$\frac{\sqrt{3}}{2}$	$\frac{\sqrt{2}}{2}$	$\frac{1}{2}$	0	-1	0	1
Tan θ	0	$\frac{\sqrt{3}}{3}$	1	$\sqrt{3}$	undefined	0	undefined	0

2. Copy and complete the table as shown.

Angle	Quadrant	Formula	Reference Angle
210°	III	210°−180°	30°
330°	IV	360−330	30°
135°	II	180−135	45°
300°	IV	360 − 300	60°
120°	II	180−120	60°
240°	III	270 − 240	30°
225°	III	270 − 225	45°

In 3–7, find the smallest positive angle that is coterminal with each angle.

3. −40° 50

4. 390° 30

5. 800° 60

6. −400° 40

7. −120° 60

In 8–22, find the exact value of each function.

8. $\sin 120°$ $\frac{\sqrt{3}}{2}$

9. $\cos 300°$ $\frac{1}{2}$

10. $\sin 315°$ $-\frac{\sqrt{2}}{2}$

11. $\tan(-60°)$ $-\sqrt{3}$

12. $\sin(-135°)$ $\frac{\sqrt{2}}{2}$

13. $\cos 90° + \tan 225°$ 1

14. $(\tan 30°)^2$ $\frac{1}{3}$

15. $\sin \dfrac{5\pi}{3}$ $-\frac{\sqrt{3}}{2}$

14. $\cos\left(-\dfrac{3\pi}{4}\right)$ $-\frac{\sqrt{2}}{2}$

17. $\cos \dfrac{3\pi}{2}$ 0

18. $\left(\cos \dfrac{5\pi}{6}\right)^2$ $\;3/4$

19. $\tan\left(-\dfrac{\pi}{4}\right)$ $\;-1$

20. $\sin \dfrac{\pi}{2}$ $\;1$

21. $\left(\sin \dfrac{3\pi}{4}\right)^2 + \left(\cos \dfrac{3\pi}{4}\right)^2$ $\;1$

22. $\sin \dfrac{7\pi}{6} + \cos \dfrac{2\pi}{3}$ $\;-1$

23. If $f(x) = \sin x$, find

   a. $f\left(-\dfrac{\pi}{4}\right)$ $\;-\sqrt{2}/2$

   b. $f\left(\dfrac{5\pi}{3}\right)$ $\;-\sqrt{3}/2$

   c. $f(\pi)$ $\;0$

24. If $g(x) = 2 \cos x$, find

   a. $g(300°)$ $\;1$

   b. $g(-45°)$ $\;\sqrt{2}$

   c. $g(0°)$ $\;2$

25. Express each function as a function of a positive acute angle.

   a. $\sin 320°$ $\;-\sin 40$

   b. $\tan (-50°)$ $\;-\tan 50$

   c. $\cos 200°$ $\;-\cos 20$

   d. $\tan 140°$ $\;-\tan 40$

   e. $\sin 400°$ $\;\sin 40$

In 26–32, select the numeral preceding the word or expression that best completes the statement or answers the question.

26. For what value of x is the expression $\dfrac{1}{1 - \sin x}$ undefined?

   (1) 1   (3) 180°

   (2) 90°   (4) 270°

27. If $f(x) = \sin 2x + \cos x$, then $f(\pi) =$

   (1) 1   (3) 0

   (2) 2   **(4)** -1

28. Evaluate $2 \sin 330° + \cos (-60°)$.

   (1) $-1\dfrac{1}{2}$ (3) $\dfrac{1}{2}$

   (2) $-\dfrac{1}{2}$ (4) $1\dfrac{1}{2}$

29. If $g(x) = 2 \sin x - \cos 2x$, find $g\left(\dfrac{\pi}{6}\right)$.

   (1) $-1\dfrac{1}{2}$ **(3)** $\dfrac{1}{2}$

   (2) $-\dfrac{1}{2}$ (4) $1\dfrac{1}{2}$

30. If θ is an angle in standard position and its terminal side passes through the point $\left(-\dfrac{1}{2}, -\dfrac{\sqrt{3}}{2}\right)$ on the unit circle, then a possible value for θ is

   (1) 60°   (3) 240°

   (2) 120°   (4) 300°

31. The expression $\cos 290°$ is equivalent to

   (1) $\cos 20°$ **(3)** $\cos 70°$

   (2) $-\cos 20°$ (4) $-\cos 70°$

32. If $\sin x = \dfrac{\sqrt{2}}{2}$, and $\cos x = -\dfrac{\sqrt{2}}{2}$, then $x =$

   (1) $\dfrac{\pi}{4}$ (3) $\dfrac{5\pi}{4}$

   (2) $\dfrac{3\pi}{4}$ (4) $\dfrac{7\pi}{4}$

12.4 Reciprocal Trigonometric Functions and Cofunctions

Each of the three basic trigonometric functions has a corresponding reciprocal function. The **secant** function (sec) is the reciprocal of the cosine function, the **cosecant** function (csc) is the reciprocal of the sine function, and the **cotangent** function is the reciprocal of the tangent function.

$$\sec \theta = \frac{1}{\cos \theta} \qquad \csc \theta = \frac{1}{\sin \theta} \qquad \cot \theta = \frac{1}{\tan \theta}$$

Note: It is easy to remember that the cotangent function is the reciprocal of the tangent function. However, it is easy to mix up the secant and cosecant functions. One way to remember that the secant function is the reciprocal of the cosine function and the cosecant function is the reciprocal of the sine function is to notice that each function and its reciprocal contain a *c* and an *s*. Thus, $\underline{s}ec\ \theta$ is the reciprocal of $\underline{c}os\ \theta$, and $\underline{c}sc\ \theta$ is the reciprocal of $\underline{s}in\ \theta$.

MODEL PROBLEMS

1. Name the quadrant in which $\angle A$ must lie if $\sec A > 0$ and $\csc A < 0$.

IV

SOLUTION

If $\sec A > 0$, then $\cos A > 0$. If $\csc A < 0$, then $\sin A < 0$.

At this point, draw a set of axes and note that $\cos A > 0$ is in Quadrants I and IV. Place check marks in Quadrants I and IV, as indicated in the figure below. Sin $A < 0$ is in Quadrants III and IV. Place check marks in Quadrants III and IV. Both conditions hold true in Quadrant IV.

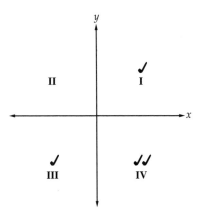

Answer: Quadrant IV

2. Find the exact value of each expression.
   a. $\sec 120°$ -2
   b. $\cot 210°$ $\sqrt{3}$
   c. $\csc \dfrac{5\pi}{3}$ $-2\sqrt{3}/3$
   d. $\cot \dfrac{3\pi}{4}$ -1
   e. $\csc \pi$ undefined

SOLUTION

a. $\sec 120° = \dfrac{1}{\cos 120°}$

$= \dfrac{1}{-\cos 60°}$ (Cosine is negative in Quadrant II.)

$= \dfrac{1}{-\dfrac{1}{2}}$

$= -2$

b. $\cot 210° = \dfrac{1}{\tan 210°}$

$\qquad\qquad = \dfrac{1}{\tan 30°}$ (Tangent is positive in Quadrant III.)

$\qquad\qquad = \dfrac{1}{\dfrac{\sqrt{3}}{3}}$

$\qquad\qquad = \dfrac{3}{\sqrt{3}}$

$\qquad\qquad = \dfrac{3}{\sqrt{3}} \cdot \dfrac{\sqrt{3}}{\sqrt{3}}$ Rationalize the denominator.

$\qquad\qquad = \dfrac{3\sqrt{3}}{3}$

$\qquad\qquad = \sqrt{3}$

c. $\csc \dfrac{5\pi}{3} = \dfrac{1}{\sin \dfrac{5\pi}{3}}$

$\qquad\qquad = \dfrac{1}{-\sin \dfrac{\pi}{3}}$ (Sine is negative in Quadrant IV.)

$\qquad\qquad = \dfrac{1}{-\dfrac{\sqrt{3}}{2}}$

$\qquad\qquad = -\dfrac{2}{\sqrt{3}}$

$\qquad\qquad = -\dfrac{2}{\sqrt{3}} \cdot \dfrac{\sqrt{3}}{\sqrt{3}}$

$\qquad\qquad = -\dfrac{2\sqrt{3}}{3}$

d. $\cot \dfrac{3\pi}{4} = \dfrac{1}{\tan \dfrac{3\pi}{4}}$

$\qquad\qquad = \dfrac{1}{-\tan \dfrac{\pi}{4}}$ (Tangent is negative in Quadrant II.)

$\qquad\qquad = \dfrac{1}{-1}$

$\qquad\qquad = -1$

e. $\csc \pi = \dfrac{1}{\sin \pi}$

$\qquad\qquad = \dfrac{1}{0}$

Therefore, $\csc \pi$ is undefined.

We have not yet illustrated the use of calculators in our study of trigonometry so we will mention it here. When you are asked to find an exact value for a trigonometric function, you may not give a decimal approximation of the answer. So, you should learn the functions of all of the special angles. However, for approximations you may use the calculator.

Your calculator has both a degree mode and a radian mode. To choose the mode you need, press (MODE). The following screen should appear.

```
Normal  Sci  Eng
Float  0123456789
Radian  Degree
Func  Par  Pol  Seq
Connected  Dot
Sequential  Simul
Real  a+bi  re^qi
Full  Horiz  G–T
```

Since there are no calculator keys for the reciprocal functions, follow this procedure to find an approximate value for csc 120°.

1. Make sure that your calculator is in degree mode.
2. Enter (1)(÷)(SIN)(()(1)(2)(0)()).
3. Press (ENTER).

The result is 1.154700538, which is an approximation for $\frac{2\sqrt{3}}{3}$.

Note: The (2nd)(SIN) button, SIN^{-1}, is the inverse of the sine function, not its reciprocal.

You may recall that if two angles are complementary, their sum is 90°. We will now expand this concept further and discuss **cofunctions**. The prefix *co-* gives us a hint about cofunctions. Sine and cosine are cofunctions, tangent and cotangent are cofunctions, and secant and cosecant are also cofunctions. The function of an acute angle is equal to the cofunction of its complement. For example, since a 30° angle is complementary to a 60° angle, sin 30° = cos 60°, tan 30° = cot 60°, and sec 30° = csc 60°.

Note: In working with cofunctions, pay attention to the prefix *co-*. Cofunctions include sine and *co*sine, tangent and *co*tangent, secant and *co*secant, and they involve *co*mplementary angles.

 **MODEL PROBLEMS**

1. Write the expression as a function of an acute angle whose measure is less than 45°.
   a. sin 70°   *cos20*
   b. tan 100° *-cot10*
   c. csc 410° *sec50*

SOLUTION
a. Since a 70° angle is complementary to a 20° angle, sin 70° = cos 20°.
b. 100° is in Quadrant II, where the tangent is negative, and the reference angle is (180° − 100°) = 80°. Therefore, tan 100° = −tan 80°. Since an 80° angle is complementary to a 10° angle, −tan 80° = −cot 10°.
c. 410° is more than one complete revolution, so we subtract 360° from it: csc 410° = csc (410° − 360°) = csc 50°. Since a 50° angle is complementary to a 40° angle, csc 50° = sec 40°.

2. If x is the measure of a positive acute angle and $\sin(x + 15) = \cos 2x$, find x.

$3x + 15 = 90$

SOLUTION
$3x = 175$ $x = 25$

Since sine and cosine are cofunctions, if the sine of one angle is equal to the cosine of another angle, the two angles must be complementary.

Thus, $x + 15 + 2x = 90$ Solve this equation and get:
$$3x + 15 = 90$$
$$3x = 75$$
$$x = 25$$

Answer: $x = 25°$

Practice

1. Copy and complete the following table

θ	0°	30°	45°	60°	90°	180°	270°	360°
Radians	(	$\frac{\pi}{6}$	$\frac{\pi}{4}$	$\frac{\pi}{3}$	$\frac{\pi}{2}$	π	$\frac{3\pi}{2}$	2π
Sec θ	(	$2\sqrt{3}$	$\sqrt{2}$	$\frac{2\sqrt{3}}{3}$	(	0	-1	0
Csc θ	undefined	2	$\sqrt{2}$	2	0	-1	0	)
Cot θ	undefined	$\sqrt{3}$	(	$\frac{\sqrt{3}}{3}$	undefined	0	undefined	0

2. In the interval $0 \le \theta \le 2\pi$, identify all values at which the function is undefined.
 a. sec θ $\pi/2$ & $3\pi/2$
 b. csc θ 0 & π
 c. cot θ 0 & π & 2π

3. Determine the quadrant in which x lies if
 a. $\sin x > 0$ and $\cot x < 0$ II
 b. $\csc x < 0$ and $\cot x < 0$ IV
 c. $\sec x > 0$ and $\sin x < 0$ IV
 d. $\cot x < 0$ and $\sec x < 0$ II
 e. $\cos x > 0$ and $\csc x > 0$ I

In 4–15, find the exact value of each expression.

4. sec 300° 2

5. csc 225° $-\sqrt{2}$

6. cot 270° undefined

7. cot 420° $\frac{\sqrt{3}}{3}$

8. csc (−210°) 2

9. (sec 150°)(cos 150°) 1

10. (tan 300°)(cot 300°) 1

11. cot $\frac{7\pi}{4}$ −1

12. sec π −1

13. csc $\frac{11\pi}{6}$ −2

14. $\left(\sec \frac{2\pi}{3} \right)\left(\sin \frac{2\pi}{3} \right)$ $-\sqrt{3}$

15. $\left(\csc \frac{3\pi}{4} \right)^2$ 2

In 16–20, write the expression as a function of an acute angle whose measure is less than 45°.

16. sin 65° cos 25

17. cot 300° −tan 30

18. csc 75° sec 15

19. tan 110° −cot 20

20. sec 47° csc 43

In 21–25, use your calculator and approximate each value to the nearest thousandth.

21. csc 238° −1.18

22. sec 410° 1.56

23. cot (−35°) −1.42

24. cot $\frac{11\pi}{7}$ −.23

25. csc $\frac{2\pi}{5}$ 1.05

In 26–33, select the numeral preceding the expression that best completes the sentence or answers the question.

26. (sec θ)(cos θ) =
 (1) 1   (3) 0
 (2) 2   (4) varies depending upon the value of θ

27. If $\tan x = \cot (2x - 15)$, then $x =$
(1) 15°
(3) 35° ⊗
(2) 25°
(4) 45°

28. Which expression is equivalent to csc 45°?
(1) $\dfrac{1}{\sin 45°}$ ⊗
(3) $\dfrac{1}{\tan 45°}$
(2) $\dfrac{1}{\cos 45°}$
(4) $\sin (-45°)$

29. If $f(x) = 2 \sec x$, find $f\left(\dfrac{\pi}{6}\right)$.
(1) $\dfrac{2\sqrt{3}}{3}$ ⊗
(3) $\sqrt{3}$
(2) 2
(4) $\dfrac{4\sqrt{3}}{3}$

30. Which expression is equivalent to sec 48°?
(1) csc 42° ⊗
(2) csc 48°
(3) cos 42°
(4) cos 48°

31. If $g(x) = \sin x + \csc x$, find $g\left(\dfrac{\pi}{2}\right)$.
(1) 1
(2) 2 ⊗
(3) 0
(4) −2

32. Which of the following is equal in value to sec π?
(1) csc π
(3) $\cot \dfrac{3\pi}{4}$
(2) tan π ⊗
(4) $\cos \dfrac{5\pi}{4}$

33. If θ is the measure of an acute angle and $\tan \theta = \cot (2\theta)$, then $\tan \theta =$
(1) $\dfrac{1}{2}$
(3) $\sqrt{3}$
(2) $\dfrac{\sqrt{3}}{3}$
(4) 30 ⊗

CHAPTER REVIEW

Select the numeral preceding the word or expression that best completes the statement or answers the question.

1. If $\csc \theta = 2$ and $\sec \theta < 0$, in what quadrant does θ terminate?
(1) I
(3) III
(2) II ⊗
(4) IV

2. If $f(\beta) = \cos 2\beta + 2 \sin \beta$, the numerical value of $f\left(\dfrac{\pi}{6}\right)$ is
(1) 1
(3) $\dfrac{3}{2}$ ⊗
(2) 0
(4) $\dfrac{\sqrt{3} + 1}{2}$

3. What is the numerical value of $\left(\tan \dfrac{3\pi}{4}\right)\left(\csc \dfrac{7\pi}{6}\right)$?
(1) −1
(3) $\dfrac{\sqrt{3}}{2}$
(2) 2 ⊗
(4) $\dfrac{2\sqrt{3}}{3}$

4. Express tan 150° as the function of a positive acute angle.
(1) tan 30°
(3) −cot 30°
(2) cot 60°
(4) −tan 30° ⊗

5. Which expression is *not* equal to $\sin \dfrac{5\pi}{3}$?
(1) $\csc \dfrac{5\pi}{3}$
(3) −sin 60°
(2) sin 60° ⊗
(4) $-\cos \dfrac{\pi}{6}$

6. If $\sin \theta < 0$ and $\tan \theta < 0$, what might be the measure of θ?
(1) 45°
(3) 135°
(2) 330° ⊗
(4) 450°

7. As angle β increases from 90° to 180°, the value of sin β
(1) decreases from 0 to −1
(2) decreases from 1 to 0 ⊗
(3) increases from −1 to 0
(4) increases from 0 to 1

8. For what value of θ is the fraction $\dfrac{2}{1 - \tan \theta}$ undefined?
(1) 0°
(3) 180°
(2) 135°
(4) 225° ⊗

9. What is the image of (1, 0) after a clockwise rotation of 60 degrees?
(1) $\left(\dfrac{1}{2}, \dfrac{\sqrt{3}}{2}\right)$
(3) $\left(\dfrac{\sqrt{3}}{2}, \dfrac{1}{2}\right)$ ⊗
(2) $\left(\dfrac{1}{2}, -\dfrac{\sqrt{3}}{2}\right)$
(4) $\left(\dfrac{\sqrt{3}}{2}, -\dfrac{1}{2}\right)$

10. Find the exact value of $\sin 150° + \cos^2 240°$.

(1) 0

(3) $\frac{1}{2}$

(2) $\frac{1}{4}$

(4) $\frac{3}{4}$

11. The expression $1 - 2\sin^2 45$ has the same value as
    (1) $\sin 90°$
    (2) $\cos 90°$
    (3) $\cos 45°$
    (4) $\sin 22.5°$

12. In the interval $0° \le \beta < 360°$, $\sin \beta = \cos \beta$ when β is
    (1) $45°$ only
    (2) $135°$ and $315°$
    (3) $225°$ only
    (4) $45°$ and $225°$

13. Express in radical form:

$$\left(\sin \frac{\pi}{2}\right)\left(\tan \frac{\pi}{6}\right) - \left(\tan \frac{\pi}{4}\right)\left(\cos \frac{\pi}{2}\right).$$

(1) $\sqrt{3}$

(3) $\frac{\sqrt{3}}{3}$

(2) $-\frac{\sqrt{3}}{3}$

(4) $-\sqrt{3}$

14. If $\tan \theta = \dfrac{-2 - \sqrt{3}}{5}$, in what quadrant(s) may this angle terminate?
    (1) I or II
    (2) I or III
    (3) II or III
    (4) II or IV

15. Rewrite $240°$ in radian measure.

(1) $\frac{2\pi}{3}$

(3) $\frac{7\pi}{6}$

(2) $\frac{4\pi}{3}$

(4) $-\frac{4\pi}{3}$

16. If placed in standard position, an angle of $\frac{7\pi}{6}$ has the same terminal ray as an angle of
    (1) $-150°$
    (2) $-30°$
    (3) $150°$
    (4) $240°$

17. If $f(\theta) = 2\tan \theta - \sin \frac{3\theta}{2}$, evaluate $f(\pi)$.
    (1) 1
    (2) -1
    (3) 3
    (4) 0

18. In circle O, the length of radius AB is 8 centimeters. If central angle AOB measures 2.5 radians, what is the length of the intercepted arc AB?
    (1) 1 cm
    (2) 2.5 cm
    (3) 3.2 cm
    (4) 20 cm

19. What is the probability that a quadrant chosen at random will contain only one positive function from $\sin A$, $\cos A$, and $\tan A$?

(1) 1

(3) $\frac{1}{2}$

(2) $\frac{3}{4}$

(4) $\frac{1}{4}$

20. What is the reference angle for $(-512°)$?
    (1) $-208°$
    (2) $-28°$
    (3) $28°$
    (4) $280°$

21. If $f(x) = \cos 2\theta + \sin \theta$, then $f\left(\frac{\pi}{2}\right)$ equals which of the following?
    (1) 1
    (2) -2
    (3) 2
    (4) 0

22. If $\sin \theta = c$, then the value of the expression $(\sin \theta)(\csc \theta)$ is equivalent to

(1) 1

(3) $\frac{1}{c^2}$

(2) c

(4) c^2

23. Solve for θ: $\sec (5\theta + 14)° = \csc (2\theta - 1)°$.
    (1) $-5°$
    (2) $11°$
    (3) $22°$
    (4) $90°$

24. Express $\sin (-107)°$ as a function of a positive acute angle less than $45°$.
    (1) $-\cos 17°$
    (2) $\cos 17°$
    (3) $-\sin 17°$
    (4) $\sin 17°$

25. Evaluate $2\csc^2 \frac{5\pi}{6} + \tan^2 \frac{2\pi}{3}$.

(1) 1

(3) $9\frac{1}{4}$

(2) $\frac{1}{2} + \sqrt{3}$

(4) 11

26. In circle O, the length of radius OB is 5 centimeters and the length of arc AB is 5 centimeters. The measure of angle AOB is
    (1) 1 radian
    (2) 60 degrees
    (3) π radians
    (4) more than 60 degrees

27. For what value of θ does $\dfrac{\tan \theta}{\cot 37°} = 1$?
    (1) $1°$
    (2) $37°$
    (3) $53°$
    (4) $63°$

28. For which of the following values is the fraction $\dfrac{4\cos \theta}{\tan^2 \theta - 3}$ undefined?
    (1) $90°$ and $270°$
    (2) $120°$ and $240°$
    (3) $210°$ and $330°$
    (4) $150°$ and $300°$

29. If the coordinates of point A are $\left(-\dfrac{\sqrt{3}}{2}, \dfrac{1}{2}\right)$, what is the value of A?

(1) $\dfrac{5\pi}{6}$

(3) $\dfrac{5\pi}{3}$

(2) $\dfrac{7\pi}{6}$

(4) $-\dfrac{\pi}{6}$

30. An angle whose measure is $(-214)°$ is co-terminal with all of the following *except*

(1) $146°$

(3) $34°$

(2) $-574°$

(4) $506°$

FYI

Since the unit circle is not a function, we cannot graph it in "function mode" on our calculators. However, the TI-83 Plus has a "parametric mode" that will enable us to graph the unit circle. Press (MODE) and you will obtain the following screen.

```
Normal Sci Eng
Float 0123456789
Radian Degree
Func Par Pol Seq
Connected Dot
Sequential Simul
Real a+bi re^θi
Full Horiz G–T
```

Scroll down and highlight Par as shown on the screen above. Now, press (ENTER) (Y =) and the following screen will appear without the functions.

```
Plot1 Plot2 Plot3
\X₁ₜ = cos (T)
 Y₁ₜ = sin (T)
\X₂ₜ =
 Y₂ₜ =
\X₃ₜ =
 Y₃ₜ =
\X₄ₜ =
```

Instead of expressing y as a function of x, in parametric mode both x and y are functions of another variable, T. Type in the information as shown in the screen above. To obtain the T, press (X,T,Θ,n). Since we are in parametric mode, the T will appear on your screen. (The x appears only when you are in function mode.) To obtain the graph of this information, we need to set a suitable window. Press (WINDOW) and set your window as shown.

```
WINDOW
 Tmin = 0
 Tmax = 6.2831853...
 Tstep = .1308996...
 Xmin = –1.5
 Xmax = 1.5
 Xscl = 1
↓Ymin = –1.5
```

```
WINDOW
↑Tstep = .1308996...
 Xmin = –1.5
 Xmax = 1.5
 Xscl = 1
 Ymin = –1.5
 Ymax = 1.5
 Yscl = 1
```

Since x and y are both functions of T, to see a complete cycle we need to set the T-values to go from 0 to 2π. Although you should type in 2π for Tmax, the calculator will convert it to its decimal equivalent. We want to plot points with increments of $\dfrac{\pi}{24}$, so we set Tstep $= \dfrac{\pi}{24}$. Again, the calculator will convert this to its decimal equivalent. When you graph the equations you will obtain a graph that looks almost elliptical. This is because your screen is wider than it is high. To adjust for the differences, press (ZOOM) (5) and you will obtain the following graph.

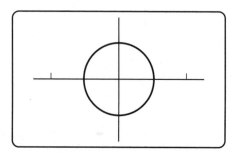

If you now check your window, you will see that the Xmin and Xmax have been adjusted to "square off" the window.

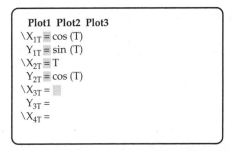

```
WINDOW
 ↑Tstep = .1308996...
  Xmin = –2.274193...
  Xmax = 2.2741935...
  Xscl  = 1
  Ymin = –1.5
  Ymax = 1.5
  Yscl  = 1
```

We can now see for ourselves how the unit circle operates. Press (TRACE) and enter various values for T. If you enter $\frac{\pi}{6}$ for T, you will obtain the following:

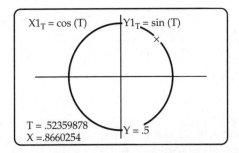

```
X1_T = cos (T)        Y1_T = sin (T)
                             ×



T = .52359878
X = .8660254          Y = .5
```

Notice that the calculator converted $\frac{\pi}{6}$ to its decimal equivalent. You should recall that $\cos\left(\frac{\pi}{6}\right) = \frac{\sqrt{3}}{2}$ and $\sin\left(\frac{\pi}{6}\right) = \frac{1}{2}$. Notice that these appear as the x- and y-values (written as their decimal equivalents). Continue moving around the unit circle, looking at the various values.

As a "sneak preview" of Chapter 13, we will now illustrate how the unit circle "unwraps" to show the graph of the sine and cosine curves as a function of the angle. Go back into (MODE) and change from Sequential graphing to Simultaneous graphing as shown below.

```
Normal Sci  Eng
Float 0123456789
Radian Degree
Func Par Pol Seq
Connected Dot
Sequential Simul
Real a+bi re^θi
Full Horiz G–T
```

We want to graph y as a function of T. First we have to set $x = $ T. Then, let $y = \cos$ (T).

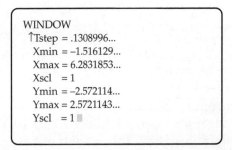

```
Plot1 Plot2 Plot3
\X_{1T} = cos (T)
 Y_{1T} = sin (T)
\X_{2T} = T
 Y_{2T} = cos (T)
\X_{3T} =
 Y_{3T} =
\X_{4T} =
```

Since $x = $ T and $y = \cos$ (T), to see the complete curve we have to adjust our window to include values of x up to 2π. Set Xmax $= 2\pi$. If we graph at this point, we will again get an elliptical shape. So, we must press (ZOOM) (5) to obtain the following window.

```
WINDOW
 ↑Tstep = .1308996...
  Xmin = –1.516129...
  Xmax = 6.2831853...
  Xscl  = 1
  Ymin = –2.572114...
  Ymax = 2.5721143...
  Yscl  = 1
```

This enables you to see the graph with its proper proportions. Notice how the circle "unwraps" to show the cosine curve. As you are graphing, press (ENTER) when the circle reaches the y-axis. (Pressing (ENTER) will pause the graph.) By looking at the cosine curve, you can see that $\cos$ (T) $= 0$. Press (ENTER) and allow the graph to continue until the circle touches the x-axis. Pause again to obtain the following graph.

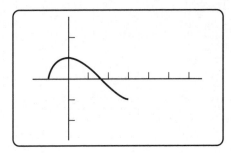

Notice how you can see that $\cos \pi = -1$. Continue along, pausing the graph to study it more closely.

Now graph $y = \sin$ (T) and follow the same procedure. This will prepare you to better understand the curves in Chapter 13.

Trigonometric Graphs

13.1 Basic Trigonometric Graphs

Just as other functions have graphs that represent them, so do trigonometric functions. When drawing trigonometric graphs by hand, we set the axes a bit differently than for other graphs. We use values of θ in radian measure.

Because π is approximately 3.14, a good way to label the horizontal axis is to use a multiple of 3 for the number of boxes that equal π. For convenience, we will keep the scales of the two axes similar by using 6 boxes on the x-axis to equal π, so 12 boxes will equal 2π. Then, $\frac{\pi}{2}$ will occur at 3 boxes to the right of the y-axis, halfway between 0 and π, while $\frac{3\pi}{2}$ is 9 boxes to the right of the y-axis, halfway between π and 2π. We use 6 boxes as a measure on the vertical axis to equal 3, so that each 2 boxes on the vertical axis equals 1 unit, as shown below.

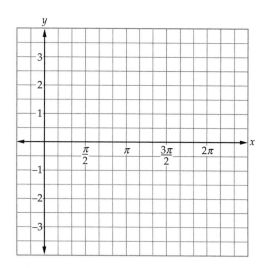

When graphing in a domain that includes values of $x \le 0$, the same process is applied.

Graph of y = sin x

To graph the function $y = \sin x$, let us explore the information the unit circle provides. Since we draw our trigonometric graphs using radians, that is the form of angle measure shown on this unit circle.

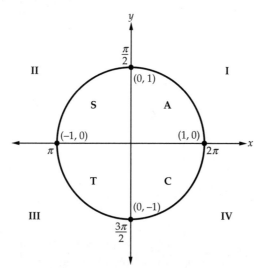

Notice the values of sin x at the quadrantal angles.

x	0	$\dfrac{\pi}{2}$	π	$\dfrac{3\pi}{2}$	2π
$\sin x$	0	1	0	−1	0

If we plot these points on a graph, we start to get an idea of the $y = \sin x$ image.

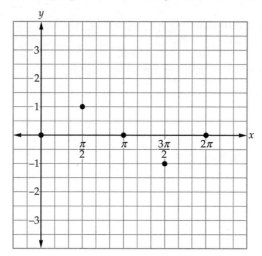

When we include other known values of sin x, such as,

$$\sin \frac{\pi}{6} = \frac{1}{2} = 0.5 \qquad\qquad \sin \frac{\pi}{3} = \frac{\sqrt{3}}{2} \approx 0.87$$

$$\sin \frac{2\pi}{3} = \frac{\sqrt{3}}{2} \approx 0.87 \qquad\qquad \sin \frac{5\pi}{6} = \frac{1}{2} = 0.5$$

$$\sin \frac{7\pi}{6} = -\frac{1}{2} = -0.5 \qquad\qquad \sin \frac{4\pi}{3} = -\frac{\sqrt{3}}{2} \approx -0.87$$

$$\sin \frac{5\pi}{3} = -\frac{\sqrt{3}}{2} \approx -0.87 \qquad\qquad \sin \frac{11\pi}{6} = -\frac{1}{2} = -0.5$$

we see the graph becoming more complete. The use of 6 boxes on the horizontal axis to equal π means that each box equals $\frac{\pi}{6}$, which makes the plotting of these points easy.

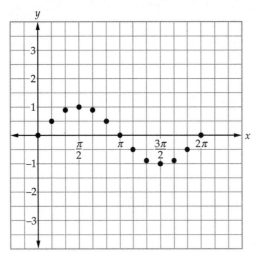

Now, look at the sine curve. In the first and second quadrants, that is, when $x \leq \pi$, the graph of $y = \sin x$ is above the x-axis, which means all values are positive, as the unit circle indicates. When $x \geq \pi$, in the third and fourth quadrants, $y = \sin \theta$ is below the x-axis and therefore negative.

Remember: A good way to recognize the sine curve when graphing by hand is to use the idea that "Sine starts at 0, ends at 0 and is at 0 halfway through."

Graph of $y = \cos x$

To graph the cosine curve by hand, again we begin by using the values shown on the unit circle.

x	0	$\frac{\pi}{2}$	π	$\frac{3\pi}{2}$	2π
$\cos x$	1	0	-1	0	1

Consider the appearance of these five points on a graph.

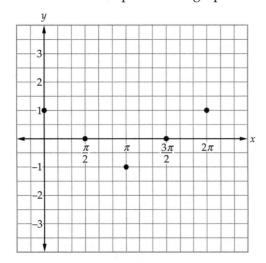

Once again, we can see more of the graph by including the cosine values of other known angles.

$$\cos \frac{\pi}{6} = \frac{\sqrt{3}}{2} \approx 0.87 \qquad\qquad \cos \frac{\pi}{3} = \frac{1}{2} = 0.5$$

$$\cos \frac{2\pi}{3} = -\frac{1}{2} = -0.5 \qquad\qquad \cos \frac{5\pi}{6} = -\frac{\sqrt{3}}{2} \approx -0.87$$

$$\cos \frac{7\pi}{6} = -\frac{\sqrt{3}}{2} \approx -0.87 \qquad\qquad \cos \frac{4\pi}{3} = -\frac{1}{2} = -0.5$$

$$\cos \frac{5\pi}{3} = \frac{1}{2} \approx 0.87 \qquad\qquad \cos \frac{11\pi}{6} = \frac{\sqrt{3}}{2} = 0.87$$

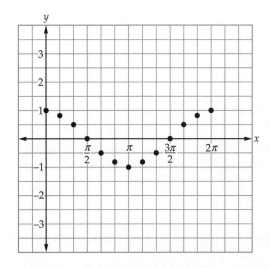

Remember: y-cosine x starts at its maximum of 1, ends at its maximum, and is at its minimum of -1 halfway through the curve. Halfway between each maximum and minimum the cosine curve is at 0.

Graph of $y = \tan x$

The graph of the tangent curve is very different from that of the sine and cosine curves because those two curves are continuous. The tangent function, however, is undefined when $x = \frac{\pi}{2}$ and again at $\frac{3\pi}{2}$ and at any other odd multiple of $\frac{\pi}{2}$. However, as x approaches $\frac{\pi}{2}$, the values of $\tan x$ continue to increase toward infinity. To indicate this on the graph, we show a dashed vertical line to represent the asymptotes at these values of x. We know that $y = \tan x$ is positive in the first and third quadrants and negative in the second and fourth. We also know certain values of $y = \tan x$ as shown in the table below.

x	0	$\frac{\pi}{6}$	$\frac{\pi}{4}$	$\frac{\pi}{3}$	$\frac{\pi}{2}$	$\frac{2\pi}{3}$	$\frac{3\pi}{4}$	$\frac{5\pi}{6}$	
$\tan x$	0	$\frac{\sqrt{3}}{3} \approx 0.58$	1	$\sqrt{3} \approx 1.7$	U	$-\sqrt{3} \approx -1.7$	-1	$\frac{-\sqrt{3}}{3} \approx -0.58$	
x	π	$\frac{7\pi}{6}$	$\frac{5\pi}{4}$	$\frac{4\pi}{3}$	$\frac{3\pi}{2}$	$\frac{5\pi}{3}$	$\frac{7\pi}{4}$	$\frac{11\pi}{6}$	2π
$\tan x$	0	$\frac{\sqrt{3}}{3} \approx 0.58$	1	$\sqrt{3} \approx 1.7$	U	$-\sqrt{3} \approx -1.7$	-1	$\frac{-\sqrt{3}}{3} \approx -0.58$	0

Now, look at the graph produced by this set of values.

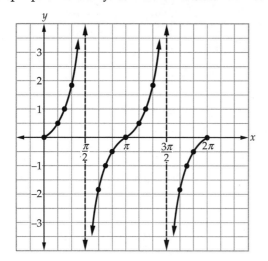

Remember: The graph of $y = \tan x$ is asymptotic to $x = \frac{\pi}{2}$ and other odd multiples of $\frac{\pi}{2}$. The graph will approach these asymptotes, growing closer and closer to them, but will never cross them. Note that $y = \tan x$ has no maximum or minimum value; we can make the values of y as large or small as we want by choosing points sufficiently close to the odd multiples of $\frac{\pi}{2}$.

Now that you have seen the process of graphing a trigonometric function by hand, let us do it using the TI-83 calculator. To graph $y = \sin x$, first go to the (MODE) screen.

```
Normal Sci  Eng
Float 0123456789
Radian Degree
Func Par  Pol  Seq
Connected Dot
Sequential Simul
Real a+bi  re^qi
Full Horiz G–T
```

Be certain that all options are highlighted on the left, particularly Radian. Go to the (Y =) screen and enter the equation $y = \sin x$. Notice the calculator gives you an open parenthesis in which you insert your argument. Now go to the (WINDOW) screen. We want the calculator to give us a trig friendly window, so we set the values as shown below.

```
WINDOW
  Xmin = 0
  Xmax = 6.2831853...
  Xscl  = π/2
  Ymin = –2
  Ymax = 2
  Yscl  = .5
  Xres  = 1
```

Notice the Xmax is a decimal value, but to get it we actually enter 2π. Once you move off that value, the calculator produces the decimal you see. Likewise, once you move the cursor off the Xscl of $\frac{\pi}{2}$, the calculator will give you a decimal equivalent. Now, hit the (GRAPH) button and you should see a graph like the one on page 131 (with labels added).

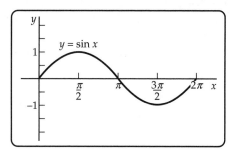

Once again, you can see how the graph of the sine function starts at 0, ends at 0, and is at 0 halfway through its curve.

To see the graph of $y = \cos(x)$, enter that equation in the (Y =) screen. Leave the (WINDOW) settings the same and hit (GRAPH).

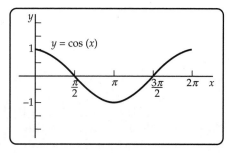

Here you can see that the graph of the cosine function starts at its maximum of 1, ends at its maximum, and is at its minimum of -1 halfway through its curve. Halfway between each of those maximum and minimum points the curve is at 0.

When you graph the tangent function, you might want to graph it in the Dot mode. As you see from the graph at the left below, in Connected mode, the calculator, in its attempt to connect points, draws rather heavy vertical lines. Someone not knowing the shape of the tan curve could be confused. In Dot mode, on the right, the graph is clearer, but specific points might be difficult to identify.

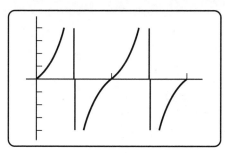

$y = \tan(x)$ in Connected mode

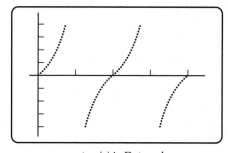

$y = \tan(x)$ in Dot mode

Practice

1. Using a domain of $\{0 \le x \le 2\pi\}$, graph the functions $y = \sin x$ and $y = \cos x$ on the same axes.
   a. At what values of x does $\sin x = \cos x$? What is this in degree measure?
   b. Translate the graph of $y = \cos x\ T_{\frac{\pi}{2},0}$. Describe what happens.
   c. In which quadrant(s) are both $y = \sin x$ and $y = \cos x$ negative?

2. Using a domain of $\{-\pi \le x \le \pi\}$, graph the functions $y = \sin x$ and $y = \cos x$ on the same axes.
   a. When does $\sin x - \cos x = 1$? (Hint: When are the two graphs one unit apart?)
   b. In which quadrant(s) do both the graphs of $y = \sin x$ and $y = \cos x$ increase? In which quadrant(s) do they both decrease?

3. Using a domain of $\left\{-\frac{\pi}{2} \le x \le \frac{\pi}{2}\right\}$, graph the functions $y = \tan x$ and $y = \cos x$ on the same axes.

a. For how many values of x does $\tan x = \cos x$?

b. For what values in the domain do the graphs of both $\tan x$ and $\cos x$ increase?

4. Graph the functions $y = \tan x$ and $y = \sin x$ on the same axes over the interval $\{-2\pi \le x \le 2\pi\}$.

a. How many full sine curves are present over this domain?

b. For how many values of x does $\tan x = \sin x$?

c. In which quadrant(s) are both $y = \tan x$ and $y = \sin x$ positive? Both negative?

5. Graph the functions $y = \sin x$ and $y = \cos x$ on the same axes over the interval $\left\{-\frac{\pi}{2} \le x \le \frac{\pi}{2}\right\}$.

a. At what value(s) of x does $\sin x = \cos x$?

b. At what value(s) of x does $|\sin x - \cos x| = 1$?

13.2 Amplitude and Period

The standard form of a trigonometric equation for the sine and cosine curves that we will be using is $y = a \sin bx$ or $y = a \cos bx$. $|a|$ represents **amplitude,** or the absolute value of half the difference between the maximum and minimum values. b represents the **frequency** (or number of whole curves in 2π). In Section 13.1, the sine and cosine curves we explored each had amplitudes and frequencies of 1.

Amplitude

The range of a trigonometric function in the form $y = a \sin bx$ is $-|a| \le y \le |a|$, while for this example, the domain remains $0 \le x \le 2\pi$. In the graph below, $f(x) = \sin x$ is drawn in bold, while $g(x) = 2 \sin x$ and $h(x) = \frac{1}{2} \sin x$ are light.

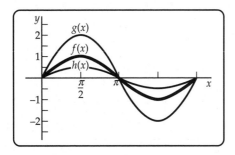

Observe the y-values of these functions in the table below. Since 0 times any value is still 0, the x-intercept does not change. Other values are the original values of the $y = \sin x$ function multiplied by the value of a.

x	0	$\frac{\pi}{2}$	π	$\frac{3\pi}{2}$	2π
$f(x)$	0	1	0	-1	0
$g(x)$	0	2	0	-2	0
$h(x)$	0	$\frac{1}{2}$	0	$-\frac{1}{2}$	0

Observe that in each case, the shape of the curve is the same. The sine curve starts at 0, ends at 0, and is at 0 halfway through its cycle. In each case, the maximum value of the sine function equals the absolute value of a, the amplitude, while the minimum value of the function equals the negative value of the amplitude.

In the graph below, $f(x) = \sin x$ is drawn in bold, while $g(x) = -\sin x$ and $h(x) = -2 \sin x$ are light.

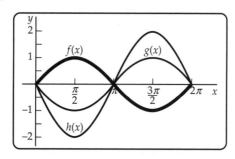

Observe that $g(x)$ is the function $f(x)$ reflected in the x-axis. Whenever a is negative, you are looking at a reflection of the original function in the x-axis.

The cosine function curves follow similar patterns. If a is negative, the curve will be at its minimum point when x equals 0 and be back at its minimum point when x equals 2π. In the graph below, $f(x) = \cos x$ is drawn in bold, while $g(x) = -\cos x$ and $h(x) = \dfrac{3}{2} \cos x$ are light.

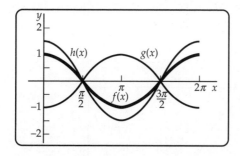

Once again, the x-intercept remains unchanged for all of the cosine curves and the basic cosine shape is present. The maximum and minimum points are achieved when a is multiplied by the value of $\cos x$.

MODEL PROBLEMS

1. Given the function $f(x) = 3 \sin x$, what is the maximum value $f(x)$ can equal?
   (1) -3
   (2) 2
   ● 3
   (4) 2π

SOLUTION
In this equation, the amplitude corresponds to the maximum value of $f(x)$. Since the amplitude is 3, the answer is choice (3).

2. In which of the following equations is the minimum value -2?
   (1) $y = \sin x$
   ● $y = 2 \sin x$
   (3) $y = -\sin x$
   (4) $y = 4 \sin x$

SOLUTION

If the minimum value in the range is to be −2, it means the equation must have an *a* value of ±2. The only equation that meets the requirement is choice (2).

3. Which of the following graphs shows a function with an amplitude of $\frac{1}{2}$?

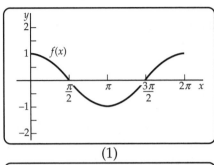

(1)

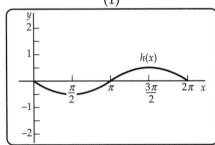

(2)

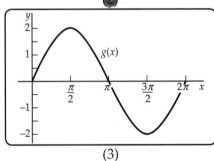

(3)

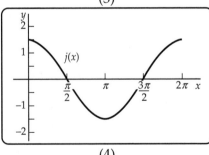

(4)

SOLUTION

An amplitude of $\frac{1}{2}$ means the range is $-\frac{1}{2} \leq y \leq \frac{1}{2}$. Looking at the graphs, the only function with that range is $h(x)$, choice (2).

Note: Since the tangent function grows to infinity, we do not discuss amplitude with regard to tangent.

Period

The **period** of a trigonometric function is the length of the interval needed to see one full curve. In all of the examples thus far, the periods of the graphs have been 2π. The formula for period is 2π divided by the frequency of the function. That is, period $= \dfrac{2\pi}{|b|}$. If we know the frequency of any function, identified in the equation as b, we can find the period by simple division.

The graph below shows the sine curve with an amplitude of 1 and periods of 2π, π, and 4π. The pertinent equations are $f(x) = \sin x$, in bold, $g(x) = \sin 2x$, and $h(x) = \sin \frac{1}{2}x$.

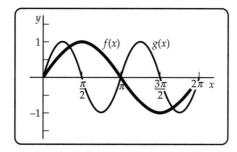 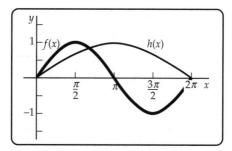

The standard sine curve, $f(x) = \sin x$, has a period of 2π. However, the graph of $g(x)$ completes two full cycles in the 2π distance, so its period is $\dfrac{2\pi}{2}$ or π. That is, one full sine curve is completed in a distance of π. The graph of $h(x)$ finishes only half of the normal sine curve in the 2π distance, so it would need a distance of 4π to finish one whole cycle. Therefore, the period of $h(x)$ is 4π.

MODEL PROBLEMS

1. Without using your graphing calculator, graph the function $y = 3 \sin 2x$ over the interval $0 \le x \le 2\pi$. On the same set of axes, graph the function $y = 2 \cos x$. Name two points of intersection.

SOLUTION

1. First explore what you know about the two equations given.

Function	$y = 3 \sin 2x$	$y = 2 \cos x$
Amplitude	3—max = 3, min = −3	2—max = 2, min = −2
Frequency	2—2 full curves in 2π	1—1 full curve in 2π
Period	π—first curve starts at $(0, 0)$ second curve starts at $(0, \pi)$	2π—first curve starts at $(0, 2)$ ends at $(2\pi, 2)$
Description	Starts at 0, ends at 0, is at 0 halfway through each cycle	Starts at max (2), ends at max; is at min (−2) halfway through the cycle

Draw the basic trigonometric axes and graph the points you know for each curve. Since the sine curve has a frequency of 2, one cycle will begin at 0, end at 0 when $x = \pi$, and be at 0 halfway through at $\frac{\pi}{2}$. The second cycle starts at $(\pi, 0)$, ends at $(2\pi, 0)$, and will also be at 0 halfway through this cycle at $\frac{3\pi}{2}$. The first maximum value of $3 \sin 2x$, which we know to be 3, will be halfway between 0 and $\frac{\pi}{2}$ when $x = \frac{\pi}{4}$. The second maximum point will be halfway between π and $\frac{3\pi}{2}$ when x equals $\frac{5\pi}{4}$. The first minimum value of $3 \sin 2x$, which we know to be -3, will occur halfway between $\frac{\pi}{2}$ and π at $\frac{3\pi}{4}$ and the second will occur halfway between $\frac{3\pi}{2}$ and 2π at $\frac{7\pi}{4}$.

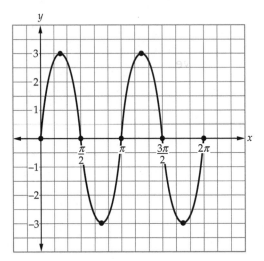

Now we draw the $y = 2 \cos x$ curve, remembering that cosine curves begin and end at their a values.

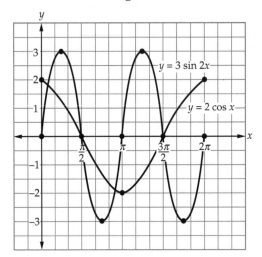

When we look at the graph of the two functions we see four points of intersection, two of which occur at $x = \frac{\pi}{2}$ and $\frac{3\pi}{2}$ while the others may be approximated at $x = \frac{\pi}{12}$ and $x = \frac{11\pi}{12}$.

2. Given the equation $y = 3 \sin 2x$, the period of the function is which of the following?
   - ● π
   - (2) 2π
   - (3) 3
   - (4) $\frac{2\pi}{3}$

SOLUTION

Divide 2π by b, in this case, $2. \dfrac{2\pi}{|2|} = \pi$. The period is π, choice (1).

3. Find the amplitude and period of the function $y = \dfrac{1}{2}\cos 4x$.

   (1) amplitude $= \dfrac{1}{2}$, period $= 4$

   (2) amplitude $= 4$, period $= \dfrac{1}{2}\pi$

   (3) amplitude $= \dfrac{1}{2}$, period $= 2\pi$

   (4) amplitude $= \dfrac{1}{2}$, period $= \dfrac{\pi}{2}$

SOLUTION

Since amplitude $= a$ and period $= \dfrac{2\pi}{|b|}$, we look first at the values of a and b in this equation. $a = \dfrac{1}{2}$ so the amplitude is $\dfrac{1}{2}$. $b = 4$ so the period is $\dfrac{2\pi}{|4|}$ or $\dfrac{\pi}{2}$, choice (4).

4. What is the greatest element in the range of the function $y = 4 \sin 2x + 3$?
   (1) 8
   (2) 7
   (3) 3
   (4) 4

SOLUTION

In this equation the traditional trigonometric equation of $y = a \sin bx$ has a numerical value being added to the y-value. This equation is $y = a \sin bx + d$ where d represents a vertical shift of the entire graph. Since the amplitude of this function is 4, normally its maximum value would be 4, but in this case, it is $4 + 3$ or 7, choice (2).

5. Using the graphing calculator, find all values of x at which $4 \sin 2x = -\cos x$ in the interval $\{0 \le x \le 2\pi\}$.

SOLUTION

Enter the two equations in Y_1 and Y_2, set your window with x-values of 0 and 2π, and hit $\boxed{\text{GRAPH}}$.

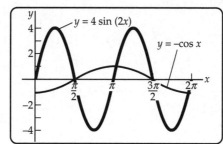

Notice that there are four points of intersection, two occurring at the quadrantal angles of $\dfrac{\pi}{2}$ and $\dfrac{3\pi}{2}$ and the other two at values you must find by using the intersect function of the calculator ($\boxed{\text{2nd}}$ $\boxed{\text{TRACE}}$ $\boxed{5}$). Remember to move your cursor close to the points whose value you want or you will keep getting the same points. The calculator will approximate the x-values in decimal form rather than in exact radian measure. The remaining x-values at the points of intersection are 3.2669205 and 6.1578575.

In 1–14, select the numeral preceding the word or expression that best completes the sentence or answers the question.

1. As angle x increases from $\frac{3\pi}{2}$ to 2π, which of the following is true?
   (1) $\sin x$ decreases from 0 to -1
   (2) $\cos x$ decreases from 0 to -1
   (3) $\cos x$ increases from 0 to 1
   (4) $\sin x$ increases from 0 to 1

2. What is the minimum element in the range of the equation $y = 5 + 2\sin\theta$?
   (1) -5 (3) 3
   (2) 2   (4) -7

3. Between -2π and 2π, the graph of the equation $y = \sin x$ is symmetric with respect to
   (1) the x-axis   (3) $y = x$
   (2) the origin   (4) the y-axis

4. How many full cycles of the function $y = 3\sin 2x$ appear in π radians?
   (1) 1   (3) 3
   (2) 2   (4) $\frac{3\pi}{2}$

5. The function $f(x) = -3\cos 2x$ reaches its minimum value when x, expressed in radians, equals
   (1) -3 (3) $\frac{\pi}{4}$
   (2) $\frac{\pi}{2}$ (4) π

6. If the graphs of the equations $y = 2\cos x$ and $y = -1$ are drawn on the same set of axes, how many points of intersection will occur between 0 and 2π?
   (1) 1   (3) 3
   (2) 2   (4) 4

7. On the same set of axes, $y = \sin x$ and $y = \cos x$ are graphed. If the translation $T_{\frac{\pi}{2},0}$ is applied to $y = \cos x$, the graphs will
   (1) intersect at only one point
   (2) intersect at only two points
   (3) coincide
   (4) not intersect at all

8. Which is an equation of the reflection of the graph of $y = \sin x$ in the y-axis?
   (1) $y = \sin(-x)$ (3) $y = -\sin(-x)$
   (2) $y = \cos x$ (4) $y = -\cos x$

9. What is the equation of the graph sketched below?

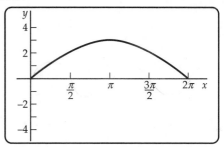

   (1) $y = 3\sin x$ (3) $y = 3\cos x$
   (2) $y = 3\sin\left(\frac{1}{2}x\right)$ (4) $y = 3\cos\left(\frac{1}{2}x\right)$

10. The graph of which equation has an amplitude of 2 and a period of π?
    (1) $y = 2\cos x$ (3) $y = 2\cos 2x$
    (2) $y = \frac{1}{2}\sin 2x$ (4) $y = -2\cos x$

11. What is the range of the function $y = 3\cos 2x + 1$?
    (1) $-3 \le y \le 3$ (3) $-2 \le y \le 4$
    (2) $-4 \le y \le 5$ (4) $-1 \le y \le 1$

12. The expression $f(x) = 3\sin\frac{1}{2}x$ reaches its maximum value when x, expressed in radians, equals
    (1) 3   (3) π
    (2) $\frac{\pi}{2}$ (4) $\frac{3\pi}{2}$

13. How many cycles of the graph of $y = \frac{2}{3}\sin 4\theta$ appear in 2π radians?
    (1) $\frac{2}{3}$ (3) π
    (2) 2   (4) 4

14. What is the equation of the graph sketched below?

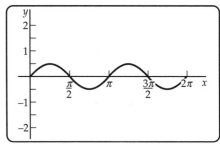

    (1) $y = 2\sin\frac{1}{2}x$ (3) $y = \frac{1}{2}\sin 2x$
    (2) $y = \frac{1}{2}\cos x$ (4) $y = \frac{1}{2}\sin\frac{1}{2}x$

In 15–18, solve each problem first by graphing by hand and then with your calculator.

15. a. On the same set of axes, sketch and label the graphs of the equations $y = -3 \cos 2x$ and $y = \frac{3}{2} \sin x$ in the interval $0 \leq x \leq 2\pi$.

   b. Use the graphs drawn in part **a** to determine at what value of x does $-3 \cos 2x + \frac{3}{2} \sin x = -3$.

16. a. Sketch the graph of the equation $y = 2 \cos x$ in the interval $0 \leq x \leq 2\pi$.

   b. On the same axes, sketch the equation of $y = 3 \sin \frac{1}{2}x$.

   c. In which quadrants does $2 \cos x = 3 \sin \frac{1}{2}x$?

17. a. On the same set of axes, sketch and label the graphs of the equations $y = -2 \cos 2x$ and $y = \frac{3}{2} \sin 2x$ in the interval $-\frac{\pi}{2} \leq x \leq \frac{\pi}{2}$.

   b. Use the graphs drawn in part **a** to determine the value of x when $-2 \cos 2x + \frac{3}{2} \sin 2x = 1$.

18. a. Sketch the graph of the equation $y = \tan x$ in the interval $-\pi \leq x \leq \pi$.

   b. On the same axes, sketch the equation $y = \frac{3}{2} \cos 2x$.

   c. For what values of x does $\tan x = \frac{3}{2} \cos 2x$?

13.3 Reflections in the Line $y = x$

Consider the function $y = \sin x$ over the interval $\{-\pi \leq x \leq \pi\}$ as shown below.

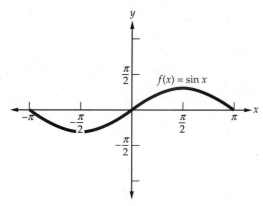

What happens if we reflect this graph in the line $y = x$? We know from our work with transformations that the equation becomes $x = \sin y$, which means "y is the angle whose sine is x." Examine the graph of $y = \sin x$ shown in bold below and its reflection in the line $y = x$.

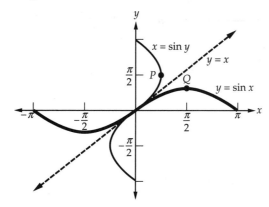

The coordinates of point P are $\left(1, \frac{\pi}{2}\right)$, the reflection of point $Q\left(\frac{\pi}{2}, 1\right)$ in the line $y = x$. We can say that $\frac{\pi}{2}$ is the angle whose sine is 1. This can also be written as $\frac{\pi}{2}$ is the arc whose sine is 1, or $\frac{\pi}{2} = $ **arc sin** 1.

The word *arc* before a function indicates that you are talking about the angle whose function value follows.

Equation	Meaning	y in the interval $-\pi \leq y \leq \pi$
$y = $ arc sin 0	y is the angle whose sine is 0.	$\pm\pi, 0$
$y = $ arc sin $\frac{1}{2}$	y is the angle whose sine is $\frac{1}{2}$.	$\frac{\pi}{6}, \frac{5\pi}{6}$
$y = $ arc sin $\frac{\sqrt{2}}{2}$	y is the angle whose sine is $\frac{\sqrt{2}}{2}$.	$\frac{\pi}{4}, \frac{3\pi}{4}$

We see that the equation $y = $ arc sin 0 has three solutions, $\pm\pi$ and 0, while each of the other equations has two solutions. When we explore arc sin, arc cos, or arc tan equations, we must remember the rules for the quadrants in which the values are positive and negative and find those solutions in the appropriate quadrants. If solving the equation $y = $ arc sin $\left(-\frac{1}{2}\right)$ whose original function had the domain $\{0 \leq x \leq 2\pi\}$, we must consider values of y in Quadrants III and IV, since sin y is negative in both. So, $y = \frac{7\pi}{6}$ or $\frac{11\pi}{6}$.

Below is a graph of $y = $ arc cos x over the interval $\{-2\pi \leq x \leq 2\pi\}$. Use it to determine the value(s) of $y = $ arc cos (-1).

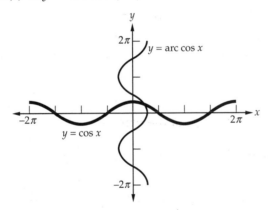

The graph demonstrates that there are two angles of y that have values of -1, $\pm\pi$. In a similar fashion, when working with $y = $ arc tan x, you must consider answers in all quadrants in which the signs are positive or negative as indicated by the problem.

1. Rewrite the expression $\theta = \arctan(-1)$.

$\tan\theta = -1$

SOLUTION

The expression $\theta = \arctan(-1)$ means θ is the angle whose tan equals -1, so it can be rewritten as $\tan\theta = -1$.

2. If $\theta = \arccos\left(-\frac{1}{2}\right)$ and $0° \leq \theta \leq 360°$, find θ.

SOLUTION

First rewrite $\theta = \arccos\left(-\frac{1}{2}\right)$ in terms of $\cos\theta$, as $\cos\theta = -\frac{1}{2}$. We know $\cos\theta$ is negative in Quadrants II and III, so we need the reference angle of $60°$ moved into these quadrants.
Quadrant II angle = $180°$ − reference angle, so $\theta = 180° - 60° = 120°$.
Quadrant III angle = $180°$ + reference angle, so $\theta = 180° + 60° = 240°$.

3. If $\theta = \arcsin\left(-\frac{\sqrt{3}}{2}\right)$ and $0 \leq \theta < 2\pi$, find θ.

SOLUTION

First rewrite $\theta = \arcsin\left(-\frac{\sqrt{3}}{2}\right)$ in terms of $\sin\theta$, as $\sin\theta = \left(-\frac{\sqrt{3}}{2}\right)$. We know $\sin\theta$ is negative in Quadrants III and IV, so we move the reference angle of $\frac{\pi}{3}$ into these quadrants.

Quadrant III angle = π + reference angle, so $\theta = \pi + \frac{\pi}{3} = \frac{4\pi}{3}$.

Quadrant IV angle = 2π − reference angle, so $\theta = 2\pi - \frac{\pi}{3} = \frac{5\pi}{3}$.

4. Evaluate $\tan\left(\arcsin\frac{1}{2}\right)$ in the interval $0 \leq \theta < 2\pi$.

SOLUTION

To evaluate $\tan\left(\arcsin\frac{1}{2}\right)$, we work from the inside of the parentheses out. The expression $\arcsin\frac{1}{2}$ means we need the angle(s) whose sine is $\frac{1}{2}$ in the interval $0 \leq \theta < 2\pi$. Recall that $\sin\theta = \frac{1}{2}$ when $\theta = \frac{\pi}{6}$ or $\frac{5\pi}{6}$. Now we need to evaluate $\tan\left(\frac{\pi}{6}\right)$ and $\tan\left(\frac{5\pi}{6}\right)$. $\tan\left(\frac{\pi}{6}\right) = \frac{\sqrt{3}}{3}$ while $\tan\left(\frac{5\pi}{6}\right) = -\frac{\sqrt{3}}{3}$, so the final answer is $\pm\frac{\sqrt{3}}{3}$.

Inverse Trigonometric Functions

Consider the graph of the function $y = \sin x$ over the interval $-\frac{\pi}{2} \leq x \leq \frac{\pi}{2}$, shown in bold in the graph below, and its reflection in the line $y = x$.

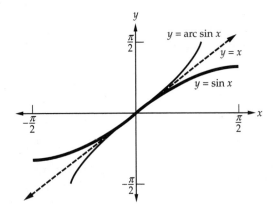

Both the original and its reflection in the line $y = x$ are functions in this case because we are looking at $y = $ arc sin x in only the first and fourth quadrants. Since the sine is positive in the first quadrant and negative in the fourth quadrant, there is no repetition of values, so the reflection is now a function. When the domain is restricted in such a manner, we now have a function whose inverse is a function as well. We write the inverse function with a capital letter A, signaling that its domain is restricted. The equation of the inverse of $y = \sin x$ is therefore $y = $ Arc sin x.

Note: $y = $ Arc sin x is a function since its graph would pass the vertical line test.

To create the inverse of $y = \cos x$, we limit the domain of the original function to be $0 \leq x \leq \pi$, keeping the cosine function in the first and second quadrants where it is first positive and then negative, as shown in the graph below.

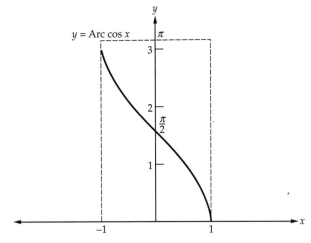

In a similar fashion, the domain of $y = \tan x$ is limited to the first and fourth quadrants to create an inverse function $y = $ Arc tan x, as shown below.

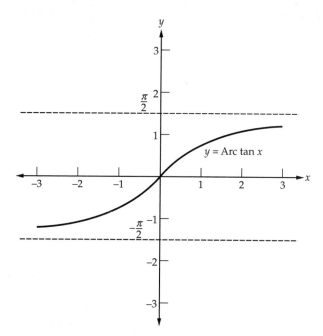

To help you remember the limited domains for the functions, review the table below.

Function	Limited Domain	Equation of Inverse
$y = \sin x$	$-\dfrac{\pi}{2} \le x \le \dfrac{\pi}{2}$	$y = \text{Arc sin } x$
$y = \cos x$	$0 \le x \le \pi$	$y = \text{Arc cos } x$
$y = \tan x$	$-\dfrac{\pi}{2} < x < \dfrac{\pi}{2}$	$y = \text{Arc tan } x$

Remember: When solving an Arc sin or Arc tan problem that contains a negative value, measure the angle in a clockwise direction to reach the fourth quadrant values.

MODEL PROBLEMS

1. The value of sin (Arc tan 1) is which of the following?
   (1) 1
   (2) $\dfrac{1}{2}$
   (3) $\dfrac{\sqrt{2}}{2}$
   (4) 45°

SOLUTION

We must work from inside the parentheses out. If $\tan \theta = 1$, then θ must lie in Quadrant I, so $\theta = 45°$. Next evaluate sin 45°, which equals $\dfrac{\sqrt{2}}{2}$, choice (3).

2. If $y = \text{Arc sin} \left(-\frac{1}{2}\right)$, then y equals

   (1) 30°

   (2) 120°

   (③) $-\frac{\pi}{6}$

   (4) $\frac{5\pi}{3}$

SOLUTION

If $\sin \theta = -\frac{1}{2}$, we are restricted to Quadrant IV, so $\theta = -30°$ or $-\frac{\pi}{6}$, choice (3).

3. In order to create an inverse of the function $y = \cos x$, in which quadrants must the function fall?

   (1) I, II, III, and IV

   (②) I and II

   (3) I and IV

   (4) II and III

SOLUTION

In order to have only one positive and one negative quadrant for the inverse function, we restrict the domain to Quadrants I and II, choice (2).

4. What would be the equation of the inverse function of $3 \cos x = -2$?

   (1) $3 \sin x = -2$

   (2) $\cos x = -\frac{2}{3}$

   (③) $x = \text{Arc cos} \left(-\frac{2}{3}\right)$

   (4) $x = \text{Arc sin} \left(-\frac{2}{3}\right)$

SOLUTION

The inverse of a trigonometric function is defined in terms of the value of the function rather than the angle measure. This eliminates choices (1) and (2). Since choice (4) switches functions, the correct answer is choice (3).

Practice

Select the numeral preceding the word or expression that best completes the sentence or answers the question.

1. The function $y = \cos x$ when reflected in the line $y = x$ corresponds to

   (1) $y = \sin x$ (③) $y = \text{arc cos } x$

   (2) $y = \text{arc sin } x$ (4) $x = \text{arc cos } y$

2. In which quadrant(s) would the θ appear if $\theta = \text{arc tan} (-1)$?

   (1) I and IV   (3) III and IV

   (②) II and IV   (4) I and III

3. If $x = \text{arc tan} (-\sqrt{3})$, x could equal

   (1) 60°   (3) 210°

   (2) 150°   (4) 300°

4. If $x = \text{arc cos} \frac{\sqrt{2}}{2}$, x cannot equal

   (1) 45°   (⑥) 225°

   (2) $\frac{\pi}{4}$ (4) $\frac{7\pi}{4}$

5. The positive value of $\cos\left(\arcsin\frac{1}{2}\right)$ is

(1) $\frac{1}{2}$

(3) $\frac{\sqrt{2}}{2}$

(2) $\frac{\sqrt{3}}{3}$

(4) $\frac{\sqrt{3}}{2}$

6. If $\theta = \arcsin 0$, θ could equal which of the following?

(1) $\{0°, 90°\}$ 　　(3) $\{90°, 270°\}$
(2) $\{0°, 180°\}$ 　　(4) $\{180°, 270°\}$

7. The graph shown below depicts which of the following?

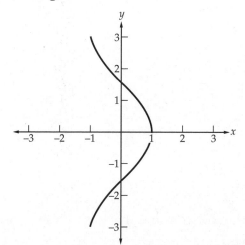

(1) $\theta = \arcsin x$ 　　(3) $\theta = \arctan x$
(2) $\theta = \arccos x$ 　　(4) $\theta = \arccos(-x)$

8. Which of the following is a true statement with regard to the reflection of the graph of $y = \sin x$ in the line $y = x$?

(1) Unless the domain of $y = \sin x$ is limited, the reflection is not a function.
(2) The graph of the reflection of $y = \sin x$ in the line $y = x$ is always a function.
(3) The equation of the graph of the reflection of $y = \sin x$ in the line $y = x$ is $y = \cos x$.
(4) The equation of the graph of the reflection of $y = \sin x$ in the line $y = x$ is $y = \sin(-x)$.

9. If $y = \arctan(-1)$ then y could equal which of the following?

(1) $\left\{\frac{\pi}{4}, \frac{5\pi}{4}\right\}$ 　　(3) $\left\{\frac{3\pi}{4}, \frac{7\pi}{4}\right\}$

(2) $\left\{\frac{3\pi}{4}, \frac{5\pi}{4}\right\}$ 　　(4) $\{0, \pi\}$

10. The value of $\tan(\arccos 1)$ is

(1) 1 　　(3) 0
(2) $\frac{1}{2}$ 　　(4) -1

11. The value of Arc tan $\left(-\frac{\sqrt{3}}{3}\right)$ + Arc sin $\left(-\frac{\sqrt{2}}{2}\right)$ is

(1) $\frac{-2\sqrt{3} - 3\sqrt{2}}{6}$ 　　(3) $-75°$

(2) $-105°$ 　　(4) $255°$

12. The value of $\cot\left(\text{Arc tan}\left(-\frac{\sqrt{5}}{2}\right)\right)$ is which of the following?

(1) $\{\ \}$ 　　(3) $\frac{2\sqrt{5}}{5}$

(2) $-\frac{2\sqrt{5}}{5}$ 　　(4) $\frac{\sqrt{5}}{2}$

13. In order for its inverse to be a function, the domain of $y = \sin x$ must be restricted to quadrants

(1) I and II 　　(3) III and IV
(2) II and IV 　　(4) I and IV

14. The value of Arc sin $\left(-\frac{\sqrt{3}}{2}\right)$ + Arc sin $\left(\frac{1}{2}\right)$ is which of the following?

(1) $-\frac{\pi}{6}$ 　　(3) $\frac{\pi}{3}$

(2) $\frac{\pi}{6}$ 　　(4) $\frac{3\pi}{2}$

15. Find the value of $\cos(\text{Arc tan}(-1))$.

(1) 1 　　(3) $-\frac{\sqrt{2}}{2}$

(2) $\frac{\sqrt{2}}{2}$ 　　(4) $\frac{1}{2}$

16. If $2\cos x = -1$, what is the equation of the inverse of this function?

(1) $\sin x = -\frac{1}{2}$ 　　(3) $-\frac{1}{2} = \text{Arc cos } x$

(2) $x = 2$ Arc sin (-1) 　　(4) $x = \text{Arc cos}\left(-\frac{1}{2}\right)$

17. Which of the following has the same value as $\sin(\text{Arc cos}(-1))$?

(1) $\cot\frac{\pi}{2}$ 　　(3) $\sec\frac{4\pi}{3}$

(2) $\csc\frac{3\pi}{2}$ 　　(4) Arc sin (1)

18. If $\theta = \text{Arc tan}(-\sqrt{3})$, the value of θ is which of the following?

(1) $-30°$ 　　(3) $120°$
(2) $-60°$ 　　(4) $150°$

19. Evaluate Arc cos (-1) + Arc sin $\left(\frac{1}{2}\right)$.

(1) 90° (3) 210°
(2) 120° (4) 240°

20. What is the inverse of the function sketched below?

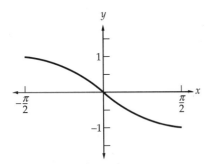

(1) $x = -\text{Arc sin } y$ (3) $x = \text{Arc sin } -y$
(2) $y = -\text{Arc sin } x$ (4) $x = \text{Arc sin } y$

21. Which of the following values does *not* appear in the range of $y = \text{Arc tan } x$?

(1) $\frac{\pi}{2}$ (3) $-\frac{1}{2}$
(2) $\frac{\pi}{4}$ (4) $\frac{\pi}{3}$

22. If $y = \sin x$ and $y = \text{arc sin } x$ are graphed on the same axes, which of the following would be a line of symmetry over the domain $-\frac{\pi}{2} < x < \frac{\pi}{2}$?

(1) $y = 0$
(2) $x = 0$
(3) $y = x$
(4) $y = \pi$

13.4 Real-World Trigonometry

Display the graph of $y = \sin x$ over the interval $\{0 \le x \le 2\pi\}$. Now consider the graph of $y = \cos x$ under a translation of $\frac{\pi}{2}, 0$. To do this on your graphing calculator rather than by hand, in Y_2 enter the equation $y = \cos\left(x - \frac{\pi}{2}\right)$ and then in Y_2 left arrow over until the cursor is at the left of the equal sign. Hit ⟨ENTER⟩ four times until your Y = screen looks like the one below. The second equation will graph as a pencil point. (Labels have been added.)

```
 Plot1  Plot2  Plot3
\Y₁ ▤ sin (X)
−0Y₂▤ cos (X−π/2)
\Y₃ =
\Y₄ =
\Y₅ =
\Y₆ =
\Y₇ =
```

Now hit the ⟨GRAPH⟩ key and look at the resulting graph.

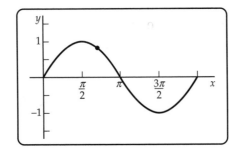

You see only one graph because a cosine curve is simply a sine curve, which has been shifted $\frac{\pi}{2}$ or 90° to the right. Therefore, sine and cosine curves are jointly called sinusoidal functions. A **sinusoid** is a function in the form $y = a \sin b(x - c) + d$, where a, b, c, and d are real numbers and $|a|$ represents amplitude, b represents frequency, c is a horizontal shift, and d is a vertical shift. $y = d$ is also known as the midline since this is a horizontal line midway through the range of the graph. The graph below shows the function $y = \cos \left(x - \frac{\pi}{2} \right)$ as well as the function $y = \cos \left(x - \frac{\pi}{2} \right) + 1$. Clearly the function $y = \cos \left(x - \frac{\pi}{2} \right) + 1$ is the original equation shifted upward one unit.

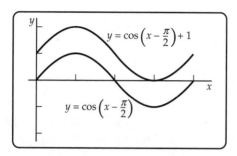

Real-life situations in which the rise and fall of values are periodic over a given interval are often modeled by sinusoidal functions.

MODEL PROBLEM

The occurrence of sunspots during the month of September can be approximated by the function $y = 148 + 44.2 \sin \left(\frac{\pi}{7.83}(x - 2.9908) \right)$ in which x represents the day of the month.

a. Graph this function for the month of September. According to this model, what is the maximum and minimum number of sunspots that occurred in September?

b. What is the average number of sunspots for the month of September? What element of the function indicates this average?

c. How many cycles of sunspots occurred in the month of September?

SOLUTION

a. Enter the graph in Y_1, graph and use (2nd) (TRACE) (CALCULATE) maximum and minimum to identify the highest and lowest values: 192.2 and 103.8.

b. The average number of sunspots is 148, the value added to the sine function, the midline. Since our sine curve begins and ends on the midline, it represents the average value of the function.

c. Look at the graph and you will see two cycles of the function (or divide 2π by the frequency to get $\frac{\pi}{7.83}$, which equals a period of 15.66). This means that there would be almost two cycles in the 30 days of September.

In 1–5, select the numeral preceding the word or expression that best completes the sentence or answers the question.

1. Art Isfun has decided to sell "designer" snow shovels in his home town of Cambridge, New York. His brother, Matt, has informed Art that he can expect his yearly sales to form a sinusoidal curve. Art has decided to graph the number of snow shovels sold as a function of the number of days since January 1. Which of the following curves could he expect to see?

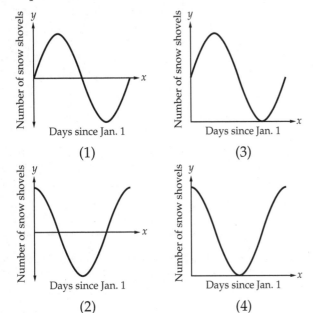

2. Liam's grandfather clock has a pendulum that moves from its central position at rest according to the trigonometric function $P(t) = -3.5 \sin\left(\frac{\pi}{2}t\right)$ where t represents the time in seconds. How many seconds does it take the pendulum to complete one full cycle from rest at the center to the left and then to the right and back to rest?
   (1) 1 second   (3) 3.5 seconds
   (2) 2 seconds   (4) 4 seconds

3. An oscilloscope is a machine which changes sound waves into electric impulses and shows their graph on a monitor. One such graph can be represented by the equation $A(t) = 12 \sin\left(\frac{2\pi}{15}t\right)$ where t represents time

in seconds. The period of this function is
   (1) 12 seconds   (3) 18 seconds
   (2) 15 seconds   (4) 30 seconds

4. Musical notes can be represented by the trigonometric function $y = \sin(2\pi qx)$ where q is the frequency of the note and x is the time in seconds that the note is played. The equation $y = 1.5 \sin(524\pi t)$, where t represents time in seconds, represents a sound wave produced by the note middle C. What is the value of q, the musical frequency of middle C?
   (1) 1.5   (3) 262
   (2) 262π (4) 524π

5. The voltage E of an alternating current electrical circuit can be represented by the sinusoidal function $E = 220 \cos(\pi t)$, where E is measured in volts and t is measured in seconds. How long does it take the alternating current to complete one full cycle?
   (1) 1 second   (3) π seconds
   (2) 2 seconds   (4) 220 seconds

6. Sales of snow removal equipment approximate a trigonometric function. If fact, sales of snow blowers, in the hundreds of units, at Jake's Hardware can be modeled by the function $j(x) = 4 \cos\left(\frac{\pi}{6}x\right) + 4$, where x represents time in months with $x = 0$ corresponding to January 1.
   a. When are Jake's sales the lowest? The highest?
   b. If Jake receives a profit of $79.00 for each snow blower he sells, what is his income from snow blowers on February 1?
   c. Jake's wife Amelia sells air conditioners and her sales can be represented by the function $a(x) = -3 \sin\left(\frac{\pi}{6}(x + 3.8197)\right) + 3.5$ where $a(x)$ represents the number of air conditioners in hundreds sold and x represents the time in months with $x = 0$ corresponding to January. When are her sales the highest and lowest?
   d. When do Amelia and Jake sell equal numbers of air conditioners and snow blowers?
   e. If the average unit that Amelia sells has a profit of $49.00, what is Amelia's maximum profit?

7. Lorna's Landscaping Limited hires employees on a seasonal basis. The number of employees on her payroll corresponds to the function $y = -12 \cos \left(\frac{\pi}{6}x\right) + 14$, where x represents time in months with $x = 0$ corresponding to January 1.
   a. If some employees are part-time, how many people are on Lorna's payroll on the first?
   b. If Lorna must pay a surcharge on her accident insurance of $26.15 for each employee on the payroll over 14 employees, when must she pay the surcharge and how much will it be for the pertinent month(s)? (Consider fractional numbers of employees as part-timers.)
   c. Lorna's brother helps her out by running a snow-shoveling service during the winter months. The number of employees for the snow-shoveling service corresponds to the function $y = 15 \cos \left(\frac{\pi}{6}(x - 1.5915)\right) + 15$, where x represents the time in months with $x = 0$ corresponding to January 1. What is his maximum number of employees? During which month are they at work?
   d. When do Lorna and her brother have the same number of employees? How many does each have on the payroll at that point?

8. Ethel Mermaid, the president of the South Hampton Swimming Pool Company, is studying the company's sales over the course of a year.
   a. If Ethel's company is located in Riverhead on Long Island, which of the following equations would you expect to be a possible model for $S(t)$, the number of swimming pools sold, as a function of time, t, in months since December 31? Explain your answer.
   (1) $S(t) = 200 \cos \left(\frac{\pi}{6}x\right) + 300$
   (2) $S(t) = -200 \cos \left(\frac{\pi}{6}x\right) + 300$
   (3) $S(t) = 200 \sin \left(\frac{\pi}{6}x\right) + 300$
   (4) $S(t) = -200 \sin \left(\frac{\pi}{6}x\right) + 300$
   b. Using your answer from part a, how many swimming pools does the company sell by January 31?
   c. When does the company sell the most pools? How many pools do they sell that month?

   d. During what month(s) does the company sell 250 pools?

9. The number of hours of daylight in New York varies sinusoidally throughout the course of a year. The equation $y = -2.786 \cos (0.017t) + 12.14$ could be used to model the number of daylight hours in New York, where t is the time in days since December 21.
   a. To the nearest tenth, approximately how many hours of daylight there are on February 22?
   b. On what day(s) are there approximately 12 hours of daylight?
   c. Based on the equation, when is there the least amount of daylight? What does this date represent? How many hours of daylight are there?

10. The depth of the water on the shore of a beach varies as the tide goes in and out. The equation $D(t) = 0.75 \cos \left(\frac{\pi}{6}x\right) + 1.5$ could be used to model the depth of the water, $D(t)$, in feet, as a function of time, t, in hours.
   a. What is the amplitude of the equation? What does that mean in terms of the tide?
   b. What is the period of the equation? What does that mean in terms of the tide?
   c. In how many hours will the tide be at its lowest?
   d. How deep will the water be 2 hours after the high tide?
   e. When will the water be 2 feet deep?

11. The temperature in Syracuse varies throughout the year. A sinusoidal equation provides a good model for the average temperature as a function of the month of the year. The equation $f(t) = -24.03206869 \cos (0.5030156t) + 47.363537$ represents the average temperature in Syracuse as a function of time, t, in months with $t = 0$ representing January 1.
   a. What is the average temperature in January? In February?
   b. During what month does the temperature reach its highest point? What does the temperature average during that month?
   c. What is the "average" temperature in Syracuse over the course of a year?
   d. During what month(s) is the temperature in Syracuse "average"?
   e. What is the amplitude of this equation? What does it represent in terms of the temperature in Syracuse?

12. Captain Freeze discovered that the profits from his neighborhood ice cream truck business were a periodic function that did best during the warm months of the year. After studying his records for a four-year period, he found that his profits could be modeled by the function $P(t) = -720 \cos\left(\frac{\pi}{26}(x - 103.45)\right) + 215$, where $P(t)$ is expressed in dollars and t represents time in weeks with $t = 0$ corresponding to the first week in January.

a. What is the range of the function? What does that mean in practical terms to Captain Freeze?

b. What is the period of the graph? What does this mean in practical terms?

c. During what week of the year does Captain Freeze earn his maximum profit? What is this maximum profit?

d. During what time period does Captain Freeze's business lose money?

e. Compare the number of weeks Captain Freeze loses money and the number of weeks he makes money. Over the course of the full year, is the Captain's business profitable? Defend your answer.

f. Based on months of profit and loss, in what part of the United States might Captain Freeze live? Why do you think so?

CHAPTER REVIEW

In 1–20 select the numeral preceding the word or expression that best completes the statement or answers the question.

1. Find the value of $\cos\left(\text{Arc}\sin\left(\frac{1}{2}\right)\right)$.

   (1) $\frac{1}{2}$ (3) $\frac{\sqrt{3}}{2}$

   (2) $\frac{\pi}{6}$ (4) $\frac{\pi}{3}$

2. Which is an equation of the graph shown below?

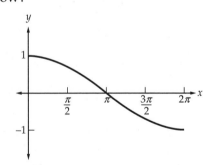

   (1) $y = \frac{1}{2}\cos x$ (3) $y = \cos\frac{1}{2}x$

   (2) $y = \frac{1}{2}\sin x$ (4) $y = \cos 2x$

3. Which of the following graphs is symmetric to the y-axis?
   (1) $y = \sin x$ (3) $y = \tan x$
   (2) $y = \cos x$ (4) $y = \log x$

4. What is the maximum value of $f(\theta)$ if $f(\theta) = 2\cos(3\theta)$?
   (1) 1   (3) 3
   (2) 2   (4) 2π

5. If $y = \cos x$ is graphed on the interval $0 \leq x \leq 2\pi$, which of the following is a line of symmetry of the graph?
   (1) $y = x$ (3) $x = \pi$
   (2) $y = \pi$ (4) $x = 2\pi$

6. What is the period of the graph whose equation is $y = 3\cos 2x$?
   (1) π (3) 3
   (2) 2   (4) 2π

7. What is the amplitude of the graph whose equation is $y = -2\sin 4x$?
   (1) π (3) -2
   (2) 2   (4) 4

8. $\text{Arc}\sin\left(\frac{1}{2}\right) + \text{Arc}\cos\left(\frac{\sqrt{3}}{2}\right) =$

   (1) $\text{Arc}\tan\left(\frac{1}{2} + \frac{\sqrt{3}}{2}\right)$ (3) $60°$

   (2) 1.366 (4) $90°$

9. What is the range for $y = 5\sin x$?
   (1) $0 \leq x \leq 2\pi$ (3) $-1 \leq y \leq 1$
   (2) $0 \leq y \leq 2\pi$ (4) $-5 \leq y \leq 5$

10. The domain for $y = \text{Arc}\sin x$ is

   (1) $-1 \leq x \leq 1$ (3) $-\frac{\pi}{2} \leq x \leq \frac{\pi}{2}$

   (2) $0 \leq x \leq \pi$ (4) $-\pi \leq x \leq \pi$

11. If the graph $y = \cos x$ is reflected in the x-axis, the equation of the image is
(1) $y = \sin x$
(2) $y = \tan x$
(3) $y = -\cos x$
(4) $y = \cos(-x)$

12. The transformation $T_{\frac{\pi}{2},0}$ maps $y = \sin x$ to
(1) $y = \cos x$
(2) $y = -\cos x$
(3) $y = -\sin x$
(4) $y = \frac{\pi}{2} \sin x$

13. What is the minimum value of the range of $y = 3 + 2 \sin x$?
(1) 1
(2) 0
(3) -1
(4) -5

14. Which of the following is equivalent to sec x?
(1) $\cos^{-1} x$
(2) $\frac{1}{\cos x}$
(3) Both (1) and (2)
(4) Neither (1) nor (2)

15. As θ increases from $\frac{\pi}{2}$ to $\frac{3\pi}{2}$, the value of $\sin \theta$
(1) increases only
(2) increases and then decreases
(3) decreases only
(4) decreases and then increases

16. For which of the following values of θ is $\tan \theta$ undefined?
(1) 0
(2) $\frac{\pi}{2}$
(3) π
(4) It is never undefined.

17. Which of the following has the same period as $y = 4 \cos 2x$?
(1) $y = 4 \cos x$
(2) $y = 4 \sin x$
(3) $y = \tan x$
(4) $y = \tan 2x$

18. What is the value of $\cos\left(\text{Arc } \cos \frac{\sqrt{2}}{2}\right)$?
(1) 1
(2) $\frac{\sqrt{2}}{2}$
(3) $\pm\frac{\sqrt{2}}{2}$
(4) $\frac{\pi}{4}$

19. If $f(x) = \sin x$ and $g(x) = \cos x$, for what value(s) of x does $f(x) = g(x)$?
(1) 0
(2) $\frac{\pi}{4}$
(3) $\frac{3\pi}{4}$
(4) $\frac{\pi}{4}$ and $\frac{3\pi}{4}$

20. The motion of a spring can be modeled by the equation $y = 1.6 \cos(\pi x) + 3$, where x represents the number of seconds the spring is oscillating and y is the distance, in inches, of the spring from the ceiling. What is the closest to the ceiling that the spring gets?
(1) 1.4 inches
(2) 1.6 inches
(3) 3 inches
(4) 0 inches

21. a. On the same set of axes, sketch the graphs of $y = 2 \cos \frac{1}{2}x$ and $y = -\sin x$ in the interval $0 \le x \le 2\pi$.
b. Give the exact value(s) for the intersection(s) of the two graphs.
c. From the graphs drawn in part a, find the exact value of x that satisfies the equation
$$2 \cos\left(\frac{1}{2}x\right) + \sin x = 0.$$

22. a. What is the period of the graph $y = 3 \cos 2x$?
b. Sketch the graph of $y = 3 \cos 2x$ for one period and label it B.
c. What are the exact values of the x-intercept(s) of the graph drawn in part b?
d. On the same set of axes, sketch the image of the graph drawn in part b under $r_{x\text{-axis}}$ and label the graph C.
e. Write an equation for the graph drawn in part c.

23. a. On the same set of axes, sketch the graphs of $y = -2 \cos x$ and $y = \tan x$ in the interval $0 \le x \le \pi$.
b. From the graphs drawn in part a, find the exact value of x that satisfies the equation $\tan x - (-2 \cos x) = 2$.
c. From the graphs drawn in part a, find the exact value of x that satisfies the equation $(-2 \cos x) - \tan x = 2$.
d. For what value(s) of x in the interval $0 \le x \le \pi$ is $\tan x$ undefined?

24. a. Sketch the graph of $y = \sin \frac{1}{2}x$ in the interval $-\pi \le x \le \pi$.
b. On the same set of axes, sketch the graph of the transformation of the graph drawn in part a under $T_{\pi,0}$ and label it B.
c. Write an equation for the graph drawn in part b.

25. Stephanie has observed that the number of squirrels she sees varies sinusoidally over the course of a year. She found that the equation
$$S(t) = -30 \cos\left(\frac{\pi}{6}x\right) + 50$$ provided a good model for the average number of squirrels, $S(t)$, Stephanie sees per month where t represents the number of months since December 1.
a. When did Stephanie see the most squirrels?
b. How many squirrels did she see then?
c. What is the average number of squirrels that Stephanie saw on March 1? On May 1?
d. During what months did Stephanie see an average of less than 1 squirrel a day?

26. The graph below shows part of a track for a roller coaster.

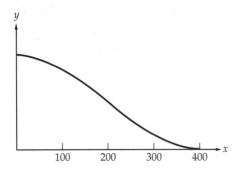

The roller coaster covers a horizontal distance of 400 feet as it descends a vertical distance of 200 feet.

a. What kind of function does this appear to be?

b. What is the period of the function? (Hint: only half the curve is shown on this graph.)

c. Since period $= \dfrac{2\pi}{\text{frequency}}$, frequency $= \dfrac{2\pi}{\text{period}}$, what is the frequency of this curve?

d. How high does the roller coaster go? Where is its midline (the line midway up the graph)?

e. If we define amplitude as the distance from the midline to the highest point on the graph, what is the amplitude?

f. To write an equation to model this graph, we use the equation: $y = a \cos(bx) + d$, where a is the amplitude, b is the frequency, and d is the vertical shift (the midline). Write an equation of the curve that will model this graph.

Sinusoidal Regression

Just as the TI-83 can perform linear and exponential regressions, it can also perform sinusoidal regressions, provided you have a minimum of four points. Obviously, the more data points you have, the more accurate the regression equation will be; however, the regression will not work without at least four points.

To do a sinusoidal regression, we will use the data below showing the average mean temperature in Fairbanks, Alaska, over a twelve-month period where month 0 corresponds to January.

Month	Temp.	Month	Temp.
0	−10	6	63
1	−4	7	57
2	11	8	46
3	31	9	25
4	49	10	3
5	60	11	−7

Enter the data into your lists, with the months in L_1 and the temperature in L_2. Turn your plots on at (2nd) (Y =). Then (ZOOM) (9) for the appropriate window and you should see the resulting graph.

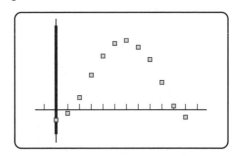

Clearly this appears to be a sinusoidal function, so now go to (STAT) and right arrow over to CALC. If you scroll all the way down, you will find SinReg as item C in the available calculations. As with other regressions, when you hit (ENTER), the type of regression is pasted on the home screen, awaiting further information.

The calculator now gives you the option of telling it how many trials or **iterations** to use in trying to find the most accurate regression. You may enter a number from 1 to 16, but the default value is 3. Be aware that the larger the number, the longer the regression will take, but the more reliable the calculations.

After the number of iterations, you enter the lists in which the data appears, and another optional entry, the period of the data you are using. You may omit the period, but again, the calculator may function faster and more accurately with this additional data. If you are not given the period, determine the distance from one maximum (or minimum) point on the graph to the next by using the (TRACE) function and subtracting the *x*-coordinates of the located max points. Finally, enter the line number from the (Y =) screen in which you'd like the equation to be pasted. Below is one command you might use.

> SinReg 6, L_1, L_2, 1
> 2, Y_1

This instruction tells the calculator to attempt to find a sinusoidal regression equation in six iterations using the data in L_1 and L_2 over a period of 12 (months) and to paste the resulting equation in Y_1. The standard form of the equation the calculator is using is $y = a \sin (bx + c) + d$ where a represents the amplitude, b the frequency, $\frac{c}{b}$ the horizontal shift, and d the vertical shift or midline.

Note: In this case, the frequency value, b, has been distributed over the parentheses, unlike the equations we used in section 13.4.

Hit (ENTER) and you should see the resulting coefficients and constants for your equation.

> SinReg
>   y=a*sin (bx+c) + d
>   a=37.718744614
>   b=.51811669252
>   c=−1.456344304
>   d=26.60647541

If your equation differs slightly from this one, it may be because you called for a different number of iterations or perhaps did not include the period and therefore the calculator found a slightly different version of the equation.

When you hit the (GRAPH) key, you should now get the sinusoidal graph you see below.

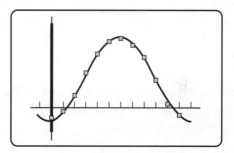

Practice

Below you will find additional average mean temperatures that will form various sinusoidal curves for your exploration. Experiment graphing two of them on the same screen to see the differences in their functions.

Average Mean Temperatures in Selected Cities

Month	0	1	2	3	4	5	6	7	8	8	10	11
Barrow, AK	−13	−18	−15	−2	19	34	39	38	31	14	−2	−11
Dodge City, KS	30	35	43	55	64	74	80	78	69	57	43	32
New York, NY	32	34	42	53	63	72	77	76	68	58	48	37
Phoenix, AZ	54	58	62	70	79	88	94	92	86	75	62	54
San Juan, PR	77	77	78	79	81	82	83	83	82	82	80	78

CHAPTER 14

Trigonometric Applications

14.1 Law of Cosines

If you were given the lengths of two sides of a right triangle, you would have no difficulty finding the length of the third side, using the Pythagorean theorem. For example, the triangle below has legs of 7 and 24, so we can find the hypotenuse using the formula $c^2 = a^2 + b^2$.

$$c^2 = a^2 + b^2$$
$$c^2 = 7^2 + 24^2$$
$$c^2 = 625$$
$$c = \pm\sqrt{625}$$
$$c = 25$$

Note: Since we are finding the length of a side of a triangle, we use only the positive square root of c, that is, 25.

However, to solve triangles that do not contain right angles, we need other methods. One formula that is very useful, if you are provided information in a Side-Angle-Side or SAS pattern, is the Law of Cosines. The Law of Cosines says: $c^2 = a^2 + b^2 - 2ab\cos C$, where C is the angle opposite the side whose length you are trying to find. This formula can be rewritten to express a similar relationship for the lengths of sides to the cosine of angle B or angle A.

1. In triangle *HAT*, $a = 6.4$, $t = 10.2$, and m$\angle H = 87$. Find the length of side *h* to the nearest tenth.

SOLUTION

Always draw a diagram when you are doing trigonometric application problems. A helpful method is to label those sides and angles you are given with a large S or A written in a different color. Sometimes this visual cue is key to deciding which formula to use and which variable corresponds to which side in the formula.

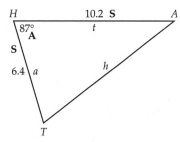

Since the diagram shows an SAS pattern, we know to use the Law of Cosines, allowing *h* to replace the original *c* of the formula while the *a* and *t* replace the *a* and *b*.

$h^2 = a^2 + t^2 - 2at\cos H$

$h^2 = (6.4)^2 + (10.2)^2 - 2(6.4)(10.2)\cos 87°$

$h^2 = 40.96 + 104.04 - 130.56 \cos 87°$

$h^2 = 138.1670176$

$h \approx 11.8$

Again we discard the negative value since we are finding the side of a triangle.

2. In isosceles triangle *QRS*, $q = s = 4.7$ centimeters. If cos $R = 0.1908$, find the length of side *r* to the nearest hundredth of a centimeter.

SOLUTION

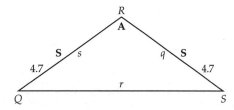

In this problem we are not given the measure of the included angle, but the value of the cosine of the angle instead. To solve, we merely substitute that value in the Law of Cosines formula.

$r^2 = q^2 + s^2 - 2qs\cos R$

$r^2 = 4.7^2 + 4.7^2 - 2(4.7)(4.7)(0.1908)$

$r^2 = 22.09 + 22.09 - 8.429544$

$r^2 = 35.750456$

$r \approx 5.98$

Answer: 5.98 cm

3. Mr. DeStefano, the art teacher, wants to make his backyard garden unusual, so he decides to design it in the shape of an obtuse triangle with white alyssum acting as the border on the two shorter sides of the triangle and purple salvia along the length of the third side. The two shorter sides measure 8 feet and 9 feet, including an angle of 105°.
   a. How long, to the nearest tenth of a foot, must the third side of the triangle be?
   b. If Mr. DeStefano needs 4 salvia plants for each foot of border, how many plants will he need?

SOLUTION

a.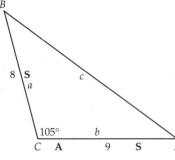

Since we are looking for the side opposite the 105° angle, that side must be c, but it really makes no difference which side we designate as a or b. Substitute the given values in the Law of Cosines formula and solve.

$$c^2 = a^2 + b^2 - 2ab\cos C$$
$$c^2 = 8^2 + 9^2 - 2(8)(9)\cos 105°$$
$$c^2 = 64 + 81 - 144 \cos 105°$$
$$c^2 = 182.2699425$$
$$c \approx 13.5$$

b. To find the number of plants needed, we multiply 13.5 by 4 and learn that Mr. DeStefano will need 54 salvia plants for his garden design.

Sometimes we are given the lengths of three sides of the triangle and asked to find the measure of an angle. In this case, it is often easier to manipulate the Law of Cosines so the cosine value is isolated.

$$c^2 = a^2 + b^2 - 2ab\cos C$$

$c^2 - a^2 - b^2 = -2ab\cos C$ Divide both sides by $-2ab$.

$\dfrac{c^2 - a^2 - b^2}{-2ab} = \cos C$ An alternate version of the Law of Cosines

or $\cos C = \dfrac{a^2 + b^2 - c^2}{2ab}$

In this format, we always subtract the square of the side opposite the angle whose measure we are trying to find.

 MODEL PROBLEM

Jed is working on a stained glass project and needs to form a triangle with sides of 8, 12, and 15 inches out of lead cane to enclose the glass. To the nearest tenth of a degree, what is the largest angle he needs to create using the lead caning?

SOLUTION

Since Jed needs to the know the largest angle, we need to let the largest side be c. We substitute the values into the formula.

$$\cos C = \frac{a^2 + b^2 - c^2}{2ab}$$

$$\cos C = \frac{(8)^2 + (12)^2 - (15)^2}{2(8)(12)}$$

$$\cos C = -0.0885416667$$

$$m\angle C = 95.1$$

Remember: When you are working with angles of a triangle, a negative cosine indicates an obtuse or second-quadrant angle.

Practice

In 1–10, select the numeral preceding the word or expression that best completes the sentence or answers the question.

1. An isosceles triangle has equal sides of 12.4 and an included angle of 93.4°. What is the length of the third side of the triangle to the nearest tenth?
   (1) 4.9   (3) 48.9
   (2) 18.0   (4) 18.5

2. In triangle ABC, $\cos A = -\frac{1}{2}$, $b = 6.5$, and $c = 7.2$. The length of a to the nearest hundredth is
   (1) 11.87   (3) 7.87
   (2) 8.87   (4) 6.78

3. In triangle MNP, $m\angle MNP = 120$, $NM = 5.8$ centimeters, and $NP = 8.3$ centimeters. The length of $\overline{MP}$ to the nearest tenth is which of the following?
   (1) 7.4 cm   (3) 12.3 cm
   (2) 11.3 cm   (4) 13.3 cm

4. Three sides of a triangle measure 5, 8, and 12. The triangle is
   (1) isosceles   (3) acute
   (2) right   (4) obtuse

5. A triangle has sides of lengths 7.1, 9.4, and 15.3. Which of the following is the measure of the largest angle of the triangle?
   (1) 135.6°   (3) 103.6°
   (2) 115.8°   (4) 25.5°

6. In $\triangle XYZ$, $x = 11.7$ inches, $y = 9.6$ inches, and $z = 5.9$ inches. What is the cosine of the smallest angle of the triangle?
   (1) -0.0876 (3) 0.5761
   (2) 0.09386   (4) 0.8647

7. In $\triangle KLM$, $k = 9$ centimeters, $l = 40$ centimeters, and $m = 41$ centimeters. What is the measure of the largest angle of the triangle?
   (1) 107°   (3) 84°
   (2) 90°   (4) 79°

8. In $\triangle PQR$, $m\angle RPQ = 131$, $q = 10.8$ inches, and $r = 8.1$ inches. What is the length of side p to the nearest tenth?
   (1) 17.2   (3) 12.9
   (2) 14.7   (4) 11.5

9. Each base angle of isosceles triangle GHI measures 57.4°, while equal sides $\overline{GH}$ and $\overline{HI}$ each measure 8.94 inches. The length of $\overline{GI}$ to the nearest hundredth of an inch is
   (1) 7.12   (3) 8.59
   (2) 8.26   (4) 9.63

10. In parallelogram $ABCD$, $AB = 11$ inches and $BC = 17$ inches. If $m\angle ABC = 102°36'$, the length of diagonal $\overline{AC}$ to the nearest tenth of an inch is
    (1) 18.1   (3) 22.2
    (2) 21.2   (4) 28.0

11. Emily and Jeff bought a beautiful slab of petrified wood that they would like to use as the top of a coffee table. Jeff is making a triangular base for the table as indicated in the diagram below. If the sides of the triangular base are 22 inches, 28.5 inches, and 30.7 inches, find the measures of the three angles, to the nearest hundredth of a degree, that Jeff must construct for the base.

12. Dimitri and Anna are in charge of setting the route for the Daffy Drivers' Bike Race at the County Fair. This is an event for children ages 8–14 in which each biker must complete the triangular course and collect souvenirs along the way. The distance from the start to the merry-go-round is 1.7 miles, the distance from the merry-go-round to the middle school field is 2.9 miles, and the angle included between them is $51°24'$. Find the total distance, to the nearest hundredth of a mile, covered by the bikers in this event.

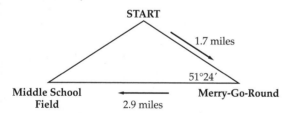

13. Two cabins are situated on Lake Happy Trails, at a distance of 800 feet apart. The owners of the cabins, the Browns and the Adlers, would like to put a wooden raft out on the lake, so that it is 1,000 feet from each of the two cabins, labeled A and B.

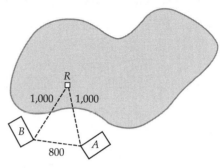

    a. What is the measure of $\angle RAB$, to the nearest tenth of a degree or nearest ten minutes?

    b. What is the measure of $\angle ARB$, to the nearest ten minutes or tenth of a degree?

14. The lighthouse on Pine Island is visible from two boats off shore. Doug's sailboat is 4.2 miles from the lighthouse while Ralph's fishing trawler is 6.7 miles from the lighthouse. If the light from the lighthouse sweeps an angle of 66.5° between the two boats, how far apart are they, to the nearest tenth of a mile?

15. Bird watchers follow a prescribed path through the nature conservation park so they do not disturb mating or nesting birds. The bird watchers start at the pond, walk 2.1 miles east to a viewing platform, turn 124° southeast, and travel 4.7 miles until they reach the nesting area. After taking all the pictures they want, the bird watchers turn northwest and return to their starting point. How long, to the nearest tenth of a mile, is the path from the nesting area to the beginning of the trail?

14.2 Law of Sines

In some problems, the information you are given for a triangle that does not include the lengths of two sides and the included angle or the lengths of three sides, the data necessary to use the Law of Cosines. As shown on page 359, the information provided about a triangle may be in an Angle-Side-Angle pattern (ASA), an Angle-Angle-Side pattern (AAS), or a Side-Side-Angle pattern (SSA).

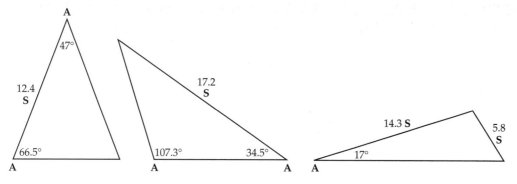

In these cases, we need to use the Law of Sines: $\dfrac{\sin A}{a} = \dfrac{\sin B}{b} = \dfrac{\sin C}{c}$.

The Law of Sines states that the sine of an angle is proportional to the side opposite that angle. When applying this rule, you should always draw a diagram to be certain you have the correct angle and side relationships.

In writing Law of Sines equations, we use only two of the possible ratios, thus producing a proportion we can solve.

 MODEL PROBLEMS

1. In triangle PQR, m$\angle PQR = 66.5$, m$\angle QRP = 47$, and $QR = 12.4$ inches. Find the length of $\overline{QP}$ to the nearest tenth of an inch.

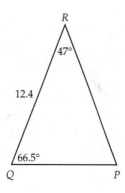

SOLUTION

Since the given information is in an ASA pattern, we need to use the Law of Sines. However, while we have the length of side $\overline{QR}$, we do not have the measure of $\angle QPR$, opposite that side. Since we do know the value of the other two angles of the triangle, we can subtract from $180°$ to learn the measure of $\angle QPR$.

$$180 - (\text{m}\angle PQR + \text{m}\angle QRP) = \text{m}\angle QPR$$
$$180 - (66.5 + 47) = \text{m}\angle QPR$$
$$180 - 113.5 = \text{m}\angle QPR$$
$$66.5 = \text{m}\angle QPR$$

Because $\triangle PQR$ is isosceles, we could use the Law of Cosines to solve this problem, but we will continue with the Law of Sines solution. Determine which ratios to use and write the equation. Then substitute the known values.

$$\frac{\sin R}{r} = \frac{\sin P}{p}$$

$$\frac{\sin 47°}{r} = \frac{\sin 66.5°}{12.4}$$

Rewriting the problem to solve for r, we find:

$$r = \frac{12.4 \sin 47°}{\sin 66.5°}$$

$$r = 9.888976909$$

$$r = 9.9 \text{ in.}$$

2. In triangle CTH, $m\angle T = 107.3$, $m\angle H = 34.5$, and $CH = 17.2$ centimeters. Find the length of $\overline{CT}$ to the nearest tenth of a centimeter.

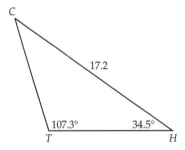

SOLUTION

Since the given information is in an AAS pattern, we use the Law of Sines.

$$\frac{\sin T}{t} = \frac{\sin H}{h}$$

$$\frac{\sin 107.3°}{17.2} = \frac{\sin 34.5°}{h}$$

$$h = \frac{17.2 \sin 34.5°}{\sin 107.3°}$$

$$h = 10.20379898$$

$$h = 10.2 \text{ cm}$$

3. Given triangle JKL in which $JK = 14.3$, $KL = 5.8$, and $m\angle LJK = 17$, find the measure of $\angle KLJ$ to the nearest tenth of a degree or nearest ten minutes.

SOLUTION

In this case, the information is in an SSA pattern, which means that we must take care to consider the possibility of two different triangles satisfying the given information. Since $JK > KL$, it follows that the measure $\angle KLJ$ must be greater than the measure of $\angle KJL$, but whether or not it must be obtuse depends on our solution. First, we set up our equation and find the value of $\sin L$.

$$\frac{\sin J}{j} = \frac{\sin L}{l}$$

$$\frac{\sin 17°}{5.8} = \frac{\sin L}{14.3}$$

$$\sin L = \frac{14.3 \sin 17°}{5.8}$$

$$\sin L = 0.720847489$$

$$\angle L = 46.1°$$

However, since the sine function is also positive in the second quadrant, it is possible that $\angle L$ is obtuse, measuring 133.9°. It is certainly just as possible to have a triangle with angles measuring 17°, 46.1°, and an obtuse angle of 116.9° as it is to have a triangle with $m\angle L = 133.9$, $m\angle J = 17$, and $m\angle K = 29.1$. This situation is often called the **ambiguous case**, because we do not know for certain which measure of ∠*L* is intended, so we must give both possible angles. The two different possible triangles are shown below.

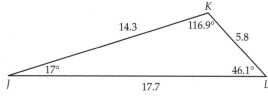

∠*L* is acute and ∠*K* is obtuse.

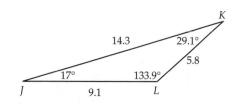

∠*L* is obtuse and ∠*K* is acute.

It may be helpful for you to remember the following relationships when you try to determine how many triangles are possible given information in an SSA pattern.

If given ∠*A* is obtuse and $a \leq c$, 0 triangles can be formed.

If given ∠*A* is obtuse and $a > c$, 1 triangle may be formed.

If given ∠*A* is acute and $c > a > c\sin A$, 2 triangles can be formed.

If given ∠*A* is acute and $a = c\sin A$, 1 triangle can be formed.

If given ∠*A* is acute and $a \geq c \geq c\sin A$, 1 triangle can be formed.

If given ∠*A* is acute and $a < c\sin A$, 0 triangles can be formed.

Practice

In 1–5, find the indicated side a to the nearest tenth or angle A to the nearest tenth of a degree for each triangle.

1.

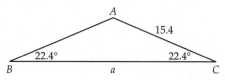

2.

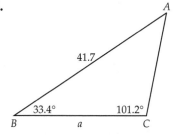

3.

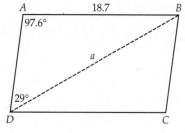

4.

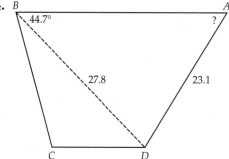

5.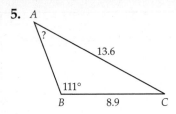

6. In $\triangle MAN$, $m\angle A = 27.6$, $m\angle N = 73.1$, and $a = 5.7$ cm. Find the length of side m to the nearest tenth.

7. In isosceles triangle YES, the vertex angle YES measures 54.6°. If the base of the triangle measures 12.7 inches, find, to the nearest tenth of an inch, the length of the two equal sides of the triangle.

8. JoAnna and Ethel are designing a triangular hopscotch board similar to the one shown in the diagram. If the equal sides of their board are to be 8.5 feet in length, and the base angles measure 71°, find the length of the base to the nearest tenth of a foot.

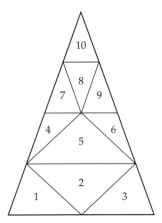

9. Kevin and Misha are going to make A-frame birdhouses as Mother's Day gifts. The basic design is shown below, but they need to know how long the base will be. If they want the sides of the A-frame to be 14.25 inches in length, with the crossbar placed 3 inches from the bottom, and the base angles will measure 65.3°, find the length of the crossbar section to the nearest hundredth of an inch.

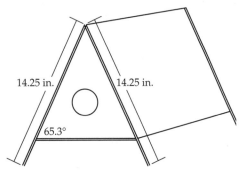

10. In parallelogram $MATH$, $MA = 9$, $MH = 6.2$, and $m\angle HAM = 38.2$. Find the measure of $\angle AMH$ to the nearest tenth of a degree. (Hint: find $m\angle AHM$ first.)

11. In $\triangle CTH$, $m\angle C = 17$, $c = 12$, and $h = 31$.
    a. How many distinct triangles CTH are possible?
    b. Find all possible measures of $\angle H$ to the nearest degree.
    c. Find all possible lengths of $\overline{CH}$ to the nearest integer.
    d. Sketch all possible triangles.

In 12–16, select the numeral preceding the word or expression that best completes the sentence or answers the question.

12. In $\triangle WXY$, $x = 8.3$ centimeters, $y = 6.4$ centimeters, and $m\angle X = 82.4$. The measure of $\angle Y$ is
    (1) 0.764°   (3) 130.2°
    (2) 49.8°   (4) 139.8°

13. In $\triangle DAY$, $\sin D = 0.6437$, $\sin A = 0.8134$, and $a = 13.2$. The length of d to the nearest tenth is
    (1) 10.4   (3) 43.8
    (2) 18.6   (4) 67.7

14. In an isosceles triangle, the base angles each measure 61° and the length of each congruent leg is 12.5. Which of the following equations can be used to find the length of the base?

    (1) $\dfrac{\sin 52°}{12.5} = \dfrac{\sin 61°}{x}$

    (2) $\dfrac{\sin 61°}{12.5} = \dfrac{\sin 58°}{x}$

    (3) $\dfrac{\sin 122°}{12.5} = \dfrac{\sin 61°}{x}$

    (4) $x^2 = (12.5)^2 + (12.5)^2 - 2(12.5)(12.5)\sin 61°$

15. In $\triangle VAL$, $v = 13.12$, $a = 11.3$, and $m\angle A = 44.5$. The triangle must be which of the following?
    (1) cannot be determined
    (2) obtuse
    (3) isosceles
    (4) right

16. If $m = 7$, $n = 10$, and $m\angle M = 85$, how many different triangles MNP can be drawn?
    (1) 1   (3) 3
    (2) 2   (4) 0

14.3 Forces and Vectors

You know from our work with complex numbers that a **vector** has both direction and magnitude (or size). Vectors are very useful in representing the properties of applied forces pushing or pulling an object in a given direction. For example, two children squabbling over ownership of a toy can be represented by vectors operating from the same given point, the toy, and moving in opposite, or differing directions, as in the diagrams below. The length of each vector represents the strength or magnitude of the force while the direction of the vector shows the movement of the force.

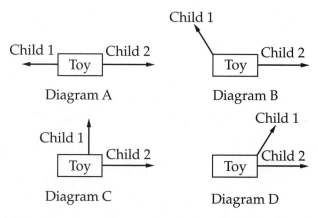

As visible in the diagrams, the force exerted by child 1 is less than that exerted by Child 2, so in Diagram A, Child 2 will win the toy. Starting in Diagram B, however, Child 1 is now using some of Child 2's strength and the force resulting from children's actions is increasing in magnitude. This new force, created by the combination of the initial forces, is called the **resultant** and will appear between the two applied forces as shown below.

In force problems, each vector represents a force applied to an object at a specific point. These vectors are used to form two consecutive sides of a parallelogram with the resultant force of the vectors forming the diagonal of the parallelogram, as shown below.

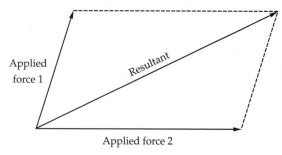

Note: The resultant does not bisect the angle between the two forces unless the forces are equal in magnitude.

Depending on what information is provided in a force problem, we will use either the Law of Cosines or the Law of Sines to solve the problem.

1. Two forces of 28 pounds and 41 pounds act on a body so that the angle between the two forces measures 72°. Find, to the nearest tenth of a pound, the magnitude of the resultant the forces produce.

SOLUTION

Remember: As in a trigonometric application problem, the first step should always be to draw a diagram.

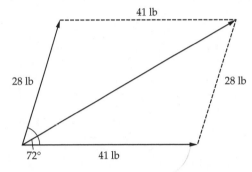

Since we have a parallelogram, we know that opposite sides are equal. With the resultant's acting as a diagonal, there are two congruent triangles present in the figure. The difficulty, however, is that the diagonal does not bisect the angle it intersects so we have no way of knowing the size of the two pieces of the divided 72° angle. But, because this is a parallelogram, consecutive angles must be supplementary, so the undivided angles of the parallelogram must equal 180° − 72°, or 108°.

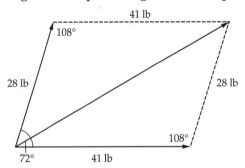

We now have information in a Side-Angle-Side or SAS pattern, so we can solve this problem using the Law of Cosines.

$$c^2 = a^2 + b^2 - 2ab\cos C$$

Substituting: $c^2 = 28^2 + 41^2 - 2(28)(41)\cos 108°$

$$c^2 = 3174.503019$$

$$c \approx 56.34272818$$

Since we wanted the answer to the nearest tenth, the magnitude of the resultant equals 56.3 pounds.

Note: When the angle between the forces is acute, the strength (magnitude) or length of the diagonal between the forces is greater than either force alone.

2. Two applied forces produce a resultant force of 18.6 pounds. The smaller force measures 15.8 pounds, and the larger force is 24.3 pounds. Find the measure of the angle between the two forces to the nearest tenth of a degree.

SOLUTION

Again, the first step is to draw the diagram of the applied forces, using vectors to form a parallelogram.

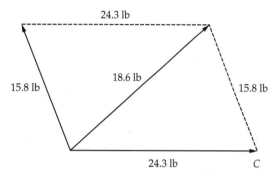

Remember: Since the diagonal does not bisect the angles of a parallelogram, we must find the angle labeled C in the diagram and determine its supplement to find the angle between the two applied forces.

The given information forms triangles in a Side-Side-Side or SSS pattern so we can use the Law of Cosines to solve the triangle.

$$\cos C = \frac{a^2 + b^2 - c^2}{2ab}$$

$$\cos C = \frac{(15.8)^2 + (24.3)^2 - (18.6)^2}{2(15.8)(24.3)}$$

$$\cos C = 0.6435510757$$

$$C = 49.9$$

Therefore, the angle between the forces must equal $180° - 49.9°$, or $130.1°$.

3. A resultant force of 162 pounds must be exerted to move a refrigerator. If the two applied forces act on the refrigerator at angles of $43.6°$ and $38.7°$ with resultant, find the magnitude of each of the two applied forces to the nearest tenth of a pound.

SOLUTION

Draw a diagram.

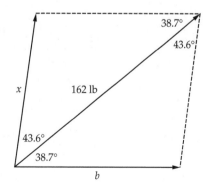

When the parallelogram is drawn, we see that the given information forms an Angle-Side-Angle or ASA pattern, meaning we need to use the Law of Sines twice to find the two applied forces. First we need to find the angle opposite the force of 162 pounds, so we add the other two angles together and subtract from 180°. $180° - (43.6° + 38.7°) = 180° - 82.3° = 97.7°$ Now, we can find the force labeled b in the diagram.

$$\frac{\sin 43.6}{b} = \frac{\sin 97.7}{162}$$

$$b = \frac{162 \sin 43.6}{\sin 97.7}$$

$$b = 112.7 \text{ pounds}$$

Having found one applied force, we could use the Law of Cosines to find the other applied force, but it is preferable to use only the information provided in the original problem to solve all parts of the problem unless otherwise instructed. So, to find x we will use the Law of Sines again.

$$\frac{\sin 38.7}{x} = \frac{\sin 97.7}{162}$$

$$x = \frac{162 \sin 38.7}{\sin 97.7}$$

$$x = 102.2 \text{ pounds}$$

Sometimes you will be asked to find the magnitude of the larger applied force or the smaller applied force. To determine which is the larger or smaller, remember that the largest side of a triangle is opposite the largest angle. In this problem the larger applied force had to be opposite the larger angle, the 43.6° angle, and it was. That force was 112.7 pounds versus the force of 102.2 pounds opposite the 38.7° angle.

Practice

Show the diagrams and work necessary to solve each problem.

1. Two forces of 21.8 pounds and 34.2 pounds act on a body with an angle of 52.6° between them. Find, to the nearest tenth of a pound, the magnitude of the resultant.

2. Two forces act on a body so the resultant is a force of 73.4 pounds. The angles between the resultant and the forces measure 56° and 47°. Find, to the nearest tenth of a pound, the magnitude of the larger applied force.

3. Find, to the nearest tenth of a degree, the angle between two applied forces of 37 newtons and 62 newtons if the resultant is 48.4 newtons.

4. If two forces of 21.8 pounds and 35.1 pounds act on a body with an angle of 110.6° between them, find the magnitude of the resultant to the nearest tenth of a pound.

5. Two forces of 37 pounds and 52 pounds act on a body forming an acute angle between them. If the angle between the smaller force and the resultant is 29°15′, find, to the nearest tenth of a pound, the magnitude of the resultant. (Hint: Find the angle between the larger force and the resultant first.)

6. Find, to the nearest minute, the measure of the angle between two applied forces of 41.6 pounds and 64.8 pounds if the resultant formed has a magnitude of 83.4 pounds.

7. Two applied forces act on a body forming angles of 18°25′ and 29°40′ between them and the resultant.
   a. If the larger force is 48.3 pounds, what is the magnitude of the resultant to the nearest tenth of a pound?
   b. What is the magnitude, to the nearest tenth of a pound, of the smaller force?

8. Two forces act on an object; the first force has a magnitude of 78 pounds and makes an angle of 31.5° with the resultant. The magnitude of the resultant is 124.7 pounds.

a. Find the magnitude of the second applied force to the nearest tenth of a pound.

b. Using the results from part **a**, find, to the nearest ten minutes or tenth of a degree, the angle the second applied force makes with the resultant.

9. A glider is moving forward at a speed of 12 miles per hour while air currents are working against the glider at a force of 8 miles per hour. The resultant speed of the glider is 10.2 miles per hour.

a. To the nearest hundredth of a degree, at what angle is the air current acting on the glider?

b. Find the measure of the angle between the air current and the resultant to the nearest minute.

14.4 Area of a Triangle

We know from previous math courses that we can find the area of a triangle using the formula Area = $\frac{1}{2}$(base)(height), but in some figures, like those shown below, we do not know both the base and the height measurements.

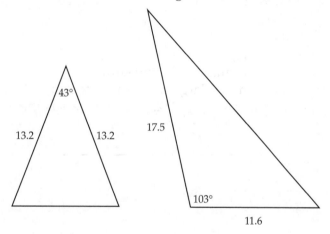

In cases like these, we need another formula, derived from the Law of Sines.

$$\text{Area} = \frac{1}{2}ab\sin C \text{ or Area} = \frac{1}{2}bc\sin A \text{ or Area} = \frac{1}{2}ac\sin B$$

In order to use this formula in any triangle to find its area, we need to know the lengths of two sides and the included angle. In other words, we need the information in a Side-Angle-Side or SAS pattern.

MODEL PROBLEMS

1. In $\triangle ABC$, $a = 16$, $b = 12$, and $\sin C = \frac{1}{2}$. Find the area of $\triangle ABC$.

SOLUTION

We have the appropriate information, so we simply substitute into the formula.

$$\text{Area} = \frac{1}{2}ab\sin C$$

$$\text{Area} = \frac{1}{2}(16)(12)\left(\frac{1}{2}\right) = 48 \text{ square units}$$

2. If the area of △*DEF* is 101 square centimeters, $d = 16$, and $e = 14$, find the measure of ∠*F* to the nearest ten minutes or tenth of a degree.

SOLUTION

In this case, we know the area but are trying to find the angle. We use the same area formula, but solve for angle *F* instead of the area.

$$\text{Area} = \frac{1}{2}de\sin F$$

$$101 = \frac{1}{2}(16)(14)\sin F$$

$$101 = 112\sin F$$

$$0.9017857 = \sin F$$

$$64.4° = ∠F$$

$$\text{or } ∠F = 115.6°$$

Note: Since sine is positive, there is an obtuse angle with this sine value, which we must also consider. Not knowing the length of side *f*, we must accept either 64.4° or 115.6° as a valid answer.

3. Find the area of the triangle, to the nearest hundredth of a square meter.

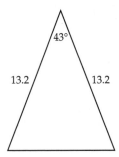

SOLUTION

In this case, we can simply substitute into the area formula.

$$\text{Area} = \frac{1}{2}(13.2)(13.2)\sin 43°$$

$$\text{Area} = 59.42 \text{ square meters}$$

4. In parallelogram *HOPE*, $HO = 16.7$ centimeters, $OP = 20.1$ centimeters, and m∠*HOP* = 108.3.
   a. Find the length of $\overline{HP}$ to the nearest tenth of a centimeter.
   b. Find the area of *HOPE* to the nearest hundredth of a square centimeter.

SOLUTION

a. First we need to use the Law of Cosines to find the length of $\overline{HP}$.

$$c^2 = a^2 + b^2 - 2ab\cos C$$

$$c^2 = (16.7)^2 + (20.1)^2 - 2(16.7)(20.1)\cos 108.3$$

$$c^2 = 893.6956954$$

$$c = 29.9 \text{ centimeters}$$

b. To find the area of the parallelogram, we double the area of a triangle.

$$\text{Area} = 2\left(\frac{1}{2}ab\sin C\right)$$

$$\text{Area} = 2\left(\frac{1}{2}\right)(16.7)(20.1)(\sin 108.3°)$$

$$\text{Area} = 318.69 \text{ square centimeters}$$

In 1–5, find the area of each triangle to the nearest hundredth of a unit.

1. In △KLM, m∠L = 78.3, k = 12.8 inches, and m = 9.7 inches.

2. In △ABC, m∠A = 58.2, b = 8.6 centimeters, and c = 7.1 centimeters.

3. In △DOG, m∠O = 123, d = 17 centimeters, and g = 11.4 centimeters.

4. In isosceles △LUV, the measure of vertex angle U = 54° and v =18 centimeters.

5. In isosceles △CAT, $\overline{CA} = \overline{AT}$, m∠C = 72, and c = 6.3 inches.

In 6–15, select the numeral preceding the expression that best completes the sentence or answers the question.

6. If the area of △END is 24 square inches, m∠E =150, and d measures 12 inches, the length of side n is how many inches?
   (1) 8   (3) 16
   (2) 12   (4) 24√3

7. If one side of an equilateral triangle measures 6, what is the exact area of the triangle?
   (1) 9   (3) 9√3
   (2) 6√3   (4) 18

8. Find the area of a parallelogram, to the nearest tenth of a square inch, if its sides measure 14 and 17 inches and an angle of the parallelogram measures 74°.
   (1) 65.6   (3) 183.2
   (2) 114.4   (4) 228.8

9. If the area of △USA is 74 square inches and side u measures 17 inches while side a measures 13 inches, which of the following is an approximation of sin ∠USA?
   (1) 0.1629   (3) 0.6697
   (2) 0.3258   (4) 0.8319

10. In rhombus LIFE, each side measures 13.6 centimeters and m∠LIF = 112.5. The area of rhombus LIFE is approximately which of the following?
    (1) 70.8   (3) 170.9
    (2) 85.4   (4) 341.8

11. In △JOG, m∠JOG = 82, j = 8.4, and g = 7.1. The area of △JOG is approximately
    (1) 14.76   (3) 59.06
    (2) 29.53   (4) 59.64

12. The base angle of an isosceles triangle measures 57.4° and the equal sides measure 10.8 inches. The area of the triangle is approximately which of the following?
    (1) 24.46   (3) 52.94
    (2) 49.13   (4) 58.32

13. If the area of an isosceles triangle is 68 and the vertex angle is 66°, what is the length of each of the equal sides of the triangle?
    (1) 5.8   (3) 10.4
    (2) 8.3   (4) 12.2

14. In △QRS, m∠Q = 102.4, r = 15.3, and s = 11.8. The area of △QRS is approximately
    (1) 176.33   (3) 44.08
    (2) 88.16   (4) 19.38

15. In parallelogram JACK, ∠JCK measures 61°15′, JC = 23.5, and KC = 18.7. The area of the parallelogram is approximately which of the following?
    (1) 192.64   (3) 423.18
    (2) 385.28   (4) 462.11

16. Given parallelogram TIME as shown in the diagram. The lengths, in centimeters, of the sides of △TIE are TI = 16.4, TE = 15.8, and EI = 21.3.

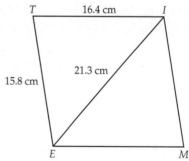

a. Find the measure of ∠TIE to the nearest tenth of a degree.

b. Find the area of parallelogram TIME to the nearest tenth of a square centimeter.

17.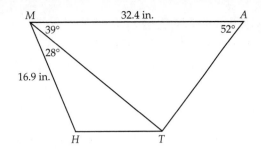

In the diagram, $\overline{MA} \parallel \overline{HT}$, $MA = 32.4$ inches, $MH = 16.9$ inches, m$\angle AMT = 39$, m$\angle MAT = 52$, and m$\angle HMT = 28$.

a. Find the length of $\overline{MT}$ to the nearest tenth of an inch.

b. Find the area of trapezoid $MATH$ to the nearest tenth of a square inch.

14.5 Mixed Trigonometric Applications

In this chapter on trigonometric applications, we have studied two different forms of the Law of Cosines, the Law of Sines, and a formula for the area of a triangle. To help you remember which formula to use under which conditions, review the following table.

Given Information	Formula to Use
Two sides and the included angle (SAS)	Law of Cosines: $c^2 = a^2 + b^2 - 2ab\cos C$
Three sides (SSS)	Law of Cosines: $\cos C = \dfrac{a^2 + b^2 - c^2}{2ab}$
Two angles and the included side (ASA)	Law of Sines: $\dfrac{\sin A}{a} = \dfrac{\sin B}{b} = \dfrac{\sin C}{c}$
Two angles and a nonincluded side (AAS)	Law of Sines: $\dfrac{\sin A}{a} = \dfrac{\sin B}{b} = \dfrac{\sin C}{c}$
Two sides and a nonincluded angle (SSA) (the ambiguous case)	Law of Sines: $\dfrac{\sin A}{a} = \dfrac{\sin B}{b} = \dfrac{\sin C}{c}$
Area of a triangle (SAS)	Area $= \dfrac{1}{2}ab\sin C$
Area of a parallelogram	Area $= ab\sin C$

In past years you have learned to solve right triangles using the SOH-CAH-TOA method. The SOH portion of this rule is merely the Law of Sines in which one of the given angles is 90°. Given right triangle ABC in which $\angle C = 90°$, we could write the equation as $\dfrac{\sin 90}{c} = \dfrac{\sin B}{b}$. Since $\sin 90° = 1$, when you want to solve for $\sin B$, this equation can be rewritten as $\sin B = \dfrac{b}{c}$ or $\sin B = \dfrac{\text{opposite leg}}{\text{hypotenuse}}$.

In solving problems that involve right triangles, if you know two sides or one acute angle and one side, it is perfectly acceptable to use the rules that tell you:

$\sin B = \dfrac{\text{opposite leg}}{\text{hypotenuse}}$ (SOH)

$\cos B = \dfrac{\text{adjacent leg}}{\text{hypotenuse}}$ (CAH)

$\tan B = \dfrac{\text{opposite leg}}{\text{adjacent leg}}$ (TOA)

It is only in nonright triangles that we must use the Law of Sines or the Law of Cosines.

To solve any trigonometric application problem, first draw and label your diagram. Then determine the pattern of the given information, and use the appropriate formula to solve.

1. An isosceles triangle has base angles of 53.4° and a base equal to 14.7 inches. Find, to the nearest tenth of an inch, the length of the equal sides of the triangle.

SOLUTION
First draw a diagram.

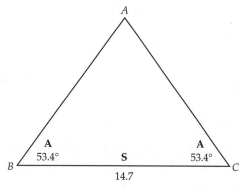

Since the information is in an angle-side-angle pattern, the problem is solved using the Law of Sines. First, however, we must find the vertex angle by subtracting the base angles from 180°: $180° - 2(53.4) = 180° - 106.8° = 73.2°$.

$$\frac{\sin A}{a} = \frac{\sin B}{b} = \frac{\sin C}{c}$$

$$\frac{\sin 73.2}{14.7} = \frac{\sin 53.4}{c}$$

$$c = \frac{14.7 \sin 53.4}{\sin 73.2}$$

$$c = 12.327$$

To the nearest tenth, each equal side of the triangle is 12.3 inches in length.

2. Dyana is working with stained glass and she needs to cut an obtuse triangle with sides of 11.6 centimeters and 8.4 centimeters to fit into her design. If the area of the triangle must measure 37.2 square centimeters, to the nearest tenth of a degree, along what obtuse angle must she cut the glass?

SOLUTION
In this case, we are given the area of the triangle and two sides and are asked for the angle between the two sides.

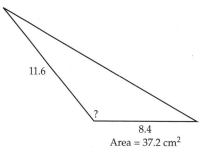

$$\text{Area} = \frac{1}{2}ab\sin C$$

$$37.2 = \frac{1}{2}(11.6)(8.4)\sin C$$

$$0.763546798 = \sin C$$

$$49.8° = \angle C$$

However, according to the problem, Dyana needs an obtuse triangle for her design. Therefore, the angle she needs is $180° - 49.8°$, or 130.2°.

3. Two forces act on a body forming a resultant force of 46 pounds. If the angle between the resultant and the smaller force of 19.8 pounds is 54.9°, what is the magnitude of the larger force, to the nearest tenth of a pound?

SOLUTION

Since the given information forms a Side-Angle-Side pattern, we use the Law of Cosines to solve this problem.

Note: Although we are looking for the length of the second vector, we use the opposite side of the parallelogram in our calculations.

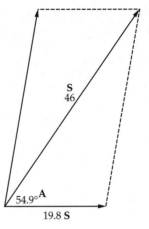

$$c^2 = a^2 + b^2 - 2ab\cos C = 46^2 + 19.8^2 - 2(46)(19.8)\cos 54.9°$$

$$c^2 = 1{,}460.610433$$

$$c = 38.2 \text{ pounds}$$

4. Katie is out with her parents at the Long Island Fair when she sees a large balloon with her name on it. Her dad tells her the angle of elevation from where she is standing to the foot of the balloon is 32° but Katie is in too much of a hurry to get closer to the balloon to listen. She runs 120 feet toward the area where the balloon is hovering before her mom, a math teacher, catches up with her and says that the angle of elevation from where she is now to the foot of the balloon is 54°. But Katie wants to know only one thing. "I want to go up there. How high up is it?" she asks. Answer Katie's question to the nearest tenth of a foot.

SOLUTION

First we must find the length of the hypotenuse, a, between the two triangles using the Law of Sines. In order to do this, we must realize that $\angle ABK$ is 126° and $\angle AKB$ is 22°.

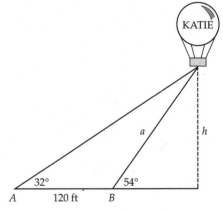

$$\frac{\sin 32°}{a} = \frac{\sin 22°}{120}$$

$$a = \frac{120 \sin 32°}{\sin 22}$$

$$a = 169.75$$

Now we can use the SOH-CAH-TOA rule to find the height of the right triangle.

$$\sin 54° = \frac{h}{169.75}$$

$$h = 137.3$$

We can tell Katie that the balloon is 137.3 feet up in the air.

In 1–10, select the numeral preceding the word or expression that best completes the sentence or answers the question.

1. In triangle ABC, $a = 6$, $b = 4.8$, and $c = 8.1$. The value of $\cos C$ is
   (1) -0.1141 (3) 0.6771
   (2) 0.1141 (4) 0.8083

2. In $\triangle VAL$, $\sin V = 0.4525$, $\sin A = 0.3128$, and $v = 7.8$. The length of side a is
   (1) 4.9 (3) 6.7
   (2) 5.4 (4) 11.3

3. If the sides of a triangle measure 5, 9, and 11, what, to the nearest tenth of a degree, is the measure of the largest angle in the triangle?
   (1) 26.6 (3) 99.6
   (2) 53.7 (4) 109.4

4. In $\triangle CTH$, $c = 12$, $h = 7$, and $m\angle T = 150$. The area of $\triangle CTH$ is
   (1) 21 (3) 42
   (2) $21\sqrt{3}$ (4) $42\sqrt{3}$

5. In $\triangle XYZ$, $m\angle X = 45$, $m\angle Y = 60$, and $XY = 8$. The measure of $\overline{XZ}$ is
   (1) 7.2
   (2) 8.9
   (3) 9.8
   (4) 10.3

6. The area of $\triangle JEN$ is 120 square centimeters. If $j = 12$ centimeters and $m\angle N = 30$, the length of side e is
   (1) 20
   (2) 30
   (3) 40
   (4) 60

7. If in $\triangle MAT$, $m\angle M = 30$, $m = 8$, and $t = 16$, which of the following must be true?
   (1) $\triangle MAT$ is a right triangle.
   (2) $\triangle MAT$ is an acute triangle.
   (3) $\triangle MAT$ is an obtuse triangle.
   (4) $\triangle MAT$ is an isosceles triangle.

8. If $m\angle A = 35$, $a = 7$, and $b = 10$, how many distinct triangles ABC can be formed?
   (1) 1
   (2) 2
   (3) 3
   (4) 0

9. In $\triangle AOK$, $a = 5$, $\sin A = 0.4$ and $k = 4$. Sin K equals
   (1) 1
   (2) 0.5
   (3) 0.32
   (4) 0.24

10. If the lengths of the sides of a triangle are 8, 15, and 17, the sine of the largest angle in the triangle is
    (1) 1
    (2) 0.8824
    (3) 0.4706
    (4) 0

In 11–20, show the diagram and equation you use to solve each problem.

11. Ms. Donal's third grade class is creating a food pyramid out of felt pieces. To fit on the bulletin board, the nutrition information will take the form of a triangle with sides of 24 inches, 24 inches, and 20 inches.
    a. Find the size of the vertex angle to the nearest degree.
    b. Find, to the nearest square inch, the area the triangle will take up on the bulletin board.

12. A surveyor is reviewing the property deed to Evelyn's triangular piece of land in Lucifer County. According to the old deed, the property has sides that measure 112 feet, 120 feet, and 96 feet, with the largest angle of the property equal to 69.98° and the smallest angle between sides of the property equal to 43.74°. If the surveyor finds the lengths of the sides of the property accurate, will she also find the angle measurements valid? Explain why or why not.

13. As Jackie and Beth bicycle to Jones Beach along the Wantagh Parkway, they take a sighting of the top of the Jones Beach Tower and find it to be 27.4°. After biking closer to the beach, they get an angle measurement of 41.2° to the top of the tower. Knowing that the Jones Beach Tower is 200 feet tall, how far, to the nearest foot, were they from the tower at each of the two locations where they took their measurements?

14. Triangle *CTH* is inscribed in circle *O* as shown below.

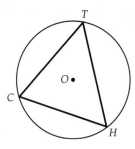

If m$\overset{\frown}{CT}$ = 98, *TH* = 12.4 centimeters, and *CT* = 11.1 centimeters,
a. Find the measure of $\angle TCH$ to the nearest tenth of a degree.
b. Find the measure of *CH* to the nearest tenth of a centimeter.
c. Find the area of $\triangle CTH$ to the nearest square centimeter.

15. A parallelogram with sides of 15 and 18 centimeters contains an angle of 57.6°.
a. Find the length of the shorter diagonal of the parallelogram to the nearest centimeter.
b. Find the area of the parallelogram to the nearest square centimeter.

16. Mike and Marie want to build a triangular lean-to in their backyard to store firewood for their fireplace. They would like to use 12-foot sheets of wood for the sides of the lean-to with a raised floor, 1 foot off the ground that measures 13 feet wide.

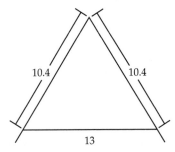

a. What must the base angles measure, to the nearest tenth of a degree, for the design?

Note: Since the floor is raised, only 10.4 feet of each congruent side will be in the lean-to.

b. What must the vertex angle measure, to the nearest tenth of a degree?

17. Janice, Molly, Ted, and Joe are hiking in the Catskill Mountains. As they hike, they take notice of their surroundings and are sur-

prised to see a fire station high above the trees. At point *T*, Ted takes a reading and finds the angle of elevation to the top of the fire station to be 11.2°. They continue hiking for another half mile and decide to make camp. As they do, Molly takes a sighting on the fire station and finds the angle of elevation to the top of the tower is now 55°.

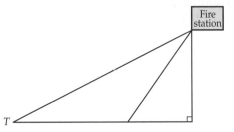

a. Find the height of the tower to the nearest foot.
b. Find the distance from point *T* to the fire tower to the nearest foot.

18. The owner of the amusement park wants to add a screening room to the Haunted House attraction, but he does not want the movie screen to be a rectangular one. Instead he has asked the designer to create a 22-foot by 12-foot screen in the shape of a parallelogram with a longer diagonal equal to 28 feet.
a. Find the measure of the angles, both acute and obtuse, between adjacent sides of the parallelogram, to the nearest tenth of a degree.
b. Find, to the nearest tenth of a square foot, the area the special-order screen will fill.

19. Two forces of 57 pounds and 43 pounds act on an object at a 65.4° angle.
a. Find the magnitude of the resultant force to the nearest tenth of a pound.
b. Find the angle, to the nearest tenth of a degree, between the resultant and the larger force.

20. Kidd's Kollege is a local day care center where the director wants to fence in the play yard to protect the children. Since the two wings of the building will serve as two sides of the play yard, fencing is needed for only the other two sides. The obtuse angle between the proposed fence and the main building is 112.8°, while the part of the main building serving as a side of the play yard is 64 feet long.

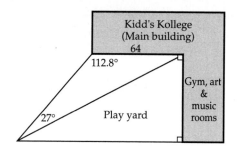

Kidd's Kollege
(Main building)
64
112.8°
27°
Play yard
Gym, art & music rooms

a. Find the length of fencing needed to the nearest tenth of a foot.

b. If fencing costs $3.85 per foot, what is the cost of the proposed fence?

CHAPTER REVIEW

1. In triangle ABC, $a = 12$, $b = 10$, and $\sin C = 0.6$. Find the area of triangle ABC.

2. In triangle DEF, $d = 20.5$, $f = 18.2$, and $\sin D = 0.345$. Find, to the nearest thousandth, $\sin F$.

3. In triangle GHI, $g = 4$, $h = 8$, and m$\angle G = 30$. Find m$\angle H$.

4. In triangle JKL, $j = 10$, $k = 6$, and m$\angle L = 60$. Find l to the nearest tenth.

5. Find the exact area of an equilateral triangle whose side is 8.

6. In triangle MNO, $m = 12$, $n = 18$, $\cos O = \frac{1}{6}$. Find o to the nearest tenth.

7. In triangle LAW, $\sin A = \frac{1}{4}$ and $\sin W = \frac{3}{7}$. If $a = 28$, find w.

8. The largest angle of a parallelogram measures 120°. If the sides measure 14 inches and 12 inches, what is the exact area of the parallelogram?

9. Find, to the nearest hundredth, the length of the base of an isosceles triangle if the sides each measure 12.42 and the vertex angle measures 64°.

In 10–18, select the numeral preceding the word or expression that best completes the statement or answers the question.

10. Find the area of triangle TRI if $t = 8$, $r = 12$, and m$\angle I = 150$.
    (1) 24   (3) 48
    (2) $24\sqrt{3}$ (4) $48\sqrt{3}$

11. In triangle PQR, m$\angle P = 30$, $p = 18$, and $r = 22$. Find $\sin R$.
    (1) $\frac{9}{22}$ (3) $\frac{18}{11}$
    (2) $\frac{11}{18}$ (4) 37

12. In triangle MAT, $m = 10$, $t = 4$, and m$\angle A = 60$. Find the length of side a.
    (1) $\sqrt{56}$ (3) $\sqrt{96}$
    (2) $\sqrt{76}$ (4) $\sqrt{156}$

13. In parallelogram $PARL$, $PA = 12$, $PL = 14$, and m$\angle P = 45$. What is the area of parallelogram $PARL$?
    (1) $42\sqrt{2}$ (3) $84\sqrt{2}$
    (2) 84   (4) 168

14. In triangle NED, $n = 6$, $e = 12$, and $d = 8$. What is the value of $\cos D$?
    (1) $-\frac{43}{48}$ (3) $\frac{29}{36}$
    (2) $-\frac{29}{36}$ (4) $\frac{43}{48}$

15. An equilateral triangle has a side of length s. Which of the following is the area of the triangle?
    (1) $\frac{s^2}{4}$ (3) $\frac{s^2}{2}$
    (2) $\frac{s^2}{4}\sqrt{3}$ (4) $\frac{s^2}{2}\sqrt{3}$

16. What is the cosine of the largest angle of a triangle whose sides measure 6, 8, and 10?
    (1) 1   (3) 0.6
    (2) 0.8   (4) 0

17. In triangle ABC, $a = 20$, $b = 16$, and m$\angle A = $ 30. Triangle ABC
    (1) must be a right triangle
    (2) must be an acute triangle
    (3) must be an obtuse triangle
    (4) could be an acute or an obtuse triangle

18. In triangle JON, side j is twice as long as side n. If m$\angle O = 30$, what is the area of triangle JON?
    (1) $\frac{n^2}{4}$ (3) n^2
    (2) $\frac{n^2}{2}$ (4) $2n^2$

19. In the accompanying diagram of circle O, $\overline{AC}$ and $\overline{DC}$ are chords, $\overline{BA}$ and $\overline{BC}$ are tangents. m$\angle ACD = 50$, m$\angle DOC = 150$, and $AB = 8$.

    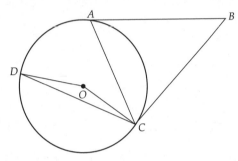

    Find:
    a. m$\widehat{AD}$
    b. m$\widehat{DC}$
    c. m$\angle ABC$
    d. BC
    e. AC (to the nearest hundredth)

20. The members of the Horticulture Club are designing a wildflower garden. They want to make it in the shape of a triangle whose sides have lengths 12 feet, 14 feet, and 18 feet.
    a. What is the measure of the largest angle in the triangle, to the nearest tenth of a degree?
    b. Using your answer to part a, find the area of the triangle to the nearest tenth of a square foot.
    c. If one package of wildflower seeds covers 25 square feet, how many packages must they buy?

21. Two forces of 36 pounds and 52 pounds act on a body at an acute angle with each other. The angle between the resultant force and the 36-pound force is 41°. Find, to the nearest degree, the angle formed by the 36-pound force and the 52-pound force.

22. Marla plans to swim across the lake from point A to point B as shown in the diagram. To determine the length of her swim, Marla has enlisted the aid of a land surveyor. The surveyor set a point at C, which is 2.6 miles from A and 3.5 miles from B. The surveyor determined that $\angle ACB$ measures 78°18'. How long is Marla's swim, to the nearest tenth of a mile?

    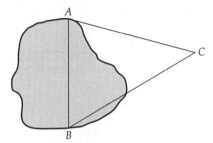

23. In triangle MAT, $a = 16$, m$\angle A = 34.6$, $t = 20$, and $\angle T$ is an obtuse angle. Find m$\angle M$ to the nearest tenth of a degree.

24. The field next to JJ Smith High School is in the shape of a parallelogram. Two consecutive sides of the field measure 340 feet and 450 feet.
    a. If the largest angle of the parallelogram measures 112.3°, to the nearest tenth of a foot, what is the longest distance from one corner of the field to the opposite corner?
    b. The school wants to replace this field with blacktop. If the blacktop company charges $4.29 per square foot, how much would it cost to install the blacktop?

25. Eddie glued together some ice cream sticks to make a square picture frame for his mother. However, he was not careful about making all of the sides perpendicular to each other, so it turned out to be a rhombus. The ice cream sticks are all 6 inches long, and he overlapped them by $\frac{1}{4}$ inch on each end when he glued them.
    a. If Eddie had made a square, exactly how long would the diagonal be?
    b. If the longer diagonal of Eddie's picture-frame is 8.5 inches, to the nearest degree, how far off are the angles?
    c. Use your answer to part b to find the length of the shorter diagonal, to the nearest tenth.

26. Tangent $\overline{PA}$ and secant $\overline{PBC}$ are drawn to circle O from external point P.
    a. If $PB = 4$ and $BC = 5$, find PA.
    b. If $\angle APC$ measures 48°58', find AC to the nearest hundredth.

CHAPTER 15

Trigonometric Identities and Equations

15.1 Basic Trigonometric Identities

An **identity** is an equation that is true for all values of the variable for which all the expressions in the equation are defined. You are already familiar with some trigonometric identities, although we did not use the term at the time. The **Reciprocal Identities** and the **Quotient Identities** are shown below.

Reciprocal Identities	Quotient Identities
$\sec \theta = \dfrac{1}{\cos \theta}$	$\tan \theta = \dfrac{\sin \theta}{\cos \theta}$
$\csc \theta = \dfrac{1}{\sin \theta}$	$\cot \theta = \dfrac{\cos \theta}{\sin \theta}$
$\cot \theta = \dfrac{1}{\tan \theta}$	

For any angle θ, in standard position on the unit circle, the x-coordinate is the cosine of the angle and the y-coordinate is the sine of the angle. In the figure below, we can see that $x^2 + y^2 = 1$.

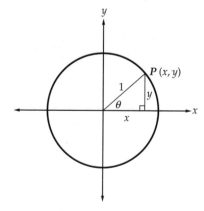

Substituting $\cos \theta$ for the x-coordinate and $\sin \theta$ for the y-coordinate, we obtain: $\cos^2 \theta + \sin^2 \theta = 1$. Since this identity is based on the Pythagorean theorem, it is

377

called a **Pythagorean Identity**. We can rewrite this identity as $\sin^2\theta + \cos^2\theta = 1$. Divide each term by $\cos^2\theta$ and simplify.

$$\sin^2\theta + \cos^2\theta = 1$$
$$\frac{\sin^2\theta}{\cos^2\theta} + 1 = \frac{1}{\cos^2\theta}$$
$$\tan^2\theta + 1 = \sec^2\theta$$

This is a second Pythagorean identity.

We can return to the original identity and divide each term by $\sin^2\theta$ and simplify to produce a third Pythagorean identity.

$$\sin^2\theta + \cos^2\theta = 1$$
$$1 + \frac{\cos^2\theta}{\sin^2\theta} = \frac{1}{\sin^2\theta}$$
$$1 + \cot^2\theta = \csc^2\theta$$

We now have three Pythagorean identities.

$$\sin^2\theta + \cos^2\theta = 1$$
$$\tan^2\theta + 1 = \sec^2\theta$$
$$1 + \cot^2\theta = \csc^2\theta$$

We can use these identities to find the values of the other trigonometric functions when the value of one function is known.

 **MODEL PROBLEMS**

1. If $\cos\theta = \frac{3}{5}$, and θ is an angle that terminates in Quadrant IV, find the values of the other five trigonometric functions.

SOLUTION
You could solve this problem using right triangle trigonometry, or by using the identities. Both methods are illustrated below.

Right Triangle Trigonometry

If $\cos\theta = \frac{3}{5}$, and θ terminates in Quadrant IV, we can sketch this as shown below, placing the 3 on the adjacent side and the 5 on the hypotenuse.

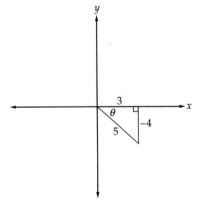

We can now use the Pythagorean theorem and find that the opposite side measures 4. Since this side is 4 in a negative direction, its *directed distance* is -4. We can now use this information to find the remaining five trigonometric functions.

$$\sin \theta = \frac{\text{opposite}}{\text{hypotenuse}} = -\frac{4}{5} \qquad \tan \theta = \frac{\text{opposite}}{\text{adjacent}} = -\frac{4}{3}$$

Then, find all of the reciprocal functions.

$$\sec \theta = \frac{1}{\cos \theta} = \frac{5}{3} \qquad \csc \theta = \frac{1}{\sin \theta} = -\frac{5}{4} \qquad \cot \theta = \frac{1}{\tan \theta} = -\frac{3}{4}$$

Identities

Since $\sin^2 \theta + \cos^2 \theta = 1$, we can substitute into this equation as follows:

$$\sin^2 \theta + \left(\frac{3}{5}\right)^2 = 1$$

$$\sin^2 \theta = 1 - \frac{9}{25}$$

$$\sin^2 \theta = \frac{16}{25}$$

$$\sin \theta = \pm\frac{4}{5}$$

Since we are in Quadrant IV, where $\sin \theta$ is negative, we pick the negative value.

$$\sin \theta = -\frac{4}{5}$$

$$\tan \theta = \frac{\sin \theta}{\cos \theta} = \frac{-\frac{4}{5}}{\frac{3}{5}} = -\frac{4}{3}$$

Then, find all of the reciprocal functions.

$$\sec \theta = \frac{1}{\cos \theta} = \frac{5}{3} \qquad \csc \theta = \frac{1}{\sin \theta} = -\frac{5}{4} \qquad \cot \theta = \frac{1}{\tan \theta} = -\frac{3}{4}$$

2. If $\sin \theta = -\frac{2}{3}$ and $\tan \theta > 0$, find $\cos \theta$.

In this case we will only illustrate the method using the identities.
Since $\sin^2 \theta + \cos^2 \theta = 1$, we can substitute into this equation.

$$\left(-\frac{2}{3}\right)^2 + \cos^2 \theta = 1$$

$$\cos^2 \theta = 1 - \frac{4}{9}$$

$$\cos^2 \theta = \frac{5}{9}$$

$$\cos \theta = \pm\frac{\sqrt{5}}{3}$$

Since $\sin \theta < 0$ and $\tan \theta > 0$, we are in Quadrant III, where $\cos \theta < 0$.

Answer: $-\dfrac{\sqrt{5}}{3}$

We can also use the identities to simplify complicated trigonometric expressions into simpler ones.

Write each expression as a single function.
a. $(\cos \theta)(\tan \theta)$ **b.** $\sec^2 \theta - 1$

SOLUTION

a. We know that $\tan \theta = \dfrac{\sin \theta}{\cos \theta}$, so we can make that substitution.

$$(\cos \theta)(\tan \theta) = (\cos \theta)\left(\dfrac{\sin \theta}{\cos \theta}\right) \quad \text{"Cancel" the } \cos \theta.$$

$$= \sin \theta$$

Answer: $\sin \theta$

b. We know that $\tan^2 \theta + 1 = \sec^2 \theta$, so we will make that substitution.

$$\sec^2 \theta - 1 = \tan^2 \theta + 1 - 1$$

$$= \tan^2 \theta$$

Answer: $\tan^2 \theta$

We can also use these basic trigonometric identities to prove other identities.

Note: When you prove an identity, you must work straight down on one or both sides of the equation. You are not solving an equation. Therefore, you cannot add, subtract, multiply or divide terms on both sides of the equation, as you would do if you were solving an equation. You are simply checking that the identity is true.

Prove that each equation is an identity.
a. $\dfrac{\cos \theta + 1}{1 + \sec \theta} = \cos \theta$ **b.** $\tan^2 \theta \,(1 - \sin^2 \theta) = 1 - \cos^2 \theta$

SOLUTION

$$\dfrac{\cos \theta + 1}{1 + \sec \theta} \stackrel{?}{=} \cos \theta \qquad \text{Use identities to substitute.}$$

$$\dfrac{\cos \theta + 1}{1 + \dfrac{1}{\cos \theta}} \stackrel{?}{=} \cos \theta \qquad \text{Simplify the complex fraction.}$$

$$\dfrac{\cos \theta + 1}{\dfrac{\cos \theta + 1}{\cos \theta}} \stackrel{?}{=} \cos \theta \qquad \text{Multiply by the reciprocal of the denominator.}$$

$$\dfrac{\cancel{\cos \theta + 1}}{1} \cdot \dfrac{\cos \theta}{\cancel{\cos \theta + 1}} \stackrel{?}{=} \cos \theta \qquad \text{"Cancel" like terms.}$$

$$\cos \theta = \cos \theta \checkmark$$

b. $\tan^2 \theta (1 - \sin^2 \theta) \overset{?}{=} 1 - \cos^2 \theta$ Work down each side separately, using identities.

$$\frac{\sin^2 \theta}{\cos^2 \theta} \cdot \frac{\cos^2 \theta}{1} \overset{?}{=} \sin^2 \theta$$

$$\sin^2 \theta = \sin^2 \theta \checkmark$$

Practice

In 1–10, write each expression as a single function or a constant.

1. $1 - \cos^2 \theta$ $\sin^2\theta$

2. $(\sin \theta)(\csc \theta)$ 1

3. $(\tan \theta)(\cot \theta)$ 1

4. $\sec^2 \theta - 1$ $\tan^2\theta$

5. $(\tan \theta)(\csc \theta)$ $\left(\frac{\sin\theta}{\cos\theta}\right)\left(\frac{1}{\sin\theta}\right) = \frac{1}{\cos\theta} = \sec\theta$

6. $\dfrac{\csc x}{\sec x}$ $\frac{1}{\sin x} / \frac{1}{\cos x} = \frac{\cos x}{\sin x} = \tan x$

7. $\cos \theta (\tan^2 \theta + 1)$ $\cos\theta\left(\frac{1}{\cos\theta}\right) = 1$

8. $\sin^2 \theta + \cos^2 \theta + \tan^2 \theta$ $1 + \tan^2\theta = \sec^2\theta$

9. $1 - \dfrac{\tan^2 \alpha}{\sec^2 \alpha}$ $1 - \frac{\sin^2\theta}{\cos^2\theta} \cdot \frac{1}{\frac{1}{\cos^2\theta}} = 1 - \sin^2\theta = \cos^2\alpha$

10. $(\sin^2 \theta)(\cos \theta)(\tan \theta)(\csc \theta)$ $\sin^2\theta \cdot \cos\theta \cdot \frac{\sin\theta}{\cos\theta} \cdot \frac{1}{\sin\theta}$ $\sin\theta$

In 11–15, prove that the equation is an identity.

11. $(1 + \cos \theta)(1 - \cos \theta) = \sin^2 \theta$

12. $\cos^2 \theta (\tan^2 \theta + 1) + \cot^2 \theta = \csc^2 \theta$

13. $\dfrac{1}{\sin^2 \beta} + \dfrac{1}{\cos^2 \beta} = (\sec^2 \beta)(\csc^2 \beta)$

14. $\csc \theta - (\cos \theta)(\cot \theta) = \sin \theta$

15. $2 - \dfrac{1 - \cos^2 \theta}{\tan^2 \theta} = \sin^2 \theta + 1$

16. If $\cos \theta = -\dfrac{5}{13}$ and θ lies in Quadrant II, find the values of the remaining five trigonometric functions.

17. If $\sin \theta = -\dfrac{7}{25}$ and $\cos \theta < 0$, find the values of the remaining five trigonometric functions.

18. If $\sec \theta = \dfrac{4}{3}$, and $\sin \theta > 0$, find the values of the remaining five trigonometric functions.

In 19–25, select the numeral preceding the expression that best completes the statement or answers the question.

19. The expression $\dfrac{\tan^2 \theta}{\sin^2 \theta}$ is equivalent to

   (1) $\sin^2 \theta$ (3) $\sec^2 \theta$
   (2) $\cos^2 \theta$ (4) $\csc^2 \theta$

20. If $\csc \theta = -\dfrac{5}{4}$ and θ is in Quadrant III, then $\cos \theta =$

   (1) $-\dfrac{4}{5}$ (3) $\dfrac{3}{5}$

   (2) $-\dfrac{3}{5}$ (4) $\dfrac{4}{5}$

21. $\sin^2 \theta + \cos^2 \theta + \tan^2 \theta =$

   (1) $\sec^2 \theta$ (3) $\cot^2 \theta$

   (2) $\csc^2 \theta$ (4) $\dfrac{1}{\cot^2 \theta}$

22. If $\sin \theta = 0.6$ and $\cos \theta < 0$, then $\tan \theta =$

   (1) -1.333 (3) 0.75
   (2) -0.75 (4) 1.333

23. If $\cos \theta = k$, then the value of $(\cos \theta)(\sin \theta)(\cot \theta) =$

   (1) 1 (3) k^2

   (2) k (4) $\dfrac{1}{k}$

24. If $\sin \theta = \dfrac{3}{4}$ and θ is an acute angle, what is the value of $(\tan \theta)(\cos \theta)$?

   (1) $\dfrac{3}{5}$ (3) $\dfrac{3}{4}$

   (2) $\dfrac{\sqrt{7}}{4}$ (4) $\dfrac{3\sqrt{7}}{7}$

25. The expression $\sec^2 \theta + \csc^2 \theta$ is equivalent to

   (1) 1 (3) $\dfrac{1}{\sin \theta \cos \theta}$

   (2) $(\sec \theta)(\csc \theta)$ (4) $\dfrac{1}{\sin^2 \theta \cos^2 \theta}$

15.2 Sum and Difference of Angles

To find the sine of the sum of two angles, we cannot simply add the sines of the two angles. For example, $\sin(30° + 60°) = \sin(90°) = 1$. We would not get the same result if we found $\sin 30° + \sin 60° = \frac{1}{2} + \frac{\sqrt{3}}{2}$. We must use the formula for the sine of the sum of two angles. The formula needed is found below.

Functions of the Sum of Two Angles

$\sin(A + B) = \sin A \cos B + \cos A \sin B$

$\cos(A + B) = \cos A \cos B - \sin A \sin B$

$\tan(A + B) = \dfrac{\tan A + \tan B}{1 - \tan A \tan B}$

Using our formula, we get

$$\sin(30°+60°) = \sin 30° \cos 60° + \cos 30° \sin 60°$$
$$= \left(\frac{1}{2}\right)\left(\frac{1}{2}\right) + \left(\frac{\sqrt{3}}{2}\right)\left(\frac{\sqrt{3}}{2}\right)$$
$$= \frac{1}{4} + \frac{3}{4}$$
$$= 1$$

Remember: $\sin(A + B) \neq \sin A + \sin B$. To compute $\sin(A + B)$, you must use the formula for the sine of the sum of two angles.

The following formulas are used to compute the functions of the difference of two angles.

Functions of the Difference of Two Angles

$\sin(A - B) = \sin A \cos B - \cos A \sin B$

$\cos(A - B) = \cos A \cos B + \sin A \sin B$

$\tan(A - B) = \dfrac{\tan A - \tan B}{1 + \tan A \tan B}$

MODEL PROBLEMS

1. If $\sin x = \frac{3}{5}$ and $\cos y = \frac{5}{13}$, and x and y are positive acute angles, find $\cos(x + y)$.

SOLUTION

$$\cos(x + y) = \cos x \cos y - \sin x \sin y$$

Since you need to use the sine and cosine functions of each of the angles, you must compute the missing functions. You could either use a trigonometric identity, or utilize the Pythagorean theorem in a right triangle. We will use a trigonometric identity here and illustrate the second option in the next example.

We know that $\sin x = \frac{3}{5}$ and x is a positive acute angle.

$$\sin^2 x + \cos^2 x = 1 \qquad \text{Use the Pythagorean identity.}$$

$$\left(\frac{3}{5}\right)^2 + \cos^2 x = 1 \qquad \text{Solve for } \cos x.$$

$$\cos^2 x = 1 - \left(\frac{3}{5}\right)^2 \qquad \text{Combine like terms.}$$

$$\cos^2 x = \frac{16}{25} \qquad \text{Take the square root of both sides.}$$

$$\cos x = \pm \frac{4}{5} \qquad \text{Since } x \text{ is a positive acute angle, choose the positive value.}$$

$$\cos x = \frac{4}{5}$$

Follow the same procedure to obtain $\sin y$.

We know that $\cos y = \frac{5}{13}$, and y is a positive acute angle.

$$\sin^2 y + \cos^2 y = 1 \qquad \text{Use the Pythagorean identity.}$$

$$\sin^2 y + \left(\frac{5}{13}\right)^2 = 1 \qquad \text{Solve for } \sin y.$$

$$\sin^2 y = 1 - \left(\frac{5}{13}\right)^2 \qquad \text{Combine like terms.}$$

$$\sin^2 y = \frac{144}{169} \qquad \text{Take the square root of both sides.}$$

$$\sin y = \pm \frac{12}{13} \qquad \text{Since } y \text{ is a positive acute angle, choose the positive value.}$$

$$\sin y = \frac{12}{13}$$

Substitute the above information into the formula.

$$\cos (x + y) = \cos x \cos y - \sin x \sin y$$
$$= \left(\frac{4}{5}\right)\left(\frac{5}{13}\right) - \left(\frac{3}{5}\right)\left(\frac{12}{13}\right)$$
$$= \frac{20 - 36}{65}$$
$$= -\frac{16}{65}$$

2. If $\cos \alpha = -\frac{2}{3}$, $\tan \beta = \frac{2}{3}$, and α and β both lie in Quadrant III, find $\sin (\alpha - \beta)$.

SOLUTION

Since you need to use the sine and cosine functions of each of the angles, you must compute the missing functions. You could either use a trigonometric identity, or a right triangle. This time we will use right triangle trigonometry.

Since α lies in Quadrant III, utilize the given information to sketch a triangle in the third quadrant. Use the Pythagorean theorem to fill in the missing side.

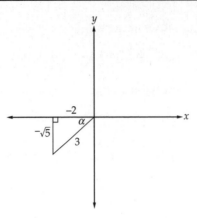

By looking at the triangle, we can see that $\sin \alpha = -\dfrac{\sqrt{5}}{3}$.

Since α lies in Quadrant III, utilize the given information to sketch a triangle in the third quadrant. Use the Pythagorean theorem to fill in the missing side. You should obtain the following:

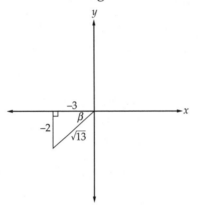

By looking at the triangle, we can see that $\sin \beta = -\dfrac{2}{\sqrt{13}} = -\dfrac{2\sqrt{13}}{13}$ and $\cos \beta = -\dfrac{3}{\sqrt{13}} = -\dfrac{3\sqrt{13}}{13}$. Substitute the above information into the formula.

$$\sin (\alpha - \beta) = \sin \alpha \cos \beta - \cos \alpha \sin \beta$$

$$= \left(-\dfrac{\sqrt{5}}{3}\right)\left(-\dfrac{3\sqrt{13}}{13}\right) - \left(-\dfrac{2}{3}\right)\left(-\dfrac{2\sqrt{13}}{13}\right)$$

$$= \dfrac{3\sqrt{65}}{39} - \dfrac{4\sqrt{13}}{39}$$

$$= \dfrac{3\sqrt{65} - 4\sqrt{13}}{39}$$

3. Prove: $\cos (180° - x) = -\cos x$.

SOLUTION
Use the formula for the cosine of the difference of two angles, $\cos (A - B) = \cos A \cos B + \sin A \sin B$, and work straight down on the left side of the equation.

$$\cos (180° - x) \overset{?}{=} -\cos x$$

$$\cos (180°) \cos x - \sin (180°) \sin x \overset{?}{=} -\cos x$$

$$(-1)\cos x - (0)\sin x \overset{?}{=} -\cos x$$

$$-\cos x - 0 \overset{?}{=} -\cos x$$

$$-\cos x = -\cos x$$

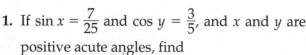

1. If $\sin x = \dfrac{7}{25}$ and $\cos y = \dfrac{3}{5}$, and x and y are positive acute angles, find
 a. $\sin (x + y)$ $^{117}/_{125}$
 b. $\cos (x - y)$ $^{4}/_{5}$
 c. $\tan (x + y)$

2. Given $\sin \theta = 0.8$ and $\tan \varphi = 0.75$, $\dfrac{\pi}{2} < \theta < \pi$, and $\pi < \varphi < \dfrac{3\pi}{2}$, find $\cos (\theta + \varphi)$.

3. Carlos would like to determine the exact value of $\cos 15°$. Since he knows the exact value of $\cos 45°$ and $\cos 30°$, he can use the formula for the cosine of the difference of two angles. What is the exact value of $\cos 15°$?

4. Marietta will use her knowledge of trigonometry to compute the exact value of $\sin 105°$.
 a. What combination of angles can she use?
 b. What is the exact value of $\sin 105°$?

5. Prove: $\sin (\pi - \theta) = \sin \theta$.

6. Prove: $\cos (360° - A) = \cos A$.

7. Prove: $\sin (180° + x) = -\sin x$.

8. Prove: $\cos \left(\dfrac{3\pi}{2} - \beta \right) = -\sin \beta$.

In 9–20 select the numeral preceding the expression that best completes the statement or answers the question.

9. If A and B are both positive acute angles and $\sin A = \dfrac{3}{5}$ and $\sin B = \dfrac{5}{13}$, then $\sin (A - B) =$
 (1) $\dfrac{16}{65}$ (3) $\dfrac{33}{65}$
 (2) $-\dfrac{16}{65}$ (4) $-\dfrac{33}{65}$

10. The expression $\tan (180° - y)$ is equivalent to
 (1) $\tan y$ (3) 0
 (2) $-\tan y$ (4) -1

11. $\sin 240° \cos 60° + \cos 240° \sin 60°$ is equivalent to
 (1) $\sin 300°$ (3) $\sin 180°$
 (2) $\cos 300°$ (4) $\cos 180°$

12. $\cos 300° \cos 30° + \sin 300° \sin 30°$ is equivalent to
 (1) $\sin 330°$ (3) $\sin 270°$
 (2) $\cos 330°$ (4) $\cos 270°$

13. $\dfrac{\tan 25° + \tan 15°}{1 - \tan 25° \tan 15°}$ is equivalent to
 (1) $\tan 10°$ (3) $\tan 40°$
 (2) $\tan 30°$ (4) $\cot 40°$

14. Which of the following is equivalent to $\cos (\pi + y)$?
 (1) $\cos y$ (3) $\sin y$
 (2) $-\cos y$ (4) $-\sin y$

15. If $\tan x = 1$, $\sin y = \dfrac{\sqrt{2}}{2}$, and x and y are positive acute angles, find $\cos (x + y)$.
 (1) 1 (3) 0
 (2) -1 (4) $1 + \dfrac{\sqrt{2}}{2}$

16. If $\sin A = \dfrac{\sqrt{3}}{2}$, $\sin B = -\dfrac{1}{2}$, $\dfrac{\pi}{2} < A < \pi$, and $\pi < B < \dfrac{3\pi}{2}$, find $\sin (A + B)$.
 (1) $\dfrac{1}{2}$ (3) $\dfrac{\sqrt{3}}{2}$
 (2) $-\dfrac{1}{2}$ (4) $-\dfrac{\sqrt{3}}{2}$

17. If $\sin A = k$, find $\sin (A + 2\pi)$.
 (1) $\sin k$ (3) k
 (2) $-\sin k$ (4) $-k$

18. Which of the following is equivalent to $\sin \left(\dfrac{\pi}{2} - y \right)$?
 (1) $\cos y$ (3) $\sin y$
 (2) $-\cos y$ (4) $-\sin y$

19. The exact value of $\sin 75°$ is
 (1) $\dfrac{1}{2} + \dfrac{\sqrt{2}}{2}$ (3) $\dfrac{\sqrt{2} + \sqrt{6}}{4}$
 (2) $\dfrac{\sqrt{2} + \sqrt{6}}{2}$ (4) $\dfrac{\sqrt{2} - \sqrt{6}}{4}$

20. The expression $\cos \left(\dfrac{\pi}{2} + \theta \right)$ is equivalent to
 (1) $\sin \theta$ (3) $\cos \theta$
 (2) $-\sin \theta$ (4) $-\cos \theta$

15.3 Double and Half Angles

We know that $\sin 30° = \frac{1}{2}$. We also know that $\sin 60° = \frac{\sqrt{3}}{2} \neq 2(\sin 30°)$. Thus, to find $\sin 60°$ from $\sin 30°$, we need to use a formula. Since $60 = 30 + 30$, we can use the formula for the sine of the sum of two angles.

$$\begin{aligned}
\sin(60°) &= \sin(30° + 30°) \\
&= \sin 30° \cos 30° + \cos 30° \sin 30° \\
&= \left(\frac{1}{2}\right)\left(\frac{\sqrt{3}}{2}\right) + \left(\frac{\sqrt{3}}{2}\right)\left(\frac{1}{2}\right) \\
&= \frac{2\sqrt{3}}{4} \\
&= \frac{\sqrt{3}}{2}
\end{aligned}$$

We can also use this technique to derive the general formula for the sine of a double angle.

$$\begin{aligned}
\sin(2A) &= \sin(A + A) \\
&= \sin A \cos A + \cos A \sin A \\
&= 2 \sin A \cos A
\end{aligned}$$

We can use this same technique to derive the formulas for the cosine of a double angle. That will be left for you to do in a practice problem.

Functions of Double Angles

$\sin 2A = 2 \sin A \cos A$

$\cos 2A = \cos^2 A - \sin^2 A$

$\cos 2A = 2 \cos^2 A - 1$

$\cos 2A = 1 - 2 \sin^2 A$

Remember: Three different formulas are given for $\cos 2A$. All three formulas are equivalent. Use whatever formula works best with the information that you are given.

MODEL PROBLEMS

1. Use the formula for $\sin 2A$ to show that $\sin 90° = 1$.

SOLUTION

$$\begin{aligned}
\sin 90° &= \sin(2 \cdot 45°) && \text{Copy the formula, replacing } A \text{ with } 45°. \\
&= 2 \sin 45° \cos 45° && \sin 45° = \cos 45° = \frac{\sqrt{2}}{2} \\
&= 2\left(\frac{\sqrt{2}}{2}\right)\left(\frac{\sqrt{2}}{2}\right) && \text{Simplify.} \\
&= \frac{2}{2} \\
&= 1
\end{aligned}$$

2. If $\cos \theta = \frac{7}{25}$, find $\cos 2\theta$.

SOLUTION

Since we are given $\cos \theta = \frac{7}{25}$, we will use the formula that contains cosine.

$$\cos 2A = 2 \cos^2 A - 1 \qquad \text{Replace } \cos A \text{ with the value of } \cos \theta.$$

$$= 2\left(\frac{7}{25}\right)^2 - 1 \qquad \text{Simplify.}$$

$$= 2\left(\frac{49}{625}\right) - 1$$

$$= \frac{98 - 625}{625}$$

$$= -\frac{527}{625}$$

3. Prove: $(\sin 2\theta)(\sec \theta) = 2 \sin \theta$.

SOLUTION

To prove an identity, we work straight down one side of the equation.

$$(\sin 2\theta)(\sec \theta) \stackrel{?}{=} 2 \sin \theta$$

$$2 \sin \theta \, \cancel{\cos \theta} \cdot \frac{1}{\cancel{\cos \theta}} \stackrel{?}{=} 2 \sin \theta$$

$$2 \sin \theta = 2 \sin \theta \checkmark$$

When we work with functions of half angles we must use the following formulas.

Functions of Half Angles

$$\sin \frac{1}{2} A = \pm \sqrt{\frac{1 - \cos A}{2}}$$

$$\cos \frac{1}{2} A = \pm \sqrt{\frac{1 + \cos A}{2}}$$

In each case, we must use either the positive or negative value depending on the quadrant in which half of the original angle lies. For example, if $0 \leq A \leq \frac{\pi}{2}$, then $0 \leq \frac{1}{2}A \leq \frac{\pi}{4}$ where both sine and cosine are positive.

The following table will help you choose the positive or negative values.

Domain of Angle	Domain of Half Angle	Quadrant of Half Angle	Sign of Function of Half Angle
$0 < A < \frac{\pi}{2}$	$0 < \frac{1}{2}A < \frac{\pi}{4}$	I	$\sin \frac{1}{2}A > 0$ $\cos \frac{1}{2}A > 0$
$\frac{\pi}{2} < A < \pi$	$\frac{\pi}{4} < \frac{1}{2}A < \frac{\pi}{2}$	I	$\sin \frac{1}{2}A > 0$ $\cos \frac{1}{2}A > 0$
$\pi < A < \frac{3\pi}{2}$	$\frac{\pi}{2} < \frac{1}{2}A < \frac{3\pi}{4}$	II	$\sin \frac{1}{2}A > 0$ $\cos \frac{1}{2}A < 0$
$\frac{3\pi}{2} < A < 2\pi$	$\frac{3\pi}{4} < \frac{1}{2}A < \pi$	II	$\sin \frac{1}{2}A > 0$ $\cos \frac{1}{2}A < 0$

For $A > 2\pi$, follow a similar pattern.

 MODEL PROBLEMS

1. Use the formula for $\sin \frac{1}{2}\theta$ to show that $\sin (45°) = \frac{\sqrt{2}}{2}$.

SOLUTION

$$\sin \frac{1}{2}A = \pm\sqrt{\frac{1 - \cos A}{2}}$$

When we use this formula we must decide whether to use the positive value or the negative value. Since 45° is in the first quadrant, where sine is positive, we will choose the positive value.

$\sin 45° = \sin \frac{1}{2}(90°)$ Copy the formula, choose the positive value, and substitute 90° for A.

$= \sqrt{\frac{1 - \cos 90°}{2}}$ $\cos 90° = 0$

$= \sqrt{\frac{1 - 0}{2}}$ Simplify.

$= \sqrt{\frac{1}{2}}$ Rationalize the denominator.

$= \frac{\sqrt{1}}{\sqrt{2}} \cdot \frac{\sqrt{2}}{\sqrt{2}}$

$= \frac{\sqrt{2}}{2}$

2. If $\cos \alpha = \frac{3}{5}$ and $\frac{3\pi}{2} < \alpha < 2\pi$, find $\cos \frac{1}{2}\alpha$.

SOLUTION

Since $\frac{3\pi}{2} < \alpha < 2\pi$, $\frac{3\pi}{4} < \frac{1}{2}\alpha < \pi$. Because $\frac{1}{2}\alpha$ lies in Quadrant II, where cosine is negative, we choose the negative value.

$$\cos \frac{1}{2}\alpha = -\sqrt{\frac{1 + \cos \alpha}{2}} \quad \text{Given } \cos \alpha = \frac{3}{5}.$$

$$= -\sqrt{\frac{1 + \frac{3}{5}}{2}} \quad \text{Simplify the numerator.}$$

$$= -\sqrt{\frac{\frac{8}{5}}{2}} \quad \text{Divide by 2.}$$

$$= -\sqrt{\frac{4}{5}} \quad \text{Simplify the radical.}$$

$$= -\frac{2}{\sqrt{5}} \quad \text{Rationalize the denominator.}$$

$$= -\frac{2\sqrt{5}}{5}$$

Practice

1. If $\sin x = \frac{4}{5}$ and x is a positive acute angle, find
   a. $\sin 2x$
   b. $\cos \frac{1}{2}x$

2. If $\cos y = \frac{1}{2}$, and $\frac{3\pi}{2} < y < 2\pi$, find
   a. $\cos 2y$
   b. $\sin \frac{1}{2}y$

3. If $\sin \theta = 0.6$, and θ lies in Quadrant II, find
   a. $\cos (2\theta)$
   b. $\cos \frac{\theta}{2}$

4. If $\tan \beta = \frac{1}{3}$, and β lies in Quadrant III, find
   a. $\sin (2\beta)$
   b. $\sin \left(\frac{\beta}{2}\right)$

5. Use the formula for sine of a double angle to find $\sin (120°)$.

6. Use the formula for cosine of half an angle to find $\cos (30°)$.

7. a. Find the exact value of $\sin 15°$.
   b. Use your answer to part **a** to approximate $\sin 15°$ to the nearest thousandth.
   c. Use your calculator to find $\sin 15°$. Does your answer agree with part **b**?

8. a. Find the exact value of $\cos 22.5°$.
   b. Use your answer to part **a** to approximate $\cos 22.5°$ to the nearest thousandth.
   c. Use your calculator to find $\cos 22.5°$. Does your answer agree with part **b**?

9. Prove the identity: $1 - \tan \theta \sin 2\theta = \cos 2\theta$.

10. Prove the identity: $\frac{\cos 2\alpha}{\sin \alpha} + 2 \sin \alpha = \csc \alpha$.

11. a. Use the fact that $\cos (2A) = \cos (A + A)$ to derive the formula $\cos 2A = \cos^2 A - \sin^2 A$.
   b. Use one of the Pythagorean identities to rewrite the formula from part **a** as $\cos 2A = 2 \cos^2 A - 1$.
   c. Use one of the Pythagorean identities to rewrite the formula from part **a** as $\cos 2A = 1 - 2 \sin^2 A$.

In 12–22, select the numeral preceding the word or expression that best completes the statement or answers the question.

12. The expression $\dfrac{\sin 2\theta}{2\cos\theta}$ is equivalent to
    (1) $\sin\theta$ (3) $\tan\theta$
    (2) $\cos\theta$ (4) $\cot\theta$

13. If $\dfrac{3\pi}{2} < \alpha < 2\pi$, in what quadrant does $\frac{1}{2}\alpha$ lie?
    (1) I   (3) III
    (2) II   (4) IV

14. Which of the following is the range of $\cos 2x$?
    (1) $-1 \le y \le 1$ (3) $-90 \le x \le 90$
    (2) $-2 \le y \le 2$ (4) $0 \le x \le 360$

15. The expression $2\sin x \cos x$ is equivalent to
    (1) $2\sin x$ (3) $\cos 2x$
    (2) $\sin 2x$ (4) $\tan 2x$

16. If $\sin x = \cos x$ and x is a positive acute angle, then $\sin 2x =$
    (1) 1   (3) 0
    (2) 2   (4) cannot be determined

17. The expression $2\cos^2(15°) - 1$ has the same value as
    (1) $\sin 15°$ (3) $\sin 30°$
    (2) $\cos 15°$ (4) $\cos 30°$

18. If $\cos\alpha = -\dfrac{5}{13}$ and $\pi < \alpha < \dfrac{3\pi}{2}$, then $\cos\frac{1}{2}\alpha =$
    (1) $-\dfrac{10}{13}$ (3) $\dfrac{2\sqrt{13}}{13}$
    (2) $-\dfrac{2\sqrt{13}}{13}$ (4) $\dfrac{10}{13}$

19. If $\sin y = -\dfrac{7}{25}$, find $\cos 2y$.
    (1) $-\dfrac{48}{25}$ (3) $\dfrac{134}{625}$
    (2) $-\dfrac{14}{25}$ (4) $\dfrac{527}{625}$

20. The expression $\dfrac{2\sin\theta\cos\theta}{\cos^2\theta - \sin^2\theta}$ is equivalent to
    (1) $\sin 2\theta$ (3) $\tan 2\theta$
    (2) $\cos 2\theta$ (4) $\cot 2\theta$

21. If $\sin\beta = 0.6$, and β terminates in Quadrant II, find $\sin 2\beta$.
    (1) -1.2 (3) 0.96
    (2) -0.96 (4) 1.2

22. The maximum value of $3\sin 2\theta$ is
    (1) 2π (3) 3
    (2) 2   (4) 6

15.4 First-Degree Trigonometric Equations

If you recall how to solve linear equations, you can use this knowledge to solve first-degree trigonometric equations.

Solve for x: $4x + 3 = 5$ Subtract 3 from both sides.
                    $4x = 2$ Divide both sides by 4.
                    $x = \dfrac{1}{2}$

Solve for θ in the interval $0° \le \theta \le 360°$.

   $4\sin\theta + 3 = 5$ Subtract 3 from both sides.
   $4\sin\theta = 2$ Divide both sides by 4.
   $\sin\theta = \dfrac{1}{2}$

Now, we have found that $\sin\theta = \dfrac{1}{2}$. However, we were not asked to find $\sin\theta$.

We were asked to find θ. First, we need to find our reference angle. Then, we must recall that $\sin\theta$ is positive in Quadrants I and II, so we need to find values of θ in Quadrants I and II.

$$\sin \theta = \frac{1}{2}$$ What angle has a sine of $\frac{1}{2}$?

Reference angle: 30°   Now, use the reference angle to find answers in Quadrants I and II.

Quadrant I: 30°   (We use the reference angle.)

Quadrant II: 150°   (180° − 30°)

Answer: 30° and 150°

 MODEL PROBLEMS

1. Solve for tan θ: $3 \tan \theta - 4 = 5 \tan \theta - 1$.

SOLUTION

$3 \tan \theta - 4 = 5 \tan \theta - 1$ Subtract 5 tan θ from both sides.

$-2 \tan \theta - 4 = -1$ Add 4 to both sides.

$-2 \tan \theta = 3$ Divide both sides by −2.

$$\tan \theta = -\frac{2}{3}$$

We were asked to find tan θ, so our answer is $\tan \theta = -\frac{2}{3}$.

2. Solve for θ in the interval $0° \le \theta \le 360°$: $8 \sec \theta - 2 = 10 + 2 \sec \theta$.

SOLUTION

$8 \sec \theta - 2 = 10 + 2 \sec \theta$ Subtract 2 sec θ from both sides.

$6 \sec \theta - 2 = 10$ Add 2 to both sides.

$6 \sec \theta = 12$ Divide both sides by 6.

$\sec \theta = 2$ Since we are more familiar with cosine, we can convert the equation to an equation containing cosine by taking the reciprocal of both sides.

$\cos \theta = \frac{1}{2}$ Find the reference angle.

Reference angle = 60°.

Cosine $\theta > 0$ in Quadrant I and IV.

Find angles in Quadrants I and IV.

Quadrant I: 60°   Quadrant IV: 300° (360° − 60°)

Answer: 60° and 300°

3. Solve for θ to the nearest degree in the interval $0° \le \theta \le 360°$: $3 (\sin \theta - 1) = -4$.

SOLUTION

$3 (\sin \theta - 1) = -4$ Distribute the 3.

$3 \sin \theta - 3 = -4$ Add 3 to both sides.

$3 \sin \theta = -1$ Divide both sides by 3.

$\sin \theta = -\frac{1}{3}$ Find a reference angle by pressing ⟨2nd⟩ ⟨SIN⟩.

Reference angle = 19.47122063; rounded to the nearest degree = 19°.

Sin $\theta < 0$ in Quadrants III and IV.

Quadrant III: 199° (180° + 19°)   Quadrant IV: 341° (360° − 19°)

Remember: Make sure that your calculator is set in Degree Mode if the question asks for an answer in degrees, and that it is set in Radian Mode if the question asks for an answer in radians.

4. Solve for exact values of θ in the interval $0 \leq \theta \leq 2\pi$: $2 \cos \theta + 3\sqrt{2} = 2\sqrt{2}$.

SOLUTION

$2 \cos \theta + 3\sqrt{2} = 2\sqrt{2}$ Subtract $3\sqrt{2}$ from both sides.

$2 \cos \theta = -\sqrt{2}$ Divide both sides by 2.

$\cos \theta = -\dfrac{\sqrt{2}}{2}$ Find the reference angle.

Reference angle: $\dfrac{\pi}{4}$

Cosine $\theta < 0$ in Quadrants II and III.

Quadrant II: $\dfrac{3\pi}{4}$ $\left(\pi - \dfrac{\pi}{4}\right)$ Quadrant III: $\dfrac{5\pi}{4}$ $\left(\pi + \dfrac{\pi}{4}\right)$

Use the following table to help you obtain your answer after you find the reference angle.

To Find an Angle in Quadrant	In Degrees (reference angle of θ)	In Radians (reference angle of θ)
I	θ	θ
II	$180° - \theta$	$\pi - \theta$
III	$180° + \theta$	$\pi + \theta$
IV	$360° - \theta$	$2\pi - \theta$

Practice

In 1–6, solve for θ in the interval 0° ≤ θ ≤ 360°.

1. $2 \tan \theta - 3 = -5$

2. $4(\csc \theta + 2) = \csc \theta + 14$

3. $2 \sin \theta + 3 = 3(\sin \theta + 1)$

4. $2 \cos \theta + 5\sqrt{3} = 4\sqrt{3}$

5. $6\left(\cot \theta - \dfrac{\sqrt{3}}{2}\right) = 5 \cot \theta - 2\sqrt{3}$

6. $3 \sin \theta - 1 = 2$

In 7–12, solve for θ in the interval 0 ≤ θ ≤ 2π.

7. $3 \tan \theta - 4 = 4 \tan \theta - 5$

8. $3 \sec \theta = \dfrac{2}{3}(3 \sec \theta - 3)$

9. $2(\sin \theta + \sqrt{2}) = \sqrt{2}$

10. $6 \cos \theta + \sqrt{3} = -4(\cos \theta + \sqrt{3})$

11. $4 \csc \theta + 5 = 3 \csc \theta + 4$

12. $4 \cos \theta + 3 = 3$

In 13–17, solve for β to the nearest tenth of a degree in the interval $0° \leq β \leq 360°$.

13. $9 \sin β - 2 = 4 \sin β - 1$

14. $-2(\tan β - 4) = 3(4 - \tan β)$

15. $3 \sec β + 12 = \frac{3}{4}(8 \sec β - 4)$

16. $\frac{1}{2} \csc β + 1 = \frac{1}{4}(\csc β + 8)$

17. $2 \tan β - \sqrt{3} = 2\sqrt{3} - \tan β$

18. Find m∠B in the interval $180° \leq B \leq 270°$ that satisfies the equation $2 \tan B - 3 = 3 \tan B - 4$.

19. In the interval $90° \leq x \leq 180°$, find the value of x that satisfies the equation $3(\sin x - 2) = \sin x - 6$.

20. If $\frac{3π}{2} \leq θ \leq 2π$, solve for θ: $5 \cos θ = 3 \cos θ + \sqrt{2}$.

In 21–27, select the numeral preceding the word or expression that best completes the statement or answers the question.

21. If θ is a positive acute angle and $2 \tan θ = 7$, what is the value of θ to the nearest degree?

(1) $\frac{2}{7}$

(3) 45

(2) $\frac{7}{2}$

(4) 74

22. One root of the equation $3 \sin β - 4 = 5 \sin β - 3$ is

(1) $\frac{π}{6}$ (3) $\frac{7π}{6}$

(2) $\frac{π}{3}$ (4) $\frac{4π}{3}$

23. In which quadrants does the solution of the equation $5 \sin x - 3 = \sin x - 6$ lie?
(1) I and II   (3) III and IV
(2) II and III   (4) I and IV

24. Which of the following is the solution set of $3 \cos α - \sqrt{2} = \cos α - 2\sqrt{2}$ in the interval $0 \leq α \leq 2π$?

(1) $\left\{ \frac{π}{4} \right\}$ (3) $\left\{ \frac{3π}{4}, \frac{5π}{4} \right\}$

(2) $\left\{ \frac{π}{4}, \frac{3π}{4} \right\}$ (4) $\left\{ \frac{5π}{4}, \frac{7π}{4} \right\}$

25. Which of the following equations does *not* have a solution?
(1) $3 \cos θ - 2 = 1$ (3) $\tan θ - 4 = 5$
(2) $4 \sin θ + 1 = 1$ (4) $2 \sin θ + 4 = 1$

26. If x is an angle in Quadrant II, which of the following is the solution of the equation $2 \cos x - \sqrt{3} = 4 \cos x$?

(1) $\frac{π}{6}$ (3) $\frac{7π}{6}$

(2) $\frac{5π}{6}$ (4) $\frac{5π}{6}$ and $\frac{7π}{6}$

27. Which of the following equations does *not* have a solution?

(1) $3 \sec θ - 2 = 1$ (3) $5 \csc θ - 2 = 1$
(2) $4 \csc θ + 6 = 1$ (4) $2 \sec θ + 4 = 1$

15.5 Second-Degree Trigonometric Equations

Just as we can solve first-degree trigonometric equations, so too can we solve second-degree trigonometric equations. Let us first review how to solve second-degree algebraic equations.

Solve for x: $x^2 - x - 1 = 1$.

$x^2 - x - 2 = 0$ Set the equation = 0 and factor.

$(x + 1)(x - 2) = 0$ If the product of two numbers is 0, one of the numbers = 0.

$x + 1 = 0$ $x - 2 = 0$ Set each factor = 0 and solve.

$x = -1$ $x = 2$

Let us solve a similar second-degree trigonometric equation.

Solve for θ in the interval $0° \leq \theta \leq 360°$: $\sin^2 \theta - \sin \theta - 1 = 1$.

$\qquad \sin^2 \theta - \sin \theta - 2 = 0$ $\qquad$ Set the equation $= 0$ and factor.

$\qquad (\sin \theta + 1)(\sin \theta - 2) = 0$ $\qquad$ If the product of two numbers is 0, one of the numbers $= 0$.

$\quad \sin \theta + 1 = 0 \quad \sin \theta - 2 = 0$ $\qquad$ Set each factor $= 0$ and solve.

$\qquad \sin \theta = -1 \qquad \sin \theta = 2$ $\qquad$ We need to find an angle whose sine is -1 and an angle whose sine is 2. There is no angle whose sine is 2.

$\qquad \theta = 270° \quad$ reject $\qquad$ (The largest value in the range of $\sin \theta$ is 1.)

If a second-degree algebraic equation cannot be solved by factoring, we can use the quadratic formula as shown below.

Solve for x: $x^2 + 2 = 4x$.

$\qquad x^2 - 4x + 2 = 0$ $\qquad$ Set the equation $= 0$.

Since the equation cannot be factored, use the quadratic formula with $a = 1$, $b = -4$, and $c = 2$ and solve.

$$x = \frac{4 \pm \sqrt{(-4)^2 - 4(1)(2)}}{2}$$

$$x = \frac{4 \pm \sqrt{8}}{2}$$

$$x = \frac{4 \pm 2\sqrt{2}}{2}$$

$$x = 2 \pm \sqrt{2}$$

We follow the same procedure for second-degree trigonometric equations.

To the nearest degree, solve for θ in the interval $0° \leq \theta \leq 360°$: $\sin^2 \theta + 2 = 4 \sin \theta$.

$\qquad \sin^2 \theta - 4 \sin \theta + 2 = 0$ $\qquad$ Set the equation $= 0$.

Since the equation cannot be factored, use the quadratic formula with $a = 1$, $b = -4$, and $c = 2$ and solve.

$$\sin \theta = \frac{4 \pm \sqrt{(-4)^2 - 4(1)(2)}}{2}$$

$$\sin \theta = \frac{4 \pm \sqrt{8}}{2}$$

$$\sin \theta = \frac{4 \pm 2\sqrt{2}}{2}$$

$$\sin \theta = 2 \pm \sqrt{2}$$

$\sin \theta = 2 + \sqrt{2}$ and $\sin \theta = 2 - \sqrt{2}$ $\qquad$ Break into two separate equations.

$\sin \theta \approx 2 + 1.41421 \quad \sin \theta \approx 2 - 1.41421 \qquad$ Approximate $\sqrt{2}$.

$\sin \theta \approx 3.41421 \qquad \sin \theta \approx 0.58579$

reject $\qquad\qquad$ Reference angle $= 35.8588°$

$(-1 \leq \sin \theta \leq 1) \qquad$ Quadrant I: $36°$

$\qquad\qquad\qquad\qquad$ Quadrant II: $144°$ ($180° - 36°$)

1. Solve for θ in the interval $0° \leq \theta \leq 360°$: $\tan^2 \theta = -\tan \theta$.

SOLUTION

$$\tan^2 \theta = -\tan \theta$$

$$\tan^2 \theta + \tan \theta = 0 \qquad \text{Set the equation} = 0.$$

$$\tan \theta \,(\tan \theta + 1) = 0 \qquad \text{Factor.}$$

$$\tan \theta = 0 \qquad\qquad \tan \theta = -1 \qquad \text{Set each factor} = 0 \text{ and solve each individual equation.}$$

$\theta = 0°, 180°, 360°$ Reference angle $= 45°$

Quadrant II: $135°$ $(180° - 45°)$

Quadrant IV: $315°$ $(360° - 45°)$

2. Solve for α in the interval $0 \leq \alpha \leq 2\pi$: $2\cos^2 \alpha + \cos \alpha + 2 = 3$

SOLUTION

$$2\cos^2 \alpha + \cos \alpha + 2 = 3$$

$$2\cos^2 \alpha + \cos \alpha - 1 = 0$$

$$(2\cos \alpha - 1)(\cos \alpha + 1) = 0$$

$$2\cos \alpha - 1 = 0 \qquad \cos \alpha + 1 = 0$$

$$2\cos \alpha = 1 \qquad\qquad \cos \alpha = -1$$

$$\cos \alpha = \frac{1}{2} \qquad\qquad \alpha = \pi$$

Reference angle $= \dfrac{\pi}{3}$

Quadrant I: $\dfrac{\pi}{3}$

Quadrant IV: $\dfrac{5\pi}{3}$

3. Solve for β in the interval $0 \leq \beta \leq 2\pi$: $\csc^2 \beta - \csc \beta + 3 = 5$.

SOLUTION

$$\csc^2 \beta - \csc \beta + 3 = 5$$

$$\csc^2 \beta - \csc \beta - 2 = 0$$

$$(\csc \beta - 2)(\csc \beta + 1) = 0$$

$$\csc \beta - 2 = 0 \qquad \csc \beta + 1 = 0$$

$$\csc \beta = 2 \qquad\qquad \csc \beta = -1 \qquad \text{Convert to } \sin \beta.$$

$$\sin \beta = \frac{1}{2} \qquad\qquad \sin \beta = -1$$

Reference angle $= \dfrac{\pi}{6}$ $\beta = \dfrac{3\pi}{2}$

Quadrant I: $\dfrac{\pi}{6}$

Quadrant II: $\dfrac{5\pi}{6}$

4. To the nearest degree, solve for x in the interval $0° \leq x \leq 360°$: $\sin x - 3 = \dfrac{-1}{\sin x}$.

SOLUTION

$$\sin x - 3 = \dfrac{-1}{\sin x}$$

$$\sin^2 x - 3\sin x = -1 \qquad \text{Multiply both sides by } \sin x.$$

$$\sin^2 x - 3\sin x + 1 = 0$$

$$\sin x = \dfrac{3 \pm \sqrt{(-3)^2 - 4(1)(1)}}{2} \qquad \text{Use the quadratic formula.}$$

$$\sin x = \dfrac{3 \pm \sqrt{5}}{2}$$

$$\sin x = \dfrac{3 + \sqrt{5}}{2} \qquad\qquad \sin x = \dfrac{3 - \sqrt{5}}{2}$$

$\sin x \approx 2.618$ $\qquad\qquad$ $\sin x \approx 0.381966$

reject $\qquad\qquad\qquad$ Reference angle: $22°$

$(-1 \leq \sin x \leq 1)$ $\qquad$ Quadrant I: $22°$

$\qquad\qquad\qquad\qquad\qquad$ Quadrant II: $158°$

Practice

In 1–5, solve for θ in the interval $0° \leq \theta \leq 360°$.

1. $3\tan^2 \theta - 2 = 1$

2. $5\cos^2 \theta - 1 = 3(1 - \cos^2 \theta)$

3. $\sin^2 \theta - 2\sin \theta = 3$

4. $\csc^2 \theta - 1 = 3$

5. $2\cos^2 \theta = \cos \theta$

In 6–10, solve for θ in the interval $0 \leq \theta \leq 2\pi$.

6. $2\cos^2 \theta = \cos \theta + 1$

7. $\tan \theta (\tan \theta + 1) = \tan \theta + 3$

8. $2\sec^2 \theta = 3\sec \theta + 2$

9. $\cos \theta = \dfrac{1}{\cos \theta}$

10. $\sin \theta = \sqrt{\sin \theta}$

In 11–16, solve for β to the nearest tenth of a degree in the interval $0° \leq \beta \leq 360°$.

11. $5\tan^2 \beta + 3\tan \beta = 2$

12. $\sec^2 \beta = 6\sec \beta + 7$

13. $3\sin^2 \beta + \sin \beta + 5 = 4(1 - \sin \beta)$

14. $6\cos^2 \beta + 6\cos \beta + 2 = 1 + \cos \beta$

15. $3(1 - \sin^2 \beta) = \sin \beta$

16. $3\tan^2 \beta - 5\tan \beta = 2$

17. Find $m\angle B$ in the interval $180° \leq B \leq 270°$ that satisfies the equation $2\sin^2 B = 6\sin B$.

18. In the interval $90° \leq x \leq 180°$, find the value of x that satisfies the equation $2\cos^2 x = 1$.

19. If $\dfrac{3\pi}{2} \leq \theta \leq 2\pi$, solve for θ: $3\tan^2 \theta + 2 = 3$.

In 20–25, select the numeral preceding the word or expression that best completes the statement or answers the question.

20. What is the total number of solutions for the equation $3\sin^2 x + \sin x = 2$ in the interval $0° \leq x < 360°$?
(1) 1 $\qquad\qquad\qquad$ (3) 3
(2) 2 $\qquad\qquad\qquad$ (4) 4

21. The number of degrees in the smallest positive angle that satisfies the equation $2\cos^2 x - 3\cos x = 2$ is
(1) 30 $\qquad\qquad\qquad$ (3) 120
(2) 60 $\qquad\qquad\qquad$ (4) 210

22. Which of the following is *not* a solution of the equation $\tan^2 \beta = 3$?

(1) $-\dfrac{\pi}{3}$

(2) $\dfrac{2\pi}{3}$

(3) $\dfrac{5\pi}{6}$

(4) $120°$

23. Which of the following equations has roots of 0 and π?

(1) $\sin^2 x - 1 = 0$ (3) $\cos^2 x + \cos x = 0$
(2) $\cos^2 x - 1 = 0$ (4) $\cos^2 x + \cos x = 2$

24. Which of the following third-quadrant angles satisfies the equation $2\cos^2 x - \cos x = 1$?

(1) 0

(2) $\dfrac{2\pi}{3}$

(3) $\dfrac{7\pi}{6}$

(4) $\dfrac{4\pi}{3}$

25. How many solutions does the equation $5\sin^2 x = 1 - 9\sin x$ have in the interval $0 \le x \le 2\pi$?

(1) 1   (3) 3
(2) 2   (4) 4

15.6 Trigonometric Equations with Different Functions or Angle Measures

Sometimes you will see a trigonometric equation with different functions or different angle measures. To solve this type of equation, use one of the trigonometric identities to convert the equation into one that you can solve.

 MODEL PROBLEMS

---

1. Solve for θ in the interval $0 \le \theta \le 360°$: $\cos^2 \theta + 2\sin \theta = 1$.

SOLUTION

$\cos^2 \theta + 2\sin \theta = 1$	Since $\sin^2 \theta + \cos^2 \theta = 1$, $\cos^2 \theta = 1 - \sin^2 \theta$.
$1 - \sin^2 \theta + 2\sin \theta = 1$	Substitute for $\cos^2 \theta$ in the equation.
$-\sin^2 \theta + 2\sin \theta = 0$	Solve the quadratic equation.
$\sin \theta(-\sin \theta + 2) = 0$	

$\sin \theta = 0 \qquad\qquad -\sin \theta + 2 = 0$

$\theta = 0°, 180°, 360° \qquad \sin \theta = -2$

$\qquad\qquad\qquad\qquad\qquad$ reject

2. Solve for θ in the interval $0 \le \theta \le 2\pi$: $2\cos \theta = \sin 2\theta$.

SOLUTION

$2\cos \theta = \sin 2\theta$	
$2\cos \theta = 2\sin \theta \cos \theta$	Use $\sin 2\theta = 2\sin \theta \cos \theta$.
$2\cos \theta - 2\sin \theta \cos \theta = 0$	Set the equation equal to 0.
$2\cos \theta (1 - \sin \theta) = 0$	Factor out $2\cos \theta$.
$2\cos \theta = 0 \qquad 1 - \sin \theta = 0$	Set each factor equal to 0 and solve.

$\cos \theta = 0 \qquad\qquad \sin \theta = 1$

$\theta = \dfrac{\pi}{2}, \dfrac{3\pi}{2} \qquad\qquad \theta = \dfrac{\pi}{2}$

Answer: $\dfrac{\pi}{2}, \dfrac{3\pi}{2}$

Note: After substituting $2\sin \theta \cos \theta$ for 2θ, the equation above contains two functions, sine and cosine. These can be separated by factoring.

3. Solve for θ, to the nearest tenth of a degree, in the interval $0 \le \theta \le 360°$: $\cos 2\theta + 3 \sin \theta = 0$.

SOLUTION

$\cos 2\theta + 3 \sin \theta = 0$ Since our equation contains $\sin \theta$, use the formula for $\cos 2\theta$ that contains $\sin \theta$: $\cos 2\theta = 1 - 2 \sin^2 \theta$.

$1 - 2 \sin^2 \theta + 3 \sin \theta = 0$ Write the equation in the form $ax^2 + bx + c = 0$.

$2 \sin^2 \theta - 3 \sin \theta - 1 = 0$ Use the quadratic formula to solve for $\sin \theta$.

$$\sin \theta = \frac{3 \pm \sqrt{9 - 4(2)(-1)}}{2(2)}$$

$$\sin \theta = \frac{3 \pm \sqrt{17}}{4}$$

$\sin \theta = \dfrac{3 + \sqrt{17}}{4}$ $\sin \theta = \dfrac{3 - \sqrt{17}}{4}$

$\sin \theta \approx 1.780776$ $\sin \theta \approx -0.280776$

reject   Reference angle: $16.30655°$

                         Quadrant III: $180° + 16.3° = 196.3°$

                         Quadrant IV: $360° - 16.3° = 343.7°$

Answer: $196.3°$ and $343.7°$

4. Solve for θ in the interval $0 \le \theta \le 2\pi$: $\sin \frac{1}{2}\theta = \sin \theta$.

SOLUTION

$$\sin \frac{1}{2}\theta = \sin \theta$$

$\sqrt{\dfrac{1 - \cos \theta}{2}} = \sin \theta$ Use the half angle formula for sine.

$\dfrac{1 - \cos \theta}{2} = \sin^2 \theta$ Square both sides of the equation.

$\dfrac{1 - \cos \theta}{2} = 1 - \cos^2 \theta$ Replace $\sin^2$ with $1 - \cos^2 \theta$.

$1 - \cos \theta = 2 - 2\cos^2 \theta$ Multiply both sides of the equation by 2.

$2\cos^2 \theta - \cos \theta - 1 = 0$ Set the equation equal to 0.

$(2 \cos \theta + 1)(\cos \theta - 1) = 0$ Factor.

$2 \cos \theta + 1 = 0$ $\cos \theta - 1 = 0$ Set each factor equal to 0 and solve.

     $\cos \theta = -0.5$ $\cos \theta = 1$

       $\theta = \dfrac{2\pi}{3}, \dfrac{4\pi}{3}$ $\theta = 0, 2\pi$

Because we had a radical equation and squared both sides of the equation, we must check our solutions.

Check: $\sin \frac{1}{2}\theta = \sin \theta$

$\theta = \dfrac{2\pi}{3}$	$\theta = \dfrac{4\pi}{3}$	$\theta = 0$	$\theta = 2\pi$
$\sin \frac{1}{2}\left(\dfrac{2\pi}{3}\right) \overset{?}{=} \sin \dfrac{2\pi}{3}$	$\sin \frac{1}{2}\left(\dfrac{4\pi}{3}\right) \overset{?}{=} \sin \dfrac{4\pi}{3}$	$\sin \frac{1}{2}(0) \overset{?}{=} \sin 0$	$\sin \frac{1}{2}(2\pi) \overset{?}{=} \sin (2\pi)$
$\sin \dfrac{\pi}{3} \overset{?}{=} \sin \dfrac{2\pi}{3}$	$\sin \dfrac{2\pi}{3} \overset{?}{=} \sin \dfrac{4\pi}{3}$	$\sin 0 \overset{?}{=} \sin 0$	$\sin \pi \overset{?}{=} \sin 2\pi$
$\dfrac{\sqrt{3}}{2} = \dfrac{\sqrt{3}}{2}$ ✓	$\dfrac{\sqrt{3}}{2} \ne \dfrac{-\sqrt{3}}{2}$	$0 = 0$ ✓	$0 = 0$ ✓

Since only three of our answers check, our solution is: $0, \dfrac{2\pi}{3}, 2\pi$.

In 1–5, solve for θ in the interval 0° ≤ θ ≤ 360°.

1. $\sin 2\theta = 0$

2. $\cos 2\theta = \cos \theta$

3. $2\cos^2 \theta + \sin \theta = 1$

4. $\sin \frac{1}{2}\theta = 1$

5. $\sin 2\theta + \cos \theta = 0$

In 6–10, solve for α in the interval 0 ≤ α ≤ 2π.

6. $\sin 2\alpha = -\sin \alpha$

7. $\cos 2\alpha + \cos \alpha = 0$

8. $\sin^2 \theta + \cos^2 \theta = \cos \theta$

9. $\cos \frac{1}{2}\theta = \cos \theta$

10. $\tan \theta = 2\sin \theta$

In 11–15, find, to the nearest tenth of a degree, all values of θ in the interval 0° ≤ θ ≤ 360° that satisfy the equation.

11. $3\cos^2 \theta - \sin \theta = 2$

12. $\tan \theta = \cos \theta$

13. $3\cos 2\theta + 2\cos \theta = 0$

14. $\cos 2\theta - \sin^2 \theta + \sin \theta + 1 = 0$

15. $\sin \frac{1}{2}\theta = \cos \theta + 1$

16. a. On the same set of axes, sketch and label the graphs of $y = 2\sin x$ and $y = \cos 2x$ for values of x in the interval $0 \le x \le 2\pi$.

   b. Based on the graphs drawn in part **a**, what value(s) of x in the interval $0 \le x \le 2\pi$ satisfy the equation $2\sin x - \cos 2x = 3$?

   c. Using algebraic techniques, solve the equation $2\sin x - \cos 2x = 3$.

17. a. On the same set of axes, sketch and label the graphs of $y = -\sin x$ and $y = 2\cos \frac{1}{2}x$ for values of x in the interval $0 \le x \le 2\pi$.

   b. Based on the graphs drawn in part **a**, find all values of x in the interval $0 \le x \le 2\pi$ that satisfy the equation $2\cos \frac{1}{2}x = -\sin x$.

   c. Using algebraic techniques, solve the equation $2\cos \frac{1}{2}x = -\sin x$.

18. a. On the same set of axes, sketch and label the graphs of $y = -\cos x$ and $y = \sin 2x$ for values of x in the interval $0 \le x \le 2\pi$.

   b. Based on the graphs drawn in part **a**, what value(s) of x in the interval $0 \le x \le 2\pi$ satisfy the equation $-\cos x = \sin 2x$? Why is it difficult to get an exact value for some of the solutions using the graph?

   c. Using algebraic techniques, solve the equation $-\cos x = \sin 2x$.

19. a. On the same set of axes, sketch and label the graphs of $y = -\cos x$ and $y = \sin \frac{1}{2}x$ for values of x in the interval $0 \le x \le 2\pi$.

   b. Based on the graphs drawn in part **a**, what value of x in the interval $0 \le x \le 2\pi$ satisfies the equation $-\cos x = \sin \frac{1}{2}x$?

   c. Using algebraic techniques, solve the equation $-\cos x = \sin \frac{1}{2}x$.

In 20–23, select the numeral preceding the expression that best completes the statement or answers the question.

20. What is the total number of solutions for the equation $5\sin^2 \theta = 7\cos \theta - 1$ in the interval $0 \le \theta \le 360°$?

   (1) 1   (3) 3

   (2) 2   (4) 4

21. Which of the following is *not* a solution of the equation $\sin 2\theta = \cos \theta$?

   (1) $\frac{\pi}{6}$ (3) $\frac{5\pi}{6}$

   (2) $\frac{\pi}{2}$ (4) π

22. The number of degrees in the smallest positive angle that satisfies the equation $3\cos 2x + 2\sin x + 1 = 0$ is

   (1) 1   (3) 90

   (2) 42   (4) 138

23. What is the total number of solutions of the equation $\frac{\sin 2\theta}{\sin \theta} = \sec \theta$ in the interval $0 \le \theta \le 2\pi$?

   (1) 1   (3) 3

   (2) 2   (4) 4

In 1–15, select the numeral preceding the word or expression that best completes the statement or answers the question.

1. The value of $\cos 64° \cos 26° - \sin 64° \sin 26°$ is
   (1) 1
   (2) 0
   (3) $\frac{1}{2}$
   (4) 0.7880

2. The expression $\cos(\pi - x)$ is equivalent to
   (1) $\cos x$
   (2) $\sin x$
   (3) $-\sin x$
   (4) $-\cos x$

3. The expression $\frac{\cos^2 \theta}{\sin \theta} + \sin \theta$ is equivalent to
   (1) $1 + \cos^2 \theta$
   (2) $\cos^2 \theta$
   (3) $\frac{1}{\csc \theta}$
   (4) $\frac{1}{\sin \theta}$

4. If θ is an acute angle and $\sin \theta = \frac{1}{2}$, the value of $\cos\left(\frac{\pi}{2} + \theta\right)$ is
   (1) $\frac{\sqrt{3}}{2}$
   (2) $\frac{1}{2}$
   (3) $-\frac{1}{2}$
   (4) $-\frac{\sqrt{3}}{2}$

5. The expression $\sin 37° \cos 83° + \cos 37° \sin 83°$ can also be written as
   (1) $\cos 120°$
   (2) $\sin 120°$
   (3) $\cos 46°$
   (4) $\sin 46°$

6. If $\tan x = -\frac{1}{4}$ and $\tan y = 2$, the value of $\tan(x + y)$ is
   (1) $\frac{7}{6}$
   (2) $\frac{9}{6}$
   (3) $\frac{7}{2}$
   (4) $\frac{9}{2}$

7. The expression $4 + \cos^2 A$ is equivalent to
   (1) $5 - \sec^2 A$
   (2) $5 - \sin^2 A$
   (3) $5 + \sin^2 A$
   (4) $\frac{5}{\sec^2 A}$

8. Which of the following is a valid identity?
   (1) $\sin^2 4x + \cos^2 4x = 1$
   (2) $\sin 4x = 4 \sin x \cos x$
   (3) $\sin^4 x + \cos^4 x = 4$
   (4) $\cos^4 x = 1 - \sin^4 x$

9. What value of x in the interval $90° \le x \le 180°$ satisfies the equation $\sin^2 x + \sin x = 0$?
   (1) 90°
   (2) 120°
   (3) 135°
   (4) 180°

10. The equation $\sqrt{4 \sin \theta + 7} = 3$ has which of the following as a possible solution?
    (1) $\frac{\pi}{2}$
    (2) $\frac{\pi}{3}$
    (3) $\frac{\pi}{4}$
    (4) $\frac{\pi}{6}$

11. The equation $\sin^2 \theta - 2 \sin \theta + 1 = 0$ has how many different solutions for θ in the interval $0 \le \theta \le 2\pi$?
    (1) 1
    (2) 2
    (3) 3
    (4) 0

12. If $\cos \theta = c$, then $\sin^2 \frac{\theta}{2}$ equals
    (1) $\frac{1 - c}{2}$
    (2) $\frac{1 + c}{2}$
    (3) $\frac{1 - c}{c + c}$
    (4) $\frac{1 - c}{4}$

13. If $f(x) = 2 \sin x - \cos 2x$, the exact value of $f\left(\frac{\pi}{2}\right)$ is
    (1) 1
    (2) 2
    (3) 3
    (4) 0

14. In the interval $0° \le x < 360°$, how many values of x satisfy the equation $\cos^2 x - 5 \cos x - 6 = 0$?
    (1) 1
    (2) 2
    (3) 3
    (4) 0

15. Which of the following is *not* a solution to the equation $2 \cos \theta - 1 = \sec \theta$?
    (1) 0°
    (2) 120°
    (3) 180°
    (4) 240°

In 16–21, demonstrate that each identity is true.

16. $\cos 2\theta (1 + \tan^2 \theta) = 2 - \frac{1}{\cos^2 \theta}$

17. $\frac{\sin 2\theta}{1 + \cos 2\theta} = \tan \theta$

18. $\cot \theta = \frac{\sin 2\theta}{2 \sin^2 \theta}$

19. $\frac{1 + \cos \theta + \cos 2\theta}{\sin \theta + \sin 2\theta} = \cot \theta$

20. $\dfrac{2 \sin \beta}{\sin 2\beta \cos \beta} = \sec^2 \beta$

21. $\sec x - \sin x \tan x = \cos x$

In 22–30, solve each equation for all values of θ, to the nearest tenth of a degree, in the interval $0° \leq \theta < 360°$.

22. $\dfrac{2}{\cos \theta} = 5 \cos \theta + 3$

23. $3 \sin^2 \theta + 2 = 7 \sin \theta$ (19.5°

24. $2 \sin^2 \theta + 5 \cos \theta = 4$

25. $3 \sec^2 \theta - 5 \tan \theta = 1$ 0 & 59

26. $3 \tan \theta - 2 \cot \theta = 3$

27. $3 \cos^2 \theta - 5 = 5 \sin \theta$

28. $2 \cos \theta - 3 = 5 \sec \theta$

29. $2 \cos 2\theta + 1 = \sin \theta$ 48.6 & 90

30. $3 \cos 2\theta = 2 - \sin \theta$

FYI

We can use the graphing capabilities of the calculator to verify trigonometric identities. Let us use the identity $\sin^2 \theta + \cos^2 \theta = 1$. In your calculator, enter the left side of the equation into Y_1 and the right side of the equation into Y_2 as shown below. Be sure to select the "path" option in your Y_2 so that you can see both graphs.

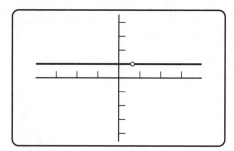

Plot1 Plot2 Plot3
\Y_1 = (sin (X))² + (cos (X))²
−oY_2 = 1
\Y_3 =
\Y_4 =
\Y_5 =
\Y_6 =

Graph the two equations. You will see that the second equation is identical to the first, as shown below.

Although this does not prove the identity, it is a graphical illustration of the identity. Be aware that, if two graphs appear identical, it does not guarantee that they are identical; an algebraic proof is still needed. However, the graphing calculator does provide a valuable illustration of identities.

Let us consider another expression.

$$\frac{\cos \theta + 1}{1 + \sec \theta} = \cos \theta$$

There is no button on your calculator for secant θ, so you have to enter secant θ as $\dfrac{1}{\cos \theta}$.

Remember: Be careful to use parentheses where needed.

Enter the left side of the equation into Y_1 as follows:

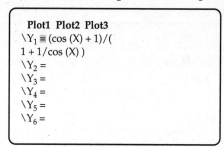

Plot1 Plot2 Plot3
\Y_1 = (cos (X) + 1)/(1 + 1/cos (X))
\Y_2 =
\Y_3 =
\Y_4 =
\Y_5 =
\Y_6 =

To obtain an appropriate viewing window, press [ZOOM] [7].

Enter $\cos \theta$ into Y_2, selecting the "path" option. When you graph the two functions you can see that they are identical.

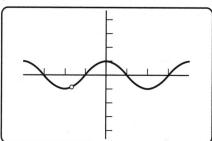

Try entering some of the other identities from section 15.1 to illustrate that they are identities.

Calculators can also be used to illustrate identities numerically. Look at the expression sin 12° cos 38° + cos 12° sin 38°. You may recognize this as the formula for sin $(A + B)$. We know that sin $(A + B)$ = sin A cos B + cos A sin B. By letting A = 12 and B = 38, we can see that the expression sin 12° cos 38° + cos 12° sin 38° is equivalent to sin $(12° + 38°)$ = sin 50°. Verify this with your calculator. Make sure that your calculator is set in degree mode, and type in sin 12 cos 38 + cos 12 sin 38. Now, type in sin 50. You can see that both expressions have a value of 0.7660444431.

Calculators are also useful for solving trigonometric equations. However, the calculator will only give approximate values. Let us revisit problem 11 from section 15.5: $5 \tan^2 \beta + 3 \tan \beta = 2$. To solve this equation using the calculator, type the left side of the equation into Y_1 and the right side of the equation into Y_2 as shown.

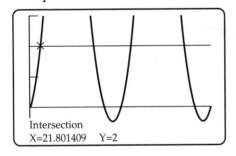

Make sure that your calculator is in degree mode. Set your window to $[0, 360] \times [-1, 3]$ and graph the two equations. Now, see where the two graphs intersect. The figure below shows the first intersection point.

The four solutions of the equation in the interval are 21.8°, 135°, 201.8°, 315°.

The calculator can also be used to solve equations containing two different functions. Problem 15 from section 15.6 asks us to solve for θ: $\sin \frac{1}{2} \theta = \cos \theta + 1$. Input the left side of the equation into Y_1 and the right side into Y_2. The figure below shows the resulting (Y =) screen.

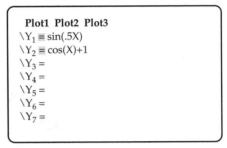

Graph the two equations in the window $[0, 360] \times [-2, 2]$ and find their points of intersection. The figure below shows one of the intersection points.

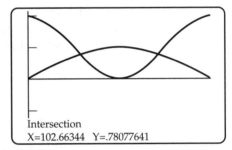

The two solutions in the interval $0° \le \theta \le 360°$ are θ = 102.7° and θ = 257.3°.

CHAPTER 16

The Binomial Theorem and Probability

16.1 Binomial Expansion

From earlier work in algebra, you are familiar with the term **binomial**, an expression consisting of two terms, such as $x + y$, $2p + 5$, or $a^2 - 1$. These are binomials because they all show two monomial terms being combined by addition or subtraction. **Binomial expansion** is taking that two-term expression and raising it to successive powers, as shown below.

$(a + b)^0 = \qquad\qquad\qquad 1$

$(a + b)^1 = \qquad\qquad\qquad 1a + 1b$

$(a + b)^2 = \qquad\qquad\qquad 1a^2 + 2ab + 1b^2$

$(a + b)^3 = \qquad\qquad\qquad 1a^3 + 3a^2b^1 + 3a^1b^2 + 1b^3$

$(a + b)^4 = \qquad\qquad\qquad 1a^4 + 4a^3b^1 + 6a^2b^2 + 4a^1b^3 + 1b^4$

$(a + b)^5 = \qquad\qquad 1a^5 + 5a^4b^1 + 10a^3b^2 + 10a^2b^3 + 5a^1b^4 + 1b^5$

Look at the coefficients of each term in the expansion above and see if you notice a pattern.

$$
\begin{array}{ccccccccccc}
 & & & & & 1 & & & & & \\
 & & & & 1 & & 1 & & & & \\
 & & & 1 & & 2 & & 1 & & & \\
 & & 1 & & 3 & & 3 & & 1 & & \\
 & 1 & & 4 & & 6 & & 4 & & 1 & \\
1 & & 5 & & 10 & & 10 & & 5 & & 1
\end{array}
$$

This arrangement of numbers is known as **Pascal's triangle** after the French mathematician and physicist Blaise Pascal who expanded the triangle in 1653, based on earlier versions developed by the Chinese. Among its interesting characteristics are

- Every outer number on the left and right will always be 1.
- The triangle has a vertical axis of symmetry which can be drawn downward through the initial one.
- Each number not on the outer edge is the sum of the two numbers immediately above it.
- The second number in each row indicates the power of the expansion being performed.

Using these facts, you can write the coefficients in the next two rows:

$$\begin{array}{ccccccccc} 1 & & 6 & & 15 & & 20 & & 15 & & 6 & & 1 \\ & 1 & & 7 & & 21 & & 35 & & 35 & & 21 & & 7 & & 1 \end{array}$$

Pascal's triangle is based on the concept of combinations that you studied in Math A. Pascal's triangle can also be written as:

$$\begin{array}{c} {}_0C_0 \\ {}_1C_0 \quad {}_1C_1 \\ {}_2C_0 \quad {}_2C_1 \quad {}_2C_2 \\ {}_3C_0 \quad {}_3C_1 \quad {}_3C_2 \quad {}_3C_3 \\ {}_4C_0 \quad {}_4C_1 \quad {}_4C_2 \quad {}_4C_3 \quad {}_4C_4 \\ {}_5C_0 \quad {}_5C_1 \quad {}_5C_2 \quad {}_5C_3 \quad {}_5C_4 \quad {}_5C_5 \end{array}$$

Each row represents the combinations of n things taken r at a time where n is the number of the row. The leftmost term in each row is $_nC_0$ while the rightmost term must be $_nC_r$. Since we know from our earlier studies of probability in Math A that $_nC_r = _cN_{n-r}$ the triangle must be symmetric over its axis of symmetry.

Note: To find the value of $_nC_r$ on the TI-83, enter the n value on your home screen. Then go to the Math window and right or left arrow over to the Probability option (PRB). Scroll down to choice 3 (or enter 3) on your keypad. The calculator will display the $_nC_r$ on the home screen to the right of your value for n. Type your value for r and hit (ENTER).

In the binomial expansion of $(a + b)^n$ the exponents of the variables change with each successive term; in the first term the exponent of a is n and the exponent of b is zero (not usually written). In successive terms, the exponent of a decreases by 1 and the exponent of b increases by 1. The sum of the exponents in each term is n. Hence, the formula for a binomial expansion can be written as:

$$(a + b)^n = {}_nC_0a^nb^0 + {}_nC_1a^{n-1}b^1 + {}_nC_2a^{n-2}b^2 + {}_nC_3a^{n-3}b^3 + {}_nC_4a^{n-4}b^4 \ldots {}_nC_na^0b^n.$$

Note: The number of terms in the complete expansion is $n + 1$. The formula above is known as the Binomial Theorem.

1. Expand $(m + 2)^3$.

SOLUTION

$$(m + 2)^3 = {}_3C_0 m^3 2^0 + {}_3C_1 m^2 2^1 + {}_3C_2 m^1 2^2 + {}_3C_3 m^0 2^3$$
$$= 1m^3(1) + 3m^2(2) + 3m^1(4) + 1(1)(8)$$
$$= m^3 + 6m^2 + 12m + 8$$

Note: After simplifying the expression, the coefficients from Pascal's triangle disappear when they are multiplied by the other terms.

2. Expand $(a - 3)^4$.

SOLUTION

In this case, the second term is negative so you must be certain to keep track of that negative value as you set up the expansion. For that reason, it is best to write the second term in its own parenthesis.

$$(a - 3)^4 = {}_4C_0 a^4(-3)^0 + {}_4C_1 a^3(-3)^1 + {}_4C_2 a^2(-3)^2 + {}_4C_3 a^1(-3)^3 + {}_4C_4 a^0(-3)^4$$
$$= 1a^4(1) + 4a^3(-3) + 6a^2(9) + 4a^1(-27) + 1(1)(81)$$
$$= a^4 - 12a^3 + 54a^2 - 108a + 81$$

3. Expand $(2x + 3y)^5$.

SOLUTION

In this example, you must take into account the coefficients of both the first and second monomial terms when raising them to the appropriate powers.

$$(2x + 3y)^5 = {}_5C_0(2x)^5(3y)^0 + {}_5C_1(2x)^4(3y)^1 + {}_5C_2(2x)^3(3y)^2 + {}_5C_3(2x)^2(3y)^3 + {}_5C_4(2x)^1(3y)^4 +$$
$${}_5C_5(2x)^0(3y)^5$$
$$= 1(32x^5)(1) + 5(16x^4)(3y) + 10(8x^3)(9y^2) + 10(4x^2)(27y^3) + 5(2x)(81y^4) + 1(1)(243y^5)$$
$$= 32x^5 + 240x^4y + 720x^3y^2 + 1{,}080x^2y^3 + 810xy^4 + 243y^5$$

4. Write the binomial expansion of $(3 - 5i)^3$. Then simplify to a binomial expression.

SOLUTION

First do the binomial expansion and then replace the various exponential i terms with their equivalents.

$$(3 - 5i)^3 = {}_3C_0 \, 3^3(-5i)^0 + {}_3C_1 3^2(-5i)^1 + {}_3C_2 3^1(-5i)^2 + {}_3C_3 3^0(-5i)^3$$
$$= 1(27)(1) + 3(9)(-5i) + 3(3)(25i^2) + 1(1)(-125i^3)$$
$$= 27 - 135i + 225i^2 - 125i^3$$
$$= -198 - 10i$$

Sometimes you are asked for only one term of a binomial expansion. Certainly, you can expand the entire expression and select the particular term, but there is a formula to help you find the needed term.

rth term of $(a + b)^n = {}_nC_{r-1}(a)^{n-(r-1)}(b)^{r-1}$

Remember: a and b can represent any monomials such as $2x$ or $-3k$.

1. Find the fourth term of the expansion $(3x + 2)^5$.

SOLUTION
Always make yourself a list of the values of the monomials that a and b represent, n, r, and $r-1$ before substituting into the formula. $a = 3x$, $b = 2$, $n = 5$, $r = 4$, and $r - 1 = 3$. Therefore the formula becomes $_5C_3(3x)^2(2)^3 = 10(9x^2)(8) = 720x^2$.

2. Find the middle term of the expansion $(2m - 5)^6$.

SOLUTION
A binomial expansion always has one more term than its highest exponent does. In this case, the expansion of $(2m - 5)^6$ has seven terms, so the fourth term is the desired middle term.
$a = 2m$, $b = -5$, $n = 6$, $r = 4$, and $r - 1 = 3$
$_6C_3(2m)^3(-5)^3 = 20(8m^3)(-125)$
$\qquad\qquad\qquad\quad = -20{,}000m^3$

 Practice

In 1–6, use the binomial theorem to write the binomial expansion for each expression. Simplify if possible.

1. $(z + 5)^3$

2. $(a - 3b)^4$

3. $(4p + 2)^5$

4. $(1 - 2i)^5$

5. $(6x - 1)^4$

6. $\left(\frac{1}{2}z + 4\right)^6$

In 7–10, find the third term of the expansion of each expression.

7. $(4 - 2i)^7$

8. $(3x + 2y)^6$

9. $(3 + \sqrt{2})^5$

10. $(7d - 2c)^4$

In 11–20, select the numeral preceding the word or expression that best completes the sentence or answers the question.

11. The third term of the expansion $(1 + \pi)^5$ is
(1) $10\pi^2$ (3) $15\pi^3$
(2) $15\pi^2$ (4) $20\pi^3$

12. The fourth term in the expansion of $(2 - \sin x)^4$ is
(1) $-4\sin^3 x$ (3) $-8\sin^3 x$
(2) $4\sin^3 x$ (4) $8\sin^3 x$

13. The third term of the expansion $(2 - 3i)^5$ is
(1) $720i$ (3) $-1{,}080i$
(2) -720 (4) $-1{,}080$

14. The last term of the expansion $(3x - 2)^8$ is
(1) -512 (3) 256
(2) -256 (4) 512

15. The middle term of the expansion $(2\tan\theta - 3)^4$ is
(1) $216\tan^2\theta$ (3) $-72\tan^2\theta$
(2) $72\tan^2\theta$ (4) $-216\tan^2\theta$

16. The fifth term of $(1 + i)^7$ is
(1) -35 (3) 21
(2) -21 (4) 35

17. The coefficient of the sixth term of $(4x + 3)^8$ can be found by which formula?
(1) $_8C_6(4x)^2(3)^6$ (3) $_8C_5(4x)^5(3)^3$
(2) $_8C_6(4x)^6(3)^2$ (4) $_8C_5(4x)^3(3)^5$

18. What is the numerical coefficient of the third term of the expansion $(1 - 2y)^7$?
(1) -672 (3) 84
(2) -280 (4) 560

19. $_{10}C_5(3a)^5(4)^5$ is a formula to find which term of the expansion $(3a + 4)^{10}$?
(1) the last term   (3) the middle term
(2) the tenth term   (4) the fifth term

20. When writing out the expansion of $(1 - 2i)^6$, the fourth term is
(1) $-160i$ (3) $160i$
(2) -160 (4) 160

16.2 Probability of Exactly *r* Successes in *n* Trials

If a fair coin is tossed 4 times, what is the probability of obtaining exactly 3 heads? To analyze the problem, list the 16 possible outcomes for the 4 coin tosses.

T T T T	*T T H H*	*H H H H*	*H H T T*
T T T H	*T H H T*	*H H H T*	*H T T H*
T T H T	*T H T H*	*H H T H*	*H T H T*
T H T T	*T H H H*	*H T H H*	*H T T T*

The list above shows the following information:

- The probability of getting 0 heads $= \dfrac{1}{16}$.   (*T T T T*)

- The probability of getting exactly 1 head $= \dfrac{4}{16}$.   (*T T T H*), (*T T H T*), (*T H T T*), (*H T T T*)

- The probability of getting exactly 2 heads $= \dfrac{6}{16}$.   (*T T H H*), (*T H H T*), (*T H T H*), (*H H T T*), (*H T T H*), (*H T H T*)

- The probability of getting exactly 3 heads $= \dfrac{4}{16}$.   (*T H H H*), (*H H H T*), (*H H T H*), (*H T H H*)

- The probability of getting 4 heads $= \dfrac{1}{16}$.   (*H H H H*)

Thus, the probability of getting exactly 3 heads is $\dfrac{4}{16} = \dfrac{1}{4}$.

It seems unreasonable to always have to create a list of all of the possibilities to determine the probability of success. Note that the list was created by taking the two possible outcomes, tails and heads, and listing all of the possibilities for $(T + H)$ for 4 tosses of the coins, or $(T + H)^4$. These terms can be found using the binomial expansion from Section 16.1. The binomial expansion of $(T + H)^4$ is:

$$_4C_0T^4H^0 + {}_4C_1T^3H^1 + {}_4C_2T^2H^2 + {}_4C_3T^1H^3 + {}_4C_4T^0H^4$$

Substituting the value for each combination gives

$$T^4 + 4T^3H + 6T^2H^2 + 4TH^3 + H^4$$

To obtain the probability of getting exactly 3 heads, look for 3 heads in the list of possibilities, that is, $4TH^3$. Since the probability of obtaining a tail on any one toss of a fair coin is $\dfrac{1}{2}$ and the probability of obtaining a head on any one toss of a fair coin is $\dfrac{1}{2}$, the final step is to substitute that information in the term $4TH^3$.

$$4TH^3 = 4\left(\dfrac{1}{2}\right)\left(\dfrac{1}{2}\right)^3 = \dfrac{4}{16} = \dfrac{1}{4}$$

This is the same answer we obtained by listing all of the possibilities.

What if you were on a ski vacation and heard that there was a 25 percent chance of snow for each of the next 3 days? What is the probability of it snowing on exactly 2 of those 3 days? Again, there are two possibilities, either it snows or it does not snow. Let F represent failure of snow and S represent success of snow.

$$(F + S)^3 = {}_3C_0F^3S^0 + {}_3C_1F^2S^1 + {}_3C_2F^1S^2 + {}_3C_3F^0S^3$$

The term that shows snow on exactly 2 of those days is ${}_3C_2F^1S^2$. The probability of snow on any one day is 25% or $\frac{1}{4}$, so the probability of it not snowing on a day is $1 - \frac{1}{4}$ or $\frac{3}{4}$. Thus, ${}_3C_2F^1S^2 = 3\left(\frac{3}{4}\right)\left(\frac{1}{4}\right)^2 = \frac{9}{64}$.

Probability problems that can be solved using binomial expansion are known as **binomial** or **Bernoulli experiments.** A binomial experiment must meet these conditions:

- There are exactly two possible outcomes for any trial, with one outcome considered success (S) and the other failure (F).
- There is a fixed number of trials, n.
- The trials are independent.
- The probability of each outcome is the same for each trial. If the probability of success is p, then the probability of failure, called q, is $1 - p$.

Sometimes, a situation must be reinterpreted to suit the binomial conditions. For example, getting a sum of 9 on a pair of dice can be defined as the successful outcome and all other sums as failures.

It is not necessary to write out the entire expansion each time that information about one term is needed. The probability of obtaining exactly r successes in n trials is:

$${}_nC_r(\text{failure})^{n-r}(\text{success})^r$$

Remember: In the given formula, "failure" and "success" are in alphabetical order to make it easier to remember. This corresponds to "first" or a and "second" or b that were used in the binomial expansion $(a + b)^n$.

Note: Instead of learning the formula in terms of "failure" and "success," you may have seen the following formula:

$${}_nC_rp^rq^{n-r}$$

This is the probability of obtaining exactly r successes in n trials when the probability of success is p and the probability of failure is $1 - p = q$. The two formulas are equivalent, so you may use either one of them.

MODEL PROBLEMS

1. Instead of studying for his social studies quiz last night, Jared went to a rock concert. He needs to get a grade of 80% on the quiz to pass for the quarter, but has no knowledge of the material that is on the quiz. If there are 5 questions on the quiz, and 5 choices for each question, what is the probability that Jason can completely guess on each question and get the 80% he needs to pass?

SOLUTION

To get 80% on the quiz, Jared needs to get 4 of the 5 questions correct. Since there are 5 choices for each question, the probability of guessing correctly (success) on any one question is $\frac{1}{5}$. The probability of not guessing correctly (failure) is $\frac{4}{5}$. Use the formula for a binomial probability.

$$_{n\ \text{trials}}C_{r\ \text{successes}}(\text{failure})^{n-r}(\text{success})^r = {}_5C_4\left(\frac{4}{5}\right)^1\left(\frac{1}{5}\right)^4 = 5\left(\frac{4}{5}\right)^1\left(\frac{1}{5}\right)^4 = \frac{4}{625} \text{ or } .0064$$

2. Marissa and Tyrone are playing a game of Yahtzee. To win the game, Marissa must get exactly 3 ones on the 5 dice that are thrown. What is the probability of Marissa winning the game?

SOLUTION

The probability of getting a one on any die is $\frac{1}{6}$. The probability of not getting a one on a die is thus $\frac{5}{6}$.

$$_{n\ \text{trials}}C_{r\ \text{successes}}(\text{failure})^{n-r}(\text{success})^r = {}_5C_3\left(\frac{5}{6}\right)^2\left(\frac{1}{6}\right)^3 = 10\left(\frac{25}{36}\right)\left(\frac{1}{6}\right)^3 = \frac{250}{7776} \text{ or } .03215$$

 **Practice**

1. A fair coin is tossed 3 times. Find the probability of getting
  a. exactly 2 heads
  b. exactly 3 heads
  c. exactly 1 tail

2. Slugger McGraw has a .300 batting average. This means that Slugger hits 3 out of every 10 times at bat. Expressed as a decimal, what is the probability of Slugger
  a. getting exactly 2 hits in his next 3 times at bat
  b. getting exactly 4 hits in his next 5 times at bat
  c. getting exactly 6 hits in his next 10 times at bat
  d. not getting a single hit in his next 4 times at bat

3. A die is rolled 4 times. What is the probability of getting
  a. exactly 2 sixes
  b. exactly 3 threes
  c. exactly 1 two
  d. all fives
  e. no fives

4. In the accompanying diagram, there is an equal probability of the spinner landing in any one of the sections.

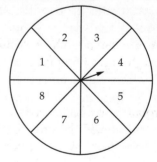

Find
  a. $P(4)$
  b. $P(\text{even number})$
  c. $P(\text{prime number})$
  d. the probability of obtaining exactly 2 fours in 3 spins
  e. the probability of obtaining exactly 3 even numbers in 5 spins
  f. the probability of obtaining all prime numbers in 4 spins

5. In the accompanying diagram of a spinner, $\overline{AD}$ is a diameter of circle O, $\overline{EO} \perp \overline{AD}$, $\overline{OF}$ bisects $\angle EOA$, $\angle AOB \cong \angle BOC \cong \angle COD$.

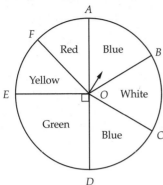

Find
a. P(red)
b. P(white)
c. P(blue)
d. P(yellow)
e. P(green)
f. the probability of obtaining exactly 2 reds in 3 spins
g. the probability of obtaining exactly 1 blue in 3 spins
h. the probability of obtaining exactly 4 greens in 5 spins
i. the probability of obtaining exactly 2 whites in 4 spins
j. The probability of obtaining all yellows in 4 spins

6. Which has a greater probability, answering 4 out of 5 questions correctly on a multiple-choice test where each question has 4 choices or answering 3 out of 5 questions correctly on a multiple-choice test where each question has 5 choices? Explain your answer.

In 7–15, select the numeral preceding the expression that best answers the question.

7. A die is rolled 3 times. What is the probability of getting no twos?

(1) $\dfrac{1}{216}$ (3) $\dfrac{125}{216}$

(2) $\dfrac{1}{6}$ (4) $\dfrac{5}{6}$

8. Ricardo has a "magic penny" that he uses in his magic show. The probability of getting heads on Ricardo's "magic penny" is $\dfrac{2}{3}$. What is the probability of getting exactly 2 heads on 3 tosses of this penny?

(1) $\dfrac{4}{27}$ (3) $\dfrac{4}{9}$

(2) $\dfrac{3}{8}$ (4) $\dfrac{5}{8}$

9. In a family of four children, what is the probability that exactly two of them are girls? (Assume P(boy) = P(girl).)

(1) $\dfrac{1}{8}$ (3) $\dfrac{3}{8}$

(2) $\dfrac{1}{4}$ (4) $\dfrac{1}{2}$

10. At the Brite Lites Manufacturing Company, the probability of a lightbulb being defective is .1%. In a sample of 10 lightbulbs, what is the probability of finding exactly one defective lightbulb?

(1) $_{10}C_1(.99)^9(.01)$

(2) $_{10}C_9(.99)(.01)^9$

(3) $_{10}C_1(.999)^9(.001)$

(4) $_{10}C_1(.9999)^9(.0001)$

11. In a true-false test of 10 questions, what is the probability of answering exactly 9 of them correctly by guessing?

(1) $\left(\dfrac{1}{2}\right)^{10}$ (3) $10\left(\dfrac{1}{2}\right)^{10}$

(2) $\left(\dfrac{1}{2}\right)^{9}$ (4) $10\left(\dfrac{1}{2}\right)^{9}$

12. Edgar is a very consistent basketball player. When he shoots a foul shot, he is successful 2 out of 3 times. If he shoots 5 foul shots, what is the probability that he will make all 5 shots?

(1) $\dfrac{1}{243}$ (3) $\dfrac{64}{243}$

(2) $\dfrac{32}{243}$ (4) $\dfrac{128}{243}$

13. The figures in the accompanying diagram are drawn one to a card. Each of three students picks a card at random and replaces it before the next pick.

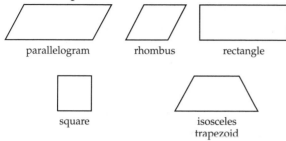

parallelogram   rhombus   rectangle

square   isosceles trapezoid

What is the probability that they all picked a card with a picture of a figure that is not a parallelogram?

(1) $\frac{1}{125}$ (3) $\frac{64}{125}$

(2) $\frac{1}{25}$ (4) $\frac{4}{5}$

14. In a car manufacturing plant, 2 out of every 10 cars manufactured are red. If 20 cars are randomly selected that come from the plant's production run, what is the probability that exactly 3 of them are red?

(1) $_{20}C_{17}\left(\frac{4}{5}\right)^3\left(\frac{1}{5}\right)^{17}$ (3) $_{20}C_3\left(\frac{4}{5}\right)^3\left(\frac{1}{5}\right)^{17}$

(2) $_{20}C_3\left(\frac{4}{5}\right)^{17}\left(\frac{1}{5}\right)^3$ (4) $_{20}C_{17}\left(\frac{3}{5}\right)^{17}\left(\frac{2}{5}\right)^3$

15. The four faces of a fair tetrahedron die are numbered 1, 2, 3, and 4. If the die is tossed 3 times, what is the probability of obtaining exactly two 2s?

(1) $\frac{3}{64}$ (3) $\frac{9}{256}$

(2) $\frac{9}{64}$ (4) $\frac{27}{256}$

16. A spinner is divided into five equal regions, numbered 1, 2, 3, 4, and 5. If the spinner is spun 4 times, what is the probability of obtaining exactly two odd numbers?

(1) $\frac{96}{625}$ (3) $\frac{6}{16}$

(2) $\frac{1}{4}$ (4) $\frac{216}{625}$

16.3 Probability of At Least or At Most *r* Successes in *n* Trials

If a friend tells you he can get *at least* two tickets for an upcoming concert that you are eager to see and he only gets one ticket, you would be really annoyed. **At least *r*** means the minimum number of successes is *r*. Other acceptable *r* values would be $r + 1, r + 2, r + 3$, and so on. In the case of your friend with the tickets, it would not have mattered to you if he had gotten 2, 3, 4, or 20 tickets as long as he had one for you. The probability of at least *r* successes in *n* trials is defined as: $P(\text{at least } r) = P(r) + P(r + 1) + P(r + 2) + P(r + 3) + \ldots + P(n)$ successes.

At most *r* out of *n*, or **no more than *r*,** however, provides the maximum allowed value and works downward from that point. That is, *r* is the maximum number permitted. If you are told at most 2 apples in a crate of 50 will be rotten and you find 5 rotten apples, you have a right to be angry. The probability of at most *r* successes out of *n* trials is defined as: $P(\text{at most } r) = P(r) + P(r - 1) + P(r - 2) + P(r - 3) + \ldots + P(0)$ successes.

1. Jack is tossing a fair coin and casually says he knows he can get at least 2 heads out of 3 tosses. What is the probability of this happening?

SOLUTION

The probability of at least 2 successes out of 3 trials must include the probability of exactly 2 heads plus the probability of exactly 3 heads. Since Jack is using a fair coin, the probability of success (heads) and failure (tails) both equal $\frac{1}{2}$.

$$P(\text{at least 2 out of 3 heads}) = {}_3C_2\left(\frac{1}{2}\right)^1\left(\frac{1}{2}\right)^2 + {}_3C_3\left(\frac{1}{2}\right)^0\left(\frac{1}{2}\right)^3$$

$$= 3\left(\frac{1}{2}\right)\left(\frac{1}{4}\right) + 1(1)\left(\frac{1}{8}\right)$$

$$= \frac{1}{2}$$

The probability of exactly 2 heads in 3 tosses is $\frac{3}{8}$ while the probability of all heads is $\frac{1}{8}$, so their sum is $\frac{4}{8}$ or $\frac{1}{2}$. Jack has an equal chance of winning or losing.

2. The wheel in the accompanying figure is divided into three equal areas.

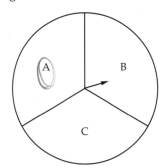

What is the probability that the spinner will land on a vowel at most twice in three spins?

SOLUTION

Since there is only one vowel among the three lettered areas, the probability of landing on a vowel is $\frac{1}{3}$ while the probability of not landing on a vowel is $\frac{2}{3}$. The probability of landing on a vowel at most 2 times, is the sum of the probabilities of exactly 2 times, exactly 1 time, and exactly 0 times in 3 spins.

$$P(\text{at most 2 times}) = P(2) + P(1) + P(0)$$

$$= {}_3C_2\left(\frac{2}{3}\right)^1\left(\frac{1}{3}\right)^2 + {}_3C_1\left(\frac{2}{3}\right)^2\left(\frac{1}{3}\right)^1 + {}_3C_0\left(\frac{2}{3}\right)^3\left(\frac{1}{3}\right)^0$$

$$= 3\left(\frac{2}{3}\right)\left(\frac{1}{9}\right) + 3\left(\frac{4}{9}\right)\left(\frac{1}{3}\right) + 1\left(\frac{8}{27}\right)(1)$$

$$= \frac{26}{27}$$

This problem can also be done by using the "back door method," that is, indirectly by figuring out the probability that the event does not occur and subtracting from 1. There is one way to fail to get at most 2 vowels in 3 spins, that is, to get 3 vowels in 3 spins.

P(at most 2 vowels) $= 1 - P$(3 vowels)

$$= 1 - {}_3C_3\left(\frac{2}{3}\right)^0\left(\frac{1}{3}\right)^3$$

$$= 1 - 1(1)\left(\frac{1}{27}\right)$$

$$= \frac{26}{27}$$

Note: Either approach will yield the same answer.

Practice

In 1–5, a fair die is tossed 4 times. Find the probability of

1. at least 2 5s

2. at most 3 even numbers

3. no more than 1 odd number

4. at least 1 prime number

5. at most 1 number greater than 4

In 6–15, select the number preceding the expression that best answers the question.

6. If the probability of the Devils winning the game against the Angels is $2x$, what is the probability of the Angels winning?
   (1) $-2x$
   (2) $1 - 2x$
   (3) $(2x)^2$
   (4) $\frac{1}{2x}$

7. Dan has a biased coin with which the probability of getting a head is $\frac{5}{8}$. What is the probability that Dan will get at least 4 heads in 5 tosses?
   (1) 1
   (2) $\frac{5}{8}$
   (3) $\frac{3,125}{8,192}$
   (4) $\frac{9,375}{32,768}$

8. Portia's Pinkettes, a dart team, and their opponent, Shaylala's Sisters, have tied the game for the championship. The probability of Portia hitting the bull's-eye is $\frac{5}{7}$. What is the probability she can do so at least 3 out of 5 times to win the trophy for the Pinkettes?
   (1) $\frac{1,625}{2,401}$
   (2) $\frac{5}{7}$
   (3) $\frac{3,125}{16,807}$
   (4) $\frac{14,375}{16,807}$

9. In the game of Monopoly, a player must go to jail if he rolls more than 2 sets of doubles with a pair of fair dice in 3 rolls. What is the probability Evan will stay out of jail by rolling no more than 2 sets of doubles in 3 rolls? (Hint: first determine the probability of rolling a double.)
   (1) $\frac{5}{216}$
   (2) $\frac{1}{6}$
   (3) $\frac{72}{216}$
   (4) $\frac{215}{216}$

10. On Saturday mornings, Mrs. Elliott allows her children to spin the chore wheel to determine who has what chore before going out to play.

Assuming John always spins first, what is the probability that during a month with 4 Saturdays, John has to vacuum at least 3 times?

(1) $\frac{1}{4}$

(2) $\frac{5}{16}$

(3) $\frac{3}{8}$

(4) $\frac{1}{2}$

11. If a letter is selected at random from the word STATISTICS in three separate trials, what is the probability an S will be selected at most twice?
(1) .27
(2) .30
(3) .672
(4) .973

12. A standardized test has multiple-choice questions, each with 5 possible choices. Mark is tired of answering questions and decides to randomly guess on a reading comprehension section, without reading the passage or the questions. Approximately what is the probability he will get no more than 3 of the 8 questions on this section correct?
(1) .94
(2) .85
(3) .50
(4) .20

13. Gary Yansick's career batting average is .293. In a game where he comes to bat 5 times, approximately what is the probability he gets at least 2 hits?
(1) .293
(2) .376
(3) .457
(4) .570

14. A supervisor at a company manufacturing lacrosse sticks knows from past production that 0.004 of the sticks shipped have a defect. If the University of Guessville orders 72 lacrosse sticks, which formula below represents the probability that at least 2 of them will be defective?
(1) 1
(2) $1 - (_{72}C_1(.996)^{71}(.004)^1 + {}_{72}C_0(.996)^{72}(.004)^0)$
(3) $_{72}C_2(.996)^{70}(.004)^2$
(4) $_{72}C_2(.996)^{70}(.004)^2 + {}_{72}C_1(.996)^{71}(.004)^1$

15.

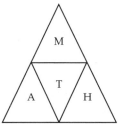

In the accompanying figure from a game called MATH, each small triangle has an equal area, so the probability of any one letter being pressed at random is equal. If 4 letters are pressed at random, what is the probability that no more than one vowel will be pressed?

(1) $\frac{81}{256}$

(2) $\frac{93}{256}$

(3) $\frac{189}{256}$

(4) $\frac{201}{256}$

16. Mr. New Teacher decides to give his first-period class a multiple-choice quiz with four choices per question and his fifth-period class a true-false quiz. Each quiz has 5 questions. The grades of the students in the fifth-period class are significantly higher than the grades of the students in the first-period class. Using probability, explain why this does not necessarily mean that the fifth-period students knew the material better than the students in the first-period class did.

17. At Snow Angel Ski Resort, the management promises that the probability of snow, man-made or natural, on every day in February is $\frac{2}{3}$. In fact, their brochure says, "If it doesn't snow at least 2 days out of the 3 days you are here, we will refund half the cost of your stay." Is this a wise marketing strategy or will the resort lose money?

18.

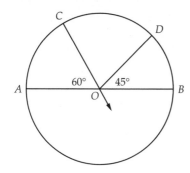

In circle O shown in the diagram, with diameter $\overline{AOB}$ and radii $\overline{OC}$ and $\overline{OD}$, $m\angle AOC = 60$ and $m\angle BOD = 45$. Find the probability that a spinner lands in

a. region AOC at least twice in 3 spins

b. region BOD no more than once in 4 spins

c. the lower semicircle at least twice in 5 spins

19. Ms. Weikman's badminton team is going to play Mr. DeStefano's team for the school intramural championship. The probability that Ms. Weikman's team will win a game is $\frac{2}{3}$. In a three-game series, find the probability that

a. Ms. Weikman's team wins at least two games

b. Mr. DeStefano's team does not lose all three games

20. A children's game Hugs & Kisses is played on a hexagonal board like the one shown below. Katie and Mavis take turns tossing X or O markers over their shoulders onto the board.

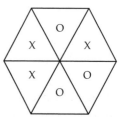

Whoever gets 3 markers on her letter first wins. Assuming all the markers hit the board, what is the probability that

a. Katie can score at least 3 X's in 4 tosses of her X markers

b. Mavis scores no more than 1 O in 3 tosses of her O markers

CHAPTER REVIEW

In 1–17, select the numeral preceding the expression that best completes the statement or answers the question.

1. What is the third term in the expansion $(x + 2y)^4$?

(1) $6x^2y^2$ (3) $12x^2y^2$

(2) $4x^2y^2$ (4) $24x^2y^2$

2. If a fair coin is tossed 3 times, what is the probability of getting at least 2 heads?

(1) $\frac{1}{2}$ (3) $\frac{1}{4}$

(2) $\frac{3}{8}$ (4) $\frac{1}{8}$

3. The weather forecaster has predicted that there is a 25% probability of rain on any of the next 4 days. What is the probability that it will rain at least twice?

(1) $\frac{66}{256}$ (3) $\frac{68}{256}$

(2) $\frac{67}{256}$ (4) $\frac{175}{256}$

4. If the probability that an event will occur is $\frac{1}{2x + 1}$, the probability that the event will not occur is

(1) $\frac{2x + 2}{2x + 1}$ (3) $\frac{1}{2x + 1}$

(2) $\frac{2x}{2x + 1}$ (4) $-\frac{1}{2x + 1}$

5. What is the fourth term in the expansion $(a + bi)^6$?

(1) $15a^2b^2$ (3) $20a^3b^3i$

(2) $20a^3b^3$ (4) $-20a^3b^3i$

6. Nicole is taking a 5-question multiple-choice test. If she completely guesses every answer, and each question has 4 choices, what is the probability that she gets at most one wrong answer?

(1) .015625

(2) .008

(3) .006945

(4) .00672

7. What is the last term in the expansion $(\sin q + \cos \theta)^3$?
   (1) 1
   (2) $\cos^3 \theta$
   (3) $\sin^3 \theta$
   (4) $\sin^3 \theta + \cos^3 \theta$

8. A spinner is divided into five equal sectors labeled 1 through 5. What is the probability of getting at most 2 prime numbers in 3 spins?
   (1) $\frac{98}{125}$
   (2) $\frac{64}{125}$
   (3) $\frac{61}{625}$
   (4) $\frac{27}{625}$

9. What is the numerical coefficient of the fourth term in the expansion $(2x - y)^5$?
   (1) -40
   (2) -20
   (3) -10
   (4) 40

10. A coin is biased so that the probability of obtaining heads is $\frac{3}{5}$. What is the probability of obtaining at least 3 heads in 4 tosses of the coin?
    (1) $\frac{81}{625}$
    (2) $\frac{135}{625}$
    (3) $\frac{216}{625}$
    (4) $\frac{297}{625}$

11. What is the middle term in the expansion $(a - 3b)^4$?
    (1) $-54a^2b^2$
    (2) $-6a^2b^2$
    (3) $6a^2b^2$
    (4) $54a^2b^2$

12. The probability of the Mets winning a game against the Diamondbacks is $\frac{3}{4}$. If they are playing a 3-game series this weekend, what is the probability that the Mets will win at least 2 out of 3 games?
    (1) $\frac{9}{64}$
    (2) $\frac{27}{64}$
    (3) $\frac{54}{64}$
    (4) $\frac{63}{64}$

13. If one letter is selected at random from the word PARALLEL and then replaced in 4 random trials, what is the probability that no more than 1 L is chosen?
    (1) $\frac{1,695}{4,096}$
    (2) $\frac{2,048}{4,096}$
    (3) $\frac{2,125}{4,096}$
    (4) $\frac{5}{6}$

14. The expansion $(3 - 2i)^6$ is equivalent to
    (1) $729 - 64i$
    (2) $729 + 64i$
    (3) $-2,035 + 828i$
    (4) $2,035 - 828i$

15. The president's press conference is being shown nationally on channels 2, 4, 7, and 8. Of the 6 television sets randomly tuned in to the news program at Ella's Electronic Expo, what is the probability that at least half are tuned to channel 8?
    (1) $\frac{162}{2,048}$
    (2) $\frac{347}{2,048}$
    (3) $\frac{1}{2}$
    (4) $\frac{1,701}{2,048}$

16. A survey of coffee drinkers found that given a choice, 5 out of 7 coffee drinkers prefer regular coffee to decaffeinated coffee. What is the probability that of the next five coffee drinkers who enter The Coffee Bean, none of them will want decaf?
    (1) $\frac{3,125}{16,807}$
    (2) $\frac{6,250}{16,807}$
    (3) $\frac{13,682}{16,807}$
    (4) $\frac{15,625}{16,807}$

17. A traffic light on Hempstead Turnpike is green for 40 seconds, yellow for 5 seconds, and red for 15 seconds out of every minute. What is the probability that at least 4 of the next 5 cars get a green light?
    (1) $\frac{32}{243}$
    (2) $\frac{80}{243}$
    (3) $\frac{112}{243}$
    (4) $\frac{201}{243}$

18. Write the binomial expansion for $(a - 2b)^3$.

19. Rosa has a reputation for usually being late. Her family has decided that there is a 90% probability of Rosa being late for any one event. If there are 4 family events coming up, what is the probability that
    a. Rosa is late for all 4 of them
    b. Rosa is on time for all 4 of them
    c. Rosa is late for *at most* 1 of them
    d. Rosa is late for *at least* 1 of them

20. What are the coefficients for the expansion of $(x + y)^4$?

21. In the accompanying diagram, a regular pentagon is divided into five equal sections.

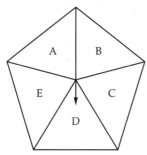

Find
a. $P(\text{B})$
b. $P(\text{vowel})$
c. the probability of obtaining *exactly* 2 B's on 3 spins
d. the probability of obtaining *at least* 1 vowel on 3 spins

22. Mrs. Superteacher has 15 students in her math class. Each time a student does something special, she writes the student's name on a piece of paper and puts it in a container. At the end of the week she randomly selects the name of one or more students to receive a "no homework night." If more than one selection is to be made, Mrs. Superteacher replaces the slip in the box before picking an additional slip. Jason has 4 slips in the box, Mandy and Mia each have 3 slips, Frank, Juanita, Kaitlyn, and Steve each have 2 slips, and all the other students have 1 slip each. What is the probability of
a. a particular student being selected who only has one slip in the box if only 1 selection is made
b. Juanita or Kaitlyn being selected if only 1 selection is made
Set up, but do not calculate, the probability of each situation.
c. Mia being selected *exactly* twice if 3 selections are made
d. Jason being selected *at least* once if 3 selections are made
e. Steve being selected *at least* twice if 3 selections are made

23. Write and simplify the binomial expansion for $(2 + i)^4$.

24. The Sweet Dreams Candy Company is putting a coupon redeemable for a free box of candy in 1 out of every 100 boxes of candy they manufacture. Set up, but do not calculate, the probability of a person receiving
a. exactly 1 coupon if he buys 6 boxes of candy
b. no coupons if she buys 10 boxes of candy
c. at least 2 coupons if he buys 8 boxes of candy
d. at most 1 coupon if she buys 10 boxes of candy

25. The American Red Cross collects approximately half of all blood needed in the United States. Different blood types occur in the U.S. population with varying probabilities.
a. Approximately 34 percent of the population has A^+ blood. To the nearest thousandth, what is the probability that of the first 5 donors at a blood drive, at least two have A^+ blood?
b. The universal donor is the person with type O blood. If 45 percent of the U.S. population has type O blood, what is the probability that exactly 4 out of 6 donors waiting to donate will have type O? (Round to nearest thousandth.)
c. Type B blood occurs in 11 percent of the population. If one of the players on the YMCA softball team of 18 players needs a transfusion of type B blood, what is the probability that none of the other players on the team have B blood to donate to him?
d. Four-day-old Baby Jones needs a transfusion of AB^+ blood, found in only 3 percent of the population. If the blood drive collected 152 pints of blood, what is the probability that at least one pint of AB^+ was collected?

The TI-83 calculator can also help you determine the probabilities of Bernoulli trials. For a single probability (exactly r successes in n trials), we use the binompdf command. Press the (2nd) (VARS) keys that correspond to DISTR (Distribution). Then press 0 (zero). This pastes the binompdf (on the screen. You must then enter three pieces of information: n, the number of trials; p, the probability of success; and r, the number of desired successes. For example, when you enter binompdf (4,.25,3), as shown below, this means you want the probability of exactly 3 out of 4 successes in a situation where the probability of success is .25 or $\frac{1}{4}$. The calculator tells you the probability is .046875 or $\frac{3}{64}$.

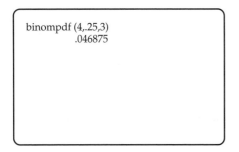

If you omit the third parameter, the calculator will give all probabilities, from 0 successes to 4 successes, in 4 trials.

Note: This is given in a horizontal line and you must use the right arrow to see all the probabilities.

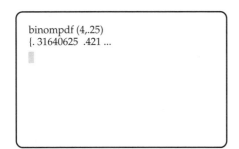

For your convenience, those probabilities are printed in the table as decimals and fractions:

Number of Successes	Probability as Decimal	Probability as Fraction
0	.31640625	$\frac{81}{256}$
1	.421875	$\frac{108}{256} = \frac{27}{64}$
2	.2109375	$\frac{54}{256} = \frac{27}{128}$
3	.046875	$\frac{12}{256} = \frac{3}{64}$
4	.00390625	$\frac{1}{256}$

If we want to find the probability of *at most* 3 out of 4 successes in a situation where the probability of success is .25 or $\frac{1}{4}$, we could add those values shown above or we can use the binomcdf command (cumulative distributive frequency). This is found as option A on the (2nd) (VARS) (DISTR) menu. Again, there are three inputs after the command: n, p, and r.

binomcdf (4,.25,3) produces the answer .99609375 or $\frac{255}{256}$.

Note: If you need to find *at least* r *of* n, use the format $1 -$ binomcdf (n,p,r) or omit the r value and add the probabilities you need.

Practice

Find the probability of obtaining

a. 3 successes in 5 trials if the probability of success is $\frac{2}{3}$

b. 2 successes in 3 trials if the probability of success is $\frac{3}{4}$

c. 1 success in 4 trials if the probability of success is .45

d. *at most* 4 successes out of 5 if the probability of success is .2

e. *at least* 3 successes out of 5 if the probability of success is .2

CHAPTER 17

Statistics

17.1 Sigma Notation

In statistics, it is very common to need the sum of a collection of data. The Greek capital letter sigma, written Σ, is the symbol used to indicate summation. The **sigma notation** $\sum\limits_{i=2}^{4} 2^i$ means find the sum of the 2^i terms for every consecutive integer i, from $i = 2$ through $i = 4$. The i in this notation represents the **index.** The lower limit or starting value of the index appears below the sigma while the upper limit or ending value of the summation is found above the sigma.

$$\sum_{i=2}^{4} 2^i = 2^2 + 2^3 + 2^4 = 4 + 8 + 16 = 26$$

Therefore, $\sum\limits_{i=2}^{4} 2^i = 26$ when calculated. Any letter can be used to represent the index, but mathematical convention usually assigns the letters $i, j, k,$ or n.

Note: When using sigma notation, i does not indicate the imaginary unit equivalent to $\sqrt{-1}$.

MODEL PROBLEMS

1. Evaluate $\sum\limits_{i=4}^{7} (3i - 2)$. 58

SOLUTION

$$\sum_{i=4}^{7} (3i - 2) = (3(4) - 2) + (3(5) - 2) + (3(6) - 2) + (3(7) - 2) = 58$$

Calculator Solution: Summation problems can also be done using the TI-83+ calculator. Go to the (2nd)(STAT) menu (LIST).

```
NAMES OPS MATH
1 : L₁
2 : L₂
3 : L₃
4 : L₄
5 : L₅
6 : L₆
7 : RESID
```

Right arrow over to MATH. The following menu appears.

```
NAMES OPS MATH
1 : min (
2 : max (
3 : mean (
4 : median (
5 : sum (
6 : prod (
7↓stdDev (
```

Down arrow to choice 5. Press (ENTER) and the sum notation, sum(, will be pasted on your home screen. Now, go back to (2nd)(STAT) menu (LIST) and right arrow over to OPS.

```
NAMES OPS MATH
1 : SortA (
2 : SortD (
3 : dim (
4 : Fill (
5 : seq (
6 : cumSum (
7↓ Δ List (
```

Down arrow to choice 5:seq(. Press (ENTER). The seq(command will now be pasted on your home screen adjacent to the sum command.

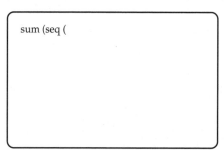

Now enter the function to be summed, followed by the variable used, the starting value, the ending value, and the distance between each value. Using the problem above, the command would look like this:

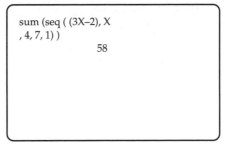
```
sum (seq ( (3X–2), X
  , 4, 7, 1) )
                    58
```

In the above command the first entry is the function enclosed in parentheses; the second is the variable in use, then the lower limit, followed by the upper limit, and finally the interval of the increase, usually 1. Notice that the same answer is obtained with hand calculation.

2. Evaluate $\displaystyle\sum_{k=1}^{6} \sin\left(\frac{k\pi}{4}\right)$. $\quad \frac{\sqrt{2}}{2}$

SOLUTION

To evaluate $\displaystyle\sum_{k=1}^{6} \sin\left(\frac{k\pi}{4}\right)$, we must replace the k in the expression $\frac{\sin \pi k}{4}$ for all values from 1 through 6.

$$\sum_{k=1}^{6} \sin\left(\frac{k\pi}{4}\right) = \left(\sin \frac{1\pi}{4} + \sin \frac{2\pi}{4} + \sin \frac{3\pi}{4} + \sin \frac{4\pi}{4} + \sin \frac{5\pi}{4} + \sin \frac{6\pi}{4}\right)$$

$$= \left(\frac{\sqrt{2}}{2} + 1 + \frac{\sqrt{2}}{2} + 0 + \left(-\frac{\sqrt{2}}{2}\right) + (-1)\right)$$

$$= \frac{\sqrt{2}}{2}$$

3. If $x_1 = 19$, $x_2 = 20$, $x_3 = 26$, $x_4 = 30$, and $\frac{1}{5}\displaystyle\sum_{i=1}^{5} x_i = 24$, what must be the value of x_5?

(1) 20
(2) 24
(3) 25
(4) 26

SOLUTION
In this problem, the data are defined with subscripted terms, $x_1 = 19$, $x_2 = 20$, $x_3 = 26$, and $x_4 = 30$. We are looking for the fifth term, x_5, having been given the information that the average of the five terms, expressed as $\frac{1}{5}\displaystyle\sum_{i=1}^{5} x_i$ equals 24. Hence, we want to find the sum of the four terms that we do know and solve for the fifth term.

$$\frac{1}{5}\sum_{i=1}^{5} x_i = \frac{1}{5}(x_1 + x_2 + x_3 + x_4 + x_5)$$

$$= \frac{1}{5}(19 + 20 + 26 + 30 + x_5)$$

$$= \frac{1}{5}(95 + x_5) \qquad \text{Based on the problem, we know this expression equals 24.}$$

$$24 = \frac{1}{5}(95 + x_5)$$

$$120 = 95 + x_5$$

$$25 = x_5$$

4. Evaluate $2 \sum_{j=1}^{3} (j^{j-1})$. *24*

SOLUTION

In this example, the 2 acts as a coefficient of the sigma term, indicating that the entire sum is to be multiplied by 2.

$$2 \sum_{j=1}^{3} (j^{j-1}) = 2(1^{1-1} + 2^{2-1} + 3^{3-1})$$
$$= 2(1^0 + 2^1 + 3^2)$$
$$= 2(1 + 2 + 9)$$
$$= 24$$

Note that $\sum_{j=1}^{3} 2(j^{j-1}) = 2(1^0) + 2(2^1) + 2(3^2) = 24.$

So, $2 \sum_{j=1}^{3} (j^{j-1}) = \sum_{j=1}^{3} 2(j^{j-1}).$

5. Using summation notation, write an expression that indicates the sum:
$$\frac{4}{3} + \frac{9}{4} + \frac{16}{5} + \frac{25}{6} + \frac{36}{7}.$$

SOLUTION

To solve this type of problem, look for patterns. Examine the numerators and denominators of these fractions separately.

$$\frac{4}{3} + \frac{9}{4} + \frac{16}{5} + \frac{25}{6} + \frac{36}{7}$$

The numerators are all perfect squares and the denominators are consecutive integers. One approach then is to set the index to begin at 3 and include all integer values through 7. Looking at the numerators again, we can observe that the numerators are the squares of 1 less than each denominator. Therefore, one way of writing this summation is $\sum_{j=3}^{7} \frac{(j-1)^2}{j}.$

This sigma notation, however, is not unique. An alternate, equally correct solution would be to let $k = j - 1$ and restate the summation as $\sum_{k=2}^{6} \frac{k^2}{(k+1)}.$ To check to see that these are equivalent summations, you may want to write them out for yourself.

Practice

In 1–12, find the value of each expression indicated in sigma notation.

1. $\sum_{i=0}^{4} (i - 2)$

2. $\sum_{j=4}^{8} (3j - 5)$

3. $\frac{1}{2} \sum_{k=1}^{4} (13 - 3k)$

4. $\sum_{k=2}^{5} \cos\left(\frac{k\pi}{2}\right)$

5. $\sum_{j=7}^{10} (j - 6)^2$

6. $\displaystyle\sum_{k=1}^{4}\left(\frac{2k+3}{k}\right)$

7. $\displaystyle\sum_{n=0}^{4}\tan(n\pi)$

8. $\displaystyle\sum_{i=1}^{5}(2i^2)$

9. $\displaystyle 2\sum_{k=4}^{5}\sin\left(\frac{k\pi}{3}\right)$

10. $\displaystyle\sum_{k=4}^{5}\sin\left(\frac{2k\pi}{3}\right)$

11. $\displaystyle\frac{1}{3}\sum_{i=0}^{3}i^3$

12. $\displaystyle\sum_{n=1}^{3}(3-n)^2$

In 13–16, use the summation symbol to write each sum in sigma notation.

13. $5 + 9 + 13 + 17 + 21 + 25$

14. $35 + 48 + 63 + 80 + 99$

15. $1 + \frac{1}{2} + 0 + \left(-\frac{1}{2}\right) + (-1)$

16. $\left(\frac{-2}{5}\right) + \left(\frac{-3}{7}\right) + \left(\frac{-4}{9}\right) + \left(\frac{-5}{11}\right)$

In 17–23, select the numeral preceding the word or expression that best answers the question.

17. Which of the following is equivalent to $\displaystyle 3\sum_{j=2}^{5}(j-4)$?

(1) $\displaystyle\sum_{j=2}^{5}3j-4$ (3) $\displaystyle\sum_{j=2}^{5}3j-12$

(2) $\displaystyle\sum_{j=2}^{5}\frac{j-4}{3}$ (4) $\displaystyle 3\sum_{j=-2}^{-5}(4-j)$

18. If $x_1 = 9$, $x_2 = 12$, $x_3 = 17$, $x_4 = 23$, and $\displaystyle\sum_{i=1}^{5}x_i = 81$, what must be the value of x_5?

(1) 30   (3) 19
(2) 20   (4) 5

19. If $x_1 = 91$, $x_2 = 72$, $x_3 = 86$, and $\displaystyle\sum_{j=1}^{4}\frac{x_j}{4} = 85$, what must be the value of x_4?

(1) 100   (3) 91
(2) 94   (4) 85

20. Which of the following represents the sum $6 + 15 + 26 + 39$?

(1) $\displaystyle\sum_{n=4}^{7}2n-2$ (3) $\displaystyle\sum_{n=2}^{5}n^2+n$

(2) $\displaystyle\sum_{n=4}^{7}n^2-10$ (4) $\displaystyle\sum_{n=2}^{5}\frac{3n^2}{2}$

21. Zach graduated from college after borrowing money to pay his tuition for 4 years. If he borrowed $20,000 the first year and increased the total borrowed by $5,000 each year thereafter, which of the following represents the total college loans he must repay?

(1) $\displaystyle\sum_{k=1}^{4}20{,}000 + 5{,}000k$

(2) $\displaystyle\sum_{k=1}^{4}25{,}000k$

(3) $\displaystyle\sum_{k=0}^{4}5{,}000k + 25{,}000$

(4) $\displaystyle\sum_{k=1}^{4}20{,}000 + (k-1)5{,}000$

22. Fiona is training to run the marathon in New York City next year. Each week she increases the distance she runs by 0.5 mile. If she initially started running a 4-mile route, which of the following expressions represents the total miles she will run in 52 weeks of training?

(1) $\displaystyle\sum_{i=0}^{51}4 + 0.5i$ (3) $\displaystyle\sum_{i=0}^{51}4.5i$

(2) $\displaystyle\sum_{i=0}^{51}0.5 + 4i$ (4) $\displaystyle\sum_{i=0}^{51}4 - 0.5i$

23. As the number of days before the holidays decreases, the number of shoppers at the mall increases. If the sigma notation $\displaystyle\sum_{n=1}^{25}300(85 + n)$ represents the total number of shoppers at the Snowy North Pole Mall from December 1 to December 25, how many additional shoppers appear at the mall each successive day?

(1) 60
(2) 85
(3) 300
(4) 25,500

17.2 Measures of Central Tendency

Mean, Median, and Mode

Measures of central tendency are summary statistics that indicate, in some way, where the typical value of a collection of data lies. Three common measures of central tendency are the **mean**, **median**, and **mode**. These were studied in Math A. The **mean** is referred to as the arithmetic average of the data and is symbolized as $\bar{x}$, read "x bar."

Note: Two different symbols are used to represent the mean of a collection of data. When the mean of a sample population is being studied, $\bar{x}$ is commonly used. When the mean of a collection of data representing an entire population is under investigation, the Greek letter mu, μ, is frequently utilized. In accord with current Regents practice, we will use only $\bar{x}$.

To find $\bar{x}$, we find the sum of all the given data and divide by the number of pieces of data. Mathematically, $\bar{x} = \dfrac{\sum\limits_{k=1}^{n} x_k}{n}$ where n is the total number of terms. For example, Priscilla has the following grades on her Math B quizzes this quarter: 74, 83, 79, 90, and 82. Then the mean value of her grades so far is

$$\bar{x} = \frac{\sum\limits_{i=1}^{5} x_i}{5} = \frac{74 + 83 + 79 + 90 + 82}{5} = 81.6.$$

The **median** of given data is the positional middle when the data is placed in numerical order, either ascending or descending. To find out which position is the median, add 1 to the total number of data values and divide by 2. The value in that position, counting from the first or last term, is the median.

MODEL PROBLEMS

---

1. Find the median of the following set of data: 11, 17, 31, 18, 25, 12, 29, 13, 15.

SOLUTION
First put the terms in order: 11, 12, 13, 15, 17, 18, 25, 29, 31. Since there are 9 terms, find $\dfrac{n+1}{2} = \dfrac{9+1}{2} = 5$. The fifth term, 17, is the median.

2. Find the median of the following set of data: 9, 11, 7, 10, 2, 17, 8, 13.

SOLUTION
In this problem, the number of terms, 8, is even. Find $\dfrac{n+1}{2} = \dfrac{8+1}{2} = 4.5$. The median will be halfway between the fourth and fifth terms once they are in order, or the mean of the fourth and fifth terms. Given 2, 7, 8, 9, 10, 11, 13, 17, the median value is 9.5, which is the arithmetic mean of 9 and 10.

---

3. Consider the frequency table shown at the right.

    a. Find the mean.   **b.** Find the median.

Data	Frequency
56	4
73	9
78	7
82	5
86	5

SOLUTION

a. To find the mean, multiply the frequency times each data value and find the sum of those products. Then divide by 30, since there is a total of 30 given values.

$$\text{mean} = \frac{2{,}267}{30} = 75.56666\ldots = 75.5\overline{6}$$

b. The median is the middle term; add 1 and divide 31 by 2. The median value is in the 15.5th position. Since both the 15th and 16th terms are 78, the median is 78.

The **mode** is the most commonly repeated data value. Some collections of data, often referred to as distributions, will have no mode and others will have multiple modes.

 **MODEL PROBLEMS**

1. Find the mode of the following data: 67, 54, 91, 67, 83, 46, 72, 54, 91, 81, 75, 67, 54, 88.

SOLUTION
Since 67 and 54 were both repeated three times, both of these values serve as modes.

2. Find the mode of the following data: 113, 154, 139, 112, 138, 129, 143, 170, 184, 206.

SOLUTION
In this set of data, there is no mode because none of the data values is repeated.

3. Gasoline prices, for self-serve regular, in Albany over a 13-week period were $1.63, $1.63, $1.60, $1.62, $1.58, $1.54, $1.49, $1.46, $1.44, $1.41, $1.38, $1.36, $1.33. Find the mean, median, and mode for this data. Which is the most representative measure of central tendency? Why?

SOLUTION
It is not usual to find the data in an approximate descending numerical order, but it does occasionally happen. This problem can be done by hand or by using the TI-83. To use the calculator, go to

(STAT), Edit (that takes you to lists) and enter the prices in L_1. To find the mean and median, go to (STAT) and right arrow over to CALC.

```
EDIT CALC TESTS
1 : 1–Var Stats
2 : 2–Var Stats
3 : Med–Med
4 : LinReg (ax+b)
5 : QuadReg
6 : CubicReg
7↓QuartReg
```

Choose 1 : 1–Var Stats, which stands for one-variable statistics. Press (ENTER), and the command 1–Var Stats is pasted onto the Home Screen. Tell the calculator which list to use, in this case, L_1.

```
1–Var Stats L₁
```

Now, press (ENTER).

```
1–Var Stats
x̄ = 1.497692308
Σx = 19.47
Σx² = 29.3025
Sx = .1089459993
σx = .1046719304
↓n = 13
```

```
1–Var Stats
↑n = 13
minX = 1.33
Q₁ = 1.395
Med = 1.49
Q₃ = 1.61
maxX = 1.63
```

These tables indicate the various statistical information for the data provided in L_1. $\bar{x} = 1.498$ and median = 1.49.

To find the mode, you can visually examine the set of data to find that $1.63 is repeated twice while no other terms are repeated. Alternately, you can enter the data into a list, sort the list, and see which terms are being repeated in the sorted group. In this problem, therefore, the mode is $1.63.

In this situation the mean and the median are very close in value and either can serve as a useful measure of average price. The mode is too high to be a meaningful average. Since the mean price is not an actual value, the median may be preferable.

Choosing Appropriate Statistical Measures

While the mean, median, and mode all indicate an "average" value of a set of data, sometimes one is preferred over another. The mean, as a mathematical average, is affected by the outliers, or extreme values. The mode, while a commonly used element, sometimes does not exist in a set of data, while at other times, there can be more than one mode. In many cases, the median seems to be the most reliable as the middle term, the halfway piece of data in a group, if it can be calculated.

 **MODEL PROBLEM**

Real estate agents often talk about the "average" house price in a neighborhood. Consider the following data, representing the prices of homes sold in a small community, and determine whether the mean, median, or mode would be most representative of the data at hand and explain why.

Selling Prices of Homes

$149,799	$158,239	$177,899	$174,599	$185,600	$195,299	$219,900
$152,599	$159,899	$174,599	$181,500	$193,799	$210,000	$335,000

SOLUTION

Enter data in L_1 and use 1:−Variable Stats to find the mean and median. Find the mode by observation. Mean = $190,623.64, median = $179,699.50, and mode = $174,599. The mean is much higher than the median and mean because of the extremely high price of the last piece of data, the $335,000. Though it is repeated, the mode represents only the prices of two houses out of 14 sold, so it is not a strongly representative value. In this case, the median would most accurately illustrate the "average" house price in this neighborhood, although unscrupulous real estate companies might prefer to use the mean price to impress some of their buyers with the higher "average" price.

Bias and Random Sample

Often it is not possible or not cost-effective to gather data from an entire population. In such cases, conclusions about the entire population may be based on results for a **sample** or subset of the population. In order for the conclusions to be accurate, the sample must fairly represent the entire population.

Sometimes in statistics, the information presented is not without bias. That is, the data collected in the sample has come from sources that have a particular interest in the impact of the statistics. The sample is therefore not representative of the general population so it is said to be biased or skewed. For example, if dairy farmers were surveyed about the average number of ounces of milk every person in the United States should drink for better health, the results would be based on a **biased sample**. The sample would be biased since the farmers have an economic interest in increasing the amount of milk drunk by the average American. On the other hand, if the College of Pediatric Surgeons or American Board of Nutritionists provided the information, it could be presumed to be relatively free of such bias. Similarly, a sample of city residents chosen from only one neighborhood would probably not mirror the characteristics or concerns of the overall population. It is important in interpreting any statistics that you explore the source of the data and the possibility of a biased sample.

MODEL PROBLEM

Car manufacturers want to explore the desirability of pre-installed infant seats in their new car designs. Which of the following groups would be most likely to provide an unbiased sample for a survey?

    (1) adult shoppers at a supermarket with young children in the shopping carts
    (2) couples signing up to win a honeymoon package at a bridal expo
    (3) adults visiting a car show
    (4) a group of teenagers playing pickup ball at the park

SOLUTION
Choice 3 is the least biased group since choice 1 contains people who already need car seats, choice 2 involves young couples who will probably have children in the future, and choice 4 involves teenagers for whom parenthood is not relevant.

Practice

In 1–10, select the numeral preceding the word or expression that best completes the sentence or answers the question.

1. The mean of 37, 54, 72, 89, 74, 83, 90, 93 is
    (1) 73
    (2) 74
    (3) 78
    (4) 81.5

2. Which of the following statements is true about the data 14, 18, 21, 19, 27, 23, 17?
    (1) mean = median   (3) mean > median
    (2) mean < median   (4) median = mode

3. Consider the frequency table below.

x_i	f_i
62	6
71	5
80	5
89	4

Which of the following is a true statement?
    (1) mean = median   (3) mode > median
    (2) mean < median   (4) mean > mode

4. If the mean of a set of data is 27 and the data includes 24, 34, 19, 22, 29, and x, the value of x is
    (1) 27   (3) 34
    (2) 29   (4) 37

5. The median height of the players on the basketball team is 6 ft 4 in. This means
    (1) the tallest player is 6 ft 4 in.
    (2) no player is shorter than 6 ft 4 in.
    (3) an equal number of players are taller than 6 ft 4 in. and shorter than 6 ft 4 in.
    (4) most of the players are 6 ft 4 in. tall

6. Which would be the most representative group of people to ask about methods of Social Security reform?
    (1) adults at a senior citizen center
    (2) college students in a sociology class
    (3) members of a children's choir
    (4) adults at a discount mall

7. Creators of a new chocolate candy bar want their ads to contain positive, favorable quotations from people who like their product. Which group would they most likely choose to survey about their candy?
    (1) people who received free samples of the candy
    (2) dentists who specialize in children's teeth
    (3) customers at a health food store
    (4) nutritionists concerned with Americans' diet

8. Reporters on a news show want to survey adults about their exercise habits. Where might they go to find an unbiased sample?
   (1) Central Park   (3) an exercise gym
   (2) a movie theater (4) a rock-climbing expo

9. The city board of directors is considering raising the cost of parking tickets. Which group would be most unbiased on this issue?
   (1) 50 citizens who have never received a parking ticket
   (2) 50 citizens who have had at least three parking tickets
   (3) the first 50 people encountered in a shopping mall
   (4) 50 citizens who do not have driver licenses

10. A radio station wants to conduct a survey to predict the winner of the mayoral election. Which method is most likely to provide an unbiased sampling?
    (1) asking for callers and using the first 50 people who call in
    (2) sending a reporter to interview commuters at a suburban train station
    (3) calling the tenth person listed on each page of the city telephone directory
    (4) surveying the opinions of protesters at a rally

11. The table below gives the top ten money winners in the PGA. Find the mean, median, and mode of this data.

Golfer	Earnings
Tiger Woods	$4,976,431
Hal Sutton	$2,485,171
Phil Mickelson	$2,478,478
Jesper Parnevik	$2,237,400
Ernie Els	$2,071,255
Davis Love III	$1,875,046
David Duval	$1,777,400
Vijay Singh	$1,775,783
Tom Lehman	$1,713,360
Robert Allenby	$1,570,874

12. One hundred senior girls were interviewed about their price limit for the "perfect" prom dress. Their responses are summarized in the table below.

Maximum Price (prom dress)	Number of Girls
$100	23
$150	22
$200	26
$250	14
$300	15

a. Determine, if possible, the mean, median, and mode of the data.

b. Which measure of central tendency should the buyer for a store at the mall use to place an order based on what price gowns will sell best?

13. Top speeds of the winners at the Indianapolis 500 from 1991 to 2000 are listed below:

Year	Speed (mph)	Year	Speed (mph)
1991	176.5	1996	148.0
1992	134.5	1997	145.8
1993	157.2	1998	145.2
1994	170.9	1999	153.0
1995	153.6	2000	177.6

Find the mean, median and mode of this data. Which, in your opinion, is most representative of the data? Why?

14. Andrew wanted a raise in his allowance for doing yard work and his father said he should find out the "average" payment others in the neighborhood received. Andrew surveyed the other families on the block and discovered they paid the following prices for cutting and raking their lawns: $18.00, $22.00, $17.50, $15.00, $25.00, $17.50, $20.00, $15.00, $26.00, $28.00. Which "average" should Andrew use to promote his increase in allowance? Which "average" might his father use to rebut Andrew's argument?

15. The data below represents the median age of Americans as per the U.S. census.

Year	1960	1970	1980	1990	2000
Age	29.4	27.9	30.0	33.0	35.7

Why would the United States Census Bureau report median ages rather than mean or modal ages? What makes the median most representative?

16. The following are the ten top-grossing films in the United States as of 11/25/01.

Movie Title and Year of Release	Money Earned
Titanic 1997	$600,788,188
Star Wars 1977	$461,038,066
The Phantom Menace 1999	$431,088,297
E.T.: The Extra-Terrestrial 1982	$399,804,539
Jurassic Park 1993	$357,267,947
Forrest Gump 1994	$329,694,499
The Lion King 1994	$312,855,561
Return of the Jedi 1983	$309,306,177
Independence Day 1996	$306,179,255
The Sixth Sense 1999	$293,506,292

Find the mean and median of this data. Explain which statistic you would use as the "average gross" of the mega-movies of the United States and why.

17.3 Measures of Dispersion

In the previous section, you studied how information can be summarized for typical data values. In this section, you will study how data differs from the typical.

For example, look at the following test grades for two students.

John: 85, 84, 83, 86, 87
Mike: 79, 98, 68, 94, 86

The mean score for both John and Mike is 85. Do you feel that the two boys are the same kind of student? Why?

Let us examine the scores of the two students. John's grades are all around 85. He is a very consistent student. Mike's grades show much more variability, going up and down from one test to the next. It would be difficult to predict Mike's next grade.

Range

A **measure of dispersion** is a number that indicates the spread, or variation, of data values about the mean. The easiest measure of dispersion is the **range**. The range is the difference between the highest score and the lowest score. If we look at the test grades above, the range in John's scores is $87 - 83 = 4$, while the range in Mike's scores is $98 - 68 = 30$. Adding this component to our study of statistics will certainly help in the understanding and analysis of data. However, the range, in this case, could be a bit deceiving. Look at the following test scores.

John: 85, 84, 83, 86, 87
Mike: 79, 98, 68, 94, 86
Ann: 68, 87, 98, 86, 86

Ann also has a mean score of 85 and a range of 30. We need to go back to the data to see that a mean score of 85 is a reasonable indication of her success in the course.

Mean Absolute Deviation

There is another measure of dispersion that will be helpful to us. The **mean absolute deviation** is just what it sounds like. It is the mean of the absolute values of how much each piece of data deviates, or differs, from the mean. The formula for the mean absolute deviation is: $\dfrac{\sum\limits_{i=1}^{n} |x_i - \bar{x}|}{n}$.

Let's look at Ann's scores above.

x_i	$\bar{x}$	$x_i - \bar{x}$	$|x_i - \bar{x}|$
68	85	-17	17
87	85	2	2
98	85	13	13
86	85	1	1
86	85	1	1
			$\dfrac{\sum |x_i - \bar{x}|}{5} = 6.8$

The mean absolute deviation of her scores is 6.8. This indicates that her scores "average" about 6.8 points from the mean.

Note: Be sure to take the absolute value of the deviation of the scores from the mean. If you found the sum of the scores from the third column, you would have found the sum to be zero. So, remember to take the absolute value of the deviations.

Look at Mike's scores.

x_i	$\bar{x}$	$x_i - \bar{x}$	$\lvert x_i - \bar{x} \rvert$
79	85	-6	6
98	85	13	13
68	85	-17	17
94	85	9	9
86	85	11	11
			$\dfrac{\sum \lvert x_i - \bar{x} \rvert}{5} = 11.2$

The fact that the mean absolute deviation is 11.2 points clearly indicates that Mike is not an "85 average" student.

Let us determine the mean absolute deviation of John's grades.

x_i	$\bar{x}$	$x_i - \bar{x}$	$\lvert x_i - \bar{x} \rvert$
85	85	0	0
84	85	-1	1
83	85	-2	2
86	85	1	1
87	85	2	2
			$\dfrac{\sum \lvert x_i - \bar{x} \rvert}{5} = 1.2$

The mean absolute deviation for John's scores is 1.2, indicating that all his scores lie close to the mean.

Since Mike's mean absolute deviation is more than 9 times John's, his scores are more widely dispersed or distributed. Ann's scores do not vary as much as Mike's.

In 1–5, select the numeral preceding the word or expression that best answers the question.

1. If the range of a set of data is 40 and the highest score is 50, what is the lowest score?
   (1) −10   (3) 10
   (2) 1.2   (4) 90

2. Given each of the following values of the mean absolute deviation, which would indicate data most closely grouped near the mean?
   (1) 102   (3) 1.2
   (2) 10.2   (4) 1.02

3. Which of the following set of scores has the smallest mean absolute deviation?
   (1) 10, 14, 2, 3, 4
   (2) 101, 202, 303, 404, 505
   (3) 2, 4, 8, 16, 32
   (4) 17, 19, 16, 18, 17

4. What is the mean absolute deviation of the data 8, 15, 18, 22, 13, 14?
   (1) $-\dfrac{10}{3}$ (3) $\dfrac{10}{3}$
   (2) 0   (4) 20

5. Which of the following sets of data has the greatest range?
   (1) 32, 65, 34, 43, 16   (3) 65, 54, 75, 45, 86
   (2) 14, 76, 56, 42, 86   (4) 21, 45, 90, 65, 54

6. Mary has been up late each night studying for her Math B Regents exam. She has kept track of the number of hours of sleep she had each night for the past week. If she has slept 6 hours, 5 hours, 6 hours, 7 hours, 3 hours, 4 hours, and 4 hours, find
   a. the mean of the number of hours of sleep she had each night
   b. the range of the number of hours of sleep she had each night
   c. to the nearest tenth, the mean absolute deviation of the number of hours of sleep she had each night

7. The heights of the 2001–2002 New York Knicks team are listed in the table below.

Name	Height
Shandon Anderson	6 ft 6 in.
Marcus Camby	6 ft 11 in.
Howard Eisley	6 ft 2 in.
Othella Harrington	6 ft 9 in.
Allan Houston	6 ft 6 in.
Mark Jackson	6 ft 3 in.
Travis Knight	7 ft 0 in.
Lavor Postell	6 ft 4 in.
Larry Robinson	6 ft 2 in.
Felton Spencer	7 ft 0 in.
Latrell Sprewell	6 ft 5 in.
Kurt Thomas	6 ft 9 in.
Charlie Ward	6 ft 2 in.
Clarence Weatherspoon	6 ft 7 in.

For the given data, find
   a. the mean, to the nearest tenth
   b. the range
   c the mean absolute deviation, to the nearest tenth

8. In Math 101 at a local college, the youngest member of the class was 18 and the oldest member was 43. What is the range in ages?

9. In Math 201 at the same college, the mean age was 19 and the mean absolute deviation was 1.2. What can you conclude about the age of the oldest member of the class?

10. The name, year of birth, and year of appointment for the Supreme Court Justices are listed in the table below.

Name	Year of Birth	Year of Appointment
William H. Rehnquist	1924	1972
Stephen Breyer	1938	1994
Ruth Bader Ginsburg	1933	1993
Anthony M. Kennedy	1936	1988
Sandra Day O'Connor	1930	1981
Antonin Scalia	1936	1986
David Hackett Souter	1939	1990
John Paul Stevens	1920	1975
Clarence Thomas	1948	1991

a. Find, to the nearest tenth, the mean age of the Supreme Court justices, the range of their ages, and the mean absolute deviation of their ages.
b. Find, to the nearest tenth, the mean number of years the Supreme Court justices have served, the range of their years of service, and the mean absolute deviation of their years of service.

11. Monica and Maurice each have a 180 bowling average.

a. If the range of Monica's scores is 50 points and her lowest score is 140, what is her highest score? What can you conclude about Monica's consistency?
b. If the mean absolute deviation of Maurice's scores is 50 points, what does this tell you about Maurice's consistency?

12. The names and of the 10 top female finishers in the 2001 New York Marathon are shown in the table below along with the time it took them to finish the race.

Name	Time (hr:min:sec)
Margaret Okayo	2:24:21
Susan Chepkemei	2:25:12
Svetlana Zakharova	2:25:13
Joyce Chepchumba	2:25:51
Esther Kiplagat	2:26:15
Ludmila Petrova	2:26:18
Deena Drossin	2:26:59
Elena Paramonova	2:30:03
Madina Biktagirova	2:31:14
Elena Meyer	2:31:43

a. Find, to the nearest tenth of a second, the mean time for the top ten female finishers of the New York City 2001 Marathon.
b. Find the range of the times in total seconds and in minutes and seconds.
c. Find the mean absolute deviation of the times to the nearest tenth of a second.

13. The highest temperature on record in New York State, 108°F, was recorded in Troy on July 22, 1926. The lowest temperature on record in New York, −52°F, was recorded on February 18, 1979, at Old Forge. What is the range in temperatures?

14. The highest point in New York State is Mount Marcy, which is located 5,344 feet above sea level. The lowest point in New York State is where New York meets the Atlantic Ocean, at sea level. What is the range in altitudes?

15. The winner of the Women's 100-meter dash in the 2000 Olympics was Marion Jones who completed the race in 10.75 seconds. The names and times of other gold medal Olympic winners in the 100-meter dash are listed in the table below.

   a. To the nearest hundredth, what is the mean time for the 100-meter dash?

   b. What is the range for these times?

   c. To the nearest hundredth, what is the mean absolute deviation for the times?

   d. Who holds the record for the 100-meter dash? How much does her time differ from the mean?

Year	Name	Time
1928	Elizabeth Robinson	12.20
1932	Stanislawa Walasiewicz	11.90
1936	Helen Stephens	11.50
1948	Fanny Blankers-Koen	11.90
1952	Marjorie Jackson	11.50
1956	Betty Cuthbert	11.50
1960	Wilma Rudolph	11.00
1964	Wyomia Tyus	11.40
1968	Wyomia Tyus	11.00
1972	Renate Stecher	11.07
1976	Annegret Richter	11.08
1980	Lyudmila Kondratyeva	11.60
1984	Evelyn Ashford	10.97
1988	Florence Griffith-Joyner	10.54
1992	Gail Devers	10.82
1996	Gail Devers	10.94
2000	Marion Jones	10.75

17.4 Variance and Standard Deviation

There are several other measures of dispersion. For the mean absolute deviation, we used the absolute values of the deviations to avoid the problem of negative and positive values summing to zero. We can also square numbers to avoid problems with negative values.

The **variance**, v, is the arithmetic average of the squares of the deviations from the mean. The formula for the variance is $v = \dfrac{\sum_{i=1}^{n} (x_i - \bar{x})^2}{n}$.

Find the variance for John's and Mike's scores from Section 17.3.

SOLUTION

John's scores are 85, 84, 83, 86, and 87.

x_i	$\bar{x}$	$x_i - \bar{x}$	$(x_i - \bar{x})^2$
85	85	0	0
84	85	−1	1
83	85	−2	4
86	85	1	1
87	85	2	4
			$\dfrac{\sum (x_i - \bar{x})^2}{5} = 2$

Mike's scores are 79, 98, 68, 94, and 86.

x_i	$\bar{x}$	$x_i - \bar{x}$	$(x_i - \bar{x})^2$
79	85	−6	36
98	85	13	169
68	85	−17	289
94	85	9	81
86	85	1	1
			$\dfrac{\sum (x_i - \bar{x})^2}{5} = 115.2$

Answer: The variance for John's scores is 2 and the variance for Mike's scores is 115.2.

One problem with the variance is that we are now dealing with squares of scores, rather than the scores themselves. To get a measure comparable to the original deviations before they were squared, we can take the square root of the variance. The square root of the variance is called the **standard deviation**, which is a widely used measure of dispersion that indicates the concentration of the scores about the mean. The symbol for standard deviation is a lowercase sigma, σ. You may also see the standard deviation written as σ_x, thus, the formula for

standard deviation is $\sigma = \sqrt{\dfrac{\sum\limits_{i=1}^{n} (x_i - \bar{x})^2}{n}}$.

Note: Many statistics books prefer to use μ (mu) instead of $\bar{x}$ in the formula for the standard deviation to indicate the mean associated with the standard deviation. The formula for the **population standard deviation** is thus symbolized as $\sigma = \sqrt{\dfrac{\sum (x - \mu)^2}{n}}$. For the measure known as the **sample standard deviation**, the formula given is usually $\sqrt{\dfrac{\sum (x - \bar{x})^2}{n - 1}}$. The sum of the squared deviations is divided by $n - 1$ instead of n to compensate for the reduced variability in a sample as compared to a whole population.

Since John and Mike's scores are all listed, we will use the population standard deviation. The standard deviation for John's scores is $\sqrt{2} \approx 1.414$. The standard deviation for Mike's scores is $\sqrt{115.2} \approx 10.733$.

MODEL PROBLEM

Find the standard deviation of Ann's scores from Section 17.3.

SOLUTION
Ann's scores are 68, 87, 98, 86, and 86.

x_i	$\bar{x}$	$x_i - \bar{x}$	$(x_i - \bar{x})^2$
68	85	-17	289
87	85	2	4
98	85	13	169
86	85	1	1
86	85	1	1
			$\sqrt{\dfrac{\sum (x_i - \bar{x})^2}{5}} = 9.63$

Answer: The standard deviation for Ann's scores is 9.63.

Sometimes we need a frequency table to determine the standard deviation. For example, if we have 4 scores of 80, 3 scores of 82, 1 score of 78, 2 scores of 81, and 2 scores of 83, a frequency table would make the calculations a bit simpler. The procedure for finding the standard deviation is outlined in the following table.

x_i	f_i	$x_i f_i$	$\bar{x}$	$x_i - \bar{x}$	$(x_i - \bar{x})^2$	$f_i(x_i - \bar{x})^2$
78	1	78	81	-3	9	9
80	4	320	81	-1	1	4
81	2	162	81	0	0	0
82	3	246	81	1	1	3
83	2	166	81	2	4	8
	$n = 12$	$\sum x_i f_i = 972$				$\sqrt{\dfrac{\sum f_i(x_i - \bar{x})^2}{12}} = \sqrt{2}$

The third column, $x_i f_i$, must be completed to find the mean: $\bar{x} = \dfrac{\sum x_i f_i}{n} = \dfrac{972}{12} = 81$. To find the variance, we divide the sum of the last column ($9 + 4 + 0 + 3 + 8 = 24$) by the total number of scores ($n = 12$): $v = \dfrac{24}{12} = 2$. To find the standard deviation, we take the square root of the variance: $\sigma = \sqrt{2} \approx 1.414$.

The TI-83+ can calculate the standard deviation for you. To do so, you must access the statistical features of your calculator. Press (STAT)(1). If there is any data in your lists, be sure to clear it by highlighting the name of the list and pressing (CLEAR) and then (ENTER).
Put the scores into L$_1$ and the frequency into L$_2$ as shown below.

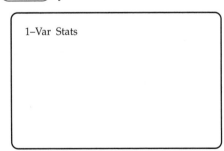

Press (STAT)(▶)(1) to take you into STAT, CALC and choice 1, which is 1−Var Stats. After you press (ENTER), you should see the following screen.

1−Var Stats

You must insert the information about the frequency of the data. Press (2nd) (1) (,) (2nd) (2) to produce the following screen.

```
1–Var Stats L₁, L
2
```

After you press (ENTER), you will see

```
1–Var Stats
 x̄ = 81
 Σx = 972
 Σx² = 78756
 Sx = 1.477097892
 σx = 1.414213562
 ↓n = 12
```

You can see that the mean is 81, the sum of the x-values is 972, the sum of the squares of the x-values is 78756. Sx, the sample standard deviation, is 1.477097892 and the population standard deviation, σx, is 1.414213562. You are also given the number of pieces of data in the sample, 12, the lowest x-value, the first quartile, the median, the third quartile, and the maximum x-value, if you scroll down. If you need any of these values at a later time, you can press (VARS) (5), and then choose what you need.

To obtain the variance using the calculator, follow the procedure as outlined above, and then square the standard deviation, as shown below.

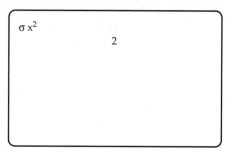

As we previously explained, the sample standard deviation is used when the entire population data is impractical to collect. In these cases, a representative sample would be used to estimate information about the entire population.

If the data in the above example represented the scores of an entire class, the population standard deviation would be used. If this data was used to estimate information for the scores in an entire school, the sample standard deviation would be used.

In 1–6, select the numeral preceding the word or expression that best completes the sentence or answers the question.

1. If the variance of a set of data is 16, what is the standard deviation?
   (1) 256
   (2) 32
   (3) 8
   (4) 4

2. If the standard deviation of a set of data is 16, what is the variance?
   (1) 256
   (2) 32
   (3) 8
   (4) 4

3. What is the sample standard deviation for the following set of data: 6, 12, 14, 19, 24, 36?
   (1) 9.622
   (2) 10.540
   (3) 18.5
   (4) 111

4. What is the population standard deviation for the following set of data: 5, 10, 20, 40, 80?
   (1) 744
   (2) 31
   (3) 27.276
   (4) 5

5. After giving a test to her class, Mrs. Statsrule has decided to raise everyone's score by 5 points. How does this affect the standard deviation?
   (1) increases it by 5 points
   (2) increases it by $\sqrt{5}$ points
   (3) no change
   (4) The change cannot be determined.

6. If each score in a set of data were multiplied by 2, the standard deviation would
   (1) be multiplied by 2
   (2) be divided by 2
   (3) not change
   (4) The change cannot be determined.

7. The table below shows the temperature in various places in New York on November 24, 2001.

Location	Temp.	Location	Temp.
Albany	57	Montgomery	57
Binghamton	57	Niagara Falls	65
Buffalo	65	Pen Yan	62
Dansville	64	Plattsburgh	55
Dunkirk	67	Poughkeepsie	57
Elmira	61	Rochester	65
Fulton	62	Saranak Lake	55
Glens Falls	48	Syracuse	64
Islip	63	Utica	51
JFK Airport	63	Watertown	64
La Guardia Airport	63	Westhampton Beach	60
Massena	62		

   a. According to the data, to the nearest tenth, what was the mean temperature in New York State on November 24, 2001?
   b. What is the standard deviation of the temperatures, to the nearest tenth?
   c. Use your calculator to determine the variance of the temperatures, to the nearest tenth.
   d. If you find the square root of your answer to part **c**, you will not obtain your answer to part **b**. Why?

8. All of the students in Mr. Consistent's math class scored a 90 on a test.
   a. What is the mean score?
   b. What is the standard deviation?

9. Both of the following sets of data have the same mean. Without doing any computation, determine which one has the smaller standard deviation. Explain how you came to your conclusion.
   A: 10, 90, 40, 5, 30, 5
   B: 32, 30, 36, 28, 24, 30

10. The PSAT scores of a group of students in Kennedy High School are given in the table below.

Score	Frequency	Score	Frequency
20	1	55	34
25	2	60	27
30	2	65	23
35	2	70	11
40	14	75	3
45	28	80	2
50	36		

   a. Based on the data given above, to the nearest hundredth, what is the mean PSAT score of these students?
   b. What is the standard deviation, to the nearest hundredth?

11. The table below contains a possible starting line-up for the New York Jets offense, the position played by each player, and the weight of each player.

Name	Position	Weight (lb)
Richie Anderson	Fullback	230
Anthony Becht	Tight End	272
Wayne Chrebet	Wide Receiver	188
Laveranues Coles	Wide Receiver	190
Jason Fabini	Tackle	304
Kerry Jenkins	Guard	295
Curtis Martin	Running Back	205
Kevin Mawae	Center	289
Vinny Testaverde	Quarterback	235
Randy Thomas	Guard	301
Ryan Young	Tackle	320

   a. To the nearest tenth of a pound, what is the mean weight of the members of the New York Jets offensive line-up?
   b. What is the standard deviation, to the nearest tenth of a pound?

12. The table below contains a possible starting line-up for the New York Jets defense, the position played by each player, and the weight of each player.

Name	Position	Weight (lb)
John Abraham	End	256
Shane Burton	End	312
Marcus Coleman	Corner Back	210
Shaun Ellis	End	294
James Farrior	Linebacker	238
Aaron Glenn	Corner Back	185
Victor Green	Safety	210
Marvin Jones	Middle Linebacker	244
Morris Lewis	Linebacker	258
Steve Martin	Tackle	319
Damien Robinson	Safety	223

a. To the nearest tenth of a pound, what is the mean weight of the members of the New York Jets defensive line-up?
b. What is the standard deviation, to the nearest tenth of a pound?

13. The table below lists the ages of people who attended the Screaming Ghouls Rock Concert.

Age (yr)	Frequency	Age (yr)	Frequency
12	23	19	11
13	46	20	10
14	56	21	6
15	65	22	3
16	43	23	2
17	38	31	2
18	21	42	1

a. What is the mean age of the rock concert attendees, to the nearest hundredth?
b. What is the sample standard deviation, to the nearest hundredth?
c. Who would be interested in this type of information?

14. The table below shows the hourly rates of various employees in the Love to Eat Bakery.

Hourly Rate	Frequency	Hourly Rate	Frequency
$5.15	2	$6.00	4
$5.25	7	$10.00	2
$5.50	8	$25.00	1

a. To the nearest cent, what is the mean hourly rate paid?
b. To the nearest cent, what is the standard deviation?

15. The table below lists the average number of days of rain or snow in Buffalo, New York, during a recent year.

Month	Days of Rain or Snow	Month	Days of Rain or Snow
January	19	July	10
February	17	August	10
March	16	September	11
April	14	October	12
May	13	November	15
June	11	December	18

a. To the nearest tenth, what is the mean number of days that it rains or snows in Buffalo per month?
b. What is the standard deviation, to the nearest tenth?
c. To the nearest integer, what is the variance?

17.5 Normal Distribution and the Bell Curve

According to the U. S. Census Bureau, the average female in her twenties is 5 feet 4 inches tall. Certainly a woman who is 5 feet 5 inches would not be considered tall, nor would a woman 5 feet 3 inches be considered short. There is a certain range of heights within which women would be considered "normal height."

If we took a large sample of twenty-year-old women and made a histogram of their heights, we could expect to see a graph similar to the one below.

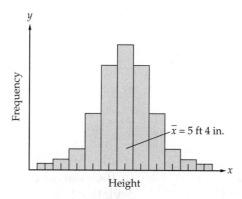

The mean height is 5 feet 4 inches. The middle bar of the histogram represents this height. If we connected the midpoints of the bars of the histogram we would obtain the frequency polygon shown below.

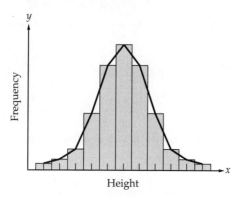

If we drew a smooth curve through the points that determine the frequency polygon, we would get a curve that resembled a bell. In statistics, this curve is called a **normal curve**. Data that can be modeled by a normal curve is said to have a **normal distribution**. People's heights, weights, temperatures, blood pressure, IQ scores, SAT scores, ACT scores, and so on, have a normal distribution. The amount of time a lightbulb burns also produces a normal distribution, as does the size of the bolts produced by a bolt manufacturer.

Note: All data is not modeled by a normal curve. For example, the test scores in your math class would probably not be modeled by a normal curve since the grades are not equally distributed around the mean.

In a normal curve, the mean is the score that occurs the most frequently. (Thus, the mean is also the mode.) Half of the scores lie above the mean and half lie below the mean. (Thus, the mean is also the median.) Since the mean occurs at the center of the curve, it is the axis of symmetry for the curve.

In a normal curve, approximately 68.2% of the scores occur within one standard deviation of the mean, 34.1% below the mean, and 34.1% above the mean. Approximately 95.4% of the scores occur within two standard deviations of the mean, 47.7% above the mean, 47.7% below the mean. Approximately 99.8% of the scores occur within three standard deviations of the mean, 49.9% above the mean, and 49.9% below the mean.

We can break up the normal curve into even smaller intervals. The graph below shows the percentage of students within 0.5, 1, 1.5, 2, 2.5, and 3 standard deviations of the mean.

In statistics, the word *percentile* is often used. A **percentile** indicates a point below which a percentage of scores fall. For example, if you are in the 75th percentile, 75 percent of the people have scores lower than your score, and 25 percent of the people have scores above your score.

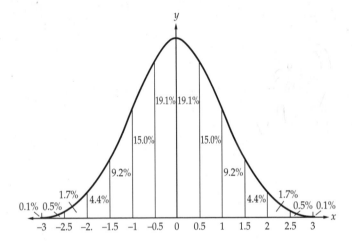

In a normal curve, the mean is the 50th percentile—half of the scores are below the mean, half are above the mean. The figure below includes the percentiles for the normal curve.

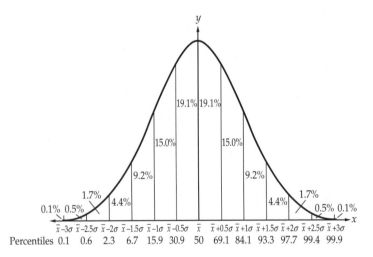

Use the following information to answer Questions 1–3.

Each year, the College Board publishes the mean SAT and the standard deviation for students taking the test. SAT scores are normally distributed. Assume for a group of students that the mean SAT score is 500 with a standard deviation of approximately 100 points.

1. Find the score that is
    a. one standard deviation above the mean
    b. one standard deviation below the mean

SOLUTION

a. One standard deviation above the mean is $500 + 100 = 600$.
b. One standard deviation below the mean is $500 - 100 = 400$.

2. Approximately what percentile would a student be in if he or she scored
    a. 500
    b. 600
    c. 450
    d. 750

SOLUTION

To determine the percentiles, we have to take our normal curve and include the SAT information. The mean is 500, so that goes in the center. Since the standard deviation is 100 points, 0.5 of a standard deviation is 50 points. Fill in the information as shown in the figure below.

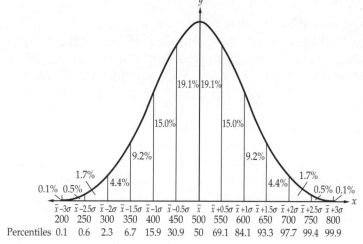

Look at the graph to answer the questions.
a. 500 is at the 50th percentile.
b. 600 is at the 84.1st percentile.
c. 450 is at the 30.9th percentile.
d. 750 is at 99.4th percentile.

3. Over 1,000,000 students took the SAT in 2000. If the standard deviation was 100 points, approximately how many of them would be expected to score
   a. between 400 and 450
   b. between 500 and 550
   c. between 300 and 400
   d. between 650 and 750
   e. above 750

SOLUTION

To answer this question we again refer back to the normal curve. The mean is 500, so that goes in the center. Since the standard deviation is 100 points, 0.5 of a standard deviation is 50 points. Fill in the information as shown in the figure below.

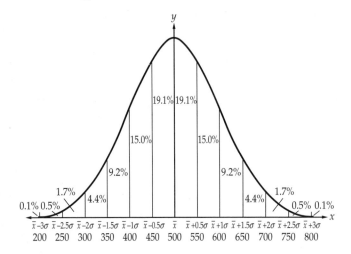

Refer to the figure to answer the questions.
a. Between 400 and 450, 15.0% of the scores occur. 15% of 1,000,000 is 150,000 students.
b. Between 500 and 550, 19.1% of the scores occur. 19.1% of 1,000,000 is 191,000 students.
c. To find the number of scores between 300 and 400, we have to add the two percentages that are given, 4.4% and 9.2%. Thus, 13.6% of the scores occur between 300 and 400. 13.6% of 1,000,000 is 136,000 students.
d. To find the number of scores between 650 and 750, we have to add the two percentages that are given, 4.4% and 1.7%. Thus, 6.1 percent of the scores occur between 650 and 750, which is 61,000 students.
e. Since 750 is at the 99.4th percentile, we can see that 100% − 99.4% = 0.6% of the scores are above 750. Alternatively, we can take the two percentages that are above 750, 0.5% and 0.1%, and add them, which also gives us 0.6%. So, 0.6% of 1,000,000 is 6,000 students.

In 1–10, select the numeral preceding the expression that best answers the question.

1. The mean is 82.75 and the standard deviation is 2.25. If the scores were normally distributed, which of the following scores would be most likely to occur?
   (1) 90   (3) 80.5
   (2) 87.25   (4) 77

2. The Brite Lites R Us Company manufactures lightbulbs. They advertise that the "average lightbulb" can burn for 1,000 hours. Tests have shown that this is the mean length of time. The times that the lights can burn are normally distributed with a standard deviation of 200 hours. What percent of the bulbs could be expected to last 600 or fewer hours?
   (1) 0.6   (3) 6.7
   (2) 2.3   (4) 30.9

3. On a standardized test with a normal distribution, the mean is 85 and the standard deviation is 5. If 1,200 students take the exam, approximately how many of them are expected to earn scores between 90 and 95?
   (1) 14   (3) 163
   (2) 98   (4) 1,172

4. If the mean of a set of normally distributed data is 14 and the standard deviation is 1.5, which of the following scores could be at the 17th percentile?
   (1) 15.6   (3) 12.6
   (2) 15.4   (4) 11.1

5. In a normal distribution, $\bar{x}$ is the mean, and σ is the standard deviation. If $\bar{x} + 0.5\sigma = 100$, and $\bar{x} - 0.5\sigma = 80$, what is the mean?
   (1) 5   (3) 20
   (2) 10   (4) 90

6. The We Go Farther Tire Company advertises a tire that lasts for 80,000 miles. The mileage for the tires is a normal distribution with a mean of 80,000 miles, and a standard deviation of 10,000 miles. If the company produces 32,000 tires, how many of them would be expected to last between 65,000 and 100,000 miles?
   (1) 27,212   (3) 30,528
   (2) 29,120   (4) 31,264

7. On a standardized test with a normal distribution, the mean was 42 and the standard deviation was 2.6. Which score could be expected to occur less than 5 percent of the time?
   (1) 50   (3) 39
   (2) 45   (4) 37

8. The NuBolt Company manufactures nuts and bolts. The size of the diameters of the bolts manufactured produces a normal distribution. The mean size of a certain bolt is 3 centimeters, with a standard deviation of 0.1 centimeter. Bolts that vary from the mean by more than 0.3 centimeter cannot be sold. If the company manufactures 150,000 of the 3-centimeter bolts, approximately how many of them cannot be sold?
   (1) 150   (3) 15,000
   (2) 300   (4) 30,000

9. On a standardized test with a normal distribution and a standard deviation of 2, a score of 35 will occur less than 5 percent of the time. Which of the following could be the mean for this test?
   (1) 32   (3) 38
   (2) 34   (4) 40

10. In a normal distribution, $\bar{x}$ is the mean, and σ is the standard deviation. If $\bar{x} + 2\sigma = 60$, and $\bar{x} - 2\sigma = 40$, what is the standard deviation?
    (1) 5   (3) 20
    (2) 10   (4) 50

11. The mean age of the entering freshman class at a certain university is 18.5, with a standard deviation of 0.75 year. If the data produces a normal distribution, find
    a. the percent of students who are between 19.25 and 17.75 years of age
    b. the percentile of a student who is 20 years old
    c. the number of students who could be expected to be younger than $\bar{x} - \sigma$ years of age, if the total number of incoming freshmen is 1,200 students

12. The average temperature in Central Park, New York, in January is given in the table below.

Year	Temp.	Year	Temp.
1870	37.5	1940	25.0
1875	23.8	1945	25.1
1880	39.6	1950	41.4
1885	29.4	1955	31.0
1890	37.6	1960	33.9
1895	29.8	1965	29.7
1900	31.8	1970	25.1
1905	29.3	1975	37.3
1910	21.1	1980	33.7
1915	34.5	1985	28.8
1920	23.4	1990	41.4
1925	28.8	1995	37.5
1930	33.3	2000	31.3
1935	28.9	2001	33.6

a. Determine the mean temperature in Central Park in January, to the nearest tenth.

b. What is the standard deviation for this data, to the nearest tenth?

c. Assume that, over a long period of time, the January Central Park temperature approximates a normal distribution. Based on your answers from parts **a** and **b**, answer the following questions.

1. What temperature is at the 50th percentile?

2. What is the range of temperatures that occur 95.4 percent of the time?

3. What is the likelihood of coming to Central Park in January and having the temperature above freezing?

4. What temperature is at the 6.7th percentile?

5. Between what two temperatures do 68.2 percent of the temperatures lie?

13. The following table shows the percentages of college freshmen that classified their political orientation as "liberal" over a twenty-year period.

Year	Percent	Year	Percent
1980	20	1996	22
1985	21	1997	22
1990	23	1998	21
1995	21	1999	22

a. Fill in the following table containing the percent and frequency of each percent.

Percent	Frequency
20	
21	
22	
23	

b. Use the information from the frequency table to determine the mean and standard deviation (to the nearest thousandth) of the percent of college freshmen that classify their political orientation as "liberal."

c. Assume that, over a long period of time, the data approximates a normal distribution. Use your answer from part **b** to answer the following questions.

1. Approximately what percent of the time would we expect to see more than 24 percent of college freshmen classify themselves as liberals?

2. Approximately what percent of the time would we expect to see between 19.768 and 23.232% of college freshmen classify themselves as liberals?

14. Scores on the ACT approximate a normal distribution. The following table contains the mean ACT score of students during several years.

Year	1987	1990	1997	1998
Scores	20.6	20.6	21.0	21.0

   a. Using the information from the table above, determine the mean and standard deviation for students taking the ACT from 1987–1998.

   b. Based on your answer to part **a**, approximate the score needed for a student to be in the 97.7th percentile.

   c. Between what two scores do approximately 68.2 percent of the scores lie?

   d. Each year, close to 1,000,000 students take the ACT. Approximately how many of them would be expected to score between 20.8 and 21.2?

CHAPTER REVIEW

In 1–20, select the numeral preceding the word or expression that best completes the sentence or answers the question.

1. $\sum_{j=0}^{5} \sin\left(\frac{j\pi}{2}\right)$ is equivalent to

(1) 1   (3) 0

(2) 2   (4) −1

2. $\frac{1}{2}\sum_{k=1}^{3} k^{k-1}$ is equivalent to

(1) 24   (3) 6

(2) 12   (4) $\frac{1}{2}$

3. Given $\sum_{i=1}^{5} x_i$ with $x_1 = 19$, $x_2 = 21$, $x_3 = 12$, and $x_4 = 18$. If the mean of this data is 19, x_5 must equal

(1) 15   (3) 20

(2) 18   (4) 25

4. What is the median for the data in the table below?

x	$f(x)$
26	8
30	5
32	6
35	3
38	3

(1) 26   (3) 32

(2) 30   (4) 38

5. A standardized test has a mean score of 86 and a standard deviation of 4.3. A student who is in the 41st percentile could have a score of

(1) 41   (3) 85

(2) 80   (4) 90.3

6. On a standardized test, the mean score is 79 and the standard deviation is 5.5. Between which two scores will approximately 15% of the scores fall?

(1) 73.5–79   (3) 79–81.75

(2) 76.25–79   (4) 81.75–84.5

7. In a normal distribution, $\bar{x} + 1.5\sigma = 73$ and $\bar{x} + 1.5\sigma = 58$ when $\bar{x}$ represents the mean and σ represents the standard deviation. The standard deviation is

(1) 5   (3) 12

(2) 10   (4) 15

8. If a set of SAT math scores has a normal distribution and its mean is 451, which score has the greatest probability of being chosen at random?

(1) 510   (3) 421

(2) 590   (4) 390

9. Scores on a calculus final examination at a local college were normally distributed and had a mean of 78.4 and a standard deviation of 8.4. If there were 240 students who took the final exam, approximately how many students could expect a grade between 74.2 and 91?

(1) 91   (3) 150

(2) 120   (4) 163

10. If the variance of a set of data is 12.8, the standard deviation is approximately
(1) 3.58
(3) 25.2
(2) 6.4
(4) 163.84

11. If the standard deviation is 5.7, the variance of the data is approximately
(1) 2.387
(3) 22.8
(2) 11.4
(4) 32.49

In 12–15, use the information in the table that gives the number of divorced individuals per 1,000 married for a 38-year period.

Year	Number of Divorcées	Year	Number of Divorcées
1960	35	1995	161
1970	47	1996	167
1980	100	1997	177
1990	142	1998	175

12. The mean number of divorced people between 1960 and 1998 is
(1) 125.5
(3) 151.5
(2) 140
(4) 158

13. The range of this data is
(1) 125.5
(3) 151.5
(2) 142
(4) 158

14. The variance of this data is
(1) 2,457
(3) 3,337
(2) 2,920
(4) 3,947

15. The standard deviation of this data is
(1) 49.568
(3) 57.767
(2) 54.03
(4) 62.825

16. The local school would like to have a stoplight near the school crossing but the town council decides it needs more information. To find an unbiased sampling of opinions, which of the following would be the best way to survey?
(1) Question parents dropping children off at school.
(2) Telephone a random group of homeowners.
(3) Hold a school meeting on this issue.
(4) Ask owners of local stores.

17. Given the following set of data:

Measure (x_i)	Frequency (f_i)
20	4
32	3
45	3
51	6

Which of the following statements is true?
(1) mean > median
(3) mode < mean
(2) median > mean
(4) mode < median

18. The owner of a business proudly tells his employees that the median salary for the company is $41,000. He doesn't tell them that he is the only person receiving an annual salary of $150,000. He would like to increase his own salary to $200,000 per year. Which of the following statements is true?
(1) The median salary would not be affected.
(2) The median salary would be increased.
(3) The mean salary would not be affected.
(4) The mode salary would be increased.

19. If the variance of a set of data is doubled, the standard deviation is
(1) doubled
(3) multiplied by $\sqrt{2}$
(2) halved
(4) divided by $\sqrt{2}$

20. If the standard deviation of a set of data is doubled, the variance is
(1) doubled
(3) multiplied by 8
(2) multiplied by 4
(4) divided by $\sqrt{2}$

21. Alexander Borbely is a professor at the University of Zurich Medical School where he is the director of the sleep laboratory. The data below comes from the sleeping patterns of 100 random subjects over a twenty-four-hour period, documented in his book *Secrets of Sleep*.

Hours Slept	Frequency	Hours Slept	Frequency
3.5	1	7.5	32
4.5	1	8.5	45
5.5	2	9.5	7
6.5	11	10.5	1

a. Find the mean of this data, to the nearest tenth.
b. Find the variance of this data, to the nearest tenth.
c. Find the standard deviation of this data, to the nearest tenth.
d. Sketch the curve showing the distribution of this data.
e. How many scores fall within $\pm 1\sigma$ of the mean?
f. What percentage of the scores fall within $\pm 1\sigma$ of the mean?
g. Compare the distribution curve for this data and the "normal" distribution. Is this sampling a normal distribution? Why or why not?

22. Gasoline prices, for self-serve regular, in Nassau County over the weeks from August 27, 2001, to November 22, 2001, were $1.54, $1.52, $1.51, $1.52, $1.50, $1.48, $1.44, $1.44, $1.39, $1.37, $1.32, $1.30, $1.28.
a. Find the mean, median, and mode of this data, to the nearest hundredth.
b. Which is the most representative measure of central tendency? Why?
c. Find the standard deviation of this data, to the nearest hundredth.

23. The grades in Mr. Bergersen's Math B class are as follows:

Grade	Frequency
60	1
65	2
70	2
75	3
80	5
85	7
90	5
95	2
100	1

a. What are the mean (to the nearest hundredth), median, and mode for these scores?
b. Without doing any further calculations, can you tell if these scores are normally distributed? Explain.
c. Find the mean absolute deviation, to the nearest hundredth.
d. Find the variance and standard deviation, to the nearest hundredth.
e. How many scores lie within one standard deviation of the mean?
f. Explain how your answer to e verifies your conclusion from b.

ASSESSMENT

Cumulative Reviews and Regents Examinations

CUMULATIVE REVIEW CHAPTERS 1–2

Part I

Answer all questions in this part. Each correct answer will receive 2 credits. No partial credit will be allowed.

1. If you are given the statement $\overline{AB} \perp \overline{CD}$ at point E, what conclusion must be true?
   (1) $\overline{AE} \cong \overline{EB}$.
   (2) $\overline{AB}$ bisects $\overline{CD}$.
   (3) $\angle AEC$ is a right angle.
   (4) $\overline{AB} \cong \overline{CD}$.

2. Given $\triangle MAP$ with $\overline{AQ}$ a perpendicular bisector of $\overline{MP}$, which of the following reasons could be used to prove $\triangle MQA \cong \triangle PQA$?
   (1) SSS $\cong$ SSS
   (2) SAS $\cong$ SAS
   (3) ASA $\cong$ ASA
   (4) Hypotenuse-Leg $\cong$ Hypotenuse-Leg

3. Given parallelogram *HOPE*, which of the following statements is invalid?
   (1) m$\angle HOP \cong$ m $\angle PEH$
   (2) $\overline{HP} \cong \overline{EO}$
   (3) $\overline{HO} \parallel \overline{EP}$
   (4) $\overline{HE} \cong \overline{OP}$

4. Given $\triangle RQN \sim \triangle PQS$.

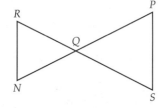

Which of the following statements must be true?
   I. $\angle RQN \cong \angle PQS$.
   II. $\overline{RQ} \cong \overline{QN}$.
   III. $\overline{RN}$ is proportional to $\overline{PS}$.
   (1) I only   (3) I, II, and III
   (2) I and II   (4) I and III

5. Which of the following is an untrue statement about line segments in a circle?
   (1) All chords in a circle are congruent.
   (2) All radii of a circle are congruent.
   (3) If a diameter is perpendicular to a chord, it bisects the chord.
   (4) Congruent central angles have congruent arcs.

6. If two tangents are drawn from a point to a circle and intercept a minor arc of 74°, the angle formed by these two tangents measures
   (1) 37   (3) 74
   (2) 53   (4) 106

7. Tangent $\overline{PA}$ and secant $\overline{PBC}$ are drawn to circle O from point P. If $PA = 12$ and $PB = 8$, the measure of $\overline{BC}$ is
   (1) 18   (3) 10
   (2) 12   (4) 4

8. △ABC is inscribed in circle O. $\overarc{AB}$ measures 124 and ∠CAB ≅ ∠ABC. What is the measure of $\overarc{BC}$?
   (1) 59   (3) 118
   (2) 62   (4) 124

9. Secants $\overline{PBC}$ and $\overline{PDE}$ are drawn to circle O from point P. If PBC = 20, PB = 5, and PDE = 25, the length of PD is

   (1) 20   (3) 5
   (2) 15   (4) 4

10. Chords $\overline{MN}$ and $\overline{PQ}$ intersect at X in circle O. If MX = 4, XN = 12, and PX = 3, the length of QX is
    (1) 16   (3) 8
    (2) 12   (4) 4

Part II

Answer all questions in this part. Each correct answer will receive 2 credits. Clearly indicate the necessary steps, including appropriate formula substitutions, diagrams, graphs, charts, etc. For all questions in this part, a correct numerical answer with no work shown will receive only 1 credit.

11. In circle O, chords $\overline{JK}$ and $\overline{GH}$ intersect at A. If $\overarc{GK}$ = 108° and $\overarc{JH}$ = 52°, determine the measures of ∠JAH and ∠GAK and explain the relationship between these angles.

12. Police detective Hendrix thinks a suspect is pretending to be deaf. How could he use indirect reasoning to prove the suspect can hear?

13. Jared and Mike have a disagreement about the definition of a square. Jared says a square is a rhombus with one right angle. Mike says a square is a rectangle with all sides equal. Who is right? Explain your reasoning.

14. In circle O, chord $\overline{CD}$ is perpendicular to diameter $\overline{AOB}$ at E. If OC = 17 and CD = 16, find the length of $\overline{OE}$.

Part III

Answer all questions in this part. Each correct answer will receive 4 credits. Clearly indicate the necessary steps, including the appropriate formula substitutions, diagrams, graphs, charts, etc. For all questions in this part, a correct numerical answer with no work shown will receive only 1 credit.

15. In circle O, tangent $\overline{PA}$, secant $\overline{PCD}$ intersects diameter $\overline{AOB}$ at M. If m$\overarc{AC}$ = 86 and m$\overarc{DB}$ = 28, find the measures of ∠APD and ∠ABD.

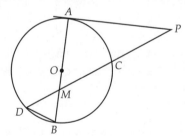

16. Given: △PQR with $\overline{TS} \parallel \overline{QP}$.
    Prove: △PQR ~ △STR.

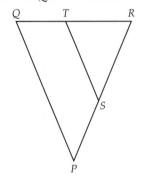

17. In circle O, chord $\overline{WE}$ intersects chord $\overline{US}$ at X. If WE = 25, UX = 18, and XS = 8, find the lengths of WX and XE if WX < XE.

18. Given circle O with diameter $\overline{COB}$, tangents $\overline{PA}$ and $\overline{PB}$, and chords $\overline{AC}$ and $\overline{AB}$ drawn; m∠APB = 58. Find the measure of ∠OAB.

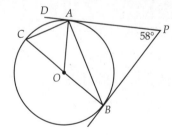

Part IV

Answer all questions in this part. Each correct answer will receive 6 credits. Clearly indicate the necessary steps, including appropriate formula substitutions, diagrams, graphs, charts, etc. For all questions in this part, a correct numerical answer with no work shown will receive only 1 credit.

19. Given: Circle O with diameters $\overline{COD}, \overline{AOB}$, chords $\overline{AD}, \overline{BC}$.
Prove: $\overline{AD} \cong \overline{BC}$.

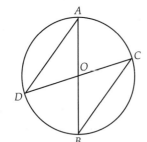

20. Given: circle O with tangent $\overline{PA}$, secant $\overline{PBC}$, diameter $\overline{DOE}$, chord $\overline{AC}$. $PA = 20$, $PB = 8$, $\overline{AF} = \overline{CF}$, m$\angle APC = 49$, m$\widehat{AB} = 41$.
Find the length of OC and the measure of $\angle COD$.

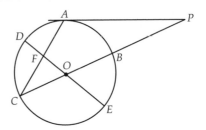

Not drawn to scale

CUMULATIVE REVIEW CHAPTERS 1–3

Part I

Answer all questions in this part. Each correct answer will receive 2 credits. No partial credit will be allowed.

1. The expression $\dfrac{1 + \sqrt{5}}{2 + \sqrt{5}}$ is equivalent to
(1) $\sqrt{5} - 3$ (3) $3 - \sqrt{5}$
(2) $\dfrac{1}{2}$ (4) $3 + \sqrt{5}$

2. $|3 + \sqrt{-16}|$ is equal to
(1) -1 (3) $3 - 4i$
(2) $4 + 4i$ (4) 5

3. Tangent $\overline{PA}$ and secant $\overline{PBC}$ are drawn to circle O from point P. If $PB = 4$ and $BC = 5$, then PA is
(1) 9 (3) 3
(2) 6 (4) 4

4. Which of the following *cannot* be used to prove two triangles congruent?
(1) SSA $\cong$ SSA
(2) AAS $\cong$ AAS
(3) ASA $\cong$ ASA
(4) Hyp-leg $\cong$ Hyp-leg

5. In what quadrant does the sum of $6 - 5i$ and $4 + 6i$ lie?
(1) I   (3) III
(2) II   (4) IV

6. In circle O, chords $\overline{AB}$ and $\overline{CD}$ intersect at point E. If m$\angle CEB = 40$ and m$\widehat{AD} = 50$, what is m$\widehat{CB}$?
(1) 10 (3) 30
(2) 20 (4) 40

7. Simplify: $3i^2 - 2i^4 + 5i^{23}$.
(1) $1 - 5i$ (3) $5 - 5i$
(2) $-5 - 5i$ (4) $5 + 5i$

8. If you are given that, in triangle ABC, $\overline{AD}$ is a median to side $\overline{BC}$, what can you conclude?
(1) $\overline{AD} \cong \overline{DB}$ (3) $\overline{AD} \cong \overline{DC}$
(2) $\overline{BD} \cong \overline{DC}$ (4) $\angle BDA$ is a right angle.

9. Two tangents are drawn to a circle from external point P. If the major arc has a measure of 240, find m$\angle P$.
(1) 60 (3) 120
(2) 100 (4) 140

10. Which of the following is *not* sufficient to prove that quadrilateral $ABCD$ is a square?
(1) All four sides are congruent.
(2) $ABCD$ is a rhombus with one right angle.
(3) $ABCD$ is a rectangle with two congruent adjacent sides.
(4) All four angles are right angles and two adjacent sides are congruent.

Part II

Answer all questions in this part. Each correct answer will receive 2 credits. Clearly indicate the necessary steps, including appropriate formula substitutions, diagrams, graphs, charts, etc. For all questions in this part, a correct numerical answer with no work shown will receive only 1 point.

11. Simplify: $(14 - 6i) - (8 + 3i)$.

12. Amanda is trying to begin an indirect proof, but doesn't know where to start. She wants to prove that: If a triangle is not isosceles then no two angles are congruent. How should she begin her proof?

13. In circle O, chords $\overline{AB}$ and $\overline{CD}$ intersect at point E. If $AE = x$, $EB = x + 2$, $CE = 8$, and $ED = 3$, find AE.

14. What is the product of $(2 + 3i)$ and its conjugate?

Part III

Answer all questions in this part. Each correct answer will receive 4 credits. Clearly indicate the necessary steps, including the appropriate formula substitutions, diagrams, graphs, charts, etc. For all questions in this part, a correct numerical answer with no work shown will receive only 1 credit.

15. Solve for x: $\sqrt{x + 14} = x + 2$.

16. Juan and Zach were studying together for their Math B test. They disagreed over whether or not a rhombus and an isosceles trapezoid are parallelograms. Explain which (if either) of the two quadrilaterals is a parallelogram. Justify your answer.

17. Given $Z_1 = 2 + 5i$ and $Z_2 = 5 + 3i$.
  a. Graph each of the numbers Z_1 and Z_2.
  b. Graph the sum of Z_1 and Z_2.
  c. Express the sum of Z_1 and Z_2 as a complex number.

18. Fill in the correct information in the following proof:
Given: Rectangle $RECT$, with M the midpoint of $\overline{EC}$.
Prove: Triangle RMT is isosceles.

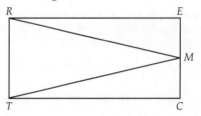

Statements	Reasons
1. Rectangle $RECT$, M the midpoint of $\overline{EC}$.	**1.** Given.
2.	**2.** Definition of midpoint.
3. $\angle E$ and $\angle C$ are right angles.	**3.**
4. $\angle E \cong \angle C$.	**4.** All right angles are congruent.
5. $\overline{RE} \cong \overline{TC}$.	**5.**
6. $\triangle REM \cong \triangle TCM$.	**6.** SAS $\cong$ SAS.
7.	**7.** CPCTC.
8. Triangle RMT is isosceles.	**8.** Definition of isosceles triangle.

Answer all questions in this part. Each correct answer will receive 6 credits. Clearly indicate the necessary steps, including appropriate formula substitutions, diagrams, graphs, charts, etc. For all questions in this part, a correct numerical answer with no work shown will receive only 1 credit.

19. Given: Triangle ABC with $\overline{AD} \perp \overline{BC}$, $\overline{DA}$ bisects $\angle BAC$.
Prove: $\angle ABC \cong \angle ACB$.

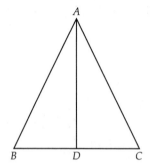

20. In the accompanying diagram of circle O, diameter $\overline{AOC}$ is extended through C to point D; tangent $\overline{DB}$; chords $\overline{AE}$ and $\overline{CE}$ are drawn; $m\overarc{BC} = 70$; $m\angle ACE = 60$.

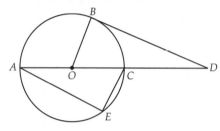

Find
a. $m\angle BOC$
b. $m\overarc{AB}$
c. $m\angle BDA$
d. $m\overarc{CE}$

CUMULATIVE REVIEW CHAPTERS 1–4

Part I

Answer all questions in this part. Each correct answer will receive 2 credits. No partial credit will be allowed.

1. If you are given $\triangle ABC$ with $\overline{AB} \cong \overline{CB}$, which statement must be true?
(1) $\overline{AC} = \overline{AB}$
(2) $\angle ABC \cong \angle BAC$
(3) $\angle BAC \cong \angle BCA$
(4) $\angle ABC \cong \angle BCA$

2. Given $\triangle NBC$ with $\overline{QC}$ an angle bisector of $\angle BCN$. Which of the following additional statements would give you sufficient information to prove $\triangle NQC \cong \triangle BQC$?
(1) Q is the midpoint of $\overline{NB}$.
(2) $\overline{QC} \perp \overline{BN}$.
(3) $\overline{QC}$ is a median to $\overline{NB}$.
(4) $\angle BCQ \cong \angle NCQ$.

3. The height y of Marla's model rocket can be represented by the equation $y = -16x^2 + 70x + 37$ where x represents the time in seconds since the rocket was launched, and height is expressed in feet. What was the maximum height of Marla's rocket to the nearest tenth of a foot?
(1) 243.6
(2) 143.4
(3) 113.6
(4) 39.4

4. Secants $\overline{PBC}$ and $\overline{PDE}$ are drawn to circle O from point P. If $PB = 9$, $BC = 15$, and $PD = 6$, what is the difference in length between the two secants?
(1) 6
(2) 12
(3) 18
(4) 36

5. Which of the following discriminants would indicate that a quadratic equation has two rational, real, unequal roots?
(1) -43
(2) 0
(3) 17
(4) 36

6. When the vectors $(3 - 2i)$ and $(-1 + 5i)$ are graphed, their sum lies in which quadrant?
(1) I
(2) II
(3) III
(4) IV

7. The solution to the equation $\sqrt{2x^2 + 1} = x + 1$ is
(1) $\{0\}$
(2) $\{2\}$
(3) $\{0, 2\}$
(4) $\{\ \}$

8. Parallelogram *CALM* is inscribed in circle *O*. If $\overset{\frown}{ALM} = 180°$, $\overset{\frown}{CAL} = 180°$, what kind of quadrilateral must *CALM* be?
(1) a trapezoid   (3) a square
(2) a rhombus   (4) a rectangle

9. The graphs of $y = 2x^2 - 5x + 2$ and $y - 4x = 13$ intersect in how many points?
(1) 1   (3) 3
(2) 2   (4) 0

10. Which equation states that the temperature of rare roast beef, *t*, is less than 5° from 140°?
(1) $|5 - t| < 140$ (3) $|5 + t| < 140$
(2) $|140 - t| < 5$ (4) $|140 + t| < 5$

Part II

Answer all questions in this part. Each correct answer will receive 2 credits. Clearly indicate the necessary steps, including appropriate formula substitutions, diagrams, graphs, charts, etc. For all questions in this part, a correct numerical answer with no work shown will receive only 1 credit.

11. Kyle cannot remember how to rationalize the denominator of the expression $\dfrac{15}{2 - \sqrt{7}}$. Explain the process to him and show him the answer he should obtain.

12. Point *P* lies outside circle *O*. The angle formed by tangents $\overline{PA}$ and $\overline{PB}$ measures 58. What is the measure of major arc $\overset{\frown}{ACB}$?

13. Find the positive root of the equation $y = 2x^2 - 3x - 4$ to the nearest hundredth.

14. Simplify $2\sqrt{54} - \dfrac{3}{2}\sqrt{24} + \sqrt{96}$.

Part III

Answer all questions in this part. Each correct answer will receive 4 credits. Clearly indicate the necessary steps, including the appropriate formula substitutions, diagrams, graphs, charts, etc. For all questions in this part, a correct numerical answer with no work shown will receive only 1 credit.

15. Convert the equation $y = 2x^2 - 8x + 13$ to vertex form and identify the axis of symmetry and turning point.

16. Rectangle *MATH* has a length of $\dfrac{x^2 - 16}{2x^2 + 11x + 12}$ and a width of $\dfrac{3 - 7x - 6x^2}{2 - 6x}$. Express the area of *MATH* in simplest form.

17. Given: Circle *O* with tangent $\overline{PD}$ and secant $\overline{PAB}$; $PD = 15$, $PB = 25$; m∠$CEB = 74$; m$\overset{\frown}{AD} = 95$.

Find the length of *PA* and the measure of $\overset{\frown}{CB}$.

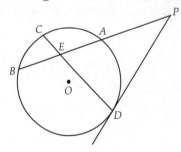

18. One root of a quadratic equation is $3 - 2i\sqrt{5}$. Explain how you know what the other root must be. Then find the equation that has these two roots as its solution.

Answer all questions in this part. Each correct answer will receive 6 credits. Clearly indicate the necessary steps, including appropriate formula substitutions, diagrams, graphs, charts, etc. For all questions in this part, a correct numerical answer with no work shown will receive only 1 credit.

19. The profits of an Internet auction company can be represented by the function $P = -t^2 + 8t + 12$ where P represents profits in hundreds of thousands of dollars and t represents the years since the company started (let 2000 be $t = 0$). According to the model, in what year will the company have maximum profits? What will the maximum profits be?

20. Given: Parallelogram $ABCD$; $AE = FC$.
    Prove: $\triangle ADF \cong \triangle CBE$.

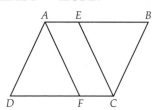

CUMULATIVE REVIEW CHAPTERS 1–5

Part I

Answer all questions in this part. Each correct answer will receive 2 credits. No partial credit will be allowed.

1. What is $|2 - 6i|$?
   (1) $4\sqrt{2}$ (3) 3
   (2) $2\sqrt{10}$ (4) 4

2. In circle O, chords $\overline{AB}$ and $\overline{CD}$ intersect at point E. If E is the midpoint of chord CD, $AE = 4$ and $BE = 16$, find CD.
   (1) 8   (3) 16
   (2) 10   (4) 20

3. If you are given that $\overline{CD}$ is an altitude to $\overline{AB}$ in triangle ABC, what can you conclude?
   (1) $\overline{AD} \cong \overline{DB}$
   (2) $\angle ACD \cong \angle BCD$
   (3) $\angle ACD$ is right angle.
   (4) $\angle ADC$ is a right angle.

4. What is the product of the roots of the equation $x^2 - 3x + 7 = 0$?
   (1) -7 (3) 3
   (2) -3 (4) 7

5. Write as a monomial in terms of i:
   $2\sqrt{-9} + 7\sqrt{-36} - 4\sqrt{-25}$.
   (1) $-62i$ (3) $28i$
   (2) $-28i$ (4) $62i$

6. Simplify: $\dfrac{\frac{1}{x} - \frac{1}{y}}{\frac{y}{x} - \frac{x}{y}}$.
   (1) $\dfrac{1}{x + y}$ (3) $-\dfrac{1}{x + y}$
   (2) $\dfrac{1}{x - y}$ (4) $-\dfrac{1}{x - y}$

7. Solve: $|2x - 3| = 5$.
   (1) $\{1, 4\}$ (3) $\{-1, 4\}$
   (2) $\{-1, -4\}$ (4) $\{1, -4\}$

8. In circle O, tangents $\overline{AB}$ and $\overline{BC}$ meet at external point B. If $m\angle ABC = 70$, what is the measure of the major arc of the circle?
   (1) 70   (3) 250
   (2) 140   (4) 260

9. If $5 - 6i$ is one root of a quadratic equation, what is another root?
   (1) $-5 - 6i$ (3) $5 + 6i$
   (2) $-5 + 6i$ (4) cannot be determined

10. What is the vertex of the parabola $y = (x - 2)^2 + 7$?
    (1) $(-2, 7)$ (3) $(2, -7)$
    (2) $(-2, -7)$ (4) $(2, 7)$

Part II

Answer all questions in this part. Each correct answer will receive 2 credits. Clearly indicate the necessary steps, including appropriate formula substitutions, diagrams, graphs, charts, etc. For all questions in this part, a correct numerical answer with no work shown will receive only 1 credit.

11. Mrs. Sheehan's math class is designing a game. They have decided to make the game board in the shape of a regular pentagon. If the length of each of the sides is $\dfrac{x}{x+1}$, what is the perimeter of the game board?

12. If you are given that $\overline{DB} \perp \overline{RH}$ at point P, what can you conclude?

13. Madeline has bought a Frisbee as a gift for her friend Tom. To disguise the shape of the Frisbee when it is wrapped, Madeline is going to inscribe it in a triangle whose sides are tangent to the circle as shown in the figure.

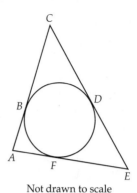

Not drawn to scale

If $AB = 6$ inches, $BC = 5$ inches, and $DE = 7$ inches, what is the perimeter of triangle ACE?

14. Solve for x: $\sqrt{x+2} = x$.

Part III

Answer all questions in this part. Each correct answer will receive 4 credits. Clearly indicate the necessary steps, including the appropriate formula substitutions, diagrams, graphs, charts, etc. For all questions in this part, a correct numerical answer with no work shown will receive only 1 credit.

15. Mary Lu is four years younger than her sister, Mary Jane. Their mother, who is a math teacher, noticed that the product of the ages of the two sisters is 32. How old are the girls? (Only an algebraic solution will be accepted.)

16. When Lauren and Johnny worked together to rake the leaves in their backyard, it took them 6 hours. The last time the leaves needed raking, Johnny worked alone, and it took him 10 hours. If Lauren raked the leaves by herself, how long would it take her?

17. Frank and Nora are driving from Huntington Station, NY, to Valley Cottage, NY, a trip that takes approximately 110 minutes. Depending on traffic, their traveling time, t, could differ from the 110 minutes by at most 20 minutes.

 a. Write an equation involving absolute value that could be used to express this information.

 b. Solve the above equation to find t.

18. In the accompanying diagram of circle O, diameter $\overline{AOC}$ is extended through C to point D; tangent $\overline{DB}$; chords $\overline{AE}$ and $\overline{CE}$ are drawn.

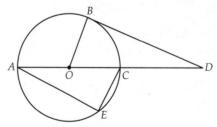

Prove that m$\angle OBD$ = m$\angle CEA$.

Part IV

Answer all questions in this part. Each correct answer will receive 6 credits. Clearly indicate the necessary steps, including appropriate formula substitutions, diagrams, graphs, charts, etc. For all questions in this part, a correct numerical answer with no work shown will receive only 1 credit.

19. Given: Quadrilateral *EASY* with *E*(1, 5), *A*(5, 7), *S*(7, 3) and *Y*(3, 1).
Prove: Quadrilateral *EASY* is a square.

20. The doorway of a new office building is in the shape of a parabolic arch. The equation which models the doorway is $y = -x^2 + 8x$. Partytime Caterers have been asked to plan a grand opening celebration. They want to hang a banner across the doorway, eight feet above the ground. To the nearest tenth of a foot, how wide can the banner be?

CUMULATIVE REVIEW CHAPTERS 1–6

Part I

Answer all questions in this part. Each correct answer will receive 2 credits. No partial credit will be allowed.

1. If $f(x) = |10 - 4x - x^2|$, the value of $f(2)$ is
(1) −2   (3) 6
(2) 2   (4) 22

2. Given $f(x) = 2x^2 - 4x + 5$, we know its roots are
(1) imaginary
(2) real, rational, and equal
(3) real, rational, and unequal
(4) real, irrational, and unequal

3. Tangent $\overline{PA}$ and secant $\overline{PBC}$ are drawn to circle *O* from the same external point *P*. If *PA* = 16 and *PB* = 8, the length of $\overline{BC}$ is which of the following?
(1) 32   (3) 16
(2) 24   (4) 8

4. An elliptically shaped pond is used by neighborhood children as a skating rink. The pond is approximately 128 feet long and 72 feet wide. Which of the following could represent the equation for the outline of this skating rink?
(1) $x^2 + y^2 = 200$ (3) $\dfrac{x^2}{64^2} + \dfrac{y^2}{36^2} = 1$

(2) $x^2 + y^2 = 10\sqrt{2}$ (4) $\dfrac{x^2}{64^2} + \dfrac{y^2}{36^2} = 100$

5. Which of the following is *not* a function?
(1) $3x + 4y = 20$ (3) $y^2 - 3y - 2 = x$
(2) $x^2 + 5x = y$ (4) $x^2 + \frac{2}{3}x + 1 = y$

6. The solution set for the equation $3 + \sqrt{2x - 3} = x$ is
(1) {−2, −6}   (3) {2, 6}
(2) {2}   (4) {6}

7. Given $\triangle KEY$ with $\angle ESY$ a right angle and $\angle K \cong \angle Y$, which of the following is *not* a true statement?

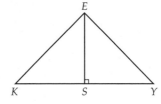

(1) $\overline{EK} \perp \overline{EY}$
(2) $\overline{KE} \cong \overline{EY}$
(3) $\triangle KEY$ is an isosceles triangle.
(4) $\triangle KES \cong \triangle YES$

8. Which of the following is true of the product of $(3 + 4i)$ and $(3 - 4i)$?
(1) The product is a real, rational number.
(2) The product is a complex number.
(3) The product is $0 + 0i$.
(4) The product is an irrational number.

9. When reduced to lowest terms, $\dfrac{6x^2 - 5x - 4}{8 - 2x - 3x^2}$ is
(1) −1   (3) $\dfrac{2x + 1}{2 + x}$

(2) 2   (4) $-\dfrac{2x + 1}{2 + x}$

10. Paul left the office and started to drive home. He was stuck in traffic for nearly twenty minutes when he realized he had forgotten an important file he would need early the next morning for a meeting with a client. He returned to the office and then headed home again. This time he encountered little traffic. Which of the graphs could represent his distance from home as a function of time?

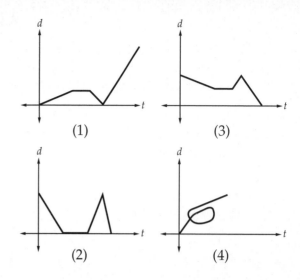

(1)   (3)

(2)   (4)

Part II

Answer all questions in this part. Each correct answer will receive 2 credits. Clearly indicate the necessary steps, including appropriate formula substitutions, diagrams, graphs, charts, etc. For all questions in this part, a correct numerical answer with no work shown will receive only 1 credit.

In 11 and 12, use the following situation.
The profits earned by PQR Corporation for the last six years can be represented by the function $p(x) = -0.89x^2 + 7x - 3$ in which $p(x)$ is given in hundreds of thousands of dollars and x represents the number of years since the company was founded in January 1996.

11. In what year did the company show its highest profit and how much was it?

12. A friend says she is thinking about investing in the PQR Corporation and asks your opinion. What would you tell her and why?

13. Ilana says the fraction $\dfrac{2x^2 - 3x + 1}{x^2 + 1}$ is never undefined but Alan does not believe her. Explain to Alan why Ilana is correct.

14. In circle O, chords $\overline{MN}$ and $\overline{PQ}$ intersect at K. If $MN = 25$, $PK = 18$, and $KQ = 8$, find the length of $\overline{MK}$ and $\overline{NK}$ if $MK < NK$.

Part III

Answer all questions in this part. Each correct answer will receive 4 credits. Clearly indicate the necessary steps, including the appropriate formula substitutions, diagrams, graphs, charts, etc. For all questions in this part, a correct numerical answer with no work shown will receive only 1 credit.

15. Given the function $g(x) = \dfrac{2x - 7}{\sqrt{x^2 - 1}}$, determine its domain and explain your answer.

16. Joanna earns money as a part-time receptionist according to the function $j(x) = 8x - 2.35$ where x is the number of hours she works. Her father suggests that Joanna invest her earnings in a company whose quarterly payout is represented by the function $p(x) = 4x + 28$. What single function would represent the quarterly value of the investment of all of Joanna's earnings in the company her father recommends?

17. One root of a quadratic equation is $3 + \sqrt{2}i$. Determine the other root and write the equation which has these values as its roots.

18. If $f(x) = x^2 - 2x - 11$ and $g(x) = 3x - 2$, find the rule which represents the expression $(f \circ g)(x)$.

Part IV

Answer all questions in this part. Each correct answer will receive 6 credits. Clearly indicate the necessary steps, including appropriate formula substitutions, diagrams, graphs, charts, etc. For all questions in this part, a correct numerical answer with no work shown will receive only 1 credit.

19. Given: Circle O with diameter $\overline{AOB}$, tangents $\overline{PC}$, $\overline{PD}$, radius $\overline{OC}$, and chords $\overline{AC}$, $\overline{AD}$.

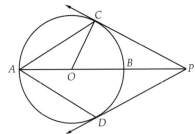

Not drawn to scale

If $m\angle CPA = 36$ and $m\widehat{AD} = 126$, find

  a. $m\angle ADP$
  b. $m\widehat{CB}$
  c. $m\angle CAP$

20. Given quadrilateral $PQRS$ with coordinates $P(0, 0)$, $Q(4, 3)$, $R(7, -1)$, and $S(3, -4)$. Prove that $PQRS$ is a square.

CUMULATIVE REVIEW CHAPTERS 1–7

Part I

Answer all questions in this part. Each correct answer will receive 2 credits. No partial credit will be allowed.

1. If $f(x) = x + 2$ and $g(x) = x^2$, find $(f \circ g)(3)$.
  (1) 11   (3) 25
  (2) 14   (4) 45

2. If x varies inversely as y and $x = 4$ when $y = 12$, when $y = 3$, $x =$
  (1) 1   (3) 13
  (2) 9   (4) 16

3. The expression $(3 + 4i)^2$ is equivalent to
  (1) $-7 - 24i$ (3) 25
  (2) $-7 + 24i$ (4) $9 + 16i$

4. If you are given that $\overrightarrow{BD}$ bisects $\angle ABC$, you can conclude that
  (1) $\overline{AB} \cong \overline{BC}$ (3) $\angle DAB \cong \angle DCB$
  (2) $\angle ABD \cong \angle CBD$ (4) $\angle ADB \cong \angle CDB$

5. The roots of the equation $x^2 - x + 10 = 0$ are
  (1) real, rational, and equal
  (2) real, rational, and unequal
  (3) real, irrational, and unequal
  (4) imaginary

6. In circle O, chords $\overline{CH}$ and $\overline{RD}$ intersect at point S. If S is the midpoint of chord $\overline{CH}$, $RS = 2$, and $SD = 8$, what is the length of chord $\overline{CH}$?
  (1) 16   (3) 8
  (2) 10   (4) 4

7. What is the solution set for $|2x - 4| < 6$?
  (1) $\{x \mid -1 < x < 5\}$ (3) $\{x \mid x < -1 \text{ or } x > 5\}$
  (2) $\{x \mid -5 < x < 1\}$ (4) $\{x \mid x < -5 \text{ or } x > 1\}$

8. The fraction $\dfrac{1 - \frac{1}{a}}{1 - \frac{1}{a^2}}$ is equivalent to
  (1) 1   (3) $\frac{1}{a}$
  (2) $-\frac{1}{a}$ (4) $\frac{a}{a + 1}$

9. In which quadrants does the graph of $xy = 4$ lie?
  (1) I and II   (3) I and III
  (2) II and III   (4) II and IV

10. If $x^2 + y^2 = 16$ and $x = 5$, then a value of y is
  (1) -3 (3) 3
  (2) $-3i$ (4) $9i$

Part II

Answer all questions in this part. Each correct answer will receive 2 credits. Clearly indicate the necessary steps, including appropriate formula substitutions, diagrams, graphs, charts, etc. For all questions in this part, a correct numerical answer with no work shown will receive only 1 credit.

11. What are the domain and range of the function $y = x^2 + 3$?

12. The length of a rectangle is $\dfrac{2x + 4}{x^2 - 9}$ and its width is $\dfrac{3}{x - 3}$. Express the perimeter of the rectangle as a single fraction in simplest form.

13. In circle O, $m\angle ABC = 50$. Find $m\angle AOC$.

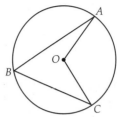

14. Write an equation for the line tangent to the circle $x^2 + y^2 = 36$ at the point whose x-coordinate is 6.

Part III

Answer all questions in this part. Each correct answer will receive 4 credits. Clearly indicate the necessary steps, including the appropriate formula substitutions, diagrams, graphs, charts, etc. For all questions in this part, a correct numerical answer with no work shown will receive only 1 credit.

15. Solve for x and express the roots in simplest $a + bi$ form: $x^2 - 2x + 10 = 0$.

16. **a.** Does the function $y = 2x - 3$ have an inverse? Explain your answer.
    b. If your answer to part **a** is "yes," write the equation for the inverse function.

17. Solve for x: $\dfrac{3}{x - 2} + \dfrac{8}{x^2 - 4} = 1$.

18. Given $Z_1 = 6 + 8i$ and $Z_2 = 2 + 5i$.
    a. Graph each of the numbers Z_1 and Z_2.
    b. Graph the difference of Z_1 and Z_2.
    c. Express the difference of Z_1 and Z_2 as a complex number.

Part IV

Answer all questions in this part. Each correct answer will receive 6 credits. Clearly indicate the necessary steps, including appropriate formula substitutions, diagrams, graphs, charts, etc. For all questions in this part, a correct numerical answer with no work shown will receive only 1 credit.

19. The track team at Conicsrule High School is designing a logo for their uniforms, as shown in the figure below.

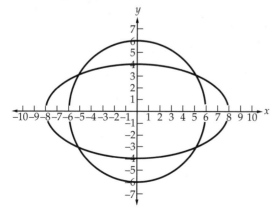

    a. Write equations for the circle and the ellipse shown in the figure.

    b. To the nearest tenth, find the coordinates of the point where the two figures intersect in Quadrant I.

20. Given: Rhombus $PARL$ with $\overline{LR}$ extended through R to point G and $\overline{AR}$ extended through R to point E; $\overline{LA} \parallel \overline{EG}$.
    Prove: $PA \cdot RG = RE \cdot PL$.

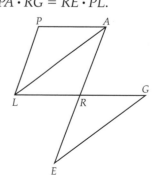

CUMULATIVE REVIEW CHAPTERS 1–8

Part I

Answer all questions in this part. Each correct answer will receive 2 credits. No partial credit will be allowed.

1. The single transformation that is equivalent to $r_{x\text{-axis}} \circ r_{y=x}$ is
   (1) $r_{y=-x}$
   (2) $R_{90°}$
   (3) $R_{270°}$
   (4) r_{origin}

2. Which of the following is *not* an appropriate method of proving by coordinate geometry that a quadrilateral is a parallelogram?
   (1) Find the slope of all four sides to prove opposite sides parallel.
   (2) Use the midpoint formula on the diagonals to prove diagonals bisect each other.
   (3) Use the distance formula to prove two pairs of opposite sides equal in length.
   (4) Use the slope formula to prove diagonals perpendicular.

3. When simplified, $\frac{1}{2}\sqrt{80} + 2\sqrt{45} - 10\sqrt{\frac{1}{5}}$ equals
   (1) $10\sqrt{5}$
   (2) $6\sqrt{5}$
   (3) $5\sqrt{6}$
   (4) $\frac{\sqrt{5}}{10}$

4. The smallest integral value of c that will produce imaginary roots in the equation $4x^2 - 7x + c = 0$ is
   (1) 0
   (2) 2
   (3) 3
   (4) 4

5. The general equation of certain conics, $ax^2 + by^2 = c$, will represent an ellipse when
   (1) $a \neq b, a > 0$ and $b > 0$
   (2) $a = b, a > 0$ and $b > 0$
   (3) $a \neq b$ and $b < 0$
   (4) $a = b$ and $b < 0$

6. The solution set of $\frac{2}{2x+1} + \frac{3x+1}{x+2} = 2$ is
   (1) $\{1\}$
   (2) $\left\{\frac{1}{2}\right\}$
   (3) $\left\{\frac{1}{2}, 1\right\}$
   (4) $\{\ \}$

7. Which of the following is a direct isometry?
   (1) D_2
   (2) $r_{x\text{-axis}}$
   (3) $r_{y=x}$
   (4) $R_{90°}$

8. The price per person of renting a limousine varies inversely to the number of people who will ride in the limousine. If 8 people rent the limo to go to the senior prom, the cost is $72 per person. What is the cost per person if 12 people rent the limo?
   (1) $72
   (2) $60
   (3) $48
   (4) $36

9. The domain of $y = \frac{x^2 - 3x + 2}{x^2 - 9}$ is
   (1) all real numbers except ± 3
   (2) $-3 < x < 3$
   (3) ± 3
   (4) all real numbers

10. The graph in the accompanying diagram shows the solution to which of the following inequalities?

   (1) $x^2 + 2x \geq 8$
   (2) $x^2 + 2x \leq 8$
   (3) $x^2 + 2x < 8$
   (4) $x^2 - 2x < 8$

Part II

Answer all questions in this part. Each correct answer will receive 2 credits. Clearly indicate the necessary steps, including appropriate formula substitutions, diagrams, graphs, charts, etc. For all questions in this part, a correct numerical answer with no work shown will receive only 1 credit.

11. Jacob decided to start saving for a car from his salary at a part-time job. His weekly earnings are represented by $S(x) = 8x + 40$, where x is the number of hours worked. If he wants to save 25 percent of salary, $S(x)$, write the composition that shows the amount Jacob will save each week.

12. Write the equation of a circle with a radius of 3 and center at $(4, -5)$.

13. Find all values of x for which $x + |3 - 2x| = 4$.

14. In circle O, secants $\overline{PAB}$ and $\overline{PCD}$ and chord $\overline{BC}$ are drawn.

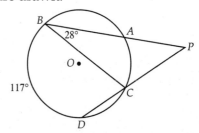

If m$\angle PBC = 28$ and m$\overset{\frown}{BD} = 117$, find m$\angle BPD$.

Part III

Answer all questions in this part. Each correct answer will receive 4 credits. Clearly indicate the necessary steps, including the appropriate formula substitutions, diagrams, graphs, charts, etc. For all questions in this part, a correct numerical answer with no work shown will receive only 1 credit.

15. If $f(x) = x^2 - 4x$ and $g(x) = 2x + 3$, find $(f \circ g^{-1})(x)$.

16. Determine whether or not the following equations represent functions.
    a. $(x + 2)^2 + (y - 3)^2 = 9$
    b. $xy = 12$
    Explain your reasoning.

17. Solve for x in simplest $a + bi$ form: $4x - 4 = \dfrac{-17}{x}$.

18. Michael says he can describe the roots of a quadratic equation without actually solving the equation. Jillian doesn't believe him and challenges him to describe the roots of the equation $y = 3x^2 - 4x - 2$. What does Michael tell her and how does he know?

Part IV

Answer all questions in this part. Each correct answer will receive 6 credits. Clearly indicate the necessary steps, including appropriate formula substitutions, diagrams, graphs, charts, etc. For all questions in this part, a correct numerical answer with no work shown will receive only 1 credit.

19. Given $\triangle ABC$ with coordinates $A(2, 5)$, $B(-4, 8)$, and $C(-1, 1)$. Graph and state the coordinates of $\triangle A'B'C'$, the image of $\triangle ABC$ under the composition $R_o \circ T_{-2, 6}$.

20. Given: In circle O, chords $\overline{MA}, \overline{MT}, \overline{AH}$, and $\overline{HT}$ are drawn.

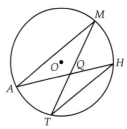

Prove: $\triangle MAQ \sim \triangle HTQ$.

CUMULATIVE REVIEW CHAPTERS 1–9

Part I

Answer all questions in this part. Each correct answer will receive 2 credits. No partial credit will be allowed.

1. The movie *Titanic* has one of the highest box office grosses at over $600 million. What is this number in scientific notation?
   (1) 6×10^9
   (2) 6×10^8
   (3) 6×10^7
   (4) 6×10^6

2. If $f(x) = 2x^0$, find $f(4)$.
   (1) 1
   (2) 2
   (3) 8
   (4) 0

3. Which element is *not* in the range of the function $f(x) = -x^2 + 10$?
   (1) 1
   (2) 5
   (3) 10
   (4) 15

4. The members of the Drama Club are going to paint the scenery for their play. They figured that it would take 4 of them 6 days to paint the scenery. If they need the scenery in 3 days, and they work at the same rate, how many members do they need to help paint?
   (1) 1
   (2) 2
   (3) 8
   (4) 12

5. When a new video game is introduced, the number of people who have it grows slowly at first. As the game catches on, more people buy it, and the rate of growth increases. Which graph could be used to model the number of people who own the game as a function of time since the game was introduced?

6. Which of the following is *not* sufficient information to prove that quadrilateral *ABCD* is a rectangle?
   (1) *ABCD* is a parallelogram with one right angle.
   (2) *ABCD* has four right angles.
   (3) *ABCD* is a parallelogram whose diagonals bisect each other.
   (4) *ABCD* is a parallelogram whose diagonals are congruent.

7. What are the real numbers a and b that make the statement $a + bi = 3 + 6i - 2 + i$ true?
   (1) $a = 1, b = 7$
   (2) $a = 5, b = 7$
   (3) $a = 1, b = 6$
   (4) $a = 5, b = 6$

8. Which of the following might be the value of the discriminant of a parabola that lies entirely above the x-axis?
   (1) -6
   (2) 0
   (3) 3
   (4) 50

9. In circle *O*, chords $\overline{CH}$ and $\overline{RD}$ intersect at point *S*. If $CS = 6$, $SH = 3$, and $RS = 2$, find *RD*.
   (1) 5
   (2) 7
   (3) 9
   (4) 11

10. Solve for x: $|x - 3| = 2x$.
    (1) {1}
    (2) {1, 3}
    (3) {−3}
    (4) {1, −3}

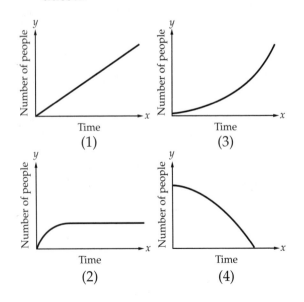

Number of people vs. Time

(1)

(3)

(2)

(4)

Part II

Answer all questions in this part. Each correct answer will receive 2 credits. Clearly indicate the necessary steps, including appropriate formula substitutions, diagrams, graphs, charts, etc. For all questions in this part, a correct numerical answer with no work shown will receive only 1 credit.

11. Solve for x: $3^{2x} = 27^{x-1}$.

12. What single transformation is equivalent to $r_{y\text{-axis}} \circ r_{x\text{-axis}}$? Explain.

13. The number of goldfish in an aquarium is represented by $\frac{x}{x+2}$ and the number of gup-

pies is represented by $\frac{2}{x^2 - x - 6}$. Express, as a single fraction, the total number of fish in the aquarium.

14. For what value of k are the roots of $3x^2 - 6x + k = 0$ equal?

Part III

Answer all questions in this part. Each correct answer will receive 4 credits. Clearly indicate the necessary steps, including the appropriate formula substitutions, diagrams, graphs, charts, etc. For all questions in this part, a correct numerical answer with no work shown will receive only 1 credit.

15. Solve the equation $x + \frac{6}{x} = 2$ and express the roots in simplest $a + bi$ form.

16. Miguel wants to buy a new rug for his bedroom. He knows that the length is 2 feet more than the width, but can't remember either dimension. If the total area of the room is 90 square feet, what are the dimensions of Miguel's room, to the nearest tenth of a foot?

17. One root of a quadratic equation is $4 - 5i$.
 a. What is the other root? Explain how you know that you are correct.
 b. Write the quadratic equation that has these two roots.

18. Given: Circle O, secants $\overline{ABE}$ and $\overline{CODE}$. Chords $\overline{AF}$ and $\overline{BF}$ are drawn. $m\angle AFB = 50$ and $m\overarc{BD} = 20$.
Find: **a.** $m\overarc{AB}$ **b.** $m\angle AEC$.

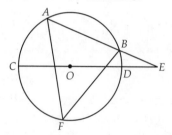

Part IV

Answer all questions in this part. Each correct answer will receive 6 credits. Clearly indicate the necessary steps, including appropriate formula substitutions, diagrams, graphs, charts, etc. For all questions in this part, a correct numerical answer with no work shown will receive only 1 credit.

19. A new television show, "The World of Mathematics," has just premiered. The number of people who watch the show can be modeled by the function $N(t) = 3(1.15)^t$, where $N(t)$ is the number of thousands of viewers, and t is the time, in months, since the show was first introduced.
 a. Evaluate $N(4)$ to the nearest thousandth and explain what this means in terms of the show.
 b. Find t, to the nearest thousandth, such that $N(t) = 4$ and explain what this means in terms of the show.

20. The coordinates of the vertices of triangle SUN are $S(1, 2)$, $U(6, 3)$, and $N(4, 6)$.
 a. Graph and label triangle SUN and its image, $\triangle S'U'N'$ after a reflection in the line $y = x$.
 b. Graph and state the coordinates of $\triangle S''U''N''$, the image of $\triangle S'U'N'$ after D_2.

CUMULATIVE REVIEW CHAPTERS 1–10

Part I

Answer all questions in this part. Each correct answer will receive 2 credits. No partial credit will be allowed.

1. If $f(x) = \log_4 x$, then $f(8)$ equals

    (1) $\dfrac{3}{2}$

    (3) 3

    (2) 2

    (4) 4

2. The graphs of $y = \log_2 x$ and $2^y = x$
    (1) intersect in only one point
    (2) intersect in two points
    (3) are the same graph
    (4) do not intersect at all

3. If $\log_a 3 = m$ and $\log_a 5 = p$, which of the following could represent $\log_a 75$?
    (1) $m + p^2$ (3) $m + 2p$
    (2) $2mp$ (4) mp^2

4. Martha has been struggling to lose weight. The first ten pounds came off quickly, but then the rate of weight loss began to slow. Which of the following graphs might represent the rate of Martha's weight loss over time?

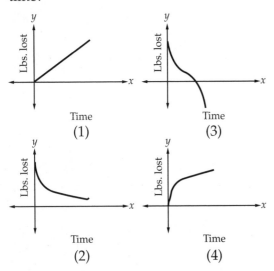

5. Under the composition $r_{y\text{-axis}} \circ R_{90°} \circ T_{-2,3}$ point $A(4, -2)$ becomes
    (1) $(1, 2)$ (3) $(0, -1)$
    (2) $(2, 1)$ (4) $(-1, 2)$

6. The value of x in the equation $4^{3x} = 16^{x+1}$ is
    (1) -2 (3) 3
    (2) 2   (4) 4

7. When simplified, $\dfrac{\dfrac{c}{2} - \dfrac{2}{c}}{1 + \dfrac{c}{2}}$ equals which of the following?

    (1) c

    (3) $\dfrac{c + 2}{2}$

    (2) $\dfrac{2 - c}{2}$

    (4) $\dfrac{c - 2}{c}$

8. Which of the following is the solution set to the equation $1 + \sqrt{3x + 1} = x$?
    (1) $\{0\}$ (3) $\{0, 5\}$
    (2) $\{5\}$ (4) $\{\ \}$

9. Chords $\overline{CH}$ and $\overline{AD}$ intersect in circle O at point T. If $CT = 8$ and $TH = 10$, the lengths of $\overline{AT}$ and $\overline{TD}$ *cannot* be which of the following?
    (1) 5 and 16   (3) 6 and 15
    (2) 4 and 20   (4) 8 and 10

10. Given parallelogram $LOVE$, which additional statements are needed to prove $LOVE$ is a rhombus?

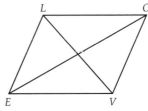

    I. $\overline{LO} \cong \overline{OV}$
    II. $\overline{LV} \perp \overline{OE}$
    III. $m\angle ELO \cong m\angle LOV$
    (1) I or II or III   (3) I or II
    (2) I, II, and III   (4) I and II

Part II

Answer all questions in this part. Each correct answer will receive 2 credits. Clearly indicate the necessary steps, including appropriate formula substitutions, diagrams, graphs, charts, etc. For all questions in this part, a correct numerical answer with no work shown will receive only 1 point.

11. Steve says $9x^2 + 4(y - 2)^2 = 36$ is the equation of an ellipse but Elise says it is the equation of a circle with a radius of 6. Explain who is correct and why.

12. The function $P(t) = 17432(0.7882)^t$ represents the population of Elvesville, North Pole, where $t = 0$ represents the year 2000. Interpret the changing population of this community. Is it increasing or decreasing and at what rate?

13. Fully describe the roots of the quadratic equation $4x^2 - 4x + 5 = 0$.

14. Given the function $f(x) = x^2 - 4$ over the interval $0 \le x \le 10$, evaluate $f^{-1}(5)$.

Part III

Answer all questions in this part. Each correct answer will receive 4 credits. Clearly indicate the necessary steps, including the appropriate formula substitutions, diagrams, graphs, charts, etc. For all questions in this part, a correct numerical answer with no work shown will receive only 1 credit.

15. Solve for x in simplest $a + bi$ form:
    $9x^2 - 6x + 2 = 0$.

16. a. Complete the table below for the function $y = \log_{\frac{1}{2}} x$.

x							
y	-3	-2	-1	0	1	2	3

   b. Sketch the graph of $y = \log_{\frac{1}{2}} x$.

   c. Reflect the graph of $y = \log_{\frac{1}{2}} x$ in the line $y = x$.

   d. What is the equation of the graph sketched in part **c**?

17. Perform the indicated operations and simplify: $\dfrac{2x^2 - 9x + 9}{2x^3 - 3x^2} \div \dfrac{3x^2 - 11x + 6}{6 - 5x - 6x^2}$.

18. Let $f(x) = 4x^2 - 1$ and $g(x) = \dfrac{x + 2}{3}$.
    a. Find the value of $(f \circ g)(7)$.
    b. Express $(g \circ f)(x)$ in simplest form.
    c. Find the value of $(g \circ g^{-1})(3)$.

Part IV

Answer all questions in this part. Each correct answer will receive 6 credits. Clearly indicate the necessary steps, including appropriate formula substitutions, diagrams, graphs, charts, etc. For all questions in this part, a correct numerical answer with no work shown will receive only 1 credit.

19. Solve the following system of equations.
    $y = x^2 - 3x - 4$
    $y = -2x^2 + x$

20. Given: Circle O with diameter $\overline{AOH}$ and chords $\overline{MA}, \overline{AT}, \overline{TH}, \overline{HM},$ and $\overline{MT}$.

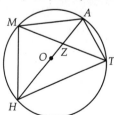

Prove: $\dfrac{MZ}{ZH} = \dfrac{AZ}{ZT}$.

Part I

Answer all questions in this part. Each correct answer will receive 2 credits. No partial credit will be allowed.

1. Keisha and her friends have started a business designing Web pages. They charge clients a $100 initial fee and $20 per hour for the time spent designing the Web page. What type of function could be used to model their business income?
   (1) exponential   (3) logarithmic
   (2) linear   (4) power

2. When the graph $y = 2^x$ is reflected over the line $y = x$, what is the equation of the resulting graph?
   (1) $y = 2^{-x}$ (3) $y = \log_x 2$
   (2) $y = -2^x$ (4) $y = \log_2 x$

3. The origin of a coordinate grid is labeled O. Line segment OP forms an angle of 30° with the x-axis. If $OP = 10$, what are the coordinates of point P?
   (1) $(5, 5\sqrt{2})$ (3) $(10\cos 30°, 10\sin 30°)$
   (2) $(5\sqrt{2}, 5)$ (4) $(10\sin 30°, 10\cos 30°)$

4. The temperature, t, in Frigidland is always within 2 degrees of freezing (which is 32°F). Which of the following equations could represent the temperature in Frigidland?
   (1) $|2 + t| < 32$ (3) $|32 + t| < 2$
   (2) $|2 - t| < 32$ (4) $|32 - t| < 2$

5. If $f(x) = 2x + 3$, and $g(x) = x^2 - x - 4$, what is $(f \circ g)(2)$?
   (1) -1 (3) 18
   (2) -38 (4) 38

6. David leaves his house to visit his friend Mark who lives 3 miles away. On the way, he stops to have lunch, and then continues to Mark's house. Which of the following could be used to model David's distance from home as a function of time?

7. Simplify: $|5 - 12i|$.
   (1) -13 (3) 13
   (2) $-13i$ (4) $13i$

8. If you are given that $\overrightarrow{BD}$ bisects $\angle ABC$, you can conclude that
   (1) $\overline{AB} \cong \overline{BC}$ (3) $\angle ACB \cong \angle ACD$
   (2) $\overrightarrow{BA} \cong \overrightarrow{BC}$ (4) $\angle ABD \cong \angle CBD$

9. If the length of a rectangle is $\frac{a}{2}$ and its width is $\frac{1}{a + 2}$, its perimeter is
   (1) $\dfrac{a^2 + 2a + 1}{a + 2}$ (3) $\dfrac{a^2 + 2a + 1}{2(a + 2)}$
   (2) $\dfrac{a^2 + 2a + 2}{a + 2}$ (4) $\dfrac{a^2 + 2a + 2}{2(a + 2)}$

10. Solve for y: $y(y - 2) < 8$.
    (1) $y < 0$ or $y < 2$ (3) $y < -2$ or $y > 4$
    (2) $y < 0$ or $y > 2$ (4) $-2 < y < 4$

Part II

Answer all questions in this part. Each correct answer will receive 2 credits. Clearly indicate the necessary steps, including appropriate formula substitutions, diagrams, graphs, charts, etc. For all questions in this part, a correct numerical answer with no work shown will receive only 1 credit.

11. Regular pentagon *PENTA* is inscribed in circle *O*. What is $\stackrel{\frown}{mPE}$?

12. Write as the logarithm of a single function: $\log x + 2\log y - \log z$.

13. The senior class has decided to rent a hall for their prom. If only 75 members of the class come to the prom, it will cost them $50 each. However, they want to keep the cost to only $25 each. How many people would have to come to the prom for this to happen?

14. Solve for x: $\dfrac{x}{2} - \dfrac{9}{x} = \dfrac{3}{2}$.

Part III

Answer all questions in this part. Each correct answer will receive 4 credits. Clearly indicate the necessary steps, including the appropriate formula substitutions, diagrams, graphs, charts, etc. For all questions in this part, a correct numerical answer with no work shown will receive only 1 credit.

15. The population of Mathland can be modeled by the equation $P(t) = 25(1.03)^t$, where $P(t)$ is the population in thousands and t is the number of years since Mathland was founded. To the nearest tenth of a year, how long will it take until there are 100,000 people in Mathland?

16. Express in simplest form:
$$\frac{3x - 9}{9 - x^2} \cdot \frac{x^2 + 7x + 12}{3x + 12}.$$

17. a. Juliet is standing on a balcony and mistakenly knocks over the flowerpot that is sitting on the ledge. If the height, in feet, of the flowerpot is represented by the equation $h = -16t^2 + 64$, where t is the time measured in seconds, in how many seconds will the flowerpot hit the ground?

b. If 6-foot-tall Romeo were standing directly under the flowerpot, to the nearest tenth of a second, how long would he have to get out of the way before the flowerpot hit him on the head?

18. Solve the equation $2x^2 = 3x - 3$ in simplest $a + bi$ form.

Part IV

Answer all questions in this part. Each correct answer will receive 6 credits. Clearly indicate the necessary steps, including appropriate formula substitutions, diagrams, graphs, charts, etc. For all questions in this part, a correct numerical answer with no work shown will receive only 1 credit.

19. Given circle O with diameter $\overline{AOB}$ extended through B to point P; secant $\overline{PCD}$ and radius $\overline{OC}$ are drawn, $m\angle COB = 40$, $m\widehat{AD} : m\widehat{DC} = 3:2$.

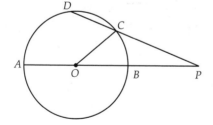

Find
a. $m\widehat{CB}$
b. $m\widehat{DC}$
c. $m\angle DPA$

20. Given: Quadrilateral $ABDC$, with $A(a, 0)$, $B(b, 0)$, $C(a + c, d)$, and $D(b + c, d)$.
Prove: Quadrilateral $ABDC$ is a parallelogram.

CUMULATIVE REVIEW CHAPTERS 1–12

Part I

Answer all questions in this part. Each correct answer will receive 2 credits. No partial credit will be allowed.

1. If $f(x) = \frac{1}{2}x^2 - x^{\frac{1}{2}} - 3x^0, f(4)$ equals

   (1) 1   (3) 3

   (2) 2   (4) 4

2. In the accompanying diagram, if $m\angle APC = 21$, the measure of $\overparen{AB}$ is

   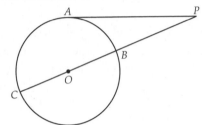

   (1) 21   (3) 69

   (2) 42   (4) 128

3. Which of the following represents the solution to $2x^2 - x - 3 < 0$?

   (1) ← ○————○ → with $-\frac{3}{2}$, 0, 1

   (2) ← ○————————○ → with -1, $\frac{3}{2}$

   (3) ← ○————○ → with -3, $\frac{1}{2}$

   (4) ← ○————○ → with $-\frac{1}{2}$, 3

4. The domain of which function below is $-1 \le x \le 1$?

   (1) $y = \frac{3x + 7}{x^2 - 1}$ (3) $y = \sqrt{1 - x^2}$

   (2) $y = x^2 - 1$ (4) $y = \frac{1}{\sqrt{1 - x^2}}$

5. The value of x in the equation $\log_{(x-1)} 9 = 2$ is

   (1) 1   (3) 3

   (2) 2   (4) 4

6. The scatterplot shown has a correlation coefficient of

   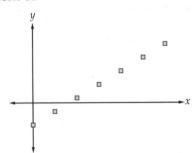

   (1) 1   (3) -0.4

   (2) 0.6   (4) -1

7. If $f(x) = 3\sin x + 2\cos 2x$, the value of $\left(\frac{\pi}{2}\right)$ is

   (1) 1   (3) 3

   (2) 2   (4) 5

8. If point $A(-1, 0)$ is rotated $60°$, the coordinates of point A' would be

   (1) $\left(-\frac{\sqrt{3}}{2}, -\frac{1}{2}\right)$ (3) $\left(\frac{\sqrt{3}}{2}, -\frac{1}{2}\right)$

   (2) $\left(-\frac{1}{2}, -\frac{\sqrt{3}}{2}\right)$ (4) $\left(\frac{1}{2}, \frac{\sqrt{3}}{2}\right)$

9. If the product of the roots of a quadratic equation is $-\frac{1}{4}$ and the sum of the roots of the same quadratic equation is $\frac{5}{2}$, the equation may be which of the following?

   (1) $2x^2 - 5x = \frac{1}{2}$ (3) $4x^2 - 1 = 0$

   (2) $5x = 1 + 2x^2$ (4) $4x^2 = 5x + 1$

10. The price a flower shop charges for roses is inversely proportional to the number of days before Valentine's Day that the order is placed. A dozen roses ordered ten days before Valentine's Day costs $12.00 while the same order placed five days before Valentine's Day costs $24.00. What is the cost of a dozen roses ordered one day before Valentine's Day?

    (1) $32.00   (3) $72.00

    (2) $36.00   (4) $120.00

Part II

Answer all questions in this part. Each correct answer will receive 2 credits. Clearly indicate the necessary steps, including appropriate formula substitutions, diagrams, graphs, charts, etc. For all questions in this part, a correct numerical answer with no work shown will receive only 1 credit.

11. If $z_1 = 3 - 2i$ and $z_2 = 5 + 3i$, show the sum of $z_1 + z_2$ graphically.

12. Jan has been offered a job that promises a salary package represented by the function $S(t) = 38,000(1.055)^t$ where t is the number of years worked.
  a. What is her starting salary?
  b. Evaluate $S(3)$ and explain its meaning.

13. Given: Circle O with diameter $\overline{AOD}$, tangent $\overrightarrow{PA}$, secant $\overline{PCD}$, $\overline{CD} \parallel \overline{AE}$, m$\angle ADC = 43$.

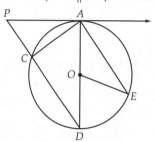

Not drawn to scale

  a. Find m$\angle APD$. **b.** Find m$\angle OEA$.

14. Solve for x: $\sqrt{3x + 1} - 1 = x - 4$.

Part III

Answer all questions in this part. Each correct answer will receive 4 credits. Clearly indicate the necessary steps, including the appropriate formula substitutions, diagrams, graphs, charts, etc. For all questions in this part, a correct numerical answer with no work shown will receive only 1 credit.

15. If the length of a rectangle is represented by $\dfrac{x^2 - 5x - 14}{2x^2 + 5x + 2}$ while the width of the rectangle is represented by $\dfrac{2x^2 + 9x + 4}{x^2 - 7x}$, express the area of the rectangle in simplest form.

16. For Independence Day, the village of Treetop is planning to launch fireworks from a barge on the lake. The rockets will achieve a height represented by the function $H(t) = -16t^2 + 96t + 4$ where $H(t)$ is measured in feet and t is time in seconds after launch.

  a. At what time, to the nearest second, is the fireworks rocket at its highest point?
  b. If the rocket is designed to explode at its highest point, to the nearest foot, how high is the rocket when it explodes?

17. Solve for x in simplest $a + bi$ form: $4x^2 + 17 = 4x$.

18. a. Graph the function $f(x) = \log_2 x$ over the interval $-3 \le y \le 3$.
  b. Graph the function $f(x) = \log_2 x$ following a rotation of $90°$ counterclockwise.

Part IV

Answer all questions in this part. Each correct answer will receive 6 credits. Clearly indicate the necessary steps, including appropriate formula substitutions, diagrams, graphs, charts, etc. For all questions in this part, a correct numerical answer with no work shown will receive only 1 credit.

19. The table below indicates the percentage of the U.S. population without high school diplomas since 1970.

Year	Percent Without Diplomas	Year	Percent without Diplomas
1970	47.7	1990	22.4
1980	33.5	1991	21.6
1985	26.1	1997	17.9
1989	23.1		

a. Determine the best-fit curve for the percent of people without diplomas as a function of time, t (let 1970 = 0). Identify the type of function you chose.

b. If this relationship continues as above, what will be the first year in which less than 10 percent of the U.S. population will be without a high school diploma?

20. Given quadrilateral *HOPE* with coordinates $H(5, -2)$, $O(9, 4)$, $P(3, 5)$, and $E(-2, 2)$. If M is the midpoint of $\overline{HO}$, A is the midpoint of $\overline{OP}$, R is the midpoint of $\overline{PE}$, and K is the midpoint of $\overline{EH}$, prove that *MARK* is a parallelogram.

CUMULATIVE REVIEW CHAPTERS 1–13

Part I

Answer all questions in this part. Each correct answer will receive 2 credits. No partial credit will be allowed.

1. If $f(x) = x^{\frac{2}{3}} + x^{-1} + 2x^0$, find $f(8)$.

(1) -3 (3) $5\frac{1}{8}$

(2) -2 (4) $6\frac{1}{8}$

2. All houses in Gridsville are located at points on a coordinate plane. One day the mayor of Gridsville announced that everyone's house would be moved according to the formula $(x, y) \rightarrow (2y, -x)$. If Mary Lu's house is presently located at $(1, 2)$, what are the coordinates of the new location of her house?

(1) $(2, 2)$ (3) $(4, 1)$
(2) $(2, -2)$ (4) $(4, -1)$

3. Evaluate $\sin\left(\arccos\frac{\sqrt{2}}{2}\right)$.

(1) 1 (3) $\frac{\sqrt{3}}{2}$

(2) $\frac{\sqrt{2}}{2}$ (4) $\sqrt{2}$

4. What is the correct arrangement of these terms, in order of value, from smallest to largest?

(1) $6\sqrt{2}, 6\frac{1}{3}, \sqrt[4]{620}, |-6.3|$

(2) $6\frac{1}{3}, 6\sqrt{2}, \sqrt[4]{620}, |-6.3|$

(3) $6\sqrt{2}, \sqrt[4]{620}, |-6.3|, 6\frac{1}{3}$

(4) $\sqrt[4]{620}, |-6.3|, 6\frac{1}{3}, 6\sqrt{2}$

5. Express $135°$ in radian measure.

(1) $\frac{\pi}{4}$ (3) $\frac{3\pi}{4}$

(2) $\frac{2\pi}{3}$ (4) $\frac{5\pi}{4}$

6. In 1998, there were 5 students who wanted to start a Key Club in their school. Each year the number of members of the club has increased by 8 percent. Which of the following equations could be used to express the number of members of the Key Club since 1998?

(1) $N(t) = 5(0.8)^t$ (3) $N(t) = 5(1.08)^t$
(2) $N(t) = 5(1.8)^t$ (4) $N(t) = 8(1.05)^t$

7. If $f(x) = a \sin(bx)$, the maximum value in the range is
   (1) a
   (2) b
   (3) $a + b$
   (4) There is no maximum.

8. When a pendulum swings, its path can be modeled by the equation $\dfrac{x^2}{4} + \dfrac{(y-2)^2}{9} = 1$. This equation produces the graph of
   (1) a circle   (3) a hyperbola
   (2) an ellipse   (4) a parabola

9. Jill drove at 50 miles per hour for 4 hours to visit her brother Jack. Jill hit traffic on her way home, and could drive at only 40 miles per hour for the entire return trip. What was Jill's average speed, in miles per hour, for the entire trip?

   (1) 42.346   (3) 45
   (2) 44.444   (4) 47.263

10. Which of the following equations could be used to model the scatterplot pictured below?

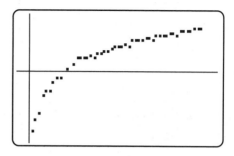

   (1) $y = 3^x$
   (2) $y = 3^{-x}$
   (3) $y = \log_3 x$
   (4) $y = 2 + 3x$

Part II

Answer all questions in this part. Each correct answer will receive 2 credits. Clearly indicate the necessary steps, including appropriate formula substitutions, diagrams, graphs, charts, etc. For all questions in this part, a correct numerical answer with no work shown will receive only 1 credit.

11. Solve: $|2n - 4| < 8$.

12. Moisha says that the roots of the equation $y = 2x^2 - x - 3$ are real, rational, and unequal. Abdul says that the roots are real, irrational, and unequal. Explain who is correct, and why.

13. Is a circle a function? Explain.

14. Name a positive acute angle that is coterminal with a $-310°$ angle.

Part III

Answer all questions in this part. Each correct answer will receive 4 credits. Clearly indicate the necessary steps, including the appropriate formula substitutions, diagrams, graphs, charts, etc. For all questions in this part, a correct numerical answer with no work shown will receive only 1 credit.

15. The graph of $y = 2\sin 3x$ is reflected in the x-axis.
   a. Sketch a graph of one period of the original curve.
   b. Sketch a graph of the curve after the reflection.
   c. Write an equation for the new curve.

16. The equation of a parabola is $y = x^2 - 2x + 7$. Show how to determine the vertex of this parabola by completing the square. What is the vertex of the parabola?

17. Express in simplest form: $\dfrac{1 - \dfrac{1}{9x^2}}{1 - \dfrac{1}{3x}}$.

18. The equation $f(t) = 100(0.98)^t$ represents the temperature in degrees Celsius of a cup of tea t minutes after it was poured. To the nearest hundredth of a minute, how long would it take before the temperature of the tea reached 90°C? (Only an algebraic solution will be accepted.)

Answer all questions in this part. Each correct answer will receive 6 credits. Clearly indicate the necessary steps, including appropriate formula substitutions, diagrams, graphs, charts, etc. For all questions in this part, a correct numerical answer with no work shown will receive only 1 credit.

19. The following table shows the number of students from Hillsdale High School who have part-time jobs.

Year	1996	1997	1998	1999	2000	2001
Number of Students	200	220	239	261	280	300

   a. What type of function does this appear to be? Why?

   b. Write an equation for the number of students, $N(t)$, who have part-time jobs as a function of the time, t, in years since 1996.

   c. Based on your equation, determine the number of students who are expected to have part-time jobs in 2005.

   d. If the trend continues, when will all 400 students at Hillsdale High School be holding part-time jobs? (Find your answer to the nearest thousandth of a year.)

20. Mrs. Smart's health class has begun a project to encourage people to break their smoking habit. Utilizing graph paper, they have designed the symbol shown below.

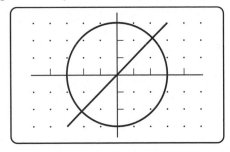

   a. Write an equation for the circle pictured.

   b. Write an equation for the line.

   c. What are the exact coordinates of the points of intersection?

CUMULATIVE REVIEW CHAPTERS 1–14

Part I

Answer all questions in this part. Each correct answer will receive 2 credits. No partial credit will be allowed.

1. Solve for x: $2x^{\frac{3}{2}} - 3 = 13$.
   (1) 16   (3) 8
   (2) 9   (4) 4

2. Coach Willful believes that the best sixth-grade soccer players are 58 inches tall and he will accept only students whose heights are within 4 inches of his ideal as players on the club team. Which of the following equations expresses the height, h, of Coach Willful's team players?
   (1) $|h - 4| > 58$ (3) $|h + 4| > 58$
   (2) $|58 - h| < 4$ (4) $|h - 58| > 4$

3. Tangent $\overline{PE}$ and secant $\overline{PAC}$ are drawn to circle O from point P. If $PE = 16$, and $PA = 8$, which of the following is the length of the radius of circle O?

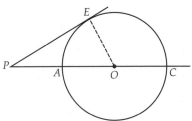

   (1) 12   (3) 20
   (2) 16   (4) 24

4. Paras is drawing a solar system display for his science class. If the equation representing Saturn is $(x-4)^2 + (y+3)^2 = 36$, which of the following equations could be used to represent Saturn's rings, which have an elliptical orbit?

(1) $\dfrac{(x-4)^2}{9} + \dfrac{(y+3)^2}{4} = 1$

(2) $\dfrac{(x-4)^2}{64} + \dfrac{(y+3)^2}{49} = 1$

(3) $\dfrac{(x+4)^2}{36} - \dfrac{(y-3)^2}{25} = 1$

(4) $\dfrac{(x+4)^2}{144} + (y-3)^2 = 1$

5. Express 330° in radian measure.

(1) $\dfrac{5\pi}{6}$ (3) $\dfrac{11\pi}{6}$

(2) $\dfrac{5\pi}{3}$ (4) $\dfrac{11\pi}{4}$

6. Mrs. Indira is the secretary at Cornwallis High School's Guidance Office, responsible for coordinating college applications. She noticed that since she starting working there in 1996, the number of girls applying to medical schools has been increasing. Her data are shown in the table below.

Year	1996	1997	1998	1999	2000	2001	2002
Number of Applications	8	11	14	17	20	23	26

Which of the following best describes the number of girls' applications to medical schools as a function of the year?

(1) The number of applications increases yearly by $3\tfrac{2}{3}$ percent.

(2) The increase in applications each year is at a constant rate.

(3) The rate of growth of applications to medical schools is increasing each year.

(4) In 2010, the number of applications will definitely be at least 51.

7. Given $\triangle XYZ$ with $\overline{XY} \cong \overline{YZ}$ and altitude $\overline{YA}$ drawn to $\overline{XZ}$, which of the following statements is invalid?

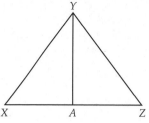

(1) $\triangle XYA$ can be proved $\cong \triangle ZYA$ by Hyp-leg $\cong$ Hyp-leg.

(2) $\triangle XYA$ can be proved $\cong \triangle ZYA$ by Angle-Side-Angle $\cong$ Angle-Side-Angle.

(3) $m\angle XYA$ can be proved $\cong m\angle ZYA$ by CPCTC.

(4) $\overline{XY} \perp \overline{YZ}$ by CPCTC.

8. If $4x^2 + 9 = kx$, what value of k will produce equal roots?

(1) -3 (3) 12

(2) 5   (4) 16

9. The scatterplot shown has a linear correlation coefficient of approximately which of the following?

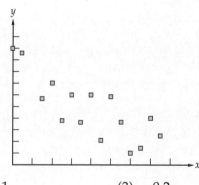

(1) 1   (3) -0.2

(2) 0.7   (4) -0.7

10. The graph of the function in the accompanying diagram can best be represented by which equation below?

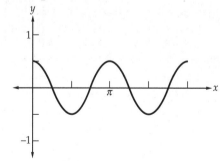

(1) $y = 2\sin(2x)$ (3) $y = 2\cos(x)$

(2) $y = \tfrac{1}{2}\sin(2x)$ (4) $y = \tfrac{1}{2}\cos(2x)$

Part II

Answer all questions in this part. Each correct answer will receive 2 credits. Clearly indicate the necessary steps, including appropriate formula substitutions, diagrams, graphs, charts, etc. For all questions in this part, a correct numerical answer with no work shown will receive only 1 credit.

11. Cody and Efrim were competing in a road rally. If Cody traveled $\dfrac{x^2 - 4}{3x - 6}$ in the first hour and Efrim traveled $\dfrac{2x^2 + 3x - 2}{8x - 4}$, who traveled farther the first hour of the race? Explain your reasoning.

12. Gabe's rabbit has a triangular hutch with two sides measuring 20 inches and 32 inches respectively. If the angle between these two sides of the hutch measures 104.2, what is the area of the rabbit's cage to the nearest square inch?

13. Solve for x: $x = 1 + \sqrt{x + 5}$.

14. The graph shown below represents the profits, y, in tens of thousands of dollars, of the Pennyworth Investment Firm over the twenty-four months since its formation in January 1999.

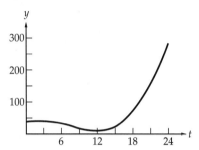

Explain to the stockholders the history of the financial returns, based on this graph.

Part III

Answer all questions in this part. Each correct answer will receive 4 credits. Clearly indicate the necessary steps, including the appropriate formula substitutions, diagrams, graphs, charts, etc. For all questions in this part, a correct numerical answer with no work shown will receive only 1 credit.

15. Melba is building a grandfather clock and needs to know the minimum width of the case. If the pendulum's arc subtends a central angle of 1.2 radians and the length of the pendulum itself is 18 inches, what is the minimum width of the clock case, to the nearest tenth of an inch, needed?

16. **a.** Sketch the function $y = 4^x$ over the interval $-2 \le x \le 2$.

    b. Now sketch the function $y = \left(\dfrac{1}{4}\right)^{-x}$ on the same set of axes over the same interval.

    c. Discuss the relationship between these two graphs.

    d. Now sketch the function $x = 4^y$ on the same set of axes over the same interval.

    e. How does the graph drawn in part **d** relate to the other two graphs? Why?

17. Express the roots of $9x^2 + 40 = 36x$ in simplest $a + bi$ form.

18. Given $\log_c 3 = 1.857$ and $\log_c 2 = 1.214$, evaluate
    a. $\log_c \sqrt{12}$
    b. $\log_c \dfrac{3}{2}$

Part IV

Answer all questions in this part. Each correct answer will receive 6 credits. Clearly indicate the necessary steps, including appropriate formula substitutions, diagrams, graphs, charts, etc. For all questions in this part, a correct numerical answer with no work shown will receive only 1 credit.

19. The Hatfields and the McCoys are still feuding over property rights in the hills of Tennessee and Sheriff Good has heard there might be trouble next Saturday night. Since the Sheriff is a distant cousin to the McCoys, she was able to get the dimensions of the McCoy land as shown below.

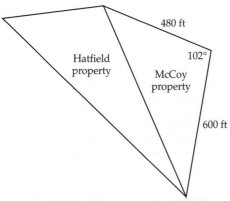

If she can determine the length of the boundary between the two pieces of property, she can request extra deputies and assign one deputy to stand every 20 feet for the night of the expected trouble. Determine how many deputies the sheriff will need to keep the peace between the Hatfields and the McCoys.

20. The table below gives the percentage of the U.S. population with 4 years of college or more between 1970 and 1997.

Year	1970	1980	1985	1989	1990	1991	1997
Percent with Degrees	10.7	16.2	19.4	21.1	21.3	21.4	23.9

a. Find the line of best fit for this data, with the number of degrees as a function of t with $t = 0$ representing 1970. (Round to the ten thousandth.)

b. What is the correlation coefficient of the function? What does this number mean?

c. If the trend continues as indicated in this data, what percent of the U.S. population would have college or postgraduate degrees in 2005? Does this seem reasonable to you? Why or why not?

CUMULATIVE REVIEW CHAPTERS 1–15

Part I

Answer all questions in this part. Each correct answer will receive 2 credits. No partial credit will be allowed.

1. The graph below shows the temperature of a chemical solution as it cools over a period of time.

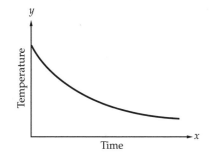

Which of the following types of functions would best model the graph?
(1) exponential   (3) logarithmic
(2) linear   (4) trigonometric

2. If $f(\theta) = \sin 2\theta - \cos \theta$, find $f(\pi)$.
(1) 1   (3) −1
(2) 0   (4) −2

3. Find x if $\log_x 9 = \frac{2}{3}$.
(1) 1   (3) 27
(2) 9   (4) 81

4. Which is *not* an element in the range of the function $y = 2 \sin x$?
   (1) 1   (3) 3
   (2) 2   (4) 0

5. The linear correlation coefficient for the data shown below would be closest to

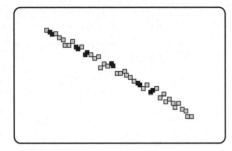

   (1) −0.9   (3) 0.5
   (2) −0.5   (4) 0.9

6. Simplify: $|7 + 24i|$.
   (1) −25   (3) 25
   (2) −25i (4) 25i

7. For which value of k are the roots of $2x^2 - 4x + k = 0$ equal?
   (1) 0   (3) 3
   (2) 2   (4) 4

8. In circle O, the length of radius $\overline{OP}$ is 2 inches, and the measure of $\overparen{PQ}$ is 4 inches. What is the measure of $\angle POQ$?

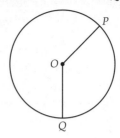

   (1) 1 radian   (3) π radians
   (2) 2 radians   (4) $\frac{1}{2}$ radian

9. Diana works for a clothing store, where employees are given a 20 percent discount on all clothing that can be worn to work. Tax on clothing is 4.25 percent. If Diana buys a blouse that is priced at d dollars, how much can she expect to pay?
   (1) 0.755d (3) 0.8425d
   (2) 0.834d (4) 1.245d

10. Which of the following is not an isometry?
    (1) rotation   (3) translation
    (2) dilation   (4) reflection

Part II

Answer all questions in this part. Each correct answer will receive 2 credits. Clearly indicate the necessary steps, including appropriate formula substitutions, diagrams, graphs, charts, etc. For all questions in this part, a correct numerical answer with no work shown will receive only 1 credit.

11. Mrs. Tightenup, the gym teacher, has listed the heights and weights of the students in her gym class as a set of ordered pairs. For example, (60, 110) would represent a person whose height is 60 inches and weight is 110 pounds. Are the weights of the members of the class a function of the heights? Explain.

12. Express in simplest form: $\dfrac{x - \frac{9}{x}}{1 + \frac{3}{x}}$.

13. Write as a single logarithm:
    $\frac{1}{2} \log a + 2 \log b - \log c$.

14. Some of the capital letters of the alphabet have horizontal line symmetry. Give an example of a letter of the alphabet that has horizontal line symmetry and explain why you believe your answer is correct.

Part III

Answer all questions in this part. Each correct answer will receive 4 credits. Clearly indicate the necessary steps, including the appropriate formula substitutions, diagrams, graphs, charts, etc. For all questions in this part, a correct numerical answer with no work shown will receive only 1 credit.

15. The members of the Delta Delta Delta Sorority want to take a picture of themselves standing in a triangle formation. They determined that the three sides of the triangle must measure 20 feet, 22 feet, and 24 feet. To the nearest hundredth of a degree, what is the measure of the largest angle of the triangle?

16. On the same set of axes, sketch and label the graph of $y = 2^x$ and its inverse. What is the equation of the inverse?

17. The angles of triangle ABC are in the ratio 1:2:3. If triangle ABC is inscribed in circle O, what is the measure of each of the arcs of circle O? If the measure of the longest side of triangle ABC is 20 inches, what are the exact measurements of each of the other two sides?

18. The Bugs Be Gone Exterminating Company specializes in ridding homes of all types of insects. As shown in the diagram below, the company's monthly income over a twelve-month period can be modeled by the equation $y = A \cos Bx + D$. Determine the values of A, B, and D and explain how you arrived at your values.

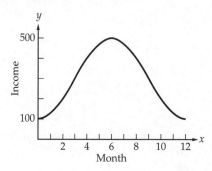

Part IV

Answer all questions in this part. Each correct answer will receive 6 credits. Clearly indicate the necessary steps, including appropriate formula substitutions, diagrams, graphs, charts, etc. For all questions in this part, a correct numerical answer with no work shown will receive only 1 credit.

19. The table below lists the number of Spanish radio stations in the United States.

Year	1994	1995	1996	1997	1998	1999	2001
Number of Stations	401	427	463	474	493	536	574

a. Write a linear equation that would express the number of Spanish radio stations, $S(t)$, as a function of time, t, in years since 1994.

b. If the number of stations continues to increase linearly, how many could we expect to be on the air in 2005?

c. Based on your equation from part **a**, when would we expect that there were 350 Spanish radio stations?

20. Quadrilateral $ABCD$ is inscribed in circle O. Prove that if $m\widehat{AB} = m\widehat{BC} = m\widehat{CD} = m\widehat{DA}$, then quadrilateral $ABCD$ is a square.

CUMULATIVE REVIEW CHAPTERS 1–16

Part I

Answer all questions in this part. Each correct answer will receive 2 credits. No partial credit will be allowed.

1. Which of the following transformations is a direct isometry?
   (1) $r_{y=x} \circ r_{x\text{-axis}}$
   (2) $R_{90°} \circ r_{y\text{-axis}}$
   (3) $T_{-4,2} \circ r_{x=3}$
   (4) $r_{y=-x} \circ D_{\frac{1}{2}}$

2. Jorge is planning his strategy for the New York City Marathon. He plans to start off at an easy pace and steadily increase the rate at which he runs over the course of the marathon. Which of the following graphs shows his distance from the starting line as a function of his running time?

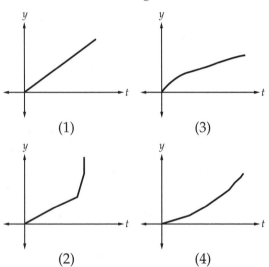

   (1)   (3)

   (2)   (4)

3. If one root of a function is $\frac{1}{2} - 2i$, what is the equation of this function?
   (1) $4x^2 - 17x + 4 = 0$
   (2) $4x^2 - 4x + 17 = 0$
   (3) $x^2 - x + 17 = 0$
   (4) $4x^2 + 4x + 17 = 0$

4. If $\sin(2\theta + 18) = \cos(5\theta - 12)$, which of the following pairs of angles are represented in this equation?
   (1) $42°, 48°$
   (2) $38°, 52°$
   (3) $12°, 68°$
   (4) $45°, 45°$

5. Crossing a wooden bridge at Letchworth Park, Melissa drops a penny into the water below for good luck. If the height of the penny is modeled by the function $h(t) = 64 - 16t^2$, where t represents time in seconds and $h(t)$ is height in feet, how many seconds did it take the penny to hit the water?
   (1) 1
   (2) 2
   (3) 3
   (4) 4

6. If $4^x = 2^y$ and $9^{x-1} = 3^{x+1}$, which of the following are the values of x and y?
   (1) $x = 2, y = 4$
   (2) $x = 3, y = 6$
   (3) $x = 4, y = 2$
   (4) $x = 6, y = 3$

7. When David was born, his grandparents deposited $1,000 in a college account that promised 4 percent interest compounded annually for 18 years. Which of the following equations shows the worth of the account when David is 18?
   (1) $y = 18(4)(1{,}000)$
   (2) $y = 18(0.04)(1{,}000)$
   (3) $y = 1{,}000(0.04)^{18}$
   (4) $y = 1{,}000(1.04)^{18}$

8. If $4.5^x = 97$, an approximate value of x is
   (1) 2.15
   (2) 3.04
   (3) 3.16
   (4) 3.47

9. If the roots of a quadratic equation are real, irrational, and unequal, which of the following might be the discriminant of that equation?
   (1) -9
   (2) 0
   (3) 14
   (4) 25

10. The pie chart below shows the preferred shopping days for U.S. shoppers who have a preference. What is the probability that of 4 people chosen at random at least 3 of them prefer to shop on Saturdays?

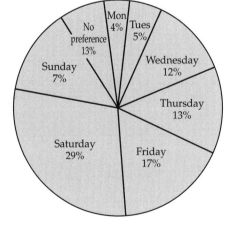

   (1) 6.9%
   (2) 7.6%
   (3) 29%
   (4) 87%

Part II

Answer all questions in this part. Each correct answer will receive 2 credits. Clearly indicate the necessary steps, including appropriate formula substitutions, diagrams, graphs, charts, etc. For all questions in this part, a correct numerical answer with no work shown will receive only 1 credit.

11. In circle O, $\overline{AB} \perp \overline{CD}$ at E. If $CD = 30$ and $OD = 17$, find the length of $\overline{EB}$.

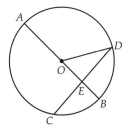

12. The number of electric blankets sold at Jenkin's Home Furnishings from January 1 through December 31 can be represented by the function $y = 680 \cos\left(\frac{\pi}{6}t\right) + 708$ in which t is time in months with $t = 0$ corresponding to January 1. Determine when the fewest electric blankets were sold and how many were sold.

13. Simplify: $\dfrac{20 + 7x - 3x^2}{x^2 - 16} \div \dfrac{6x + 10}{2x^2 + 5x - 12}.$

14. If $\cos \gamma = -\dfrac{4}{5}$ when $90° < \gamma < 180°$, find the value of $\sin (2\gamma)$.

Part III

Answer all questions in this part. Each correct answer will receive 4 credits. Clearly indicate the necessary steps, including the appropriate formula substitutions, diagrams, graphs, charts, etc. For all questions in this part, a correct numerical answer with no work shown will receive only 1 credit.

15. Given: $\triangle CTH$ with coordinates $C(8, -3)$, $T(0, 3)$, and $H(4, 5)$.
Prove: $\triangle CTH$ is a right triangle.

16. Preston will win the All County Billiards Championship if he sinks the last ball. Analyzing the position of the balls, he is going to try a bank shot as shown in the diagram below. To the nearest degree, at what angle must the cue ball hit the side of the table to sink the last ball?

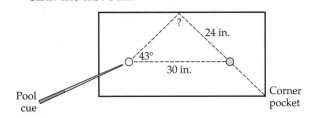

17. If $3\sin^2 \theta - 4\sin \theta + 1 = 0$, find all values of θ to the nearest minute in the interval $0 \le x \le 360$.

18. Show the expansion of $(3 - 2i)^5$. Give the final answer in simplest terms.

Part IV

Answer all questions in this part. Each correct answer will receive 6 credits. Clearly indicate the necessary steps, including appropriate formula substitutions, diagrams, graphs, charts, etc. For all questions in this part, a correct numerical answer with no work shown will receive only 1 credit.

19. The following table provides the average cost per No-fault Claim in New York State.

Year	Average Cost	Year	Average Cost
1990	$3,360	1995	$4,862
1991	$3,788	1996	$4,969
1992	$4,197	1997	$5,675
1993	$4,396	1998	$6,064
1994	$4,623	1999	$6,700

a. Determine the linear and exponential functions that best fit this data. (Remember to let $t = 0$ represent 1990.)
b. Which function do you think is most accurate? Which would you prefer to be most accurate? Explain your reasoning.

20. Given: Rectangle *MATH* with diagonal $\overline{MT}$ and segment $\overline{HX}$ drawn such that $\overline{MT} \perp \overline{HX}$.

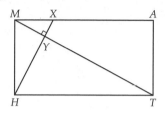

Prove: $\dfrac{MX}{MT} = \dfrac{XY}{HM}$.

CUMULATIVE REVIEW CHAPTERS 1–17

Part I

Answer all questions in this part. Each correct answer will receive 2 credits. No partial credit will be allowed.

1. According to the 2002 *World Almanac,* New York State had approximately $31,650,180,000 in public school revenue. Expressed in scientific notation, this number is approximately
(1) 3.165×10^8 (3) 31.65×10^9
(2) 3.165×10^9 (4) 3.165×10^{10}

2. What is the fourth term in the expansion of $(x - y)^4$?
(1) $4x^3y$ (3) $4xy^3$
(2) $-4x^3y$ (4) $-4xy^3$

3. The expression $\dfrac{\sin^2 x + \cos^2 x}{\cos x}$ is equivalent to
(1) $\sin x$ (3) $\sec x$
(2) $\cos x$ (4) $\csc x$

4. If the probability that an event will occur is $\dfrac{x}{y}$, what is the probability that it will not occur?
(1) $\dfrac{y}{x}$ (3) $\dfrac{y - x}{y}$
(2) $-\dfrac{x}{y}$ (4) $\dfrac{1 - x}{y}$

5. If $\cos \theta < 0$ and $\tan \theta < 0$, in what quadrant does θ terminate?
(1) I   (3) III
(2) II   (4) IV

6. The test scores in Mrs. Kaste's Math B class are normally distributed with a mean of 85 and a standard deviation of 5. Between what two scores would 95.4 percent of the scores fall?
(1) 70−100   (3) 80−90
(2) 75−95   (4) 85−90

7. The heights of the tides at Jones Beach, New York, are a function of the time of day. The time from one high tide to another is approximately 12 hours. Which of the following types of functions would best model this situation?
(1) exponential   (3) logarithmic
(2) linear   (4) trigonometric

8. Solve for x: $(3 + 2i) + (4 + xi) = 7 - 5i$.
(1) -7 (3) 3
(2) -3 (4) 7

9. Which of the following is not sufficient to prove that a quadrilateral is a parallelogram?
(1) opposite sides are congruent
(2) opposite angles are congruent
(3) diagonals are congruent
(4) consecutive angles are supplementary

10. Johnney has taken four math tests, and has a mean score of 89 points. What does he need to earn on his fifth test to make the mean score exactly 90 points?
(1) 90   (3) 94
(2) 92   (4) 95

Part II

Answer all questions in this part. Each correct answer will receive 2 credits. Clearly indicate the necessary steps, including appropriate formula substitutions, diagrams, graphs, charts, etc. For all questions in this part, a correct numerical answer with no work shown will receive only 1 credit.

11. Evaluate: $2 \sum_{k=1}^{3} k^2$.

12. Solve for x: $\sin x = \cos (2x + 15)$.

13. Write an equation that has a root of $3 + i$.

14. Maxine left her home for school, walking at a steady pace. She stopped at a snack shop for some hot chocolate, and then continued on to school, walking at a steady pace but a little faster to make up for the time she spent at the snack shop. Sketch a graph of Maxine's distance from home as a function of time.

Part III

Answer all questions in this part. Each correct answer will receive 4 credits. Clearly indicate the necessary steps, including the appropriate formula substitutions, diagrams, graphs, charts, etc. For all questions in this part, a correct numerical answer with no work shown will receive only 1 credit.

15. The table below shows domestic retail car sales in the United States for ten years.

Year	Millions of Cars	Year	Millions of Cars
1991	6.1	1996	7.3
1992	6.3	1997	6.9
1993	6.7	1998	6.8
1994	7.3	1999	7.0
1995	7.1	2000	6.8

a. To the nearest tenth of a million, what is the mean number of domestic cars sold in the United States for these ten years?
b. What is the standard deviation, to the nearest tenth?

16. Lucy and Ricky are pushing on a desk forming a 55° angle with each other. If Lucy exerts a 110-pound force on the desk while Ricky exerts a 160-pound force, what is the magnitude of the resultant force, to the nearest tenth of a pound?

17. Mrs. Mathsgreat has spent her entire life teaching mathematics to grateful students. She has now saved $1,000 and plans to deposit it into a fund that will pay her 10 percent interest each year. Her husband, Mr. Mathsgreat, says that it will take ten years for the money to double. Is this correct? Explain how you would determine how long it would take.

18. The We Make Widgets Company manufactures widgets. They find that when they charge d dollars for each widget, their income, $I(d)$, can be expressed by the formula $I(d) = -120d^2 + 14{,}400d + 100$. What price should they charge to maximize their income? If this price is charged, what is their maximum income?

Part IV

Answer all questions in this part. Each correct answer will receive 6 credits. Clearly indicate the necessary steps, including appropriate formula substitutions, diagrams, graphs, charts, etc. For all questions in this part, a correct numerical answer with no work shown will receive only 1 credit.

19. a. Sketch the graph of $f(x) = 3 \sin 2x$ in the interval $-\pi \le x \le \pi$.
    b. If $g(x) = T_{(0,1)}f(x)$, sketch the graph of $g(x)$ on the same set of axes.
    c. Write an equation for $g(x)$.
    d. If $h(x) = r_{x\text{-axis}}f(x)$, sketch the graph of $h(x)$ on the same set of axes.
    e. Write an equation for $h(x)$.

20. In a package of candy-coated chocolates, 30 percent of the candies are brown, 20 percent of them are yellow, and 20 percent of them are red. There are 10 percent each of orange, green, and blue. If Ronan reaches into a package and pulls out 12 candies, what is the probability that
    a. exactly 2 of them would be red
    b. at most 2 of them would be red
    c. none of them would be blue
    (Round answers to the nearest tenth of a percent.)

Sources

Throughout *Preparing for the Regents Examination: Mathematics B*, we have tried to create problems using real-world data. The following list shows the sources of data for the problems indicated. Teachers and students can use these sources to create additional projects and practice problems.

Chapter/Section	Page(s)	Problem	Source
Ch. 4, Chapter Review	102	7	www.esbnyc.com
		20	www.nycroads.com
5.2	111	Model Problem 2	U. S. Census Bureau, *Statistical Abstract of the United States: 2000*, Washington, DC, 2000, Table 230.
9.1	224	Text	pds.jpl.nasa.gov
	227	31	www.forbes.com/finance/lists/setters/listHomeSetter.jhtml?passsListId=10
		32	www.publicdebt.treas.gov/opd/opdpenny.htm
9.3	234	Model Problem 1	www.collegeboard.com/press/cost00/html/exhitbit2.html
	236	1	www.census.gov/prod/99pubs/p20-522.pdf
Ch. 9, Chapter Review	249	23	*Newsday*, August 31, 1997.
10.6	269	4	*The New York Times Almanac 2001*, Penguin Putnam, Inc., New York, 2000.
11.2	280–282	5, 6, 8	*The World Almanac and Book of Facts 2001*.
		9; 11	*The New York Times Almanac 2001*.
11.3	283	Model Problem 2	www.empire.state.ny.us/nysdc/ftp/StateCountyPopests/CountyPopHistory.pdf; http://aging.state.ny.us/explore/projections/page10.htm
	287–288	6	*Statistical Abstract of the United States: 2000*, Table 919.
		10	*The World Almanac and Book of Facts 2001*.
11.4	289	Text	pubs.usgs.gov/gip/earthq4/severitygip.html
Ch. 11, Chapter Review	294	13	*The Universal Almanac 1994*; *Statistical Abstract of the United States: 2000*, Table 311.
	296–297	17	*The World Almanac and Book of Facts 2001*.
		18; 20	*The World Almanac and Book of Facts 1997*.
		19	*The New York Times Almanac 2001*.
Ch. 11, FYI	298	A	*The World Almanac and Book of Facts 2001*.
		B	*The New York Times Almanac 2001*.
13.4	347	Model Problem	www.nasa.gov/soho
	349	11	www.met.utah.edu/jhorel/html/wx/climate/normtemp.html
Ch. 13, FYI	352–353		*The World Almanac and Book of Facts 2001*.
17.2	425–426	Model Problem 3	*Newsday*, November 23, 2001.
	429–430	11, 13, 15	*The New York Times Almanac 2001*.
		16	www.boxofficemojo.com
17.3	433–435	7	www.nba.com/knicks/roster
		10	www.usscplus.com/info/justices/htm
		12	www.nyrrc.org/race/2001/ma1top.htm
		13, 14	www.netstate.com/states/geography/ny_geography.htm
		15	www.info1988please.com/00olympicsmedalt.html; *The New York Times Almanac 2000*.

Chapter/Section	Page(s)	Problem	Source
17.4	440–442	7	http://twister.sbs.ohio-state.edu/text/obs/summaries/abus21.kaly
		11, 12	www.nfl.com/rosters/2001/nyj.html
		15	www.worldbookonline.com/na/ta/cp/ta389200e.ht12m
17.5	443	Text	*Statistical Abstract of the United States: 2000*, Table 230.
	445	Model Problem	www.collegeboard.org/sat/cbsenior/yr2001/2001reports.html; www.collegeboard.org/sat/cbsenior/yr2000/nat/natbk300.html
	448–449	12	www.erh.noaa.gov/er/okx/climate/records/monthannualtemp.html
		13	*Statistical Abstract of the United States: 2000*, Table 302.
		14	*The New York Times Almanac 2000.*
Ch. 17, Chapter Review	450–451	12	*The New York Times Almanac 2001.*
		22	*Newsday*, November 23, 2001.
Cumulative Review 1–9	466	1	*The Time Almanac 2002 with Information Please*, Family Education Company, Boston, MA.
Cumulative Review 1–12	474	19	*The Amazing Almanac*, Black Birch Press, Woodbury, 2000.
Cumulative Review 1–14	479	20	*The Amazing Almanac.*
Cumulative Review 1–15	481	19	*The World Almanac and Book of Facts 2002.*
Cumulative Review 1–16	482–484	10	*The Amazing Almanac.*
		19	*Newsday*, January 20, 2002.
Cumulative Review 1–17	484–485	1, 15	*The World Almanac and Book of Facts 2002.*
		20	http://www.m-ms.com/cai/mms/faq.html

Mathematics B
Regents Examinations

Part I

Answer all questions in this part. Each correct answer will receive 2 credits. No partial credit will be allowed. For each question, write on the separate answer sheet the numeral preceding the word or expression that best completes the statement or answers the question. [40]

1. What is the value of $\sum_{n=1}^{5}(-2n + 100)$?

    (1) 70   (2) 130   (3) 470   (4) 530

2. The effect of pH on the action of a certain enzyme is shown on the accompanying graph.

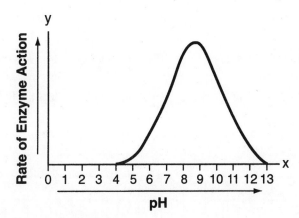

   What is the domain of this function?
   (1) $4 \le x \le 13$ (2) $4 \le y \le 13$ (3) $x \ge 0$ (4) $y \ge 0$

3. Which graph shows that soil permeability varies inversely to runoff?

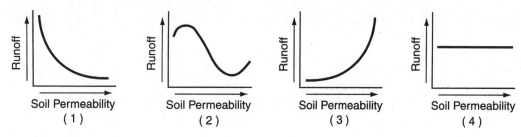

4. On a standardized test, a score of 86 falls exactly 1.5 standard deviations below the mean. If the standard deviation for the test is 2, what is the mean score for this test?
   (1) 84   (2) 84.5   (3) 87.5   (4) 89

5. Which transformation of the graph of $y = x^2$ would result in the graph of $y = x^2 + 2$?
   (1) D_2 (2) $T_{0, 2}$ (3) $r_{y=2}$ (4) $R_{0, 90}$

6. A sound wave is modeled by the curve $y = 3 \sin 4x$. What is the period of this curve?

    (1) π (2) $\frac{\pi}{2}$ (3) 3   (4) 4

7. If $\sqrt{2x - 1} + 2 = 5$, then x is equal to
   (1) 1   (2) 2   (3) 5   (4) 4

8. The expression $(1 + \cos x)(1 - \cos x)$ is equivalent to
   (1) 1   (2) $\sec^2 x$ (3) $\sin^2 x$ (4) $\csc^2 x$

9. If θ is a positive acute angle and $\sin 2\theta = \dfrac{\sqrt{3}}{2}$, then $(\cos \theta + \sin \theta)^2$ equals

   (1) 1   (2) $1 + \dfrac{\sqrt{3}}{2}$ (3) $30°$ (4) $60°$

10. What is the solution of the inequality $|y + 8| > 3$?
    (1) $y > -5$ or $y < -11$ (3) $-11 < y < -5$
    (2) $y > -5$ (4) $-5 < y < 11$

11. The speed of sound, v, at temperature T, in degrees Kelvin, is represented by the equation $v = 1087\sqrt{\dfrac{T}{273}}$. Which expression is equivalent to $\log v$?

    (1) $1087 + \dfrac{1}{2} \log T - \log 273$ (3) $\log 1087 + \dfrac{1}{2} \log T - \dfrac{1}{2} \log 273$

    (2) $1087\left(\dfrac{1}{2} \log T - \dfrac{1}{2} \log 273\right)$ (4) $\log 1087 + 2 \log (T + 273)$

12. In physics class, Eva noticed the pattern shown in the accompanying diagram on an oscilloscope.

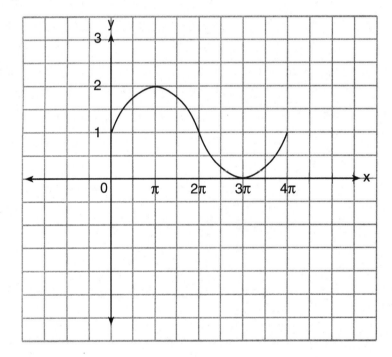

Which equation best represents the pattern shown on this oscilloscope?

(1) $y = \sin\left(\dfrac{1}{2}x\right) + 1$ (3) $y = 2 \sin x + 1$

(2) $y = \sin x + 1$ (4) $y = 2 \sin\left(-\dfrac{1}{2}x\right) + 1$

13. The expression $\dfrac{5}{\sqrt{5}-1}$ is equivalent to

(1) $\dfrac{5}{4}$ (2) $\dfrac{5\sqrt{5}+5}{4}$ (3) $\dfrac{5\sqrt{5}-5}{4}$ (4) $\dfrac{5\sqrt{5}-5}{6}$

14. The roots of the equation $2x^2 - 5 = 0$ are
    (1) imaginary
    (2) real, rational, and equal
    (3) real, rational, and unequal
    (4) real and irrational

15. What is the radian measure of the angle formed by the hands of a clock at 2:00 p.m.?

(1) $\dfrac{\pi}{2}$ (2) $\dfrac{\pi}{3}$ (3) $\dfrac{\pi}{4}$ (4) $\dfrac{\pi}{6}$

16. If θ is an angle in standard position and $P(-3, 4)$ is a point on the terminal side of θ, what is the value of $\sin \theta$?

(1) $\dfrac{3}{5}$ (2) $-\dfrac{3}{5}$ (3) $\dfrac{4}{5}$ (4) $-\dfrac{4}{5}$

17. When simplified, the expression $\left(\sqrt[3]{m^4}\right)\left(m^{-\frac{1}{2}}\right)$ is equivalent to

(1) $\sqrt[3]{m^{-2}}$ (2) $\sqrt[4]{m^3}$ (3) $\sqrt[5]{m^{-4}}$ (4) $\sqrt[6]{m^5}$

18. What are the coordinates of point A', the image of point $A(-4, 1)$ after the composite transformation $R_{90°} \circ r_{y=x}$ where the origin is the center of rotation?
    (1) $(-1, -4)$ (2) $(-4, -1)$ (3) $(1, 4)$ (4) $(4, 1)$

19. The accompanying diagram shows a 24-foot ladder leaning against a building. A steel brace extends from the ladder to the point where the building meets the ground. The brace forms a right angle with the ladder.

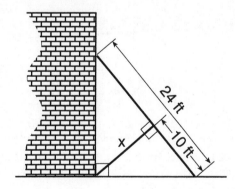

If the steel brace is connected to the ladder at a point that is 10 feet from the foot of the ladder, which equation can be used to find the length, x, of the steel brace?

(1) $\dfrac{10}{x} = \dfrac{x}{14}$ (2) $\dfrac{10}{x} = \dfrac{x}{24}$ (3) $10^2 + x^2 = 14^2$ (4) $10^2 + x^2 = 24^2$

20. The center of a circle represented by the equation $(x - 2)^2 + (y + 3)^2 = 100$ is located in Quadrant
    (1) I (2) II (3) III (4) IV

Part II

Answer all questions in this part. Each correct answer will receive 2 credits. Clearly indicate the necessary steps, including appropriate formula substitutions, diagrams, graphs, charts, etc. For all questions in this part, a correct numerical answer with no work shown will receive only 1 credit. [12]

21. If $f(x) = 5x^2 - 1$ and $g(x) = 3x - 1$, find $g(f(1))$.

22. On the accompanying diagram, draw a mapping of a relation from set *A* to set *B* that is *not* a function. Explain why the relationship you drew is *not* a function.

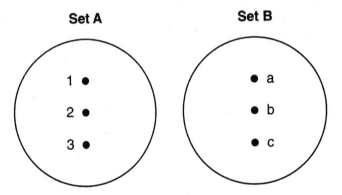

23. In the accompanying diagram, $\overline{PA}$ is tangent to circle *O* at *A*, secant $\overline{PBC}$ is drawn, $PB = 4$, and $BC = 12$. Find *PA*.

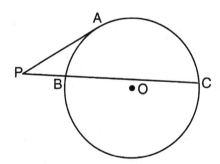

24. The time it takes to travel to a location varies inversely to the speed traveled. It takes 4 hours driving at an average speed of 55 miles per hour to reach a location. To the *nearest tenth of an hour*, how long will it take to reach the same location driving at an average speed of 50 miles per hour?

25. During a recent survey, students at Franconia College were asked if they drink coffee in the morning. The results showed that two-thirds of the students drink coffee in the morning and the remainder do not. What is the probability that of six students selected at random, *exactly* two of them drink coffee in the morning? Express your answer as a fraction or as a decimal rounded to *four decimal places*.

26. Solve algebraically for *x*: $8^{2x} = 4^6$

Part III

Answer all questions in this part. Each correct answer will receive 4 credits. Clearly indicate the necessary steps, including appropriate formula substitutions, diagrams, graphs, charts, etc. For all questions in this part, a correct numerical answer with no work shown will receive only 1 credit. [24]

27. In physics class, Taras discovers that the behavior of electrical power, x, in a particular circuit can be represented by the function $f(x) = x^2 + 2x + 7$. If $f(x) = 0$, solve the equation and express your answer in simplest $a + bi$ form.

28. On the accompanying grid, sketch the graphs of $y = 2^x$ and $3y = 7x + 3$ over the interval $-3 \le x \le 4$. Identify and state the coordinates of all points of intersection.

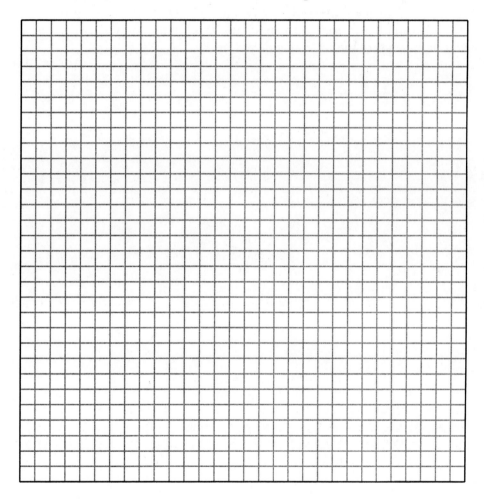

29. Simplify completely:

$$\dfrac{\dfrac{1-m}{m}}{m - \dfrac{1}{m}}$$

30. An architect is using a computer program to design the entrance of a railroad tunnel. The outline of the opening is modeled by the function $f(x) = 8 \sin x + 2$, in the interval $0 \le x \le \pi$, where x is expressed in radians.

    Solve algebraically for all values of x in the interval $0 \le x \le \pi$, where the height of the opening, $f(x)$, is 6. Express your answer in terms of π.

    If the x-axis represents the base of the tunnel, what is the maximum height of the entrance of the tunnel?

31. The Vietnam Veterans Memorial in Washington, D.C., is made up of two walls, each 246.75 feet long, that meet at an angle of 125.2°. Find, to the *nearest foot*, the distance between the ends of the walls that do not meet.

32. The current population of Little Pond, New York, is 20,000. The population is *decreasing*, as represented by the formula $P = A(1.3)^{-0.234t}$, where P = final population, t = time, in years, and A = initial population.

What will the population be 3 years from now? Round your answer to the *nearest hundred people*.

To the *nearest tenth of a year*, how many years will it take for the population to reach half the present population? [The use of the grid below is optional.]

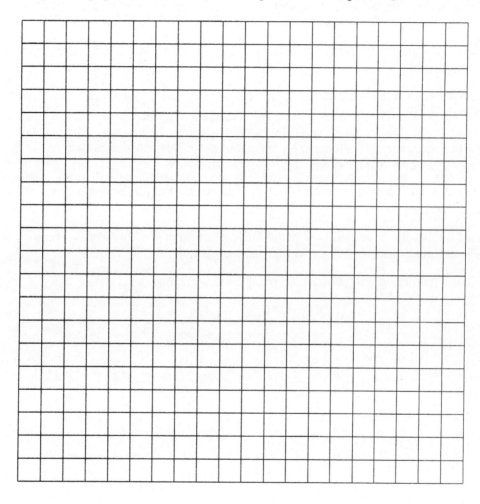

Part IV

Answer all questions in this part. Each correct answer will receive 6 credits. Clearly indicate the necessary steps, including appropriate formula substitutions, diagrams, graphs, charts, etc. For all questions in this part, a correct numerical answer with no work shown will receive only 1 credit. [12]

33. Since 1990, fireworks usage nationwide has grown, as shown in the accompanying table, where t represents the number of years since 1990, and p represents the fireworks usage per year, in millions of pounds.

Number of Years Since 1990 (t)	0	2	4	6	7	8	9	11
Fireworks Usage per Year, in Millions of Pounds (p)	67.6	88.8	119.0	120.1	132.5	118.3	159.2	161.6

Find the equation of the linear regression model for this set of data, where t is the independent variable. Round values to *four decimal places.*

Using this equation, determine in what year fireworks usage would have reached 99 million pounds.

Based on this linear model, how many millions of pounds of fireworks would be used in the year 2008? Round your answer to the *nearest tenth.*

34. Given: parallelogram *FLSH*, diagonal $\overline{FGAS}$, $\overline{LG} \perp \overline{FS}$, $\overline{HA} \perp \overline{FS}$

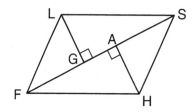

Prove: $\triangle LGS \cong \triangle HAF$

Part I

Answer all questions in this part. Each correct answer will receive 2 credits. No partial credit will be allowed. For each question, write on the separate answer sheet the numeral preceding the word or expression that best completes the statement or answers the question. [40]

1. Each graph below represents a possible relationship between temperature and pressure. Which graph does *not* represent a function?

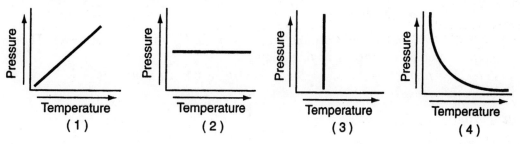

2. If $f(x) = x^{-\frac{3}{2}}$, then $f\left(\frac{1}{4}\right)$ is equal to

   (1) 8   (2) –2   (3) $-\frac{1}{8}$ (4) –4

3. In the accompanying diagram of circle O, chord $\overline{AY}$ is parallel to diameter $\overline{DOE}$, $\overline{AD}$ is drawn, and $m\widehat{AD} = 40$.

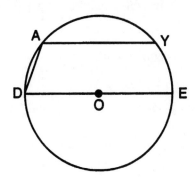

   What is $m\angle DAY$?
   (1) 90   (2) 110   (3) 130   (4) 150

4. If x is a positive acute angle and $\sin x = \frac{1}{2}$, what is $\sin 2x$?

   (1) $-\frac{1}{2}$ (2) $\frac{1}{2}$ (3) $-\frac{\sqrt{3}}{2}$ (4) $\frac{\sqrt{3}}{2}$

5. The temperature generated by an electrical circuit is represented by $t = f(m) = 0.3m^2$, where m is the number of moving parts. The resistance of the same circuit is represented by $r = g(t) = 150 + 5t$, where t is the temperature. What is the resistance in a circuit that has four moving parts?
   (1) 51   (2) 156   (3) 174   (4) 8,670

6. If the equation $x^2 - kx - 36 = 0$ has $x = 12$ as one root, what is the value of k?
   (1) 9   (2) –9   (3) 3   (4) –3

7. The height, f(x), of a bouncing ball after x bounces is represented by f(x) = $80(0.5)^x$. How many times higher is the first bounce than the fourth bounce?
   (1) 8   (2) 2   (3) 16   (4) 4

8. A radio transmitter sends a radio wave from the top of a 50-foot tower. The wave is represented by the accompanying graph.

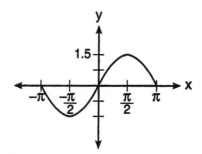

   What is the equation of this radio wave?
   (1) $y = \sin x$ (2) $y = 1.5 \sin x$ (3) $y = \sin 1.5x$ (4) $y = 2 \sin x$

9. If $\tan \theta = 2.7$ and $\csc \theta < 0$, in which quadrant does θ lie?
   (1) I   (2) II   (3) III   (4) IV

10. The expression $\dfrac{1 - \cos^2 x}{\sin^2 x}$ is equivalent to
    (1) 1   (2) –1   (3) $\sin x$ (4) $\cos x$

11. The graph of $y = (x - 3)^2$ is shifted left 4 units and down 2 units. What is the axis of symmetry of the transformed graph?
    (1) $x = -2$ (2) $x = -1$ (3) $x = 1$ (4) $x = 7$

12. The solution set of $2^{x^2+2x} = 2^{-1}$ is
    (1) $\{1\}$ (2) $\{-1\}$ (3) $\{-1, 1\}$ (4) $\{\ \}$

13. Which transformation best describes the relationship between the functions f(x) = 2^x and g(x) = $\left(\dfrac{1}{2}\right)^x$?

    (1) reflection in the line $y = x$ (3) reflection in the x-axis
    (2) reflection in the origin   (4) reflection in the y-axis

14. What is the multiplicative inverse of $3i$?

    (1) $-3i$ (2) -3 (3) $\frac{1}{3}$ (4) $-\frac{i}{3}$

15. Mrs. Donahue made up a game to help her class learn about imaginary numbers. The winner will be the student whose expression is equivalent to $-i$. Which expression will win the game?
    (1) i^{46} (2) i^{47} (3) i^{48} (4) i^{49}

16. Which equation represents a hyperbola?

    (1) $y^2 = 16 - x^2$ (2) $y = 16 - x^2$ (3) $y = 16x^2$ (4) $y = \frac{16}{x}$

17. The solution set of which inequality is represented by the accompanying graph?

    (1) $|x - 2| > 7$ (2) $|x - 2| < 7$ (3) $|2 - x| > -7$ (4) $|2 - x| < -7$

18. According to Boyle's Law, the pressure, p, of a compressed gas is inversely proportional to the volume, v. If a pressure of 20 pounds per square inch exists when the volume of the gas is 500 cubic inches, what is the pressure when the gas is compressed to 400 cubic inches?
    (1) 16 lb/in^2 (2) 25 lb/in^2 (3) 40 lb/in^2 (4) 50 lb/in^2

19. What is the fourth term in the expansion of $(y - 1)^7$?
    (1) $35y^4$ (2) $35y^3$ (3) $-35y^4$ (4) $-35y^3$

20. Sam needs to cut a triangle out of a sheet of paper. The only requirements that Sam must follow are that one of the angles must be 60°, the side opposite the 60° angle must be 40 centimeters, and one of the other sides must be 15 centimeters. How many different triangles can Sam make?
    (1) 1 (2) 2 (3) 3 (4) 0

Part II

Answer all questions in this part. Each correct answer will receive 2 credits. Clearly indicate the necessary steps, including appropriate formula substitutions, diagrams, graphs, charts, etc. For all questions in this part, a correct numerical answer with no work shown will receive only 1 credit. [12]

21. Find the sum of $-2 + 3i$ and $-1 - 2i$.
    Graph the resultant on the accompanying set of axes.

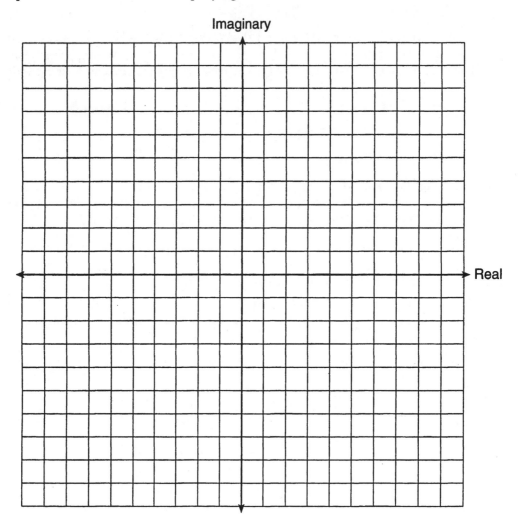

22. In $\triangle ABC$, $m\angle A = 53$, $m\angle B = 14$, and $a = 10$. Find b to the *nearest integer.*

23. Solve for x: $\log_2 (x + 1) = 3$

24. Evaluate: $\displaystyle\sum_{k=1}^{2} \frac{(-1)^{k-1}}{(2k-1)!}$

25. Ginger and Mary Anne are planning a vacation trip to the island of Capri, where the probability of rain on any day is 0.3. What is the probability that during their five days on the island, they have *no* rain on *exactly* three of the five days?

26. The pendulum of a clock swings through an angle of 2.5 radians as its tip travels through an arc of 50 centimeters. Find the length of the pendulum, in centimeters.

Part III

Answer all questions in this part. Each correct answer will receive 4 credits. Clearly indicate the necessary steps, including appropriate formula substitutions, diagrams, graphs, charts, etc. For all questions in this part, a correct numerical answer with no work shown will receive only 1 credit. [24]

27. Solve the following system of equations algebraically:

$$9x^2 + y^2 = 9$$
$$3x - y = 3$$

28. Simplify for all values of a for which the expression is defined: $\dfrac{1 - \dfrac{2}{a}}{\dfrac{4}{a^2} - 1}$

29. Solve algebraically for x: $\sqrt{3x + 1} + 1 = x$

30. The number of children of each of the first 41 United States presidents is given in the accompanying table. For this population, determine the mean and the standard deviation to the *nearest tenth*.

   How many of these presidents fall within one standard deviation of the mean?

Number of Children (x_i)	Number of Presidents (f_i)
0	6
1	2
2	8
3	6
4	7
5	3
6	5
7	1
8	1
10	1
15	1

31. A factory is producing and stockpiling metal sheets to be shipped to an automobile man-ufacturing plant. The factory ships only when there is a minimum of 2,050 sheets in stock. The accompanying table shows the day, x, and the number of sheets in stock, f(x).

Day (x)	Sheets in Stock (f(x))
1	860
2	930
3	1000
4	1150
5	1200
6	1360

Write the linear regression equation for this set of data, rounding the coefficients to *four decimal places.*

Use this equation to determine the day the sheets will be shipped.

32. A small rocket is launched from a height of 72 feet. The height of the rocket in feet, h, is represented by the equation $h(t) = -16t^2 + 64t + 72$, where t = time, in seconds. Graph this equation on the accompanying grid.

Use your graph to determine the number of seconds that the rocket will remain at or above 100 feet from the ground. [Only a graphic solution can receive full credit.]

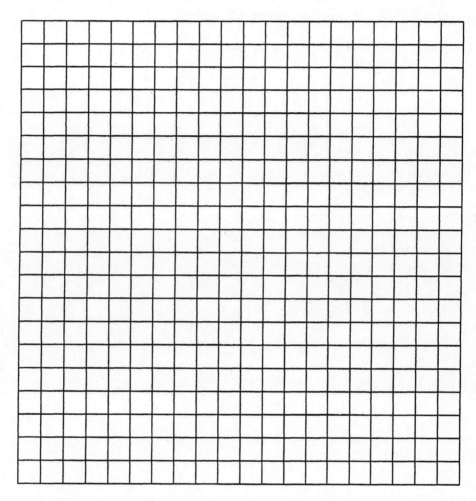

Part IV

Answer all questions in this part. Each correct answer will receive 6 credits. Clearly indicate the necessary steps, including appropriate formula substitutions, diagrams, graphs, charts, etc. For all questions in this part, a correct numerical answer with no work shown will receive only 1 credit. [12]

33. Given: $A(-2, 2)$, $B(6, 5)$, $C(4, 0)$, $D(-4, -3)$

    Prove: *ABCD* is a parallelogram but not a rectangle. [The use of the grid provided is optional.]

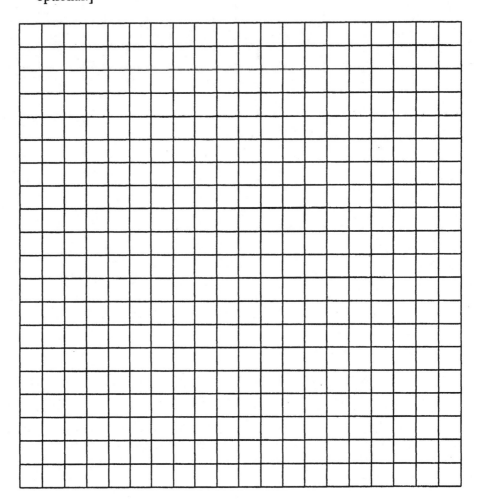

34. A triangular plot of land has sides that measure 5 meters, 7 meters, and 10 meters. What is the area of this plot of land, to the *nearest tenth of a square meter*?

Part I

Answer all questions in this part. Each correct answer will receive 2 credits. No partial credit will be allowed. For each question, write on the separate answer sheet the numeral preceding the word or expression that best completes the statement or answers the question.   [40]

1. The expression $4^{\frac{1}{2}} \cdot 2^3$ is equal to

    (1) $4^{\frac{3}{2}}$ (2) $8^{\frac{3}{2}}$ (3) 16   (4) 4

2. What is the solution of the equation $\sqrt{2x-3} - 3 = 6$?
    (1) 42   (2) 39   (3) 3   (4) 6

3. What is the minimum point of the graph of the equation $y = 2x^2 + 8x + 9$?
    (1) $(2, 33)$ (2) $(2, 17)$ (3) $(-2, -15)$ (4) $(-2, 1)$

4. If x is a positive acute angle and $\cos x = \dfrac{\sqrt{3}}{4}$, what is the exact value of $\sin x$?

    (1) $\dfrac{\sqrt{3}}{5}$ (2) $\dfrac{\sqrt{13}}{4}$ (3) $\dfrac{3}{5}$ (4) $\dfrac{4}{5}$

5. Which equation does *not* represent a function?
    (1) $x = \pi$ (2) $y = 4$ (3) $y = |x|$ (4) $y = x^2 + 5x$

6. The expression $\dfrac{12}{3 + \sqrt{3}}$ is equivalent to

    (1) $12 - \sqrt{3}$ (2) $6 - 2\sqrt{3}$ (3) $4 - 2\sqrt{3}$ (4) $2 + \sqrt{3}$

7. The function $y = 2^x$ is equivalent to
    (1) $x = y \log 2$ (2) $x = \log_2 y$ (3) $y = x \log 2$ (4) $y = \log_2 x$

8. In $\triangle ABC$, D is a point on $\overline{AC}$ such that $\overline{BD}$ is a median. Which statement must be true?
    (1) $\triangle ABD \cong \triangle CBD$ (2) $\angle ABD \cong \angle CBD$ (3) $\overline{AD} \cong \overline{CD}$ (4) $\overline{BD} \perp \overline{AC}$

9. A designer who is planning to install an elliptical mirror is laying out the design on a coordinate grid. Which equation could represent the elliptical mirror?
    (1) $x^2 = 144 + 36y^2$ (2) $x^2 + y^2 = 144$ (3) $x^2 + 4y^2 = 144$ (4) $y = 4y^2 + 144$

10. A solution set of the equation $5 \sin \theta + 3 = 3$ contains all multiples of
    (1) $45°$ (2) $90°$ (3) $135°$ (4) $180°$

11. What is the total number of points of intersection for the graphs of the equations $y = x^2$ and $y = -x^2$?
    (1) 1   (2) 2   (3) 3   (4) 0

12. For which equation is the sum of the roots equal to the product of the roots?
    (1) $x^2 + x + 1 = 0$ (2) $x^2 + 3x - 6 = 0$ (3) $x^2 - 8x - 4 = 0$ (4) $x^2 - 4x + 4 = 0$

13. If the perimeter of an equilateral triangle is 18, the length of the altitude of this triangle is
    (1) 6   (2) $6\sqrt{3}$ (3) 3   (4) $3\sqrt{3}$

14. Jonathan's teacher required him to express the sum $\frac{2}{3} + \frac{3}{4} + \frac{4}{5} + \frac{5}{6} + \frac{6}{7}$ using sigma notation. Jonathan proposed four possible answers. Which of these four answers is *not* correct?

    (1) $\sum_{k=3}^{7} \frac{k-1}{k}$ (2) $\sum_{k=1}^{5} \frac{k}{k+1}$ (3) $\sum_{k=1}^{5} \frac{k+1}{k+2}$ (4) $\sum_{k=2}^{6} \frac{k}{k+1}$

15. What is the period of the graph of the equation $y = 2 \sin \frac{1}{3} x$?

    (1) $\frac{2}{3}\pi$ (2) 2π (3) 6π (4) $\frac{3\pi}{2}$

16. What is the solution set of the equation $|x^2 - 2x| = 3x - 6$?
    (1) $\{2, \pm 3\}$ (2) $\{2\}$ (3) $\{\pm 3\}$ (4) $\{2, 3\}$

17. The expression $\frac{\sin 2\theta}{\sin^2 \theta}$ is equivalent to

    (1) $\frac{2}{\sin \theta}$ (2) $2 \cos \theta$ (3) $2 \cot \theta$ (4) $2 \tan \theta$

18. The accompanying diagram shows unit circle O, with radius $OB = 1$.

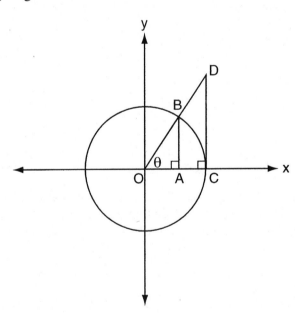

Which line segment has a length equivalent to $\cos \theta$?
(1) $\overline{AB}$ (2) $\overline{CD}$ (3) $\overline{OC}$ (4) $\overline{OA}$

19. The expression $\dfrac{3y^2 - 12y}{4y^2 - y^3}$ is equivalent to

(1) $\dfrac{3}{y}$ (2) $-\dfrac{3}{y}$ (3) $-\dfrac{9}{4}$ (4) $\dfrac{3}{4} - \dfrac{12}{y^2}$

20. Which graph represents a quadratic function with a negative discriminant?

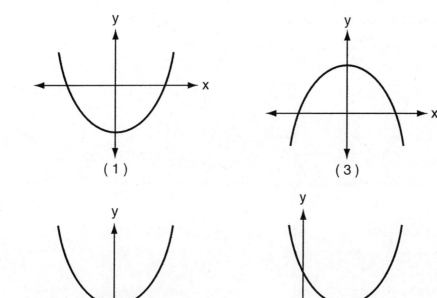

(1) (3)

(2) (4)

Part II

Answer all questions in this part. Each correct answer will receive 2 credits. Clearly indicate the necessary steps, including appropriate formula substitutions, diagrams, graphs, charts, etc. For all questions in this part, a correct numerical answer with no work shown will receive only 1 credit. [12]

21. The complex number $c + di$ is equal to $(2 + i)^2$. What is the value of c?

22. The volume of any spherical balloon can be found by using the formula $V = \dfrac{4}{3}\pi r^3$.

Write an equation for r in terms of V and π.

23. What is the number of degrees in an angle whose radian measure is $\dfrac{7\pi}{12}$?

24. Solve for x: $\log_b 36 - \log_b 2 = \log_b x$

25. Beth's scores on the six Earth science tests she took this semester are 100, 95, 55, 85, 75, and 100. For this population, how many scores are within one standard deviation of the mean?

26. Given point $A(-2, 3)$. State the coordinates of the image of A under the composition $T_{-3,\,-4} \circ r_{x\text{-axis}}$. [The use of the accompanying grid is optional.]

Part III

Answer all questions in this part. Each correct answer will receive 4 credits. Clearly indicate the necessary steps, including appropriate formula substitutions, diagrams, graphs, charts, etc. For all questions in this part, a correct numerical answer with no work shown will receive only 1 credit. [24]

27. In the accompanying diagram of circle O, diameter $\overline{AOB}$ is drawn, tangent $\overline{CB}$ is drawn to the circle at B, E is a point on the circle, and $\overline{BE} \| \overline{ADC}$.

    Prove: $\triangle ABE \sim \triangle CAB$

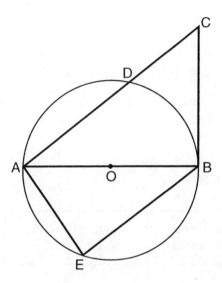

28. The accompanying diagram shows a triangular plot of land that is part of Fran's garden. She needs to change the dimensions of this part of the garden, but she wants the area to stay the same. She increases the length of side AC to 22.5 feet. If angle A remains the same, by how many feet should side AB be *decreased* to make the area of the new triangular plot of land the same as the current one?

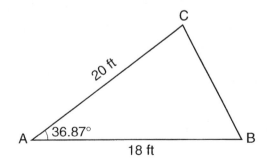

29. A machine part consists of a circular wheel with an inscribed triangular plate, as shown in the accompanying diagram. If $\overline{SE} \cong \overline{EA}$, $SE = 10$, and $m\overset{\frown}{SE} = 140$, find the length of $\overline{SA}$ to the *nearest tenth*.

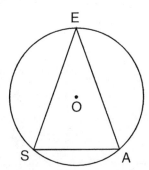

30. On mornings when school is in session in January, Sara notices that her school bus is late one-third of the time. What is the probability that during a 5-day school week in January her bus will be late *at least* three times?

31. Jean invested $380 in stocks. Over the next 5 years, the value of her investment grew, as shown in the accompanying table.

Years Since Investment (x)	Value of Stock, in Dollars (y)
0	380
1	395
2	411
3	427
4	445
5	462

Write the exponential regression equation for this set of data, rounding all values to *two decimal places*.

Using this equation, find the value of her stock, to the *nearest dollar*, 10 years after her initial purchase.

32. After an oven is turned on, its temperature, T, is represented by the equation $T = 400 - 350(3.2)^{-0.1m}$, where m represents the number of minutes after the oven is turned on and T represents the temperature of the oven, in degrees Fahrenheit.

How many minutes does it take for the oven's temperature to reach 300°F? Round your answer to the *nearest minute*. [The use of the grid below is optional.]

Part IV

Answer all questions in this part. Each correct answer will receive 6 credits. Clearly indicate the necessary steps, including appropriate formula substitutions, diagrams, graphs, charts, etc. For all questions in this part, a correct numerical answer with no work shown will receive only 1 credit. [12]

33. In the accompanying diagram, circle O has radius $\overline{OD}$, diameter $\overline{BOHF}$, secant $\overline{CBA}$, and chords $\overline{DHG}$ and $\overline{BD}$; $\overline{CE}$ is tangent to circle O at D; $m\overset{\frown}{DF} = 80$; and $m\overset{\frown}{BA} : m\overset{\frown}{AG} : m\overset{\frown}{GF} = 3 : 2 : 1$.

    Find $m\overset{\frown}{GF}$, $m\angle BHD$, $m\angle BDG$, $m\angle GDE$, $m\angle C$, and $m\angle BOD$.

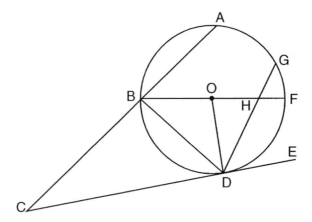

34. Barb pulled the plug in her bathtub and it started to drain. The amount of water in the bathtub as it drains is represented by the equation $L = -5t^2 - 8t + 120$, where L represents the number of liters of water in the bathtub and t represents the amount of time, in minutes, since the plug was pulled.

    How many liters of water were in the bathtub when Barb pulled the plug? Show your reasoning.

    Determine, to the *nearest tenth of a minute*, the amount of time it takes for all the water in the bathtub to drain.

Part I

Answer all questions in this part. Each correct answer will receive 2 credits. No partial credit will be allowed. For each question, write on the separate answer sheet the numeral preceding the word or expression that best completes the statement or answers the question. [40]

1. Which equation best represents the accompanying graph?
   (1) $y = 2^x$ (2) $y = x^2 + 2$ (3) $y = 2^{-x}$ (4) $y = -2^x$

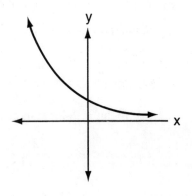

2. The accompanying diagram shows the approximate linear distances traveled by a sailboat during a race. The sailboat started at point S, traveled to points E and A, respectively, and ended at point S.

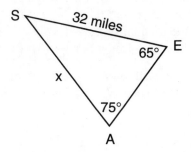

   Based on the measures shown in the diagram, which equation can be used to find x, the distance from point A to point S?

   (1) $\dfrac{x}{\sin 65°} = \dfrac{\sin 75°}{32}$ (2) $\dfrac{\sin 65°}{x} = \dfrac{\sin 75°}{32}$ (3) $\dfrac{x}{65} = \dfrac{32}{75}$ (4) $\dfrac{65}{x} = \dfrac{32}{75}$

3. If $\sqrt{x - a} = b, x > a$, which expression is equivalent to x?
   (1) $b^2 - a$ (2) $b^2 + a$ (3) $b - a$ (4) $b + a$

4. What is the total number of points of intersection of the graphs of the equations $xy = 12$ and $y = -x^2 + 3$?
   (1) 1   (2) 2   (3) 3   (4) 4

5. The expression i^{25} is equivalent to
   (1) 1   (2) −1   (3) i (4) $-i$

6. The expression $\dfrac{\dfrac{1}{3}+\dfrac{1}{3x}}{\dfrac{1}{x}+\dfrac{1}{3}}$ is equivalent to (1) $\dfrac{x+1}{x+3}$ (2) 2 (3) $\dfrac{3x+3}{x+3}$ (4) $\dfrac{1}{3}$

7. The term "snowstorms of note" applies to all snowfalls over 6 inches. The snowfall amounts for snowstorms of note in Utica, New York, over a four-year period are as follows:

7.1, 9.2, 8.0, 6.1, 14.4, 8.5, 6.1, 6.8, 7.7, 21.5, 6.7, 9.0, 8.4, 7.0, 11.5, 14.1, 9.5, 8.6

What are the mean and population standard deviation for these data, to the *nearest hundredth*?
(1) mean = 9.46; standard deviation = 3.74
(2) mean = 9.46; standard deviation = 3.85
(3) mean = 9.45; standard deviation = 3.74
(4) mean = 9.45; standard deviation = 3.85

8. The expression $\dfrac{4}{5-\sqrt{13}}$ is equivalent to

(1) $\dfrac{5+\sqrt{13}}{3}$ (2) $\dfrac{5-\sqrt{13}}{3}$ (3) $\dfrac{2\left(5+\sqrt{13}\right)}{19}$ (4) $\dfrac{2\left(5-\sqrt{13}\right)}{19}$

9. What is the value of b in the equation $4^{2b-3}=8^{1-b}$?

(1) $\dfrac{-3}{7}$ (2) $\dfrac{7}{9}$ (3) $\dfrac{9}{7}$ (4) $\dfrac{10}{7}$

10. What is the solution set of the inequality $|2x-1|<9$?
(1) $\{x|{-4}<x<5\}$ (2) $\{x|x<{-4}\text{ or }x>5\}$ (3) $\{x|x<5\}$ (4) $\{x|x<{-4}\}$

11. Which transformation could be used to make the graph of the equation $y=\sin x$ coincide with the graph of the equation $y=\cos x$?
(1) translation (2) rotation (3) dilation (4) point reflection

12. Data collected during an experiment are shown in the accompanying graph. What is the range of this set of data?
(1) $2.5\le y\le 9.5$
(2) $2.5\le x\le 9.5$
(3) $0\le y\le 100$
(4) $1\le x\le 10$

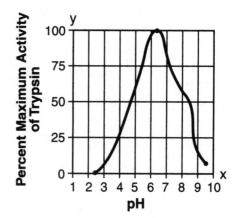

13. Which is a true statement about the graph of the equation $y=x^2-7x-60$?
(1) It is tangent to the x-axis.
(2) It does not intersect the x-axis.
(3) It intersects the x-axis in two distinct points that have irrational coordinates.
(4) It intersects the x-axis in two distinct points that have rational coordinates.

14. Which quadratic equation has the roots $3 + i$ and $3 - i$?
    (1) $x^2 + 6x - 10 = 0$ (2) $x^2 + 6x + 8 = 0$ (3) $x^2 - 6x + 10 = 0$ (4) $x^2 - 6x - 8 = 0$

15. What is the amplitude of the function shown in the accompanying graph?
    (1) 1.5   (2) 2   (3) 6   (4) 12

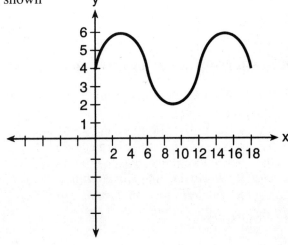

16. Which equation represents the circle shown in the accompanying graph?
    (1) $(x - 1)^2 - (y + 2)^2 = 9$ (3) $(x + 1)^2 - (y - 2)^2 = 9$
    (2) $(x - 1)^2 + (y + 2)^2 = 9$ (4) $(x + 1)^2 + (y - 2)^2 = 9$

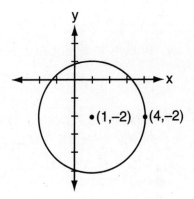

17. A black hole is a region in space where objects seem to disappear. A formula used in the study of black holes is the Schwarzschild formula, $R = \dfrac{2GM}{c^2}$.

    Based on the laws of logarithms, $\log R$ can be represented by
    (1) $2 \log G + \log M - \log 2c$ (3) $\log 2 + \log G + \log M - 2 \log c$
    (2) $\log 2G + \log M - \log 2c$ (4) $2 \log GM - 2 \log c$

18. In the unit circle shown in the accompanying diagram, what are the coordinates of (x, y)?

    (1) $\left(-\dfrac{\sqrt{3}}{2}, -0.5\right)$

    (2) $\left(-0.5, -\dfrac{\sqrt{3}}{2}\right)$

    (3) $(-30, -210)$

    (4) $\left(-\dfrac{\sqrt{2}}{2}, -\dfrac{\sqrt{2}}{2}\right)$

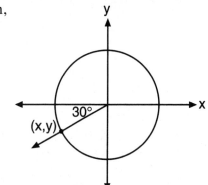
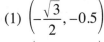

19. Which transformation represents a dilation?
    (1) $(8, 4) \rightarrow (11, 7)$ (2) $(8, 4) \rightarrow (-8, 4)$ (3) $(8, 4) \rightarrow (-4, -8)$ (4) $(8, 4) \rightarrow (4, 2)$

20. In $\triangle ABC$, $m\angle A = 30$, $a = 14$, and $b = 20$. Which type of angle is $\angle B$?
    (1) It must be an acute angle.
    (2) It must be a right angle.
    (3) It must be an obtuse angle.
    (4) It may be either an acute angle or an obtuse angle.

Part II

Answer all questions in this part. Each correct answer will receive 2 credits. Clearly indicate the necessary steps, including appropriate formula substitutions, diagrams, graphs, charts, etc. For all questions in this part, a correct numerical answer with no work shown will receive only 1 credit. [12]

21. In the accompanying diagram of circle O, diameter $\overline{AOB}$ is extended through B to external point P, tangent $\overline{PC}$ is drawn to point C on the circle, and $\overparen{mAC}:\overparen{mBC} = 7{:}2$. Find $m\angle CPA$.

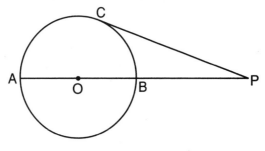

(Not drawn to scale)

22. The accompanying diagram shows a revolving door with three panels, each of which is 4 feet long. What is the width, w, of the opening between x and y, to the *nearest tenth of a foot*?

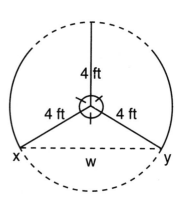

23. In $\triangle ABC$, $AC = 18$, $BC = 10$, and $\cos C = \dfrac{1}{2}$. Find the area of $\triangle ABC$ to the *nearest tenth of a square unit*.

24. On the accompanying set of axes, graphically represent the sum of $3 + 4i$ and $-1 + 2i$.

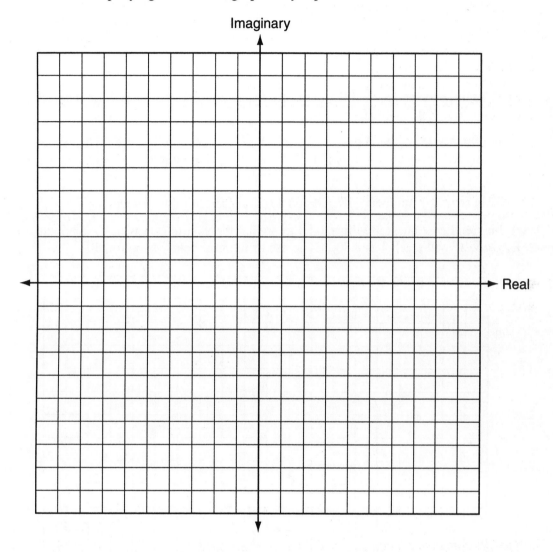

25. As shown in the accompanying diagram, a dial in the shape of a semicircle has a radius of 4 centimeters. Find the measure of θ, in radians, when the pointer rotates to form an arc whose length is 1.38 centimeters.

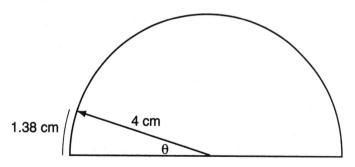

26. What is the fourth term in the expansion of $(2x - y)^5$?

Part III

Answer all questions in this part. Each correct answer will receive 4 credits. Clearly indicate the necessary steps, including appropriate formula substitutions, diagrams, graphs, charts, etc. For all questions in this part, a correct numerical answer with no work shown will receive only 1 credit. [24]

27. Find, to the *nearest degree*, all values of θ in the interval $0° \leq \theta \leq 180°$ that satisfy the equation $8 \cos^2 \theta - 2 \cos \theta - 1 = 0$.

28. Since January 1980, the population of the city of Brownville has grown according to the mathematical model $y = 720{,}500(1.022)^x$, where x is the number of years since January 1980.

    Explain what the numbers 720,500 and 1.022 represent in this model.

    If this trend continues, use this model to predict the year during which the population of Brownville will reach 1,548,800. [The use of the grid below is optional.]

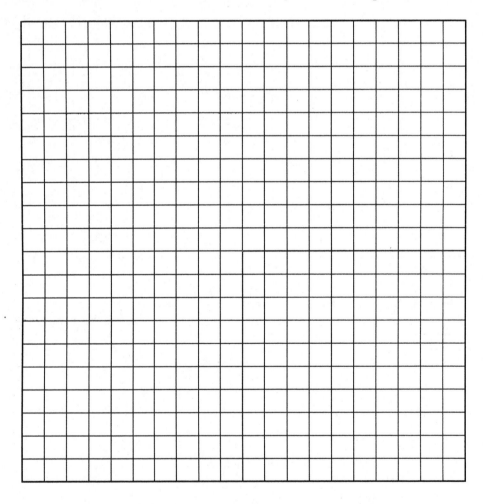

29. Matt's rectangular patio measures 9 feet by 12 feet. He wants to increase the patio's dimensions so its area will be twice the area it is now. He plans to increase both the length and the width by the same amount, x. Find x, to the *nearest hundredth of a foot*.

30. The accompanying table shows the number of new cases reported by the Nassau and Suffolk County Police Crime Stoppers program for the years 2000 through 2002.

Year (x)	New Cases (y)
2000	457
2001	369
2002	353

If $x = 1$ represents the year 2000, and y represents the number of new cases, find the equation of best fit using a power regression, rounding all values to the *nearest thousandth*.

Using this equation, find the estimated number of new cases, to the *nearest whole number*, for the year 2007.

31. Dr. Glendon, the school physician in charge of giving sports physicals, has compiled his information and has determined that the probability a student will be on a team is 0.39. Yesterday, Dr. Glendon examined five students chosen at random.

Find, to the *nearest hundredth*, the probability that *at least* four of the five students will be on a team.

Find, to the *nearest hundredth*, the probability that *exactly* one of the five students will *not* be on a team.

32. In the accompanying diagram, $m\widehat{BR} = 70$, $m\widehat{YD} = 70$, and $\overline{BOD}$ is the diameter of circle O. Write an explanation or a proof that shows $\triangle RBD$ and $\triangle YDB$ are congruent.

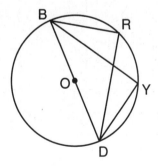

Part IV

Answer all questions in this part. Each correct answer will receive 6 credits. Clearly indicate the necessary steps, including appropriate formula substitutions, diagrams, graphs, charts, etc. For all questions in this part, a correct numerical answer with no work shown will receive only 1 credit. [12]

33. Perform the indicated operations and simplify completely:

$$\frac{x^2 - 9}{x^2 - 5x} \cdot \frac{5x - x^2}{x^2 - x - 12} \div \frac{x - 4}{x^2 - 8x + 16}$$

34. Two forces of 40 pounds and 20 pounds, respectively, act simultaneously on an object. The angle between the two forces is 40°.

    Find the magnitude of the resultant, to the *nearest tenth of a pound*.

    Find the measure of the angle, to the *nearest degree*, between the resultant and the larger force.

Index